If you're wondering why you should buy this new edition of *International Relations,* here are 5 good reasons!

1. New "Policy Perspectives" boxes consider the **complex policy decisions** that world leaders face.

2. Eight new "Big Picture" boxes and podcasts show how to use **three core principles**—dominance, reciprocity, and identity—to interpret current events.

3. **Revised theory chapters**—Chapter 2, "Realist Theories" and Chapter 3, "Liberal and Social Theories"—review all the major schools of thought in international relations.

4. Coverage of **current world political events**—the wars in Iraq and Afghanistan, Russia's reemergence as a global power, the worldwide financial crisis, and more—provides more relevant and immediate examples of key political science concepts.

5. Every chapter is updated to include the **latest scholarship and data**.

PEARSON

NEW! For International Relations

This state-of-the-art online learning companion features book-specific assessment and interactive/multimedia activities to help students connect concepts and current events and to help instructors follow students' learning.

MyPoliSciKit includes:

 Assessment Review each chapter using learning objectives, chapter summaries, practice tests, and more.

 Flashcards Learn the key terms in your textbook; you can test yourself by term or definition.

 Videos Analyze recent world affairs by watching streaming video from major news providers.

 Simulations Play the role of an IR decision-maker and experience how IR concepts work in practice.

 World Politics News Review Look beyond today's headlines in this blog's analysis of world politics.

 Financial Times News Feeds Get hourly updates of U.S. and world news to keep up with current events.

This Week's Current Events Quiz Master the headlines in this review of the week's most important news.

 Mapping Exercises Test your geographical knowledge of regions around the world.

Online Administration With Grade Tracker, instructors can easily follow students' work on the site and their progress on each activity.

Log onto www.mypoliscikit.com today to see a demo, redeem your access code, or purchase a subscription.

Questions? Contact your Longman representative for more information at www.pearsonhighered.com/replocator.

Goldstein/Pevehouse's Open-Access Companion Website

Integrated with *International Relations* via marginal icons, this website offers a set of learning tools that take advantage of the Web's resources. As students read through a chapter, icons direct them to www.IRtext.com where, by entering the page number on which an icon appears, they can easily call up the following features.

Podcast. These icons prompt students to download and listen to podcasts on www.IRtext.com in which the authors discuss a key topic from the chapter using an example in international politics.

Video. These icons direct students to www.IRtext.com where they will find links to video clips. Critical-thinking questions for each video tie these real-world examples to concepts discussed in the book.

ONLINE PRACTICE TEST
Take an online practice test at www.IRtext.com.

- ☐ A
- ☐ B
- ☑ C
- ☐ D

Online Practice Tests. This icon at the end of each chapter refers students to the practice tests available at the Companion Website.

Visit www.IRtext.com

International Relations

BRIEF FIFTH EDITION

Joshua S. Goldstein
American University, Washington, D.C.
University of Massachusetts, Amherst

Jon C. Pevehouse
University of Wisconsin, Madison

Longman
New York   San Francisco   Boston
London   Toronto   Sydney   Tokyo   Singapore   Madrid
Mexico City   Munich   Paris   Cape Town   Hong Kong   Montreal

IN MEMORY OF PROF. DEBORAH J. "MISTY" GERNER

Editor-in-Chief: Eric Stano
Acquisitions Editor: Vikram Mukhija
Associate Editor: Donna Garnier
Editorial Assistant: Toni Magyar
Senior Media Editor: Regina Vertiz
Marketing Manager: Lindsey Prudhomme
Production Manager: Eric Jorgensen
Project Coordination, Text Design, and Electronic Page Makeup: Elm Street Publishing Services
Cover Designer/Manager: Wendy Ann Fredericks
Cover Photo: Muslim women in Indonesia look at a mosaic of Barack Obama, 2008, © Dadang
    Tri/Reuters/Corbis.
Cartographer: Maps.com
Photo Researcher: Julie Tesser
Senior Manufacturing Buyer: Alfred C. Dorsey
Printer and Binder: Courier Corporation—Kendallville
Cover Printer: Lehigh-Phoenix Color Corp.

For permission to use copyrighted material, grateful acknowledgment is made to the
copyright holders on p. 361, which are hereby made part of this copyright page.

Library of Congress Cataloging-in-Publication Data

Goldstein, Joshua S., 1952–
    International relations / Joshua S. Goldstein, Jon C. Pevehouse. — Brief 5th ed.
        p. cm.
    Includes index.
    ISBN-13: 978-0-205-72391-1
    ISBN-10: 0-205-72391-8
    1. International relations—Textbooks.   I. Pevehouse, Jon C.   II. Title.
    JZ1242.G652 2009
    327—dc22
                                                        2009011651

Please visit us at www.IRtext.com.

1 2 3 4 5 6 7 8 9 10—CRK—12 11 10 09

Longman
is an imprint of

www.pearsonhighered.com   ISBN-13: 978-0-205-72391-1
                           ISBN-10: 0-205-72391-8

Brief Contents

Detailed Contents

Note: Each chapter ends with a summary, key terms, and critical thinking questions.

Using the Icons in This Book
www.IRtext.com

 Podcast This icon represents the podcast for each chapter in which the authors discuss a key topic in the chapter using an example from recent history.

 Video These icons in each chapter direct you to the book's Companion Website, where you will find links to video clips. In addition, critical thinking questions follow each clip.

Online Practice Tests This icon at the end of each chapter refers students to the practice tests available at the Companion Website.

ONLINE PRACTICE TEST	
Take an online practice test at www.IRtext.com	❏ A ❏ B 🔑 C ❏ D

Preface

Today's students will graduate in an era of globalization in which no national economy stands alone. No event has made this clearer than the financial downturn that began in 2008 in the United States and quickly spread throughout the globe. Interconnections among states, societies, and individuals form an increasingly complex web of factors including identity, information, technology, and natural resources. But these interconnections involve more than just economic issues. The broader global phenomenon we are witnessing is the blurring of the traditional line between domestic and international issues. International issues increasingly pervade domestic politics and vice versa, whether the topic is immigration, global warming, the spread of disease, terrorism, or the wars in Iraq and Afghanistan.

Despite these increasing interconnections, many students begin college misinformed about basic facts of international relations (IR), such as the extent of poverty in the global South, levels of foreign assistance given to the global South, and the trend toward fewer wars over the past two decades. An introductory textbook plays a key role in students' education about international affairs, and we have worked hard to make this one timely, accurate, visually appealing, and intellectually engaging. We hope this textbook can help a generation develop knowledge and critical thinking in order to find its voice and place in the changing world order.

IR is not only an important topic but also a fascinating one. The rich complexity of international relationships—political, economic, and cultural—provides a puzzle to try to understand. The puzzle is not only an intellectual challenge but also emotionally powerful. It contains human-scale stories in which the subject's grand themes—war and peace, intergroup conflict and community, integration and division, poverty and development—play out.

New to the Fifth Edition

This fifth edition includes important updates and a new feature while building on the new concepts and material from the fourth edition.

We retain our focus on streamlining and clarifying the most important points in the book. We begin with three "core principles"—dominance, reciprocity, and identity—that offer potential solutions to the central recurring problem in IR, the collective goods problem in which autonomous actors have no government to regulate their interactions. We have increased the integration of the core principles throughout the book. In particular, each "Big Picture" feature now focuses on an issue relating to one of the principles. This feature focuses attention on the key point of each chapter. The related podcasts are completely new and continue to discuss key current events through the lens of these core principles, providing students real-world applications of the ideas presented in each chapter.

We have retained the insert section from the previous update, authored by the relief agency Oxfam America. Because poverty, development, and the state of the developing world continue to play a central part in debates over globalization, we wanted to add another voice to the discussion of this key topic. With the Oxfam insert, students can engage some of the key issues of IR, such as trade, aid, and poverty, from the perspective of an NGO with decades of practical experience working in the global South.

We have added a new Policy Perspectives box—Luis Moreno-Ocampo, chief prosecutor at the International Criminal Court. We have completely updated all tables and figures with the most recently available data. This is particularly important for this edition since over the past year, international institutions continued to change their methodologies for generating data. To take two important examples: UNAIDS revised their estimates of HIV/AIDS prevalence rates across the globe, adjusting their figures by as much as 30 percent; and last year the World Bank adjusted how Purchasing Power Parity (PPP) rates were calculated, leading to changes in GDP and per capita GDP in the developing world. Students will now have the most accurate and up-to-date information on these important topics.

This new edition updates key current events in the world, including the global economic downturn and its implications for global trade and development; the new policy directions of the Obama administration; the terrorist attacks in Mumbai, India; continued violence and strife in Afghanistan and Iraq; Iran's confrontation with the UN Security Council over nuclear weapons; the long-delayed deployment of UN peacekeepers in Darfur (Sudan); the stalled negotiations over world trade issues; the continuing efforts to adopt a new EU constitution; and renewed violence between Israel and Palestinians.

Structure of the Book

This book's aim is to present the current state of knowledge in IR in a comprehensive and accessible way—to provide a map of the subject covering its various research communities in a logical order. Common core principles—dominance, reciprocity, and identity—unify the book by showing how theoretical models apply across the range of topics in international security and political economy.

The overall structure of this book follows substantive topics, first in international security and then in international political economy. Chapter 1 introduces the study of IR; explains the collective goods problem and the core principles of dominance, reciprocity, and identity; and provides some geographical and historical context for the subject. Chapters 2 and 3 lay out the various theoretical approaches to IR: realist theories, liberal theories, and social theories (constructivist, postmodern, Marxist, peace studies, and gender theories). Chapter 4 introduces the main sources of international conflict and the conditions and manner in which such conflicts lead to war, terrorism, and other forms of violence. Chapter 5 introduces theoretical concepts in political economy (showing how theories of international security translate into IPE issue areas) and discusses trade relations and the politics of international money, banking, and multinational business operations. Chapter 6 shows how international organizations and law, especially the United Nations and the European Union, have evolved to become major global and regional influences and how human rights have become increasingly important. Chapter 7 addresses global North-South relations and population growth and considers alternatives for third world economic development in the context of international business, debt, and foreign aid. Chapter 8 shows how environmental politics, telecommunications, and cultural exchange expand international bargaining and interdependence.

Pedagogical Elements

In a subject such as IR, in which knowledge is tentative and empirical developments can overtake theories, critical thinking is a key skill for college students to develop. At various points in the text, conclusions are left open-ended to let students reason their way through an issue, and in addition to the critical thinking questions at the end of each chapter, the boxed features support deeper and more focused critical thinking.

The one-page "Policy Perspectives" feature in each chapter places students in the decision-making perspective of a national leader. This feature bridges international relations theory to policy problems while demonstrating the trade-offs often present in political decision making and highlighting the interconnectedness of foreign and domestic politics. The "Careers in International Relations" feature at the beginning of this book (pp. xviii–xxi) helps students think about job possibilities in the field. These pages, devoted to careers in nongovernmental organizations, government and diplomacy, international business, and teaching and research, respond to the question "How will this class help me find a job?" and include books and Web sites to further pursue the issue.

Many people find information—especially abstract concepts—easier to grasp when linked with pictures. Thus, the book uses color photographs extensively to illustrate important points. Photo captions reinforce main themes from each section of the text and link them with the scenes pictured, including in this edition many 2008 and 2009 photos.

Students use different learning styles. Students who are visual learners should find not only the photos but also the many color graphics especially useful. They can also learn well from this book's extensive video program. Aural learners may learn especially well from the podcasts for each chapter, and those who learn well through interactive exercises can use the extensive resources on the book's Web site, especially the practice tests for each chapter. For book learners, this book incorporates an integrated study guide at each chapter's end. This guide includes a chapter summary, list of key terms, critical thinking questions, and a reminder to try the practice tests on the text's Companion Website and to listen to the authors' podcast for the chapter.

The use of quantitative data also encourages critical thinking. Basic data, presented simply and appropriately at a global level, allow students to form their own judgments and to reason through the implications of different policies and theories. The text uses global-level data (showing the whole picture), rounds off numbers to highlight what is important, and conveys information graphically where appropriate. In addition, we make available through this book's Web site the CIA's authoritative *World Factbook*, with extensive data on each country's economy, demography, government, and society.

Companion Website

By following the icons in the margins, students can use the online learning resources that are integrated with this book and available on the Companion Website at **www.IRtext.com** or **www.ablongman.com/goldstein.** There, they can take practice tests, go to videos illustrating key concepts, and download CIA data on the world's countries. To use these learning resources, go to **www.IRtext.com** and enter the page number from this book where an icon appears to automatically bring up the indicated materials. Instructors will also have access to downloadable instructor supplements, recommendations for using videos, and guides to incorporating Longman's many international relations readers and casebooks with this book.

Supplements

Longman is pleased to offer several resources to qualified adopters of *International Relations* and their students that will make teaching and learning from this book even more effective and enjoyable.

For Instructors and Students

MyPoliSciKit for International Relations This premium online learning companion features multimedia and interactive activities to help students make connections between concepts and current events. The book-specific assessments, video case studies, role-playing simulations, mapping exercises, *Financial Times* newsfeeds, current events quizzes, and politics blog encourage comprehension and critical thinking. With GradeTracker, instructors can easily follow students' work on the site and their progress on each activity. MyPoliSciKit is available at no additional charge when packaged with this book. To learn more, please visit **www.mypoliscikit.com**.

For Instructors

MyPoliSciKit Video Case Studies This DVD series contains video clips featured in the MyPoliSciKit case studies for this and other Longman political science titles. Featuring video from major news sources and providing reporting and insight on recent world affairs, this DVD helps instructors integrate current events into their courses by letting them use the clips as lecture launchers or discussion starters.

Instructor's Manual/Test Bank Written by Robert Breckinridge of Mount Aloysius College, this resource includes up-to-date chapter summaries, learning objectives, multiple-choice questions, true/false questions, and essay questions for classroom discussions. To download, please visit the Instructor Resource Center at **www.pearsonhighered.com/irc**.

Pearson MyTest is a powerful assessment generation program that includes all of the items in the instructor's manual/test bank. Questions and tests can be easily created, customized, and saved online and then printed, allowing instructors ultimate flexibility to manage assessments anytime and anywhere. To start using, please visit **www.pearsonmytest.com**.

PowerPoint Presentation Organized around a lecture outline, these electronic presentations contain photos, maps, figures, and tables from each chapter. To download, please visit the Instructor Resource Center at **www.pearsonhighered.com/irc**.

Transparency Masters This set of downloadable transparency masters contains all of the book's photos, maps, tables, and figures in full color.

For Students

Longman Atlas of World Issues Introduced and selected by Robert J. Art of Brandeis University and excerpted from the acclaimed Penguin Atlas Series, the *Longman Atlas of World Issues* is designed to help students understand the geography and major issues facing the world today, such as terrorism, debt, and HIV/AIDS. These thematic, full-color maps examine forces shaping politics today at a global level. Explanatory information accompanies each map to help students better grasp the concepts being shown and how they affect our world today. Available at no additional charge when packaged with this book.

The Penguin Dictionary of International Relations This indispensable reference by Graham Evans and Jeffrey Newnham includes hundreds of cross-referenced entries on the enduring and emerging theories, concepts, and events that are shaping the academic discipline of international relations and today's world politics. Available at a discount when packaged with this book.

Research and Writing in International Relations Written by Laura Roselle and Sharon Spray of Elon University, this brief and affordable guide provides the basic step-by-step process and essential resources that are needed to write political science papers that go beyond simple description and into more systematic and sophisticated inquiry. This text focuses on the key areas in which students need the most help: finding a topic, developing a question, reviewing literature, designing research, analyzing findings, and last, actually writing the paper. Available at a discount when packaged with this book.

Acknowledgments

Many scholars, colleagues, and friends have contributed ideas that influenced the various editions of this book. The book owes a special debt to the late Robert C. North, who suggested many years ago that the concepts of bargaining and leverage could be used to integrate IR theory across four levels of analysis. For help with military data issues, we thank the late Randall Forsberg. For suggestions, we thank our colleagues, and the students in our world politics classes. For help with the glossary, thanks to Louis Cooper. For help with data research, we thank Tana Johnson and Felicity Vabulas. Thanks to Mark Lilleleht for his assistance on the Careers feature. Finally, we appreciate the years of support we received from our colleague, teacher, and friend Deborah "Misty" Gerner, who passed away in 2006 and to whom this edition is dedicated.

The following reviewers made many useful suggestions:

Abdallah M. Battah, *Minnesota University*; Philip Baumann, *Minnesota State University Moorhead*; Robert G. Blanton, *University of Memphis*; Robert E. Breckinridge, *Mount Aloysius College*; Brian Champion, *Brigham Young University*; Gregory A. Cline, *Michigan State University*; Myles Clowers, *San Diego City College*; Cynthia Combs, *University of North Carolina at Charlotte*; Paul D'Anieri, *University of Florida*; Rekha Datta, *Monmouth University*; Louise K. Davidson-Schmich, *University of Miami*; Patricia Davis, *University of Notre Dame*; Debra DeLaet, *Drake University*; Elizabeth DeSombre, *Colby College*; June Teufel Dreyer, *University of Miami*; Larry Elowitz, *George College and State University*; Mark Elrod, *Harding University*; George Emerson, *Miami Dade Community College*; Mark Everingham, *University of Wisconsin–Green Bay*; Jonathan Galloway, *Lake Forest College*; Marc Genest, *University of Rhode Island*; the late Deborah J. Gerner, *University of Kansas*; Emily O. Goldman, *University of California, Davis*; Vicki Golich, *California State University, San Marcos*; Todd A. Good, *Grand View College*; Robert Gregg, *School of International Service, American University*; Louis Hayes, *University of Montana*; Max Hilaire, *Morgan State University*; Wolfgang Hirczy, *University of Houston*; Piper Hodson, *Saint Joseph's College*; Steven W. Hook, *University of Missouri*; Ted Hopf, *Ohio State University*; Mir Zohair Husain, *University of South Alabama*; Akira Ichikawa, *University of Lethbridge*; Matthias Kaelberer, *University of Memphis*; Joyce Kaufman, *University of Maryland at College Park*; John Keeler, *University of Washington*; Michael Kelley, *University of Central Arkansas*; Jane K. Kramer, *University of Oregon*; Mark Lagon, *Georgetown University*; William Lamkin, *Glendale Community College*; Wei-Chin Lee, *Wake Forest University*; Renée Marlin-Bennett, *Johns*

Hopkins University; James Meernick, University of North Texas; Karen Mingst, University of Kentucky; Richard Moore, Lewis-Clark State College; Layna Mosley, University of North Carolina; John W. Outland, University of Richmond; Mary Pettenger, Western Oregon University; Salvatore Prisco, Stevens Institute of Technology; David Rapkin, University of Nebraska at Lincoln; Edward Rhodes, Rutgers University; Leonard Riley, Pikes Peak Community College; Henry Schockley, Boston University; Vaughn Shannon, Wright State University; Paul Vicary, Florida International University; Thomas J. Volgy, University of Arizona; and David Wilsford, Institute of American Universities, France.

The errors, of course, remain our responsibility.

JOSHUA S. GOLDSTEIN
JON C. PEVEHOUSE

To the Student

The topics studied by scholars are like a landscape with many varied locations and terrains. This textbook is a map that can orient you to the main topics, debates, and issue areas in international relations. Scholars use specialized language to talk about their subjects. This text is a phrase book that can translate such lingo and explain the terms and concepts that scholars use to talk about international relations. However, IR is filled with many voices speaking many tongues. The text translates some of those voices—of presidents and professors, free traders and feminists—to help you sort out the contours of the subject and the state of knowledge about its various topics. In this fifth edition, we have especially tried to streamline and clarify this complex subject to help you not just understand but deeply understand International Relations. But ultimately the synthesis presented in this book is the authors' own. Both you and your professor may disagree with many points. Thus, this book is only a starting point for conversations and debates.

With map and phrase book in hand, you are ready to explore a fascinating world. The great changes in world politics in the past few years have made the writing of this textbook an exciting project. May you enjoy your own explorations of this realm.

J. S. G.
J. C. P.

A Note on Nomenclature

In international relations, names are politically sensitive: different actors may call a territory or an event by different names. This book cannot resolve such conflicts; it has adopted the following naming conventions for the sake of consistency. The United Kingdom of Great Britain (England, Scotland, Wales) and Northern Ireland is called Britain. Burma, renamed Myanmar by its military government, is referred to as Burma. The 1991 U.S.-led multinational military campaign that retook Kuwait after Iraq's 1990 invasion is called the Gulf War. The war between Iran and Iraq in the 1980s is called the Iran-Iraq War. The country of Bosnia and Herzegovina is generally shortened to Bosnia (with apologies to Herzegovinians). The former Yugoslav Republic of Macedonia is called Macedonia. The People's Republic of China is referred to as China. We refer to the Democratic Republic of the Congo, or DRC (formerly Zaire), simply as Democratic Congo. Elsewhere, country names follow common usage, dropping formal designations such as "Republic of."

Jobs in Government and Diplomacy

BENEFITS AND COSTS Both governments and intergovernmental organizations (IGOs) play key roles in international relations and employ millions of people with interests in IR.

Despite differences between IGOs and governments, there are many similarities. Both are hierarchical organizations, with competitive and regulated working environments. Whether in the U.S. State Department or the UN, entrance into and promotion in these organizations is regulated by exams, performance evaluations, and tenure with the organization.

Another similarity lies in the challenges of being pulled in many directions concerning policies. Governments face competing pressures of public opinion, constituencies, and interests groups—each with distinct policy opinions. IGOs also deal with interest groups (such as NGOs), but an IGO's constituents are states, which in many cases disagree among themselves.

Many employees of IGOs or governments thrive on making decisions that influence policies. Both work environments also attract co-workers with deep interests in international affairs, and the resulting networks of contacts can bring professional and intellectual rewards. Finally, jobs in governments or IGOs may involve travel or living abroad, which many enjoy.

However, promotion can be slow and frustrating. Usually, only individuals with advanced degrees or technical specializations achieve non-entry level positions. It can take years to climb within the organization and the process may involve working in departments far from your original interests. In addition, both IGOs and governments are bureaucracies with formal rules and procedures, requiring great patience. Employees often express frustration that initiative and "thinking outside the box" are not rewarded.

SKILLS TO HONE The key to working in IGOs or government is to get your foot in the door. Be flexible and willing to take entry positions that are not exactly in your area of interest. For example, the State Department is only one of many parts of the U.S. government that deal with IR. Do not assume that to work in foreign affairs, one must be a diplomat.

Foreign language training is also important, especially for work in large IGOs with many field offices. The ability to work well in groups and to network within and across organizations is an important asset. People who can strengthen lines of communication can gain support from many places in an organization.

Finally, strong analytical and writing abilities are extremely important. Both IGOs and governments deal with massive amounts of information daily. The ability to analyze information (even including mathematical or computational analysis) and to write clear, concise interpretations will make one invaluable.

RESOURCES

Shawn Dorman. *Inside a U.S. Embassy: How the Foreign Service Works for America*. 2nd ed. Washington, DC: American Foreign Service Assoc., 2003.

Linda Fasulo. *An Insider's Guide to the UN*. New Haven: Yale University Press, 2005.

http://jobs.un.org
http://www.state.gov/p/io/empl/
http://www.usajobs.opm.gov/EI10.asp

Jobs in International Business

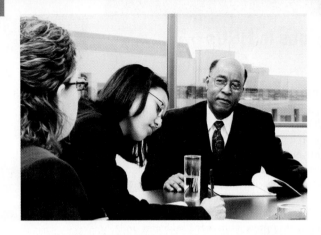

BENEFITS AND COSTS As the pace and scope of globalization have accelerated, opportunities to work in international business have blossomed. For many large companies, the domestic/global distinction has ceased to exist. This new context provides opportunities and challenges for potential employees.

Careers in international business offer many advantages. Business jobs can pay substantially more than those in governments or NGOs and can open opportunities to travel extensively and network globally. Foreign-based jobs mean relocation to another country to work and immerse oneself in another culture.

However, such a career choice also has potential costs. Many jobs require extensive hours, grueling travel, and frequent relocation. As with any job, promotion and advancement may fall victim to external circumstances such as global business cycles. And these jobs can be especially hard on families.

International opportunities arise in numerous business sectors. Banking, marketing (public relations), sales, and computing/telecommunications have seen tremendous growth in recent years. These jobs fall into three broad categories: (1) those located domestically, yet involving significant interactions with firms abroad; (2) domestic jobs working for foreign-based companies; and (3) those based abroad, for foreign or domestic firms.

SKILLS TO HONE One key to landing in the international business world is to develop two families of skills: those related to international relations and those related to business operations. Traditional MBA (Masters in Business Administration) and business school programs will be helpful for all three types of jobs, yet for jobs based abroad, employers often also look for a broader set of skills taught in economics, political science, and communications. Thus, not only traditional business skills, but language and cultural skills, are essential. Employers look for those who have knowledge of a country's human and economic geography as well as its culture. Experience with study abroad, especially including working abroad, can help show an ability to adapt and function well in other cultures. Strong analytical and especially writing abilities also matter greatly to employers.

Research also helps in landing a job. Employers often look for knowledge of a particular industry or company, in order to make the best use of an employee's language and cultural skills. Of course, while experience in non-international business never hurts, be mindful that the practices, customs, and models of business in one country may not apply well abroad. Cross-cultural skills combined with substantive business knowledge in order to translate the operational needs of companies from the business world to the global realm are highly valued.

RESOURCES

Edward J. Halloran. *Careers in International Business*. 2nd ed. NY: McGraw-Hill, 2003.

Deborah Penrith, ed. *The Directory of Jobs and Careers Abroad*. 12th ed. Oxford, UK: Vacation Work Publications, 2005.

http://www.rileyguide.com/internat.html
http://www.jobsabroad.com/search.cfm
http://www.transitionsabroad.com/listings/work/careers/index.shtml

Jobs in NGOs

BENEFITS AND COSTS Nearly 30,000 NGOs exist and that number grows daily. Thousands of individuals are interested in working in these organizations. Although all NGOs are different, many perform multiple functions: working in developing countries regarding a variety of issues; public outreach at home and abroad; lobbying governments to change their policies; designing projects to solve problems and attempting to find funding for their implementation.

Working for an NGO has many benefits. Workers often find themselves surrounded by others with similar concerns: improving the environment, protecting human rights, advancing economic development, or promoting better health. The spirit of camaraderie can be exhilarating and rewarding.

While working for an NGO can be extremely rewarding personally, it is rarely rewarding financially. Most NGOs are nonprofit operations that pay workers meagerly for long hours. Moreover, many smaller NGOs engage in a constant fight for funding from governments, think tanks, private foundations, or individuals. The process of fundraising can be quite time consuming.

Despite the large number of NGOs, relatively low pay, and long hours, finding a job with an NGO can be difficult. One key is to be specific. Try to narrow down your interests in terms of substantive areas (for example, human rights, environment) and geographic region. Also think about whether you want to work in your own country or abroad. Positions abroad may be more rewarding but are in lower supply and higher demand.

SKILLS TO HONE NGOs are looking for self-starters. Most have few resources for training. Basic office skills (for example, computer expertise) are essential, but employees also need to cover a range of duties. Anything and everything is in your job description. Writing and communication skills are key, especially when fundraising is part of the job. Foreign language skills also matter since many NGOs maintain or work with field offices abroad.

Often, NGOs ask potential employees to volunteer for a period while they train, before being hired. Increasingly, some companies place workers in an NGO or volunteer opportunity for a price. By paying to work, you can gain a probationary period to develop your skills and familiarize yourself with the operation before going on the payroll.

Finally, in cities where NGOs cluster (for example, Washington, D.C.), personal networks play an important role in finding good opportunities. Workers often move from one organization to another. For this reason, many volunteer or accept jobs with NGOs not in their immediate area of interest to gain experience and contacts, which can help future career advancement.

RESOURCES

Sherry Mueller. Careers in Nonprofit and Educational Organizations. In *Careers in International Affairs*, 7th ed. Washington, DC: Georgetown School of Foreign Service, 2003.

Richard M. King. *From Making a Profit to Making a Difference: How to Launch Your New Career in Nonprofits*. River Forest, IL: Planning/ Communications, 2000.

www.internships-usa.com
www.idealist.org
www.wango.org/resources/NGO_directory.htm

Jobs in Education and Research

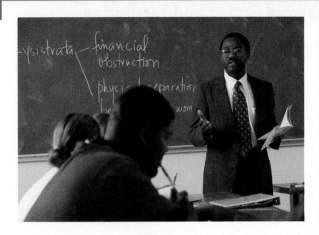

BENEFITS AND COSTS People follow various paths to an interest in teaching and researching in the field of International Relations. Your own professor or instructor is likely to have a unique story about how he or she became interested in international affairs.

One advantage of an academic and research career, whether at a teaching-oriented institution or a large research university, is intellectual freedom. One can spend a career approaching a variety of topics that are interesting and constantly evolving, that may involve travel abroad for fieldwork, and that may let you network with hundreds of colleagues interested in similar topics.

Most research positions (for example, in think tanks) are different in two respects. First, these jobs often give more direction to an individual in terms of the research to be performed. Second, there is little or no teaching involved. Still, for those interested in IR research, such jobs can result in a wider dissemination of one's work to a broader audience that often includes policy makers.

To teach IR at an advanced level or to perform research for think tanks and government agencies usually requires an advanced degree—nearly always a master's degree, often a doctorate (Ph.D.). Master's degree programs often take between one and two years, while a Ph.D. in international relations usually takes a minimum of five years. Often, students take time off between their undergraduate and graduate educations to travel internationally or get work experience to hone their interests. Of course, many students never return to extend their education if they find a job that allows them to achieve their personal and career goals.

Finally, in completing most advanced degrees, a large amount of self-direction is necessary. Coursework is only one part of master's or Ph.D. programs: a thesis is also required. Writing a thesis requires you to work on your own time schedule, balancing other duties (such as work as a teaching or research assistant) that can easily crowd out your own work. Many who complete the coursework for an advanced degree do not finish their thesis or take many years to do so.

SKILLS TO HONE Whether one wants to pursue an advanced degree for the purposes of teaching in an academic setting or engaging in applied research, there are important skill sets to develop. First and foremost is critical thinking. Scholars and researchers must consider many alternatives as answers to questions, while being able to evaluate the validity or importance of those alternatives. Second is writing. Before, during, and after producing a thesis, writing is a key skill for academics and researchers. Finally, think about developing a set of applied skills to use as a toolbox while analyzing questions. The contents of this toolbox might include other languages to facilitate fieldwork abroad. It could include statistics and data skills to facilitate quantitative analysis. Or it could include mathematics to use game theoretic models. No matter which tools you emphasize, specialized skills will help you answer research questions, whether as part of the academy or in a private or governmental research organization.

RESOURCES

The Chronicle of Higher Education (weekly). Online at chronicle.com/.

American Political Science Association. *Earning a PhD in Political Science.* 4th ed. Washington, DC, 2004.

Ernest J. Wilson. Is There Really a Scholar-Practitioner Gap? An Institutional Analysis. *PS: Political Science and Politics,* January 2007.

http://www.apsanet.org
http://www.apsia.org
http://www.isanet.org

World States and Territories

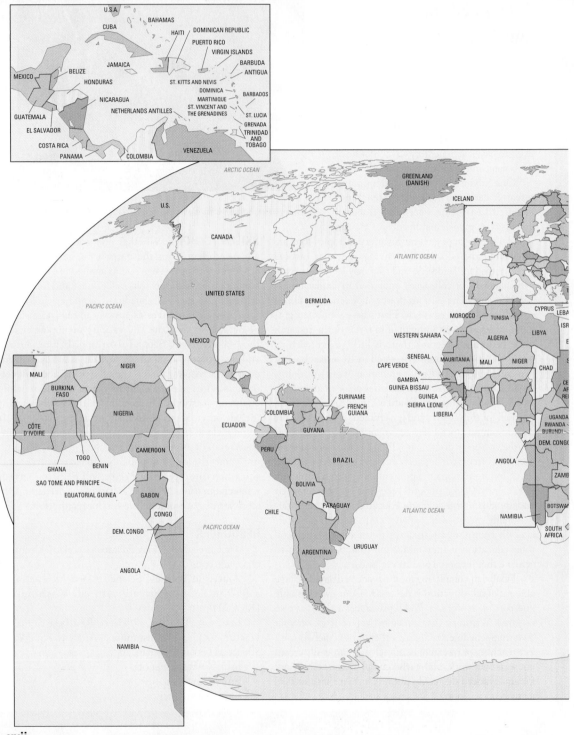

U.S.A.
BAHAMAS
CUBA
HAITI
DOMINICAN REPUBLIC
PUERTO RICO
VIRGIN ISLANDS
JAMAICA
BARBUDA
BELIZE
ANTIGUA
MEXICO
HONDURAS
ST. KITTS AND NEVIS
DOMINICA
NICARAGUA
MARTINIQUE
BARBADOS
GUATEMALA
NETHERLANDS ANTILLES
ST. VINCENT AND THE GRENADINES
ST. LUCIA
EL SALVADOR
GRENADA
TRINIDAD AND TOBAGO
COSTA RICA
PANAMA
COLOMBIA
VENEZUELA

ARCTIC OCEAN
GREENLAND (DANISH)
ICELAND
U.S.
CANADA
ATLANTIC OCEAN
PACIFIC OCEAN
UNITED STATES
BERMUDA
CYPRUS
LEBA
MOROCCO
TUNISIA
ISR
WESTERN SAHARA
ALGERIA
LIBYA
E
MEXICO
SENEGAL
MAURITANIA
CAPE VERDE
MALI
NIGER
CHAD
MALI
NIGER
GAMBIA
GUINEA BISSAU
CE
AF
GUINEA
RE
SIERRA LEONE
SURINAME
BURKINA FASO
LIBERIA
FRENCH GUIANA
UGANDA
CÔTE D'IVOIRE
NIGERIA
COLOMBIA
RWANDA
BURUNDI
DEM. CONGO
ECUADOR
GUYANA
TOGO
CAMEROON
BENIN
ANGOLA
GHANA
PERU
BRAZIL
ZAMB
SAO TOME AND PRINCIPE
EQUATORIAL GUINEA
GABON
CONGO
BOLIVIA
BOTSWA
DEM. CONGO
PARAGUAY
NAMIBIA
CHILE
ATLANTIC OCEAN
SOUTH AFRICA
ANGOLA
PACIFIC OCEAN
URUGUAY
NAMIBIA
ARGENTINA

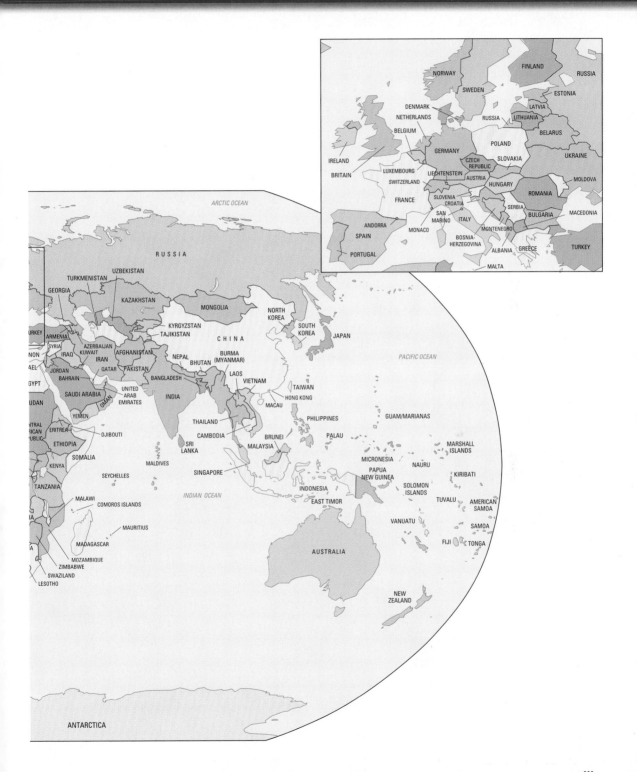

ARCTIC OCEAN

RUSSIA

TURKMENISTAN UZBEKISTAN
GEORGIA
KAZAKHSTAN
MONGOLIA
NORTH KOREA
TURKEY KYRGYZSTAN SOUTH KOREA
ARMENIA TAJIKISTAN JAPAN
SYRIA AZERBAIJAN C H I N A
NON IRAQ KUWAIT AFGHANISTAN
AEL IRAN NEPAL BURMA (MYANMAR)
JORDAN QATAR PAKISTAN BHUTAN
EGYPT BAHRAIN BANGLADESH LAOS
SAUDI ARABIA UNITED ARAB EMIRATES INDIA VIETNAM TAIWAN
UDAN OMAN HONG KONG
YEMEN MACAU
CENTRAL RICAN PUBLIC ERITREA THAILAND PHILIPPINES
ETHIOPIA DJIBOUTI CAMBODIA BRUNEI
SOMALIA SRI LANKA MALAYSIA
KENYA MALDIVES
SEYCHELLES SINGAPORE
TANZANIA INDONESIA
INDIAN OCEAN EAST TIMOR
MALAWI
COMOROS ISLANDS
MAURITIUS
MADAGASCAR
MOZAMBIQUE AUSTRALIA
ZIMBABWE
SWAZILAND
LESOTHO

PACIFIC OCEAN

GUAM/MARIANAS

PALAU MARSHALL ISLANDS
MICRONESIA NAURU KIRIBATI
PAPUA NEW GUINEA
SOLOMON ISLANDS
TUVALU AMERICAN SAMOA
VANUATU SAMOA
FIJI TONGA

NEW ZEALAND

ANTARCTICA

NORWAY FINLAND RUSSIA
SWEDEN ESTONIA
DENMARK LATVIA
NETHERLANDS RUSSIA LITHUANIA
BELGIUM POLAND BELARUS
GERMANY UKRAINE
IRELAND CZECH REPUBLIC SLOVAKIA
BRITAIN LUXEMBOURG LIECHTENSTEIN AUSTRIA HUNGARY MOLDOVA
SWITZERLAND SLOVENIA ROMANIA
FRANCE CROATIA SERBIA
SAN MARINO ITALY BULGARIA MACEDONIA
ANDORRA MONACO MONTENEGRO
SPAIN BOSNIA-HERZEGOVINA ALBANIA GREECE TURKEY
PORTUGAL MALTA

xxiii

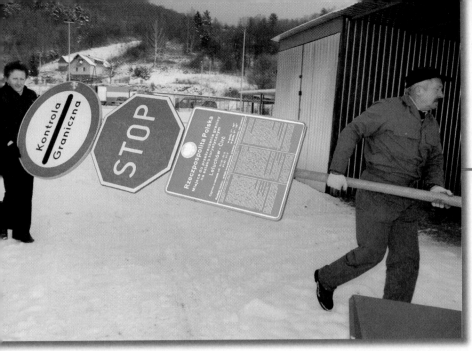

Dismantling Polish-Slovakian border checkpoints as Europe integrates, 2007.

CHAPTER 1

The Globalization of International Relations

Globalization, International Relations, and Daily Life

International relations is a fascinating topic because it concerns peoples and cultures throughout the world. The scope and complexity of the interactions among these groups make international relations a challenging subject to master.

Narrowly defined, the field of **international relations (IR)** concerns the relationships among the world's governments. But these relationships cannot be understood in isolation. They are closely connected with other actors (such as international organizations, multinational corporations, and individuals); with other social structures (including economics, culture, and domestic politics); and with geographical and historical influences. These elements together power the central trend in IR today—globalization.

CHAPTER OUTLINE

- **Globalization, International Relations, and Daily Life**

- **Actors and Influences**

- **Global Geography**

- **The Evolving International System**

THE BIG PICTURE

DOMINANCE

RECIPROCITY

IDENTITY

Each chapter of this book contains many facts, theories, and examples. To help you sort out the most important points in this mass of information, these "big picture" boxes at the start of each chapter highlight a key central theme.

This first chapter discusses the actors in IR, the world's regions, and the history that shapes present-day IR. In explaining conflicts in IR, the central concept is the "collective goods problem" (p. 3). This recurring problem results when two or more members of a group share an interest in some outcome of value to them all, but have conflicting individual interests when it comes to achieving that valued outcome. For example, the world's countries share a desire to avoid global warming, but each one benefits from burning fossil fuels to run its economy. Within domestic societies, governments solve collective goods problems by forcing the members of society to contribute to common goals, such as by paying taxes. In international affairs, no such government exists. Three core principles—dominance, reciprocity, and identity—offer different alternatives to solve the collective goods problem.

To hear the authors of this book discuss this issue, download the "IR Talk" podcast for Chapter 1 from www.IRtext.com.

PODCAST

VIDEO

Ground Zero Third Anniversary

This icon indicates videos on the Companion Website (see p. ii).

Two key events of recent years reflect globalization. The terrorists who plotted and carried out the September 11, 2001, attacks used the Internet to assist in planning, coordination, and fundraising for the attacks. And the global economic recession of 2008–2009, which began with a collapse of the U.S. home mortgage market, spread quickly to other nations. Highly integrated global financial markets created a ripple effect across the globe. Thus, two hallmarks of globalization—expanding communications technology and integrated markets—facilitated events that directly impacted our daily lives.

Not only large-scale events influence our daily lives. The prospects for getting jobs after graduation depend on the global economy and international economic competition. Those jobs also are more likely than ever to entail international travel, sales, or communication. And the rules of the world trading system affect the goods that students consume every day, such as electronics, clothes, and gasoline.

Globalization has distinct positive impacts on our daily lives as well. As technology advances, the world is shrinking year by year. Better communication and transportation capabilities constantly expand the ordinary person's contact with people, products, and ideas from other countries. Globalization is internationalizing us.

In addition to feeling the influence of globalization and international relations on our daily lives, individual citizens can influence the world as well. Often, international relations is portrayed as a distant and abstract ritual conducted by a small group of people such as presidents, generals, and diplomats. Although leaders do play a major role in international affairs, many other people participate as well. College students and other citizens participate in international relations every time they vote in an election or work on a political campaign, buy a product or service traded on world markets, and watch the news. The choices we make in our daily lives ultimately affect the world we live in.

The purpose of this book is to introduce the field of IR, to organize what is known and theorized about IR, and to convey the key concepts used by political scientists to discuss relations among nations. This first chapter defines IR as a field of study, introduces the actors of interest, and reviews the geographical and historical aspects of globalization within which IR occurs.

Core Principles

The field of IR reflects the world's complexity, and IR scholars use many theories, concepts, and buzzwords in trying to describe and explain it. Underneath this complexity, however, lie a few basic principles that shape the field. We will lay out the range of theories and approaches in Chapters 2 and 3, but here we will present the most central ideas as free from jargon as possible.

TOUCHED BY WAR

IR affects our lives in many ways. This woman's boyfriend died in Iraq in 2006.

IR revolves around one key problem: How can a group—such as two or more nations—serve its *collective* interests when doing so requires its members to forgo their *individual* interests? For example, every country has an interest in stopping global warming, a goal that can be achieved only by many countries acting together. Yet each country also has an individual interest in burning fossil fuels to keep its economy going. Similarly, all members of a military alliance benefit from the strength of the alliance, but each member separately has an interest in minimizing its own contributions in troops and money. Individual nations can advance their own short-term interests by seizing territory militarily, cheating on trade agreements, and refusing to contribute to international efforts such as peacekeeping or vaccination campaigns. But if all nations acted this way, they would find themselves worse off, in a chaotic and vicious environment where mutual gains from cooperating on issues of security and trade would disappear.

This problem of shared interests versus conflicting interests among members of a group goes by various names in various contexts—the problem of "collective action," "free riding," "burden sharing," the "tragedy of the commons," or the "prisoner's dilemma." We will refer to the general case as the **collective goods problem,** that is, the problem of how to provide something that benefits all members of a group regardless of what each member contributes to it.

VIDEO

Climate Change and the Collective Goods Problem

ALL TOGETHER NOW

Collective goods are provided to all members of a group regardless of their individual contributions, just as these migrant workers crossing the Sahara desert in Niger in 2006 all depend on the truck's progress even while perhaps jostling for position among themselves. In many issue areas, such as global warming, the international community of nations is similarly interdependent. However, the provision of collective goods presents difficult dilemmas as players seek to maximize their own share of benefits.

In general, collective goods are easier to provide in small groups than in large ones. In a small group, the cheating (or free riding) of one member is harder to conceal, has a greater impact on the overall collective good, and is easier to punish. The advantage of small groups helps explain the importance of the great power system in international security affairs and of the G8 (Group of Eight) industrialized countries in economic matters.[1]

The collective goods problem occurs in all groups and societies, but is particularly acute in international affairs because each nation is sovereign, with no central authority such as a world government to enforce on individual nations the necessary measures to provide for the common good. By contrast, in domestic politics *within* countries, a government can force individuals to contribute in ways that do not serve their individual self-interest, such as by paying taxes or paying to install antipollution equipment on vehicles and factories. If individuals do not comply, the government can punish them.

Although this solution is far from perfect—cheaters and criminals sometimes are not caught, and governments sometimes abuse their power—it mostly works well enough to keep societies going.

Three basic principles—which we call dominance, reciprocity, and identity—offer possible solutions to the core problem of getting individuals to cooperate for the common good without a central authority to make them do so (see Table 1.1). These three principles are fundamental across the social sciences, and recur in disciplines as diverse as the study of animal societies, child development, social psychology, anthropology, and economics, as well as political science. To explain each principle, we will apply the three principles to a small-scale human example and an IR example.

---

[1] The G8 meets without Russia as the G7 when foreign ministers discuss economic and financial matters, and as the G8 when state leaders meet on political issues. For simplicity, we refer only to the "G8" throughout this book.

TABLE 1.1 Core Principles for Solving Collective Goods Problems

Principle	Advantages	Drawbacks
⬍ Dominance	Order, Stability, Predictability	Oppression, Resentment
⇄ Reciprocity	Incentives for Mutual Cooperation	Downward Spirals, Complex Accounting
⤙ Identity	Sacrifice for Group, Redefine Interests	Demonizing an Out-Group

Dominance   The principle of **dominance** solves the collective goods problem by establishing a power hierarchy in which those at the top control those below—a bit like a government but without an actual government. Instead of fighting constantly over who gets scarce resources, the members of a group can just fight occasionally over position in the "status hierarchy." Then social conflicts such as who gets resources are resolved automatically in favor of the higher-ranking actor. Fights over dominance position have scripted rules that minimize, to some extent, the harm inflicted on the group members. Symbolic acts of submission and dominance reinforce an ever-present status hierarchy. Staying on top of a status hierarchy does not depend on strength alone, though it helps. Rather, the top actor may be the one most adept at forming and maintaining alliances among the group's more capable members. Dominance is complex, and not just a matter of brute force.

In international relations, the principle of dominance underlies the great power system, in which a handful of countries dictate the rules for all the others. Sometimes a so-called *hegemon* or superpower stands atop the great powers as the dominant nation. The UN Security Council, in which the world's five strongest military powers hold a veto, reflects the dominance principle.

The advantage of the dominance solution to the collective goods problem is that, like a government, it forces members of a group to contribute to the common good. It minimizes open conflict within the group. However, the disadvantage is that this stability comes at a cost of constant oppression of, and resentment by, the lower-ranking members in the status hierarchy. Also, conflicts over position in the hierarchy can occasionally harm the group's stability and well-being, such as when challenges to the top position lead to serious fights. In the case of international relations, the great power system and the hegemony of a superpower can provide relative peace and stability for decades on end but then can break down into costly wars among the great powers.

Reciprocity   The principle of **reciprocity** solves the collective goods problem by rewarding behavior that contributes to the group and punishing behavior that pursues self-interest at the expense of the group. Reciprocity is very easy to understand and can be "enforced" without any central authority, making it a robust way to get individuals to cooperate for the common good.

But reciprocity operates in both the positive realm ("You scratch my back and I'll scratch yours") and the negative ("An eye for an eye, a tooth for a tooth"). A disadvantage of reciprocity as a solution to the collective goods problem is that it can lead to a downward spiral as each side punishes what it believes to be negative acts by the other. Psychologically, most people overestimate their own good intentions and underestimate the value of the actions of their opponents or rivals. To avoid tit-for-tat escalations of conflict, one or both parties must act generously to get the relationship moving in a good direction.

In international relations, reciprocity forms the basis of most of the norms (habits; expectations) and institutions in the international system. Many central arrangements in IR, such as World Trade Organization agreements, explicitly recognize reciprocity as the linchpin of cooperation. For instance, if one country opens its markets to another's goods, the other opens its markets in return. On the negative side, reciprocity fuels arms races as each side responds to the other's buildup of weapons. But it also allows arms control agreements and other step-by-step conflict-resolution measures, as two sides match each other's actions in backing away from the brink of war.

Identity   A third potential solution to the collective goods problem lies in the identities of participants as members of a community. Although the dominance and reciprocity principles act on the idea of achieving individual self-interest (by taking what you can, or by mutually beneficial arrangements), the **identity** principle does not rely on self-interest. On the contrary, members of an identity community care about the interests of others in the community enough to sacrifice their own interests to benefit others. The roots of this principle lie in the family, the extended family, and the kinship group. But this potential is not limited to the close family; it can be generalized to any identity community that one feels a part of. As members of a family care about each other, so do members of an ethnic group, a gender group, a nation, or the world's scientists. In each case, individual members will accept solutions to collective goods problems that do not give them the best deal as individuals, because the benefits are "all in the family," so to speak. A biologist retiring from a rich American university may give away lab equipment to a biologist in a poor country because they share an identity as scientists. A computer scientist from India may return home to work for lower pay after receiving training in Canada, in order to help the community he or she cares about. Millions of people contribute to international disaster relief funds after tsunamis, earthquakes, or hurricanes because of a shared identity as members of the community of human beings.

In IR, identity communities play important roles in overcoming difficult collective goods problems, including the issue of who contributes to development assistance, world health, and UN peacekeeping missions. The relatively large foreign aid contributions of Scandinavian countries, or the high Canadian participation in peacekeeping, cannot be explained well by self-interest, but arise from these countries' self-defined identities as members of the international community. Even in military force and diplomacy (where dominance and reciprocity, respectively, rule the day), the shared identities of military professionals and of diplomats—each with shared traditions and expectations—can take the edge off conflicts. And military alliances also mix identity politics with raw self-interest, as shown by the unusual strength of the U.S.-British alliance, which shared interests alone cannot explain as well as shared identity does.

Nonstate actors, such as nongovernmental organizations or terrorist networks, also rely on identity politics to a great extent. The increasing roles of these actors—which include feminist organizations, churches, jihadists, and multinational corporations—have brought the identity principle to greater prominence in IR theory in recent years.

An Everyday Example   To sum up the three core principles, imagine that you have two good friends, a man and a woman, who are in a romantic relationship. They love each other and enjoy the other's company, but they come to you for help with a problem: When they go out together, the man likes to go to the opera, whereas the woman enjoys going to boxing matches. (This is loosely based on a game theory scenario called "Battle of the Sexes.") Because of your training in international relations, you quickly recognize this as a collective goods problem in which the shared interest is spending time together and the conflicting individual interests are watching opera and watching boxing. (Of course, you know that the behavior of states is more complicated than that of individuals, but put that aside for a moment.) You might approach this problem in any of three ways.

First, you could say, "Traditionally, relationships work best when the man wears the pants. For thousands of years the man has made the decision and the woman has followed it. I suggest you do the same, and buy season tickets to the opera." This would be a dominance solution. It could be a very stable solution, if the woman cares more about spending time with her true love than she cares about opera or boxing. It would be a simple solution that would settle all future conflicts. It would give one party everything he wants, and the other party some of what she wants (love, company, a stable relationship). This might be better for both of them than spending all their evenings arguing about where to go out. On the other hand, this solution might leave the woman permanently resentful at the manifestly unequal nature of the outcome. She might feel her love for her partner diminished, over time, by a longing for respect and a nostalgia for boxing. She might even meet another man who likes her *and* likes boxing.

Second, you could say, "Look, instead of fighting all the time, why don't you establish a pattern and trade off going to boxing one time and opera the next." This would be a reciprocity solution. You could set up agreements, accounting systems, and shared expectations to govern the implementation of this seemingly simple solution. For example, they could go to boxing on Friday nights and opera on Saturday nights. But what if opera season is shorter than boxing season? Then perhaps they would go to opera more often during its season and boxing more often when opera is out of season. What if one of them is out of town on a Friday night? Does that night count anyway or does it earn a credit for later? Or does the one who is in town go out alone? What if the man *hates* boxing but the woman only mildly dislikes opera? Do you set up a schedule of two operas for each boxing match to keep each side equally happy or unhappy? Clearly, reciprocity solutions can become very complicated (just look at the world trade rules in Chapter 5, for example), and they require constant monitoring to see if obligations are being met and cheating is being avoided. Your friends might find it an irritant in their relationship to keep close track of who owes whom a night at the opera or the boxing match.

Third, you could say, "Who cares about opera or boxing? The point is that you love each other and want to be together. Get past the superficial issues and strengthen the core feelings that brought you together. Then it won't matter where you go or what you're watching." This would be an identity solution. This approach could powerfully resolve your friends' conflict and leave them both much happier. Over time, one partner might actually begin to prefer the other's favorite activity after more exposure—leading to a change in identity. On the other hand, after a while self-interest could creep back in, because that loving feeling might seem even happier with a boxing match or opera to watch. Indeed, one partner can subtly exploit the other's commitment to get past the superficial conflicts. "What's it matter as long as we're together," she says, "and oh, look, there's a good boxing match tonight!" Sometimes the identity principle operates more powerfully in the short term than the long term: the soldier who volunteers to defend the homeland might begin to feel taken advantage of after months or years on the front line, and the American college student who gives money once to tsunami victims may not want to keep giving year after year to malaria victims.

An IR Example   Now consider the problem of nuclear proliferation. All countries share an interest in the collective good of peace and stability, which is hard to achieve in a world where more and more countries make more and more nuclear weapons. Within a society, if individuals acquire dangerous weapons, the government can take them away to keep everyone safe. But in the society of nations, no such central authority exists. In 2006, North Korea tested its first nuclear bomb and Iran continues uranium enrichment that could lead to one—defying UN resolutions in both cases.

One approach to nuclear proliferation legitimizes these weapons' ownership by just the few most powerful countries. The "big five" with the largest nuclear arsenals hold veto power on the UN Security Council. Through agreements like the Non-Proliferation Treaty (NPT) and the Proliferation Security Initiative, the existing nuclear powers actively try to keep their exclusive hold on these weapons and prevent smaller nations from getting them. This is a dominance approach. In 2003, when the United States thought Iraq's Saddam Hussein might have an active nuclear weapons program, as he had a decade earlier, it invaded Iraq and overthrew its government. Similarly, in 1982, when Iraq had begun working toward a nuclear bomb, Israel sent jets to bomb Iraq's nuclear facility, setting back the program by years. One drawback to these dominance solutions is the resentment they create among the smaller countries. Those countries point to an unenforced provision of the NPT stating that existing nuclear powers should get rid of their own bombs as other countries refrain from making new ones. And they ask what gives Israel the right to bomb another country, or the United States the right to invade one. They speak of a "double standard" for the powerful and the weak.

Reciprocity offers a different avenue for preventing proliferation. It is the basis of the provision in the NPT about the existing nuclear powers' obligation to disarm in exchange for smaller countries' agreement to stay nonnuclear. Reciprocity also underlies arms control agreements, used extensively in the Cold War to manage the buildup of nuclear bombs by the superpowers, and used currently to manage the mutual reduction of their arsenals. Deterrence also relies on reciprocity. The United States warned North Korea in 2006 against selling its bombs (an action that would be in North Korea's short-term self-interest), threatening to retaliate against North Korea if any other actor used such a bomb against the United States. And when Libya gave up its nuclear weapons program in 2003, the international community gave it various rewards, including the ending of economic sanctions, in exchange.

The identity principle has proven equally effective against nuclear proliferation, if less newsworthy. Many nations that have the technical ability to make nuclear weapons have *chosen* not to do so. They have constructed their national identities in ways that shape their self-interests so as to make nuclear bombs undesirable. Some, like Sweden, do not intend to fight wars. Others, like Germany, belong to alliances in which they come under another nation's nuclear "umbrella" and do not need their own bomb. South Africa actually developed nuclear weapons in secret but then dismantled the program before apartheid ended, keeping the bomb out of the hands of the new majority-rule government. Nobody forced South Africa to do this (as in dominance), nor did it respond to rewards and punishments (reciprocity). Rather, South Africa's identity shifted. Similarly, Japan's experience of the catastrophic results of militarism, culminating in the destruction of two of its cities by nuclear bombs in 1945, continues generations later to shape Japan's identity as a country that does not want nuclear weapons, even though it has the know-how and even the stockpile of plutonium to make them.

Collective goods problems fascinate social scientists, and especially scholars of IR, precisely because they have no easy solutions. In later chapters, we will see how these three core principles shape the responses of the international community to various collective goods problems across the whole range of IR issues.

IR as a Field of Study

As a part of political science, IR is about *international politics*—the decisions of governments about foreign actors, especially other governments. To some extent, however, the field is interdisciplinary, relating international politics to economics, history, sociology, and other disciplines. Some universities offer separate degrees or departments for IR. Most, however, teach IR in political science classes, in which the focus is on the *politics* of economic relationships, or the *politics* of environmental management, to take two examples. (The domestic politics of foreign countries, although overlapping with IR, generally makes up the separate field of *comparative politics*.)

Political relations among nations cover a range of activities—diplomacy, war, trade relations, alliances, cultural exchanges, participation in international organizations, and so forth. Particular activities within one of these spheres make up distinct **issue areas** on which scholars and foreign policy makers focus attention. Examples of issue areas include global trade, the environment, and specific conflicts such as the Arab-Israeli conflict. Within each issue area, and across the range of issues of concern in any international relationship, policy makers of one nation can behave in a cooperative manner or a conflictual manner—extending either friendly or hostile behavior toward the other nation. IR scholars often look at international relations in terms of the mix of **conflict and cooperation** in relationships among nations.

The scope of the field of IR may also be defined by the *subfields* it encompasses. Some scholars treat topics such as this book's chapters (for example, international law or international development) as subfields, but here we will reserve the term for two macro-level topics. Traditionally, the study of IR has focused on questions of war and peace—the subfield of **international security** studies. The movements of armies and of diplomats, the crafting of treaties and alliances, and the development and deployment of military capabilities were subjects that dominated the study of IR in the past, especially in the 1950s and 1960s, and they continue to hold a central position in the field. Since the Cold War, regional conflicts and ethnic violence have received more attention, while interdisciplinary peace studies programs and feminist scholarship have sought to broaden concepts of "security" further.

The subfield of **international political economy (IPE),** a second main subfield of IR, concerns trade and financial relations among nations, and focuses on how nations have cooperated politically to create and maintain institutions that regulate the flow of international economic and financial transactions. Although these topics previously centered on relations among the world's richer nations, the widening of globalization and multilateral economic institutions such as the World Trade Organization have pushed IPE scholars to focus on developing states as well. In addition, they pay growing attention to relations between developed and developing nations (often labeled North-South relations), including such topics as economic dependency, debt, foreign aid, and technology transfer. Also newly important are problems of international environmental management and of global telecommunications. The subfield of IPE is expanding accordingly.

The same principles and theories that help us understand international security (in the first half of this book) also help us understand IPE (in the second half). Economics is important in security affairs, and vice versa.

Actors and Influences

The principal actors in IR are the world's governments. Scholars of IR traditionally study the decisions and acts of those governments in relation to other governments. The international stage is crowded with actors large and small who are intimately interwoven with the decisions of governments. These actors are individual leaders and citizens. They are bureaucratic agencies in foreign ministries. They are multinational corporations and terrorist groups. But the most important actors in IR are states.

State Actors

A **state** is a territorial entity controlled by a government and inhabited by a population. The locations of the world's states and territories are shown in the reference map at the front of this book, after the preface.

A state government answers to no higher authority; it exercises *sovereignty* over its territory (to make and enforce laws, to collect taxes, and so forth). This sovereignty is recognized (acknowledged) by other states through diplomatic relations and usually by membership in the United Nations (UN). (The concepts of state sovereignty and territoriality are elaborated in Chapter 2.) The population inhabiting a state forms a *civil society* to the extent that it has developed institutions to participate in political or social life. All or part of the population that shares a group identity may consider itself a *nation* (see p. 116). The state's government is a *democracy* to the extent that the government is controlled by the members of the population rather than imposed on them. (Note that the word *state* in IR does not mean a state in the United States.) In political life, and to some extent in IR scholarship, the terms *state*, *nation*, and *country* are used imprecisely, usually to refer to state governments.

With few exceptions, each state has a capital city—the seat of government from which it administers its territory—and often a single individual who acts in the name of the state. We will refer to this person simply as the "state leader." Often he or she is the *head of government* (such as a prime minister) or the *head of state* (such as a president, or a king or queen). In some countries, the same person is head of state and government. In other countries, the prime minister or the president or royalty is a symbolic leadership position. In any case, the most powerful political figure is the one we mean by "state leader," and these figures

POWERS THAT BE

States are the most important actors in IR. A handful of states are considered great powers and one a "superpower." Here, the leaders of the Group of 20 countries meet to coordinate their response to the global economic recession, 2009.

have been the key individual actors in IR. The state actor includes the individual leader as well as bureaucratic organizations (such as foreign ministries) that act in the name of the state.

The **international system** is the set of relationships among the world's states, structured according to certain rules and patterns of interaction. Some such rules are explicit, some implicit. They include who is considered a member of the system, what rights and responsibilities the members have, and what kinds of actions and responses normally occur between states.

The modern international system has existed for less than 500 years. Before then, people were organized into more mixed and overlapping political units such as city-states, empires, and feudal fiefs. In the past 200 years the idea has spread that nations—groups of people who share a sense of national identity, usually including a language and culture—should have their own states. Most large states today are such **nation-states.** But since World War II, the decolonization process in much of Asia and Africa has added many new states, some not at all nation-states. A major source of conflict and war at present is the frequent mismatch between perceived nations and actual state borders. When people identify with a nationality that their state government does not represent, they may fight to form their own state and thus to gain sovereignty over their territory and affairs. This substate nationalism is only one of several growing trends that undermine today's system of states. Other such trends include the globalization of economic processes, the power of telecommunications, and the proliferation of ballistic missiles.

The independence of former colonies and, more recently, the breakup into smaller states of large multinational states (the Soviet Union and Yugoslavia) have increased the number of states in the world. The exact total depends on the status of a number of quasi-state political entities. The UN had 192 members in 2009.

Some other political entities are often referred to as states or countries although they are not formally recognized as states. Taiwan is the most important of these. It operates independently in practice but is claimed by China (a claim recognized formally by outside powers), and is not a UN member. Formal colonies and possessions still exist; their status may change in the future. They include Puerto Rico (U.S.), Bermuda (British), Martinique (French), French Guiana, the Netherlands Antilles (Dutch), the Falkland Islands (British), and Guam (U.S.). Hong Kong reverted from British to Chinese rule in 1997 and retains a somewhat separate economic identity under China's "one country, two systems" formula. The status of the Vatican (Holy See) in Rome is ambiguous. Including various such territorial entities with states brings the world total to about 200 state or quasi-state actors. Other would-be states (such as Kurdistan and Western Sahara) do not fully control the territory they claim and are not widely recognized.

The population of the world's states varies dramatically, from China and India with more than 1 billion people each, to microstates such as San Marino with fewer than 100,000. With the creation of many small states in recent decades, the majority of states now have fewer than 10 million people each, and more than half of the rest have 10 to 50 million each. But the 15 states with populations of more than 70 million people together contain about two-thirds of the world's population.

States also differ tremendously in the size of their total annual economic activity— **Gross Domestic Product (GDP)**[2]—from the $14 trillion U.S. economy to the economies of tiny states such as the Pacific island of Tonga ($350 million). The world economy is dominated by a few states, just as world population is. Figure 1.1 lists the largest countries by population and economy. Each is an important actor in world affairs.

A few of these large states possess especially great military and economic strength and influence, and are called *great powers* (see Chapter 2). The most powerful of great powers, those with truly global influence, have been called *superpowers*. This term generally meant the United States and the Soviet Union during the Cold War, and now refers to the United States alone.

---

[2] GDP is the total of goods and services produced by a nation; it is very similar to the gross national product (GNP). Such data are difficult to compare across nations with different currencies, economic systems, and levels of development. In particular, comparisons of GDP in capitalist and socialist economies, or in rich and poor countries, should be treated cautiously. GDP data used in this book are mostly from the World Bank. GDP data are adjusted through time and across countries for "purchasing-power parity" (how much a given amount of money can buy). See Summers, Robert, and Alan Heston. The Penn World Table (Mark 5): An Expanded Set of International Comparisons, 1950–1988. *Quarterly Journal of Economics* 106 (2), 1991: 327–68. GDP and population data are for 2006 unless otherwise noted.

FIGURE 1.1   Largest Countries, 2008

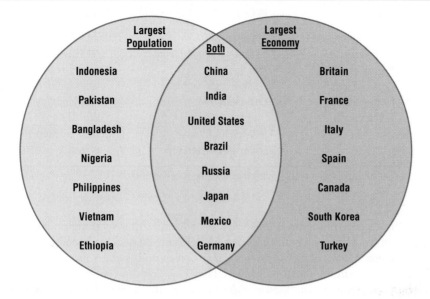

Note: *Left and center columns listed in population order, right column in GDP order. GDP calculated by purchasing parity.*

Source: CIA. *World Factbook.*

Nonstate Actors

National governments may be the most important actors in IR, but they are strongly influenced by a variety of **nonstate actors** (see Table 1.2). These actors are also called *transnational actors* when they operate across international borders.

First, states often take actions through, within, or in the context of **intergovernmental organizations (IGOs)**—organizations whose members are national governments. IGOs fulfill a variety of functions and vary in size from just a few states to virtually the whole UN membership. The Organization of Petroleum Exporting Countries (OPEC), the World Trade Organization (WTO), military alliances such as NATO, and political groupings such as the African Union (AU) are all IGOs. Another type of transnational actor, **nongovernmental organizations (NGOs),** are private organizations, some of considerable size and resources. Increasingly NGOs are being recognized, in the UN and other forums, as legitimate actors along with states, though not equal to them. Some of these groups have a political purpose, some a humanitarian one, some an economic or technical one. Sometimes NGOs combine efforts through transnational advocacy networks. There is no single pattern to NGOs. Together, IGOs and NGOs are referred to as international organizations (IOs). By one count there are more than 25,000 NGOs and 5,000 IGOs. IOs are discussed in detail in Chapter 6.

TABLE 1.2   Types of Nonstate Actors

Type		Who Are They?	Examples
IGOs[a]	Intergovernmental Organizations	Members are national governments	United Nations, NATO, Arab League
NGOs[a]	Nongovernmental Organizations	Members are individuals & groups	Amnesty International, Lions Clubs, Red Cross
MNCs	Multinational Corporations	Companies that span borders	ExxonMobil, Toyota, Wal-Mart
Others		Individuals, Cities, Constituencies, etc.	Bono, Iraqi Kurdistan, al Qaeda

[a]Note: IGOs and NGOs together make up International Organizations (IOs).

Multinational corporations (MNCs) are companies that span multiple countries. The interests of a large company doing business globally do not correspond with any one state's interests. MNCs often control greater resources, and operate internationally with greater efficiency, than many small states. They may prop up (or even create) friendly foreign governments, as the United Fruit Company did in the "banana republics" of Central America a century ago. But MNCs also provide poor states with much-needed foreign investment and tax revenues. MNCs in turn depend on states to provide protection, well-regulated markets, and a stable political environment. MNCs as international actors receive special attention in Chapters 5 and 7.

Various other nonstate actors interact with states, IOs, and MNCs. For example, the terrorist attacks since September 11, 2001, have demonstrated the increasing power that technology gives terrorists as nonstate actors. Just as Greenpeace can travel to a remote location and then beam video of its environmental actions there to the world, so too can al Qaeda place suicide bombers in world cities, coordinate their operations and finances through the Internet and global banking system, and reach a global audience with videotaped appeals. "Global reach," once an exclusive capability of great powers, now is available to many others, for better or worse.

Some nonstate actors are *substate actors:* they exist within one country but either influence that country's foreign policy or operate internationally, or both. For instance, the state of Ohio is entirely a U.S. entity but operates an International Trade Division to promote exports and foreign investment, with offices in Belgium, Japan, China, Canada, Israel, India, Australia, and Mexico. The actions of substate economic actors—companies, consumers, workers, investors—help create the context of economic activity against which international political events play out, and within which governments must operate.

In this world of globalization, of substate actors and transnational actors, states are still important. But to some extent they are being gradually pushed aside as companies, groups, and individuals deal ever more directly with each other across borders, and as the world economy becomes globally integrated. Now more than ever, IR extends beyond the interactions of national governments. Both state and nonstate actors are strongly

POLICY PERSPECTIVES

Overview

International policy makers confront a variety of problems every day. Solving these problems requires difficult decisions and choices. "Policy Perspectives" is a box feature in each chapter that places you in a particular decision-making perspective (for example, the prime minister of Great Britain) and asks you to make choices concerning an important international relations issue.

Each box contains four sections. The first, "Background," provides information about a political problem faced by the leader. This background information is factual and reflects real situations faced by these decision makers.

The second section, "Domestic Considerations," reflects on the implications of the situation for domestic politics within the leader's government and society. How will the lives of ordinary citizens be affected?

The third section, "Scenario," suggests a new problem or crisis confronting the leader. Although these crises are hypothetical, all are within the realm of possibility and would require difficult decisions by the leaders and their countries.

The fourth section, "Choose Your Policy," asks you to make a choice responding to the Scenario. With each decision, think about the trade-offs between your options. What are the risks and rewards in choosing one policy over another? Could alternative options effectively address the problem within the given constraints? Does one option pose bigger costs in the short term, but fewer in the long term? Can you defend your decision to colleagues, the public, and other world leaders? How will your choice affect your citizens' lives and your own political survival?

As you consider each problem faced by the decision maker, try to reflect on the process and logic by which you have reached the decision. Which factors seem more important and why? Are domestic or international factors more important in shaping your decision? Are the constraints you face based on limited capability (for example, money or military power), or do international law or norms influence your decision as well? How do factors such as lack of time influence your decision?

You will quickly discover that there are often no "right" answers. At times, it is difficult to choose between two good options; at other times, one has to decide which is the least bad option.

---

affected by the revolution in information technologies now under way. The new information-intensive world promises to reshape international relations profoundly. Technological change dramatically affects actors' relative capabilities and even preferences. Telecommunications and computerization allow economics, politics, and culture alike to operate on a global scale as never before.

Levels of Analysis

The many actors involved in IR contribute to the complexity of competing explanations and theories. One way scholars of IR have sorted out this multiplicity of influences, actors, and processes is to categorize them into different *levels of analysis* (see Table 1.3). A level of analysis is a perspective on IR based on a set of similar actors or processes that suggests possible explanations to "why" questions. IR scholars have proposed various level-of-analysis schemes, most often with three main levels (and sometimes a few sublevels between).

TABLE 1.3   Levels of Analysis

Many influences affect the course of international relations. Levels of analysis provide a framework for categorizing these influences and thus for suggesting various explanations of international events. Examples include:

Global Level

North-South gap	Religious fundamentalism	Information revolution
World regions	Terrorism	Global telecommunications
European imperialism	World environment	Worldwide scientific and
UN	Technological change	business communities

Interstate Level

Power	Wars	Diplomacy
Balance of power	Treaties	Summit meetings
Alliance formation	Trade agreements	Bargaining
and dissolution	IGOs	Reciprocity

Domestic Level

Nationalism	Dictatorship	Gender
Ethnic conflict	Domestic coalitions	Economic sectors and industries
Type of government	Political parties and elections	Military-industrial complex
Democracy	Public opinion	Foreign policy bureaucracies

Individual Level

Great leaders	Psychology of perception and decision	Citizens' participation (voting,
Crazy leaders	Learning	rebelling, going to war, etc.)
Decision making in crises	Assassinations, accidents of history	

The *individual* level of analysis concerns the perceptions, choices, and actions of
individual human beings. Great leaders influence the course of history, as do individual
citizens, thinkers, soldiers, and voters. Without Lenin, it is said, there might well have
been no Soviet Union. If a few more people had voted for Nixon rather than Kennedy in
the razor-close 1960 election, the Cuban Missile Crisis might have ended differently.
The study of foreign policy decision making, discussed in Chapter 3, pays special attention to individual-level explanations of IR outcomes because of the importance of
psychological factors in the decision-making process.

The *domestic* (or *state* or *societal*) level of analysis concerns the aggregations of individuals within states that influence state actions in the international arena, such as interest
groups, political organizations, and government agencies. These groups operate differently
(with different international effects) in different kinds of societies and states. Democracies
may act differently from dictatorships, and democracies may act differently in an election
year from the ways they do at other times. The politics of ethnic conflict and nationalism
plays an increasingly important role in the relations among states. Economic sectors within

states, including the military-industrial sector, can influence their governments to take actions in the international arena that are good for business. Within governments, foreign policy agencies often fight bureaucratic battles over policy decisions.

The *interstate* (or *international* or *systemic*) level of analysis concerns the influence of the international system upon outcomes. Thus it focuses on the interactions of states themselves, without regard to their internal makeup or the particular individuals who lead them. This level pays attention to states' relative power positions in the international system and the interactions among them. It has been traditionally the most important of the levels of analysis.

To these three levels can be added a fourth, the *global* level of analysis, which seeks to explain international outcomes in terms of global trends and forces that transcend the interactions of states. The evolution of human technology, of certain worldwide beliefs, and of humans' relationship to the natural environment are all processes at the global level that influence international relations. The global level is also increasingly the focus of IR scholars studying transnational integration through worldwide scientific, technical, and business communities (see Chapter 8). Another pervasive global influence is the lingering effect of historical European imperialism.

Although IR scholars often focus their study mainly on one level of analysis, other levels bear on a problem simultaneously. There is no single correct level for a given "why" question. Rather, levels of analysis help suggest multiple explanations and approaches in trying to explain a given event. They remind scholars and students to look beyond the immediate and superficial aspects of an event to explore the possible influences of more distant causes. Note that the processes at higher levels tend to operate more slowly than those at the lower levels. Individuals go in and out of office often; the structure of the international system changes rarely.

Globalization

Globalization encompasses many trends, including expanded international trade, telecommunications, monetary coordination, multinational corporations, technical and scientific cooperation, cultural exchanges of new types and scales, migration and refugee flows, and relations between the world's rich and poor countries. Although globalization clearly is very important, it is also rather vaguely defined and not well explained by any one theory. One popular conception of globalization is as "the widening, deepening and speeding up of worldwide interconnectedness in all aspects of contemporary social life...." But at least three conceptions of this process compete.

VIDEO

Globalization and the Domino Effect

One view sees globalization as the fruition of liberal economic principles (see Chapter 5). A global marketplace has brought growth and prosperity (not to all countries but to those most integrated with the global market). This economic process has made traditional states obsolete as economic units. States are thus losing authority to supranational institutions such as the International Monetary Fund (IMF) and the European Union (EU), and to transnational actors such as MNCs and NGOs. The values of technocrats and elite, educated citizens in liberal democracies are becoming global values, reflecting an emerging global civilization. The old North-South division is seen as less important, because the global South is moving in divergent directions depending on countries' and regions' integration with world markets.

A second perspective is skeptical of these claims about globalization. These skeptics note that the world's major economies are no more integrated today than before World War I (when British hegemony provided a common set of expectations and institutions). The skeptics also doubt that regional and geographic distinctions such as the North-South divide are disappearing in favor of a single global market. Rather, they see the North-South gap as increasing with globalization. Also, the economic integration of states may be leading not to a single world free trade zone, but to distinct and rival regional blocs in America, Europe, and Asia. The supposed emerging world civilization is disproved by the fragmenting of larger units (such as the Soviet Union) into smaller ones along lines of language, religion, and other such cultural factors.

A third school of thought sees globalization as more profound than the skeptics believe, yet more uncertain than the view of supporters of liberal economics. These "transformationalists" see state sovereignty as being eroded by the EU, the WTO, and other new institutions, so that sovereignty is no longer an absolute but just one of a spectrum of bargaining leverages held by states. The bargaining itself increasingly involves nonstate actors. Thus globalization diffuses authority. State power is not so much strengthened or weakened by globalization, but transformed to operate in new contexts with new tools.

THINK GLOBALLY

As the world becomes more integrated, markets and production are becoming global in scope. Here, in 2005, the Chinese car maker Chery (no relation to the U.S. trademark "Chevy") introduces its first right-hand-drive car in Malaysia, where people drive on the left as a legacy of British imperialism. The marketing technique seems a legacy of American automotive tradition.

While scholars debate these conceptions of globalization, popular debates focus on the growing power of large corporations operating globally, the disruptive costs associated with joining world markets (for example, job loss and environmental impacts), the perception of growing disparities between the rich and the poor, and the collusion of national governments in these wrongs through their participation in IOs such as the WTO and the IMF. Policies to expand free trade are a central focus of antiglobalization protesters (see pp. 187–188). Street protests have turned host cities into besieged fortresses in Seattle (1999); Washington, D.C. (2000 IMF and World Bank meetings); Quebec (2001 summit working toward a Free Trade Area of the Americas); and Genoa, Italy (2001 G8 summit). The key 2001 WTO meeting to launch a new trade round was held in Qatar, where protesters had little access. At the 2003 WTO meeting in Cancun, Mexico, thousands of protesters marched against the talks and the economic elites conducting them, but were kept away from the WTO conference center. At the 2005 Hong Kong WTO meeting, protesters blocked nearby roads and some even tried to swim across Hong Kong harbor to disrupt the meeting. Just as scholars disagree on conceptions of globalization, so do protesters disagree on their goals and tactics. Union members from the global North want to stop globalization from shipping their jobs south. But workers in impoverished countries in the global South may desperately want those jobs as a first step toward decent wages and working conditions (relative to other options in their countries). Window-smashing anarchists meanwhile steal media attention from environmentalists seeking to amend the trade agenda. Thus, neither globalization nor the backlash to it is simple.

Globalization is changing both international security and IPE, as we will see in the coming chapters, but it is changing IPE more quickly and profoundly than security. The coming chapters address this broad range of topics, each affected by globalization. Chapter 3 shows how nonstate actors influence foreign policies of states. Chapter 5 looks at economic globalization, in trade, finance, and business, where globalization's influences are most apparent. Chapter 6 discusses global institutions, international law, and human rights, all of growing importance as globalization continues. Chapter 7 covers the global North-South divide, which is central to the concept of globalization. And Chapter 8 considers the information technology side of globalization as the world becomes wired in new ways, as well as the influence of globalization on our physical environment.

The rest of *this* chapter takes up two contextual aspects of globalization that shape the issue areas discussed in subsequent chapters—(1) the relations among the world's major regions, especially the rich North and poor South; and (2) the evolution of the international system over the past century, especially the past two decades of the post–Cold War era.

Global Geography

To highlight the insights afforded by a global level of analysis, this book divides the world into nine regions. These *world regions* differ from each other in the number of states they contain and in each region's particular mix of cultures, geographical realities, and languages. But each represents a geographical corner of the world, and together they reflect the overall larger divisions of the world.

The global **North-South gap** between the industrialized, relatively rich countries of the North and the relatively poor countries of the South (see Chapter 7) is the most important geographical element at the global level of analysis. The regions used in this book have been drawn so as to separate (with a few exceptions) the rich countries from the poor ones. The North includes both the West (the rich countries of North America, Western Europe, and Japan) and the old East (the former Soviet Union and its bloc of allies).[3] The South includes Latin America, Africa, the Middle East, and much of Asia.

---

[3] Note that geographical designations such as the "West" and the "Middle East" are European-centered. From Korea, for example, China and Russia are to the west and Japan and the United States are to the east.

FIGURE 1.2 Nine Regions of the World

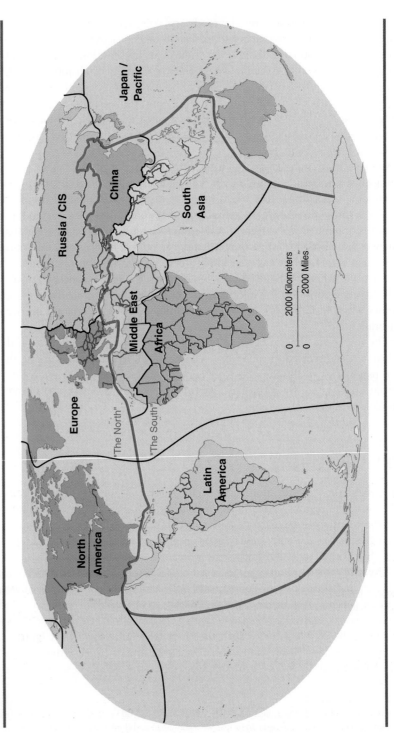

The South is often called the *third world* (third after the West and East)—a term that is still widely used despite the second world's collapse. Countries in the South are also referred to as "developing" countries or "less-developed" countries (LDCs), in contrast to the "developed" countries of the North. The overall world regions are shown in Figure 1.2.

Most of these regions correspond with commonly used geographical names, but a few notes may help. *East Asia* refers to China, Japan, and Korea. *Southeast Asia* refers to countries from Burma through Indonesia and the Philippines. Russia is considered a European state although a large section (Siberia) is in Asia. The *Pacific Rim* usually means East and Southeast Asia, Siberia, and the Pacific coast of North America and Latin America. *South Asia* only sometimes includes parts of Southeast Asia. Narrow definitions of the *Middle East* exclude both North Africa and Turkey. The *Balkans* are the states of southeastern Europe, bounded by Slovenia, Romania, and Greece.

Table 1.4 shows the approximate population and economic size (GDP) of each region in relation to the world as a whole. As the table shows, income levels per capita are, overall, more than five times as high in the North as in the South. *The North contains only 20 percent of the world's people but 60 percent of its goods and services.* The other 80 percent of the world's people, in the South, have only 40 percent of the goods and services. For individual countries within each world region, Table 1.5 shows total GDP. IR scholars have no single explanation of the huge North-South income gap (see Chapter 7).

TABLE 1.4   Comparison of World Regions, 2007

Region	Population (Millions)	GDP (Trillion $)	GDP per Capita (Dollars)
The North			
North America	350	$15	$47,000
Western Europe	525	15	29,500
Japan/Pacific	225	7	29,000
Russia/CIS	275	3	10,000
The South			
China	1,350	8	6,000
Middle East	425	4	10,000
Latin America	575	6	9,500
South Asia	2,100	7	3,300
Africa	775	2	3,000
Total North	**1,375 (20%)**	**40 (60%)**	**29,000**
Total South	**5,225 (80%)**	**27 (40%)**	**5,850**
World Total	**6,600**	**$67**	**$10,000**

Note: Data adjusted for purchasing-power parity. 2007 GDP estimates (in 2008 dollars) are from Table 1.5; those for Russia, CIS, and China should be treated especially cautiously.

North America

United States	14,000	Canada	1,200	Bahamas	9

Europe

Germany[a]	2,800	Denmark[a]	200	Estonia[a]	30
Britain[a]	2,100	Finland[a]	200	Bosnia and Herzegovina	30
France[a]	2,100	Czech Republic[a]	200	Albania	20
Italy[a]	1,800	Hungary[a]	200	Cyprus[a]	20
Spain[a]	1,400	Norway	200	Macedonia	20
Netherlands[a]	600	Ireland[a]	200	Iceland	10
Poland[a]	600	Slovakia[a]	100	Malta[a]	10
Belgium[a]	400	Bulgaria[a]	90	Montenegro	7
Greece[a]	400	Serbia	80	Liechtenstein	4
Sweden[a]	300	Croatia	70	Andorra	3
Switzerland	300	Lithuania[a]	60	Monaco	1
Romania[a]	300	Slovenia[a]	60	San Marino	1
Austria[a]	300	Luxembourg[a]	40		
Portugal[a]	200	Latvia[a]	40		

Japan/Pacific

Japan	4,400	Fiji	4	Nauru	0
South Korea	1,200	Guam/Marianas[b]	3	Marshall Islands	0
Australia	800	Solomon Islands	1	Palau	0
New Zealand	100	Samoa	1	Kiribati	0
North Korea	30	Vanuatu	1	Tuvalu	0
Papua New Guinea	10	Tonga	0	Micronesia	0

Russia/CIS

Russia	2,100	Azerbaijan	70	Kyrgyzstan	10
Ukraine	400	Turkmenistan	40	Tajikistan	10
Kazakhstan	200	Armenia	20	Moldova	10
Belarus	100	Georgia	20	Mongolia	9
Uzbekistan	70				

China

China	7,200	Hong Kong[b]	300	Macau[b]	20
Taiwan[b]	800				

Middle East

Turkey	900	Kuwait	200	Oman	70
Iran	800	Iraq	100	Yemen	50
Saudi Arabia	600	Morocco/W. Sahara	100	Lebanon	40
Egypt	400	Syria	90	Jordan	30
Algeria	300	Libya	90	Bahrain	30
Israel/Palestine	200	Tunisia	80		
United Arab Emirates	200	Qatar	80		

Latin America

Brazil	1,900	El Salvador	40	Suriname	4
Mexico	1,400	Uruguay	40	Netherlands Antilles[b]	3
Argentina	500	Bolivia	40	Guyana	2
Colombia	300	Panama	40	Belize	2
Venezuela	300	Paraguay	30	Virgin Islands[b]	2
Chile	200	Honduras	30	French Guiana[b]	2
Peru	200	Trinidad & Tobago	30	St. Lucia	2
Cuba	100	Jamaica	20	Antigua & Barbuda	2
Ecuador	100	Nicaragua	20	Grenada	1
Puerto Rico[b]	70	Haiti	10	St. Vincent & Grenadines	1
Dominican Republic	70	Martinique[b]	7	St. Kitts & Nevis	1
Guatemala	60	Barbados	5	Dominica	1
Costa Rica	50	Bermuda[b]	5		

South Asia

India	3,300	Vietnam	200	Brunei	20
Indonesia	900	Singapore	200	Laos	10
Thailand	500	Sri Lanka	90	Bhutan	3
Pakistan	500	Burma (Myanmar)	60	Maldives	2
Malaysia	400	Nepal	40	East Timor	1
Philippines	300	Cambodia	30		
Bangladesh	200	Afghanistan	30		

Africa

South Africa	500	Mauritius	20	Somalia	6
Nigeria	300	Gabon	20	Sierra Leone	4
Angola	100	Burkina Faso	20	Central African Republic	3
Sudan	80	Zambia	20	Eritea	3
Ethiopia	60	Chad	20	Lesotho	3
Kenya	60	Mali	20	Burundi	3
Tanzania	50	Congo Republic	10	Reunion[b]	3
Cameroon	40	Niger	10	Cape Verde	2
Botswana	30	Rwanda	10	Djibouti	2
Ghana	30	Namibia	10	Gambia	2
Côte d'Ivoire (Ivory Coast)	30	Benin	10	Liberia	1
Uganda	30	Zimbabwe	10	Seychelles	1
Democratic Congo	20	Guinea	10	Comoros Islands	1
Mozambique	20	Malawi	10	Guinea-Bissau	1
Equatorial Guinea	20	Mauritania	6	São Tomé & Principe	0
Senegal	20	Swaziland	6		
Madagascar	20	Togo	6		

[a]European Union.

[b]Nonmember of UN (colony or territory).

Note: GDP data are inexact by nature. Estimates for Russia, CIS, China, and other nonmarket or transitional economies are particularly suspect and should be used cautiously. Numbers below 0.5 are listed as 0.
Sources: Data are authors' estimates based on World Bank. Data are at purchasing-power parity. See footnote 2 on p. 12.

Geography provides one context in which IR takes place; history provides another. The remainder of this chapter reviews the historical development of the international system since World War II.

The Evolving International System

The basic structures and principles of international relations are deeply rooted in historical developments. The past 500 years, known as the "modern age," saw the rise of the international system of sovereign states. That era was dominated by recurring great power wars in Europe—in particular, the Thirty Years' War (1618–1648), the Napoleonic Wars (1803–1815), and the two World Wars (1914–1918 and 1939–1945). Such all-out wars among the world's most powerful armies, leaving whole continents in ruin, have not happened in the past 65 years and might never happen again. The history of these most recent 65 years is of particular importance to today's international system.

The Cold War, 1945–1990

The United States and the Soviet Union were the two superpowers of the post–World War II era: Each had its ideological mission (capitalist democracy versus communism), its networks of alliances and third world clients, and its deadly arsenal of nuclear weapons. Europe was divided, with massive military forces of the United States and its *North Atlantic Treaty Organization (NATO)* allies on one side and massive forces of the Soviet Union and its *Warsaw Pact* allies on the other. Germany itself was split, with three-quarters of the country—and three-quarters of the capital city of Berlin—occupied by the United States, Britain, and France. The remainder, surrounding West Berlin, was occupied by the Soviet Union. In 1961, East Germany built the Berlin Wall separating East from West Berlin. It symbolized the division of Europe by what Winston Churchill had called the "iron curtain."

Despite the hostility of East-West relations during the **Cold War,** a relatively stable framework of relations emerged, and conflicts never escalated to all-out war between the largest states (see Figure 1.3). Although the Soviet bloc did not join Western economic institutions, all the world's major states joined the United Nations (unlike the ill-fated League of Nations).

The central concern of the West during the Cold War was that the Soviet Union might gain control of Western Europe—either through outright invasion or through communists' taking power in the war-weary and impoverished countries of Western Europe. This could have put the entire industrial base of the Eurasian landmass (from Europe to Siberia) under one state. The *Marshall Plan*—U.S. financial aid to rebuild European economies—responded to these fears, as did the creation of the NATO alliance. Half of the entire world's military spending was devoted to the European standoff. Much spending was also devoted to a superpower nuclear arms race, in which each superpower produced tens of thousands of nuclear weapons (see pp. 156–158).

Through the policy of **containment,** adopted in the late 1940s, the United States sought to halt the expansion of Soviet influence globally on several levels at once—military,

FIGURE 1.3

FIGURE 1.3   The Cold War, 1945–1990

Timeline: 1940 — 1950 — 1960 — 1970 — 1980 — 1990

Soviet Union (leaders): Stalin | Khrushchev | Brezhnev | Andropov | Chernenko | Gorbachev

Soviet Union events: (WW II alliance) · A-bomb · Sputnik · Warsaw Pact · NATO · nuclear arms race · (nuclear superiority over USSR) · nuclear parity with U.S. · reforms (perestroika, glasnost) · student protests

United States (presidents): F. D. Roosevelt | Truman | Eisenhower | Kennedy | Johnson | Nixon | Ford | Carter | Reagan | Bush

United States events: containment policy · human rights · (Iran crisis) · military buildup · "Star Wars" (SDI)

China
- civil war (Nationalists–Communists)
- People's Republic (Taiwan nationalist)
- Sino-Soviet alliance
- Taiwan Straits crises (vs. U.S.)
- Sino-Soviet split
- A-bomb
- Cultural Revolution
- Soviet border clashes
- joins UN
- U.S.-China rapprochement
- death of Mao
- neutral to pro-U.S.

Confrontations
- Berlin crisis
- Korean War
- Soviet invasion of Hungary
- U-2 incident
- Berlin Wall
- Berlin crisis
- Cuban Missile Crisis
- Vietnam War
- USSR invades Czechoslovakia
- Afghanistan War
- U.S. invasion of Grenada

Proxy Wars
- Greek civil war
- Suez crisis
- Cuban revolution
- Chile coup
- Indonesia
- Arab-Israeli wars
- Somalia vs. Ethiopia
- Cambodia
- Nicaragua →
- El Salvador →
- Angola →

Co-operation
- Yalta summit
- Geneva summit
- Limited Test Ban Treaty
- Non-Proliferation Treaty
- SALT I
- détente
- SALT II
- START talks
- Paris summit (CFE)
- INF treaty

political, ideological, economic. The United States maintained an extensive network of military bases and alliances worldwide. Virtually all of U.S. foreign policy in subsequent decades, from foreign aid and technology transfer to military intervention and diplomacy, came to serve the goal of containment.

The *Chinese communist revolution* in 1949 led to a Sino-Soviet alliance (*Sino* means "Chinese"). But China became fiercely independent in the 1960s following the **Sino-Soviet split,** when China opposed Soviet moves toward *peaceful coexistence* with the United States. In the late 1960s, young radicals, opposed to both superpowers, ran China during the chaotic and destructive *Cultural Revolution*. But feeling threatened by Soviet power, China's leaders developed a growing affiliation with the United States during the 1970s, starting with a dramatic visit to China by U.S. president Richard Nixon in 1972. During the Cold War, China generally tried to play a balancer role against whichever superpower seemed most threatening at the time.

In 1950, the *Korean War* broke out when communist North Korea attacked and overran most of U.S.-allied South Korea. The United States and its allies (under UN authority obtained after the Soviets walked out of the Security Council in protest) counterattacked and overran most of North Korea. China sent "volunteers" to help North Korea, and the war bogged down near the original border until a 1953 truce. The Korean War hardened U.S. attitudes toward communism.

The Cold War thawed after Stalin died in 1953. The first **summit meeting** between superpower leaders took place in Geneva in 1955. But the Soviet Union sent tanks to crush a popular uprising in Hungary in 1956 (an action it repeated in 1968 in Czechoslovakia), and the Soviet missile program that orbited *Sputnik* in 1957 alarmed the United States. In Cuba, after Fidel Castro's communist revolution in 1959, the United States attempted a counterrevolution in the botched 1961 *Bay of Pigs* invasion.

The **Cuban Missile Crisis** of 1962 ensued when the Soviet Union installed medium-range nuclear missiles in Cuba. The Soviet aims were to reduce the Soviet Union's strategic nuclear inferiority, to counter the deployment of U.S. missiles on Soviet borders in Turkey, and to deter another U.S. invasion of Cuba. U.S. leaders, however, considered the missiles threatening and provocative. As historical documents later revealed, nuclear war was quite possible. Some U.S. policy makers favored military strikes before the missiles became operational, when in fact some nuclear weapons in Cuba were already operational and commanders were authorized to use them in the event of a U.S. attack. Instead, President John F. Kennedy imposed a naval blockade to force their removal. The Soviet Union backed down, and the United States promised not to invade Cuba in the future. Leaders on both sides were shaken, however, by the possibility of nuclear war. They signed the *Limited Test Ban Treaty* in 1963, prohibiting atmospheric nuclear tests, and began to cooperate in cultural exchanges, space exploration, aviation, and other areas.

The two superpowers often jockeyed for position in the third world, supporting **proxy wars** in which they typically supplied and advised opposing factions in civil wars. The alignments were often arbitrary. For instance, the United States backed the Ethiopian government and the Soviets backed next-door rival Somalia in the 1970s; when an Ethiopian revolution caused the new government to seek Soviet help, the United States switched its support to Somalia.

One flaw of U.S. policy in the Cold War period was to see all regional conflicts through East-West lenses. Its preoccupation with communism led the United States to support unpopular pro-Western governments in a number of poor countries, nowhere more disastrously than in the *Vietnam War* in the 1960s. The war divided the U.S. public and ultimately failed to prevent a communist takeover. The fall of South Vietnam in 1975 appeared to signal U.S. weakness, especially combined with U.S. setbacks in the Middle East—the 1973 Arab oil embargo and the 1979 overthrow of the U.S.-backed shah of Iran.

In this period of apparent U.S. weakness, the Soviet Union invaded Afghanistan in 1979. Like the United States in Vietnam, the Soviet Union could not suppress rebel armies supplied by the opposing superpower. The Soviets withdrew after almost a decade of war that considerably weakened the Soviet Union. Meanwhile, President Ronald Reagan built up U.S. military forces to record levels and supported rebel armies in the Soviet-allied states of Nicaragua and Angola (and one faction in Cambodia) as well as Afghanistan. Superpower relations slowly improved after Mikhail Gorbachev, a reformer, took power in the Soviet Union in 1985. But some of the third world battlegrounds (notably Afghanistan and Angola) continued to suffer from brutal civil wars into the new century.

In June 1989, massive pro-democracy demonstrations in China's capital of Beijing (Tiananmen Square) were put down violently by the communist government. Around 1990, as the Soviet Union stood by, one Eastern European country after another replaced its communist government after mass demonstrations. The toppling of the Berlin Wall in late 1989 symbolized the end of the Cold War division of Europe. Germany formally reunified in 1990. The Soviet leader, Gorbachev, allowed these losses of power in hopes of concentrating on Soviet domestic restructuring under *perestroika* (economic reform) and *glasnost* (openness in political discussion). China remained a communist, authoritarian government but liberalized its economy and avoided military conflicts. In contrast to the Cold War era, China developed close ties with both the United States and Russia and joined the world's liberal trading regime.

Scholars do not agree on the important question of why the Cold War ended. One view is that U.S. military strength under President Reagan forced the Soviet Union into bankruptcy as it tried to keep up in the arms race. Others claim that the Soviet Union suffered from internal stagnation over decades and imploded because of weaknesses that had little to do with external pressure.

The Post–Cold War Era, 1990–2009

The post–Cold War era began with a bang while the Soviet Union was still disintegrating. In 1990, perhaps believing that the end of the Cold War had left a power vacuum in its region, Iraq occupied its neighbor Kuwait in an aggressive grab for control of Middle East oil. Western powers were alarmed—both about the example that unpunished aggression could set in a new era and about the direct threat to energy supplies for the world economy. The United States mobilized a coalition of the world's major countries (with almost no opposition) to counter Iraq. Working through the UN, the U.S.-led coalition applied escalating sanctions against Iraq.

When Iraq did not withdraw from Kuwait by the UN's deadline, the United States and its allies easily smashed Iraq's military and evicted its army from Kuwait in the *Gulf War*. But the coalition did not occupy Iraq or overthrow its government. The costs of the Gulf War were shared among the participants in the coalition, with Britain and France making military commitments while Japan and Germany made substantial financial contributions. This pass-the-hat financing was an innovation, one that worked fairly well.

The final collapse of the Soviet Union followed only months after the Gulf War. The 15 republics of the Union—Russia was just one—had begun taking power from a weakened central government, declaring themselves sovereign states. This process raised complex problems ranging from issues of national self-determination to the real-location of property. In 1991, however, the Soviet Union itself broke apart. Russia and many of the other former republics struggled throughout the 1990s against economic and financial collapse, inflation, corruption, war, and military weakness. A failed Russian military coup attempt in 1991—and the role of Russian president Boris Yeltsin in opposing it—accelerated the collapse of the Soviet Union. Soon both capitalism and democracy were adopted as the basis of the economies and political systems of the former Soviet states. The republics became independent states and formed a loose coordinating structure—the *Commonwealth of Independent States (CIS)*. Of the former Soviet republics, only the three small Baltic states were nonmembers, although Georgia announced its intention to withdraw in 2008.

Western relations with Russia and the other republics have been mixed since the 1990s. Because of their own economic problems and a sense that Russia needed internal reform more than external aid, Western countries provided only limited aid for the region's harsh economic transition, which had drastically reduced living standards. Russia's brutal suppression of its secessionist province of Chechnya in 1995 and 1999 provoked Western fears. Russian leaders feared NATO expansion into Eastern Europe that placed threatening Western military forces on Russia's borders.

Despite these problems, the world's great powers increased their cooperation after the Cold War. Russia was accepted as the successor state to the Soviet Union and took its seat on the United Nations Security Council. Russia and the United States carried out major reductions in their nuclear weapons.

Just after the Gulf War in 1991, the former Yugoslavia broke apart, with several of its republics declaring independence. Ethnic Serbs, who were minorities in Croatia and Bosnia, seized territory to form a "Greater Serbia." With help from Serbia, which controlled the Yugoslav army, they killed hundreds of thousands of non-Serb Bosnians and Croatians and expelled millions more, to create an ethnically pure state.

The international community recognized the independence of Croatia and Bosnia, admitting them to the UN and passing dozens of Security Council resolutions to protect their territorial integrity and their civilian populations. But in contrast to the Gulf War, the great powers showed no willingness to bear major costs to protect Bosnia. Instead, they tried to contain the conflict by assuming a neutral role as peacekeeper and intermediary. The UN sent almost 40,000 peacekeepers to Bosnia and Croatia, at a cost of more than $1 billion per year. NATO threatened military actions repeatedly, only to back down when costs appeared too high.

In 1995, Serbian forces overran two UN-designated "safe areas" in eastern Bosnia, expelling the women and slaughtering thousands of the men. Finally, two weeks of NATO airstrikes (the alliance's first-ever military engagement), along with losses to Croatia on the ground, induced Serb forces to come to terms. The treaty to end the war (authored by U.S. negotiators) formally held Bosnia together but granted Serbian forces autonomy on half of their territory, while placing about 60,000 heavily armed (mostly NATO) troops on the ground to maintain a cease-fire.

In contrast to their indecision early in the Bosnia crisis, the Western powers acted decisively in 1999 when Serbian forces carried out "ethnic cleansing" in the Serbian province of Kosovo, predominantly populated by ethnic Albanians. NATO launched an air war that escalated over ten weeks. NATO came under criticism from Russia and China for acting without explicit UN authorization and for interfering in Serbia's internal affairs. (The international community and the UN considered Kosovo, unlike Bosnia, to be a part of Serbia.) In the end, Serbian forces withdrew from Kosovo and the UN has controlled the province ever since. In 2008, with the UN Security Council still deadlocked over its status, Kosovo declared independence, bringing protests from Serbia and its allies. Meanwhile, Serbian strongman Slobodan Milosevic was indicted for war crimes by the UN tribunal for the former Yugoslavia, was delivered to the tribunal in 2001, and died in 2006 near the end of a lengthy trial.

Other Western military intervention decisions since 1990 were less effective. In Somalia, a U.S.-led coalition sent tens of thousands of troops to suppress factional fighting and deliver relief supplies to a large population that was starving. However, when those forces were drawn into the fighting and sustained casualties, the United States abruptly pulled out. In Rwanda in 1994, the genocide of more than half a million civilians in a matter of weeks was virtually ignored by the international community. The great powers, burned by failures in Somalia and Bosnia, decided that their vital interests were not at stake. In 1997, the Rwanda conflict spilled into neighboring Zaire (now Democratic Congo), where rebels overthrew a corrupt dictator. Neighboring countries were drawn into the fighting, but the international community steered clear even as conditions worsened and millions of civilians died. The U.S. military intervened in Haiti to restore the elected president, but today Haiti remains mired in poverty and political instability.

New rifts opened in 2001 between the United States and both China and Europe. The United States stood nearly alone against the rest of the international community on a range of issues—missile defenses, the Kyoto treaty on global warming, a treaty to enforce the prohibition on biological weapons, a proposal to curb international small-arms sales, the proposed International Criminal Court, and a proposal to curb tobacco marketing in poor countries. Russia and China signed a treaty of friendship in 2001, and European countries helped vote the United States off two important UN commissions.

These divisive issues receded when the United States was attacked by terrorists on September 11, 2001. The attacks destroyed the World Trade Center in New York and a wing of the Pentagon in Washington, D.C., killing thousands of Americans and citizens of about 60 other countries. The attacks mobilized support for the United States by a very broad coalition of states, out of a realization that terrorism threatens the interstate system itself. President Bush declared a "war on terrorism" that was expected to last years

AS GOES PAKISTAN...

Peaceful trends mark the post–Cold War era, but war and terrorism continue. Pakistan embodies many of the key issues on which the future of the post–Cold War era will hinge—democracy, Islamic fundamentalism, nuclear weapons, terrorism, poverty, and corruption. Here, campaigners hold a picture of recently assassinated opposition leader Benazir Bhutto as parties opposed to Pakistan's longtime military ruler swept elections in 2008.

and span continents, employing both conventional and unconventional means. In late 2001, U.S. and British forces and their Afghan allies ousted the Taliban regime in Afghanistan, which had harbored and supported the al Qaeda network (led by Osama bin Laden) responsible for attacks on the United States.

The great power divisions reappeared, however, as the United States and Britain tried to assemble a coalition to oust Iraq's Saddam Hussein by force. France and Germany (along with Russia and China) bitterly opposed the war, as did millions of protesters around the world. As the U.S. secretary of defense called France and Germany "old Europe"—in contrast to the more pro-American "new Europe" states of Eastern Europe just joining NATO—the dispute brought the Atlantic alliance to a low point and wrecked France's dream of leading a unified European foreign policy. The Iraq War also weakened the UN's post–Cold War security role, because the U.S.-led coalition went forward despite its failure to win Security Council authorization for war.

The invasion itself was brief and decisive. A U.S. military force of 250,000 troops with advanced technology overpowered the Iraqi army in three weeks. Many Iraqis welcomed the end of a dictatorial regime, as had most Afghans in late 2001, but the war inflamed anti-American sentiment, especially in Muslim countries such as Egypt and Pakistan. Insurgent forces in Iraq gained strength as the U.S. occupation stretched on for years, and by 2006 U.S. public opinion had turned against the war as violence continued. Sectarian violence between Shi'ite and Sunni communities (rival wings of Islam) pushed the country to the brink of all-out civil war by early 2007. After a U.S. troop surge in 2007, and the arming of Sunni communities fed up with foreign Islamic radicals, violence in Iraq fell. U.S. forces then began turning over control of portions of the country to the Iraqi government by mid-2008. Still, violence does continue and estimates of Iraqi deaths caused by the war range from tens of thousands to more than 600,000. Spain, Italy, Australia, and several other coalition partners withdrew their troops from Iraq in 2007 and 2008. By late 2008, Iraq agreed to allow American military forces to remain in the country until 2011, but U.S. combat forces were to begin withdrawing from Iraqi towns beginning in 2009. The new Obama administration worked to draw down U.S. forces in 2009, both to fulfill campaign promises and to make troops available for a worsening fight in Afghanistan.

At the same time, the United States faced new crises involving nuclear weapons programs. North Korea restarted its program, producing possibly a half-dozen nuclear bombs in 2003 and testing one in 2006. Iran, in an agreement with Europe, suspended enriching uranium that could be used to build nuclear weapons, but then in 2006 began enrichment again—causing the UN Security Council to demand, backed by minor sanctions and the threat of more, that Iran stop its enrichment program. In 2009, barring a military attack by Israel or the United States, Iran appeared within a few years of obtaining nuclear weapons.

The post–Cold War era may seem a conflict-prone period in which savage wars flare up with unexpected intensity around the world, in places such as Bosnia and Rwanda— even New York City. In fact, however, *the post–Cold War era has been more peaceful than the Cold War* (see pp. 24–27). World military spending decreased by about one-third from its peak in the 1980s, although it has risen partway back since 2001. Old wars have ended faster than new ones have begun. Latin America and Russia/CIS have nearly extinguished wars in their regions, joining a zone of peace already encompassing North America, Europe, Japan/Pacific, and China.

Warfare is diminishing even in the arc of conflict from Africa through the Middle East to South Asia. Since 1990, long, bloody wars have ended in South Africa, Mozambique, Angola, southern Sudan, and Ethiopia-Eritrea, as did the Cold War conflicts in Central America. More recent wars in Sri Lanka, Ivory Coast, Rwanda, and Indonesia have also largely wound down. After the Cold War, world order did not spiral out of control with rampant aggression and war. However, the Israeli-Palestinian conflict, which saw rising expectations of peace in the 1990s, worsened in 2000 after a proposed deal fell through. With the 2006 Palestinian election victory of the militant Islamist party Hamas, responsible for many terrorist bombings in Israel, hopes for a durable peace faded. In 2006 Israel fought a brief but intense war with Hezbollah guerrillas in southern Lebanon, and in 2009 it attacked Hamas in Gaza with equal intensity.

VIDEO

Hamas Wins Palestinian Election

In international economic relations, the post–Cold War era is one of globalization. New hubs of economic growth are emerging, notably in parts of Asia with remarkable economic growth. At the same time, disparities between the rich and poor are growing, globally and within individual countries. Globalization has created backlashes among people who are adversely affected or who believe their identities are threatened by foreign influences. The resurgence of nationalism and ethnic-religious conflict—occasionally in brutal form—results partly from that backlash. So does the growing protest movement against capitalist-led globalization.

With increasing globalization, transnational concerns such as environmental degradation and disease have become more prominent as well. Global warming looms as an ever more present danger, underscored in 2005 by the toll of Hurricane Katrina on New Orleans and the accelerating melting of arctic ice. In 2006, a virulent bird flu spread worldwide, faster than expected, and triggered panicky efforts to prepare for a possible human pandemic if the flu virus mutates and spreads person to person.

China is becoming more central to world politics in the new century. Its size and rapid growth make China a rising power—a situation that some scholars liken to Germany's rise a century earlier. Historically, such shifts in power relations have caused instability in the international system. China's poor record on human rights makes it a frequent target of Western criticism from both governments and NGOs.

China holds (but seldom uses) veto power in the UN Security Council, and it has a credible nuclear arsenal. China adjoins several regional conflict areas and affects the global proliferation of missiles and nuclear weapons. It claims disputed territory in the re-source-rich South China Sea, but has not fought a military battle in 25 years. China is the only great power from the global South. Its population size and rapid industrializa-tion make China a big factor in the future of global environmental trends such as global warming. All these elements make China an important actor in the coming decades. The 2008 Olympic games in Beijing, a successful coming-of-age party for China on the world stage, focused attention on these issues.

The transition to the post–Cold War era has been a turbulent time, full of changes and new possibilities both good and bad. It is likely, however, that the basic rules and principles of IR—those that scholars have long struggled to understand—will continue to apply, though their contexts and outcomes may change. Most central to those rules and principles is the concept of power, to which we now turn.

CHAPTER REVIEW

SUMMARY

- IR affects daily life profoundly; we all participate in IR.
- IR is a field of political science concerned mainly with explaining political out-comes in international security affairs and international political economy.
- Theories complement descriptive narratives in explaining international events and outcomes, and although scholars do not agree on a single set of theories or methods, three core principles shape various solutions to collective goods problems in IR.
- States are the most important actors in IR; the international system is based on the sovereignty of about 200 independent territorial states of varying size.
- Nonstate actors such as intergovernmental organizations (IGOs), nongovernmen-tal organizations (NGOs), and multinational corporations (MNCs) exert a grow-ing influence on international relations.
- Four levels of analysis—individual, domestic, interstate, and global—suggest mul-tiple explanations (operating simultaneously) for outcomes observed in IR.
- Globalization is conceived differently by various scholars, but generally refers to the growing scope, speed, and intensity of connectedness worldwide. The process may be weakening, strengthening, or transforming the power of states. Antiglobalization activists oppose growing corporate power but disagree on goals and tactics.
- For nearly 50 years after World War II, world politics revolved around the East-West rivalry of the Cold War. This standoff created stability and avoided great power wars, including nuclear war, but turned poor states into proxy battlegrounds.

- The post–Cold War era holds hope of general great power cooperation despite the appearance of new ethnic and regional conflicts.

- A "war on terrorism" of uncertain scope and duration began in 2001 after terrorist attacks on the United States.

- The U.S. military campaign in Iraq overthrew a dictator, but divided the great powers, heightened anti-Americanism worldwide, and led to years of insurgency and sectarian violence.

KEY TERMS

international relations (IR) 1
collective goods problem 3
dominance 5
reciprocity 5
identity 6
issue areas 9
conflict and cooperation 9
international security 10

international political economy (IPE) 10
state 10
international system 11
nation-states 11
Gross Domestic Product (GDP) 12
nonstate actors 13
intergovernmental organizations (IGOs) 13

nongovernmental organizations (NGOs) 13
globalization 17
North-South gap 19
Cold War 24
containment 24
Sino-Soviet split 26
summit meeting 26
Cuban Missile Crisis 26
proxy wars 26

ONLINE PRACTICE TEST

Take an online practice test at
www.IRtext.com

❏ A
🔲 B
❏ C
❏ D

CRITICAL THINKING QUESTIONS

1. Pick a current area in which interesting international events are taking place. Can you think of possible explanations for those events from each of the four levels of analysis? (See Table 1.3, p. 16.) Do explanations from different levels provide insights into different aspects of the events?

2. The Cold War is long over, but its influences linger. Can you think of three examples in which the Cold War experience continues to shape the foreign policies of today's states?

3. What do you expect will be the character of the 21st century? Peaceful? War-prone? Orderly? Chaotic? Why do you have the expectations you do, and what clues from the unfolding of events in the world might tell you whether your guesses were correct?

BACK TO THE BIG PICTURE

To hear a discussion of the "big picture" for this chapter, raised on p. 2, along with an example from recent history, consult the "IR Talk" podcast for Chapter 1 at *www.IRtext.com*

PODCAST

Israeli artillery firing on Gaza, 2009.

CHAPTER 2

Realist Theories

Realism

No single theory reliably explains the wide range of international interactions, but one theoretical framework has historically held a central position in the study of IR. This approach, called realism, is favored by some IR scholars and vigorously contested by others, but almost all take it into account. Realism's foundation is the principle of dominance; alternatives based on reciprocity and identity will be reviewed in Chapter 3.

Realism (or *political realism*) is a school of thought that explains international relations in terms of power. The exercise of power by states toward each other is sometimes called *realpolitik,* or just *power politics*.

Modern realist theory developed in reaction to a liberal tradition that realists called **idealism.** Idealism emphasizes international law, morality, and international organization, rather than power alone, as key influences on international events. Idealists think that human nature is basically good. They see the international system as one based on a community of states that have the potential to work together to overcome mutual problems (see Chapter 3). For idealists, the principles of IR must flow from morality.

Idealists were particularly active between World War I and World War II, following the painful experience of World War I. U.S. president Woodrow Wilson led the effort to create the **League of Nations,** a forerunner of today's

35

THE BIG PICTURE

DOMINANCE

In a world of sovereign states and no central government, how can each state achieve its interests, indeed its survival? Traditionally, the theory of *realism,* based on the dominance principle, holds that each state must rely on its own power and, less reliably, on its alliances to influence the behavior of other states. Forms of power vary, but the threat and use of military force traditionally rank high in realists' power calculations.

The nature of the international system reflects this emphasis on power. A few "great powers" and their military alliances define the world order. Two superpowers with their allies defined the system during the Cold War, and a lone-superpower world order, still evolving, shapes the post–Cold War era.

To hear the authors of this book discuss this issue, with an example from recent history, download the "IR Talk" podcast for Chapter 2 from www.IRtext.com.

PODCAST

United Nations. But the U.S. Senate did not approve, and the League proved ineffective. U.S. isolationism between the world wars, along with declining British power and a Russia crippled by its own revolution, left a power vacuum in world politics that Germany and Japan filled in the 1930s. In an effort to appease German ambitions, Britain and France agreed in the **Munich Agreement** of 1938 to let Germany occupy part of Czechoslovakia. This "appeasement" seemed only to encourage Hitler's further conquests. Yet the lessons of the two world wars seem contradictory. From the failure of the Munich Agreement in 1938 to appease Hitler, many people have concluded that only a hard-line foreign policy with preparedness for war will deter aggression and prevent war. Yet in 1914 it was just such hard-line policies that apparently led Europe into a disastrous war, which might have been avoided by appeasement. Evidently the best policy would be sometimes harsh and at other times conciliatory.

After World War II, realists blamed idealists for looking too much at how the world *ought* to be instead of how it *really* is. Sobered by the experiences of World War II, realists set out to understand the principles of power politics without succumbing to wishful thinking.

Realists ground themselves in a long tradition. The Chinese strategist *Sun Tzu,* who lived 2,000 years ago, advised the rulers of states how to survive in an era when war had become a systematic instrument of power for the first time. Sun Tzu argued that moral reasoning was not very useful to the state rulers of the day, faced with armed and dangerous neighbors. He showed rulers how to use power to advance their interests and protect their survival.

At roughly the same time, in Greece, *Thucydides* wrote an account of the Peloponnesian War (431–404 B.C.) focusing on relative power among the Greek city-states. He stated that "the strong do what they have the power to do and the weak accept what they have to accept." Much later, in Renaissance Italy (around 1500), *Niccolò Machiavelli* urged princes to concentrate on expedient actions to stay in power, including the manipulation of the public and military alliances. Realists see in these historical figures evidence that the importance of power politics is timeless and cross-cultural.

TABLE 2.1   Assumptions of Realism and Idealism

Issue	Realism	Idealism
Human Nature	Selfish	Altruistic
Most Important Actors	States	States and others including individuals
Causes of State Behavior	Rational pursuit of self-interest *Rational action*	Psychological motives of decision makers
Nature of International System	Anarchy	Community

After World War II, scholar *Hans Morgenthau* argued that international politics is governed by objective, universal laws based on national interests defined in terms of power (not psychological motives of decision makers). He reasoned that no nation had "God on its side" (a universal morality) and that all nations had to base their actions on prudence and practicality. He opposed the Vietnam War, arguing in 1965 that a communist Vietnam would not harm U.S. national interests.

Similarly, in 2002, before the U.S. invasion of Iraq, leading realists figured prominently among the 33 IR scholars signing a *New York Times* advertisement warning that "war with Iraq is *not* in America's national interest." Thus realists do not always favor using military power, although they recognize the necessity of doing so at times. The target of the IR scholars' ad was the group of foreign policy makers in the Bush administration known as *neoconservatives,* who advocated more energetic use of American power, especially military force, to accomplish ambitious and moralistic goals such as democratizing the Middle East.

For realists, ideologies do not matter much, nor do religions or other cultural factors with which states may justify their actions. Realists see states with very different religions, ideologies, or economic systems as quite similar in their actions with regard to national power.

Thus, realists assume that IR can be best (though not exclusively) explained by the choices of states operating as autonomous actors rationally pursuing their own interests in an international system of sovereign states without central authority. Table 2.1 summarizes some major differences between the assumptions of realism and idealism.

Power

Power is a central concept in international relations—*the* central one for realists—but it is surprisingly difficult to define or measure.

Defining Power

Power is often defined as the ability to get another actor to do what it would not otherwise have done (or not to do what it would have done). A variation on this idea is that actors are powerful to the extent that they affect others more than others affect them.

VIDEO

U.S. Influence on Iran's Nuclear Program

POWER AS INFLUENCE

Power is the ability to influence the behavior of others. Military force and economic sanctions are among the various means that states and nonstate actors use to try to influence each other. Russia's position as a major energy supplier to Europe has increased its power in recent years, even though its military threat to Europe has decreased. In 2009 Russia shut off natural gas supplies during a price dispute with Ukraine, a dispute shadowed by Russian anger at Ukraine's efforts to join NATO. The shutoff, visible here in a pressure gauge reading zero, left customers across Europe without heat.

These definitions treat power as influence. If actors get their way a lot, they must be powerful. One problem with this definition is that we seldom know what a second actor would have done in the absence of the first actor's power. There is a danger of circular logic: power explains influence, and influence measures power.

Power is not influence itself, however, but the ability or potential to influence others. Many IR scholars believe that such potential is based on specific (tangible and intangible) characteristics or possessions of states—such as their sizes, levels of income, and armed forces. This is power as *capability*. Capabilities are easier to measure than influence and less circular in logic.

Measuring capabilities to explain how one state influences another is not simple, however. It requires summing up various kinds of potentials. States possess varying amounts of population, territory, military forces, and so forth. The best single indicator of a state's power may be its total GDP, which combines overall size, technological level, and wealth. But even GDP is at best a rough indicator, and economists do not even agree how to measure it. The method followed in this book adjusts for price differences among countries, but an alternative method gives GDP estimates that are on average about 50 percent higher for countries in the global North and about 50 percent lower for the global South including China (see footnote 2 on p. 12). So GDP is a useful estimator of material capabilities but not a precise one.

Power also depends on nonmaterial elements. Capabilities give a state the potential to influence others only to the extent that political leaders can mobilize and deploy these capabilities effectively and strategically. This depends on national will, diplomatic skill, popular support for the government (its legitimacy), and so forth. Some scholars emphasize the *power of ideas*—the ability to maximize the influence of capabilities through a psychological process. This process includes the domestic mobilization of capabilities—often through religion, ideology, or (especially) nationalism. International influence is also gained by forming the rules of behavior to change how others see their own national interests. If a state's own values become widely shared among other states, that state will easily influence others. This has been called *soft power*. For example, the United States has influenced many other states to accept the value of free markets and free trade.

As the concept of soft power illustrates, dominance is not the only way to exert power (influence others). The core principles of reciprocity and (in the case of soft power) identity can also work. For example, a father who wants his toddler to stop screaming in a supermarket might threaten or actually administer a spanking (dominance); he might promise a candy bar at the checkout as a reward for good behavior (reciprocity); or he could invoke such themes as "Be a big boy/girl" or "You want to help Daddy, don't you?" (identity). Although realists emphasize dominance approaches, they do not dispute that states sometimes achieve their interests in other ways. Furthermore, even realists recognize that power provides only a general understanding of outcomes. Real-world outcomes depend on many other elements, including accidents or luck.

Because power is a relational concept, a state can have power only relative to other states' power. *Relative power* is the ratio of the power that two states can bring to bear against each other. It matters little to realists whether a state's capabilities are rising or declining in absolute terms, only whether they are falling behind or overtaking the capabilities of rival states.

Estimating Power

The logic of power suggests that in wars the more powerful state will generally prevail. Thus, estimates of the relative power of the two antagonists should help explain the outcome of each war. These estimates could take into account the nations' relative military capabilities and the popular support for each one's government, among other factors. But most important is the total size of each nation's economy—the total GDP. With a healthy enough economy, a state can buy a large army, popular support (by providing consumer goods), and even allies.

Elements of Power

State power is a mix of many ingredients. Elements that an actor can draw on over the *long term* include total GDP, population, territory, geography, and natural resources. These attributes change only slowly. Less tangible long-term power resources include political culture, patriotism, education of the population, and strength of the scientific and technological base. The credibility of its commitments (reputation for keeping its word) is also a long-term power base for a state. So is the ability of one state's culture and values to consistently shape the thinking of other states (the power of ideas).

Other capabilities allow actors to exercise influence in the *short term*. Military forces are such a capability—perhaps the most important kind. The size, composition, and preparedness of two states' military forces matter more in a short-term military confrontation than their respective economies or natural resources. Another capability is the military-industrial capacity to quickly produce weapons. The quality of a state's bureaucracy is another type of

VIDEO

Counterinsurgency Warfare in Iraq

THE ECONOMICS OF POWER

Military power such as tanks rests on economic strength, roughly measured by GDP. The large U.S. economy supports U.S. military predominance. In the 2003 U.S. invasion of Iraq, the United States could afford to send a large and technologically advanced military force to the Middle East. Here, U.S. forces enter Iraq, March 2003.

capability, allowing the state to gather information, regulate international trade, or participate in international conferences. Less tangibly, the *support* and *legitimacy* that an actor commands in the short term from constituents and allies are capabilities that the actor can use to gain influence. So is the *loyalty* of a nation's army and politicians to their leader.

Given the limited resources that any actor commands, trade-offs among possible capabilities always exist. Building up military forces diverts resources that might be put into foreign aid, for instance. Or buying a population's loyalty with consumer goods reduces resources available to the military. To the extent that one element of power can be converted into another, it is *fungible*. Generally, money is the most fungible capability because it can buy other capabilities.

Realists tend to see *military force* as the most important element of national power in the short term, and other elements such as economic strength, diplomatic skill, or moral legitimacy as being important to the extent that they are fungible into military power. Yet, depending on the nature of the conflict in question, military power may be only one of many elements of power. A major theme of the Obama administration in 2009 was the use of multiple avenues of power, such as diplomacy and economic aid, to solve problems previously approached from mainly a military angle.

Morality can contribute to power, by increasing the will to use power and by attracting allies. States have long clothed their actions, however aggressive, in rhetoric about their peaceful and defensive intentions. Of course, if a state overuses moralistic rhetoric to cloak self-interest too often, it loses credibility even with its own population.

The use of geography as an element of power is called **geopolitics.** It is often tied to the logistical requirements of military forces. In geopolitics, as in real estate, the three most important considerations are location, location, location. States increase their power to the extent they can use geography to enhance their military capabilities, such as by securing allies and bases close to a rival power, or by controlling key natural resources. Today, control of oil pipeline routes, especially in Central Asia, is a major geopolitical issue.

The International System

States interact within a set of long-established "rules of the game" governing what is considered a state and how states treat each other. Together these rules shape the international system.

The modern international system is sometimes dated from the _Treaty of Westphalia_ in 1648, which ended the Thirty Years' War. It set out the basic rules that have defined the international system ever since—the sovereignty and territorial integrity of states as equal and independent members of an international system. Since then, states defeated in war might have been stripped of some territories but were generally allowed to continue as independent states rather than being subsumed by the victor. Key to this system was the ability of one state, or a coalition, to balance the power of another state so that it could not gobble up smaller units and create a universal empire.

Anarchy and Sovereignty

Realists believe that the international system exists in a state of **anarchy**—a term that implies not chaos or absence of structure and rules, but rather the lack of a central government that can enforce rules. In domestic society within states, governments can enforce contracts, deter citizens from breaking rules, and carry out laws. Both democracies and dictatorships provide central government enforcement of a system of rules. Realists contend that no such central authority exists to enforce rules and ensure compliance with norms of conduct. This makes collective goods problems especially acute in IR. The power of one state is countered only by the power of other states. States must therefore rely on _self-help,_ which they supplement with allies and the (sometimes) constraining power of international norms. In this anarchic world, realists emphasize prudence as a great virtue in foreign policy. Thus states should pay attention not to the _intentions_ of other states but rather to their _capabilities._

Despite its anarchy, the international system is far from chaotic. The great majority of state interactions closely adhere to **norms** of behavior—shared expectations about what behavior is considered proper. Norms change over time, slowly, but the most basic norms of the international system have changed little in recent centuries.

Sovereignty—traditionally the most important norm—means that a government has the right, in principle, to do whatever it wants in its own territory. States are separate and autonomous and answer to no higher authority. In principle, all states are equal in status, if not in power. Sovereignty also means that states are not supposed to interfere in the internal affairs of other states. Although states do try to influence each other (exert power) on matters of trade, alliances, war, and so on, they are not supposed to meddle in the internal politics and decision processes of other states. More controversially, some states claim that sovereignty gives them the right to treat their own people in any fashion, including behavior that other states call genocide.

The lack of a "world police" to punish states if they break an agreement makes enforcement of international agreements difficult. For example, in the 1990s, North Korea announced it would no longer allow inspections of its nuclear facilities by other states, which put it in violation of the Non-Proliferation Treaty (NPT). The international community used a mix of positive incentives and threats to persuade North Korea to stop producing nuclear material. But in 2002 North Korea withdrew from the NPT and built perhaps a half-dozen

TERRITORIAL LACK OF INTEGRITY

Sovereignty and territorial integrity are central norms governing the behavior of states. Terrorism and secessionist movements present two challenges to these norms. In 2008, Russia and Georgia fought a brief war over pro-Russian breakaway regions of Georgia, which ended up firmly in Russian control. Here, during the war, a tank from the region passes a billboard declaring Russia's Vladimir Putin "our president."

nuclear bombs, one of which it exploded in 2006 (the world's first nuclear test in a decade). After reaching an agreement with the United States to stop producing nuclear weapons in 2008, North Korea refused to allow physical inspection of some of its nuclear facilities, arguing "it is an act of infringing upon sovereignty." These examples show the difficulty of enforcing international norms in the sovereignty-based international system.

In practice, most states have a hard time warding off interference in their affairs. Such "internal" matters as human rights or self-determination are, increasingly, concerns for the international community. Also, the integration of global economic markets and telecommunications makes it easier than ever for ideas to penetrate state borders.

States are based on territory. Respect for the territorial integrity of all states, within recognized borders, is an important principle of IR. Many of today's borders are the result of past wars or were imposed arbitrarily by colonizers.

The territorial nature of the interstate system developed long ago when agrarian societies relied on agriculture to generate wealth. In today's world, in which trade and technology rather than land create wealth, the territorial state may be less important. Information-based economies are linked across borders instantly, and the idea that the state has a hard shell seems archaic. The accelerating revolution in information technologies may dramatically affect the territorial state system in the coming years.

States have developed norms of diplomacy to facilitate their interactions. Yet the norms of diplomacy can be violated. In 1979, Iranian students took over the U.S. embassy in Tehran, holding many of its diplomats hostage for 444 days—an episode that has soured American-Iranian relations ever since.

Realists acknowledge that the rules of IR often create a **security dilemma**—a situation in which actions taken by states to ensure their own security (such as deploying more military forces) threaten the security of other states. The responses of those other states (such as deploying more of their own military forces) in turn threaten the first state. The dilemma is a negative consequence of anarchy in the international system. If a world government could reliably detect and punish aggressors who arm themselves, states would not need to guard against this possibility. Yet the self-help system requires that states prepare for the worst. Realists tend to see the dilemma as unsolvable, whereas liberals think it can be solved through the development of norms and institutions (see Chapters 3 and 6).

VIDEO

The Global Arms Trade

Balance of Power

In the anarchy of the international system, the most reliable brake on the power of one state is the power of other states. The term **balance of power** refers to the general concept of one or more states' power being used to balance that of another state or group of states. Balance of power can refer to any ratio of power capabilities between states or alliances, or it can mean only a relatively equal ratio. Alternatively, balance of power can refer to the *process* by which counterbalancing coalitions have repeatedly formed in history to prevent one state from conquering an entire region. The theory of balance of power argues that such counterbalancing occurs regularly and maintains the stability of the international system. The system is stable in that its rules and principles stay the same: state sovereignty does not collapse into a universal empire. This stability does not, however, imply peace; it is rather a stability maintained by means of recurring wars that adjust power relations.

Alliances (to be discussed shortly) play a key role in the balance of power. Building up one's own capabilities against a rival is a form of power balancing, but forming an alliance against a threatening state is often quicker, cheaper, and more effective. Sometimes a particular state deliberately becomes a balancer (in its region or the world), shifting its support to oppose whatever state or alliance is strongest at the moment. Britain played this role on the European continent for centuries, and China played it in the Cold War.

In the post–Cold War era of U.S. dominance, balance-of-power theory would predict closer relations among Russia, China, and even Europe to balance U.S. power. These predictions appear to be on the mark. Russian-Chinese relations have improved dramatically in such areas as arms trade and demilitarization of the border. French leaders have criticized U.S. "hyperpower." Europe and Japan opposed U.S. positions on a range of proposed treaties in 2001 on such subjects as missile defense, biological weapons, small-arms trade, and global warming. In 2003, world public opinion revealed widespread anti-American sentiment. In Indonesia, Pakistan, Turkey, and Nigeria—containing half of the world's Muslims—more than 70 percent worried that the United States could become a threat to their own countries, a worry shared by 71 percent of Russians. A survey of 38,000 people in 44 nations showed a dramatic drop in support for the United States from 2002 to 2003. As Figure 2.1 illustrates, this decline in favorable views of the United States worldwide continued through 2007. Yet, 2008 brought a slight upturn in opinions of the United States. A survey of 24,000 people in 24 countries found a more positive view of America in ten of those countries. The survey noted that optimism over the 2008 presidential elections (the survey was completed before the outcome was known) accounted for some of the change in viewpoints. Still, the predominance of U.S. power has led to counterbalancing, as predicted by balance-of-power theory.

FIGURE 2.1   Views of the United States in Nine Countries, 2000–2008
(Percent favorable view in public opinion polls)

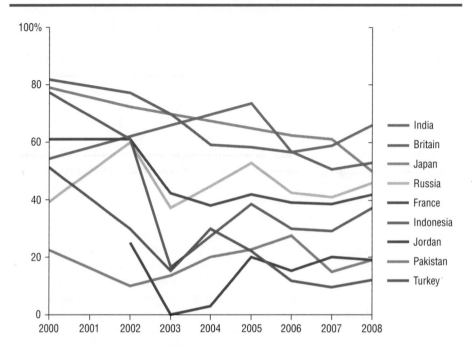

Source: *New York Times* from data of Pew Global Attitudes Project. 2000 data from State Department surveys.

Great Powers and Middle Powers

The most powerful states in the world exert most of the influence on international events and therefore get the most attention from IR scholars. By almost any measure of power, a handful of states possess the majority of the world's power resources.

Although there is no firm dividing line, **great powers** are generally considered the half-dozen or so most powerful states. A system of great power relations has existed since around A.D. 1500, and the structure and rules of that system have remained fairly stable through time, although the particular members change. The structure is a balance of power among the six or so most powerful states, which form and break alliances, fight wars, and make peace, letting no single state conquer the others. Until the past century the great power club was exclusively European. Sometimes great powers' status is formally recognized in an international structure such as the 19th-century Concert of Europe or today's UN Security Council. In general, great powers are often defined as states that can be defeated militarily only by another great power. Great powers also tend to share a global outlook based on national interests far from their home territories.

The great powers generally have the world's strongest military forces and the strongest economies to pay for them. These large economies in turn rest on some combination of large populations, plentiful natural resources, advanced technology, and educated labor forces.

Because power is based on these underlying resources, membership in the great power system changes slowly. Only rarely does a great power—even one defeated in a massive war—lose its status as a great power, because its size and long-term economic potential change slowly. Thus Germany and Japan, decimated in World War II, are powerful today.

In the *Concert of Europe* that dominated IR in the 19th century, the five most powerful states tried, with some success, to cooperate on major issues to prevent war—a possible precedent for today's UN Security Council. In this period, Britain became a balancer, joining alliances against whichever state emerged as the most powerful in Europe.

After World War II, the United States and the Soviet Union, allies in the war against Germany, became adversaries for 40 years in the Cold War. Europe was split into rival blocs—East and West—with Germany split into two states. The rest of the world became contested terrain where each bloc tried to gain allies or influence, often by sponsoring opposing sides in regional and civil wars. The end of the Cold War around 1990, when the Soviet Union collapsed, returned the international system to a more cooperative arrangement of the great powers somewhat similar to the Concert of Europe.

What states are great powers today? Although definitions vary, seven states appear to meet the criteria: the United States, China, Russia, Japan, Germany, France, and Britain. Together they account for more than half of the world's total GDP (see Figure 2.2). They include the five permanent members of the UN Security Council, who are also the members of the "club" openly possessing large nuclear weapons arsenals.

FIGURE 2.2   Great Power Shares of World GDP and Military Expenditures, 2007

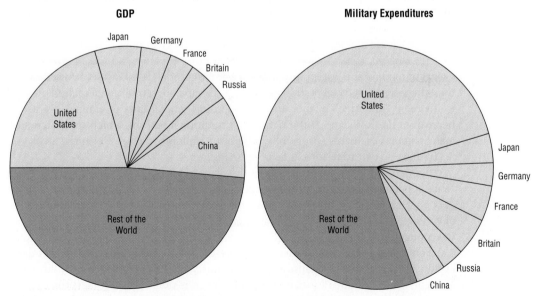

Note: GDP calculated by purchasing-power method. China's GDP using alternate method would be about half as large.
Data sources: World Bank, World Development Indicators 2007; SIPRI, SIPRI Yearbook 2007

Notable on this list are the United States and China. The United States is considered the world's only superpower because of its historical role of world leadership (especially in and after World War II) and its predominant military might. China has the world's largest population, rapid economic growth (8–10 percent annually over 15 years), and a large though not very modern military including a credible nuclear arsenal. Indeed, in 2008, the U.S. National Intelligence Council's long-range planning report noted that China is poised to have a profound effect on the world over the next 20 years—perhaps more than any other state. Japan and Germany are economic great powers, but both countries have played constrained roles in international security affairs since World War II. Nonetheless, both have large and capable military forces, which they have begun to deploy abroad, especially in peacekeeping operations. Russia, France, and Britain were winners in World War II and have been active military powers since then. Although much reduced in stature from their colonial heydays, they still qualify as great powers.

Middle powers rank somewhat below the great powers in terms of their influence on world affairs. A list of middle powers (not everyone would agree on it) might include midsized countries of the global North such as Canada, Italy, Spain, the Netherlands, Poland, Ukraine, South Korea, and Australia. It could also include large or influential countries in the global South such as India, Indonesia, Brazil, Argentina, Mexico, Nigeria, South Africa, Israel, Turkey, Iran, and Pakistan. Middle powers have not received as much attention in IR as have great powers.

Power Distribution

With each state's power balanced by other states, the most important characteristic of the international system in the view of some realists is the *distribution* of power among states. Power distribution as a concept can apply to all the states in the world or to just the states in one region, but most often it refers to the great power system.

Neorealism, sometimes called *structural realism*, explains patterns of international events in terms of the system structure—the international distribution of power—rather than the internal makeup of individual states. Compared to traditional realism, neorealism is more "scientific" in the sense of proposing general laws to explain events, but neorealism has lost some of the richness of traditional realism, which took account of many complex elements (geography, willpower, diplomacy, etc.). Recently, *neoclassical realists* have sought to restore some of these lost aspects.

Sometimes an international power distribution (world or regional) is described in terms of polarity (a term adopted from physics), which refers to the number of independent power centers in the system. This concept encompasses both the underlying power of various participants and their alliance groupings. Figure 2.3 illustrates several potential configurations of great powers.

Some might argue that peace is best preserved by a relatively equal power distribution (multipolarity) because then no country has an opportunity to win easily. The empirical evidence for this theory, however, is not strong. In fact, the opposite proposition has more support: peace is best preserved by hegemony, and next best by bipolarity.

FIGURE 2.3   Power Distribution in the International System

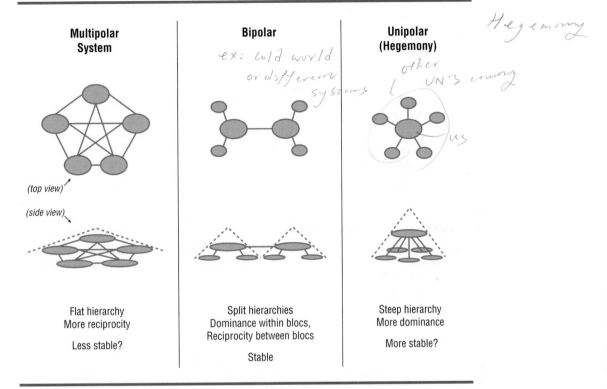

Power transition theory holds that the largest wars result from challenges to the top position in the status hierarchy, when a rising power is surpassing (or threatening to surpass) the most powerful state. At such times, power is relatively equally distributed, and these are the most dangerous times for major wars. Status quo powers that are doing well under the old rules will try to maintain them, whereas challengers that feel locked out by the old rules may try to change them. When a rising power's status (formal position in the hierarchy) diverges from its actual power, the rising power may suffer from relative deprivation: its people may feel they are not doing as well as others or as well as they deserve, even though their position may be improving in absolute terms. Germany's rise in the 19th century gave it great power capabilities even though it was left out of colonial territories and other signs of status; this tension may have contributed to the two world wars. China may face a similar problem in the future.

Hegemony

Hegemony is one state's holding a preponderance of power in the international system, allowing it to single-handedly dominate the rules and arrangements by which international political and economic relations are conducted. Such a state is called a *hegemon*.

Sometimes the term is used to refer to the complex of ideas that rulers use to gain consent for their legitimacy and keep subjects in line, reducing the need to use force to accomplish the same goal. By extension, such a meaning in IR refers to the hegemony of ideas such as democracy and capitalism, and to the global predominance of U.S. culture (see p. 339).

Most studies of hegemony point to two examples: Britain in the 19th century and the United States after World War II. Britain's predominance followed the defeat of its archrival France in the Napoleonic Wars. Both world trade and naval capabilities were firmly in British hands, as "Britannia ruled the waves." U.S. predominance followed the destruction caused by World War II. In the late 1940s, the U.S. GDP was more than half the world's total; U.S. vessels carried the majority of the world's shipping; the U.S. military could single-handedly defeat any other state or combination of states; and only the United States had nuclear weapons. Over time, and as rival states rebuild after wars, hegemonic decline may occur, particularly when hegemons have overextended themselves with costly military commitments.

Hegemonic stability theory holds that hegemony provides some order similar to a central government in the international system: reducing anarchy, deterring aggression, promoting free trade, and providing a hard currency that can be used as a world standard. Hegemons can help resolve or at least keep in check conflicts among middle powers or small states. When one state's power dominates the world, that state can enforce rules and norms unilaterally, avoiding the collective goods problem. In particular, hegemons can maintain global free trade and promote world economic growth, in this view.

From the perspective of less powerful states, of course, hegemony may seem an infringement of state sovereignty, and the order it creates may seem unjust or illegitimate. For instance, China chafed under U.S.-imposed economic sanctions for 20 years after 1949, at the height of U.S. power, when China was encircled by U.S. military bases and hostile alliances led by the United States. To this day, Chinese leaders use the term *hegemony* as an insult, and the theory of hegemonic stability does not impress them.

Even in the United States there is considerable ambivalence about U.S. hegemony. U.S. foreign policy has historically alternated between *internationalist* and *isolationist* moods. In World War I, the country waited three years to weigh in and refused to join the League of Nations afterward. U.S. isolationism peaked in the 1930s; public opinion polls late in that decade showed 95 percent of the U.S. public opposed to participation in a future great European war, and about 70 percent opposed to joining with other nations to stop aggression.

Internationalists, such as Presidents Theodore Roosevelt and Woodrow Wilson, favored U.S. leadership and activism in world affairs. These views seemed vindicated by the failure of isolationism to prevent or avoid World War II. U.S. leaders after that war feared Soviet (and then Chinese) communism and pushed U.S. public opinion toward a strong internationalism during the Cold War. The United States became an activist, global superpower.

A second area of U.S. ambivalence is *unilateralism* versus *multilateralism* when the United States does engage internationally. Multilateral approaches—working through international institutions—augment U.S. power and re- duce costs, but they limit U.S. freedom of action. In 2001, the George W. Bush administration declined to participate in such international efforts as a treaty on global warming (see pp. 312–313), a conference on racism, and an International Criminal Court (see p. 253). Unilateralist U.S. policies drew resistance from Europe and Canada. The international community's united front against terror- ism pushed these disputes to the back burner, but they soon reemerged. The 2003 U.S.-led war in Iraq, with few allies and no UN stamp of approval, marked the peak of U.S. unilateralism. The Obama administration, however, has taken a more multilateral approach in these issue areas.

Alliances

An *alliance* is a coalition of states that coordinate their actions to accomplish some end. Most alliances are formal- ized in written treaties, concern a common threat and related issues of international security, and endure across a range of issues and a period of time. If actors' purposes in banding together were shorter-term, less formal, or more issue-specific, the association might be called a *coalition* rather than an alliance. Informal but enduring strategic *alignments* in a region are discussed shortly. But these terms are somewhat ambiguous. Two countries may have a formal alliance and yet be bitter enemies, as are Greece and Turkey. Or, two countries may create the practical equivalent of an alliance without a formal treaty.

Purposes of Alliances

Alliances generally have the purpose of augmenting their members' power by pooling capabilities. For smaller states, alliances can be their most important power element, and for great powers the structure of alliances shapes the configu- ration of power in the system. Of all the elements of power,

PRICE OF HEGEMONY

The United States is the world's most power- ful single actor. Its ability and willingness to resume a role as hegemon—as after World War II—are important factors that will shape world order, but the U.S. role is still uncertain. America's willingness to absorb casualties will affect its role. Here, soldiers return from Afghanistan, 2004.

none can change as quickly and decisively as alliances. Most alliances form in response to a perceived threat. When a state's power grows and threatens that of its rivals, the lat- ter often form an alliance to limit that power. This happened to Iraq when it invaded Kuwait in 1990, as it had to Hitler's Germany in the 1940s and to Napoleon's France in the 1800s.

MARRIAGE OF CONVENIENCE

Alliances generally result from a convergence of practical interests, not sentimental or ideological reasons. Here, a U.S. general gets rival Afghan warlords to patch up relations, 2002.

Realists emphasize the fluidity of alliances. They are not marriages of love, but marriages of convenience. Alliances are based on national interests, and can shift as national interests change. This fluidity helps the balance-of-power process operate effectively. Examples of fluid alliances are many. Anticommunist Richard Nixon could cooperate with communist Mao Zedong in 1972. Joseph Stalin could sign a nonaggression pact with a fascist, Adolf Hitler, and then cooperate with the capitalist West against Hitler. The United States could back the Islamic militants in Afghanistan against the Soviet Union in the 1980s, then attack them in 2001. Every time history brings another such reversal in international alignments, many people are surprised. Realists are not so surprised.

The fluidity of alliances deepens the security dilemma (see p. 42). If there were only two states, each could match capabilities to have adequate defense but an inability to attack successfully. But if a third state is free to ally with either side, then each state has to build adequate defenses against the potential alliance of its enemy with the third state. The threat is greater and the security dilemma is harder to escape.

Alliance cohesion is the ease with which the members hold together an alliance. Cohesion tends to be high when national interests converge and when cooperation within the alliance becomes institutionalized and habitual. When states with divergent interests form an alliance against a common enemy, the alliance may come apart if the threat subsides. It did, for instance, with the World War II U.S.-Soviet alliance. Even when alliance cohesion is high, as in NATO during the Cold War, conflicts may arise over **burden sharing** (who bears the costs of the alliance).

Great powers often form alliances (or less formal commitments) with smaller states, sometimes called *client states*. Extended deterrence refers to a strong state's use of threats to deter attacks on weaker clients—such as the U.S. threat to attack the

Partnership for Peace—which almost all Eastern European and former Soviet states including Russia joined.

Other Alliances

The second most important alliance is the **U.S.-Japanese Security Treaty,** a bilateral alliance. Under this alliance the United States maintains nearly 35,000 troops in Japan (with weapons, equipment, and logistical support). Japan pays the United States several billion dollars annually to offset about half the cost of maintaining these troops. The alliance was created in 1951 against the potential Soviet threat to Japan.

Because of its roots in the U.S. military occupation of Japan after World War II, the alliance is very asymmetrical. The United States is committed to defend Japan if it is attacked, but Japan is not similarly obligated to defend the United States. The United States maintains troops in Japan, but not vice versa. The United States belongs to several other alliances, but Japan's only major alliance is with the United States. The U.S. share of the total military power in this alliance is also far greater than its share in NATO.

Japan's constitution renounces the right to make war and maintain military forces, although interpretation has loosened this prohibition over time. Japan maintains military forces, called the Self-Defense Forces, which is a powerful army by world standards but much smaller than Japan's economic strength could support. Japanese public opinion restrains militarism and precludes the development of nuclear weapons (after Japanese cities were destroyed by nuclear weapons in World War II). Nonetheless, some Japanese leaders believe that Japan's formal security role should expand commensurate with its economic power.

For its part, the United States has used the alliance with Japan as a base to project U.S. power in Asia, especially during the wars in Korea (1950–1953) and Vietnam (1965–1975), when Japan was a key staging area. However, these U.S. forces have been drawn down somewhat in the past decade in response to high costs, reduced threats, and some opposition by local residents (especially on Okinawa). As the U.S. focuses more on the Middle East, further cuts in troops may follow.

Parallel with the U.S.-Japan treaty, the United States maintains military alliances with several other states, including South Korea and Australia. Close U.S. collaboration with militaries in other states such as Israel make them de facto U.S. allies.

The 12 members of the *Commonwealth of Independent States (CIS)* comprise the former Soviet republics except the Baltic states (Estonia, Latvia, and Lithuania). Russia, the official successor state to the Soviet Union, is the leading member and Ukraine the second largest. Although some military coordination takes place through the CIS, initial plans for a joint military force instead of 12 independent armies did not succeed. Among the largest CIS members, Kazakhstan and Belarus are the most closely aligned with Russia, while Ukraine is the most independent (and in fact never officially ratified the CIS agreement). In 2008, Georgia declared it would withdraw from the CIS, effective in August 2009, over its conflict with Russia.

POLICY PERSPECTIVES

Prime Minister of India, Manmohan Singh

PROBLEM   *How do you confront a fluid security environment by managing current and formal rivals?*

BACKGROUND   As the world's largest democracy, your country faces many challenges both at home and abroad. In particular, in the past 50 years, you have fought wars against your two largest neighbors, China and Pakistan. Both states possess nuclear weapons, as do you. China and Pakistan have cooperated with each other in the past, including on sales of high technology military goods such as missiles.

Your generally hostile relationship with Pakistan grows from a territorial dispute over half of the region of Kashmir, which both of you claim, but India maintains control over. The territory is coveted not only by your respective governments but by the publics in each country as well. While there has been cooperation between each country, tensions still run high over Kashmir. In the aftermath of the November 2008 terrorist attacks in Mombai, many in your country blamed Pakistan since it is home to Islamic militant groups.

Your hostilities with China have cooled over the years, but China remains a major rival in the region and you still maintain competing claims over territory. Like your own country, China is large economically as well as militarily, and it attempts to exert strong leadership in your region. In the past two years, however, you have increased ties with China and you personally visited China at the beginning of 2008 to open discussions on future trade and military cooperation. In December 2007, your armies (the two largest in the world) held joint training exercises.

DOMESTIC CONSIDERATIONS   Within your country, neither Pakistan nor China are popular choices for allies. Your population is still angered by the Chinese victory in the 1962 Sino-Indian war and the disputed border territory that gave rise to the conflict. Yet your largely Hindu population is also angry at repeated attempts by Muslim Pakistan to gain control of Kashmir.

Your advisors also remind you that China still has a healthy relationship with Pakistan, including sales of advanced weapons and large flows of military assistance. Indeed the main political opposition parties argue that you have been too "soft" on both Pakistan and China in your time as prime minister. Any public backlash against your foreign policy on these issues could be widespread and bring calls for new elections that could unseat your government.

SCENARIO   Imagine that the government of Pakistan begins to suffer from large-scale instability. Islamist militants are close to overthrowing the government there, giving them control of Pakistan's nuclear weapons. They are also calling for Muslims in Kashmir to rise up against Indian control, promising to openly assist a rebellion in that province by providing weapons and intelligence. Your own intelligence service considers the collapse of the current Pakistani government "likely."

CHOOSE YOUR POLICY   Do you push for closer relations with China as a result of instability in Pakistan? Can you trust China to support you in a dispute with Pakistan, given those countries' close relationship? Do you ask China to help mediate between your government and Pakistan in the event of hostilities? Or do you continue your course as independently as possible, not trusting Chinese intentions toward your country?

FIGURE 2.5   Current Alignment of Great and Middle Powers

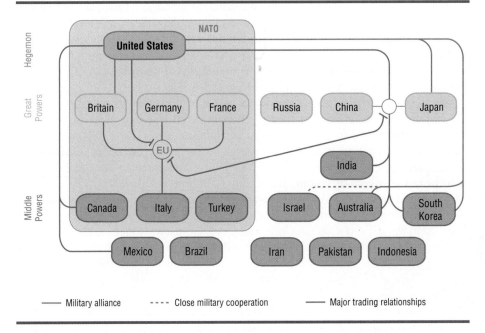

—— Military alliance   - - - - Close military cooperation   —— Major trading relationships

For the present, international alignments—both military alliances and trade relationships—center on the United States (see Figure 2.5). Although several independent-minded states such as China, Russia, and France keep U.S. hegemony in check, little evidence exists of a coherent or formal rival power alignment emerging to challenge the United States.

Strategy

Actors use strategy to pursue good outcomes in bargaining with one or more other actors. States deploy power capabilities as leverage to influence each other's actions. Bargaining is interactive, and requires an actor to take account of other actors' interests even while pursuing its own. Sometimes bargaining communication takes place through actions rather than words.

Statecraft

Classical realists emphasize *statecraft*—the art of managing state affairs and effectively maneuvering in a world of power politics among sovereign states. Power strategies are plans actors use to develop and deploy power capabilities to achieve their goals.

A key aspect of strategy is choosing the kinds of capabilities to develop, given limited resources, in order to maximize international influence. This requires foresight because the capabilities required to manage a situation may need to be developed years before that situation presents itself. Yet the capabilities chosen often will not be fungible in the short term. Central to this dilemma is what kind of standing military forces to maintain in peacetime—enough to prevent a quick defeat if war breaks out, but not so much as to overburden one's economy (see pp. 165–168).

Strategies also shape policies for when a state is willing to use its power capabilities. The *will* of a nation or leader is hard to estimate. Even if leaders make explicit their intention to fight over an issue, they might be bluffing.

VIDEO

Chinese President's U.S. Visit

The strategic actions of China in recent years exemplify the concept of strategy as rational deployment of power capabilities. China's central foreign policy goal is to prevent the independence of Taiwan, which China considers an integral part of its territory (as does the United Nations and, at least in theory, the United States). China may not have the military power to invade Taiwan successfully, but it has declared repeatedly that it will go to war if Taiwan declares independence. So far, even though such a war might be irrational on China's part, the threat has deterred Taiwan from formally declaring independence. China also breaks diplomatic relations with countries that recognize Taiwan. Chinese strategies mobilize various capabilities, including missiles, diplomats, and industrial conglomerates, in a coherent effort to influence the outcome of China's most important international issue. Strategy thus amplifies China's power.

The strategy of **deterrence** uses a threat to punish another actor if it takes a certain negative action (especially attacking one's own state or one's allies). If deterrence works, its effects are almost invisible; its success is measured in attacks that did not occur.

Most advocates of deterrence believe that conflicts are more likely to escalate into war when one party to the conflict is weak. In this view, building up military capabilities usually convinces the stronger party that a resort to military leverage would not succeed, so conflicts are less likely to escalate into violence. A strategy of **compellence,** sometimes used after deterrence fails, refers to the use of force to make another actor take some action (rather than refrain from taking an action). Generally it is harder to get another state to change course (the purpose of compellence) than it is to get it to refrain from changing course (the purpose of deterrence).

One strategy used to try to compel compliance by another state is *escalation*—a series of negative sanctions of increasing severity applied in order to induce another actor to take some action. In theory, the less severe actions establish credibility—showing the first actor's willingness to exert its power on the issue—and the pattern of escalation establishes the high costs of future sanctions if the second actor does not cooperate. These actions should induce the second actor to comply, assuming that it finds the potential costs of the escalating punishments greater than the costs of compliance. But escalation can be quite dangerous. During the Cold War, many IR scholars worried that a conventional war could lead to nuclear war if the superpowers tried to apply escalation strategies.

An **arms race** is a reciprocal process in which two (or more) states build up military capabilities in response to each other. Because each wants to act prudently against a threat, the attempt to reciprocate leads to a runaway production of weapons

by both sides. The mutual escalation of threats erodes confidence, reduces cooperation, and makes it more likely that a crisis (or accident) could cause one side to
strike first and start a war rather than wait for the other
side to strike. The arms race process was illustrated
vividly in the U.S.-Soviet nuclear arms race, which
created arsenals of tens of thousands of nuclear weapons
on each side.

Rationality

Most realists (and many nonrealists) assume that those
who wield power while engaging in statecraft behave as
rational actors in their efforts to influence others. This
view has two implications for IR.

First, the assumption of rationality implies that states
and other international actors can identify their interests
and put priorities on various interests: A state's actions
seek to advance its interests. Many realists assume that
the actor (usually a state) exercising power is a single entity that can "think" about its actions coherently and
make choices. This is called the *unitary actor* assumption,
or sometimes the *strong leader* assumption. The assumption
is a simplification, because the interests of particular
politicians, parties, economic sectors, or regions of a country often conflict. Yet realists assume that the exercise of
power attempts to advance the **national interest**—the interests of the state itself.

But what are the interests of a state? Are they the
interests of domestic groups (see Chapter 3)? The need to
prevail in conflicts with other states (see Chapter 4)? The
ability to cooperate with the international community for
mutual benefit (see Chapter 6)? There is no simple
answer. Some realists simply define the national interest as
maximizing power—a debatable assumption. Others
compare power in IR with money in economics—a
universal measure. In this view, just as firms compete for
money in economic markets, states compete for power in
the international system.

Second, rationality implies that actors are able to
perform a **cost-benefit analysis**—calculating the costs
incurred by a possible action and the benefits it is likely
to bring. Applying power incurs costs and should
produce commensurate gains. As in the problem of esti-
mating power, one has to add up different dimensions in
such a calculation. For instance, states presumably do

INTERNAL DIVISIONS

The unitary actor assumption holds that states
make important decisions as though they were
single individuals able to act in the national interest. In truth, factions and organizations with differing interests put conflicting pressures on state
leaders. Iraq is badly split among Shi'ite, Sunni,
and Kurdish factions, which could not agree on
the shape of a government for months after the
elections of December 2005. Here, one faction
campaigns in the election.

not initiate wars that they expect to lose, except when they stand to gain political benefits, domestic or international, that outweigh the costs of losing the war. But it is not easy to tally intangible political benefits against the tangible costs of a war. Even victory in a war may not be worth the costs paid. Rational actors can miscalculate costs and benefits, especially when using faulty information (although this does not mean they are irrational). Finally, human behavior and luck can be unpredictable.

These assumptions about rationality and the actors in IR are simplifications that not all IR scholars accept. But realists consider these simplifications useful because they allow scholars to explain in a general way the actions of diverse actors.

The Prisoner's Dilemma

Game theory is a branch of mathematics concerned with predicting bargaining outcomes. A game is a setting in which two or more players choose among alternative moves, either once or repeatedly. Each combination of moves (by all players) results in a set of payoffs (utility) to each player. The payoffs can be tangible items such as money or any intangible items of value. Game theory aims to deduce likely outcomes (what moves players will make), given the players' preferences and the possible moves open to them. Games are sometimes called formal models.

Game theory was first used extensively in IR in the 1950s and 1960s by scholars trying to understand U.S.-Soviet nuclear war contingencies. Moves were decisions to use nuclear weapons in certain ways, and payoffs were outcomes of the war. The use of game theory to study international interactions has become more extensive among IR scholars in recent years, especially among realists, who accept the assumptions about rationality. To analyze a game mathematically, one assumes that each player chooses a move rationally, to maximize its payoff.

Different kinds of situations are represented by different classes of games, as defined by the number of players and the structure of the payoffs. One basic distinction is between **zero-sum games,** in which one player's gain is by definition equal to the other's loss, and *non-zero-sum games*, in which it is possible for both players to gain (or lose). In a zero-sum game there is no point in communication or cooperation between the players because their interests are diametrically opposed. But in a non-zero-sum game, coordination of moves can maximize the total payoff to the players, although each may still maneuver to gain a greater share of that total payoff.

The game called **Prisoner's Dilemma (PD)** captures the kind of collective goods problem common to IR. In this situation, rational players choose moves that produce an outcome in which all players are worse off than under a different set of moves. They all could do better, but as individual rational actors they are unable to achieve this outcome. How can this be?

The original story tells of two prisoners questioned separately by a prosecutor. The prosecutor knows they committed a bank robbery but has only enough evidence to convict them of illegal possession of a gun unless one of them confesses. The prosecutor tells each prisoner that if he confesses and his partner doesn't confess, he will go free. If his partner confesses and he doesn't, he will get a long prison term for bank robbery (while the partner goes free). If both confess, they will get a somewhat reduced term. If neither confesses, they will be convicted on the gun charge and serve a short sentence. The story assumes that neither prisoner will have a chance to retaliate later, that only the immediate outcomes matter, and that each prisoner cares only about himself.

This game has a single solution: both prisoners will confess. Each will reason as follows: "If my partner is going to confess, then I should confess too, because I will get a slightly shorter sentence that way. If my partner is not going to confess, then I should still confess because I will go free that way instead of serving a short sentence." The other prisoner follows the same reasoning. The dilemma is that by following their individually rational choices, both prisoners end up serving a fairly long sentence when they could have both served a short one by cooperating (keeping their mouths shut).

In IR, the PD game has been used to gain insight into arms races. Consider the decisions of India and Pakistan about whether to build sizable nuclear weapons arsenals. Both have the ability to do so. Neither side can know whether the other is secretly building up an arsenal unless they reach an arms control agreement with strict verification provisions. To analyze the game, we assign values to each possible outcome—often called a *preference ordering*—for each player. This is not simple: if we misjudge the value a player puts on a particular outcome, we may draw wrong conclusions from the game.

The following preferences regarding possible outcomes are plausible: the best outcome would be that oneself but not the other player had a nuclear arsenal (the expense of building nuclear weapons would be worth it because one could then use them as leverage); second best would be for neither to go nuclear (no leverage, but no expense); third best would be for both to develop nuclear arsenals (a major expense without gaining leverage); worst would be to forgo nuclear weapons oneself while the other player developed them (and thus be subject to blackmail).

The game can be summarized in a *payoff matrix* (see Figure 2.6). The first number in each cell is India's payoff, and the second number is Pakistan's. To keep things simple, 4 indicates the highest payoff, and 1 the lowest. As is conventional, a decision to refrain from building nuclear weapons is called "cooperation," and a

FIGURE 2.6 Payoff Matrix in India-Pakistan PD Game

		Pakistan	
		Cooperate	Defect
India	Cooperate	(3,3)	(1,4)
	Defect	(4,1)	(2,2)

Note: First number in each group is India's payoff, second is Pakistan's. The number 4 is highest payoff, 1 lowest.

decision to proceed with nuclear weapons is called "defection." The dilemma here parallels that of the prisoners just discussed. Each state's leader reasons: "If they go nuclear, we must; if they don't, we'd be crazy not to." The model seems to predict an inevitable Indian-Pakistani nuclear arms race, although both states would do better to avoid one.

This India-Pakistan example appeared in the first edition of this textbook in 1993. Since then, as predicted by the model, both sides have built nuclear weapons. In 1998, India detonated underground nuclear explosions to test weapons designs, and Pakistan promptly followed suit. In 2002, the two states nearly went to war, with projected war deaths of up to 12 million. A costly and dangerous arms race continues, and both sides now have dozens of nuclear missiles, and counting. This example illustrates why realists tend to be pessimistic about cooperative solutions to collective goods problems such as the one that the PD game embodies.

This chapter has focused on the concerns of realists—the interests of states, distribution of power among states, bargaining between states, and alliances of states. The chapter has treated states as unitary actors, much as one would analyze the interactions of individual people. The actions of state leaders have been treated as more or less rational in terms of pursuing definable interests through coherent bargaining strategies. But realism is not the only way to frame the major issues of international security. Chapter 3 reexamines these themes critically, relying less on the core principle of dominance and more on reciprocity and identity.

CHAPTER REVIEW

SUMMARY

- Realism explains international relations in terms of power. Power can be conceptualized as influence or as capabilities that can create influence.
- The most important single indicator of a state's power is its GDP.
- Short-term power capabilities depend on long-term resources, both tangible and intangible. Realists consider military force the most important power capability.
- International anarchy—the absence of world government—means that each state is a sovereign and autonomous actor pursuing its own national interests.
- Seven great powers account for half of the world's GDP as well as the great majority of military forces and other power capabilities.
- Power transition theory says that wars often result from shifts in relative power distribution in the international system.
- Hegemony—the predominance of one state in the international system—can help provide stability and peace in international relations, but with some drawbacks.

- States form alliances to increase their effective power. Alliances can shift rapidly, with major effects on power relations. The world's main alliances, including NATO and the U.S.-Japanese alliance, face uncertain roles in a changing world order.

- International affairs can be seen as a series of bargaining interactions in which states use power capabilities as leverage to influence the outcomes.

- Rational-actor approaches treat states as though they were individuals acting to maximize their own interests. These simplifications are debatable but allow realists to develop concise and general models and explanations.

- Game theory draws insights from simplified models of bargaining situations, such as the Prisoner's Dilemma.

KEY TERMS

realism 35	great powers 44	U.S.-Japanese Security
idealism 35	middle powers 46	Treaty 53
League of	neorealism 46	deterrence 56
Nations 35	hegemony 47	compellence 56
Munich Agreement 36	hegemonic stability	arms race 56
power 37	theory 48	rational actors 57
geopolitics 40	alliance cohesion 50	national interest 57
anarchy 41	burden sharing 50	cost-benefit analysis 57
norms 41	North Atlantic Treaty	game theory 58
sovereignty 41	Organization	zero-sum games 58
security dilemma 42	(NATO) 51	Prisoner's Dilemma
balance of power 43	Warsaw Pact 51	(PD) 58

ONLINE PRACTICE TEST

Take an online practice test at
www.IRtext.com

❏ **A**
❏ **B**
❏ **C**
❏ **D**

CRITICAL THINKING QUESTIONS

1. Using Table 1.5 on pp. 22–23 (with GDP as a measure of power) and the maps at the front of the book, pick a state and speculate about what coalition of nearby states might form with sufficient power to oppose the state if it became aggressive.

2. Choose a recent international event and list the power capabilities that participants used as leverage in the episode. Which capabilities were effective, and why?

3. The modern international system came into being at a time when agrarian societies relied primarily on farmland to create wealth. Now that most wealth is no longer created through farming, is the territorial nature of states obsolete? How might the diminishing economic value of territory change how states interact?

BACK TO THE BIG PICTURE

To hear a discussion of the "big picture" for this chapter, raised on p. 36, along with an example from recent history, consult the "IR Talk" podcast for Chapter 2 at *www.IRtext.com*

PODCAST

Greek and Turkish leaders of divided Cyprus with UN mediator, 2008.

CHAPTER **3**   # Liberal and Social Theories

Liberal Traditions

If realism offers mostly dominance solutions to the collective goods problems of IR, several alternative theoretical approaches discussed in this chapter draw mostly on the reciprocity and identity principles (see Figure 3.1). Among other common elements, these approaches generally are more optimistic than realism about the prospects for peace.

The Waning of War

Although realists see the laws of power politics as relatively timeless and unchanging, liberal theorists generally see the rules of IR as slowly, incrementally evolving through time and potentially becoming more and more peaceful. This evolution results primarily from the gradual buildup of international organizations and mutual cooperation (reciprocity) and secondarily from changes in norms and public opinion (identity). The main theories discussed in this chapter all hold that we are not doomed to a world of recurring war but can achieve a more peaceful world.

CHAPTER OUTLINE

- **Liberal Traditions**
- **Domestic Influences**
- **Making Foreign Policy**
- **Social Theories**
- **Peace Studies**
- **Gender Theories**

THE BIG PICTURE

RECIPROCITY

Is realism realistic? Contrary to its predictions, much more cooperation than conflict occurs in IR, and cooperation is increasing year by year and decade by decade. Notwithstanding brutal conflicts in Iraq and Sudan, the world overall has become more and more peaceful.

Liberal theories of IR, following the philosopher Kant, explain this in two major ways. First, based on the reciprocity principle, states learn to cooperate and build international institutions to achieve mutual gains. Second, based on the identity principle, certain kinds of society or government type will make societies decide not to go to war. In common with this second liberal approach, social theories and gender theories explain IR outcomes at the domestic and individual levels of analysis.

To hear the authors of this book discuss this issue, with an example from recent history, download the "IR Talk" podcast for Chapter 3 from www.IRtext.com.

PODCAST

In recent years, a strong trend toward fewer wars has become evident. To many Americans, the world seems more war-prone and violent than ever, because the country is at war on a scale not seen since Vietnam. Yet for the world as a whole, the current period is one of the least warlike ever, with fewer and smaller wars than in the past.

First consider the long-term trend. In the first half of the 20th century, world wars killed tens of millions and left whole continents in ruin. In the second half of that century, during the Cold War, proxy wars killed millions, and the world feared a nuclear war that could have wiped out our species. Now, in the early 21st century, wars like those in Iraq and Sudan kill hundreds of thousands. We fear terrorist attacks that could destroy a city, but not life on the planet. Generation by generation, the world has moved forward, unevenly but inexorably, from tens of millions killed, to millions, to hundreds of thousands. This is still a large number and the impacts of war are still catastrophic. Perhaps if we could understand and sustain this trend, major wars might fade away altogether, though minor wars and terror attacks may continue to kill thousands of people.

Events in the post–Cold War era continue this long-term trend toward smaller wars. The late 1990s and early 21st century saw the termination of lingering Cold War–era conflicts such as in Angola, Northern Ireland, Guatemala, and southern Sudan (following South Africa and Mozambique earlier in the 1990s). Most of the wars that flared up after the Cold War ended, such as in Bosnia, Kosovo, Algeria, Rwanda, Burundi, and Uganda, have also come to an end. This waning of war continues in recent years. Liberia and Ivory Coast established power-sharing governments and brought in international peacekeepers—following in the path of Sierra Leone (which in 2003 held democratic elections). In 2005, the Irish Republican Army finished permanently dismantling its weaponry. India and Pakistan began their first cease-fire in a decade, as did Burma's government and its largest rebel militia.

Today's most serious conflicts consist mainly of skirmishing rather than all-out battles. The last battles between heavily armed forces on both sides (with, for example, artillery,

FIGURE 3.1   Theories of IR

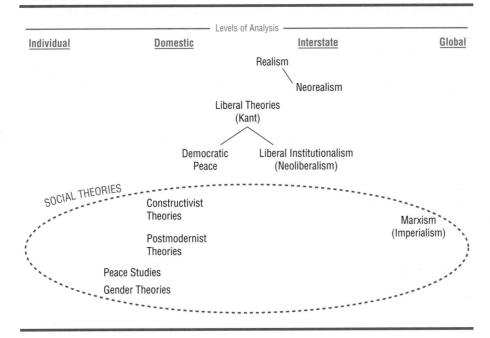

tanks, and airplanes) were the 2003 invasion of Iraq and the 2008 Russian-Georgian war, both short and one-sided affairs. The last sustained interstate war, between Ethiopia and Eritrea, ended in 2000. The last great power war (with great powers fighting each other) ended more than 50 years ago.

In 2008, war abated in Iraq and worsened in Afghanistan while sporadic but serious fighting continued in Sudan and Sri Lanka. In Democratic Congo, small-scale but brutal fighting among various factions has flared since the devastating war there ended (and UN peacekeepers arrived) in 1999.

Kant and Peace

What accounts for this positive trend toward peace in a world still feeling insecure and still violence prone in many ways and places? Liberal theories of IR try to explain how peace and cooperation are possible.

The German philosopher Immanuel Kant 200 years ago gave three answers. The first, based on the reciprocity principle, was that states could develop the organizations and rules to facilitate cooperation, specifically by forming a world federation resembling today's United Nations. This answer forms the foundation of present-day liberal institutionalism, discussed shortly.

Kant's second answer, operating at a lower level of analysis, was that peace depends on the internal character of governments. He reasoned that republics, with a legislative branch that can hold the monarch in check, will be more peaceful than autocracies. This answer, along with Kant's related point that citizens of any country deserve hospitality in any other country, is consistent with the reciprocity principle, but also relies on the identity principle. Like the social theories discussed later in this chapter, it explains states' preferences based on the social interactions within the state. A variation on Kant's answer, namely that *democracies* do not fight *each other,* is the basis of present democratic peace theory, discussed later in this chapter. (Kant himself distrusted democracies as subjecting policy to mob rule rather than rationality, a view influenced by his witnessing the French Revolution.)

Kant's third answer, that trade promotes peace, relies on the assumption that trade increases wealth, cooperation, and global well-being—all while making conflict less likely in the long term because governments will not want to disrupt any process that adds to the wealth of their state. Realists are skeptical, however, arguing that one state's reliance on another creates *more* tensions in the short term because states are nervous that another actor has an important source of leverage over them. We will return to this argument in Chapter 5.

Liberal Institutionalism

Now let us return to Kant's first answer to the question of how peace can evolve, namely the ability of states to develop and follow mutually advantageous rules, with international institutions to monitor and enforce them. Liberal theories treat rational actors as capable of forgoing short-term individual interests in order to further the long-term well-being of a community to which they belong—and hence indirectly their own well-being. The core principle of reciprocity lies at the heart of this approach, because international institutions operate by reciprocal contributions and concessions among formally equal members (peers). Indeed, in several important trade institutions, such as the World Trade Organization and the European Union, decisions require *consensus* among all members, making them all equal in governance. Kant argued that states, although autonomous, could join a worldwide federation like today's UN and respect its principles even at the cost of forgoing certain short-term individual gains. To Kant, international cooperation was a more rational option for states than resorting to war. Thus, in realist conceptions of rationality, war and violence appear rational (because they often advance short-term state interests), but in liberal theories war and violence appear as irrational deviations that result from defective reasoning and that harm the (collective, long-term) interests of warring states.

The **neoliberal** approach differs from earlier liberal approaches in that it concedes to realism several important assumptions—among them, that states are unitary actors rationally pursuing their self-interests in a system of anarchy. Neoliberals say to realists, "Even if we grant your assumptions about the nature of states and their motives, your pessimistic conclusions do not follow." States achieve cooperation because it is in their interest to do so, and they can learn to use institutions to ease the pursuit of mutual gains and the reduction of possibilities for cheating or taking advantage of another state.

Neoliberals use the *Prisoner's Dilemma (PD)* game (see pp. 58–60) to illustrate their argument that cooperation is possible. Each actor can gain by individually defecting, but both lose when both defect. Similarly, in IR, states often have a mix of conflicting and mutual interests. The dilemma can be resolved if the game is played over and over again—an accurate model of IR, in which states deal with each other in repeated interactions. In that case, a strategy of strict reciprocity after an initial cooperative move (nicknamed *tit for tat*) can bring about mutual cooperation in a repeated PD game, because the other player must conclude that any defection will merely provoke a like defection in response.

Thus, reciprocity in IR helps international cooperation emerge despite the absence of central authority. Through reciprocity, not a world government, norms and rules are enforced. But side by side with the potential for eliciting cooperation, reciprocity contains a danger of runaway hostility. When two sides both reciprocate but never manage to put relations on a cooperative footing, the result can be a drawn-out, nasty, tit-for-tat exchange of punishments. This characterizes Israeli relations with Palestinian militants over the years, for instance.

Building on the reciprocity principle, many norms mediate states' interactions. For example, diplomatic practices and participation in international organizations (IOs) are both strongly governed by shared expectations about the rules of correct behavior. As collective goods problems crop up in IR, states rely on a context of rules, norms, habits, and institutions that make it rational for all sides to avoid the self-defeating outcomes that would result from pursuing narrow, short-term self-interest. Neoliberals study historical and contemporary cases in IR to see how institutions and norms affect the possibilities for overcoming dilemmas and achieving international cooperation. Thus, for neoliberals the emergence of international institutions is key to understanding how states achieve a superior rational outcome that includes long-term self-interest and not just immediate self-interest.

International Regimes

Achieving good outcomes is not simple, though. Because of the contradictory interpretations that parties to a conflict usually have, it is difficult to resolve conflicts without a third party to arbitrate or an overall framework to set common expectations for all parties. These considerations underlie the creation of IOs.

An **international regime** is a set of rules, norms, and procedures around which the expectations of actors converge in a certain issue area (whether arms control, international trade, or Antarctic exploration). The convergence of expectations means that participants in the international system have similar ideas about what rules will govern their mutual participation: each expects to play by the same rules. (This meaning of *regime* is not the same as that referring to the domestic governments of states, as in *regime change*.)

Regimes can help solve collective goods problems by increasing transparency—everyone knows what everyone else is doing, so cheating is riskier. The current revolution in information technologies is strengthening regimes particularly in this aspect. Also, with better international communication, states can identify conflicts and negotiate solutions through regimes more effectively.

The most common conception of regimes combines elements of realism and liberalism. States are seen as autonomous units maximizing their own interests in an anarchic

VIDEO

The Climate Change Challenge

context. Regimes do not play a role in issues in which states can realize their interests directly through unilateral applications of leverage. Rather, regimes come into existence to overcome collective goods dilemmas by coordinating the behaviors of individual states. Although states continue to seek their own interests, they create frameworks to coordinate their actions with those of other states if and when such coordination is necessary to realize self-interest (that is, in collective goods dilemmas).

Regimes do not substitute for the basic calculations of costs and benefits by states; rather, they open up new possibilities with more favorable benefit-cost ratios. Regimes facilitate and empower national governments faced with issues in which collective goods problems would otherwise prevent governments from achieving their ends. Regimes can be seen as *intervening variables* between the basic causal forces at work in IR—for realists, the relative power of state actors—and the outcomes such as international cooperation (or lack thereof). For realists in particular, regimes do not negate the effects of power; more often they codify and normalize existing power relations in accordance with the dominance principle. For example, the nuclear nonproliferation regime protects the status quo in which only a few states have nuclear weapons.

HEALTHY REGIME

International regimes are sets of rules, norms, and procedures, not always codified into institutions, that govern the behavior of actors in IR. The world health regime includes states, IGOs such as the World Health Organization, nonprofit organizations such as the Gates Foundation, and others, all working with common expectations about activities to improve health and stem epidemics. Here, UNICEF vaccinates a child in Democratic Congo, 2007.

Because regimes depend on state power for their enforcement, some IR scholars argue that regimes are most effective when power in the international system is most concentrated—when there is a hegemon to keep order (see pp. 47–49). Yet regimes do not always decline with the power of hegemons that created them. Rather, they may take on a life of their own. Although hegemony may be crucial in *establishing* regimes, it is not necessary for *maintaining* them. Once actors' expectations converge around the rules embodied in a regime, the actors realize that the regime serves their own interests. Working through the regime becomes a habit, and national leaders may not seriously consider breaking out of the established rules.

In part, the survival of regimes rests on their embedding in permanent *institutions* such as the UN, NATO, and the International Monetary

Fund. These institutions become the tangible manifestation of shared expectations as well as the machinery for coordinating international actions based on those expectations. Formal institutions gain greater stability and weight than do noninstitutionalized regimes. With a staff and headquarters, an international institution can actively promote adherence to the rules in its area of political or economic life. These bureaucracies, however, can also promote policies that were not intended by the states that created the institutions (a problem noted by constructivist scholars; see pp. 87–90).

The culmination of liberal institutionalism to date is the European Union (EU), which receives in-depth discussion in Chapter 6. After centuries of devastating wars, European states now enjoy a stable peace among themselves with strong international institutions to bind them.

Collective Security

The concept of **collective security,** which grows out of liberal institutionalism, refers to the formation of a broad alliance of most major actors in an international system for the purpose of jointly opposing aggression by any actor. Kant laid out the rationale for this approach. Because past treaties ending great power wars had never lasted permanently, Kant proposed a federation (league) of the world's states. Through such a federation, Kant proposed, the majority of states could unite to punish any one state that committed aggression, safeguarding the collective interests of all the nations while protecting the self-determination of small nations that all too easily became pawns in great power games.

After the horrors of World War I, the *League of Nations* was formed to promote collective security. But it was flawed in two ways. Its membership did not include all the great powers (and not the most powerful one, the United States), and its members proved unwilling to bear the costs of collective action to oppose aggression when it did occur in the 1930s. After World War II, the United Nations was created as the League's successor to promote collective security (see Chapter 6). Several regional IGOs also currently perform collective security functions (deterring aggression) as well as economic and cultural ones—the *Organization of American States (OAS)*, the *Arab League*, and the *African Union.*

The success of collective security depends on two points. First, the members must keep their alliance commitments to the group (that is, members must not free-ride on the efforts of other members). When a powerful state commits aggression against a weaker one, it often is not in the immediate interest of other powerful states to go to war over the issue. Suppressing a determined aggressor can be very costly.

A second requisite for collective security is that enough members must agree on what constitutes aggression. The UN Security Council is structured so that aggression is defined by what all five permanent members, in addition to at least four of the other ten members, can agree on (see "The Security Council" on pp. 218–221). This collective security system does not work against aggression by a great power. When the Soviet Union invaded Afghanistan, or the United States mined the harbors of Nicaragua, or France blew up the Greenpeace ship *Rainbow Warrior,* the UN could do nothing—because those states can veto Security Council resolutions.

Collective security worked in 1990–1991 to reverse Iraq's conquest of Kuwait because the aggression brought all the great powers together and because they were willing to bear the costs of confronting Iraq. It was the first time since the founding of the UN that one member state had invaded, occupied, and annexed another—attempting to erase it as a sovereign state. The invasion was so blatant a violation of Kuwaiti sovereignty and territorial integrity that the Security Council had little trouble labeling it aggression and authorizing the use of force by a multinational coalition. The threat Iraq posed to the world's oil supplies provided incentive for coalition members to contribute money or troops to solve the problem.

In 2002–2003, by contrast, the Security Council repeatedly debated Iraq's failure to keep the agreements it had made at the end of the Gulf War, in particular the promise to disclose and destroy all its weapons of mass destruction. But the great powers split and a proposed U.S.-British resolution authorizing military force was withdrawn after France promised to veto it. Germany, Russia, and China also strongly opposed it. Public opinion around the world, especially in predominantly Muslim countries, also opposed the war. When the UN did not act, the United States, Britain, and Australia sent military forces to overthrow Saddam Hussein by force, comparing the UN to the toothless League of Nations (see pp. 35–36). However, the United States found no weapons of mass destruction in Iraq and then found itself in a prolonged counterinsurgency war. In retrospect, although the world's collective security system is creaky and not always effective, bypassing it to take military action also holds dangers.

The Democratic Peace

Kant argued that lasting peace would depend on states' becoming republics, with legislatures to check the power of monarchs (or presidents) to make war. He thought that checks and balances in government would act as a brake on the use of military force—as compared to autocratic governments in which a single individual (or small ruling group) could make war without regard for the effect on the population.

Somewhat similarly, IR scholars have linked democracy with a kind of foreign policy fundamentally different from that of authoritarianism. One theory they considered was that democracies are generally *more peaceful* than authoritarian governments (fighting fewer, or smaller, wars). This turned out not to be true. Democracies fight as many wars as do authoritarian states. Indeed, the three most war-prone states of the past two centuries (according to political scientists who count wars) were France, Russia, and Britain. Britain was a democracy throughout, France for part of the period, and Russia not at all.

What *is* true about democracies is that although they fight wars against authoritarian states, *democracies almost never fight each other.* No major historical cases contradict this generalization, which is known as the **democratic peace.** Why this is so is not entirely clear. As there have not been many democracies for very long, the generalization could be just a coincidence, though this seems unlikely. It may be that democracies do not tend to have severe conflicts with each other, as they tend to be capitalist states whose trade relations create strong interdependence (war would be costly because it would disrupt trade). Or, citizens of democratic societies (whose support is necessary for wars to be waged) may simply not see the citizens of other democracies as enemies.

By contrast, authoritarian governments of other states can be
seen as enemies. Note that the
peace among democracies gives
empirical support to a long-
standing liberal claim that,
because it is rooted in the domestic level of analysis, contra-
dicts realism's claim that the
most important explanations are
at the interstate level.

Over the past two centuries,
democracy has become more
widespread as a form of government, and this trend is changing
the nature of the foreign policy
process worldwide. Many states
do not yet have democratic governments (the most important of
these is China). And existing
democracies are imperfect in
various ways—from political
apathy in the United States and
corruption in Japan to autocratic traditions in Russia.
Nonetheless, the trend is toward
democratization in most of the
world's regions.

In the past two decades the
trend has accelerated in several
ways. New democracies emerged

DEMOCRATIC PEACE

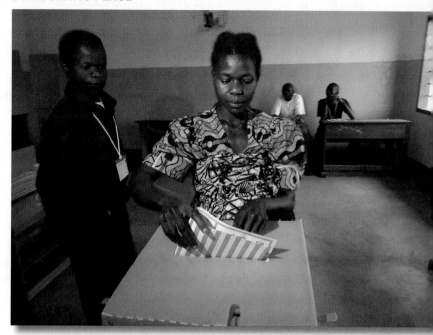

Upsurges of democratic movements throughout the world in recent years
testify to the power of the idea of democracy. Because democracies rarely
fight each other, worldwide democratization might lead to lasting peace.
This voter participates in Democratic Congo's first elections after decades
of war, 2006. Some fighting remains in part of the country but the war has
mainly ended and the government has been stable since the elections.

in several (though not all) states of the old Soviet bloc. Military governments were replaced
with democratically elected civilian ones throughout most of Latin America as well as in several African and Asian countries. South Africa, the last white-ruled African country, adopted
majority rule in 1994. In the late 1990s, long-standing dictatorships and military governments gave up power peacefully to democratic governments in Indonesia and Nigeria, both
regional giants. In late 2004 and early 2005, pro-democracy forces won a string of victories in
Ukraine, Palestine, Afghanistan, Iraq, and Kyrgyzstan. In 2006 in Nepal, massive popular
protests forced the king to reverse his seizure of absolute power and reinstate democracy,
ultimately leading Maoist rebels to join the political process and win power through elections. In 2008, Pakistan's military-run government stepped down to make way for a new
democratically elected government, as did Bangladesh's military government. However,
movement in the other direction still occurs. Military coups took place in Thailand in 2006.
Guinea in 2008, and Madagascar in 2009, while Russia's government has constrained democracy in recent years and China's communist party has maintained its iron grip on politics.

VIDEO

President
Bush on
Democracy
and Peace

We do not know where these trends toward democracy will lead, but it is now conceivable that someday nearly all of the world's states will be democratically governed. As Kant envisaged, an international community based on peaceful relations may emerge. However, although mature democracies almost never fight each other, a period of *transition* to democracy may be more prone to war than either a stable democracy or a stable authoritarian government. Therefore the process of democratization does not necessarily bode well for peace in the short term. This theory gained support in early 2006 when the first Iraqi elections were followed by a rise in sectarian violence, and then Palestinian elections brought to power the militant faction Hamas, which rejects Israel's right to exist.

Domestic Influences

Liberal institutionalism operates at the interstate level of analysis, but the democratic peace relies on the domestic level to explain IR events. In reality, a state's actions result from individual human choices—by citizenry, political leaders, diplomats, and bureaucrats—aggregated through the state's internal structures. Continuing in this vein, the next two sections examine the state from the inside out, trying to understand the processes and structures within states that make them behave as they do. We begin by examining the institutions that shape state behavior.

Bureaucracies

Of the many substate actors that influence states' actions in the international arena, those closest to the action are the bureaucratic agencies that states maintain to develop and carry out foreign policy. Different states maintain different foreign policy bureaucracies but share some common elements. Virtually all states maintain a *diplomatic corps,* or *foreign service,* of diplomats working in *embassies* in foreign capitals (and in *consulates* located in noncapital foreign cities), as well as diplomats who remain at home to coordinate policy. States appoint *ambassadors* as their official representatives to other states and to international organizations. Diplomatic activities are organized through a *foreign ministry* or the equivalent (for example, the U.S. State Department). In many democracies, some diplomats are *political appointees* who come and go with changes in government leaders, while others are *career diplomats* who come up through the ranks of the foreign service and tend to outlast changes in administration.

Diplomats provide much of the information that goes into making foreign policies, but their main role is to carry out rather than create policies. Nonetheless, foreign ministry bureaucrats often make foreign relations so routine that top leaders and political appointees can come and go without greatly altering the country's relations. The national interest is served, the bureaucrats believe, by the stability of overall national goals and positions in international affairs.

Tension is common between state leaders and foreign policy bureaucrats. Career diplomats try to orient new leaders and their appointees and to control the flow of information they receive (creating information screens). Politicians struggle to exercise power over the formal bureaucratic agencies because the latter can be too "bureaucratic" (cumbersome, routinized, conservative) to easily control. Also, these agencies are often staffed (at lower levels) mostly by career officials who may not owe loyalty to political leaders.

Sometimes state leaders appoint a close friend or key advisor to manage the foreign policy bureaucracy. President George H. W. Bush did this with his closest friend, James Baker, as did President George W. Bush in his second term with his former NSC chief and confidante, Condoleezza Rice. Chinese leader Mao Zedong put his loyal ally Zhou Enlai in charge of foreign policy. At other times, state leaders may appoint rivals with differing views of foreign policy—as President Barack Obama did with his former political rival Hillary Clinton.

Interagency tension also affects the formulation of foreign policy. Certain agencies traditionally clash, and an endless tug-of-war shapes the foreign policies that emerge. In an extreme example of interagency rivalry, the U.S. State Department and the CIA backed opposite sides in a civil war in Laos in 1960. In general, bureaucracies promote policies under which their own capabilities will be effective and their power will increase. Of special concern in many states is the institutional interest that military officers have in maintaining a strong military. If civilian state leaders allow officers' salaries to fall or the size of the military forces to be cut, they may well face institutional resistance from the military—in the extreme case a military takeover of the government (see pp. 159–160). These issues were factors in attempted military coups in the Philippines, Venezuela, and Paraguay in the 1990s.

In general, bureaucratic rivalry as an influence on foreign policy challenges the notion of states as unitary actors in the international system. Such rivalries suggest that a state does not have any single set of goals—a national interest—but that its actions may result from the bargaining of subunits, each with its own set of goals. Furthermore, such a perspective extends far beyond bureaucratic agencies because other substate actors have their own goals, which they seek to advance by influencing foreign policy.

Interest Groups

Foreign policy makers operate not in a political vacuum but in the context of the political debates in their society. In all states, societal pressures influence foreign policy, although these pressures are aggregated and made effective through different channels in different societies. In pluralistic democracies, interested parties influence foreign policy through interest groups and political parties. In dictatorships, similar influences occur but less visibly. Thus foreign policies adopted by states generally reflect some kind of process of domestic coalition formation. Of course, international factors also affect domestic politics.

Interest groups are coalitions of people who share a common interest in the outcome of some political issue and who organize themselves to try to influence the outcome. For instance, French farmers have a big stake in international negotiations in the European Community (which subsidizes agriculture) and in world trade talks (which set agricultural tariffs). French farmers have turned out in large numbers to block roads, stage violent street demonstrations, and threaten to grind the national economy to a halt unless the government adopts their position. Similarly (but often less dramatically), interest groups form around businesses, labor unions, churches, veterans, senior citizens, members of an occupation, or citizens concerned about an issue such as the environment.

Lobbying is the process of talking with legislators or officials to influence their decisions on some set of issues. Three important elements that go into successful lobbying are the ability to gain a hearing with busy officials, the ability to present cogent arguments for one's case, and the ability to trade favors in return for positive action on an issue. These favors—legal and illegal—include campaign contributions, dinners at nice restaurants, trips to golf resorts, illicit sexual liaisons, and bribes. In many states, corruption is a major problem in governmental decision making (see p. 289), and interest groups may induce government officials by illegal means to take certain actions.

VIDEO

**Arab-
American
Reactions
to Obama**

Ethnic groups within one state often become interest groups concerned about their ancestral nation outside that state. Many members of ethnic groups feel strong emotional ties to their relatives in other countries; because the rest of the population generally does not care about such issues one way or the other, even a small ethnic group can have considerable influence on policy toward a particular country. Such ethnic ties are emerging as a powerful foreign policy influence in various ethnic conflicts in poor regions. The effect is especially strong in the United States, which is ethnically mixed and has a pluralistic form of democracy. For example, Cuban Americans organize to influence U.S. policy toward Cuba, as do Greek Americans on Greece, Jewish Americans on Israel, and African Americans on Africa. But whether or not a foreign country has a large constituency of ethnic nationals within another country, it can lobby that country's government.

Clearly, interest groups have goals and interests that may or may not coincide with the national interest as a whole (if indeed such an interest can be identified). As with bureaucratic agencies, the view of the state as a unitary actor can be questioned. Defenders of interest-group politics argue that various interest groups tend to push and pull in different directions, with the ultimate decisions generally reflecting the interests of society as a whole. But according to *Marxist* theories of international relations, the key domestic influences on foreign policy in capitalist countries are rich owners of big businesses. For instance, European imperialism benefited banks and big business, which made huge profits from exploiting cheap labor and resources in overseas colonies. During the Cold War, Marxists argued that Western foreign policies were driven by the profit motive of arms manufacturers.

Public Opinion

Many domestic actors seek to influence **public opinion**—the range of views on foreign policy issues held by the citizens of a state. Public opinion has greater influence on foreign policy in democracies than in authoritarian governments. But even dictators must pay attention to what citizens think. No government can rule by force alone: it needs legitimacy to survive. It must persuade people to accept (if not to like) its policies, because in the end policies are carried out by ordinary people—soldiers, workers, and bureaucrats.

Because of the need for public support, even authoritarian governments spend great effort on *propaganda*—the public promotion of their official line—to win support for foreign policies. States use television, newspapers, and other information media in this effort. In many countries, the state owns or controls major mass media such as television and newspapers, mediating the flow of information to its citizens; however, new information technologies with multiple channels (such as the Internet) make this harder to do.

Journalists serve as the gatekeepers of information passing from foreign policy elites to the public. The media and government often conflict, because of the traditional role of the press as a watchdog and critic of government actions and powers. The media try to uncover and publicize what the government wants to hide. Foreign policy decision makers also rely on the media for information about foreign affairs.

VIDEO

Reporting on the Iraq War

Yet the media also depend on government for information; the size and resources of the foreign policy bureaucracies dwarf those of the press. These advantages give the government great power to *manipulate* journalists by feeding them information, to shape the news and influence public opinion. Government decision makers can create dramatic stories in foreign relations—through summit meetings, crises, and so forth. Bureaucrats can also *leak* secret information to the press to support their point of view and win bureaucratic battles. Finally, the military and the press have a running battle about journalists' access to military operations, but both sides gained from the open access given to journalists "embedded" with U.S. forces in Iraq in 2003.

In democracies, where governments must stand for election, an unpopular war can force a leader or party from office, as happened to U.S. president Lyndon Johnson in 1968 during the Vietnam War. Or a popular war can help secure a government's mandate to continue in power, as happened to Margaret Thatcher in Britain after the 1982 Falkland Islands War. During the war in Bosnia, officials in the U.S. State Department said privately that the main goal of U.S. policy was often just to keep the conflict there off of the front pages of U.S. newspapers (an elusive goal, as it turned out).

In democracies, public opinion generally has less effect on foreign policy than on domestic policy. National leaders traditionally have additional latitude to make decisions in the international realm. This derives from the special need of states to act in a unified way to function effectively in the international system, as well as from the traditions of secrecy and diplomacy that remove IR from the realm of ordinary domestic politics. The *attentive public* in a democracy is the minority of the population that stays informed about international issues. This segment varies somewhat from one issue to another, but there is also a core of people who care in general about foreign affairs and follow them closely. The most active members of the attentive public on foreign affairs constitute a foreign policy *elite*—people with power and influence who affect foreign policy. This elite includes people within governments as well as outsiders such as businesspeople, journalists, lobbyists, and professors. Public opinion polls show that elite opinions sometimes (but not always) differ considerably from those of the general population, and sometimes from those of the government as well.

Governments sometimes adopt foreign policies for the specific purpose of generating public approval and hence gaining domestic legitimacy. This is the case when a government undertakes a war or foreign military intervention at a time of domestic difficulty, to

FIGURE 3.2   The "Rally 'Round the Flag" Syndrome

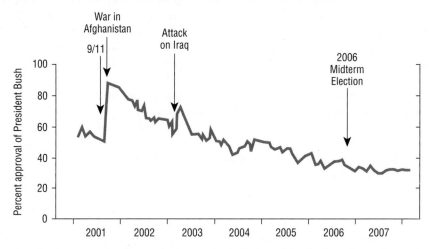

President Bush's approval rating demonstrates the "rally 'round the flag" syndrome, in which war triggers a short-term boost in public approval.

Source: Gallup Poll.

distract attention and gain public support. Such a strategy takes advantage of the **"rally 'round the flag" syndrome**—the public's increased support for government leaders during wartime, at least in the short term. Citizens who would readily criticize their government's policies on education or health care often refrain from criticism when the government is at war and the lives of the nation's soldiers are on the line. Policies of this sort are often labeled *diversionary foreign policy*. Unfortunately, it is always difficult to tell whether a state adopts a foreign policy to distract the public, because leaders would never admit to trying to divert public attention.

However, wars that go on too long or are not successful can turn public opinion against the government and even lead to a popular uprising to overthrow the government. In Argentina, the military government in 1982 led the country into war with Britain over the Falkland Islands. At first, Argentineans rallied around the flag, but after losing the war they rallied around the cause of getting rid of the military government and prosecuting its leaders. In 2006, President Bush's popularity, which had soared early in the Iraq War, plummeted as the war dragged on (see Figure 3.2), and voters threw his party out of power in Congress.

Legislatures

One conduit through which interest groups and public opinion may wield influence is legislatures. Some democracies, such as the United States, have presidential systems, in which legislative bodies are elected apart from the president (also referred to as

POLICY PERSPECTIVES

Prime Minister of Japan, Taro Aso

PROBLEM *How do you decide what foreign policy tools best balance domestic and international concerns?*

BACKGROUND Imagine that you are the prime minister of Japan. Since the end of the Korean War in 1953, relations with your neighbor to the west, North Korea, have been tense. Military tensions have persisted as North Korea has made and then broken several agreements regarding its nuclear program. North Korea tested a nuclear weapon in 2006, and it has also test-fired its short-range ballistic missiles directly over Japan in an effort to intimidate your country. Most analysts believe North Korea does possess the ability to produce at least a few nuclear weapons.

For its part, North Korea has long demanded reparations for Japan's 35-year colonization of the Korean peninsula and for Japan's actions in Korea during World War II. Japan has refused such reparations in the past, but has provided limited aid in an attempt to encourage North Korea to denuclearize. You have held talks with North Korea in the past two years, but no agreements on any political or economic issues have been reached.

In the summer of 2008, the United States removed North Korea from its list of states that sponsor terrorism. This angered many in your country, who see this as giving in to North Korean demands for more aid in exchange for giving up its nuclear program. Your government vehemently protested this move by the United States, which your finance minister called "extremely regrettable."

DOMESTIC CONSIDERATIONS Public opinion in Japan is very sensitive to relations with North Korea. In 2002, North Korea admitted to secretly abducting Japanese citizens in the 1970s and 1980s, transporting them to North Korea, and using them to train North Korean spies. North Korea claims that all 13 abductees have either returned to Japan or died, but many in Japan are skeptical of this claim. Many in Japan suspect more than 13 were abducted and have even demanded that North Korea return the bodies of the deceased. These abductions are an extremely sensitive issue in Japanese public opinion and past Japanese governments have demanded a resolution to the abduction issue before opening formal diplomatic relations with North Korea.

SCENARIO Now imagine that the United States is negotiating a new nuclear weapons agreement with North Korea. The United States asks that Japan contribute extensive foreign aid to North Korea to help ensure that a deal is reached. In return, North Korea will agree to allow increased inspections of all key nuclear sites and will rejoin the Non-Proliferation Treaty (see p. 156). The United States is placing extensive pressure on your government to provide what it feels is critical aid.

CHOOSE YOUR POLICY How do you respond to U.S. pressure for more foreign aid? Do you risk a backlash from your public by increasing aid without having the abduction issue resolved? Do you resist pressure from the United States, your most important ally, and withhold the requested aid? Can you trust the North Korean government to hold up its end of the bargain after you give the economic aid? How do you balance a sensitive domestic political issue with a delicate set of international negotiations?

executives). In these systems, legislatures play a direct role in making foreign policy by passing budgets, regulating bureaucratic rules, creating trade law, even controlling immigration policy. Although executives may attend summits and talks, any agreement they sign must be approved by their domestic legislature.

Although few would argue that legislatures in presidential democracies do not influence foreign policy generally, different rules may apply to the use of military force. Some contend that legislatures, like public opinion, rally around the flag during times of international crises. For example, three days after the September 11, 2001, terrorist attacks, the U.S. Congress voted to give President Bush full authority to prosecute a war in Afghanistan. In October 2002, Congress passed a resolution authorizing the use of force in Iraq. Thus, legislatures rarely if ever challenge an executive on important military matters.

Others point to a different dynamic in which legislatures do stand up to executive power regarding military force. For example, because legislatures hold the "purse strings" (the ability to approve or reject new spending), they have the ability to stop a war in its tracks. In the United States, the War Powers Act, enacted during the close of the Vietnam War, requires the president to notify Congress when U.S. troops are deployed for combat. After this notification, the president has 60 days (plus a possible 30-day extension) to recall the troops unless Congress explicitly approves the military action.

In parliamentary systems, such as Great Britain, executives (for example, prime ministers) are chosen by the political parties that hold a dominant position in the legislative bodies. Often parliamentary executives do not need to submit treaties or policies for formal approval by the legislature, yet legislatures still hold power regarding foreign policy. Great Britain's Parliament is not required to vote on international agreements, but it must approve any change to British laws that such agreements entail. Because most international agreements do involve these types of changes, Parliament effectively exercises a right of ratification over international agreements. In many parliamentary systems, if a foreign (or domestic) policy is particularly controversial, parties that do not have a majority in the legislature can try to call elections—meaning that the country votes again on which parties will hold seats in the legislature. If a different group of parties wins a majority of seats, a new executive is appointed. Thus, in parliamentary systems, legislatures play a key role in designing and implementing foreign policy.

Making Foreign Policy

Foreign policies are the strategies governments use to guide their actions in the international arena. Foreign policies spell out the objectives state leaders have decided to pursue in a given relationship or situation. But in general, IR scholars are less interested in specific policies than in the **foreign policy process**—how policies are arrived at and implemented.

States establish various organizational structures and functional relationships to create and carry out foreign policies. Officials and agencies collect information about a situation through various channels; they write memoranda outlining possible options for action; they hold meetings to discuss the matter; they sometimes meet privately to decide how to steer the meetings. Such activities, broadly defined, are what is meant by "the foreign policy process." IR scholars are especially interested in exploring whether certain kinds of policy processes lead to certain kinds of decisions—whether certain processes produce better outcomes (for the state's self-defined interests) than do others.

Foreign policy outcomes result from multiple forces at various levels of analysis. While the previous section discussed the state-level institutions, here the focus is on individual decision makers and the groups they operate within. Whether at the institutional or individual level of analysis, the study of foreign policy processes runs counter to realism's assumption of a unitary state actor.

Models of Decision Making

The foreign policy process is a process of *decision making*. States take actions because people in governments—*decision makers*—choose those actions. Decision making is a *steering* process in which adjustments are made as a result of feedback from the outside world. Decisions are carried out by actions taken to change the world, and then information from the world is monitored to evaluate the effects of these actions. These evaluations—along with information about other, independent changes in the environment—go into the next round of decisions (see Figure 3.3).

A common starting point for studying the decision-making process is the **rational model.** In this model, decision makers set goals, evaluate their relative importance, calculate the costs and benefits of each possible course of action, and then choose the one with the highest benefits and lowest costs (see Figure 3.4).

The choice may be complicated by *uncertainty* about the costs and benefits of various actions. In such cases, decision makers must attach probabilities to each possible outcome of an action. For example, will pressuring a rival state to give ground in peace talks work or backfire? Some decision makers are relatively *accepting of risk*, whereas others are

FIGURE 3.3   Decision Making as Steering

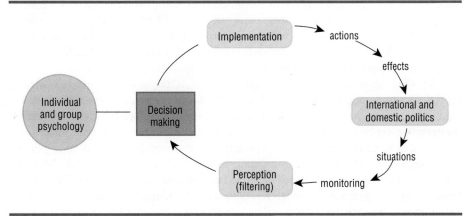

FIGURE 3.4   Rational Model of Decision Making

Clarify Your Goals in the situation

↓

Order Them by importance

↓

List the Alternatives for achieving your goals

↓

Investigate the Consequences of each alternative

↓

Choose the alternative that best achieves your goals

averse to risk. These factors affect the importance that decision makers place on various alternative outcomes that could result from an action.

The goals of different individuals involved in making a decision may diverge, as may the goals of different state agencies. For example, the U.S. secretary of state may have a different goal than the secretary of defense, just as the Central Intelligence Agency may view a situation differently than the National Security Council does. The rational model of decision making thus is somewhat complicated by uncertainty and the multiple goals of decision makers. The rational model may imply that decision making is simpler than is actually the case.

An alternative to the rational model of decision making is the **organizational process model.** In this model, foreign policy decision makers generally skip the labor-intensive process of identifying goals and alternative actions, relying instead for most decisions on standardized responses or *standard operating procedures*. For example, the U.S. State Department every day receives more than a thousand reports or inquiries from its embassies around the world and sends out more than a thousand instructions or responses to those embassies. Most are never seen by the top decision makers (the secretary of state or the president); instead, they are handled by low-level decision makers who apply general principles—or who simply try to make the least controversial, most standardized decision. The organizational process model implies that much of foreign policy results from "management by muddling through."

Another alternative to the rational model is the **government bargaining** (or *bureaucratic politics*) **model,** in which foreign policy decisions result from the bargaining process among various government agencies with somewhat divergent interests in the outcome. In 1992, the Japanese government had to decide whether to allow sushi from California to be imported—a weakening of Japan's traditional ban on importing rice (to maintain self-sufficiency in its staple food). The Japanese Agriculture Ministry, with an interest in the well-being of Japanese farmers, opposed the imports. The Foreign Ministry, with an interest in smooth relations with the United States, wanted to allow the imports. The final decision to allow imported sushi resulted from the tug-of-war between the ministries. Thus, according to the government bargaining model, foreign policy decisions reflect (a mix of) the interests of state agencies.

Individual Decision Makers

Every international event is the result, intended or unintended, of decisions made by individuals. IR does not just happen. President Harry Truman, who decided to drop U.S. nuclear bombs on two Japanese cities in 1945, had a sign on his desk: "The buck stops here." As leader of the world's greatest power, he had nobody to pass the buck to. If he chose to use the bomb (as he did), more than 100,000 civilians would die. If he chose not to, the war might drag on for months with tens of thousands of U.S. casualties. Truman had to choose. Some people applaud his decision; others condemn it. But for better or worse, Truman as an individual had to decide, and take responsibility for the consequences. Similarly, the decisions of individual citizens, although they may not seem important when taken one by one, create the great forces of world history.

The study of individual decision making revolves around the question of rationality. To what extent are national leaders (or citizens) able to make rational decisions in the national interest—if indeed such an interest can be defined? Individual rationality is not equivalent to state rationality: states might filter individuals' irrational decisions so as to arrive at rational choices, or states might distort individually rational decisions and end up with irrational state choices. But realists tend to assume that both states and individuals are rational and that the goals or interests of states correlate with those of leaders.

The most simplified rational-actor models assume that interests are the same from one actor to another. If this were so, individuals could be substituted for each other in various roles without changing history very much. States would all behave similarly to each other (or rather, the differences between them would reflect different resources and geography, not differences in the nature of national interests). Individual decisions would reflect the *values* and *beliefs* of the decision maker.

Individual decision makers not only have differing values and beliefs, but also have unique personalities—their personal experiences, intellectual capabilities, and personal styles of making decisions. Some IR scholars study individual psychology to understand how personality affects decision making.

Beyond individual *idiosyncrasies* in goals or decision-making processes, individual decision making diverges from the rational model in at least three *systematic* ways. First, decision makers suffer from **misperceptions** and **selective perceptions** (taking in only some kinds of information) when they compile information on the likely consequences of their choices. Decision-making processes must reduce and filter the incoming information on which a decision is based; the problem is that such filtration often is biased. **Information screens** are subconscious filters through which people put the information coming in about the world around them. Often they simply ignore any information that does not fit their expectations. Information is also screened out as it passes from one person to another in the decision-making process. For example, prior to the September 2001 terrorist attacks, U.S. intelligence agencies failed to adequately interpret available evidence because too few analysts were fluent in Arabic.

MADMAN?

Foreign policies often deviate from rationality as a result of the mispercep-tions and biases of decision makers and populations. Here, South Korea's president meets the reclusive and eccentric dictator of North Korea, Kim Jong Il, in 2007 as international negotiations seek to curtail Kim's nuclear weapons. These weapons would pose a much greater threat if Kim were an irrational madman, as some believe, than if he were a shrewdly rational actor, as others believe.

Misperceptions can affect the implementation of policy by low-level officials as well as its formulation by high-level officials. For example, in 1988, officers on a U.S. warship in the Persian Gulf shot down a civilian Iranian jet that they believed to be a military jet attacking them. The officers were trying to carry out policies established by national leaders, but because of misperceptions their actions instead damaged their state's interests.

Second, the rationality of in-dividual cost-benefit calculations is undermined by emotions that decision makers feel while think-ing about the consequences of their actions—an effect referred to as *affective bias*. (*Positive* and *negative affect* refer to feelings of liking or disliking someone.) As hard as a decision maker tries to be rational in making a decision, the decision-making process is bound to be influenced by strong feelings held about the person or state toward which a decision is directed.

Third, *cognitive biases* are systematic distortions of rational calculations based not on emotional feelings but simply on the limitations of the human brain in making choices. The most important bias seems to be the attempt to produce *cognitive balance*—or to reduce *cognitive dissonance*. These terms refer to the tendency people have to try to maintain mental models of the world that are logically consistent (this seldom succeeds entirely).

One implication of cognitive balance is that decision makers place greater value on goals that they have put much effort into achieving—the *justification of effort*. This is es-pecially true in a democracy, in which politicians must face their citizens' judgment at the polls and so do not want to admit failures. The Vietnam War trapped U.S. decision makers in this way in the 1960s. After sending half a million troops halfway around the world, U.S. leaders found it difficult to admit to themselves that the costs of the war were greater than the benefits.

Decision makers also achieve cognitive balance through *wishful thinking*—an overestimate of the probability of a desired outcome. A variation of wishful thinking is to assume that an event with a *low probability* of occurring will *not* occur. This could be a dangerous way to think about catastrophic events such as accidental nuclear war or a terrorist attack.

Cognitive balance often leads decision makers to maintain a hardened image of an *enemy* and to interpret all of the enemy's actions in a negative light (because the idea of bad people doing good things would create cognitive dissonance). A *mirror image* refers to two sides in a conflict maintaining very similar enemy images of each other ("we are defensive, they are aggressive," etc.). A decision maker may also experience psychological *projection* of his or her own feelings onto another actor.

Another form of cognitive bias, related to cognitive balance, is the use of *historical analogies* to structure one's thinking about a decision. This can be quite useful or quite misleading, depending on whether the analogy is appropriate. As each historical situation is unique in some way, when a decision maker latches onto an analogy and uses it as a shortcut to a decision, the rational calculation of costs and benefits may be cut short as well. In particular, decision makers often assume that a solution that worked in the past will work again—without fully examining how similar the situations really are. For example, U.S. leaders incorrectly used the analogy of Munich in 1938 to convince themselves that appeasement of communism in the Vietnam War would lead to increased communist aggression in Asia. Vietnam in turn became a potent analogy that made U.S. leaders shy of involvement in overseas conflicts such as Bosnia; this was called the "Vietnam syndrome."

All of these psychological processes—misperception, affective biases, and cognitive biases—interfere with the rational assessment of costs and benefits in making a decision. Two specific modifications to the rational model of decision making have been proposed to accommodate psychological realities.

First, the model of *bounded rationality* takes into account the costs of seeking and processing information. Nobody thinks about every single possible course of action when making a decision. Instead of **optimizing**, or picking the very best option, people usually work on the problem until they come up with a "good enough" option that meets some minimal criteria; this is called **satisficing** (finding a satisfactory solution). The time constraints faced by top decision makers in IR—who are constantly besieged with crises—generally preclude their finding the very best response to a situation. These time constraints were described by U.S. Defense Secretary William Cohen in 1997: "The unrelenting flow of information, the need to digest it on a minute-by-minute basis, is quite different from anything I've experienced before.... There's little time for contemplation; most of it is action."

Second, **prospect theory** provides an alternative explanation (rather than simple rational optimization) of decisions made under risk or uncertainty. According to this theory, decision makers go through two phases. In the *editing phase*, they frame the options available and the probabilities of various outcomes associated with each option. Then, in the *evaluation phase*, they assess the options and choose one. Prospect theory holds that evaluations take place by comparison with a *reference point*, which is often the status quo but might be some past or expected situation.

Individual decision making thus follows an imperfect and partial kind of rationality at best. Not only do the goals of different individuals vary, but decision makers face a series of obstacles in receiving accurate information, constructing accurate models of the world, and reaching decisions that further their own goals. The rational model is only a simplification at best and must be supplemented by an understanding of individual psychological processes that affect decision making.

Group Psychology

In one respect, groups promote rationality by balancing out the blind spots and biases of any individual. Advisors or legislative committees may force a state leader to reconsider a rash decision. And the interactions of different individuals in a group may result in the formulation of goals that more closely reflect state interests rather than individual idiosyncrasies. However, group dynamics also introduce new sources of irrationality into the decision-making process.

Groupthink refers to the tendency for groups to reach decisions without accurately assessing their consequences, because individual members tend to go along with ideas they think the others support. The basic phenomenon is illustrated by a simple psychology experiment. A group of six people is asked to compare the lengths of two lines projected onto a screen. When five of the people are secretly instructed to say that line A is longer—even though anyone can see that line B is actually longer—the sixth person is likely to agree with the group rather than believe his or her own eyes.

Unlike individuals, groups tend to be overly optimistic about the chances of success and are thus more willing to take risks. Participants suppress their doubts about dubious undertakings because everyone else seems to think an idea will work. Also, because the group diffuses responsibility from individuals, nobody feels accountable for actions.

FIGURE 3.5   Some Psychological Pitfalls of Decision Making

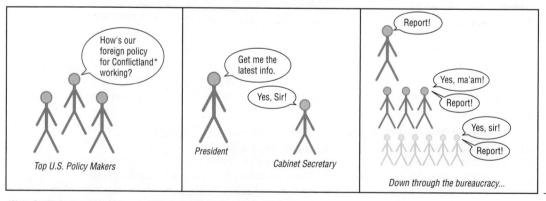

*Note: Conflictland could be Vietnam in 1968, Bosnia in 1994, or Iraq in 2006.

In a spectacular case of groupthink, President Ronald Reagan's close friend and director of the U.S. Central Intelligence Agency (CIA) bypassed his own agency and ran covert operations spanning three continents using the National Security Council (NSC) staff in the White House basement. The NSC sold weapons to Iran in exchange for the freedom of U.S. hostages held in Lebanon, and then used the Iranian payments to illegally fund Nicaraguan Contra rebels. The *Iran-Contra scandal* resulted when these operations, managed by an obscure NSC aide named Oliver North, became public.

The U.S. war in Iraq may also provide cautionary examples to future generations about the risks of misinformation, misperception, wishful thinking, and groupthink in managing a major foreign policy initiative. Some of the problems of individual and group psychology in the policy process—be they in Vietnam, Bosnia, or Iraq—are illustrated in Figure 3.5.

The *structure of a decision-making process*—the rules as to the decision makers, how voting is conducted, and so forth—can affect the outcome, especially when no single alternative appeals to a majority of participants. Experienced participants in foreign policy formation are familiar with the techniques for manipulating decision-making processes to favor outcomes they prefer. The structure of decision making also reflects the composition of a decision group.

State leaders often rely on an inner circle of advisors in making foreign policy decisions. The composition and operation of the inner circle vary across governments. Some groups depend heavily on *informal* consultations in addition to formal meetings. Some leaders create a "kitchen cabinet"—a trusted group of friends who discuss policy issues with the leader even though they have no formal positions in government. Russian president Boris Yeltsin relied on the advice of his bodyguard, who was a trusted friend.

Crisis Management

The difficulties in reaching rational decisions, both for individuals and for groups, are heightened during a crisis. *Crises* are foreign policy situations in which outcomes are very

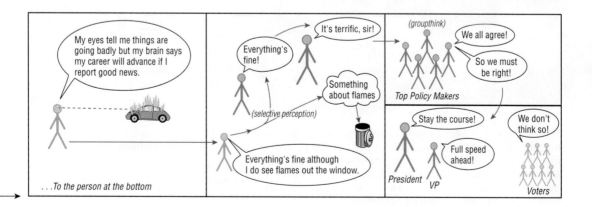

important and time frames are compressed. Crisis decision making is harder to understand and predict than is normal foreign policy decision making.

In a crisis, decision makers operate under tremendous time constraints. The normal checks on unwise decisions may not operate. Communications become shorter and more stereotyped, and information that does not fit a decision maker's expectations is more likely to be discarded simply because there is no time to consider it. In framing options, decision makers tend to restrict the choices, again to save time, and tend to overlook creative options while focusing on the most obvious ones.

Groupthink occurs easily during crises. During the 1962 Cuban Missile Crisis, President John F. Kennedy created a small, closed group of advisors who worked together intensively for days on end, cut off from outside contact. Even the president's communication with Soviet leader Nikita Khrushchev was rerouted through Kennedy's brother Robert and the Soviet ambassador, cutting out the State Department. Recognizing the danger of groupthink, Kennedy left the room from time to time—removing the authority figure from the group—to encourage free discussion. The group managed to identify an option (a naval blockade) between their first two choices (bombing the missile sites or doing nothing).

WORKING UNDER STRESS

Crisis management takes a high toll psychologically and physiologically. President Eduard Shevardnadze of Georgia seems to show this strain in 1992—just the beginning of years of civil war and perpetual crisis in that country. Shevardnadze, formerly a Soviet foreign minister, had returned to lead his native Georgia when the Soviet Union dissolved. He left office in 2003 after a popular uprising against corruption.

Participants in crisis decision making not only are rushed, but experience severe psychological *stress* amplifying the biases just discussed. Decision makers tend to overestimate the hostility of adversaries and to underestimate their own hostility toward those adversaries. More and more information is screened out in making decisions.

Whether in crisis mode or normal routines, individual decisions are shaped by the government and society in which they work. Foreign policy is constrained and shaped by substate actors such as government agencies, political interest groups, and industries. Foreign policy is a complex outcome of a complex process. It results from the struggle of competing themes, competing domestic interests, and competing government agencies. No single individual, agency, or guiding principle determines the outcome.

Beyond the challenges to realist theories from liberal theories and foreign policy analysis, several more sweeping critiques have emerged. These include constructivism, postmodernism, peace studies, Marxist theories, and gender theories of IR.

Social Theories

Several distinct approaches in IR theory may be grouped together as *social theories*, meaning that they rely on social interaction to explain individuals' and states' preferences. These theories contrast with the assumption of fixed, timeless preferences in most theories based on realism (states want more power) and liberalism (states, interest groups, and individuals want peace and prosperity).

Constructivism

Constructivism, a fast-growing approach in IR, is best described as an approach rather than a theory. When stripped to its core, it says nothing about IR per se, but its lessons about the nature of norms, identity, and social interaction can provide powerful insights into the world of IR. In fact, most constructivist explanations draw heavily on the identity principle to explain international behavior.

Constructivism is interested in how actors define their national interests, threats to those interests, and relationships to one another. Realists (and neoliberals) tend to simply take state interests as given. Thus, constructivism puts IR in the context of broader social relations. States decide what they want based not only on material needs, but "social" interaction. Just as a shopper may decide to buy a particular mp3 player because it will be perceived as cool (that is, more socially acceptable), so states may chose policies based on what they perceive will be "popular" with other states. Yet, just as shoppers may have limits placed on which music player they can afford to buy (limited resources), constructivists also recognize that power is not absent from international relations.

For example, why is the United States concerned when North Korea builds nuclear weapons, but not when Great Britain does? Realists would quickly answer that North Korea poses a bigger threat, yet from a pure military power perspective, Great Britain is a *far* superior military force to North Korea. Yet no one would argue that Great Britain is a threat to the United States no matter how many nuclear weapons it builds and no matter how deep disagreements about foreign policy become. Constructivist scholars would point out the shared history, shared alliances, and shared norms that tell Americans and the British they are not a threat to one another although they are very powerful militarily. The identity of the potential adversary matters, not just its military capabilities and interests.

Constructivists hold that these state identities are complex and changing and arise from interactions with other states—often through a process of *socialization*. Some constructivist scholars contend that over time, states can conceptualize one another in such a way that there is no danger of a security dilemma, arms races, or the other effects of anarchy. They point to Europe as an example—a continent that was the center of two military conflicts in the first half of the 20th century that killed millions. By the end of that century, war had become unthinkable. European identities are now intertwined with the European Union, not with the violent nationalism that led to two world wars. For constructivists, power politics, anarchy, and military force cannot explain this change. Institutions, regimes, norms, and changes in identity are better explanations.

Societies as a whole also change over time in what they consider to be threatening. Two hundred years ago, pirates were the scourge of the high seas. These nonstate actors invaded ports, pillaged goods, committed murder, and flaunted all international authority. It would not be hard to consider such behavior terrorism even though the pirates had no political goals in their violence. Even if not terrorism, no one would doubt the costs associated with piracy. Many states, including the United States, used their navies in attempts to eradicate pirates. Yet, despite the danger and harm historically caused by these actors, today we celebrate pirates by making them sports mascots, naming amusement rides after them, and glorifying them in movies.

Of course, one could argue that pirates are no longer a threat—even though numerous acts of piracy still occur on the high seas. Even apart from the high-profile pirate hijackings near Somalia in 2008–2009, the threat from piracy has remained high for many years. Yet, we find it acceptable to play down the piracy threat by incorporating them into popular culture. No doubt someone from two centuries ago would find such acceptance odd.

NEW IDENTITY

Constructivist theories, based on the core principle of identity, see actors' preferences as constructed by the actors rather than given "objectively." These theories may do better than realist or liberal approaches in explaining major changes in a state's foreign policy goals and image in the world that arise from internal changes and new self-concepts rather than external constraints or opportunities. Examples might include the breakup of the Soviet Union and the election of Barack Obama as U.S. president. Here, the new face of American power is reflected in Brazilian masks being prepared for Carnival, 2009.

How odd? Imagine in 200 years your great-great-grandchildren riding a terrorist-themed ride at Disneyland or watching the latest *Terrorists of the Persian Gulf* movie. Constructivists are quick to point out that what societies or states consider dangerous is not universal or timeless. Social norms and conventions change and these changes can have tremendous implications for foreign policy.

Another field of constructivist research also relies heavily on international norms and their power to constrain state action. Although realists (and neoliberals) contend that states make decisions based on a *logic of consequences* ("What will happen to me if I behave a certain way?"), constructivist scholars note that there is a powerful *logic of appropriateness* ("How should I behave in this situation?"). For example, some cases of humanitarian intervention—military intervention by a state or states to protect citizens or subjects of another state—seem difficult to explain in realist or liberal terms. Why, for example, did the United States in 1992 send troops to Somalia—a country of minimal strategic and economic importance to the United States—as Somalia descended into political chaos and faced the possibility of mass starvation (see p. 29)? A constructivist explanation might point to changing norms about which kinds of people are worthy of protection. In the 19th century, European powers occasionally intervened to protect Christian subjects of the Ottoman Empire from massacres, but generally ignored non-Christian victims. However, as decolonization enshrined the principle of self-determination and as human rights became widely valued, the scope of humanitarian intervention expanded. Although the international community does not always respond effectively to humanitarian crises, it is no longer acceptable to view only Christians as deserving protection.

Examples of identity principles can be found in the developing world as well. Some constructivists have argued that countries in Latin America, Africa, and the Middle East have adopted or changed policies in response to international norms—not because it provided large benefits, but rather because it was perceived as the appropriate course of action. For example, many developing states have raced to create science bureaucracies and/or begin technological modernization of their militaries. Constructivists point out that the reason developing states choose to spend their limited resources on such projects is their desire to be perceived as "modern" by the international system. Ironically, many states that build science bureaucracies have few scientists and many states that build advanced militaries have few enemies. Thus, constructivists emphasize that identities and norms must be used to explain this seemingly puzzling behavior.

How are these international norms spread around the world? In an age of global communication and relative ease of transportation, many possibilities exist. Some contend that individuals labeled *norm entrepreneurs,* through travel, writing, and meeting with elites, change ideas and encourage certain types of norms. Some point to broad-based social movements and nongovernmental organizations, such as the anti-apartheid movement encouraging the development of a global norm of racial equality. Others show how international organizations (such as the UN and NATO) can diffuse norms of what is appropriate and inappropriate behavior. In each case, however, new ideas and norms, rather than power and self-interest, drive state behavior.

Research in the constructivist tradition has expanded rapidly in recent years. Scholars have examined the role of the European Union in socializing elites in new member states as well as the role of the United Nations in conferring legitimacy on the use of force as a source of its power. Others have investigated how international organizations gain authority through their expertise (for example, the IMF on international financial issues) to make decisions that run counter to what their member states desire. Finally, constructivist scholars have begun to investigate how notions of identity and symbolism are important for understanding terrorist movements and counterterrorism policy.

Of course, like any approach or theory of IR, constructivism has its critics. Realists suggest that norms are simply covers for state (or personal) interests. Liberals argue that some constructivist scholars pay too little attention to the formal institutions and the power politics within them. Moreover, both realists and liberals criticize that it is difficult to tell when a person's beliefs or identity are genuine or adopted strategic reasons to bring material benefits (such as more aid, trade, or membership into an exclusive organization). Despite these criticisms, constructivist thinking and its emphasis on the identity principle will continue to be at the core of IR research for years to come.

Postmodernism

Postmodernism is a broad approach to scholarship that has left its mark on various academic disciplines, especially the study of literature. Because of their literary roots, postmodernists pay special attention to *texts* and to *discourses*—how people talk and write about their subject (IR). Postmodern critiques of realism thus center on analyzing realists' words and arguments. A central idea of postmodernism is that there is no single, objective reality but a multiplicity of experiences and perspectives that defy easy categorization. For this reason, postmodernism itself is difficult to present in a simple or categorical way. Postmodern scholarship in IR preceded, set the stage for, and has largely been supplanted by, constructivism.

From a postmodern perspective, realism cannot justify its claim that states are the central actors in IR and that states operate as unitary actors with coherent sets of objective interests (which they pursue through international power politics). Postmodern critics of realism see nothing objective about state interests, and certainly nothing universal (in that one set of values or interests applies to all states).

More fundamentally, postmodernism calls into question the whole notion of states as actors. States have no tangible reality; they are "fictions" that we (as scholars and citizens) construct to make sense of the actions of large numbers of individuals. For postmodernists, the stories told about the actions and policies of states are just that—stories. They are filtered through an interpretive process that distorts the actual experiences of those involved.

Contrary to realism's claim that states are unitary actors, postmodernists see multiple realities and experiences lurking below the surface of the fictional entities that realists construct (states). The Soviet Union, for example, was treated by realists as a single actor with a single set of objective interests. Indeed, it was considered the second most important actor in the world. Realists were amazed when the Soviet Union split into 15 pieces, each containing its own fractious groups and elements. It became clear that the "unitary state" called the Soviet Union had masked (and let realists ignore) the divergent experiences of constituent republics, ethnic groups, and individuals.

Postmodernists seek to "deconstruct" such constructions as states, the international system, and the associated stories and arguments (texts and discourses) with which realists portray the nature of international relations. To *deconstruct* a text—a term borrowed from literary criticism—means to tease apart the words in order to reveal hidden meanings, looking for what might be omitted or included only implicitly. The hidden meanings not explicitly addressed in the text are often called the **subtext.** Omissions are an aspect of subtext, as when realist theories of IR omit women and gender, for example. In its emphasis on states, realism omits the roles of individuals, domestic politics, economic classes, MNCs, and other nonstate actors. In its focus on the great powers, realism omits the experiences of poor countries. In its attention to military forms of leverage, it omits the roles of various nonmilitary forms of leverage. By contrast, postmodernists celebrate the diversity of experiences that make up IR without needing to make sense of them by simplifying and categorizing.

Marxism

Historically most important among social theories, Marxist approaches to IR hold that both IR and domestic politics arise from unequal relationships between **economic classes.** This emphasis on classes—implying that the domestic and economic attributes of societies shape the society's external relations with other states—contrasts with the realist approach to IR with its separation of domestic and international politics. We will discuss Marxist theories of IR in Chapter 7, as they primarily concern the global divisions of North and South arising from the history of imperialism. Here we will show, briefly, how Marxist theories as social theories contrast with the realist paradigm.

Marxism is a branch of socialism that holds that the more powerful classes oppress and exploit the less powerful by denying them their fair share of the surplus they create. The oppressed classes try to gain power in order to seize more of the wealth for themselves. This process, called *class struggle*, is one way of looking at the political relationships between richer and poorer people, and ultimately between richer and poorer world regions.

Marxism includes both communism and other approaches. In the mid-19th century, *Karl Marx* emphasized labor as the source of economic surplus. At that time, the Industrial Revolution was accompanied by particular hardship among industrial workers (including children) in Europe. Marxists still believe that the surplus created by labor should be recaptured by workers through political struggle. Today, Marxism is most influential in countries of the global South, where capital is scarce and labor conditions are wretched.

One important class in revolutions during the past century (contrary to Marx's expectations) has been *peasants*. Marxists traditionally consider peasants backward, ignorant, individualistic, and politically passive as compared to the better-educated and class-conscious proletariat. But in practice, the successful third world revolutions have been peasant rebellions (often led by Marxists talking about the proletariat). The largest was the Chinese revolution in the 1930s and 1940s.

Marx's theories of class struggle were oriented toward *domestic* society in the industrializing countries of his time, not toward poor countries or international relations. Traditional Marxists looked to the advanced industrialized countries for revolution and socialism, which would grow out of capitalism. In their view, the third world would have to develop through its own stages of accumulation from feudalism to capitalism before taking the revolutionary step to socialism. What actually happened was the opposite. Proletarian workers in industrialized countries enjoyed rising standards of living and did not make revolutions. Meanwhile, in the backward third world countries, oppressed workers and peasants staged a series of revolutions, successful and failed.

Why did revolutions occur in backward rather than advanced countries? The answer largely shapes how one sees North-South relations today. Marxists have mostly (but not exclusively) followed a line of argument developed by *V. I. Lenin,* founder of the Soviet Union, before the Russian Revolution of 1917. Russia was then a relatively backward state, as the global South is today, and most Marxists considered a revolution there unlikely (looking instead to Germany).

Lenin's theory of imperialism argued that European capitalists were investing in colonies where they could earn big profits and then using part of these profits to *buy off* the working class at home. But Lenin saw that after the scramble for colonies in the 1890s, few areas of the world remained to be colonized. Imperialist expansion could occur only at the expense of other imperialist states, leading to interimperialist competition and wars such as World War I. Seizing on Russia's weakness during that war, Lenin led the first successful communist revolution there in 1917.

Lenin's general idea still shapes a major approach to North-South relations—the idea that industrialized states exploit poor countries (through both formal and informal colonization) and buy off their own working classes with the profits. Through this *globalization of class relations,* world accumulation concentrates surplus toward the rich parts of the world and away from the poor ones. Revolutions, then, would be expected in poor regions.

Many revolutionaries in poor countries sought to break loose from exploitation by the European colonizers. After European colonization ended, the United States as the world's richest country (with large investments in the global South and a global military presence) became the target of revolutionaries agitating against exploitation in poor countries. In a number of countries, imperialists were thrown out (often violently, sometimes not) and revolutionary nationalists took power.

One of the most important such revolutions was in China, where Mao Zedong's communists took power in 1949 on a Leninist platform adapted to the largely peasant-based movement they led. Mao declared that "China has stood up"—on its own feet, throwing off foreign domination and foreign exploitation. In India at the same time, the movement led by Gandhi used a different means (nonviolence) to achieve similar ends—national independence from colonialism. Indonesia threw out the Dutch. Lebanon threw out the French. Cuba threw out the Americans. This pattern was repeated, with variations, in dozens of countries.

According to the revolutionaries in these countries, exploitation of poor countries by rich ones takes away the economic surplus of the global South and concentrates the accumulation of wealth toward the rich parts of the world. By breaking free of such exploitation, poor states can then retain their own surplus and begin to accumulate their own wealth. Eventually they can generate their own self-sustaining cycles of accumulation and lift themselves out of poverty.

Such an approach has not worked well. A policy of self-reliance does not foster growth (see p. 171). And within a single poor country, trade-offs arise between concentrating or distributing wealth. For former colonies, the realities of economic development after independence have been complex. These realities are discussed in Chapter 7.

Not all Marxist approaches favor a policy of self-reliance after revolution. *Leon Trotsky,* a Russian revolutionary, believed that after the 1917 revolution Russia would never be able to build socialism alone and should make its top priority the spreading of revolution to other countries to build a worldwide alliance. Trotsky's archrival

Stalin wanted to build "socialism in one country," and he prevailed (and had Trotsky killed). Most revolutions since then, including China's, have had a strongly national-ist flavor.

Marxist theories in IR entered a low-visibility phase after the collapse of the Soviet Union and China's turn toward capitalism—events that seemed to discredit Marxist theories. However, in recent years Marxists and former Marxists have taken power in a number of Latin American countries. Venezuela and Bolivia, as a result, have become active allies of Cuba, forming an anti-American coalition. In Nicaragua, the former com-munist leader whom U.S.-organized rebels fought in the 1980s won election as president in 2006. In Nepal, Maoists reached a peace deal and then won national elections. These events, along with China's continuing formal adherence to Marxism, suggest that Marxist theories of IR have ongoing importance in the post–Cold War era.

Peace Studies

Peace studies, like other identity-based approaches to IR, challenges fundamental con-cepts behind both realism and neoliberalism. In particular, peace studies seeks to shift the focus of IR away from the interstate level of analysis and toward a broad conception of social relations. Peace studies connects war and peace with individual responsibility, economic inequality, gender relations, cross-cultural understanding, and other aspects of social relationships. Peace studies seeks the potentials for peace not in the transactions of state leaders but in the transformation of entire societies (through social revolution) and in transnational communities (bypassing states and ignoring borders to connect people and groups globally).

Another way in which peace studies seeks to broaden the focus of inquiry is to reject the supposed objectivity of traditional (realist and liberal) approaches. Most scholars of peace studies think that a good way to gain knowledge is to participate in action—not just to observe objectively. This lack of objectivity has been criticized as *normative bias* because scholars impose their personal norms and values on the subject. Scholars in peace studies respond, however, that realism itself has normative biases and makes pol-icy prescriptions.

The development and implementation of peaceful strategies for settling conflicts— using alternatives to violent forms of leverage—are known by the general term **conflict resolution.** These methods are at work, competing with violent methods, in virtually all international conflicts. Recently the use of conflict resolution has been increasing, becoming more sophisticated, and succeeding more often.

Most conflict resolution uses a third party whose role is **mediation** between two conflicting parties. If both sides agree in advance to abide by a solution devised by a mediator, the process is called *arbitration*. In that case, both sides present their arguments to the arbitrator, who decides on a "fair" solution. Arbitration often uses a panel of three people, one chosen by each side and a third on whom both sides agree. In 2002, such a panel (with the UN choosing the third member) delineated the Ethiopian-Eritrean border following a costly war.

Conflicting parties (and mediators) can also use *confidence-building* measures to gradually increase trust. By contrast, *linkage* lumps together diverse issues so that compromises on one can be traded off against another in a grand deal.

Peace studies scholars argue that war is not just a natural expression of power, but one closely tied to *militarism*, the glorification of war, military force, and violence through TV, films, books, political speeches, toys, games, sports, and other such avenues. Militarism also refers to the structuring of society around war—for example, the dominant role of a military-industrial complex in a national economy. Militarism may underlie the propensity of political leaders to use military force. Historically, militarism has had a profound influence on the evolution of societies. War has often been glorified as a "manly" enterprise that ennobles the human spirit (especially before World War I, which changed that perspective). Not only evil acts but also exemplary acts of humanity are brought forth by war—sacrifice, honor, courage, altruism on behalf of loved ones, and bonding with a community larger than oneself.

Examples of less militarized cultures show that realism's emphasis on military force is not universal or necessary. Costa Rica has had no army for 50 years (just lightly armed forces), even during the 1980s when wars occurred in neighboring Nicaragua and Panama. Japan since World War II has developed strong norms against war and violence.

SHADOW OF WAR

Militarism in a culture, or the lack thereof, can influence foreign policy. In societies at war, children's psychological trauma contributes to intergroup conflicts decades later. Generations of Pakistanis have grown up in a society affected by violent conflict. This boy holds a toy gun at an Islamist party rally, 2008.

Positive peace refers to a peace that resolves the underlying reasons for war—peace that is not just a cease-fire but a transformation of relationships. Under positive peace, not only do state armies stop fighting each other, they stop arming, stop forming death squads against internal protest, and reverse the economic exploitation and political oppression that scholars in peace studies believe are responsible for social conflicts that lead to war.

Proponents of this approach see broad social and economic issues—assumed by realists to be relatively unimportant—as inextricably linked with positive peace. Some scholars define poverty, hunger, and oppression as forms of violence—which they call *structural violence* because it is caused by the structure of social relations rather than by direct actions such as shooting people. Structural violence in this definition kills and harms many more people each year than do war and other forms of direct political violence. Positive peace is usually defined to include the elimination of structural violence because it is considered a source of conflict and war.

Positive peace encompasses a variety of approaches to social change. These include alternative mechanisms for conflict resolution to take the place of war; popular pressure on governments through peace movements and political activism; strengthening of norms against the use of violence; the development of international or global identity transcending national, ethnic, and religious divisions; and egalitarian relations within societies in the economic, social, and political realms. Positive peace is usually defined to include political equality and human rights as well. When a small ruling group or dictator holds political power, fewer checks on government violence operate than when democratic institutions exist (see pp. 70–72). And when avenues of legitimate political participation are open, citizens are less likely to turn to violence.

The creation of a **world government** has long been debated by scholars and pursued by activists. Some scholars believe progress is being made (through the UN) toward the eventual emergence of a world government. Others think the idea is impractical or even undesirable (merely adding another layer of centralized control, when peace demands decentralization and freedom).

FOR PEACE

Peace demonstrators play a role in many international conflicts. Here, marchers in Spain protest the U.S. war in Iraq, 2007.

Scholars in peace studies also study how to achieve the conditions for positive peace. Most peace studies scholars share a skepticism that state leaders left to themselves would ever achieve positive peace. Rather, they believe the practice of IR will change only as a result of pressures from individuals and groups. The most commonly studied method of exerting such pressure is through **peace movements**—people taking to the streets in protest against war and militarism.

Peace activists often disagree on goals. In the U.S. peace movement since World War I, an *internationalist* wing has seen international organizations (today, the UN) as the best hope for peace and has supported wars against aggression. A *pacifist* wing has opposed all wars, distrusted international organizations whose members are state governments, and favored more radical social change to achieve positive peace.

The philosophies of *nonviolence* and *pacifism* are based on a unilateral commitment to refrain from using any violent forms of leverage in bargaining. No state today follows such a strategy; indeed, it is widely believed that in today's world, a state that adopted a nonviolent philosophy would risk exploitation or conquest. The term *pacifism* has fallen

VIDEO

Lessons from the Saffron Revolution

into disfavor because it has been taken to imply passivity in the face of aggression. The more popular term, *nonviolence*, reflects especially the philosophy and practice of *Mahatma Gandhi,* who emphasized that nonviolence must be *active* in seeking to prevent violence, to resolve conflicts without violence, and especially to stand up against injustice enforced violently.

Gender Theories

Scholarship on gender has cut a broad swath across academic disciplines, from literature to psychology to history. In recent years, it has made inroads in international relations, once considered one of the fields most resistant to feminist arguments.

VIDEO

Women and AIDS

Why Gender Matters

Gender scholarship encompasses a variety of strands of work, but all have in common the insight that gender matters in understanding how IR works—especially in issues relating to war and international security. *Feminist scholarship* in various disciplines seeks to uncover hidden assumptions about gender in how we study a subject. What scholars traditionally claim to be universal often turns out to be true only of males. Some feminist IR scholars argue that the core assumptions of realism—especially of anarchy and sovereignty—reflect the ways in which *males* tend to interact and to see the world. In this view, the realist approach simply assumes male participants when discussing foreign policy decision making, state sovereignty, or the use of military force.

This critique is somewhat complex. Because the vast majority of heads of state, diplomats, and soldiers *are* male, it may be realistic to study them as males. What the feminist critics then ask is that scholars explicitly recognize the gendered nature of their subject (rather than implicitly assuming all actors are male). In this

A GUY THING

Feminists from various theoretical traditions agree that the gender makeup of international summits is important. Here, leaders of the G20 states—the major economies of the global North and South—meet to respond to the world financial crisis in November 2008. Of the 24 participants, only Germany's chancellor is female.

From this difference-feminist perspective, neoliberalism has gone backward from traditional liberalism by accepting the realist assumption of separate unitary states as the important actors and downplaying substate and transnational actors including women. Neoliberalism's conception of cooperation as rule-based interactions among autonomous actors also reflects masculinist assumptions.

Gender in War and Peace

In addition to its emphasis on autonomy and anarchy, realism stresses military force as the key form of leverage in IR. Here, too, many difference feminists see in realism a hidden assumption of masculinity. They see war as not only a male occupation, but the quintessentially male occupation. In this view, men are inherently the more warlike sex, and women the more peaceful. Thus, although realism may accurately portray the importance of war and military force in IR, it merely reflects the male domination of the international sphere to date—not a necessary, eternal, or inescapable logic of relations among states.

VIDEO

Gender, Terror, and War in Sri Lanka

Difference feminists find much evidence to support the idea of war as a masculine pursuit. Anthropologists have found that in all known cultures, males are the primary (and usually the only) combatants in warfare, despite the enormous diversity of those cultures in so many other ways. One supposed link between war and masculinity is the male sex hormone testosterone (along with related hormones), which some biologists have connected with aggressive behavior in animals. However, complex behaviors such as aggression and war cannot be said to be biologically *driven* or predetermined, because humanity's most striking biological capability is flexibility.

Difference feminists emphasize women's unique abilities and contributions as *peacemakers*. They stress women's roles as *mothers* and potential mothers. Because of such caregiving roles, women are presumed to be more likely than men to oppose war and more likely to find alternatives to violence in resolving conflicts. Both biologically and anthropologically, no firm evidence connects women's caregiving functions (pregnancy and nursing) with any particular kinds of behavior such as reconciliation or nonviolence. The role of women varies considerably from one society to another. Although they rarely take part in combat, women often provide logistical support to male warriors and sometimes help drive the men into a war frenzy by dancing, shaming nonparticipating males, and other activities supportive of war.

Nonetheless, the idea of women as peacemakers has a long history. In ancient Athens, the (male) playwright Aristophanes, in the play *Lysistrata*, speculated about how women might end the unpopular Peloponnesian War with Sparta, then in progress (in part by withholding sex from men). Women have formed their own organizations to work for peace on many occasions. In 1852, *Sisterly Voices* was published as a newsletter for women's peace societies. During World War I, Jane Addams and other feminists founded the Women's Peace Party (now called the Women's International League for Peace and Freedom).

After World War I, the *suffrage* movement won the right for women to vote. Difference feminists thought that women would vote for peace and against war, changing the nature of foreign policy, but women generally voted as their husbands did.

Nonetheless, U.S. public opinion on foreign policy issues since the 1930s partially vindicates difference feminists. A **gender gap** in polls finds women about 10 percentage points lower than men on average in their support for military actions. This gender gap shrinks, however, when broad consensus on a military action exists, as when U.S. forces attacked terrorist supporters in Afghanistan in late 2001. In 1995, the UN-sponsored Beijing conference on women brought together women activists from around the world and helped deepen feminists' engagement with global issues such as North-South inequality. Through these various actions, difference feminists began developing a feminist practice of international relations that could provide an alternative to the masculine practice of realism.

In 2000, the UN Security Council passed Resolution 1325, mandating greater inclusion of women and attention to gender in UN peacekeeping and reconstruction. But in several locations UN peacekeepers participated in local prostitution, rape, and even sex trafficking. In 2004, Secretary-General Annan called "shameful" the reported behavior of UN troops from several countries serving in Democratic Congo. Investigators there found hundreds of cases of sexual crimes by UN personnel.

As a result of Resolution 1325, "gender advisors" have begun to accompany international peacekeeping and relief operations to provide practical advice on more effective operations in the context of local cultures' gender relations. For example, the head of a group of Swedish men sent to build a bridge in Sri Lanka initially said, "Our task is to build a bridge, we don't need to worry about gender issues." When asked how it would be used, he replied, "By car mostly," but when asked, "The women too?" he said, "No, they'll probably walk." As a result of this gender perspective, the bridge was redesigned to include a pedestrian walkway.

Women in IR

Liberal feminists are skeptical of difference-feminist critiques of realism. They believe that when women are allowed to participate in IR, they play the game basically the same way men do, with similar results. They think that women can practice realism—based on autonomy, sovereignty, anarchy, territory, military force, and all the rest—just as well as men can. Thus liberal feminists tend to reject the critique of realism as masculine. Liberal feminism focuses on the integration of women into the overwhelmingly male preserves of foreign policy making and the military. (In practice, many feminist scholars draw on both difference feminists' and liberal feminists' views in various proportions.)

Female state leaders do not appear to be any more peaceful, or any less committed to state sovereignty and territorial integrity, than are male leaders (see Table 3.1). Of course, women in traditionally male roles may have been selected (or self-selected) on the basis of their suitability to such roles: they may not act the way "average" women would act. Some have even suggested that women in power tend to be more warlike to compensate for being females in traditionally male roles. But overall, women state leaders, like men, seem capable of leading in war or in peace as circumstances demand.

In the U.S. Congress, it is hard to compare men's and women's voting records on foreign policy issues because there have been so few women. The U.S. Senate, which approves treaties and foreign policy appointments, was 98–99 percent male until 1992

TABLE 3.1   Notable Women State Leaders of Recent Decades

Leader	Country	Record in Office	Time Frame
Sheikh Hasina Wajed	Bangladesh	Attempting to consolidate democratic transition	2008–
Angela Merkel	Germany	Only current woman leader of a great power; put limits on German troops with NATO forces in Afghanistan	2005–
Ellen Johnson-Sirleaf	Liberia	Struggling to keep country calm after civil war	2006–
Margaret Thatcher	Britain	First woman to lead a great power in a century; went to war to recover Falkland Islands from Argentina	1982
Indira Gandhi	India	Led war against Pakistan	1971
Golda Meir	Israel	Led war against Egypt and Syria	1973
Benazir Bhutto	Pakistan	Struggled to control own military	late 1980s
Corazon Aquino	Philippines	Struggled to control own military	late 1980s
Tansu Çiller	Turkey	Led a harsh war to suppress Kurdish rebels	mid-1990s
Violetta Chamorro	Nicaragua	Kept the peace between factions after civil war	1980s
Chandrika Kumaratunga	Sri Lanka	Tried to make peace with separatists, but returned to war	1990s and since
Megawati Sukarnoputri	Indonesia	Struggled to keep country calm; lost re-election bid	2004

Note: Other states, such as Finland, Norway, New Zealand, and Iceland, have had women leaders when war and peace were not major political issues in those countries.

(but dropped to 84 percent male in 2007). Women have never chaired the key foreign policy committees (Armed Services and Foreign Relations) in the Senate or House.

Globally, the number of women serving in legislatures is increasing. A 2008 UN report found that women comprised over 18 percent of members of parliaments across the world, up from 7 percent in 1995. Some nations set aside a certain number of seats for females in parliament. Yet, female candidates often capture more seats than are set aside. In Rwanda, for example, women make up over 50 percent of the lower house of parliament, even though the law requires only 30 percent female representation. Although more women find themselves in politics, the UN report pointed to global shortcomings as well. For example, even though women are increasingly represented in legislatures, they do not hold correspondingly equal numbers in political party leadership positions.

Liberal feminists also believe that women soldiers, like women politicians, have a range of skills and abilities comparable to men's. About 200,000 women soldiers serve in the U.S. military (15 percent of the total) and more than 1 million women are veterans. Women perform well in a variety of military roles, including logistical and medical support, training, and command. Women have had success in other countries that have allowed them into the military (or, in a few cases, drafted them).

Although women have served with distinction in military forces, they have been excluded from combat roles in almost all those forces. In some countries, military women are limited to traditional female roles such as nurses and typists. Even when women may hold nontraditional positions such as mechanics and pilots (as in the United States), most women remain in the traditional roles. And certain jobs still remain off-limits; for instance, women cannot serve on U.S. submarines or in combat infantry. Thus relatively few cases exist to judge women's abilities in combat.

Those cases include historical examples of individual women who served in combat (sometimes disguised as men, sometimes not). In the 15th century, Joan of Arc rallied French soldiers to defeat England, turning the tide of the Hundred Years' War. (The English burned her at the stake as a witch after capturing her.) Women have often participated in combat in rebel forces fighting guerrilla wars in Vietnam, Nicaragua, and elsewhere, as well as in terrorist or paramilitary units in countries such as Peru, Germany, Italy, and Palestine. Women in Eritrea's guerrilla forces became part of that country's regular army after independence and then served in frontline combat units during Eritrea and Ethiopia's trench warfare in the late 1990s. In recent years, U.S. women soldiers have found themselves in combat (present mobile tactics and fluid front lines make it hard to separate combat from support roles). In the 2003 Iraq War, women flew all types of airplanes and helicopters, and one woman was in the first group of U.S. POWs captured early in the war. During the subsequent years of war in Iraq, U.S. women military police have acquitted themselves well in numerous firefights. All these cases suggest that (at least some) women are able to hold their own in combat.

The main reason that military forces exclude women from combat seems to be fear about what effect their presence might have on the male soldiers, whose discipline and loyalty have traditionally been thought to depend on male bonding and single-minded focus. Liberal feminists reject such arguments and argue that group bonding in military units does not depend

COMBAT HERO

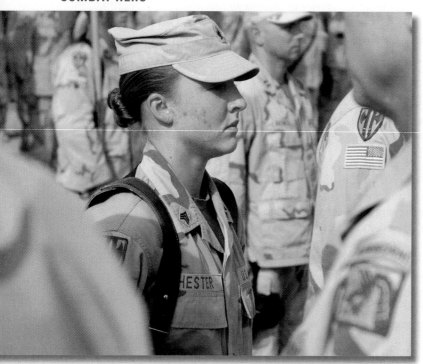

Women soldiers have performed as well as men in military tasks, as predicted by liberal feminists. But in state armies, women are barred from virtually all infantry combat units worldwide. Guerrilla forces more often include women, and female U.S. military police in Iraq often participate in fighting. Here, in 2005, a sergeant from the Kentucky National Guard receives the silver star for heroism in combat after fighting off an ambush in Iraq.

on gender segregation. (After all, similar rationales were once given for racial segregation in U.S. military forces.)

The effect of war on noncombatant women has also received growing attention. Attacks on women in Algeria, Rwanda, Bosnia, Afghanistan, Democratic Congo, and Sudan pointed to a possible new trend toward women as military targets. Systematic rape was used as a terror tactic in Bosnia and Rwanda, and the Japanese army in World War II operated an international network of sex slaves known as "comfort women." Rape has long been treated as a normal if regrettable by-product of war, but recently certain instances of rape were declared war crimes (see pp. 255–256).

In sum, liberal feminists reject the argument that women bring uniquely feminine assets or liabilities to foreign and military affairs. They do not critique realism as essentially masculine in nature but do criticize state practices that exclude women from participation in international politics and war.

Difference Feminism versus Liberal Feminism?

The arguments of difference feminists and liberal feminists may seem totally at odds. But the evidence in favor of both positions can be reconciled to some extent by bearing in mind that the character and ability of an individual are not the same as that of his or her group. Rather, the qualities of individuals follow a bell curve distribution, with many people clustered in the middle and fewer people very high or low on a given capability.

Gender differences posited by difference feminists mean that one bell curve is shifted from the other, even though the two may still overlap quite a bit (see Figure 3.6).

FIGURE 3.6   Overlapping Bell Curves

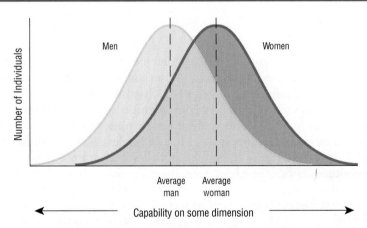

Bell curves show that individuals differ in capabilities such as physical strength or peacemaking ability. Although the genders differ on average, for most individuals (in the area of overlap) such differences do not come into play. Liberal feminists emphasize the area where the curves overlap; difference feminists emphasize the overall group differences.

To take a simple example, a few women are physically larger than almost all men, and a few men are smaller than almost all women. But, on average, men are somewhat larger than women. On different dimensions of capability, the women's curve is above the men's on average, but there is still much overlap.

Liberal feminists emphasize the overlap of the two bell curves. They say that individual women—*most* women on most relevant dimensions—are well within the male curve and thus can perform equally with the men. Indeed, women in nontraditional gender roles may well perform better than their male counterparts, because presumably women who self-select into such roles (such as by joining the military or running a government) are near the high end of the female bell curve, whereas the men are closer to the middle of the male curve.

Difference feminists are more interested in the shift in the two bell curves, not their overlap. On average, in this perspective, women tend to see international relations in a somewhat different way than men do. So although *individuals* selected to participate in foreign policy and the military may not differ from their male counterparts, women as a group differ. Women voters display different concerns regarding IR than men (as shown by the gender gap in opinion polls and voting patterns).

By this logic, then, profound differences in IR—and a shift away from the utility of realism in explaining state behavior—would occur only if many women participated in key foreign policy positions. A *few* women politicians or women soldiers do not change the masculine foundations of IR. But a world in which *most* politicians or soldiers were female might be a different story. Of course, these theories of difference feminists have never been tested, because women have never attained predominance in foreign policy making in any country—much less in the international system as a whole.

In addition to the liberal and difference strands of feminism, a third strand, postmodern feminism, is connected with the rise of postmodernism.

Postmodern Feminism

One line of criticism directed at realism combines feminism and postmodernism. *Postmodern feminism* seeks to deconstruct realism with the specific aim of uncovering the pervasive hidden influences of gender in IR while showing how arbitrary the construction of gender roles is. Feminist postmodernists agree with difference feminists that realism carries hidden meanings about gender roles, but deny that there is any fixed, inherent meaning in either male or female genders. Rather, feminist postmodernists look at the interplay of gender and power in a more open-ended way. Postmodern feminists criticize liberal feminists for trying merely to integrate women into traditional structures of war and foreign policy. They criticize difference feminists as well, for glorifying traditional feminine virtues.

Postmodern feminists have tried to deconstruct the language of realism, especially when it reflects influences of gender and sex. For instance, the first atomic bombs had male gender (they were named "Fat Man" and "Little Boy"). The plane that dropped the atomic bomb on Hiroshima (the *Enola Gay*) had female gender; it was named after the pilot's mother. Similarly, pilots have pasted pinup photos of nude women onto conventional bombs before dropping them. In all these cases, postmodern feminists would note that the feminine gender of vehicles, targets, or decorations amplifies the masculinity of the weapon itself.

All three strands of feminist theories provide explanations that often differ from both realist and liberal theories. For example, in the case of response to aggression, feminists might study the need for state leaders to prove their manhood by standing up to the bad guys. This is connected with the male role as protector of the orderly domestic sphere (home, family, country) against the dangerous and anarchic outside world. Since 2001, gender roles have become increasingly visible on both sides of the "war on terror," with both women's positions in society and men's concepts of masculinity becoming contested territory between the West and armed Islamic groups. Traditional theories of IR that ignore these issues may lack explanatory power as a result.

Each of these alternatives to realism has certain advantages and disadvantages as they attempt to explain world events. However, all of these theories and approaches must try to understand international conflicts and the use of military force. Chapter 4 takes up these issues.

CHAPTER REVIEW

SUMMARY

- Liberals dispute the realist notion that narrow self-interest is more rational than mutually beneficial cooperation. Neoliberalism argues that even in an anarchic system of autonomous rational states, cooperation can emerge through the building of norms, regimes, and institutions.

- Reciprocity can be an effective strategy for reaching cooperation in ongoing relationships but carries a danger of turning into runaway hostility or arms races.

- Collective goods are benefits received by all members of a group regardless of their individual contribution. Shared norms and rules are important in getting members to pay for collective goods.

- International regimes—convergent expectations of state leaders about the rules for issue areas in IR—help provide stability in the absence of a world government.

- In a collective security arrangement, a group of states agrees to respond together to aggression by any participating state.

- Foreign policies are strategies governments use to guide their actions toward other states. The foreign policy process is the set of procedures and structures that states use to arrive at foreign policy decisions and to implement them.

- Domestic constituencies (interest groups) have distinct interests in foreign policies and often organize politically to promote those interests.

- Public opinion influences governments' foreign policy decisions (more so in democracies than in authoritarian states), but governments also manipulate public opinion.

- Democracies have historically fought as many wars as authoritarian states, but democracies have almost never fought wars against other democracies. This is called the democratic peace.

- In the rational model of decision making, officials choose the action whose consequences best help meet the state's established goals. By contrast, in the organizational process model, decisions result from routine administrative procedures; in the government bargaining (or bureaucratic politics) model, decisions result from negotiations among governmental agencies with different interests in the outcome.

- The actions of individual decision makers are influenced by their personalities, values, and beliefs as well as by common psychological factors that diverge from rationality.

- Foreign policy decisions are also influenced by the psychology of groups (including groupthink), the procedures used to reach decisions, and the roles of participants. During crises, the potentials for misperception and error are amplified.

- Constructivists reject realist assumptions about state interests, tracing those interests in part to social interactions and norms.

- Postmodern critics reject the entire framework and language of realism, with its unitary state actors. Postmodernists argue that no simple categories can capture the multiple realities experienced by participants in IR.

- Marxists view international relations, including global North-South relations, in terms of a struggle between economic classes (especially workers and owners) that have different roles in society and different access to power.

- Peace studies programs are interdisciplinary and seek to broaden the study of international security to include social and economic factors ignored by realism.

- Mediation and other forms of conflict resolution are alternative means of exerting leverage on participants in bargaining.

- Positive peace implies not just the absence of war but addressing conditions that scholars in peace studies connect with violence—especially injustice and poverty.

- Feminist scholars of IR agree that gender is important in understanding IR but diverge into several strands regarding their conception of the role of gender.

- Difference feminists argue that real (not arbitrary) differences between men and women exist. Men think about social relations more often in terms of autonomy (as do realists), but women think in terms of connection. Difference feminists argue that men are more warlike on average than women.

- Liberal feminists disagree that women have substantially different capabilities or tendencies as participants in IR. They argue that women are equivalent to men in virtually all IR roles. As evidence, liberal feminists point to historical and present-day women leaders and women soldiers.

- Postmodern feminists seek to uncover gender-related subtexts implicit in realist discourse, including sexual themes connected with the concept of power.

KEY TERMS

neoliberal   66
international regime   67
collective security   69
democratic peace   70
interest groups   73
public opinion   74
"rally 'round the flag" syndrome   76
foreign policy process   78
rational model   79
organizational process model   80

government bargaining model   80
misperceptions   81
selective perceptions   81
information screens   81
optimizing   83
satisficing   83
prospect theory   83
groupthink   84
constructivism   87
postmodernism   90
subtext   90

economic classes   91
Marxism   91
conflict resolution   93
mediation   93
positive peace   94
world government   95
peace movements   95
difference feminism   97
liberal feminism   97
postmodern feminism   98
gender gap   100

ONLINE PRACTICE TEST

Take an online practice test at
www.IRtext.com

❑ A
🖰 B
❑ C
❑ D

CRITICAL THINKING QUESTIONS

1. Inasmuch as democracies almost never fight wars with each other, do existing democracies have a national security interest in seeing democratization spread to China and other authoritarian states? If so, how can that interest be reconciled with the long-standing norm of noninterference in the internal affairs of other sovereign states?

2. India and Pakistan are neighbors and enemies. Given the problems of misperception and bias in foreign policy decision making, what steps could you propose that each government adopt to keep these problems from interfering in the rational pursuit of national interests?

3. Peace studies claims that internal characteristics of states (at the domestic level of analysis) strongly affect the propensity for war or potential for lasting peace. For one society, show how internal characteristics—social, economic, and/or cultural—influence that society's external behavior.

4. Would IR operate differently if most state leaders were women? What would the differences be? What evidence (beyond gender stereotypes) supports your answer?

BACK TO THE BIG PICTURE

To hear a discussion of the "big picture" for this chapter, raised on p. 64, along with an example from recent history, consult the "IR Talk" podcast for Chapter 3 at *www.IRtext.com*

PODCAST

CHAPTER **4**

Conflict, War, and Terrorism

The Wars of the World

Chapter 3 discussed the decreasing number and size of wars in the world (see pp. 64–65). This chapter will focus on the remaining wars, and historical cases, to explain the causes of international conflicts.

Figure 4.1 shows the 13 wars in progress in 2009. The largest are in Iraq, western Sudan (Darfur), and Afghanistan. All 13 wars are in the global South. All but Colombia and the Philippines are in a zone of active fighting spanning parts of Africa, South Asia, and the Middle East.

In five smaller zones (dotted lines on the map), dozens of wars of recent decades have ended. Some of the countries in these zones still face difficult postwar years with the possibility of sliding back into violence as Democratic Congo did in 2007 after a 1999 cease-fire. But most peace agreements in the world's postwar zones are holding up.

CHAPTER OUTLINE

- **The Wars of the World**
- **Conflicts of Ideas**
- **Conflicts of Interest**
- **Conventional Military Forces**
- **Terrorism**
- **Weapons of Mass Destruction**
- **States and Militaries**

THE BIG PICTURE

IDENTITY

What are state and nonstate armed forces fighting about? Currently, ethnic and religious antagonisms stand out as the most important forces shaping most of the world's armed conflicts in the post–Cold War era. The identity principle underlies in-group/out-group psychology, which can lead to dehumanization and even genocide.

In a shorter-term, more immediate sense, most armed conflicts center on control of territory and of national governments, whatever the underlying conflicts. Sometimes these assets themselves are the points of contention; at other times they play out less tangible causes of conflict. Conflicts over material interests such as territory and governments allow for compromise (the reciprocity principle) more readily than do conflicts over ethnicity and religion (the identity principle).

To hear the authors of this book discuss this issue, with an example from recent history, download the "IR Talk" podcast for Chapter 4 from www.IRtext.com.

PODCAST

Types of War

Many different activities are covered by the general term *war*. Consequently, it is not easy to say how many wars are going on in the world at the moment. But most lists of wars set some minimum criteria—for instance, a minimum of a thousand battle deaths—to distinguish war from lower-level violence such as violent strikes or riots.

Wars are diverse. Wars tend to arise from different situations and play different sorts of roles in bargaining over conflicts. Starting from the largest wars, we may distinguish the following main categories.

Hegemonic war is a war over control of the entire *world order*—the rules of the international system as a whole, including the role of world hegemony (see p. 47). This class of wars (with variations in definition and conception) is also known as *world war*, *global war*, *general war*, or *systemic war*. The last hegemonic war was World War II. This kind of war probably cannot occur any longer without destroying civilization.

Total war is warfare by one state waged to conquer and occupy another. The goal is to reach the capital city and force the surrender of the government, which can then be replaced with one of the victor's choosing. Total war as we know it began with the mass destruction of the Napoleonic Wars, which introduced large-scale conscription and geared the entire French national economy toward the war effort. In total war, with the entire society mobilized for the struggle, the entire society of the enemy is considered a legitimate target.

Limited war includes military actions carried out to gain some objective short of the surrender and occupation of the enemy. For instance, the U.S.-led war against Iraq in 1991 retook the territory of Kuwait but did not go on to Baghdad to topple Saddam Hussein's government. Many border wars have this character: after occupying the land it wants, a state may stop and defend its gains, as Russia did after expelling Georgian troops from disputed Georgian provinces in 2008, for example.

FIGURE 4.1   Wars in Progress, May 2009

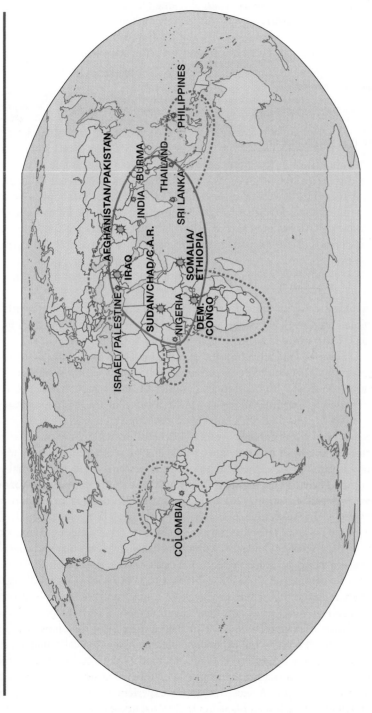

☀ Estimated deaths to date over 100,000

❀ Estimated deaths to date under 100,000

— Zone of active wars

··· Zones of transition from wars in recent decades

Raids are limited wars that consist of a single action—a bombing run or a quick incursion by land. In 2007, Israeli warplanes bombed a facility in Syria that Israel believed to be a nuclear research facility. Raids fall into the gray area between wars and nonwars because their destruction is limited and they are over quickly. Raiding that is repeated or fuels a cycle of retaliation usually becomes a limited war or what is sometimes called *low-intensity conflict.*

Civil war refers to war between factions within a state trying to create, or prevent, a new government for the entire state or some territorial part of it. (The aim may be to change the entire system of government, to merely replace the people in it, or to split a region off as a new state.) The U.S. Civil War of the 1860s is a good example of a secessionist civil war. The war in El Salvador in the 1980s is an example of a civil war for control of the entire state (not secessionist). Civil wars often seem to be among the most brutal wars. The 50,000 or more deaths in the civil war in El Salvador, including many from massacres and death squads, were not based on ethnic differences. Of course, many of today's civil wars emerge from ethnic conflicts as well. In Chad, for example, a rebel group composed of rival clans to the president's nearly overthrew the government in 2007. Sustaining a civil war usually requires a source of support for rebels, from neighboring states, diaspora ethnic communities, or revenue from natural resources or illegal drugs.

Guerrilla war, which includes certain kinds of civil wars, is warfare without front lines. Irregular forces operate in the midst of, and often hidden or protected by, civilian populations. The purpose is not to directly confront an enemy army but rather to harass and punish it so as to gradually limit its operation and effectively liberate territory from its control. Iraqi paramilitary forces used such methods in the Iraq War after 2003. U.S. military forces in South Vietnam fought against Vietcong guerrillas in the 1960s and 1970s, with rising frustration. Efforts to combat a guerrilla army—counterinsurgency—are discussed on pp. 140–142. Without a fixed front line, there is much territory that neither side controls; both sides exert military leverage over the same places at the same time. Thus, guerrilla wars hurt civilians, who suffer most when no military force firmly controls a location, opening the door to banditry, personal vendettas, sexual violence, and other such lawless behavior. The situation is doubly painful because conventional armies fighting against guerrillas often cannot distinguish them from civilians and punish both together. In one famous case in South Vietnam, a U.S. officer who had ordered an entire village burned to deny its use as a sanctuary by the Vietcong commented, "We had to destroy the village to save it." Warfare increasingly is irregular and guerrilla-style; it is less and less often an open conventional clash of large state armies.

In all types of war, the abstractions and theories of IR scholars hardly capture the horrors experienced by those on the scene, both soldiers and civilians. War suspends basic norms of behavior and, especially over time, traumatizes participants and bystanders. Soldiers see their best friends blown apart before their eyes; they must kill and maim their fellow human beings; some experience lifelong psychological traumatic stress as a result. Civilians experience terror, violence, and rape; they lose loved ones and homes; they too often live with trauma afterward. The violence of war does not resemble war movies, but instead creates a nearly psychotic experience of overwhelming confusion, noise, terror, and adrenaline. Soldiers in professional armies train to keep functioning in these conditions—but still have an incredibly difficult job—whereas those in irregular forces and civilian populations caught in civil wars have little hope of coping. The horrors of all war are magnified in cases of genocide and massacre, of child soldiers, and of brutal warfare that continues over years.

Scholars and policy makers are paying more attention in recent years to the difficult transitions from war to peace around the world—postwar reconciliation, conflict resolution, transitional governments representing opposing factions, economic reconstruction, and so forth. These efforts often address collective goods problems among the parties, as when Somali clan elders in 2007 agreed that all would be better off by giving up their guns to the new central government but none wanted to go first. After the shooting stops, international peacekeepers and NGOs focus on Security Sector Reform (SSR) to create professional military and police forces instead of warlord militias. The process of Disarmament, Demobilization, and Reintegration (DDR) deals with the common problem of what to do with irregular forces after civil wars end.

In several countries where long internal wars in the 1990s had led to dehumanization and atrocities—notably in South Africa—new governments used **truth commissions** to help the society heal and move forward. The commissions' role was to hear honest testimony from the period, to bring to light what really happened during these wars, and in exchange to offer most of the participants asylum from punishment. Sometimes international NGOs helped facilitate the process. However, human rights groups objected to a settlement in Sierra Leone in 1999 that brought into the government a faction that had routinely cut off civilians' fingers as a terror tactic. (Hostilities did end, however, in 2001.) Thus, after brutal ethnic conflicts give way to complex political settlements, most governments try to balance the need for justice and truth with the need to keep all groups on board.

VIDEO

Truth and Reconciliation in Guatemala

Experts have debated how much truth and reconciliation is necessary after long conflicts. Some now argue that in some circumstances, tribunals and government-sponsored panels to investigate past crimes could lead to political instability in transitional states. Other experts disagree, noting that the work of such panels can be essential to building trust, which is essential for democracy.

Causes of War

The Roman writer Seneca said nearly 2,000 years ago: "Of war men ask the outcome, not the cause." This is not true of political scientists. They want to know why countries fight.

The term **conflict** in IR generally refers to armed conflict. Conflict itself is ever present in the international system—the condition against which bargaining takes place. In conflict bargaining, states develop capabilities that give them leverage to obtain more favorable outcomes than they otherwise would achieve. Whether fair or unfair, the ultimate outcome of the bargaining process is a settlement of the particular conflict. Rarely do conflicts lead to violence, however.

The question of why war breaks out can be approached in different ways. Descriptive approaches, favored by historians, tend to focus narrowly on specific, direct causes of the outbreak of war, which vary from one war to another. For example, one could say that the assassination of Archduke Franz Ferdinand in 1914 "caused" World War I. More theoretical approaches, favored by many political scientists, tend to focus on the search for general explanations, applicable to a variety of contexts, about why wars break out. For example, one can see World War I as caused by shifts in the balance of power among European states, with the assassination being only a catalyst.

Broad generalizations about the causes of war have been elusive. Wars do not have a single or simple cause. Many theories about war have been put forward, but few have universal validity. Levels of analysis can help us organize these theories.

The Individual Level   On the *individual* level of analysis, theories about war center on rationality. One theory, consistent with realism, holds that the use of war and other violent means of leverage in international conflicts is normal and reflects *rational* decisions of national leaders.

An opposite theory holds that conflicts often escalate to war because of *deviations* from rationality in the individual decision-making processes of national leaders (see Chapter 3)—information screens, cognitive biases, groupthink, and so forth. A related theory holds that the education and mentality of whole populations of individuals determine whether conflicts become violent. Here, public nationalism or ethnic hatred—or even an innate tendency toward violence in human nature—may pressure leaders to solve conflicts violently.

Neither theory holds up very well. Some wars clearly reflect rational calculations of national leaders, whereas others clearly were mistakes and cannot be considered rational. Certainly some individual leaders seem prone to turn to military force to try to settle conflicts on favorable terms. But a maker of war can become a maker of peace, as did Egypt's Anwar Sadat. Individuals of many cultural backgrounds and religions lead their states into war, as do both male and female leaders.

The Domestic Level   The *domestic* level of analysis draws attention to the characteristics of states or societies that may make them more or less prone to use violence in resolving conflicts. During the Cold War, Marxists frequently said that the aggressive and greedy *capitalist* states were prone to use violence in international conflicts, whereas Western leaders claimed that the expansionist, ideological, and totalitarian nature of *communist* states made them especially prone to using violence. In truth, both types of society fought wars regularly.

Likewise, rich industrialized states and poor agrarian ones both go to war. Anthropologists have found that a wide range of *preagricultural* hunter-gatherer societies were much more prone to warfare than today's societies. Thus the potential for warfare seems to be universal across cultures, types of society, and time periods—although the importance and frequency of war vary greatly from case to case.

Some argue that domestic political factors shape a state's outlook on war and peace. For example, the democratic peace suggests that democracies almost never fight other democracies (see Chapter 3), although both democracies and authoritarian states fight wars. Others claim that domestic political parties, interest groups, and legislatures play an important role in whether international conflicts become international wars.

Few useful generalizations can tell us which societies are more prone or less prone to war. The same society may change greatly over time. For example, Japan was prone to using violence in international conflicts before World War II, but has been averse to such violence since then. If general principles explain why some societies at some times are more peaceful than others and why they change, political scientists have not yet identified them.

(handwritten margin notes:)
① individual
② Domestic
③ interstate
④ global

The Interstate Level   Theories at the *interstate* level explain wars in terms of power relations among major actors in the international system. *Power transition theory* holds that conflicts generate large wars at times when power is relatively equally distributed and a rising power is threatening to overtake a declining hegemon (see pp. 47–49). At this level, too, incompatible theories compete. Deterrence is supposed to stop wars by building up power and threatening its use. But the theory of arms races holds that wars are caused, not prevented, by such actions. No general formula has been discovered to tell us in what circumstances each of these principles holds true.

Some political scientists study war from a statistical perspective, analyzing data on types of wars and the circumstances under which they occurred. Current research focuses on the effects of such factors as democracy, government structure, trade, and international organizations in explaining the escalation or settlement of "militarized interstate disputes."

The Global Level   At the *global* level of analysis, a number of theories of war have been proposed. Of the several variations on the idea that major warfare in the international system is *cyclical*, one approach links large wars with *long economic waves* (also called *Kondratieff cycles*) in the world economy, of about 50 years' duration. Another approach links the largest wars with a 100-year cycle based on the creation and decay of world orders (see pp. 47–49). These *cycle theories* at best can explain only general tendencies toward war in the international system over time.

Thus, on all the levels of analysis, competing theories offer different explanations for why some conflicts become violent and others do not. Political scientists cannot yet confidently

WHY WAR?

Political scientists do not agree on a theory of why great wars like World War II occur and cannot predict whether they could happen again. The city of Stalingrad (Volgograd) was decimated during Germany's invasion of the Soviet Union, 1943.

predict which of the world's many international conflicts will lead to war. We can gain insight, however, by studying various types of conflicts to understand better what states fight about.

Conflicts of Ideas

The following sections discuss six types of international conflict: ethnic, religious, ideological, territorial, governmental, and economic. The first three are conflicts over ideas, the last three conflicts over interests. These six types of conflict are not mutually exclusive, and they overlap considerably in practice. For example, the conflicts between Russia and Ukraine after the 1991 Soviet breakup were complex. *Ethnic* Russians living in Ukraine, and ethnic Ukrainians in Russia, experienced ethnic conflict. There are *religious* differences between Ukrainian and Russian forms of Christianity. In addition, the two new states had a *territorial* dispute over the Crimean peninsula, which Soviet leader Nikita Khrushchev had transferred to Ukraine in the 1950s. The two states also had *economic* conflicts over trade and money after the Soviet breakup, which created new borders and currencies. These multiple conflicts did not lead to the use of military force, however. In 2005, the opposition took control of Ukraine's government (after a flawed election was rerun in response to weeks of mass street protests). Russian president Vladimir Putin, who had campaigned for the incumbent party in Ukraine, protested vigorously but did not seriously consider military force. So the types of conflict discussed here come into play in combination rather than separately.

We will look first at the most difficult types of conflict in which intangible elements such as ethnic hatred, religious fervor, or ideology come into play—conflicts of ideas. These identity-based sources of international conflict today have been shaped historically by nationalism as the link between identity and internationally recognized statehood. Therefore we will briefly review the development of nationalism before examining the three types of conflicts of ideas.

Nationalism

Nationalism—devotion to the interests of one's own nation over the interests of other states—may be the most important force in world politics in the past two centuries. A nation is a population that shares an identity, usually including a language and culture. But nationality is a difficult concept to define precisely. To some degree, the extension of political control over large territories such as France created the commonality necessary for nationhood—states created nations. At the same time, however, the perceived existence of a nation has often led to the creation of a corresponding state as a people win sovereignty over their own affairs—nations create states.

Around A.D. 1500, countries such as France and Austria began to bring entire nations together into single states. These new nation-states were very large and powerful and they overran smaller neighbors. Over time, they conquered and incorporated many small territorial units. Eventually the idea of nationalism itself became a powerful force and ultimately contributed to the disintegration of large, multinational states such as Austria-Hungary (in World War I), the Soviet Union, and Yugoslavia.

The principle of *self-determination* implies that people who identify as a nation should have the right to form a state and exercise sovereignty over their affairs. Self-determination is a widely praised principle in international affairs today (not historically). But it is generally secondary to the principles of sovereignty (noninterference in other states' internal affairs) and territorial integrity, with which it frequently conflicts. Self-determination does not give groups the right to change international borders, even those imposed arbitrarily by colonialism, in order to unify a group with a common national identity. Generally, though not always, self-determination has been achieved by violence. When the borders of (perceived) nations do not match those of states, conflicts almost inevitably arise. Today such conflicts are widespread—in Northern Ireland, Quebec, Israel-Palestine, India-Pakistan, Sri Lanka, Tibet, Sudan, and many other places.

VIDEO

Self-Determination and South Ossetia

The process of popular mobilization intensified greatly in the French Revolution and the subsequent Napoleonic Wars, when France instituted a universal draft and a centrally run "command" economy. Its motivated citizen armies, composed for the first time of Frenchmen rather than mercenaries, marched longer and faster. People participated in part because they were patriotic. Their nation-state embodied their aspirations, and brought them together in a common national identity.

The United States meanwhile had followed the example of the Netherlands by declaring independence from Britain in 1776. Latin American states gained independence early in the 19th century, and Germany and Italy unified their nations out of multiple political units (through war) later in that century.

Before World War I, socialist workers from different European countries had banded together as workers to fight for workers' rights. In that war, however, most abandoned such solidarity and instead fought for their own nation; nationalism thus proved a stronger force than socialism. Before World War II, nationalism helped Germany, Italy, and Japan build political orders based on *fascism*—an extreme authoritarianism girded by national chauvinism. And in World War II it was nationalism and patriotism (not communism) that rallied the Soviet people to sacrifice by the millions to turn back Germany's invasion.

In the past 50 years, nations by the dozens have gained independence and statehood. Jews worked persistently in the first half of the 20th century to create the state of Israel, and Palestinians aspired in the second half to create a Palestinian state. While multinational states such as the Soviet Union and Yugoslavia have fragmented in recent years, ethnic and territorial units such as Ukraine, Slovenia, and East Timor have established themselves as independent nation-states. Others, such as Kosovo and Kurdistan, seek to do so and already run their own affairs. The continuing influence of nationalism in today's world is evident. It affects several of the main types of conflict that occupy the rest of this chapter.

Ethnic Conflict

Ethnic conflict is quite possibly the most important source of conflict in the numerous wars now occurring throughout the world. **Ethnic groups** are large groups of people who share ancestral, language, cultural, or religious ties and a common *identity* (individuals identify with the group). Although conflicts between ethnic groups often have material aspects—notably over territory and government control—ethnic conflict itself entails a dislike or hatred that members of one ethnic group systematically feel toward another ethnic group. In this regard, ethnic conflict is based not on tangible causes (what someone does) but on intangible ones (who someone is).

Ethnic groups often form the basis for nationalist sentiments. Not all ethnic groups identify as nations; for instance, within the United States various ethnic groups coexist (sometimes uneasily) with a common *national* identity as Americans. But in locations where millions of members of a single ethnic group live as the majority population in their ancestors' land, they usually think of themselves as a nation. In most such cases they aspire to have their own state with its formal international status and territorial boundaries.

Territorial control is closely tied to the aspirations of ethnic groups for statehood. All states' borders deviate to some extent (sometimes substantially) from the actual location of ethnic communities. Members of the ethnic group are left outside its state's borders, and members of other ethnic groups are located within the state's borders. The resulting situation can be dangerous, with part of an ethnic group controlling a state and another part living as a minority within another state controlled by a rival ethnic group.

Other ethnic groups lack any home state. Kurds share a culture, and many aspire to create a state of Kurdistan. But Kurds live in four states—Turkey, Iraq, Iran, and Syria—all of which strongly oppose giving up part of their own territory for a new Kurdish state (see Figure 4.2). Kurds enjoyed autonomy in part of northern Iraq under U.S. protection in the 1990s, and quasi-autonomous status in a post-Saddam Iraq. The Kurds' success in the 2006 Iraqi elections gave them a strong position to retain this status.

Ethnic conflicts often involve pressures to redraw borders by force. When ethnic populations are minorities in territories controlled by rival ethnic groups, they may even be driven from their land or (in rare cases) systematically exterminated. By driving

FIGURE 4.2   Kurdish Areas

Ethnic populations often span international borders. Shaded region shows the approximate area of Kurdish settlements.

out the minority ethnic group, a majority group can assemble a more unified, more contiguous, and larger territory for its nation-state, as ethnic Serbs did through "ethnic cleansing" after the breakup of Yugoslavia.

Outside states often worry about the fate of "their people" living as minorities in neighboring states. For instance, Albania is concerned about ethnic Albanians who are the majority population in the Serbian province of Kosovo. But as Kosovo moved toward independence from Serbia, Serbia worried about the minority of ethnic Serbs living in Kosovo. Similar problems have fueled wars between Armenia and Azerbaijan and between India and Pakistan. The dangerous combination of ethnic conflict and territorial disputes could lead to more wars in the future.

In extreme cases, governments use **genocide**—systematic extermination of ethnic or religious groups in whole or in part—to try to destroy scapegoated groups or political rivals. Under its fanatical policies of racial purity, Nazi Germany exterminated 6 million Jews and millions of others, including homosexuals, Roma, and communists. The mass murders, now known as the Holocaust, along with the sheer scale of war unleashed by Nazi aggression, are considered among the greatest *crimes against humanity* in history. Responsible German officials faced justice in the *Nuremberg Tribunal* after World War II (see p. 252). The pledges of world leaders after that experience to "never again" allow genocide have been found wanting as genocide recurred in the 1990s in Bosnia and Rwanda, and most recently in Darfur, Sudan.

In Rwanda, where the Hutu group is the majority and the Tutsi group the minority, a Hutu-nationalist government in 1994 slaughtered an estimated 800,000 Tutsis (and Hutus opposed to the government) in a matter of weeks. The weak international response to this atrocity reveals how frail are international norms of human rights compared to norms of noninterference in other states' internal affairs—at least when no strategic interests are at stake. The Hutu ultranationalists quickly lost power when Tutsi rebels defeated the government militarily, but the war spread into Democratic Congo, where the ultranationalists took refuge and where fighting continues 15 years later.

In Sudan, the warring sides (largely northern Muslims versus southern Christians) in a decades-long civil war signed a peace agreement in 2003, ending a war that had killed more than a million people. The agreement called for withdrawing government forces from the south of the country, establishing a power-sharing transitional government and army, and holding a referendum in the rebel areas in six years. But following this peace agreement, rebels in the western Darfur region began to protest their exclusion from the peace agreement. In response, the government helped Arab (Muslim) militias raid black African (also Muslim) Darfur villages, wantonly killing, raping, and burning. In late 2004, the government and some of the Darfur rebels reached a tentative peace agreement to be monitored by the African Union and the United Nations, but Sudan blocked a UN peacekeeping force, and the war crimes continued. While Sudan finally approved UN peacekeepers, their promised deployment in 2008 was frustrated by continual delays, usually orchestrated by the Sudanese government. The international community's ineffective response to the mass murders in Darfur, like that in Rwanda in 1994, shows the limited reach of international norms in today's state-based international system.

In cases of both genocide and less extreme scapegoating, ethnic hatreds do not merely bubble up naturally. Rather, politicians provoke and channel hatred to strengthen their own

VIDEO

**Ethnic
Conflict and
Globalization**

power. Often, in ethnically divided countries, political parties form along ethnic lines and party leaders consolidate their positions in their own populations by exaggerating the dangers from the other side. The existence of a threat from an out-group promotes the cohesion of an in-group, thereby creating a somewhat self-reinforcing process of ethnic division.

Causes of Ethnic Hostility   Why do ethnic groups frequently dislike each other? Often long-standing historical conflicts exist over specific territories or natural resources, or over one ethnic group's economic exploitation or political domination of another. They become driven not by tangible grievances (though these may well persist) but by processes described by social psychology. The ethnic group is a kind of extended *kinship* group—a group of related individuals sharing some ancestors. Even when kinship relations are not very close, a *group identity* makes a person act as though the other members of the ethnic group were family. Perhaps as technology allows far-flung groups to congregate in cyberspace, there will be less psychological pressure to collect ethnic groups physically in a territorial nation-state.

Ethnocentrism, or *in-group bias,* is the tendency to see one's own group in favorable terms and an *out-group* in unfavorable terms. No *minimum criterion* of similarity or kin relationship is needed to evoke the group identity process, including in-group bias. In psychological experiments, even trivial differentiations can evoke these processes. If people are assigned to groups based on a known but unimportant characteristic (such as preferring circles to triangles), before long the people in each group show in-group bias and begin to dislike the other group's members. Just as the reciprocity principle has its negative side (see pp. 5–6), so does the identity principle. The same forces that allow sacrifice for a group identity, as in the European Union, also allow the formation of in-group bias.

In-group biases are stronger when the other group looks different, speaks a different language, or worships in a different way (or all three). All too easily, an out-group can be *dehumanized* and stripped of all human rights. This dehumanization includes the common use of animal names—"pigs," "dogs," and so forth—for members of the out-group. U.S. propaganda in World War II depicted Japanese people as apes. Especially in wartime, dehumanization can be extreme. The restraints on war that have evolved in regular interstate warfare, such as not massacring civilians (see pp. 252–256), are easily discarded in interethnic warfare.

Experience in Western Europe shows that education over time can overcome ethnic animosities between traditionally hostile nations, such as France and Germany. After World War II, these states' governments rewrote the textbooks for a new generation. Previously, each state's textbooks had glorified its past deeds, played down its misdeeds, and portrayed its traditional enemies in unflattering terms. In a continent-wide project, new textbooks that gave a more objective and fair rendition were created. By contrast, present-day Japanese textbooks that gloss over Japan's crimes in World War II continue to inflame relations with both China and Korea.

Ethnic groups are only one point along a spectrum of kinship relations—from nuclear families through extended families, villages, provinces, and nations, up to the entire human race. Loyalties fall at different points along the spectrum. It is unclear why people identify most strongly at one level of group identity. In Somalia, loyalties are to clans; in Serbia, they are to the ethnic group; in the United States and elsewhere, multi-ethnic countries command people's primary loyalty. States reinforce their citizens'

POLICY PERSPECTIVES

President of Liberia, Ellen Johnson-Sirleaf

PROBLEM *How do you prevent civil war while retaining control of your government?*

BACKGROUND Imagine you are the president of Liberia. Your election in the spring of 2006 as the first woman president in Africa was hailed as a breakthrough for Liberia. The election ended decades of political violence that devastated your own country as well your neighbors Ivory Coast and Sierra Leone. The violence ended when former Liberian president Charles Taylor went into exile in Nigeria. Tens of thousands of people lost their lives or were subject to human rights abuses, including torture and mutilation, in the wars begun under Taylor's rule.

Recently, however, there is optimism within your country and from the international community. Rebel groups have remained quiet, and Charles Taylor was arrested in 2006 and faces trial in a war crimes tribunal. Economic aid has begun to stream into your country to assist in development. Your country is resource rich and has the potential to become a middle-income country owing to its vast natural agricultural and mineral resources.

DOMESTIC CONSIDERATIONS Tremendous challenges, however, lie ahead. Economically, your country is underdeveloped, with years of civil war leading to increases in corruption and economic stagnation. Many of the powerful economic actors in your country benefit from the corruption and graft, which you have pledged to end. Unemployment is very high, with hundreds of thousands of young men unemployed. Until recently, arms had been embargoed to your country, meaning no weapons could be given to your armed forces, leading to roving bands of fighters controlling pockets of territory. Armed police have occasionally returned to the streets to restore order, and in late 2008, a mass breakout from the country's only maximum security prison allowed over 100 criminals to escape.

SCENARIO Now imagine that a group that was involved in the civil war begins to reopen the war. The group has taken refuge in Sierra Leone and now begins to make cross-border raids against your country. Although Sierra Leone does not support the group, its government has limited resources to devote to the issue.

One option is to negotiate directly with the group. Negotiations could lead to peace, but might require power sharing in your government, which could derail your attempts to lessen corruption.

Another option is to use military force against the rebels. But international donors would discourage you from endangering the fragile peace in Liberia, with the implicit threat of an aid cutoff if you are perceived to be too hard-line. In addition, the reemergence of a civil war would make your proposed democratic and economic reforms more difficult to implement. Your military is not well trained and you are very uncertain about the possibility of success against the rebels. A strong military response to the rebels, however, could discourage future aggression and establish that you are a tough leader.

CHOOSE YOUR POLICY How do you handle this new threat from the rebels? Do you adopt a hard-line policy against them in hopes of defeating them? Or do you attempt reconciliation in hopes of minimizing the prospect of further bloodshed, but at the price of bringing your enemies into the government and thus undermining some of your goals?

identification with the state through flags, anthems, pledges of allegiance, and so forth. Perhaps someday people will shift loyalties further, developing a *global identity* as humans first and members of states and ethnic groups second.

Religious Conflict

One reason ethnic conflicts often transcend material grievances is that they find expression as *religious* conflicts. Because religion is the core of a community's value system in much of the world, people whose religious practices differ are easily disdained and treated as unworthy or even inhuman. When overlaid on ethnic and territorial conflicts, religion often surfaces as the central and most visible division between groups. For instance, most people in Azerbaijan are Muslims; most Armenians are Christians.

Nothing inherent in religion mandates conflicts—in many places members of different religious groups coexist peacefully. But religious differences hold the potential to make existing conflicts more intractable, because religions involve core values, which are held as absolute truth. This is increasingly true as *fundamentalist* movements have gained strength in recent decades. (The reasons for fundamentalism are disputed, but it is clearly a global-level phenomenon.) Members of these movements organize their lives and communities around their religious beliefs; many are willing to sacrifice, kill, and die for those beliefs. Fundamentalist movements have become larger and more powerful in recent decades in Christianity, Islam, Judaism, Hinduism, and other religions. Such movements challenge the values and practices of **secular** political organizations—those created apart from religious establishments.

Among the secular practices threatened by fundamentalist movements include the rules of the international system, which treat states as formally equal and sovereign whether they are "believers" or "infidels." As transnational belief systems, religions often are taken as a higher law than state laws and international treaties. This runs counter to the norms of the international system and to the assumptions of realism.

Islamist Movements
Currently, violent conflicts are being prosecuted in the name of all the world's major religions. But special attention is due to conflicts involving Islamic groups and states. Islamist actors are active participants in 8 of the world's 13 wars in progress (see p. 111). In addition, the U.S. "war on terror" is directed against a network of Islamic terror groups. To understand these groups, we must start, by contrast, with a broader understanding of Islamist movements, most of which are not violent.

Islam, the religion practiced by **Muslims,** is broad and diverse. Its divergent populations include Sunni Muslims (the majority), Shi'ite Muslims (concentrated in Iran, southern Iraq, southern Lebanon, and Bahrain), and many smaller branches and sects. Most countries with mainly Muslim populations belong to the Islamic Conference, an IGO. The world's predominantly Islamic countries stretch from Nigeria to Indonesia, centered historically in the Middle East (see Figure 4.3) but with the largest populations in South and Southeast Asia. Many international conflicts around this zone involve Muslims on one side and non-Muslims on the other, as a result of geographical and historical circumstances including colonialism and oil.

Islamist groups advocate basing government and society on Islamic law. These groups vary greatly in the means they employ to pursue this goal. Most are nonviolent—charities

FIGURE 4.3 Members of the Islamic Conference and Areas of Conflict

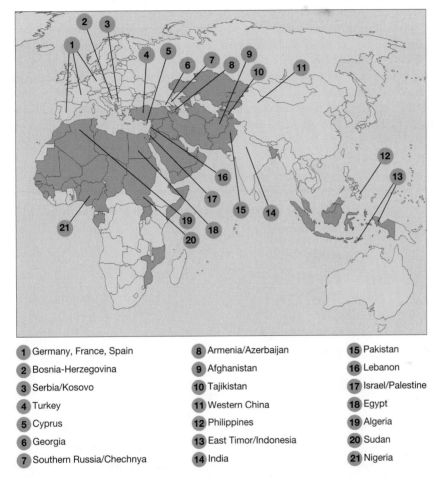

1 Germany, France, Spain	8 Armenia/Azerbaijan	15 Pakistan
2 Bosnia-Herzegovina	9 Afghanistan	16 Lebanon
3 Serbia/Kosovo	10 Tajikistan	17 Israel/Palestine
4 Turkey	11 Western China	18 Egypt
5 Cyprus	12 Philippines	19 Algeria
6 Georgia	13 East Timor/Indonesia	20 Sudan
7 Southern Russia/Chechnya	14 India	21 Nigeria

Shaded countries are members of the conference; numbered regions are areas of conflict between Muslims and non-Muslims or secular authorities.

and political parties. Some are violent—militias and terrorist networks. To start with the former, Islamist political movements are active throughout the Muslim world. In Jordan, Islamic parties won the largest bloc of seats in Parliament without violence. In the 1990s Islamic parties gained ground in Turkey—a fiercely secular state in which the military has intervened repeatedly to prevent religious expression in politics—and a former Islamist leader has been prime minister since 2003. Islamist parties have also played leading roles in Iraq's government since 2003.

If Islamist movements seek changes primarily in domestic policies, why do they matter for IR? Islamist politics may lead to different foreign policies, but the more important answer is that some Islamist movements have become a transnational force shaping world order and global North-South relations in important ways.

In several countries, Islamists reject Western-oriented secular states in favor of governments more explicitly oriented to Islamic values. These movements reflect long-standing *anti-Western* sentiment in these countries—against the old European colonizers who were Christian—and are in some ways *nationalist* movements expressed through religious channels. In some Middle Eastern countries with authoritarian governments, religious institutions (mosques) have been the only available avenue for political opposition. Religion has therefore become a means to express opposition to the status quo in politics and culture.

Public opinion in both Muslim and non-Muslim countries shows some misconceptions and differences in opinion (see Figure 4.4). Support for Islamist radicals varies

FIGURE 4.4   Public Opinion in Muslim and Non-Muslim Countries, 2005

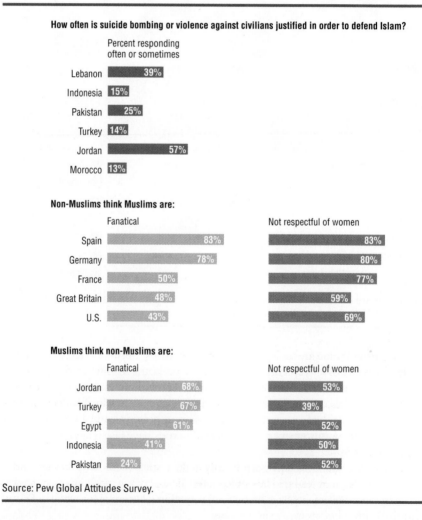

How often is suicide bombing or violence against civilians justified in order to defend Islam?

Percent responding often or sometimes

Country	Percent
Lebanon	39%
Indonesia	15%
Pakistan	25%
Turkey	14%
Jordan	57%
Morocco	13%

Non-Muslims think Muslims are:

	Fanatical	Not respectful of women
Spain	83%	83%
Germany	78%	80%
France	50%	77%
Great Britain	48%	59%
U.S.	43%	69%

Muslims think non-Muslims are:

	Fanatical	Not respectful of women
Jordan	68%	53%
Turkey	67%	39%
Egypt	61%	52%
Indonesia	41%	50%
Pakistan	24%	52%

Source: Pew Global Attitudes Survey.

greatly among countries, from a majority in Jordan down to 14 percent and 13 percent in Turkey and Morocco, respectively. A 2005 poll recalls "mirror image" perceptions (see p. 83). In five Western industrialized countries, 40–80 percent thought Muslims were "fanatical" and 60–80 percent thought Muslims did not respect women. But in three of five *Muslim* countries, more than 60 percent thought non-Muslims were "fanatical" and in four of those five countries, a majority thought non-Muslims did not respect women.

The more radical Islamist movements not only threaten some existing governments—especially those tied to the West—but also undermine traditional norms of state sovereignty. They reject Western political conceptions of the state (based on individual autonomy) in favor of a more traditional Islamic orientation based on community. Some aspire to create a single political state encompassing most of the Middle East, as existed in the *caliphate* of A.D. 600–1200. Such a development would create a profound challenge to the present international system—particularly to its current status quo powers—and would therefore be opposed at every turn by the world's most powerful states.

Islamist movements follow in a long tradition of global North-South conflict—the struggle against colonialism and for the world's poor countries and people. Although revolutions almost always advocate for the poor versus the rich and for nationalism versus imperialism, the particular character of these movements varies across regions and time periods. In Africa, where colonialism left behind state boundaries at odds with ethnic divisions, many revolutionary movements have a strong tribal and provincial base; this may fuel secessionism by a province (such as Eritrea from Ethiopia). Asian revolutionary movements tapped into general anticolonial sentiments, as when Vietnamese communists fought to oust the French colonizers and then saw the war against the United States as a continuation of the same struggle. In Latin America, where national independence was won long ago, revolutions tended to be couched in terms of class struggle against rich elites and their foreign allies (states and MNCs).

In the post–Cold War era, the most potent revolutionary movements are Islamist, not communist. Islamists in Middle Eastern countries, like revolutionaries elsewhere, derive their main base of strength from championing the cause of the poor masses against rich elites. Like other revolutionaries throughout the global South, Islamist movements in countries such as Turkey, Egypt, and Lebanon draw their base of support from poor slums, where the Islamists sometimes provide basic services unmet by the government.

In a public opinion poll in 2006 in Egypt, Morocco, Saudi Arabia, and Jordan, a plurality of respondents identified primarily as Muslims, more than identified primarily as citizens of their states or as Arabs. But in Lebanon and the UAE, the pattern was reversed, with large majorities identifying primarily as citizens of their states. Islamist movements tap into the public's identification with issues that may not materially affect them but affect their identities as Muslims, across national borders—especially the Arab-Israeli conflict. The public in Muslim countries also cared about wars in the 1990s in Bosnia, Azerbaijan, and Chechnya, where Christian armed forces attacked Muslim civilians. Islamists see all these conflicts as part of a broad regional (or even global) struggle of Islam against Western, Christian imperialism—a struggle dating back to the Crusades almost a thousand years ago. From the perspective of some outsiders, the religious conflicts boiling and simmering at the edges of the Islamic world look like an expansionist threat to be contained. The view from within looks more like being surrounded and repressed from several directions.

The Iraq War since 2003 greatly inflamed anti-American feeling and helped radicalize politics across the Muslim world, especially in Arab countries that saw the U.S. invasion as a humiliation to Arab dignity and a parallel to Israel's occupation of Arab land. In the 2006 Arab public opinion poll, citizens in all six countries showed extremely high levels of distrust of U.S. motives and disagreement with U.S. actions in the region. However, the presidency of Barack Hussein Obama, whose middle name reflects Muslim family roots in Kenya and who grew up partly in Muslim Indonesia, may alter this anti-American dynamic.

Armed Islamist Groups Anti-American and anti-Western sentiments in predominantly Islamic countries have accelerated the growth of violent Islamist groups as well. Although they are in the minority, they have disproportionate effects on IR and receive the most public attention.

Armed Islamist groups vary tremendously, and in some cases violently disagree with each other (see Table 4.1). In particular, divisions between the Sunni and Shi'ite wings of Islam have led to violence, especially in and around Iraq—a Shi'ite-majority country ruled by Sunnis under Saddam Hussein. Iraq's war against Shi'ite Iran killed a million people, and Saddam's repression of a Shi'ite uprising after the 1991 Gulf War killed tens of thousands at the least. Under the U.S. occupation of Iraq since 2003, Shi'ite parties took power and Shi'ite militias exacted revenge, while some Sunnis waged a relentless and brutal insurgency. In 2006, after the bombing of a revered Shi'ite mosque in Iraq, a wave of sectarian violence killed tens of thousands of Iraqis. In the subsequent two years, violence among rival factions in Iraq increased and then lessened, but the long-term relationship of Iraqi Sunnis and Shi'ites remains unsettled.

In the worldwide picture as well, armed Islamist groups divide into Sunni and Shi'ite wings that do not cooperate much. On the Shi'ite side, the most important groups are Iran's Revolutionary Guards, the Mahdi Army in Iraq (and other Shi'ite militias there), and Hezbollah in southern Lebanon. These groups are all relatively successful—in Iran the religious leadership controls the state, and in Lebanon Hezbollah controls territory and holds seats in the national legislature.

In Iran, a popular uprising in 1979 overthrew the U.S.-backed shah and installed an Islamic government in which the top religious leaders (ayatollahs) can overturn the laws passed by the parliament. The rejection of international norms by some Islamists was dramatically illustrated when, after its revolution, Iran refused to protect U.S. diplomats and the U.S. embassy in Iran (see "Laws of Diplomacy" on pp. 246–248). For Iran, religion was an important motivator for the nation in fighting the Iran-Iraq War from 1980 to 1988: teenaged soldiers expected to go to heaven as martyrs if they died in battle. Defying the UN Security Council, Iran is currently developing nuclear technology that could produce nuclear weapons within about five years.

Iran strongly supports—with money, arms, and training—the Hezbollah militia in Lebanon. Hezbollah runs hundreds of schools, hospitals, and other charities, but is also included on the U.S. list of terrorist organizations. Hezbollah claimed that its attacks induced Israel to withdraw from southern Lebanon in 2000. Then in 2006, Hezbollah

TABLE 4.1   Major Armed Islamist Groups

Group	Country	Branch of Islam	Actions
Islamic Republic of Iran	Iran	Shi'ite	Only Islamic revolution to successfully control a state (since 1979); held off secular Iraq in 1980s war; now attempting to build nuclear weapons.
Hezbollah	Lebanon	Shi'ite	Fought well against Israeli army in 2006 war. Previously claimed credit for driving Israel from southern Lebanon in 2000. Popular even with Sunnis.
Mahdi Army	Iraq	Shi'ite	Has clashed with U.S. forces in Iraq; major faction in Iraqi government.
Various	Iraq	Sunni	Insurgent forces have inflicted many casualties on U.S. forces in Iraq. Foreign fighters also active in Iraq.
Hamas	Palestine (Gaza)	Sunni	Forces have killed hundreds of Israeli civilians and fought a war against Israel in 2008. Won Palestinian elections in 2006. Controls Gaza Strip.
Islamic Courts	Somalia	Sunni	Took control of the capital and most of the country in 2006, but was ousted within months.
Moro Islamic Liberation Front	Philippines	Sunni	Forces have fought for independence of certain regions in the Muslim-populated southern Philippine islands.
al Qaeda	World (Pakistan?)	Sunni	9/11 attacks and European bombings. Is among major insurgent groups in Iraq.
Taliban	Afghanistan	Sunni	Controlled Afghanistan and gave sanctuary to al Qaeda until ousted after 9/11. Regrouped in remote Pakistan and staged many attacks from 2006–2009.

Islamist guerrilla fighters/terrorists are also active in Chechnya (Russia), Kashmir (India), Central Asia, Indonesia, and Europe.

showed itself to be a competent military force, putting up a stiff fight in a brief but destructive war with Israel. Hezbollah's success in "standing up to Israel" won it popular support throughout the Arab world, even among Sunnis. But it raised old divisions within Lebanon, leading to more political instability there.

Iran also supports Shi'ite militias in southern Iraq, but they operate independently. (Although both Iranians and southern Iraqis are Shi'ites, the first are Persians and the latter Arabs.) Two of the largest such militias are the virulently anti-American Mahdi Army, led by Moqtada al-Sadr, and the Supreme Council for Islamic Revolution in Iraq (SCIRI), which is less anti-American. The Mahdi Army's influence has diminished since the Iraqi government fought for and won military control of the main southern Iraqi city and the U.S. army cleared Mahdi fighters from Baghdad.

On the Sunni side, the major radical Islamist groups adhere to some version of Wahhabism, a fundamentalist interpretation of Islamic law with roots in Saudi Arabia. The most important center of this fundamentalist movement currently is in Afghanistan and the next-door tribal areas of western Pakistan.

An Islamic government was established in Afghanistan in 1992 after a civil war (and following a decade of ill-fated Soviet occupation). Rival Islamic factions then continued the war with even greater intensity for several years. By 1997, a faction called Taliban had taken control of most of Afghanistan and imposed an extreme interpretation of Islamic law. With beatings and executions, the regime forced women to wear head-to-toe coverings, girls to stay out of school, and men to grow beards, among other repressive policies.

The incendiary mixture in Afghanistan in the 1990s—unending war, grinding poverty, Islamic fundamentalism, and an ideologically driven government—allowed Afghanistan to become a base for worldwide terrorist operations, culminating in the September 11, 2001, attacks. In response, the United States exerted its power to remove the Taliban from power in Afghanistan and disrupt the al Qaeda terrorist network headquartered there. Despite U.S. successes in the 2001 war, the Taliban continues daily attacks on NATO forces. Attacks on civilians also continue in Afghanistan.

The defeat of fundamentalists in Afghanistan in 2001 put pressure on its much larger next-door neighbor, nuclear-armed Pakistan, whose military ruler tried, after 2001, to smother Islamic extremists and hold together a stable, relatively secular government. Radically anti-American Islamists have gained control of Pakistan's autonomous "tribal areas" bordering Afghanistan, using them to launch attacks on Afghanistan, on Pakistan's cities, and in late 2008 on Mumbai, India. Pro-democracy forces in Pakistan ousted the military ruler and installed an

THE FUTURE OF ISLAM

In some Muslim-populated countries, Islam is a political rallying point with anti-Western connotations—especially in authoritarian countries in which the mosque is a rare permitted gathering point. Islamic radicals frequently attack Western concepts of politics and culture, including some of the underpinnings of the international system. Elsewhere, Islam remains fairly separate from politics. This Indonesian girl, preparing for the Ramadan fast in 2008, will grow up in a world where Islam's role is changing.

elected government in 2008, though not until after the movement's leader, Benazir Bhutto, had been assassinated.

In the tribal areas of Pakistan, Osama bin Laden and others are believed to continue to direct al Qaeda. Al Qaeda is an international group—more a network or movement than a central organization in recent years—that recruits fighters from various countries, possibly trains them in other countries, and perhaps sends them on missions to fight in foreign conflicts (such as Afghanistan in the 1980s or Iraq today). It is one of many similarly minded groups, but has been the most prominent, partly because of its sophisticated use of media; the fame of its leader, bin Laden; and the spectacular horror of the September 11 attacks.

Elsewhere in Asia, Islamic extremist groups connected with al Qaeda continue to operate. In 2002 terrorists killed hundreds—mostly Australians—in a nightclub bombing in Bali, Indonesia. U.S. advisors meanwhile began helping to counter Islamist guerrillas on Philippine islands. In 2003, al Qaeda and related groups carried out terror bombings worldwide—in Morocco, Saudi Arabia, Russia, the Philippines, Indonesia, Iraq, and Turkey—and called on followers to go to Iraq to fight the Americans and their allies. In 2004, they bombed trains in Madrid, killing hundreds and apparently tipping an election against the pro-American Spanish government—and thus inducing Spain to pull its troops out of Iraq. In 2005, their followers—Muslims who had grown up in Britain—bombed the London subway and bus system. In 2008, armed attackers from Pakistan stormed hotels and public places in Mumbai, India, and killed about 150 people, mostly in random shootings. The attack heightened tensions between India and Pakistan, raising the possibility that Pakistan would divert military forces from the fight in the tribal areas to the Indian border. Cooler heads prevailed, however, and the nuclear-armed rivals did not move toward war.

In Saudi Arabia—home to the world's largest oil reserves, Islam's holiest sites, and the roots of Wahhabism—al Qaeda has long sought to overthrow the monarchy, which stays in power through a combination of repression, cooptation, and oil-funded economic development. In 1979, Islamist militants briefly seized control of the Grand Mosque in Mecca, and in 2003 al Qaeda suicide bombers attacked several residential compounds in the kingdom. In 2007, Saudi authorities broke up what they called a major al Qaeda network in that country, which had planned major attacks on oil facilities. The plots, although disrupted, showed that Iraq had become a new training ground for al Qaeda fighters who were brought in from other countries, battle-trained in Iraq, and then sent elsewhere to stage attacks.

In Palestine, the radical Islamist faction Hamas is another important Sunni Islamist militia, not closely connected with al Qaeda or Taliban. Centered in the Gaza Strip, Hamas sent suicide bombers that killed hundreds of Israelis after 2000, then won free parliamentary elections in 2006 because it was seen as less corrupt than the dominant secular Fatah party. However, the Palestinian presidency remains in Fatah control, and rival security organizations have occasionally fought street battles. In 2009 Palestine remained divided, with Fatah controlling the West Bank and Hamas controlling the Gaza Strip, which Israel heavily attacked in early 2009.

Sudan's civil war between the mainly Muslim north (government-run) and the mainly Christian and animist south dragged on for two decades and killed millions. A 2005 peace agreement ended the war, giving the south autonomy for six years, positions in Sudan's government, and a referendum on the region's future. However, Sudan's government then sponsored brutal attacks in Darfur in the west of the country.

In Algeria, Islamic revolutionaries organized against the ruling party that had kicked out the French colonizers in 1962 but had then become, in their view, corrupt and inept. The Islamic parties won preliminary parliamentary elections in 1991 and were assured of coming to power in the final elections. Instead, the military took over, canceled the elections, and touched off eight years of violence and as many as 100,000 deaths before a new president reached a peace agreement with the main rebel faction.

The predominantly Sunni Muslim republic of Chechnya, a Russian province, tried to split away from Russia in the early 1990s after the Soviet Union collapsed. In 1994–1995, Russia sent in a huge military force that destroyed the Chechen capital but faced fierce resistance from Chechen nationalist guerrillas and withdrew in defeat. In 1999–2000, another destructive Russian campaign won power in the province. But Chechen guerrillas continued to fight and in 2004, hundreds of children died after Chechen terrorists took over a school and held them hostage. In 2005, Russian forces killed the Chechen separatist leader they held responsible, and the war in Chechnya has now all but ended.

Overall, conflicts involving Islamist movements are more complex than simply religious conflicts; they concern power, economic relations, ethnic chauvinism, and historical empires as well.

Ideological Conflict

To a large extent, ideology like religion symbolizes and intensifies conflicts between groups and states more than it causes them. But ideologies have a somewhat weaker hold on core values and absolute truth than religions do.

For realists, ideological differences among states do not matter much, because all members of the international system pursue their national interests in the context of relatively fluid alliances. Over the long run, even countries that experience revolutions based on strong ideologies tend to lose their ideological fervor—be it Iran's Islamic fundamentalism in 1979, China's Maoist communism in 1949, Russia's Leninist communism in 1917, or even U.S. democracy in 1776. In each case, the revolutionaries expected that their assumption of power would dramatically alter their state's foreign policy, because in each case their ideology had profound international implications. Yet within a few decades, each of these revolutionary governments turned to the pursuit of national interests above ideological ones.

Sometimes even self-proclaimed ideological struggles are not really ideological. In Angola in the 1980s, the United States backed a rebel army called UNITA against a Soviet-aligned government—supposedly a struggle of democracy against Marxism. In truth, the ideological differences were quite arbitrary. The government mouthed Marxist rhetoric to get the Soviet Union to give it aid (a policy it reversed as soon as Soviet aid dried up). The rebels who used democratic rhetoric to get U.S. support had earlier received Chinese support and mouthed Maoist rhetoric. This conflict, which finally ended in 2002, really had nothing to do with ideology. It was a power struggle between two armed, ethnically based factions fighting to control Angola's oil, diamonds, and other wealth.

In the short term, revolutions *do* change international relations—they make wars more likely—but not because of ideology. Rather, the sudden change of governments can alter alliances and change the balance of power. With calculations of power being revised by all parties, it is easy to miscalculate or to exaggerate threats on both sides. Saddam Hussein, for example, miscalculated Iran's power after its revolution and attacked with the expectation of a quick victory. But revolutions are seldom exported to other states.

Ideology and political philosophies do play some role in international politics. Ideologies can help mobilize national populations, such as in war. And in some proxy wars of the Cold War era—such as Nicaragua in the 1980s—the rebels and governments had real ideological differences.

IDEOLOGICAL SPLIT

Ideology plays only a limited role in most international conflicts. After revolutions, ideologies such as Marxism may affect foreign policy, but over the following decades countries such as China or the Soviet Union typically revert to a foreign policy based more on national interests than ideology. Nonetheless, ideological clashes still occur, as between the United States and Venezuela today, which have a strong trading relationship but suffer from political antagonism. Here the leftist Venezuelan president, Hugo Chavez, addresses Venezuelans while visiting Cuba, in front of a poster of communist icon Che Guevara, 2007.

Conflicts of Interest

If conflicts of ideas can be intractable because of psychological and emotional factors, conflicts about material interests are somewhat easier to settle based on the reciprocity principle. In theory, given enough positive leverage—a payment in some form—any state should agree to another state's terms on a disputed issue.

Territorial Disputes

Among the international conflicts that concern tangible "goods," those about territory have special importance because of the territorial nature of the state (see pp. 40–43).

Conflicts over control of territory are really of two varieties: territorial disputes (about where borders are drawn) and conflicts over control of entire states within existing borders (discussed next under "Control of Governments"). Consider first differences over where borders between two states should be drawn—that is, who controls a disputed piece of land. Because states value home territory with an almost fanatical devotion, border disputes tend to be among the most intractable in IR. States seldom yield territory in exchange for money or any other positive reward. Nor do states quickly forget territory that they lose involuntarily. For example, in 2002, Bolivian public opinion opposed a gas export pipeline through Chile to the sea because Chile had seized the coastline from Bolivia in 1879. The goal of regaining territory lost to another state is called **irredentism.** This form of nationalism often leads directly to serious interstate conflicts.

Because of their association with the integrity of states, territories are valued far beyond any inherent economic or strategic value they hold. For example, after Israel and Egypt made peace in 1978, it took them a decade to settle a border dispute at Taba, a tiny plot of beachfront on which Israeli developers had built a hotel just across the old border. The two states finally submitted the issue for binding arbitration, and Egypt ended up in possession. For Egypt, regaining every inch of territory was a matter of national honor and a symbol of its sovereignty and territorial integrity.

The value states place on home territory seems undiminished despite the apparent reduction in the inherent value of territory as technology has developed. Historically, territory was the basis of economic production—agriculture and the extraction of raw materials. Winning wars meant gaining territory, which meant increasing wealth. Today, however, much more wealth derives from trade and technology than from agriculture. The costs of most territorial disputes appear to outweigh any economic benefits that the territory in question could provide. Exceptions exist, however, such as the capture of diamond-mining areas in several African countries by rebels who use the diamond revenues to finance war. (In 2002, 40 states created a program of UN certification for legitimate diamonds, trying to keep the "conflict diamonds" off the international market.)

Means of Controlling Territory   Historically, military means have been the most effective leverage for controlling territory, and wars have often redrawn the borders of states. Military forces can seize control on the ground in a way that is hard to contest by any means except other military forces. Since World War II, however, a strong norm has arisen in the international system *against* trying to alter borders by force. By contrast, it is considered a lesser offense for one state merely to topple another's government and install a puppet regime, even if done violently. The principle is that governments come and go but borders remain.

Secession   Efforts by a province or region to secede from an existing state are a special type of conflict over borders—not the borders of two existing states but the efforts to draw international borders around a new state. Dozens of secession movements exist around the world, of varying sizes and political effectiveness, but they succeed in seceding only rarely. The existing state almost always tries to hold on to the area in question. For example, in the 1990s, the predominantly Albanian population of the Serbian province of Kosovo fought a war to secede from Serbia. NATO intervention, including sustained bombing of Serbia (not approved by the UN), led to the withdrawal of Serbia's army from Kosovo and its replacement with European and American peacekeeping troops who have been there ever since. Most of the Kosovo population wants to secede and feels the international system should give them self-determination. But Serbians argue that Kosovo is historically and presently under Serbian sovereignty. Throughout 2007, the UN and the great powers negotiated over the future of Kosovo, with Russia insisting there be no promise of independence. Kosovars, however, took matters into their own hands in 2008, declaring their independence without UN approval. Several countries, including the United States and the largest EU states, recognized Kosovo's independence, angering Serbia, Russia, and China.

Wars of secession can be large and deadly, and they can easily spill over international borders or draw in other countries. This spillover is particularly likely if members of an ethnic or a religious group span two sides of a border, constituting the majority group in one state and a majority in a nearby region of another state, but a minority in the other state as a whole. In the Kosovo case, Albanian Muslims are the majority in Albania and in Kosovo but the minority in Serbia. The same pattern occurs in Bosnia-Serbia, Moldova-Russia, and India-Pakistan. In some cases, secessionists want to merge their territories with the neighboring state, which amounts to redrawing the international border. International norms frown on such an outcome.

The strong international norms of sovereignty and territorial integrity treat secession movements as domestic problems of little concern to other states. The general principle seems to be this: "We existing states all have our own domestic problems and disaffected groups or regions, so we must stick together behind sovereignty and territorial integrity." Thus, for instance, Russia and China

NEWBORN AND ALREADY MAKING WAVES

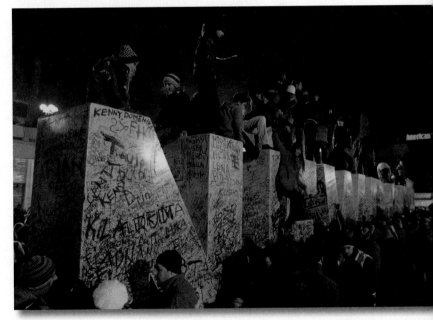

Efforts by a region to secede from a state are a frequent source of international conflict, but international norms generally treat such conflicts as internal matters unless they spill over borders. Increasingly, autonomy agreements are resolving secession conflicts. Here, however, citizens of Kosovo celebrate a unilateral declaration of independence from Serbia (recognized by some great powers and opposed by others) by signing a "Newborn" sculpture, 2008.

opposed the secession of Kosovo from Serbia because of its implications for Chechnya and Taiwan, respectively.

This principle does have limits, however. In 2008, Russia was quick to recognize the breakaway provinces of Abkhazia and South Ossetia, both part of the Republic of Georgia. In August of 2008, after fighting broke out between the Georgian military and South Ossetia, Russia intervened militarily on behalf of South Ossetia and Abkhazia, resulting in a brief war between Russia and Georgia. Russia then recognized both Georgian provinces as independent, a move denounced by the United States and the EU and not accepted by the UN.

Messy border problems can result when multinational states break up into pieces. In such cases, borders that had been internal become international; because these borders are new they may be more vulnerable to challenge. This was the case in the former Yugoslavia, where ethnic groups had intermingled and intermarried, leaving mixed populations in most of the Yugoslav republics. When Yugoslavia broke up in 1991–1992, several republics declared their independence as separate states. Two of these, Croatia and Bosnia, contained minority populations of ethnic Serbs. Serbia seized effective control of significant areas of Croatia and Bosnia that contained Serbian communities or linked such populations geographically. Non-Serbian populations in these areas were driven out or massacred—**ethnic cleansing.** Then, when Croatia reconquered most of its territory in 1995, Serbian populations fled. Ethnic nationalism, whipped up by opportunistic politicians, proved stronger than multiethnic tolerance in both Serbia and Croatia.

The breakup of a state need not lead to violence, however. Serbia split peacefully from Montenegro (a former Yugoslav republic) in 2006. Czechoslovakia split into the Czech Republic and Slovakia in a cooperative manner. And the breakup of the Soviet Union mostly did not lead to violent territorial disputes between republics even when ethnic groups spanned new international borders (such as Ukraine-Russia).

The norm against forceful redrawing of borders does not apply to cases of decolonization. Only the territorial integrity of existing, recognized states is protected by international norms. Colonies and other territorial possessions historically had value only as property to be won, lost, sold, or traded in political deals and wars. The transfer of Hong Kong from British to Chinese control in 1997 illustrates how colonial territory is dispensable (Britain's perspective) while home territory is nearly sacred (China's perspective). From neither perspective do the views of the inhabitants carry much weight.

Increasingly, autonomy for a region has become a realistic compromise between secession and full control by a central government. In 2005, spurred partly by the devastating tsunami a year earlier, separatists in Aceh province, Indonesia, disbanded, giving up on independence and instead participating in regional elections in 2006. The Indonesian government withdrew its 24,000 troops from Aceh and offered the province limited self-rule along with 70 percent of the oil, gas, and mineral wealth earned there.

Interstate Borders   Border disputes between existing states are taken more seriously by the international community, but are less common than secessionist conflicts. Because of the norm of territorial integrity, few important border conflicts remain among long-established states. At one time, huge chunks of territory passed between states at the stroke of a pen. Since the end of World War II, however, only a minuscule amount of territory has changed hands between established states through force (this does not apply to the formation of new states and the fragmenting of old ones).

Furthermore, when territorial disputes do occur between established states, they *can* be settled peacefully. In 2006, Nigeria withdrew its troops from the potentially oil-rich Bakassi Peninsula, which it ceded to Cameroon's sovereignty. The resolution of the dispute, dating from colonial times, followed more than a decade of painstaking progress through the World Court, the personal mediation of the UN secretary-general when Nigeria initially rejected the Court's decision, and the promise of outside powers to monitor implementation of the agreement. Why would Nigeria—a country with nine times Cameroon's population, more than triple its GDP, and a much stronger military— voluntarily cede territory? Doing so would seem to run counter to the predictions of realism in particular and the dominance principle in general. Liberal theories would do better at explaining this outcome: Nigeria acted in its own self-interest, because turning the dispute over to the World Court and bringing in the UN to assist with implementation brought the kind of stability needed for foreign investment to develop the area's resources, primarily oil.

Lingering Disputes   Today, the few remaining interstate border disputes generate important international conflicts. Among the most difficult are the borders of *Israel*, which have never been firmly defined and recognized by its neighbors. The 1948 cease-fire lines resulting from Israel's war of independence expanded in the 1967 war, then contracted again on the Egyptian border after the Camp David peace treaty of 1978. The remaining territories occupied in 1967—the *West Bank* near Jordan, the *Gaza Strip* near Egypt, and the *Golan Heights* of Syria—are central to the Arab-Israeli conflict.

Another serious border dispute is in the *Kashmir* area where India, Pakistan, and China intersect. The Indian-held part of Kashmir is predominantly inhabited by Muslims, a group that is the majority in Pakistan but a minority in India. A *Line of Control* divides the disputed province. Pakistan accuses India of oppressing Kashmiris and thwarting an international agreement to decide Kashmir's future by a popular referendum. India accuses Pakistan of aiding and infiltrating Islamic radicals who carry out attacks in Indian-occupied Kashmir. The two countries went to war twice before over the issue, and nearly did so again in 2002—but this time with both sides holding dozens of nuclear-armed missiles that some experts estimated would kill more than 10 million people in an India-Pakistan war. Perhaps chastened by this experience, the two countries improved relations in 2003 and 2004, maintaining a cease-fire that stopped the incessant low-level fighting along the Line of Control, though not the fighting between Indian authorities and insurgents. In 2004, India agreed to begin a slow withdrawal of troops, and in 2005 a major earthquake helped relations as relief efforts need coordination. In late 2008, Indian-administered elections were held, and despite separatists' calls for a boycott, turnout was high.

Many of the world's other remaining interstate territorial disputes—and often the most serious ones—concern the control of small islands, which often provide strategic advantages, natural resources (such as offshore oil), or fishing rights. International law now gives an island's owner fishing and mineral rights in surrounding seas for 200 miles

FIGURE 4.5   Disputed Islands

The Spratly Islands exemplify contemporary conflicts over territory and natural resources around islands. All or part of the Spratlys are claimed by China, Vietnam, Malaysia, Brunei, the Philippines, and Taiwan.

in each direction. Six countries claim the tiny *Spratly Islands* in the South China Sea (see Figure 4.5). In 2002, they agreed to avoid confrontations over the islands, and they remain calm. Japan and China also dispute tiny islands, as do Japan and South Korea, Iran and the United Arab Emirates, Spain and Morocco, Argentina and Britain, and Russia and Japan. In 2005, Japan and China argued over whether Okinotori—an uninhabited coral reef with two tiny protrusions smaller than a house—was an "island" (with surrounding economic rights) or just a "rock."

Territorial Waters   States treat **territorial waters** near their shores as part of their national territory. Definitions of such waters are not universally agreed upon, but norms have developed in recent years, especially since the UN *Convention on the Law of the Sea (UNCLOS)* (see p. 317). Waters within three miles of shore have traditionally been recognized as territorial, but there are disputes about how far out national sovereignty extends and for what purposes. UNCLOS generally allows a 12-mile limit for shipping and a 200-mile *exclusive economic zone (EEZ)* covering fishing and mineral rights (but allowing for free navigation). The EEZs together cover a third of the world's oceans.

Because of the EEZs, sovereignty over a single tiny island can now bring with it rights to as much as 100,000 square miles of surrounding ocean. But these zones overlap greatly, and shorelines do not run in straight lines; numerous questions of interpretation arise about how to delineate territorial and economic waters. In the Sea of Okhotsk, Russia's EEZ includes all but a small "doughnut hole" of international waters in the middle. Non-Russian boats have fished intensively in the "hole," which depletes fish stocks in Russia's EEZ.

Airspace   The **airspace** above a state is considered the territory of the state. To fly over a state's territory an airplane must have that state's permission. For example, in a 1986 raid on Libya, U.S. bombers based in Britain had to fly a long detour over the Atlantic Ocean because France (between Britain and Libya) would not let U.S. planes use its airspace.

LOCATION, LOCATION, LOCATION

Control of islands, and of the large exclusive economic zone (EEZ) that surrounds them under the law of the sea, has created a number of complicated interstate conflicts. Japan claims Okinotori, shown here in 2005, as an island with an EEZ, but China calls it merely a "rock" without surrounding economic rights.

Outer space, by contrast, is considered international territory like the oceans. International law does not define exactly where airspace ends and outer space begins. However, orbiting satellites fly higher than airplanes, move very fast, and cannot easily change direction to avoid overflying a country. And very few states can shoot down satellites. Because satellites have become useful to all the great powers as intelligence-gathering tools, and because all satellites are extremely vulnerable to attack, a norm of demilitarization of outer space has developed. No state has ever attacked the satellite of another.

Control of Governments

Despite the many minor border disputes that continue to plague the world, most struggles to control territory do not involve changing borders or fighting over islands. Rather, they are conflicts over which governments will control entire states within their existing borders.

In theory, states do not interfere in each other's governance, because of the norm of sovereignty. In practice, however, states often have strong interests in other states' governments and try to influence who holds power in those states. Conflicts over governments take many forms, some mild and some severe, some deeply entwined with third parties and some more or less bilateral. Sometimes a state merely exerts subtle influences on another state's elections; at other times, a state supports rebel elements seeking to overthrow the second state's government.

Occasionally, one state invades another in order to change its government. The Soviet Union did this in Czechoslovakia in 1968; the United States did not do so in Iraq in 1991 but did in 2003. The international community frowns on such overt violations of national sovereignty.

Economic Conflict

Economic competition is the most pervasive form of conflict in international relations because economic transactions are pervasive. Every sale made and every deal reached across international borders entails a resolution of conflicting interests. Costa Rica wants the price of coffee, which it exports, to go up; Canada, which imports coffee, wants it to go down. In a global capitalist market, all economic exchanges involve some conflict of interest.

However, such economic transactions also contain a strong element of mutual economic gain in addition to the element of conflicting interests (see Chapters 3 and 5). These mutual gains provide the most useful leverage in bargaining over economic exchanges: states and companies enter into economic transactions because they profit from doing so. The use of violence would usually diminish such profit by more than could be gained as a result of the use of violence. Thus, economic conflicts do not usually lead to military force and war.

Many states' foreign policies are influenced by *mercantilism*—a practice of centuries past in which trade and foreign economic policies were manipulated to build up a monetary surplus that could be used to finance war (see pp. 165–168). Because a trade surplus confers an advantage in international security affairs over the long run, trade conflicts have implications for international security relations.

Another kind of economic conflict that affects international security concerns *military industry*—the capacity to produce military equipment, especially high-technology weapons such as fighter aircraft or missiles. There is a world trade in such items, but national governments try (not always successfully) to control such production—to try to ensure that national interests take priority over those of manufacturers and that the state is militarily self-sufficient in case of war. Economic competition (over who profits from such sales) is interwoven with security concerns (over who gets access to the weapons). In 2009, proponents of a bailout for the U.S. automobile industry argued that the industry could provide vital production capacity in time of war, as it had during World War II. The transfer of knowledge about high-tech weaponry and military technologies to potentially hostile states is a related concern.

Economic competition also becomes a security issue when it concerns trade in *strategic materials* needed for military purposes, such as special minerals or alloys for aircraft production and uranium for atomic weapons. Few countries are self-sufficient in these materials; the United States imports about half the strategic materials it uses. Nearly every country must import at least some strategic materials for its economy to function.

Drug Trafficking   As a form of illegal trade across international borders, drug trafficking is smuggling, which deprives states of revenue and violates states' legal control of their borders. But smuggling in general is an economic issue rather than a security one (see p. 182). Unlike other smuggled goods, however, drugs are treated as a security threat because of their effect on national (and military) morale and efficiency. Drug trafficking also has become linked with security concerns because military forces participate regularly in operations against the heavily armed drug traffickers.

The U.S. government is trying to prevent *cocaine cartels* based in Colombia from supplying cocaine to U.S. cities. Such cocaine derives mostly from coca plants grown by peasants in mountainous areas of Peru, Bolivia, and Colombia itself. For poor peasants, the cocaine trade may be their only access to a decent income. More importantly for international security, rebel armies in two of the world's 13 active wars—Afghanistan and Colombia—fund their operations primarily through control of the trade in illicit drugs. Afghanistan, the central front in the West's struggle against Islamist extremism (specifically the Taliban), supplies most of the raw material for heroin in the world.

In Latin America, the long history of U.S. military intervention makes state cooperation with U.S. military forces a sensitive political issue. In 1989, U.S. forces invaded Panama; arrested its leader, dictator Manuel Noriega; and convicted him in U.S. courts of complicity in drug trafficking through Panama.

All six types of conflict discussed in this chapter can be pursued through peaceful or violent means. The rest of this chapter examines how states and armed nonstate groups use capabilities of violence to pursue their goals in international conflicts.

Conventional Military Forces

A state leader in a conflict can apply various kinds of leverage to influence an outcome (see Figure 4.6). One set of levers represents nonviolent means of influencing other states, such as foreign aid, economic sanctions, and personal diplomacy (less tangible means are the use of norms, morality, and other ideas). A second set of levers—the subject of the rest of this chapter—makes violent actions occur. They set armies marching or missiles flying.

Great powers continue to dominate the makeup of world military forces. Table 4.2 summarizes the most important forces of the great powers. Together, they account for about two-thirds of world military spending, a third of the world's soldiers, a third of the weapons, 99 percent of nuclear weapons, and 85 percent of arms exports. (The table also indicates the sizable military forces maintained by Germany and Japan despite their nontraditional roles in international security since World War II.)

Military capabilities divide into three types: conventional forces, irregular forces (terrorism, militias), and weapons of mass destruction (nuclear, chemical, and biological weapons). Conventional forces are most important—they are active in all 13 wars currently in progress.

FIGURE 4.6   Military and Nonmilitary Means of Leverage

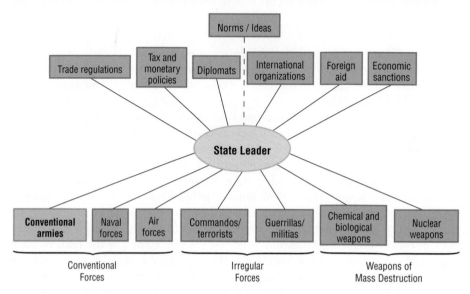

Conventional armed force is the most commonly used military form of leverage.

Armies

Whatever their ultimate causes and objectives, most wars involve a struggle to *control territory*. Territory holds a central place in warfare because of its importance in the international system, and vice versa. Borders define where a state's own military forces and rival states' military forces are free to move. *Armies* are adapted to take, hold, or defend territory. Military forces with armed foot soldiers can *occupy* a territory militarily. Although inhabitants may make the soldiers' lives unhappy through violent or nonviolent resistance, generally only another organized military force can displace occupiers.

Foot soldiers are called the *infantry*. They use assault rifles and other light weapons (such as mines and machine guns) as well as heavy artillery of various types. Artillery is extremely destructive and not very discriminating: it usually causes the most damage and casualties in wars. *Armor* refers to tanks and armored vehicles. In open terrain, such as desert, mechanized ground forces typically combine armor, artillery, and infantry. In close terrain, such as jungles and cities, however, foot soldiers are more important.

Counterinsurgency has received growing attention in recent years because of Iraq, but it is central to all 13 wars currently in progress worldwide. Counterinsurgency warfare often includes programs to try to "win the hearts and minds" of populations so that they stop sheltering the guerrillas.

VIDEO

The War in Afghanistan

TABLE 4.2   Estimated Great Power Military Capabilities, 2001–2008

| | Military Expenditures[b] (Billions of US $) | Active Duty Soldiers[b] (Millions) | Heavy Weapons[a] | | | Nuclear Weapons[c] | Arms Exported[b] (Billions of US $) |
			Tanks	Carriers/ Warships/ Submarines	Combat Airplanes		
United States	575	1.5	10,000	11 / 112 / 74	3,600	10,300*	13
Russia	80*	1.0	20,000*	0 / 40 / 69	1,800	16,000*	5
China	140*	2.2	10,000	0 / 29 / 6	2,100*	400	1
France	50	0.3	1,000	0 / 19 / 12	300	350	3
Britain	55	0.2	1,000	0 / 35 / 16	300	200	3
Germany	35	0.2	3,000	0 / 14 / 0	400	0	1
Japan	40	0.2	1,000	0 / 39 / 20	300	0	0
Approximate % of world total	70%	30%	25%	100 / 60 / 50%	40%	99%	85%

*Problematic data: Russian and Chinese military expenditure estimates vary. Many Chinese aircraft and Russian tanks are old and of limited military use. U.S. and Russian nuclear warheads include deployed strategic weapons (6,000 U.S., 6,000 Russian) with the remainder held in reserve or retired (awaiting destruction).

Notes: Data are for 2007 unless otherwise noted, and are in 2008 dollars. In the 1990s, the military forces of many of these states—Russia above all—were profoundly restructured. Numbers of weapons or soldiers do not indicate quality (levels of technology) or predict how armed forces would actually perform in combat. Russian forces are disorganized and in disrepair, with nonoperational equipment and low morale. Chinese forces are lower-tech than the others. Expenditure data are notoriously unreliable for Russia and China.

Data on soldiers exclude reserves. Tanks include only main battle tanks. Carriers include only supercarriers. Warships are major surface combat ships over 3,000 tons. Nuclear warheads include both strategic and tactical weapons. Arms exports are deliveries, not orders, for 2007.

Sources: Author's estimates based on data provided by the following sources: [a] 2001 data from the Institute for Defense and Disarmament Studies (IDDS) World Arms Database 2001 (www.idds.org). [b] 2008 data from Institute for International and Strategic Studies. *The Military Balance 2008*. [c] Carnegie Endowment for International Peace (www.ceip.org).

In some ways, because counterinsurgency warfare is as much about political gains as military strategy, it is the most complex type of warfare. While battling armed factions of an insurgency, a government must essentially conduct a public relations campaign to persuade the population to abandon the movement, providing public services (such as education and welfare programs) to show its responsiveness to the population. A government must be strong militarily, but cannot be too brutal in the application of force, lest more of the population begin to support the guerrillas.

Land mines are simple, small, and cheap containers of explosives with a trigger activated by contact or sensor. These mines were a particular focus of public attention in the 1990s because in places such as Angola, Afghanistan, Cambodia, and Bosnia, they were used extensively by irregular military forces that never disarmed them. Long after such a war ends, land mines continue to maim and kill civilians who try to reestablish their lives in former war zones. Public opinion and NGOs have pressured governments to restrict the future use of land mines. A treaty to ban land mines was signed by more than 100 countries at a 1997 conference organized by Canada. Russia and Japan signed on shortly afterward, but not China or the United States (which said mines would be needed to slow any North Korean invasion of South Korea). By 2007, more than 40 million land mines had been destroyed under the treaty, with 80 countries eliminating their stockpiles.

PROJECTING POWER

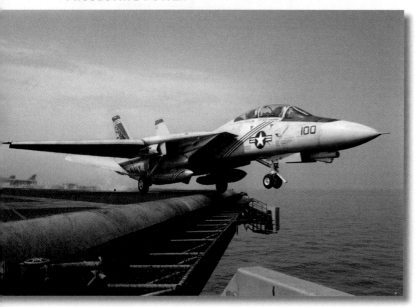

Different types of military forces are adapted to different purposes. Aircraft carriers are used for power projection in distant regions, such as in the Afghanistan and Iraq campaigns.

Navies

Navies are adapted primarily to control passage through the seas and to attack land near coastlines. Controlling the seas in wartime allows states to move their own goods and military forces by sea while preventing enemies from doing so.

Recently, navies of the Western powers began facing a new mission, responding to the rapid growth of piracy in two of the world's vital shipping lanes—the waters off Somalia south of the Suez Canal, and the Straits of Malacca in Indonesia connecting the Indian Ocean with East Asia. The Somali pirates, taking advantage of near-anarchy in that country, established safe havens onshore and ventured out to capture dozens of ships, holding the vessels, cargoes, and crews for

FIGURE 4.7   Pirate Attacks Near Somalia, January to September, 2008

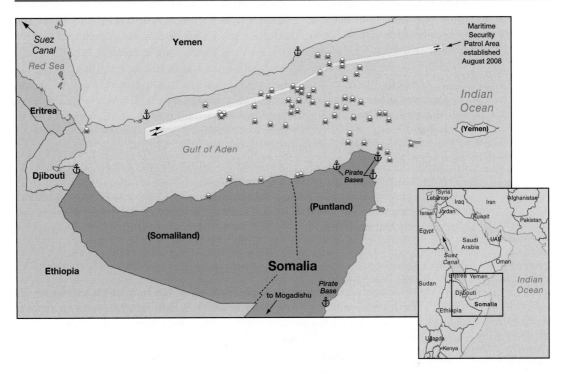

Source: UNOSAT map, October 2, 2008.

ransom (see Figure 4.7). Shipping companies generally paid up, first hundreds of thousands and eventually millions of dollars per ship, rather than lose valuable goods and people. In the fall of 2008, the pirates pushed the limits by capturing first a Ukrainian freighter loaded with tanks and weapons and then a huge Saudi oil tanker with $100 million of oil. The pirates' methods are simple but effective. Racing to ships in very small, fast boats, and armed with automatic rifles and grenade launchers, they throw up grappling hooks, climb the sides, and subdue the crew, typically within about five minutes. Western navies have organized patrols in the area to deter piracy, but with limited success because of the huge stretches of sea in which the pirates could operate (more than a million square miles) and the tens of thousands of commercial ships passing through it each year. The problem illustrates a main challenge facing navies, namely the sheer size of the oceans and the inability of ships to be everywhere, even in the relative confines of major shipping lanes.

Aircraft carriers—mobile platforms for attack aircraft—are instruments of **power projection** that can attack virtually any state in the world. Merely sending an aircraft carrier sailing to the vicinity of an international conflict implies a threat to use force.

VIDEO

Collective Security and the Problem of Piracy

For example, in 1996 the United States dispatched two carriers to the Taiwan area when Chinese war games there threatened to escalate. In 2001, however, during a tense standoff when a U.S. reconnaissance airplane crash-landed in China, the United States pointedly refrained from sending aircraft carriers, signaling an intent to settle the conflict diplomatically. Aircraft carriers are extremely expensive and typically require 20 to 25 supporting ships for protection and supply. Only the United States currently operates large carriers (11 of them, costing more than $5 billion each). Eight other countries (France, India, Russia, Spain, Brazil, Italy, Thailand, and the United Kingdom) maintain smaller carriers that use helicopters or small airplanes.

Surface ships, which account for the majority of warships, rely increasingly on guided missiles and are in turn vulnerable to attack by missiles (fired from ships, planes, submarines, or land). Because the ranges of small missiles now reach from dozens to hundreds of miles, naval warfare emphasizes detection at great distances without being detected oneself—a cat-and-mouse game of radar surveillance and electronic countermeasures.

Air Forces

Air forces serve several purposes—strategic bombing of land or sea targets; "close air support" (battlefield bombing); interception of other aircraft; reconnaissance; and airlift of supplies, weapons, and troops. Missiles—whether fired from air, land, or sea—are increasingly important. In the Soviet war in Afghanistan, the U.S.-made portable Stinger missiles used by guerrillas took a heavy toll on the Soviet air force. In 2003, the threat from shoulder-fired missiles kept the Baghdad airport closed to commercial air traffic for more than a year.

Traditionally, and still to some extent, aerial bombing resembles artillery shelling in that it causes great destruction with little discrimination. This has changed somewhat as smart bombs improve accuracy. Laser-guided bombs follow a sensor pointed at the target from the air or ground. Other bombs use GPS navigation (see p. 151) to hit targets through clouds, smoke, or sandstorms. Most of the bombing in the 1991 Gulf War was high-altitude saturation bombing using dumb bombs. But in the 2003 Iraq War, the massive air campaign early in the war entirely used smart bombs, hitting far more targets with fewer bombs.

The increasing sophistication of electronic equipment and the high-performance requirements of attack aircraft make air forces expensive—totally out of reach for some states. Thus, rich states have huge advantages over poor ones in air warfare. Despite the expense, air superiority is often the key to the success of ground operations, especially in open terrain. The U.S. bombings of Iraq (1991 and 2003), Serbia (1999), and Afghanistan (2001) demonstrated a new effectiveness of air power, applied not against the morale of enemy populations (as in World War II), but directly at battlefield positions. The U.S. ability to decimate distant military forces while taking only very light casualties is historically unprecedented. The 2003 attack on Iraq demonstrated the usefulness of air power, but also its limits. A massive precision bombing raid on Baghdad a few days into the war destroyed hundreds of targets of value to Saddam Hussein's government. It was designed to "shock and awe" enemy commanders into giving up. However, U.S. forces still had to slug it out on the ground to get to Baghdad. Clearly this war could not have been won from the air. As ground soldiers have pointed out, "Nobody ever surrendered to an airplane."

Logistics and Intelligence

All military operations rely heavily on logistical support such as food, fuel, and ordnance (weapons and ammunition). Military logistics is a huge operation, and in most armed forces the majority of soldiers are not combat troops. Global reach capabilities combine long-distance logistical support with various power-projection forces. These capabilities allow a great power to project military power to distant corners of the world and to maintain a military presence in most of the world's regions simultaneously. Only the United States today fully possesses such a capability—with worldwide military alliances, air and naval bases, troops stationed overseas, and aircraft carriers.

Space forces are military forces designed to attack in or from outer space. Ballistic missiles, which travel through space briefly, are not generally included in this category. Only the United States and Russia have substantial military capabilities in space. China put an astronaut in orbit in 2003, successfully tested an antisatellite missile in 2007, and launched a lunar orbiter in 2007, but it has fewer space capabilities overall. The development of space weapons has been constrained by the technical challenges and expenses of space operations, and by norms against militarizing space.

Satellites are used extensively for military purposes, but these purposes do not include attack. Satellites perform military surveillance and mapping, communications, weather assessment, and early warning of ballistic missile launches. Satellites also provide navigational information to military forces—army units, ships, planes, and even guided missiles in flight. Locations are calculated to within about 50 feet by small receivers, which pick up beacons transmitted from a network of 18 U.S. satellites known as a *Global Positioning System* (GPS). Handheld receivers are available commercially, so the military forces of other countries can free-ride on these satellite navigation beacons. Analysts pore over masses of satellite reconnaissance data every day in Washington, D.C., and other capitals. Poorer states can buy satellite photos on the commercial market—including high-resolution pictures that Russia sells for hard currency. In fact, access to such information has diffused to the point that the terrorists who attacked Mumbai, India, in 2008 planned their attack using satellite images available through Google Earth, and coordinated it in real time from Pakistan using satellite phones. But generally, in outer space great powers have the advantage over smaller or poorer states.

Intelligence gathering also relies on various other means such as electronic monitoring of telephone lines and other communications, reports from embassies, and information in the open press. The U.S. military operates a massive intelligence-gathering operation, especially for information relevant to battlefield deployments and other tactical matters. Satellite intelligence is supplemented by monitoring of a very high volume of electronic communications, such as radio and telephone conversations. Terrorists in remote Afghanistan had to use couriers because the U.S. military could monitor their electronic communications.

The largest U.S. military intelligence agency is the National Security Agency (NSA), whose mission is encoding U.S. communications and breaking the codes of foreign communications. The NSA employs more mathematics Ph.D.s than anyone else in the world, is the second largest electricity consumer in the state of Maryland, has a budget larger than the CIA's, and is believed to have the most powerful computer facility in the world. The various intelligence operations taken together are very large and are growing in importance as the information revolution proceeds and as the war on terrorism makes their mission more central.

Evolving Technologies

Technological developments have changed the nature of military force in several ways. First, the resort to force in international conflicts now has more profound costs and consequences. Great powers in particular can no longer use force to settle disputes among themselves without risking massive destruction and economic ruin. Also, military engagements now occur across greater standoff distances between opposing forces. Missiles of all types are accelerating this trend. These technological advances undermine the territorial basis of war and of the state itself. The state once had a hard shell of militarily protected borders, but today borders offer far less protection. For example, Israel's successful defense of its borders did not stop Hamas from hitting Israeli cities with missiles in 2008, leading to an Israeli military offensive against Hamas forces in Gaza.

In recent decades, the technological revolution in electronics has profoundly affected military forces, especially their command and control. **Electronic warfare** (now broadened to *information warfare*) refers to the uses of the electromagnetic spectrum (radio waves, radar, infrared, etc.) in war—employing electromagnetic signals for one's own benefit while denying their

REVOLUTIONARIES

The information revolution is making smaller weapons and smaller dispersed units more potent. A "revolution in military affairs" is driving changes in U.S. military strategy, as exemplified by the use of special forces with local armies in Afghanistan. Here U.S. and Afghan soldiers work together, 2006.

use to an enemy. Electromagnetic signals are used for sensing beyond the normal visual range through radar, infrared, and imaging equipment to see in darkness, through fog, or at great distances. These and other technologies have illuminated the battlefield so that forces cannot be easily hidden. Electronic countermeasures try to counteract enemy electronic systems such as radar and radio communications. *Stealth technology* uses special radar-absorbent materials and unusual shapes in the design of aircraft, missiles, and ships to scatter enemy radar. However, stealth is extremely expensive (the B-2 stealth bomber costs about $2 billion, about three times its weight in gold) and is prone to technical problems.

Strategies for *cyberwar*—disrupting enemy computer networks to degrade command and control, or even hacking into bank accounts electronically—were developed by NATO forces during the 1999 Kosovo war. Russian hackers apparently disabled Georgian Web sites during the 2008 war between those countries. Though mostly not implemented, these strategies will probably figure in future wars. Some experts fear that terrorist attacks also could target computer networks, including the Internet.

Terrorism

The U.S. State Department lists 44 foreign terrorist organizations as of 2008. Some are motivated by religion (for example, al Qaeda) but others by class ideology (for example, Shining Path in Peru) or by ethnic conflict and nationalism (for example, Basque Fatherland and Liberty). Earlier in this chapter (pp. 126–130) we discussed conflicts involving armed Islamist militias and terrorist networks. Here we discuss terrorism itself as a tactic. Since September 2001, governments and citizens have paid much more attention to terrorism than before. But terrorism itself is not new.

Terrorism refers to political violence that targets civilians deliberately and indiscriminately. Beyond this basic definition, other criteria can be applied, but the definitions become politically motivated: one person's freedom fighter is another's terrorist. More than guerrilla warfare, terrorism is a shadowy world of faceless enemies and irregular tactics marked by extreme brutality.

Traditionally, the purpose of terrorism is to demoralize a civilian population in order to use its discontent as leverage on national governments or other parties to a conflict. Related to this is the aim of creating drama in order to gain media attention for a cause. Terrorism is seldom mindless; rather it is usually a calculated use of violence as leverage. However, motives and means of terrorism vary widely, having in common only that some actor is using violence to influence other actors.

Traditionally, the primary effect of terrorism is psychological. In part the effectiveness of terrorism in capturing attention is due to the dramatic nature of the incidents, especially as shown on television news. Terrorism also gains attention because of the randomness of victims. Although only a few dozen people may be injured by a bomb left in a market, millions of people realize "it could have been me," because they, too, shop in markets. Attacks on airplanes augment this fear because many people already fear flying. Terrorism thus amplifies a small amount of power by its psychological effect on large populations; this is why it is usually a tool of the weak. However, al Qaeda's attacks follow a somewhat different pattern, planned less to create fear than simply to kill as many Americans and their allies as possible—and ultimately to touch off apocalyptic violence that al Qaeda followers believe will bring about God's intervention. The psychological effect is aimed at Muslim populations worldwide rather than at Americans.

In the shockingly destructive attack on the World Trade Center, tangible damage was far greater than in previous terrorist attacks—reaching into thousands of lives and tens of billions of dollars. The psychological impact was even stronger than the physical damage—changing the U.S. political and cultural landscape instantly. And the same terrorist network was trying to obtain nuclear weapons (see pp. 150–151) with which to kill not thousands but hundreds of thousands of Americans.

The classic cases of terrorism—from the 1970s to the 2001 attacks—are those in which a *nonstate* actor uses attacks against *civilians* by secret *nonuniformed* forces, operating across *international borders*, as a leverage against state actors. Radical political factions or separatist groups hijack or blow up airplanes or plant bombs in cafés, clubs, or other crowded places. For example, Chechen radicals seized a school in Beslan, a small city in the Caucasus region in 2004. For three days, they held nearly 1,200 children, parents, and teachers without food or water. When Russian troops stormed the school, more than 300 people died, including 172 children. Such tactics create spectacular incidents that draw attention to the terrorists' cause. Often terrorism is used by radical factions of movements that have not been able to get attention or develop other effective means of leverage. It is often a tactic of desperation, and it almost always reflects weakness in the power position of the attacker.

ASYMMETRICAL CONFLICT

Terrorist attacks often reflect the weakness of the perpetrators and their lack of access to other means of leverage. Terror can sometimes amplify a small group's power and affect outcomes. Al Qaeda's September 11, 2001, attacks, staged by a relatively small nonstate actor, ultimately led to the withdrawal of U.S. troops from Saudi Arabia, drew the United States into a counterinsurgency war in Iraq, and brought al Qaeda itself a surge of recruits for new attacks worldwide.

Yet, the persistence of terrorism is in some ways puzzling because the tactic has a mixed record of success. Suicide bombers were arguably effective at convincing the United States to leave Lebanon in 1983, but the Chechen terrorists' 2004 school attack marked their end as a serious force in Chechnya. The Palestinians did not win a state through terrorism. Al Qaeda affiliates in Iraq so alienated the Sunni tribes that had sheltered them that the tribes turned against them. In addition, even large numbers of suicide bombers have yet to be effective at gaining a state for the Tamils in Sri Lanka or providing leverage for Hamas or Islamic Jihad against Israel. Clearly, terrorist activities do not reliably achieve political ends.

Terrorists are more willing than states are to violate the norms of the international system because, unlike states, they do not have a stake in that system. Conversely, when a political group gains some power or legitimacy, its use of terrorism usually diminishes.

Some research has attempted to systematically analyze when particular types of terrorism, such as suicide bombings, are effective at achieving the goals of terrorist organizations. According to one study, suicide bombings, rather than an irrational use of violence by terrorist groups, seem to follow strategic patterns. In particular, they occur most frequently against democracies rather than autocracies, presumably because they are thought to strongly influence public opinion. Still, this same study concludes that this terror tactic has not been particularly successful at achieving significant goals.

States themselves carry out acts designed to terrorize their own populations or those of other states, but scholars tend to avoid the label "terrorism" for such acts, preferring to call them repression or war. In fact, no violent act taken during a civil or international war—by or toward a warring party—can necessarily fit neatly into the category of terrorism. The narrowest definition of terrorism would exclude acts either by or against *uniformed military forces* rather than civilians. This definition would exclude the killing of 243 U.S. Marines by a car bomb in Lebanon in 1983, and the 2001 attack on the Pentagon, because they were directed at military targets. It would also exclude the bombing of German cities in World War II although the purpose was to terrorize civilians. But in today's world of undeclared war, guerrilla war, civil war, and ethnic violence, a large gray zone surrounds clear cases of terrorism. Disagreements about whether terrorism included Palestinian attacks on Israel, and Pakistani attacks in Kashmir, scuttled efforts to pass a UN treaty on terrorism in late 2001.

State-sponsored terrorism refers to the use of terrorist groups by states—usually under control of the state's intelligence agency—to achieve political aims. In 1988, a bomb scattered pieces of Pan Am flight 103 over the Scottish countryside. Combing the fields for debris, investigators found fragments of a tape recorder with a sophisticated plastic explosive bomb. The U.S. and British governments identified the Libyan intelligence agents responsible and, in 1992, backed by the UN Security Council, they demanded that Libya turn over the two agents for trial. When Libya refused, the UN imposed economic sanctions. In 1999, Libya turned over the suspects for trial—two received life in prison while a third was acquitted—and the UN suspended its sanctions. In 2003, Libya formally took responsibility for the bombing, struck a multibillion-dollar compensation deal with victims' families, and regained a normal place in the international community.

As of 2009, the United States accuses four states of supporting international terrorism—Iran, Syria, Sudan, and Cuba. All have been on the list for more than a decade. The U.S. government has barred U.S. companies from doing business in those states. However, these kinds of unilateral U.S. sanctions are of limited effect. Cuba can do business with Canada, as can Iran with Russia. North Korea was removed from the list in 2008 in exchange for halting its nuclear weapons program.

Weapons of Mass Destruction

Weapons of mass destruction comprise three general types: nuclear, chemical, and biological weapons. They are distinguished from conventional weapons by their enormous potential lethality, given their small size and modest costs, and by their relative lack of discrimination in whom they kill. When deployed on ballistic missiles, they can be fired from the home territory of one state and wreak great destruction on the home territory of another state. Until now this has never happened. But the mere threat of such an action undermines the territorial integrity and security of states in the international system. Of central concern today are the potentials for proliferation—the possession of weapons of mass destruction by more and more states and nonstate actors.

Nuclear Weapons

VIDEO

How to Make Nuclear Weapons

Nuclear weapons are, in sheer explosive power, the most destructive weapons available to states. A single weapon the size of a refrigerator can destroy a city. Defending against nuclear weapons is extremely difficult at best. To understand the potentials for nuclear proliferation, one has to know something about how nuclear weapons work. There are two types. *Fission* weapons (atomic bombs or A-bombs) are simpler and less expensive than **fusion weapons** (also called thermonuclear bombs, hydrogen bombs, or H-bombs).

When a fission weapon explodes, one type of atom (element) is split into new types with less total mass. The lost mass is transformed into energy according to Albert Einstein's famous formula, $E = mc^2$, which shows that a little bit of mass is equivalent to a great deal of energy. In fact, the fission bomb that destroyed Nagasaki, Japan, in 1945 converted to energy roughly the amount of mass in a penny.

The two elements that can be split in this way, uranium-235 (U-235) and plutonium, are known as **fissionable material.** Fission weapons work by taking subcritical masses of the fissionable material—amounts not dense enough to start a chain reaction—and compressing them into a critical mass, which explodes. In the simplest design, one piece of uranium is propelled down a tube (by conventional explosives) into another piece of uranium. A more efficient but technically demanding design arranges high explosives precisely around a hollow sphere of plutonium so as to implode the sphere and create a critical mass.

Although these designs require sophisticated engineering, they are well within the capabilities of many states and some private groups. The obstacle is obtaining fissionable material. Only 10 to 100 pounds or less are required for each bomb, but even these small amounts are not easily obtained. U-235, which can be used in the simplest bomb designs, is especially difficult to make. Extracting the fissionable U-235, referred to as enriching the uranium up to weapons grade (or high grade), is slow, expensive, and technically complex—a major obstacle to proliferation. But North Korea, Iran, Iraq, and Libya all built infrastructure to do so in recent years. North Korea promised to end its uranium program and dismantle its nuclear complex (after testing a plutonium bomb in 2006). It made progress in this direction in 2007–2008, albeit behind schedule. But Iran defied several UN Security Council demands to stop enriching uranium in 2006–2009, insisting on its sovereign right to enrich uranium for what it calls "peaceful purposes."

Plutonium is more easily produced, from low-grade uranium in nuclear power reactors. But a plutonium bomb is more difficult to build than a uranium one—another obstacle to proliferation. Plutonium is also used in commercial breeder reactors, which Japan and other countries have built recently—another source of fissionable material.

Fusion weapons are extremely expensive and technically demanding; they are for only the richest, largest, most technologically capable states. Here, two small atoms (variants of hydrogen) fuse together into a larger atom, releasing energy. This reaction occurs only at very high temperatures (the sun "burns" hydrogen through fusion). Weapons designers use fission weapons to create these high energies and trigger an explosive fusion reaction. The explosive power of most fusion weapons is a hundred times that of fission nuclear weapons. In the post–Cold War era, fusion weapons have become irrelevant, since they are too powerful for any actor to use productively and too difficult for terrorists or small states to build.

Ballistic Missiles and Other Delivery Systems

Delivery systems for getting nuclear weapons to their targets—much more than the weapons themselves—are the basis of states' nuclear arsenals and strategies (discussed shortly). Inasmuch as nuclear warheads can be made quite small—weighing a few hundred pounds or even less—they are adaptable to a wide variety of delivery systems.

During the Cold War, nuclear delivery systems were divided into two categories. *Strategic* weapons could hit an enemy's homeland. *Tactical* nuclear weapons were designed for battlefield use. Both superpowers integrated tactical nuclear weapons into their conventional air, sea, and land forces using a variety of delivery systems—gravity bombs, artillery shells, short-range missiles, land mines, depth charges, and so forth.

However, the tens of thousands of nuclear warheads integrated into superpower conventional forces posed dangers such as theft or accident. Their actual use would have entailed grave risks of escalation to strategic nuclear war, putting home cities at risk. Thus, both superpowers phased out tactical nuclear weapons almost entirely when the Cold War ended.

The main strategic delivery vehicles are **ballistic missiles;** unlike airplanes, they are extremely difficult to defend against. Ballistic missiles carry a warhead up along a trajectory—typically out of the atmosphere, at least 50 miles high—before descending. In addition, some missiles fire from fixed sites (silos), whereas others are mobile, firing from railroads or large trailer trucks (making them hard to target). The longest-range missiles are **intercontinental ballistic missiles (ICBMs),** with ranges of more than 5,000 miles.

Of special interest today are short-range ballistic missiles (SRBMs), with ranges under 1,000 miles. In regional conflicts, the long range of more powerful missiles may not be necessary. The largest cities of Syria and Israel are only 133 miles from each other; the capital cities of Iraq and Iran are less than 500 miles apart, as are those of India and Pakistan (see Figure 4.8). All of these states are among the 33 that own ballistic missiles. Short-range and some medium-range ballistic missiles are cheap enough to be bought or made by small middle-income states.

Many short-range ballistic missiles are highly inaccurate but still very difficult to defend against. With conventional warheads, they have more psychological than military utility (demoralizing an enemy population). With nuclear, chemical, or biological warheads, however, these missiles could be deadlier. The **cruise missile** is a small winged missile that can navigate across thousands of miles of previously mapped terrain to reach a target. Cruise missiles can be launched from ships, submarines, airplanes, or land.

FIGURE 4.8   Expanding Ranges of Indian and Pakistani Missiles, 1998–2003

Source: *The Washington Post,* May 29, 1999: A32, Table 6.3.

The proliferation of ballistic missiles has been difficult to control. Through the **Missile Technology Control Regime,** industrialized states try to limit the flow of missile-relevant technology to states in the global South, but with limited success. Short- and medium-range missiles (with ranges up to about 2,000 miles) apparently are being developed by Iran, Israel, Saudi Arabia, Pakistan, India, North Korea, and possibly Argentina and Brazil. In 2008, Iran alarmed the West by testing a space rocket that could be adapted as an ICBM.

Small states or terrorists that may acquire nuclear weapons in the future could deliver them through innovative means. Because nuclear weapons are small, one could be smuggled into a target state by car, by boat, or in diplomatic pouches. Since 2001, the United States has begun a Container Security Initiative aimed at preventing weapons of mass destruction from reaching U.S. shores in seaborne shipping containers. But doing so without impeding the prosperity-inducing flow of international trade is a daunting challenge—nearly 8 million shipping containers pass through U.S. ports every year.

Chemical and Biological Weapons

A *chemical weapon* releases chemicals that disable and kill people. The chemicals vary from lethal ones such as nerve gas to merely irritating ones such as tear gas. Different chemicals interfere with the nervous system, blood, breathing, or other body functions. Some can be absorbed through the skin; others must be inhaled. Some persist in the target area long after their use; others disperse quickly.

It is possible to defend against most chemical weapons by dressing troops in protective clothing and gas masks and following elaborate procedures to decontaminate equipment. But protective suits are hot, and antichemical measures reduce the efficiency of armies. Civilians are much less likely to have protection against chemicals than are military forces. Chemical weapons are by nature indiscriminate about whom they kill. Several times, chemical weapons have been deliberately used against civilians (notably by the Iraqi government against Iraqi Kurds in the 1980s).

Use of chemical weapons in war has been rare. Mustard gas, which produces skin blisters and lung damage, was widely used in World War I. After the horrors of that war, the use of chemical weapons was banned in the 1925 Geneva protocol, which is still in effect today. In World War II, both sides were armed with chemical weapons but neither used them, for fear of retaliation (the same was true in the Gulf War). Since then (with possibly a few unclear exceptions) only Iraq has violated the treaty—against Iran in the 1980s. Unfortunately, Iraq's actions not only breached a psychological barrier against using chemical weapons, but showed such weapons to be cheap and effective against human waves of attackers without protective gear. This stimulated dozens more poor states to begin acquiring chemical weapons.

Chemical weapons are a cheap way for states to gain weapons of mass destruction. Production of chemical weapons can use similar processes and facilities as for pesticides, pharmaceuticals, and other civilian products, which makes it difficult to find chemical weapons facilities in suspect countries, or to deny those states access to the needed chemicals and equipment.

The 1925 treaty did not ban the production or possession of chemical weapons, only their use, and several dozen states built stockpiles of them. The United States and the Soviet Union maintained large arsenals of chemical weapons during the Cold War but have reduced them greatly in the past decade. The 1992 **Chemical Weapons Convention** to ban the production and possession of chemical weapons has been signed by all the great powers and nearly all other states, with a few exceptions including Egypt, Syria, and North Korea. The new treaty includes strict verification provisions and the threat of sanctions against violators including (an important extension) those who are nonparticipants in the treaty. From 1997 to 2008, the treaty organization oversaw the elimination of more than a third of the world's chemical weapons.

VULNERABLE

Civilians are more vulnerable to chemical weapons than soldiers are. A treaty aims to ban chemical weapons worldwide. Here, Israeli kindergarteners prepare against a chemical warfare threat from Iraqi Scud missiles during the Gulf War, 1991.

Biological weapons resemble chemical ones, but use deadly microorganisms or biologically derived toxins. Some use viruses or bacteria that cause fatal diseases, such as smallpox, bubonic plague, and anthrax. Others cause nonfatal, but incapacitating, diseases or diseases that kill livestock. Theoretically, a single weapon could spark an epidemic in an entire population, but this would pose too great a danger so less contagious microorganisms are preferred.

Biological weapons have virtually never been used in war (Japan tried some on a few Chinese villages in World War II). Their potential strikes many political leaders as a Pandora's box that could let loose uncontrollable forces if opened. Thus, the development, production, and possession of biological weapons are banned by the 1972 **Biological Weapons Convention,** signed by more than 100 countries including the great powers. The superpowers destroyed their stocks of biological weapons and had to restrict their biological weapons complexes to defensive research rather than the development of weapons. However, because the treaty makes no provision for inspection and because biological weapons programs are, like chemical ones, relatively easy to hide, several states remain under suspicion of having biological weapons. UN inspections of Iraq in the mid-1990s uncovered an active biological weapons program. Evidence surfaced after the collapse of the Soviet Union that a secret biological weapons program had been under way there as well. Today, the United States and perhaps a dozen other countries maintain biological weapons research (not banned by the treaty). Researchers try to ascertain the military implications of advances in biotechnology.

Proliferation

Proliferation is the spread of weapons of mass destruction—nuclear weapons, ballistic missiles, and chemical or biological weapons—into the hands of more actors. The implications of proliferation for international relations are difficult to predict but clearly profound. Ballistic missiles with weapons of mass destruction remove the territorial protection offered by state borders and make each state vulnerable to others. Some realists, who believe in rationality, reason that in a world where the use of military force could lead to mutual annihilation, there would be fewer wars—just as during the arms race of the Cold War, the superpowers did not blow each other up. Other IR scholars who put less faith in the rationality of state leaders are much more alarmed by proliferation. They fear that with more and more nuclear (or chemical/biological) actors, miscalculation or accident—or fanatical terrorism—could lead to disaster.

The leaders of the great powers tend to side with the second group. They have tried to restrict weapons of mass destruction to the great powers. Proliferation erodes the great powers' advantage relative to middle powers. There is also a widespread fear that these weapons may fall into the hands of terrorists or other nonstate actors who would be immune from threats of retaliation (with no territory or cities to defend). Evidence captured during the 2001 war in Afghanistan showed that al Qaeda was trying to obtain weapons of mass destruction and would be willing to use them. Lax security at the vast, far-flung former Soviet nuclear complex increased fears that fissionable materials could reach terrorists.

Nuclear proliferation could occur simply by a state or nonstate actor's buying (or stealing) one or more nuclear weapons or the components to build one. The means to prevent this include covert intelligence, tight security measures, and safeguards to prevent a stolen weapon from being used. In 2007, two teams of armed assailants broke into the South African nuclear facility where atomic bombs had once been designed and produced. After reaching the control room and shooting one guard, they were repelled, leaving a mystery along with doubts about the security of such nuclear facilities. As political unrest occurs in nuclear states, notably Pakistan, thoughts often turn toward the safety of nuclear weapons.

A stronger form of nuclear proliferation is the development by states of nuclear complexes to produce their own nuclear weapons on an ongoing basis. Here larger numbers of weapons are involved and strong potentials exist for arms races in regional conflicts and rivalries. The relevant regional conflicts are those between Israel and the Arab states, Iran and its neighbors, India and Pakistan, the two Koreas, and possibly Taiwan and China. India and Pakistan each have dozens of nuclear weapons and the missiles to deliver them. North Korea tested one in 2006, but has negotiated an end to its program. In addition, South Africa reported in 1993 that it had built several nuclear weapons but then dismantled them in the 1980s (before white minority rule ended).

Israel has never officially admitted it has nuclear weapons but is widely believed to have a hundred or more. Israel wants these capabilities to convince Arab leaders that military conquest

SOMETHING TO HIDE

The most important hurdle in making nuclear weapons is access to fissionable materials (plutonium and uranium). Iran's enrichment of uranium could give that country nuclear bombs within the decade. Fueling Western suspicions, Iran has not been forthcoming with international inspectors. Iran bulldozed this large site and removed its topsoil in 2004 before letting inspectors in. In 2006 and 2007 the UN Security Council applied mild sanctions against Iran over its refusal to stop enriching uranium.

of Israel is impossible. In 2007, Israeli warplanes destroyed a site in Syria thought to be a nuclear reactor of North Korean design. Syria quickly cleared all traces of the building after the attack.

VIDEO

Pakistan's Nuclear Sales

The **Non-Proliferation Treaty (NPT)** of 1968 created a framework for controlling the spread of nuclear materials and expertise. The International Atomic Energy Agency (IAEA), a UN agency based in Vienna, is charged with inspecting the nuclear power industry in member states to prevent secret military diversions of nuclear materials. However, a number of potential nuclear states (such as Israel) have not signed the NPT, and even states that have signed may sneak around its provisions by keeping some facilities secret (as Iraq and Iran did). In 2006, a deal between the United States and India to share nuclear technology led many states to question the NPT, because those benefits were supposedly reserved for signatories only. Nonetheless the deal received final U.S. and Indian approval in 2008.

North Korea withdrew from the IAEA in 1993, then bargained with Western leaders to get economic assistance, including safer reactors, in exchange for freezing its nuclear program. North Korea's leader died months later, but the compromise held up. In 1999 North Korea allowed inspection of a disputed underground complex and agreed to suspend missile tests, in exchange for aid and partial lifting of U.S. trade sanctions. Then, in 2002, the United States confronted North Korea with evidence of a secret uranium enrichment program, which the North Koreans then admitted. As relations deteriorated, North Korea pulled out of the agreement and out of the IAEA, restarted its nuclear reactor, and apparently turned its existing plutonium into a half-dozen bombs within months, one of which was tested in 2006. U.S., Chinese, Japanese, and Korean leaders continued to negotiate and in 2008 North Korea again agreed to give up its program, only to renege on this promise yet again in 2009.

Iran denies, but appears to be, working to develop nuclear weapons. Since 2003, Iran first agreed to suspend its uranium enrichment program and allow surprise IAEA inspections, then restarted enrichment, suspended it again, and restarted it again. In 2005, U.S.-backed efforts by Europe to offer Iran economic incentives to dismantle its program, and by Russia to enrich Iran's uranium on Russian soil with safeguards, both faltered. In 2006–2008, the UN Security Council condemned Iran's actions and imposed mild sanctions. Iran insisted on its right to enrich uranium for what it called peaceful purposes.

Nuclear Strategy and Arms Control

The term *nuclear strategy* refers to decisions about how many nuclear weapons to deploy, what delivery systems to put them on, and what policies to adopt regarding their possible use. The main reason for possessing nuclear weapons is to deter another state from a nuclear or conventional attack by threatening ruinous retaliation. Under **mutually assured destruction (MAD),** neither side can prevent the other from destroying it. The acronym implies that the strategy, though "rational," is actually insane (mad) because it could destroy both sides.

Defense has played little role in nuclear strategy to date because no effective defense against missile attack exists. However, the United States is spending billions of dollars a year to try to develop defenses that could shoot down incoming ballistic missiles. The program is called the **Strategic Defense Initiative (SDI), or "Star Wars."**

In 2004, the United States began deploying both a prototype missile intercept system based in Alaska and a destroyer in the Sea of Japan that could try to shoot down a North Korean missile in its boost phase. It also moved to put in place— against strong Chinese opposition—a missile-defense collaboration in Asia that would include Japan, Australia, possibly India, and Taiwan. Four Japanese destroyers are to join the U.S. one, and Patriot missiles based in Japan would try to shoot down incoming missiles. But North Korea has more than 600 ballistic missiles capable of hitting Japan.

As of 2009, the United States is deploying a multilayer system with 24 ground-based interceptor missiles in Alaska and California (directed toward the North Korean threat), 21 ship-based interceptors, about 500 Patriot missiles for short-range ballistic missile threats, and a series of radars and control centers. It had begun testing an airplane-based laser system, and had concluded agreements with Poland and the Czech Republic to build missile defenses in those former Soviet-bloc countries, along the potential flight path of missiles fired from Iran. Russian objections to this plan were the subject of ongoing negotiations in 2009.

During the Cold War, the superpowers' nuclear forces grew and technologies developed. These evolving force structures were codified by a series of arms control agreements. *Arms control* is an effort by two or more states to regulate by formal agreement their acquisition of weapons, using the reciprocity principle to solve the collective goods problem of expensive arms races that ultimately benefit neither side (see pp. 5–6). Arms control is broader than just nuclear weapons—for instance, after World War I the great powers negotiated limits on sizes of navies—but in the Cold War, nuclear weapons were the main focus of arms control. Arms control agreements typically require long, formal negotiations with many technical discussions, culminating in a treaty. Some arms control treaties are multilateral, but during the Cold War most were bilateral (U.S.-Soviet). Some stay in effect indefinitely; others have a limited term.

Several treaties in the 1970s locked in the superpowers' basic parity in nuclear capabilities under MAD. The U.S. arsenal peaked in the 1960s at more than 30,000 warheads; the Soviet arsenal peaked in the 1980s at more than 40,000. More recent arms control agreements substantially reduced nuclear forces after the end of the Cold War. Under the 2002 U.S.-Russian Strategic Offensive Reductions Treaty, each side is to reduce deployed warheads from about 6,000 to 2,200. Overall the U.S. and Russian nuclear arsenals are down to one-third of their peak levels and dropping, and the majority of remaining warheads are not deployed. The reciprocity principle that helped fuel the arms race also enables its step-by-step reversal.

China, France, and Britain each have several hundred weapons—France's and Britain's mostly on submarine-launched missiles and China's mostly on long-range bombers and intermediate-range missiles.

A **Comprehensive Test Ban Treaty (CTBT)** to halt all nuclear test explosions was signed in 1996 after decades of stalemate. It aims to impede the development of new types of nuclear weapons. However, the treaty does not take effect until signed and ratified by all 44 states believed capable of building at least a crude nuclear weapon. India did not sign the CTBT and defied it in 1998 with five nuclear tests. Pakistan followed suit with its own tests. The U.S. Senate voted in 1999 against ratifying the CTBT, and the Bush administration opposed it. Russia ratified it in 2000. Although no nuclear tests occurred worldwide in 1999–2005, North Korea's nuclear test in 2006 dealt another setback to the CTBT.

Efforts to control *conventional* arms trade through arms control treaties have had little success. In the early 1990s, the five permanent members of the Security Council, which account for most weapons sales in the Middle East, tried to negotiate limits on the supply of weapons to that region. But no participant wanted to give up its own lucrative arms sales in the region, which each naturally saw as justified (again, showing the difficulty of overcoming collective goods problems).

All the weapons of mass destruction are relatively difficult and expensive to build, yet provide only specialized capabilities that are rarely if ever actually used. This is why most states that could technically acquire them have decided not to do so. Such cost-benefit thinking also applies more broadly to states' decisions about the acquisition of all kinds of military forces.

States and Militaries

Given the range of military capabilities available to states (at various costs), how much and what types should state leaders choose to acquire? This question confronts all states but they answer it in different ways.

Military Economics

States vary widely in military spending, from Costa Rica, with virtually no military spending at all, to North Korea, which devotes 20 percent or more of all economic activity to military purposes. If military budgets are too low, states may be unprepared to meet a security threat. But if leaders set military budgets too high, they will overburden the national economy in the long run.

World military spending is about 2 percent of the total goods and services in the world economy—about $1.2 trillion every year, or roughly $1 million every 30 seconds. Most is spent by a few big states, nearly half by the United States alone. World military spending is a vast flow of money that could, if redirected to other purposes, change the world profoundly and improve major world problems. Of course, "the world" does not spend this money or choose how to direct it; states do. World military spending decreased by about one-third overall in the 1990s, although it slowly began to increase again after 1998 and has jumped back up by one-quarter since 2001.

Arms imports by states of the global South make up more than half of all arms sales. In recent years, about half of the South's arms imports have been in the Middle East, where oil exports create a ready source of funding, but in 2004 India and China took a larger share. Worldwide, the top arms exporter is the United States and the top three—the United States, Russia, and Britain—together account for three-quarters of international arms sales. Still, globally, arms sales have declined in the post–Cold War era.

Activists have called attention to the sales of small arms, especially assault rifles, to unstable conflict zones where irregular armies commit brutalities. In 2001, 140 states agreed to a voluntary pact to curb small-arms sales to conflict zones. The United States, by far the largest exporter of small arms, blocked proposals to restrict sales of military weapons to rebel movements and to civilians. In 2006 the UN General Assembly voted to begin work on an Arms Trade Treaty, although the United States opposed it and its success is doubtful.

THE WAR IS OVER

U.S. and Russian nuclear forces were greatly reduced in the 1990s. Here, U.S. B-52 bombers are being chopped up, under the eye of Russian satellites, to bring force levels down.

Control of Military Forces

Although militaries are instruments of state power, in many states the military forces themselves control the government. These **military governments** are mostly in the global South, where the military may be the only large modern institution in a country. A **coup d'état** is the seizure of political power by domestic military forces—a change of political power outside the state's constitutional order. In late 2008, military leaders took control of Guinea after the death of the civilian president. Coup leaders move quickly to seize centers of power—official state buildings as well as television stations and transmitters—before other units of the military can put down the coup attempt or unleash a civil war. Civilian politicians in power and uncooperative military officers are arrested or killed. The coup leaders try to create a sense of inevitability around the change in government while claiming their actions will bring long-term stability.

Even in nonmilitary governments, the interaction of civilian with military leaders—called *civil-military relations*—is an important factor in how states use force. Military officers want autonomy of decision once force is committed, in order to avoid the problems created in the Vietnam War when President Johnson sat in the

HIGHLY IRREGULAR

A coup is a change of government carried out by domestic military forces operating outside the state's constitution. The number of military governments is declining, but dozens remain. Here, tanks guard a highway in Bangkok, Thailand, after a coup in 2006.

White House situation room daily picking targets for bombing raids. Worse yet, in NATO's 1999 bombing of Serbia, specific targets had to be approved by politicians in multiple countries.

Covert operations can also get out of the control of governments. Several thousand such operations were mounted during the Cold War, when the CIA and its Soviet counterpart, the KGB, waged an ongoing worldwide secret war. CIA covert operations in the 1950s overthrew unfriendly foreign governments in Iran and Guatemala by organizing coups against them. The CIA-organized Bay of Pigs invasion in Cuba, in 1961, was its first big failure, followed by other failed efforts against the Castro government (including eight assassination attempts). CIA covert activities were sharply scaled back after congressional hearings in the 1970s revealed scandals. Such covert operations now must be reported to special congressional *oversight* committees through an elaborate set of procedures. After September 2001, the executive branch enjoyed greater authority in conducting covert operations without congressional scrutiny, although the limits returned after Democrats won Congress in 2006.

Another factor in controlling military forces is the increasing reliance on private companies to provide services that militaries themselves used to provide, such as logistical support, maintaining bases, and even bodyguards and virtual private armies that operate in war zones. In the U.S. operation in Iraq, a very large contract with the company Halliburton came under criticism, and investigators found financial problems with the operation. Private contractors do not necessarily follow military discipline, nor the laws of either their home or host governments.

Overall, states face complex choices regarding the configuration of their military forces. Yet, despite the threat of conflict or war and the importance of security concerns, trade, money, and business are playing more and more powerful roles in international relations. In the next chapter we move to a discussion of the politics of international economic activities, the world monetary system, and the role of private companies as nonstate actors in the world economy.

CHAPTER REVIEW

SUMMARY

- Wars vary greatly in size and character, from guerrilla wars and raids to hegemonic war for leadership of the international system. Currently 13 wars are in progress, mostly small to intermediate size, all pitting a regular state army against local rebels or militias.

- Many theories have been offered as general explanations of the causes of war, but political scientists cannot reliably predict the outbreak of war.

- Ethnic conflicts, especially when linked with territorial disputes, are very difficult to resolve because of psychological biases.

- Fundamentalist religious movements pose a broad challenge to the rules of the international system in general and state sovereignty in particular.

- Territorial disputes are among the most serious international conflicts because states place great value on territorial integrity. With a few exceptions, however, almost all the world's borders are now firmly fixed and internationally recognized.

- Military spending tends to stimulate economic growth in the short term but reduce growth over the long term. In the 1990s, military forces and expenditures of the great powers—especially Russia—were reduced and restructured. Since then U.S. defense spending has risen back to Cold War–era levels.

- Control of territory is fundamental to state sovereignty and is accomplished primarily with ground forces.

- Air war, using precision-guided bombs against battlefield targets, proved extremely effective in the U.S. campaigns in Iraq in 1991, Serbia in 1999, Afghanistan in 2001, and Iraq in 2003.

- A "revolution in military affairs" uses new information technologies to enhance the power of small units.

- The 2001 attacks differed from earlier terrorism both in their scale of destruction and in the long reach of the global al Qaeda terrorist network.

- The production of nuclear weapons is technically within the means of many states and some nonstate actors, but the necessary fissionable material (uranium-235 or plutonium) is very difficult to obtain. Most industrialized states, and many poor ones, have refrained voluntarily from acquiring nuclear weapons.

- Slowing the proliferation of ballistic missiles and weapons of mass destruction in the global South is a central concern of the great powers.

- The United States is testing systems to defend against ballistic missile attack, although none has yet proven feasible, and withdrew from the ABM treaty with Russia to pursue this program.

- The United States and Russia have arsenals of thousands of nuclear weapons; China, Britain, and France have hundreds; Israel, India, and Pakistan each have scores.
- North Korea apparently has a half-dozen nuclear weapons and tested one in 2006. Iran appears to be moving forward to develop them. Iran's case was referred to the UN Security Council in 2006.

KEY TERMS

hegemonic war   110
total war   110
limited war   110
civil war   112
guerrilla war   112
truth commissions   113
conflict   113
nationalism   116
ethnic groups   117
genocide   119
ethnocentrism   120
secular   122
Islam   122
Muslims   122
Islamist   122
irredentism   132
ethnic cleansing   134
territorial waters   136

airspace   137
counterinsurgency   140
land mines   142
power projection   143
electronic warfare   146
state-sponsored
    terrorism   149
weapons of mass
    destruction   149
fusion weapons   150
fissionable material   150
ballistic missiles   151
intercontinental
    ballistic missiles
    (ICBMs)   151
cruise missile   151
Missile Technology
    Control Regime   152

Chemical Weapons
    Convention   153
Biological Weapons
    Convention   154
proliferation   154
Non-Proliferation Treaty
    (NPT)   156
mutually assured destruc-
    tion (MAD)   156
Strategic Defense
    Initiative (SDI)   157
Comprehensive Test Ban
    Treaty (CTBT)   158
military
    governments   159
coup d'état   159

ONLINE PRACTICE TEST

Take an online practice test at
www.IRtext.com

❏ A
❏ B
❏ C
❏ D

CRITICAL THINKING QUESTIONS

1. How many of the six types of international conflict discussed in this chapter can you connect with the phenomenon of nationalism discussed on pp. 116–117? What are the connections in each case?

2. The rise of fundamentalism among the world's major religions challenges traditional notions of state sovereignty. How might this trend strengthen, or weaken, the United Nations and other attempts to create supranational authority (which also challenge state sovereignty)?

3. Most of the great powers are reconfiguring their military forces in the post–Cold War era. What kinds of capabilities do you think your own country needs in this period? Why?

BACK TO THE BIG PICTURE

To hear a discussion of the "big picture" for this chapter, raised on p. 110, along with an example from recent history, consult the "IR Talk" podcast for Chapter 4 at *www.IRtext.com*

PODCAST

Paris stock market display, October 2008.

CHAPTER 5

Trade and Finance

CHAPTER OUTLINE

- Theories of Trade

- Trade Regimes

- Economic Globalization

- Globalization, Financial Markets, and the Currency System

- State Financial Positions

- Multinational Business

Theories of Trade

International trade amounts to about a sixth of the total economic activity in the world. About $17 trillion worth of goods and services cross international borders each year.[1] This is a very large number, about 12 times the world's military spending. The great volume of international trade reflects the fact that trade is profitable.

The role of trade in the economy varies somewhat from one nation to another, but overall, it is at least as important in the global South as in the industrialized North. Although the global South accounts for a relatively small part of all trade in the world economy, this is because its economic activity itself is only 40 percent of the world total (see p. 26).

Trade is not only an economic issue but a highly political one. It crosses state-defined borders, is regulated by states that are pressured by interest groups, and occurs within trade regimes maintained and negotiated among states.

Scholars of *international political economy (IPE)* study the politics of international economic activities. The most frequently studied of these

---

[1] Data in this chapter are calculated from World Trade Organization statistics; and United Nations. *World Economic and Social Survey 2006: Trends and Policies in the World Economy.* United Nations.

THE BIG PICTURE

RECIPROCITY

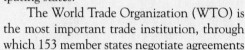

How do countries gain the great wealth created from international trade without getting stuck on their conflicting interests? Trade is a collective goods problem, and reciprocity is the primary principle used to solve it. States negotiate, through institutions they have created for this purpose, complex trade deals based on reciprocal benefits to the participating states.

The World Trade Organization (WTO) is the most important trade institution, through which 153 member states negotiate agreements and resolve disputes about their implementation. The WTO operates by consensus so every member is equal and all must approve a deal for any of them to enjoy its benefits. That this works at all shows the strength of the principle of reciprocity in IPE.

To hear the authors of this book discuss this issue, with an example from recent history, download the "IR Talk" podcast for Chapter 5 from www.IRtext.com.

PODCAST

activities are trade, monetary relations, and multinational corporations. Most scholars of IPE focus on the industrialized regions of the world, where most of the world's economic activity occurs. However, the global South has received growing attention as globalization integrates parts of the South into the world economy more intensely (see Chapter 7).

The core principles laid out in Chapter 1 and the concepts of power and bargaining developed initially in Chapter 2 apply to IPE. States are the most important actors in IPE, but not as important as in international security. Actors in IPE, as in security affairs, tend to act in their own interests. As Brazil's foreign minister explained in 2001, his country shared with the United States the same guiding principle in negotiating a hemisphere-wide free trade area: "What's in it for us?"

Liberalism and Mercantilism

Two major approaches within IPE differ on their views of trade. One approach, called **mercantilism,** generally shares with realism the belief that each state must protect its own interests at the expense of others—not relying on international organizations to create a framework for mutual gains. Mercantilists therefore emphasize relative power (as do realists): what matters is not so much a state's absolute amount of well-being as its position relative to rival states.

In addition, mercantilism (like realism) holds that the importance of economic transactions lies in their implications for the military. States worry about relative wealth and trade because these can be translated directly into military power. Thus, although military power is generally not useful in economic negotiations, mercantilists believe that the outcome of economic negotiations matters for military power.

Economic liberalism, an alternative approach, generally shares with liberal internationalism a belief in the possibility of cooperation to realize common gains (see pp. 6–7 and pp. 66–67). It holds that by building international organizations, institutions, and

VIDEO

Resource Wars in the Congo

norms, states can mutually benefit from economic exchanges. It matters little to liberals whether one state gains more or less than another—just whether the state's wealth is increasing in *absolute* terms.

Liberalism and mercantilism are *theories* of economics and also *ideologies* that shape state policies. Liberalism is the dominant approach in Western economics, though more so in *microeconomics* (the study of firms and households) than in *macroeconomics* (the study of national economies). Marxism is often treated as a third theoretical/ideological approach to IPE, along with mercantilism and liberalism (see Chapter 3). Marxist approaches are attuned to economic exploitation as a force that shapes political relations. Chapter 7 explores Marxist theories in depth, as they find their greatest explanatory power in North-South relations.

Most international economic exchanges (as well as security relationships) contain some element of mutual interests—joint gains that can be realized through cooperation—and some element of conflicting interests. Game theorists call this a "mixed interest" game. In international trade, even when two states both benefit from a trade (a shared interest), one or the other will benefit more (a conflicting interest). Liberalism emphasizes the shared interests in economic exchanges, whereas mercantilism emphasizes the conflicting interests. For liberals, the most important goal of economic policy is to create a maximum of total wealth by achieving optimal *efficiency* (maximizing output, minimizing waste). For mercantilists, the most important goal is to create the most favorable possible *distribution* of wealth.

Liberalism sees individual households and firms as the key actors in the economy and views government's most useful role as one of noninterference in economics except to regulate markets in order to help them function efficiently (and to create infrastructure such as roads, which also help the economy function efficiently). Politics, in this view, should serve the interests of economic efficiency. With the hand of government removed from markets, the "invisible hand" of supply and demand can work out the most efficient patterns of production, exchange, and consumption (through the mechanism of prices). Because of the benefits of **free trade** among countries, liberals disdain realists' obsession with international borders, because borders constrain the maximum efficiency of exchange.

When two or more states are simultaneously dependent on each other, they are *interdependent*. **Interdependence** is a political and not just an economic phenomenon. States that trade become mutually dependent on each other's *political* cooperation in order to realize economic gains through trade. In IPE, interdependence refers less often to a *bilateral* mutual dependence than to a *multilateral* dependence in which each state depends on the political cooperation of most or all of the others to keep world markets operating efficiently. Trade-based wealth depends on international political cooperation, and violence usually does not work well in pursuing such wealth. Thus, liberals argue that interdependence inherently promotes peace, an idea introduced earlier (pp. 70–72). (Then again, some observers saw similar trends in international interdependence just before World War I, but war occurred anyway.)

The distribution of benefits from trade may not be divided equally among participating states. Liberal economists are interested in maximizing the overall (joint) benefits from exchange, rather than how total benefits are distributed among the parties (see Figure 5.1).

FIGURE 5.1   Joint and Individual Benefits

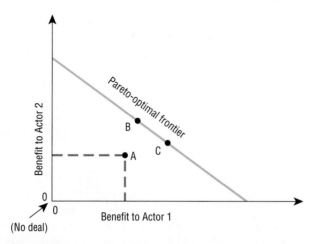

Any deal struck, such as at point A, yields certain benefits to each actor (dotted lines). Joint benefits are maximized at the Pareto-optimal frontier, but the distribution of those benefits, as between points B and C (both of which are better than A for both actors), is a matter for bargaining. Liberalism is more concerned with joint benefits, mercantilism more with the relative distribution.

Mercantilists' preferred means of making trade serve a state's political interests—even at the cost of some lost wealth that free markets might have created—is to create a favorable balance of trade. The **balance of trade** is the value of a state's imports relative to its exports. A state that exports more than it imports has a *positive balance of trade*, or *trade surplus*. A state that imports more than it exports has a *negative balance of trade* (*trade deficit*). A trade deficit is different from a budget deficit in government spending. Since the late 1990s, the U.S. trade deficit has grown steadily to hundreds of billions of dollars per year, more than $800 billion in 2008, with about a quarter (and more each year) accounted for by China and another quarter by oil imports. China has run a large trade surplus for years, passing $250 billion per year (see Figure 5.2).

States must ultimately reconcile the balance of trade. It is tracked financially through the system of national accounts (see p. 198). In the short term, a state can trade for a few years at a deficit and then for a few years at a surplus. The imbalances are carried on the national accounts as a kind of loan. But a trade deficit that persists for years becomes a problem. In recent years, to balance its trade deficit, the United States has "exported" currency (dollars) to China, Japan, Europe, and other countries, which use the dollars to buy such things as shares of U.S. companies, U.S. Treasury bills, or U.S. real estate. Economists worry that if foreigners lose their taste for investments in the United States, the U.S. economy could suffer.

This is one reason why mercantilists favor national economic policies to create a trade surplus. Then, rather than being unable to find the money it might need to cope

FIGURE 5.2   China's Growing Trade Surplus

Source: *New York Times* 9/12/06: U.S. Census, *Foreign Trade Statistics.*

with a crisis or fight a war, the state sits on a pile of money representing potential power. Historically, mercantilism literally meant stockpiling gold (gained from running a trade surplus) as a fungible form of power (see Figure 5.3). Such a strategy is attuned to realism's emphasis on relative power. For one state to have a trade surplus, another must have a deficit. With the global recession in 2009, world leaders eyed each other warily to see if mercantilism would again make a comeback.

Comparative Advantage

The overall success of liberal economics is due to the substantial gains that can be realized through trade. These gains result from the **comparative advantage** that different states enjoy in producing different goods (a concept pioneered by economists Adam Smith and David Ricardo 200 years ago). States differ in their abilities to produce certain goods because of differences in natural resources, labor force characteristics, technology, and other such factors. In order to maximize the overall creation of wealth, each state should specialize in producing the goods for which it has a comparative advantage and then trade for goods that another state produces best. Of course,

FIGURE 5.3   Balance of Trade

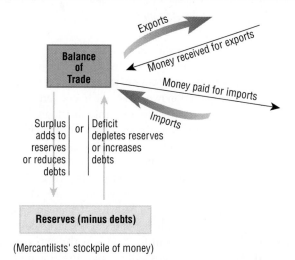

the costs of transportation and of processing the information in the trade (called *transaction costs*) must be included in the costs of producing an item. But increasingly, as globalization proceeds, both of these are low relative to the differences in the cost of producing items in different locations.

Two commodities of great importance in the world are oil and cars. It is much cheaper to produce oil (or another energy source) in Saudi Arabia than in Japan, and much cheaper to produce cars in Japan than in Saudi Arabia. Japan needs oil to run its industry (including its car industry), and Saudi Arabia needs cars to travel its vast territory (including reaching its remote oil wells). Even with shipping and transaction costs, shipping Japanese cars to Saudi Arabia and Saudi oil to Japan saves a huge amount of money, compared to the costs if each tried to be self-reliant.

A state need not have an absolute advantage (that is, be the most efficient producer in the world) in producing one kind of good to make specialization pay. It need only specialize in producing goods that are relatively lower in cost than other goods. Imagine that Japan discovered a way to produce synthetic oil using the same mix of labor and capital that it now uses to produce cars, and that this synthetic oil could be produced a bit more cheaply than what it costs Saudi Arabia to produce oil, but that Japan could still produce cars *much* more cheaply than can Saudi Arabia. It might seem intuitive that Japan should produce synthetic oil rather than pay extra for Saudi oil. But this is wrong. From a strictly economic point of view, Japan should keep producing cars (where it has a huge comparative advantage) and not divert capital and labor to make synthetic oil (where it has only a slight advantage). The extra profits Japan would make from exporting more cars would more than compensate for the slightly higher price it would pay to import oil.

Thus, international trade allocates global resources to states that have the greatest comparative advantage in producing each kind of commodity. As a result, prices are both lower overall and more consistent worldwide. Increasingly, production is oriented to the world market.

The economic benefits of trade, however, come with some political drawbacks. First, long-term benefits may incur short-term costs. When a state begins to import goods that it had been producing domestically, its economy may be disrupted; workers may need to retrain and find new jobs, and capital may not be easy to convert to new uses.

Also, the benefits and costs tend to be unevenly distributed *within* a state. Some industries or communities may benefit at the expense of others. For example, if a U.S. manufacturing company moves its factory to Mexico to take advantage of cheaper labor there and exports its goods back to the United States, the workers at the old U.S. factory lose their jobs, but U.S. consumers enjoy cheaper goods. The costs of such a move fall heavily on a few workers, but the benefits are spread thinly across many consumers. This kind of unequal distribution of costs and benefits often creates political problems for free trade even when the *overall* economic benefits outweigh the costs. Worker or industry interest groups (see pp. 180–182) will form against the concentrated costs (losing jobs) far more often than consumer groups will form against the diffuse losses (such as a $20 increase for many).

Political Interference in Markets

A free and efficient market requires many buyers and sellers with fairly complete information about the market. Also, the willingness of participants to deal with each other should not be distorted by personal (or political) preferences but should be governed only by price and quality considerations. Deviation from these conditions, called *market imperfections*, reduce efficiency.

International trade occurs more often at world market prices than does *domestic* economic exchange. No world government owns industries, provides subsidies, or regulates prices. Nonetheless, world markets are often affected by politics. When states are the principal actors in international economic affairs, the number of participants is often small. When there is just one supplier of an item—a *monopoly*—the supplier can set the price quite high. An *oligopoly* is a monopoly shared by just a few large sellers—often allowing for tacit or explicit coordination to force the price up. To the extent that companies band together along national lines, monopolies and oligopolies are more likely.

Another common market imperfection in international trade is *corruption;* individuals may receive payoffs to trade at nonmarket prices. The government or company involved may lose some of the benefits being distributed, but the individual government official or company negotiator gets increased benefits (see p. 289). Politics provides a *legal framework* for markets—ensuring that participants keep their commitments, buyers pay for goods they purchase, counterfeit money is not used, and so forth. As in security affairs, rules can be codified in international treaties, but enforcement depends on practical reciprocity (see pp. 242–243).

Taxation is another political influence on markets. Taxes generate revenue for the government and regulate economic activity by incentives. For instance, a government may keep taxes low on foreign companies in hopes of attracting them to locate and invest in the country. Taxes applied to international trade itself, called *tariffs*, are a frequent source of international conflict (see p. 173).

Sanctions   Political interference in free markets is most explicit when governments apply *sanctions* against economic interactions of certain kinds or between certain actors. Political power then prohibits an economic exchange that would otherwise have been mutually beneficial. In 2009, the United States had trade restrictions on 13 states in response to those states' political actions, such as human rights violations.

Enforcing sanctions is always a difficult task, because participants have a financial incentive to break the sanctions through black markets or other means. Without broad, multilateral support for international sanctions, they generally fail. Refusing to participate in mutually profitable economic trade often harms oneself more than the target of one's actions, unless nearly all other states follow suit (note that enforcement of sanctions is a form of the collective goods problem).

Autarky   One obvious way to avoid becoming dependent on other states, especially for a weak state whose trading partners would tend to be more powerful, is to avoid trading and instead try to produce everything it needs by itself. Such a strategy is called *self-reliance* or **autarky.** As the theory of comparative advantage suggests, such a policy has proven ineffective. A self-reliant state pays a very high cost to produce goods for which it does not have a comparative advantage. As other states cooperate among themselves to maximize their joint creation of wealth, the relative power of the autarkic state in the international system tends to fall.

China's experience illustrates the problems with autarky. China's economic isolation in the 1950s and 1960s, resulting from an economic embargo imposed by the United States and its allies, deepened during its Cultural Revolution in the late 1960s

PLAY BALL

Economic sanctions, such as the U.S. restrictions on trade with Cuba, are among the most obvious ways that politics interferes in markets. But sanctions are hard to enforce, especially when not all countries participate, because doing business is profitable. The U.S. government first tried to exclude Cuba from the World Baseball Classic in 2006 but backed down after strong complaints from other countries that do not apply sanctions to Cuba. Here, Japan's Ichiro Suzuki and Cuban players celebrate after Japan beat Cuba in the championship game in San Diego.

when it broke ties with the Soviet Union as well. In that period, China rejected all things foreign. When China opened up to the world economy in the 1980s, the pattern reversed. The rapid expansion of trade, along with some market-oriented reforms in its domestic economy, resulted in rapid economic growth.

Protectionism

Although few states pursue strategies of autarky, many states try to manipulate international trade to strengthen one or more domestic industries and shelter them from world markets. Such policies are broadly known as **protectionism**—protection of domestic industries from international competition. Although this term encompasses a variety of trade policies arising from various motivations, all are contrary to liberalism in that they seek to distort free markets to gain an advantage for the state (or for substate actors within it), generally by discouraging imports of competing goods or services.

A state's motivation to protect domestic industry can arise from several sources. Often governments simply cater to the political demands of important domestic industries and interests, regardless of the overall national interest. An industry may lobby or give campaign contributions in order to win special tax breaks, subsidies, or restrictions on competing imports (see pp. 202–204). Sometimes, states attempt to protect an *infant industry* as it starts up in the state for the first time, until it can compete on world markets. Another motivation for protection is to give a domestic industry breathing room when market conditions shift or new competitors arrive on the scene.

Governments also protect industries considered vital to national security. In the 1980s, U.S. officials sought to protect the U.S. electronics and computer industries against being driven out of business by Japanese competitors, because those industries were considered crucial to military production. The government sponsored a consortium of U.S. computer chip companies to promote the

KING COTTON

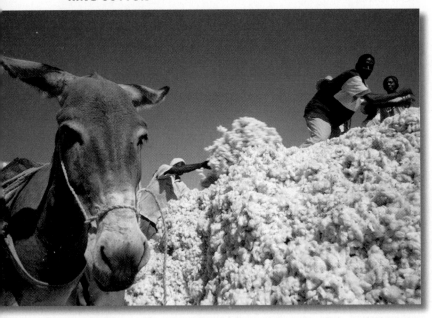

Protectionism uses various means to keep foreign imports from competing with domestic products. Agricultural producers in the global South complain that subsidies and other protectionist measures in Europe and the United States prevent poor farmers in developing countries from exporting to world markets. Here, cotton awaits processing in Mali, where low prices for cotton, the country's most important cash crop, have hurt farmers badly (2006).

U.S. capability to produce chips cheaply (ordinarily the government would discourage such a consortium as an antitrust violation). Autarky may not pay in most economic activities, but for military goods, states will sacrifice some economic efficiency for the sake of self-sufficiency, to reduce vulnerability in the event of war.

Finally, protection may be motivated by a defensive effort to ward off predatory practices by foreign companies or states. *Predatory* generally refers to efforts to unfairly capture a large share of world markets, or even a near-monopoly, so that eventually the predator can raise prices without fearing competition. Most often these efforts entail **dumping** products in foreign markets at prices below the minimum necessary to make a profit. Great disagreements occur about whether a given price level is predatory or merely competitive. These conflicts now generally are resolved through the WTO (see pp. 174–178).

Just as there are several motivations for protectionism, so too governments use several tools to implement this policy. The simplest is a **tariff** (or *duty*)—a tax imposed on certain types of imported goods, usually as a percentage of their value, as they enter the country. Tariffs not only restrict imports but also can be an important source of state revenues. If a state is to engage in protectionism, international norms favor tariffs as the preferred method of protection because they are straightforward and not hidden (see pp. 174–176). Most states maintain a long, complex list of tariffs on thousands of categories of goods.

Other means to discourage imports are **nontariff barriers** to trade. Imports can be limited by a *quota*. Quotas are ceilings on how many goods of a certain kind can be imported; they are imposed to restrict the growth of such imports. The extreme version is a flat prohibition against importing a certain type of good (or goods from a certain country). The U.S. government used quotas to restrict the number of Japanese-made cars that could enter the United States in the 1980s, when the U.S. automobile industry was losing ground rapidly to Japanese imports. Most of those quotas were *voluntary* in that Japan and the United States negotiated a level that both could live with.

A more complex nontariff barrier is to give *subsidies* to a domestic industry, which allow it to lower its prices without losing money. Such subsidies are extensive in, but not limited to, state-owned industries. Subsidies to an industry struggling to get established or facing strong foreign competition include *tax breaks*, *loans* (or guarantee private loans) on favorable terms, and high *guaranteed prices* paid by governments. Subsidies to farmers have been the major sticking point between rich and poor countries in the Doha Round trade talks, and are a frequent source of U.S.-European conflict.

Imports can also be restricted by *regulations* that make it hard to distribute and market a product even when it can be imported. In marketing U.S. products in Japan, U.S. manufacturers complain of complex bureaucratic regulations and a tight system of corporate alliances funneling the supply of parts from Japanese suppliers to Japanese manufacturers. Environmental and labor regulations can function as nontariff barriers as well. This has caused great controversy in the WTO, such as when Europe banned genetically modified crops that happened to come mostly from the United States. Finally, when a state nationalizes an entire industry, such as oil production or banking, foreign competition is shut out.

VIDEO

**Dubai Ports
Deal Fallout**

Sometimes a country's culture, rather than state action, discourages imports. Citizens may (with or without government encouragement) follow a philosophy of *economic nationalism*—use of economics to influence international power and relative standing in the international system (a form of mercantilism). For example, U.S. citizens sometimes ignore the advice of liberal economists to buy the best product at the best price, and instead "buy American" even if it means paying a bit more for an equivalent product. Although such a bias reduces the overall efficiency of world production, it does benefit U.S. workers.

Protectionism has both positive and negative effects on an economy, most often helping producers but hurting consumers. Another problem with protectionism is that domestic industry may use protection to avoid needed improvements and may therefore remain inefficient and uncompetitive—especially if protection continues over many years.

Trade Regimes

As information technologies link the world across space, a global integration process based on free trade is shaping the international economic agenda. The World Trade Organization plays the central role in this process.

The World Trade Organization

The **World Trade Organization (WTO)** is a global, multilateral IGO that promotes, monitors, and adjudicates international trade. Together with the regional and bilateral arrangements described shortly, the WTO shapes the overall expectations and practices of states regarding international trade. The WTO is the successor organization to the **General Agreement on Tariffs and Trade (GATT),** which was created in 1947 to facilitate freer trade on a multilateral basis. The GATT was more of a negotiating framework than an administrative institution. It did not actually regulate trade. Before the GATT, proposals for a stronger institutional agency had been rejected because of U.S. fears that overregulation would stifle free trade. In addition to its main role as a negotiating forum, the GATT helped arbitrate trade disputes, clarifying the rules and helping states observe them.

In 1995, the GATT became the WTO, which incorporated the GATT agreements on manufactured goods and extended the agenda to include trade in services and intellectual property. The WTO has some powers of enforcement and an international bureaucracy (600 people), which monitors trade policies and practices in each member state and adjudicates disputes among members. The WTO wields some power over states, but as with many international institutions, this power is limited. An ongoing public backlash against free trade (see pp. 187–188) reflects uneasiness about the potential power of a foreign and secretive organization to force changes in democratically passed national laws. But the WTO is the central international institution governing trade and therefore one that almost all countries want to participate in and develop.

Over time, the membership of the WTO has grown. By 2009, 153 countries—almost all of the world's major trading states except Russia—had joined the WTO. In 2006, Russia and the United States reached an agreement expected to lead to Russia's admission in the coming years. Vietnam joined in 2007, and Ukraine in 2008. More than 25 states are seeking admission, the most important of which after Russia are Iran and Iraq. After more than a decade of contentious negotiations, China joined in 2001. The United States and other countries usually demand, as a condition of membership, liberalization of the trading practices of would-be members. These new practices have affected China's economic and political development (see pp. 280–283).

The WTO framework rests on the principle of reciprocity—matching states' lowering of trade barriers to one another. It also uses the concept of nondiscrimination, embodied in the **most-favored nation (MFN)** concept, which says that trade restrictions imposed by a WTO member on its most-favored trading partner must be applied equally to all WTO members. If Australia applies a 20 percent tariff on auto parts imported from France, it must not apply a 40 percent tariff on auto parts imported from the United States. Thus, the WTO does not get rid of barriers to trade altogether but equalizes them in a global framework to create a level playing field for all member states. States are not prevented from protecting their own industries but cannot play favorites among their trading partners. States may also extend MFN status to others that are not WTO members, as the United States did with China before it joined the WTO.

An exception to the MFN system is the **Generalized System of Preferences (GSP),** by which rich states give trade concessions to poor ones to help their economic development. Preferences amount to a promise by rich states to allow imports from poor ones under lower tariffs than those imposed under MFN.

The WTO continues the GATT's role as a negotiating forum for multilateral trade agreements that lower trade barriers on a fair and reciprocal basis. These detailed and complex agreements specify commitments to lower certain trade barriers by certain amounts on fixed schedules. Almost every commitment entails domestic political costs, because domestic industries lose protection against foreign competition. Even when other states agree to make similar commitments in other areas, lowering trade barriers is often hard for national governments.

As a result, negotiations on these multilateral agreements are long and difficult, typically stretching on for years in a *round of negotiations.* Among the five rounds of GATT negotiations from 1947 to 1995, the most important was the *Uruguay Round,* which started in 1986 in Uruguay. Although the rough outlines of a new GATT agreement emerged after a few years, closure eluded five successive G7 summit meetings in 1990–1994. A successful conclusion to the round would add more than $100 billion to the world economy annually. But that money was a collective good, to be enjoyed both by states that made concessions in the final negotiations and by those that did not. Agreement was finally reached in late 1994.

From 1947, the GATT encouraged states to use import tariffs rather than nontariff barriers to protect industries, and to lower those tariffs over time. The GATT concentrated on manufactured goods and succeeded in substantially reducing the average tariffs, from 40 percent of the goods' value decades ago to 3 percent by 2002 (under the Uruguay Round agreement). Tariff rates in the global South are much higher, around 30 percent (reflecting the greater protection that industry there apparently needs).

Agricultural trade is politically more sensitive than trade in manufactured goods and came into play only in the Uruguay Round. Trade in services, such as banking and insurance, is another current major focus of the WTO. Such trade approached one-fifth of the total value of world trade in 2007. Trade in telecommunications is a related area of interest. In 1997, 70 states negotiating through the WTO agreed on a treaty to allow telecommunications companies to enter each other's markets.

The problems in expanding into these and other sensitive areas became obvious at a 1999 Seattle WTO conference, where trade ministers had hoped to launch a new post-Uruguay round of trade negotiations. Representatives of poor countries argued that they needed trade to raise incomes and could not meet the standards of industrialized countries (which, after all, had allowed low wages, harsh working conditions, and environmental destruction when *they* began industrializing). Environmental and labor activists, joined by window-smashing anarchists, staged street protests that delayed the conference opening by a day. The meeting ended in failure.

Recovering from Seattle, in 2001 trade ministers meeting in Doha, Qatar, agreed to launch a new round of trade negotiations, the **Doha Round.** The issues under negotiation include agriculture, services, industrial products, intellectual property, WTO rules (including how to handle antidumping cases), dispute settlement, and some trade and environmental questions. WTO members worked to conclude the Doha Round before President Bush's congressional "fast-track" authorization (which commits Congress to vote on trade deals in full without amending them) expired in July 2007. But no agreement materialized and the deadline passed. The main obstacle remains the resistance of the industrialized West to cut agricultural subsidies as demanded by countries in the global South.

In general, states continue to participate in the WTO because the benefits, in terms of global wealth creation, outweigh the costs, in terms of harm to domestic industries and painful adjustments in national economies. States try to change the rules in their favor during the rounds of negotiations (never with complete success), and between rounds they may evade the rules in minor ways. But the overall benefits are too great to jeopardize by nonparticipation or by allowing frequent trade wars to occur.

Bilateral and Regional Agreements

Although the WTO provides an overall framework for multilateral trade in a worldwide market, most international trade also takes place in more specific international agreements—bilateral trade agreements and regional free trade areas.

Bilateral Agreements   Bilateral treaties covering trade are reciprocal arrangements to lower barriers to trade between two states. Usually they are very specific. For instance, one country may reduce its prohibition on imports on product X (which the second country exports at competitive prices) while the second country lowers its tariff on product Y (which the first country exports). A sweeping agreement, such as the new U.S.-Korean free trade deal or that between Canada and India in 2007, generally contains mind-numbing levels of detail concerning specific industries and products.

As with most agreements based on the reciprocity principle, trade treaties involve great complexity and constant monitoring.

Part of the idea behind the GATT/WTO was to strip away the maze of bilateral agreements on trade and simplify the system of tariffs and preferences. This effort has only partially succeeded. Bilateral trade agreements continue to play an important role. They have the advantages of reducing the collective goods problem inherent in multilateral negotiations and facilitating reciprocity as a means to achieve cooperation. When WTO negotiations bog down, bilateral agreements can keep trade momentum going.

Free Trade Areas   Regional free trade areas also matter in the structure of world trade. In such areas, groups of neighboring states agree to remove most or all trade barriers within their area. Beyond free trade areas, states may reduce trade barriers *and* adopt a common tariff toward states that are not members of the agreement. This is known as a *customs union*. If members of a customs union decide to coordinate other policies such as monetary exchange, the customs union becomes a *common market*. The creation of a regional trade agreement (of any type) allows a group of states to cooperate in increasing their wealth without waiting for the rest of the world.

The most important free trade area is in Europe; it is connected with the European Union but has a somewhat larger membership. Europe contains a number of small industrialized states living close together, so the creation of a single integrated market allows these states to gain the economic advantages that come inherently to a large state such as the United States. The European free trade experiment has been a great success overall, contributing to Europe's accumulation of wealth (see Chapter 6).

The United States, Canada, and Mexico signed the **North American Free Trade Agreement (NAFTA)** in 1994, following a U.S.-Canadian free trade agreement in 1988. In NAFTA's first decade, U.S. imports from both Mexico and Canada more than doubled, then fell back somewhat (after 1999). Canada and Mexico were the largest and third-largest U.S. trading partners, respectively (Japan was second). Initially, Mexico's currency dropped drastically relative to the dollar in 1994–1995. But over 15 years, neither the great benefits predicted by NAFTA supporters nor the disasters predicted by opponents have materialized.

Politicians in North and South America have long spoken of creating a single free trade area in the Western Hemisphere, from Alaska to Argentina—the *Free Trade Area of the Americas (FTAA)*. After President Bush won fast-track authority from Congress, FTAA negotiations began in 2003 with a target date of 2005. But by then several factors had created pressures against the FTAA. The 2001 recession and post–September 11 security measures reduced trade; China provided U.S. companies with a better source of cheap labor; and left-leaning governments, wary of liberal economic advice, came to power in most of the Latin American countries. Those countries cared most about tariff-free trade, while the U.S. position emphasized a range of other issues such as services, intellectual property, and financial openness. In late 2005, trade talks failed at a summit meeting in Argentina, where one participant, Venezuelan president Hugo Chavez, led a 25,000-person anti-American rally in the streets. Currently, the FTAA talks remain in hibernation, and the weight of trade negotiations fall to the Doha Round. Meanwhile, however, the United States reached free trade agreements with Chile and with five Central American countries.

Efforts to create a free trade area in Asia began in the late 1980s but moved slowly. Unlike the European and North American arrangements, an Asian bloc would include very different kinds of states—rich ones such as Japan, poor ones such as the Philippines; and democracies, dictatorships, and communist states. It is unclear how well such diverse states could coordinate their common interests, especially because their existing trade patterns are not focused on each other but spread out among other states including the United States. But despite these problems, in 2007 the ten ASEAN countries met with China, Japan, India, Australia, and New Zealand to begin negotiating an East Asian free trade area. The group, unlike some other Asia-Pacific IGOs, does not include the United States, but it does include half the world's population and some of its most dynamic economies. If the concept succeeds, it will create a third great regional trading bloc after the European Union and the North American (or future all-American) free trade area.

The Southern Cone Common Market (Mercosur) began in the early 1990s with Brazil, Argentina, Uruguay, and Paraguay. Venezuela later joined. Chile, Bolivia, Colombia, Ecuador, and Peru have joined as associate members. Still, Mercosur members trade more with the United States than they do with each other. In 2002, the countries agreed to allow their 250 million citizens free movement and residency across countries. Other agreements exist in Latin America, but none have been particularly successful at increasing trade or growth.

If regional free trade areas such as those in Europe and North America gain strength and new ones arise, the WTO may be weakened. The more that states meet the political requirements of economic growth through bilateral and regional agreements, the less they may depend on the worldwide agreements developed through the WTO.

Cartels

A **cartel** is an association of producers or consumers, or both, of a certain product—formed to manipulate its price on the world market. It is an unusual but interesting form of trade regime. Most often producers and not consumers form cartels, because there are usually fewer producers than consumers, and it seems possible for them to coordinate to keep prices high. Cartels can use a variety of means to affect prices; the most effective is to coordinate limits on production by each member so as to lower the supply, relative to demand, of the good.

The most prominent cartel in the international economy is the **Organization of Petroleum Exporting Countries (OPEC).** Its member states together control hundreds of billions of dollars in oil exports annually—about 40 percent of the world total and enough to significantly affect the price. (A cartel need not hold a monopoly on production of a good to affect its price.) At OPEC's peak of strength in the 1970s, the proportion was even higher. OPEC maintains a headquarters in Vienna, Austria, and holds negotiations several times a year to set quotas for each country's production of oil in order to keep world oil prices in a target range. Saudi Arabia is by far the largest oil exporter and therefore occupies a unique position in the world economy (see Table 5.1).

TABLE 5.1   OPEC Members and Oil Production, December 2008

Member State	Millions of Barrels/Day
Saudi Arabia	8.7
Iran	3.9
United Arab Emirates	2.6
Kuwait	2.5
Venezuela	2.4
Iraq	2.3
Nigeria	1.9
Angola	1.9
Libya	1.7
Algeria	1.4
Indonesia	0.9
Qatar	0.8
Ecuador[a]	0.5
Total OPEC	31.0
Percent of World	40%

[a]Ecuador re-joined OPEC in 2007 after suspending its membership in 1992.

Note: Major oil exporters not in OPEC include Russia, Kazakhstan, Mexico, China, Britain, and Norway. Gabon left OPEC in 1995. The United States, until several decades ago a major oil exporter, is now a major importer.

Source: Data adapted from Middle East Economic Survey. www.mees.com/Energy_Tables/crude-oil.htm.

OPEC illustrates the potential that a cartel creates for collective goods problems. Individual members of OPEC can cheat by exceeding their production quotas while still enjoying the collective good of high oil prices. The collective good breaks down when too many members exceed their quotas, as has happened repeatedly to OPEC. Then world oil prices drop. (Iraq's accusations that fellow OPEC member Kuwait was exceeding production quotas and driving oil prices down was one factor in Iraq's invasion of Kuwait in 1990.)

OPEC may work as well as it does only because one member, Saudi Arabia, has enough oil to unilaterally manipulate supply enough to drive prices up or down—a form of hegemonic stability (see p. 5) within the cartel. Saudi Arabia can take up the slack from some cheating in OPEC (cutting back its own production) and keep prices up. Or if too many OPEC members are cheating on their quotas, it can punish them by flooding the market with oil and driving prices down until the other OPEC members collectively come to their senses.

In general, the idea of cartels runs counter to liberal economics because cartels deliberately distort free markets. Cartels usually are not as powerful as market forces in determining overall world price levels: too many producers and suppliers exist, and too many substitute goods can replace ones that become too expensive, for a cartel to corner the market.

Industries and Interest Groups

Industries and other domestic political actors often seek to influence a state's foreign economic policies (see pp. 73–74). These pressures do not always favor protectionism. Industries that are advanced and competitive in world markets try to influence their governments to adopt free trade policies. This strategy promotes a global free trade system in which such industries can prosper. By contrast, industries that lag behind their global competitors tend to seek government protection.

Means to influence foreign economic policy include lobbying, forming interest groups, paying bribes, and even encouraging coups. Actors include industry-sponsored groups, companies, labor unions, and individuals. Within an industry, such efforts usually work in a common direction because, despite competition among companies and between management and labor, all share common interests regarding the trade policies. However, a different industry may be pushing in a different direction. For instance, some U.S. industries support the North American Free Trade Agreement (NAFTA); others oppose it.

Interest groups not organized along industry lines also have particular interests in state trade policies. U.S. environmentalists, for example, do not want U.S. companies to use NAFTA to avoid pollution controls by relocating to Mexico (where environmental laws are less strict). U.S. labor unions do not want companies to use NAFTA to avoid paying high wages. However, Mexican American citizens' groups in the United States tend to support NAFTA because it strengthens ties to relatives in Mexico.

Several industries are particularly important in trade negotiations currently. Atop the list is the agricultural sector. Traditionally, agriculture has been protected since self-sufficiency in food reduces national vulnerability (especially in time of war). Although such security concerns have now faded somewhat, farmers are well-organized and powerful domestic political actors in Europe, the United States, Japan, and other countries. In the Doha Round of WTO negotiations that began in 2001, agricultural subsidies were a key sticking point. The talks collapsed in 2003 in Cancun, Mexico, over the subsidies, but were revived the next year after U.S. promises to cut farm subsidies 20 percent. At the 2005 Hong Kong talks, wealthy countries agreed to end all farm export subsidies by 2013.

Cotton Subsidies

Cambodian Textiles after Quotas

A second important focus in recent years has been the textile and garment sector. As of 2005, textile quotas worldwide were dropped as a part of previously negotiated WTO deals. At the same time, China began dominating world clothing exports, with whole cities specializing in one type of garment produced for mass export to giant retailers. With vast pools of cheap and disciplined labor, China threatened to drive U.S. textile and clothing producers out of business and give stiff, new competition to exporters such as Pakistan and Bangladesh, where textiles make up 70 percent of exports. Later in 2005, the European Union and the United States each reached bilateral agreements with China to reimpose textile quotas for a few years.

Intellectual property rights are a third contentious area of trade negotiations. Intellectual property rights are the rights of creators of books, films, computer software, and similar products to receive royalties when their products are sold. The United States has a major conflict with some states in the global South over piracy of computer software, music, films, and other creative works—products in which the United States has a strong comparative advantage globally. It is technically easy and cheap to copy such works and sell them in violation of the copyright, patent, or trademark. Because U.S. laws cannot be enforced in foreign countries, the U.S. government wants foreign governments to prevent and punish such violations. Countries that reportedly pirate large amounts of computer software, music, and entertainment products include China, Taiwan, India, Thailand, Brazil, and the former Soviet republics. The Russian government estimated in 2002 that more than 80 percent of films sold in Russia on video and DVD were produced illegally. The worldwide piracy rate was estimated at 40 percent in 2001. Infringement of intellectual property rights is widespread in many countries of the global South, on products such as DVDs and prescription drugs.

In response, the international community has developed an extensive IGO with 184 member states, the World Intellectual Property Organization (WIPO), which tries to regularize patent and copyright law across borders. The WTO oversees the world's most important multilateral agreement on intellectual property, called TRIPS (Trade-Related Aspects of Intellectual Property Rights). The 2001 WTO meeting at Doha led to a declaration that states could exempt certain drugs from TRIPS rules to deal with serious domestic health crises, such as an HIV/AIDS epidemic. (The U.S. government supported this move after it had threatened to take over production of a powerful antibiotic drug, Cipro, during the post–9/11 anthrax scare.) Although procedures were established for these exceptions, only a few developing countries have used them. For several years, these disputes slowed the effective distribution of medicines to millions of Africans with AIDS, though progress picked up after 2004.

A fourth key trade issue is the openness of countries to trade in the **service sector** of the economy. This sector includes many services, especially those concerning information, but the key focus in international trade negotiations is on banking, insurance, and related financial

J'ACCUSE!

Intellectual property rights have been an important focus of recent trade negotiations. In many countries, pirated copies of videos, music, and software sell on the street with no royalty payments. Here, the U.S. Trade Representative holds a pirated DVD from China as she files a copyright complaint against China in the World Trade Organization, 2007.

services. In general, as telecommunications becomes cheaper and more pervasive, services offered by companies in one country can be efficiently used by consumers in other countries. U.S. consumers phoning customer service at U.S. companies and connecting to India or another English-speaking developing country engage in a long-distance trade in services.

Another especially important industry in international trade is the arms trade, which operates largely outside the framework of normal commercial transactions because of its national security implications. Governments in industrialized countries want to protect their domestic arms industries rather than rely on imports to meet their weapons needs. And those domestic arms industries become stronger and more economically viable by exporting their products (as well as supplying their own governments). Governments usually participate actively in the military-industrial sector of the economy, even in countries such as the United States that lack industrial policy in other economic sectors. For example, fighter jets are a product in which the United States enjoys a global comparative advantage (see pp. 73–74). The Middle East has been the leading arms-importing region of the global South, with India and China increasing recently.

A different problem is presented by the "industry" of illicit trade, or *smuggling*. Illicit trade often creates conflicts of interest among states and leads to complex political bargaining among governments, each looking after its own interests.

Enforcement of Trade Rules

As with international law generally, economic agreements among states depend strongly on reciprocity for enforcement (see pp. 56–57, 242–244). If one state protects its industries, or puts tariffs on the goods of other states, or violates the copyright on works produced in other countries, the main resort that other states have is to apply similar measures against the offending state.

Enforcement of equal terms of trade is complicated by differing interpretations of what is "fair." States generally decide which practices of other states they consider unfair (often prodded by affected domestic industries) and then take (or threaten) retaliatory actions to punish those practices. A U.S. law, the Super 301 provision, mandates retaliation against states that restrict access to their markets. One disadvantage of reciprocity is that it can lead to a downward spiral of noncooperation, popularly called a trade war. Third-party arbitration can help resolve trade disputes. Currently, the World Trade Organization (see pp. 174–176) hears complaints and sets levels of acceptable retaliation. In some cases, regional trade agreements establish mechanisms to hear and resolve complaints as well.

Retaliation for unfair trade practices usually tries to match the violation in type and extent. Under WTO rules, a state may impose retaliatory tariffs equivalent to the losses caused by another state's unfair trade practices (as determined by WTO hearings). In 2001, the European Union threatened the United States with sanctions on an unprecedented $4 billion of goods in response to U.S. tax credits to exporters such as Microsoft and Boeing (which the WTO had ruled unfair). Usually, at the last minute, negotiators agree to avert large-scale retaliatory sanctions or trade wars, but in 2004 Europe imposed the retaliatory tariffs, and lifted them in 2005, only after the U.S. Congress repealed the tax breaks.

In cases of dumping, retaliation aims to offset the advantage enjoyed by goods imported at prices below the world market. Retaliatory tariffs raise the price back to market levels. In 2001, the weakened U.S. steel industry pleaded for U.S. government protection from cheap foreign steel, under an antidumping rationale. The Bush administration, although usually favoring free trade, agreed to offer relief (scoring points with labor unions and swing voters in Pennsylvania and West Virginia). Before such tariffs are imposed, a U.S. government agency, the International Trade Commission (ITC), decides whether the low-priced imports have actually hurt the U.S. industry. The ITC ruled that U.S. steelmakers had indeed been hurt, and suggested tariffs of 5–40 percent. President Bush imposed 30 percent tariffs in 2002, and other countries challenged them in the WTO, which ruled against the United States in 2003. The WTO gave other countries the right to impose $2 billion in retaliatory tariffs against the United States. As Europeans drew up their list of tariffs, targeting maximum damage to swing electoral states in 2004, President Bush backed down and abolished the steel tariffs (declaring them successful and no longer needed). By making the cost of tariffs higher than the benefits, the WTO effectively changed U.S. policy—an indication of the WTO's growing power. This example also shows how closely international trade connects with domestic politics.

Trade disputes and retaliatory measures are common. States keep close track of the exact terms of trade. Large bureaucracies monitor international economic transactions (prices relative to world market levels, tariffs, etc.) and develop detailed policies to reciprocate any other state's deviations from cooperation. The role and operation of the major trade regimes and institutions are the focus of the next section.

Economic Globalization

We introduced the process of *globalization* in Chapter 1 (see pp. 17–19) in general terms, and will now consider some specifically economic aspects of globalization. The expansion of trade is a central aspect of globalization in the international political economy, but hardly the only one. Globalization is transforming not only trade but money, business, integration, communication, environmental management, and the economic development of poor countries—the subjects of the remaining chapters of this book. Today's accelerating pace of economic activity grows out of a long history of world economic expansion, which serves as the foundation for globalization.

VIDEO

Trade for Development

The World Economy, 1750–Present

In 1750, Britain, the world's most advanced economy, had a GDP of about $1,200 per capita (in today's dollars). That is less than the present level of most of the global South. However, today Britain produces more than ten times that much per person (and with a much larger population than in 1750). This accomplishment is due to **industrialization**—the use of energy to drive machinery and the accumulation of such machinery along with the products created by it. The Industrial Revolution started in Britain in the 18th century and underpinned Britain's emerging leadership role in the world economy, and spread to the other advanced economies (see Figure 5.4).

By around 1850, the wooden sailing ships of earlier centuries had given way to larger and faster coal-powered iron steamships. Coal-fueled steam engines also drove

FIGURE 5.4 The World Economy, 1750–2000

	1750	1800	1850	1900	1950	2000
Production		industrialization →		WWI / world depression / Soviet industrialization	WWII → postwar prosperity / Cold War arms race / Japanese & German growth	globalization / Soviet collapse →
Energy	coal →	steam engine / cotton gin		oil →	nuclear power →	nat. gas →
Leading Sectors		iron & steam → / textiles →	steel →	electricity → / motor vehicles →	plastics → / electronics → / jets	computers → / biotech → / freeways → / high-speed rail →
Transportation		(wooden sailing ships) / iron steamships →	railroads → / Suez Canal	airplanes → / Trans-Siberian Railroad / Panama Canal / automobiles →		
Trade		British dominance	(free trade) →	protectionism	U.S. dominance / GATT → / European integration →	WTO / NAFTA
Money			pound sterling (British) as world currency →	post-WWI inflation	U.S. dollar as world currency / Keynes / Marshall Plan / IMF → / Bretton Woods	U.S. drops gold standard / IMF debt crises / Russia joins IMF
Communication			telegraph → / transoceanic cables / telephone invented	radio →	communication satellites / information revolution →	Internet / fax, modem, cellular, etc.

184

factories producing textiles and other commodities. The great age of railroad building was taking off. These developments not only increased the volume of world production and trade, but also tied distant locations more closely together economically. The day trip across France by railroad contrasted with the same route a hundred years earlier, which took three weeks to complete. In this period of mechanization, however, factory conditions were extremely harsh, especially for women and children operating machines.

Britain dominated world trade in this period. Because Britain's economy was the most technologically advanced in the world, its products were competitive worldwide. Thus British policy favored free trade. In addition to its central role in world trade, Britain served as the financial capital of the world, managing an increasingly complex world market in goods and services in the 19th century. The British currency, pounds sterling (silver), became the world standard. International monetary relations were still based on the value of precious metals, as they had been in the 16th century when Spain bought its armies with Mexican silver and gold.

By the outset of the 20th century, however, the world's largest and most advanced economy was no longer Britain but the United States. The industrialization of the U.S. economy was fueled by territorial expansion throughout the 19th century, adding vast natural resources. The U.S. economy attracted huge pools of immigrant labor from Europe as well. The United States led the world in converting from coal to oil and from horse-drawn transportation to motor vehicles. New technical innovations, from electricity to airplanes, also helped push the U.S. economy into a dominant world position.

In the 1930s, the U.S. and world economies suffered a severe setback in the Great Depression. The protectionist Smoot-Hawley Act adopted by the United States in 1930, which imposed tariffs on imports, contributed to the severity of the depression by provoking retaliation and reducing world trade. Adopting the principles of *Keynesian economics*, the U.S. government used deficit spending to stimulate the economy, paying itself back from new wealth generated by economic recovery. The government's role in the economy intensified during World War II.

Following World War II, the capitalist world economy was restructured under U.S. leadership. Today's international economic institutions, such as the World Bank and the International Monetary Fund (IMF), date from this period. The United States provided massive assistance to resuscitate the Western European economies (through the Marshall Plan) as well as Japan's economy. World trade greatly expanded, and the world market became ever more closely woven together through air transportation and telecommunications. Electronics emerged as a new leading sector, and technological progress accelerated throughout the 20th century.

Standing apart from this world capitalist economy, the economies of the Soviet Union and Eastern Europe followed communist principles of central planning and state ownership. In a **centrally planned economy** (or *command economy*), political authorities set prices and decide on quotas for production and consumption of each commodity according to a long-term plan. This type of economy was for decades the standard in the communist states of the former Soviet Union, Eastern Europe, China, and several smaller countries (it is still in place in Cuba and North Korea). Within the Soviet economic bloc (which included Eastern Europe and Mongolia), international trade also took place at government-controlled prices.

The Soviet economy had some notable successes in rapidly industrializing the country in the 1930s, surviving the German assault in the 1940s, and developing world-class aerospace and military production capability in the 1950s and 1960s. The Soviet Union launched the world's first satellite (*Sputnik*) in 1957, and in the early 1960s its leaders boasted that communist economies would outperform capitalist ones within decades. Instead, the Soviet-bloc economies stagnated under the weight of bureaucracy, ideological rigidity, environmental destruction, corruption, and extremely high military spending. Centrally planned economies proved hopelessly inefficient.

Now the former Soviet republics and Eastern Europe are almost all **transitional economies** trying to make the change to a market-based economy connected to the world capitalist economy. This transition proved difficult. In the first half of the 1990s, the total GDP of the region *shrank* by about 35 percent—a depression worse than the Great Depression the United States experienced in the early 1930s. Living standards dropped dramatically. In Boris Yeltsin's administration (1991–1999), Russia's economy remained dysfunctional, owing to depression, corruption, tax delinquency, and the vast differences between the old communist and new capitalist models. President Vladimir Putin (2000–2008) brought new energy to economic reform, and high prices for crude oil, a major Russian export, buoyed its economy in the new century, but Putin's centralization of political power could choke off capitalist growth in the long run.

China, whose government continues to follow a Marxist *political* line (central control by the Communist party), has shifted substantially toward a *market economy*. (The state still controls major industries.) This transition has dramatically increased China's economic growth ever since the 1980s. Growth reached a sustained annual rate of about 10 percent throughout the 1990s and nearly as fast in recent years (see pp. 280–283).

Today, the world's economic activity follows the principles of free markets more than central planning but often falls somewhere between the extremes. Many governments control domestic prices on some goods (for instance, subsidizing certain goods to win political support). Many states *own* (all or part of) industries thought to be vital for the national economy—**state-owned industries** such as oil production companies or national airlines. And, the government sector of the economy (military spending, road building, Social Security, and so on) makes up a substantial fraction of the industrialized countries' economies. Because they contain both some government control and some private ownership, the economies of the industrialized West are often called **mixed economies.**

Today there is a single integrated world economy that almost no country can resist joining. At the same time, the imperfections and problems of that world economy are evident in periodic crises and recessions and in the sharpening of disparities between the richest and poorest world regions. At no time have these imperfections been more glaring than during the 2008 global financial crisis and ensuing world recession. Starting with the sub-prime mortgage collapse in the United States, economic troubles quickly spread to Europe as major banks and investment companies lost hundreds of billions of dollars. These losses led to a global slowdown in consumer spending and production that caused large job losses in the United States, China, India, and other countries. The subsequent fall in consumer demand for goods led to declines in global trade of nine percent—the largest decline since World War II.

Resistance to Trade

The globalization of the world economy has fueled a countercurrent of growing nationalism in several world regions where people believe their identities and communities to be threatened by the penetration of foreign influences. In addition, the material dislocations caused by globalization directly affect the self-interests of certain segments of countries' populations.

Workers in industrialized countries in industries that face increasing competition from low-wage countries in the global South—such as steel, automobiles, electronics, and clothing—are among the most adversely affected by free trade. The competition from low-wage countries holds down wages in those industries in the industrialized countries. It also creates pressures to relax standards of labor regulation, such as those protecting worker safety, and it can lead to job losses if manufacturers close down plants in high-wage countries and move operations to the global South. Not surprisingly, labor unions have been among the strongest political opponents of unfettered trade expansion. (Although the United States stands at the center of these debates, other industrialized countries face similar issues.)

Human rights NGOs have joined labor unions in pushing for trade agreements to include requirements for improving working conditions in low-wage countries; these could include laws regarding minimum wage, child labor, and worker safety. The U.S. Congress in 1997 banned U.S. imports of goods manufactured by South Asia's 15 million indentured (slave) child laborers. Clothing manufacturers such as Nike and Reebok, meanwhile, stung by criticism of "sweatshop" conditions in its Asian factories, adopted a voluntary program to end the worst abuses. More than 200 million children under age 14 work in the global South, more than half of them in hazardous labor, according to the UN-affiliated International Labor Organization. That total represents about 5 percent of 5- to 14-year-olds in Latin America, 20 percent in Asia, and 25 percent in Africa. Much of the chocolate consumed in the global North originates in Ivory Coast, where tens of thousands of children work for low wages, or even as slaves, on cocoa plantations.

Environmental groups also have actively opposed the unrestricted expansion of trade, which they see as undermining environmental laws in industrialized countries and promoting environmentally harmful

CHEAP LABOR

Labor, environmental, and human rights organizations have all criticized unrestricted free trade. They argue that free trade agreements encourage MNCs to produce goods under unfair and unhealthy conditions, including the use of child labor. This boy in India makes soccer balls, 2002.

practices worldwide (see p. 314). For example, U.S. regulations require commercial shrimp boats to use devices that prevent endangered species of sea turtles from drowning in shrimp nets. Indonesia, Malaysia, Thailand, and Pakistan, whose shrimp exports to the United States were blocked because they do not require the use of such devices, won a ruling from the World Trade Organization that the U.S. regulation unfairly discriminated against them. Sea turtles became a symbol of environmentalist opposition to the WTO. (In 2001, the WTO ruled the U.S. law acceptable after changes had made application of the law more even-handed.)

Labor, environmental, and consumer groups all portray the WTO as a secretive bureaucracy outside democratic control that serves the interests of big corporations at the expense of ordinary people in both the global North and South. More fundamentally, these critics distrust the corporate-driven globalization of which the WTO is just one aspect.

The benefits of free trade are much more diffuse than the costs. U.S. consumers enjoy lower prices on goods imported from low-wage countries. Consumers may therefore spend more money on other products and services, eventually employing more U.S. workers. Cheap imports also help keep inflation low, which benefits citizens and politicians. However, the costs of free trade fall disproportionately on smaller groups (for example, steel workers) who are likely to put up resistance.

Globalization, Financial Markets, and the Currency System

Globalization has led to momentous changes in many areas of international relations. So far, we have discussed how globalization has influenced global security and international trade relations. Globalization has had its most profound influence in the way states, businesses, and individuals deal with financial markets.

Today, global financial markets are as integrated as they have ever been. Investors in one country buy and sell assets or exchange currency with a few clicks of a mouse. Banks' investment portfolios often contain millions of dollars in assets (real estate, land, stocks) located in other countries. Nearly a trillion and a half dollars a day is exchanged on currency markets as investors need various currencies to do business in other countries, but also to bet on the rise and fall of currencies, which we discuss momentarily.

This financial integration has tremendous advantages. It offers investors and businesses access to overseas markets to spur economic growth. It allows for the possibility of better returns on investments for individuals investing for college tuition or retirement. But as we have witnessed in the past two years, financial integration also carries risks. An economic crisis in one state can quickly spread to another, then another. The spread of economic difficulties can quickly lead to a global economic crisis affecting small and large economies alike.

Such was the case in 2008. As an economic downturn began in the United States, many Americans who had taken out loans on their homes found themselves unable to pay these loans back. At the same time, the value of their homes began to fall, so that even if banks were to reclaim them, the banks could not recover the money they had loaned. Moreover, these loans had been resold by the banks to other businesses as investments, often in other countries. Several large U.S. banks then announced that they were on the verge of failing because they had too much money tied up in these bad home loans. This was a problem not only for the banks and the individuals who could not pay for their homes, but also for those businesses who had purchased these loans as investments.

Given the global integration of financial markets, this housing crisis led quickly to a global banking crisis. Several British banks then announced they were near bankruptcy. The U.S. government responded with a rescue package of $800

SIGN OF THE TIMES

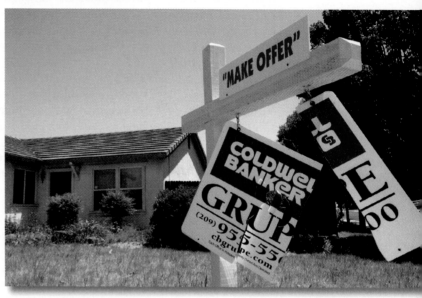

Finance in different countries and world regions has become globally interwoven. The problems of the U.S. housing and mortgage market in 2008 triggered an economic shock wave that quickly crossed international borders and economic sectors, contributing to bank failures, corporate bankruptcies, and higher unemployment around the world. This house in California sits on the market in 2008.

billion to help shore up failing banks. Britain also created a rescue package of nearly $450 billion. The entire banking sector of Iceland was taken over by the government, and Iceland, a prosperous country, needed a loan from the International Monetary Fund (IMF) to rescue the government from bankruptcy.

Global stock markets tumbled dramatically as a result of this financial crisis. Unemployment increased worldwide. What began as trouble in the U.S. housing market ended as a global financial meltdown. The remainder of this chapter investigates two central pillars of our global financial markets: the politics of the world monetary system and the role of private companies as nonstate actors in the world economy.

VIDEO

The Global Economic Crisis

The Currency System

Nearly every state prints its own money. Because of the nature of state sovereignty, the international economy is based on national currencies, not a world currency. One of the main powers of a national government is to create its own currency as the sole legal currency in the territory it controls. The national currencies are of no inherent value in another country, but can be exchanged one for another.

For centuries, the European state system used precious metals as a global currency, valued in all countries. Gold was most important, and silver second. These metals had inherent value because they looked pretty and were easily molded into jewelry or similar objects. They were relatively rare, and the mining of new gold and silver was relatively slow. These metals lasted a long time, and they were difficult to dilute or counterfeit.

Over time, gold and silver became valuable *because* they were a world currency—because other people around the world trusted that the metals could be exchanged for future goods—and this overshadowed any inherent functional value of gold or silver. Bars of gold were held by states as a kind of bank account denominated in an international currency.

In recent years the world has not used such a **gold standard** but has developed an international monetary system divorced from any tangible medium such as precious metals. Even today, some private investors buy stocks of gold or silver at times of political instability, as a haven that would reliably have future value. But gold and silver have now become basically like other commodities, with unpredictable fluctuations in price. The change in the world economy away from bars of gold to purely abstract money makes international economics more efficient; the only drawback is that without tangible backing in gold, currencies may seem less worthy of people's confidence.

Today, national currencies are valued against each other, not against gold or silver. Each state's currency can be exchanged for a different state's currency according to an **exchange rate.** These exchange rates affect almost every international economic transaction. In particular, currency policies directly affect trade issues, but are not governed by the WTO regime.

International Currency Exchange

Most exchange rates are expressed in terms of the world's most important currencies—the U.S. dollar, the Japanese yen, and the EU's euro. Thus, the rate for exchanging Danish kroner for Brazilian reals depends on the value of each relative to these world currencies. Exchange rates that most affect the world economy are those *within* the G8 states—U.S. dollars, euros, yen, British pounds, and Canadian dollars.

The relative values of currencies at a given point in time are arbitrary; only the *changes* in values over time are meaningful. For instance, the euro happens to be fairly close to the U.S. dollar in value, whereas the Japanese yen is denominated in units closer to the U.S. penny. In itself this says nothing about the desirability of these currencies or the financial positions of their states. However, when the value of the euro rises (or falls) *relative* to the dollar, because euros are considered more (or less) valuable than before, the euro is said to be strong (or weak).

Some states do not have *convertible* currencies. The holder of such money has no guarantee of being able to trade it for another currency. Such is the case in states cut off from the world capitalist economy, such as the former Soviet Union. In practice, even nonconvertible currency can often be sold, in black markets or by dealing directly with the government issuing the currency, but the price may be extremely low.

TABLE 5.2   Inflation Rates by Region, 1993–2008

Region	Inflation Rate (percent per year)		
	1993	2001	2008[a]
Industrialized West	3	2	2
Russia/CIS	1,400	22	15
China	15	7	6
Middle East	27	17	8
Latin America	750	6	8
South Asia	6	6	9
Africa	112	6	12

[a]Data are estimates based on partial data for 2008.

Note: Regions are not identical to those used elsewhere in this book.

Source: Adapted from United Nations. *World Economic Situation and Prospects 2008*. United Nations, 2008.

Some currencies are practically nonconvertible because they are inflating so rapidly that holding them for even a short period means losing money. The industrialized West has kept inflation relatively low—mostly below 5 percent annually—since 1980. Inflation in the global South is lower than a decade ago (see Table 5.2). Latin America brought inflation from 750 percent to below 15 percent, while China and South Asia got inflation rates below 5 percent. Most dramatically, in Russia and other former Soviet republics, inflation rates of more than 1,000 percent came down to less than 10 percent. Extremely high, uncontrolled inflation—more than 50 percent per month, or 13,000 percent per year—is called **hyperinflation.** The 100-trillion-dollar notes introduced by Zimbabwe in 2009 quickly lost most of their initial value (about 30 U.S. dollars) under hyperinflation exceeding 200 million percent per year. Even at less extreme levels, currencies can lose 95 percent of their value in a year, and it becomes hard to conduct business domestically, let alone internationally.

By contrast with nonconvertible currency, **hard currency** is money that can be readily converted to leading world currencies (which now have relatively low inflation). For example, a Chinese computer producer can export its products and receive payment in dollars, euros, or another hard currency, which it can use to pay for components it needs to import from abroad. But a Chinese farmer paid in Chinese currency for rice could not simply take that currency to buy imported goods. Rather, the exchange for foreign currency would be controlled by the Chinese government at rates the government set.

States maintain **reserves** of hard currency. These are the equivalent of the stock-piles of gold in centuries past. National currencies are now backed by hard-currency reserves, not gold. Some states continue to maintain gold reserves as well. The industrialized countries have financial reserves roughly in proportion to the size of their economies.

One form of currency exchange uses **fixed exchange rates.** Here governments decide, individually or jointly, to establish official rates of exchange for their currencies. The Canadian and U.S. dollars were for many years equal in value; a fixed rate of one-to-one was maintained (this is no longer true). States have various means for trying to maintain, or modify, such fixed rates in the face of changing economic conditions (see pp. 193–196).

Floating exchange rates are now more common and are used for the world's major currencies. Rates are determined by global currency markets in which private investors and governments alike buy and sell currencies. There is a supply and demand for each state's currency, with prices constantly adjusting in response to market conditions. Just as investors might buy shares of Apple Computer stock if they expected its value to rise, so they would buy a pile of Japanese yen if they expected that currency's value to rise in the future. Through short-term speculative trading in international currencies, exchange rates adjust to changes in the longer-term supply and demand for currencies.

Major international currency markets operate in a handful of cities—the most important being New York, London, Zurich (Switzerland), Tokyo, and Hong Kong—linked by instantaneous computerized communications. These markets are driven in the short term by one question: What will a state's currency be worth in the future relative to what it is worth today? These international currency markets involve huge amounts of money—a trillion and a half dollars every day—moving around the world (of course, only the computerized information actually moves). They are private markets, not as strongly regulated by governments as are stock markets.

National governments periodically intervene in financial markets, buying and selling currencies in order to manipulate their value. (These interventions may also involve changing interest rates paid by the government; see pp. 198–199.) Such government intervention to manage the otherwise free-floating currency rates is called a **managed float** system. The leading industrialized states often, but not always, work together in such interventions. If the price of the U.S. dollar, for instance, goes down too much relative to other important currencies (a political judgment), governments step into the currency markets, side by side with private investors, and buy dollars. With this higher demand for dollars, the price may then stabilize and perhaps rise again. (If the price gets too high, governments step in to sell dollars, increasing supply and driving the price down.) Such interventions usually happen quickly and may be repeated several times in order to have the desired effect. In their interventions in international currency markets, governments are at a disadvantage because even acting together, they control only a small fraction of the money moving on such markets; most of it is privately owned.

A successful intervention can make money for governments at the expense of private speculators. If, for example, the G8 governments step in to raise the price of U.S. dollars by buying them around the world (selling other hard currencies), and if they succeed, the governments can then sell again and pocket a profit. However, if the intervention fails and the price of dollars keeps falling, the governments *lose* money and may have to keep buying and buying in order to stop the slide. In fact, if investors become aware of such moves, they may interpret this action as a signal that the currency being bought is weak, which could depress the price even further. In extreme cases, the governments may run out of their stockpiles of hard currencies before then and have to absorb a huge loss. Thus governments must be realistic about the limited effects they can have on currency prices.

These limits were well illustrated in the 2001 Argentine financial collapse. Argentina in the 1990s had pegged the value of its currency at a fixed rate to the U.S. dollar—a wonderfully effective way to stop the runaway inflation that had recently wreaked devastation on Argentina's economy. Tying the peso to the dollar, however, represented a loss of sovereignty over monetary policy, one of the key levers to control an economy. Argentina accumulated $132 billion in foreign loans and could not service its debts. IMF assistance in restructuring debt was contingent on a tight financial policy of tax increases and spending cuts—a mistake during a major multiyear recession, according to critics. In 2001, as the United States and the IMF stood by, Argentina's economy collapsed; two presidents resigned in short order; and a populist took power, defaulted on foreign debts, and devalued the peso to create jobs—an embarrassing chapter for the IMF and a painful one for Argentina. In 2003, Argentina defaulted on a $3 billion payment to the IMF, the largest default in IMF history. Its economy turned around and it paid the IMF off in 2006, though negotiations with foreign government creditors continued.

More recently, pressures built up in a vastly more important case—China's currency. As in Argentina in 2001, the current policy of pegging China's currency to the dollar did not adjust to different economic conditions in the two countries. China runs a big trade surplus and the United States a big trade deficit—more than $240 billion with China alone in 2008 and over $700 billion in total. Critics charge that the dollar-yuan ratio is held artificially high, making China's exports to the United States cheaper and contributing to the trade imbalance and the loss of U.S. manufacturing jobs—an issue in U.S. domestic politics. As the economic position of the United States has worsened in the past two years, pressure on China to reform its currency has grown. Yet, China has also experienced an economic downturn and is reluctant to undertake reform that could lead to job losses. China has only slowly allowed its currency to appreciate in value modestly, and will not allow it to float freely.

Why Currencies Rise or Fall

In the short term, exchange rates depend on speculation about the future value of currencies. But over the long term, the value of a state's currency tends to rise or fall relative to others because of changes in the long-term supply and demand for the currency. *Supply* is determined by the amount of money a government prints. Printing money is a quick way to generate revenue for the government, but the more money printed, the lower its price. *Demand* for a currency depends on the state's economic health and political stability. People do not want the currency of an unstable country because political instability leads to the breakdown of economic efficiency and of trust in the currency.

PRICES SUBJECT TO CHANGE

Changes in the value of the dollar—reflecting underlying trends in U.S. and foreign economies as well as governments' monetary policies—directly affect the prices of imported goods such as gasoline, here rising in 2008.

A *strong* currency increases its value relative to other currencies—not just in day-to-day fluctuations on currency markets, but in a longer-term perspective. A weak currency is the opposite. The strength of a state's currency tends to reflect that state's monetary policy and economic growth rate. Investors seek a currency that will not be watered down by inflation and that can be profitably invested in a growing economy.

To some extent, states have *common* interests—opposed to those of private investors—in maintaining stable currency exchange rates. Despite these shared interests, states also experience conflicts over currency exchange. States often prefer a low value for their own currency relative to others, because a low value promotes exports and helps turn trade deficits into surpluses—as mercantilists especially favor (see pp. 167–168).

Exchange rates and trade surpluses or deficits tend to adjust automatically toward equilibrium (the preferred outcome for liberals). An *overvalued* currency is one whose exchange rate is too high, resulting in a chronic trade deficit. The deficit can be covered by printing more money, which in turn waters down the currency's value and brings down the exchange rate (if it floats freely). Because they see adjustments as harmless, liberals do not mind exchange rate changes, which they view as mechanisms for the world economy to work out inefficiencies and maximize growth.

A unilateral move to reduce the value of one's own currency by changing a fixed or official exchange rate is called a **devaluation.** Generally, devaluation is a quick fix for financial problems in the short term, but it can create new problems. It causes losses to foreigners who hold one's currency (which suddenly loses value). This reduces the trust people place in the currency. As a result, demand for the currency drops, even at the new lower rate. Investors become wary of future devaluations, and indeed such devaluations often follow one after another in unstable economies. In the first three weeks of 2009, Russia devalued its ruble six times, after the price of its main export, oil, plummeted. A currency may be devalued by being allowed to float freely after a period of fixed exchange rates, often bringing a single sharp drop in values.

States also share an interest in the integrity of their currencies against counterfeiting, but "rogue" states may feel otherwise. In 2006, the Unites States accused North Korea of

POLICY PERSPECTIVES

President of China, Hu Jintao

PROBLEM *How do you balance international political pressures with domestic economics?*

BACKGROUND Imagine that you are the president of China. The Chinese economy has grown rapidly in the past decade. Growth rates rose to near 11 percent as of 2007, exceeding nearly all countries in the developing world. In particular, China's exports have boomed during this period. In 2008, because of the world financial crisis, exports fell but still stood at nearly $1 trillion. China's trade surplus exceeded $250 billion in 2008.

Your position in the international economy is unique, because China's currency, the yuan, has been pegged to the U.S. dollar for nearly a decade (and to a basket of currencies, with just small adjustments, starting in mid-2005). Thus, even though the demand for the yuan may rise and fall, China's exchange rate does not change much.

Many feel that your pegged currency is one explanation for your country's tremendous economic growth and trade surplus. The demand for the yuan is high (to pay for your exports), but the peg keeps the yuan low. The result is that Chinese exports are much cheaper on the world market, making your goods very attractive.

DOMESTIC CONSIDERATIONS This economic growth is important for your country. Given the country's large population, increases in jobs are important to keep unemployment low. Higher wages help ensure low birthrates (see pp. 326–328). Exports are a key part of this picture, contributing heavily to economic growth by generating hard currency and creating jobs.

Recently, however, two dangers have appeared on the horizon. The first is economic. The global economic downturn has led to a decrease in demand for your exports. In 2008, your exports experienced their largest decline in a decade. This led to waves of layoffs and you instituted a nearly $600 billion economic stimulus package in response. The second danger is political. Both Europe and the United States have complained bitterly about your pegged exchange rate and your trade surplus. The United States recently blamed the yuan-dollar peg for costing America 1.5 million jobs, further exacerbating political tensions.

SCENARIO Now imagine that the advanced-economy countries approach you with possible membership in the G8. Their condition is that you allow the yuan to float freely on international currency markets. Such a move would be very popular in international political circles and would lessen the chances that your own economy will "overheat" and become inflationary. In the long run, such a move will ensure your further integration into the international economy. In addition, a closer link to G8 states would provide significant prestige to your government.

Of course, there are also dangers in this course of action. If the yuan rises rapidly in value, your exports will be less competitive internationally, risking a stall in a key engine of your economy. You also become more vulnerable to international currency shocks, such as the 1997 Asian economic crisis, which you avoided in large part due to your pegged exchange rate.

CHOOSE YOUR POLICY Do you remove the yuan-dollar peg? If yes, how do you make sure your economy stays on a moderate growth rate and your exports stay competitive? If no, how do you deal with the political pressure arising from your fixed exchange rate?

passing off tens of millions of dollars in extremely realistic counterfeit $100 bills—a direct gain for the North Korean regime at the expense of the U.S. Treasury.

Central Banks

Governments control the printing of money. In some states, the politicians or generals who control the government directly control the amounts of money printed. It is not surprising that inflation tends to be high in those states, because political problems can often be solved by printing more money. But in most industrialized countries, politicians know they cannot trust themselves with day-to-day decisions about printing money. To enforce self-discipline and enhance public trust in the value of money, these decisions are turned over to a **central bank.**

The economists and technical experts who run the central bank seek to maintain the value of the state's currency by limiting the amount of money printed and not allowing high inflation. Politicians appoint the people who run the bank, but generally for long terms that do not coincide with those of the politicians. Thus, central bank managers try to run the bank in the national interest, a step removed from partisan politics. If a state leader orders a military intervention, the generals obey, but if the leader orders an intervention in currency markets, the central bank does not have to comply. In practice, the autonomy of central banks varies.

In the United States, the central bank is the *Federal Reserve,* or the Fed. The Fed can affect the economy by releasing or hoarding its money. Internationally, it does this by intervening in currency markets as described earlier. Multilateral interventions are usually coordinated by the heads of central banks and treasury (finance) ministries in the leading countries. The long-term, relatively nonpartisan perspective of central bankers makes it easier for states to achieve the collective good of a stable world monetary system.

Domestically, the Fed exercises its power mainly by setting the **discount rate**—the interest rate the government charges when it loans money to private banks. In effect, this rate controls how fast money is injected into the economy. If the Fed sets too low a discount rate, too much money will enter into circulation and inflation will result. If the rate is set too high, too little money will circulate and consumers and businesses will find it hard to borrow as much or as cheaply from private banks; economic growth will be depressed.

Although central banks control sizable reserves of currency, they are constrained by the limited share of world money they own. Most wealth is controlled by private banks and corporations. As economic actors, states do not drive the direction of the world economy; in many ways they follow it, at least over the long run. Yet, as we have seen in the current global economic crises, states still play a key role in the global economy. In the short run, states can adopt massive financial stimulus packages, can rescue private banks and corporations that teeter on bankruptcy, and can prosecute individuals that act illegally to cause economic hardship.

The World Bank and the IMF

Because of the importance of international cooperation for a stable world monetary system and because of the need to overcome collective goods problems, international regimes and institutions have developed around norms of behavior in monetary relations. Just as the UN institutionally supports regimes based on norms of behavior in international security affairs, the same is true in the world monetary regime.

As in security affairs, the main international economic institutions were created near the end of World War II. The **Bretton Woods system** was adopted at a conference of the winning states in 1944 (at Bretton Woods, New Hampshire). It established the *International Bank for Reconstruction and Development (IBRD)*, more commonly called the **World Bank,** as a source of loans to reconstruct the European economies after the war and to help states through future financial difficulties. (Later, the main borrowers were developing countries and, in the 1990s, Eastern European ones.) Closely linked with the World Bank is the **International Monetary Fund (IMF).** The IMF coordinates international currency exchange, the balance of international payments, and national accounts (discussed shortly). The World Bank and the IMF continue to be the pillars of the international financial system. (The roles of the World Bank and the IMF in international development are taken up in Chapter 7.)

VIDEO

The
International
Monetary
Fund

To replace gold as a world standard after 1971, the IMF created a new world currency, the **Special Drawing Right (SDR).** The SDR has been called "paper gold" because it is created in limited amounts by the IMF, is held as a hard-currency reserve by states' central banks, and can be exchanged for various international currencies. The SDR is today the closest thing to a world currency that exists, but it cannot buy goods—only currencies. And it is owned only by states (central banks), not by individuals or companies. SDRs are linked in value to a basket of several key international currencies. Since the 1970s, the major national currencies have been governed by the managed float system. Transition from the dollar-gold regime to the managed float regime was difficult. States had to bargain politically over the targets for currency exchange rates in the meetings now known as G8 summits. The technical mechanisms of the IMF are based on each member state's depositing financial reserves with the IMF, based on the size and strength of a state's economy. A state can then borrow to stabilize its economy in difficult times and repay the IMF in subsequent years. In 2009, world leaders pledged an additional one trillion dollars to be paid to the IMF so it could help developing countries cope with the global financial crisis.

Unlike the WTO or UN General Assembly, the IMF and the World Bank use a *weighted voting system*—each state has a vote equal to its deposits. Thus the G8 states control the IMF, although nearly all the world's states are members. The United States has the single largest vote (17 percent), and its capital city is headquarters for both the IMF and the World Bank. In 2006 and 2008, the IMF adjusted the voting formula, increasing modestly the voting power of China (from about 3 to 3.7 percent of the total) along with other developing countries.

Since 1944, the IMF and the World Bank have tried to accomplish three major missions. First they sought to provide stability and access to capital for states ravaged by World War II, especially Japan and the states of Western Europe. This mission was a great success, leading to growth and prosperity in those states. Then, especially in the 1970s and 1980s, the World Bank and the IMF have tried to promote economic development in developing countries. That mission was far less successful—as seen in the lingering poverty in much of the global South (see Chapter 7). The third mission, in the 1990s, was the integration of Eastern Europe and Russia into the world capitalist economy. This effort posted a mixed record but has had general success overall.

State Financial Positions

As currency rates change and state economies grow, the overall positions of states relative to each other shift.

National Accounts

The IMF maintains a system of *national accounts* statistics to keep track of the overall monetary position of each state. A state's **balance of payments** is like the financial statement of a company: it summarizes all the flows of money into and out of the country. The system itself is technical and not political in nature. Essentially, three types of international transactions go into the balance of payments.

The *current account* is basically the balance of trade discussed earlier. *Capital flows* are foreign investments in, and by, a country. *Changes in foreign exchange reserves* make the national accounts balance. Any difference between the inflows and outflows of money is made up by an equal but opposite change in reserves (purchases and sales of SDRs, gold, and hard currencies other than its own, and changes in its deposits with the IMF). Thus, national accounts always balance in the end.

International Debt

In one sense, an economy is constantly in motion, as money moves through the processes of production, trade, and consumption. But economies also contain *standing wealth*. The hard-currency reserves owned by governments are one form of standing wealth, but not the most important. Most standing wealth is in the form of homes and cars, farms and factories, ports and railroads. In particular, *capital* goods (such as factories) are products that can be used as inputs for further production. Nothing lasts forever, but standing wealth lasts for enough years to be treated differently from goods that are quickly consumed. The main difference is that capital can be used to create more wealth: factories produce goods, railroads support commerce, and so forth. Standing wealth creates new wealth, so the economy tends to grow over time. As it grows, more standing wealth is created. In a capitalist economy, money makes more money.

If the state's economy is healthy, it can borrow money from foreign governments, banks, or companies and create enough new wealth to repay the debts a few years later. But states, like businesses, sometimes operate at a loss; then their debts mount up. In a vicious circle, more and more of the income they generate goes to paying interest, and more money must be borrowed to keep the state in operation.

Why do states go into debt? One major reason is a trade deficit. In the balance of payments, a trade deficit must be made up somehow. It is common to borrow money to pay for a trade deficit. A second reason is the income and consumption pattern among households and businesses. If people and firms spend more than they take in, they must borrow to pay their bills. The credit card they use may be from a local bank, but that bank may be getting the money it lends to them from foreign lenders.

A third reason for national debt is government spending relative to taxation. Under the principles of **Keynesian economics** (named for economist John Maynard Keynes), governments sometimes spend more on programs than they accrue in tax revenue—*deficit spending*—to stimulate economic growth. This has been the strategy adopted by many G8 countries in the 2009 financial crisis, especially the United States. If the strategy works,

DON'T PAY!

Failure to make payments on international debt, called a default, is a very serious action because it can cut off a country's access to future investment and loans. Nonetheless, several states have defaulted on debts rather than inflict painful budget cuts that would hurt the population. These protesters in late 2008 supported the president of Ecuador as he decided to default on Ecuador's $3 billion international debt in the face of the world financial meltdown, which had hit the country hard.

increased economic growth eventually generates higher tax revenues to make up the deficit. If it does not, a state finds itself with a poor economy and even deeper in debt.

Government decisions about spending and taxation are called **fiscal policy;** decisions about printing and circulating money are called **monetary policy.** These are the two main tools available for government to manage an economy. There is no free lunch: high taxation chokes off economic growth, printing excess money causes inflation, and borrowing to cover a deficit places a mortgage on the state's standing wealth. This is why, for all the complexities of governmental economic policies and international economic transactions, a state's wealth and power ultimately depend more than anything on the underlying health of its economy—the education and training of its labor force, the amount and modernity of its capital goods, the morale of its population, and the skill of its managers. In the long run, international debt reflects these underlying realities.

Multinational Business

Although states are the main rule makers for currency exchange and other international economic transactions, those transactions are carried out mainly by private firms and individuals, not governments. Most important among these private actors are MNCs.

Multinational Corporations

Multinational corporations (MNCs) are companies based in one state with affiliated branches or subsidiaries operating in other states. There is no exact definition, but the clearest case of an MNC is a large corporation that operates on a worldwide basis in many countries simultaneously, with fixed facilities and employees in each. There is also no exact count of the total number of MNCs, but most estimates are in the tens of thousands worldwide.

Most important are *industrial corporations*, which make goods in factories in various countries and sell them to businesses and consumers in various countries. The automobile, oil, and electronics industries have the largest MNCs. Almost all of the largest MNCs are based in G8 states. *Financial corporations* (the most important being banks) also operate multinationally—though often with more restrictions than industrial MNCs. Money moves across borders at the rate of $1.5 trillion per day. In this context, financial corporations are becoming more internationalized. Some MNCs sell *services*. The McDonald's fast-food chain and American Telephone and Telegraph (AT&T) are good examples.

Some scholars see MNCs as virtually being agents of their home national governments. This view resonates with mercantilism, in which economic activity ultimately serves political authorities; thus MNCs have clear national identities and act as members of their national society under state authority. A variant of this theme (from a more revolutionary world view) considers national governments to be agents of their MNCs; state interventions (economic and military) serve private, monied interests.

Others see MNCs as citizens of the world beholden to no government. The head of Dow Chemical once said he dreamed of buying an island beyond any state's territory and putting Dow's world headquarters there. In such a view, MNCs act globally in the interests of their (international) stockholders and owe loyalty to no state. In any case, MNCs are motivated by the need to maximize profits. Only in the case of state-owned MNCs—an important exception but a small minority of the total companies worldwide—do MNC actions reflect state interests. Even then, managers of state-owned MNCs have won greater autonomy to pursue profit in recent years (as part of the economic reforms instituted in many countries), and in many cases state-owned enterprises are being sold off (privatized).

As independent actors in the international arena, MNCs are increasingly powerful. Dozens of industrial MNCs have annual sales of tens of billions of dollars each (hundreds of billions for the top corporations such as ExxonMobil, Wal-Mart, and GM). Only about 35 states have more economic activity per year (GDP) than does the largest MNC in 2008, Wal-Mart. However, the largest *government* (the United States) has government revenues of $2 trillion—about seven times that of Wal-Mart. Thus the power of MNCs does not rival that of the largest states but exceeds that of many poorer states (see pp. 290–291).

Giant MNCs contribute to global interdependence. They are so deeply entwined in so many states that they have a profound interest in the stable operation of the international system—in security affairs as well as in trade and monetary relations. MNCs prosper in a stable international atmosphere that permits freedom of trade, of movement, and of capital flows (investments)—all governed by market forces with minimal government interference. Thus MNCs are, overall, a strong force for liberalism in the world economy, despite the fact that particular MNCs in particular industries push for certain mercantilist policies to protect their own interests.

Foreign Direct Investment

MNCs do not just operate in foreign countries, they also own capital there—buildings, factories, cars, and so forth. For instance, U.S. and German MNCs own some of the capital located in Japan, and Japanese MNCs own capital located in the United States and Germany. Investments in foreign countries are among the most important, and politically sensitive, activities of MNCs. Figure 5.5 illustrates the growth of foreign direct investment.

Unlike portfolio investment (on paper), *foreign direct investment* involves tangible goods such as factories and office buildings (including ownership of a sizable fraction of a company's total stock, as opposed to a portfolio with little bits of many companies). Paper can be traded on a global market relatively freely, but direct investments cannot be freely moved from one state to another when conditions change. Direct investment is long term, and it is more visible than portfolio investment. Investments in the manufacturing sector usually entail the greatest investment in fixed facilities and in training workers and managers. Investments in the service sector tend to be less expensive and easier to walk away from if conditions change.

Mercantilists tend to view foreign investments in their own country suspiciously. In developing countries, foreign direct investment often evokes concerns about a loss of sovereignty, because governments may be less powerful than the MNCs that invest in their country. These fears also reflect the historical fact that most foreign investment in the global South once came from colonizers. Furthermore, although such investments create jobs, they also bring dislocations of traditional ways of life and cultures. Many poor and transitional states desperately need capital from any source to stimulate

DOING BUSINESS WORLDWIDE

Multinational corporations (MNCs) play important roles in international relations and are powerful actors with considerable resources in negotiating with governments. Here, Airbus, a division of a European MNC, shows off its new super-jumbo jet at the Singapore Airshow, 2008.

FIGURE 5.5   Foreign Direct Investment, World Total, 1970–2007

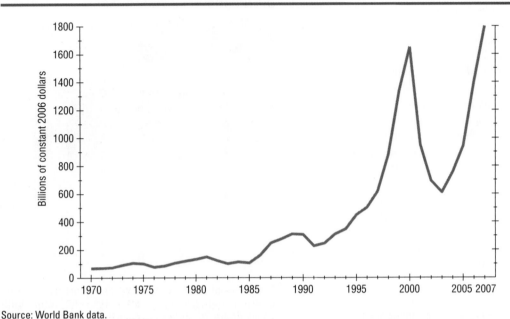

Source: World Bank data.

economic growth, so foreign direct investment is generally welcomed and encouraged despite the fears of economic nationalists (on North-South investment, see pp. 290–291). Most foreign direct investment (like most portfolio investment) is not in the global South, however, but in industrialized countries.

Host and Home Government Relations

A state in which a foreign MNC operates is called the *host country*; the state where the MNC has its headquarters is called its *home country*. Because host governments can regulate activities on their own territories, an MNC cannot operate in a state against the wishes of the host country's government. Conversely, because MNCs have many states to choose from, a host government cannot generally force an MNC to do business in the country against the MNC's wishes. Both the MNC and the host government benefit— the MNC from profits, the government directly by taxation and indirectly through economic growth (generating future taxes and political support).

However, conflicts also arise in the relationship. One obvious conflict concerns the distribution of new wealth between the MNC and the host government. This distribution depends on the rate at which MNC activities or profits are taxed, as well as on the ground rules for MNC operations. Before an MNC invests or opens a subsidiary in a host country, it sits down with the government to negotiate these issues. Threats of violent leverage are largely irrelevant. Rather, the government's main leverage is to promise a

VIDEO

Chinese Investments in Africa

favorable climate for doing business and making money; the MNC's main leverage is to threaten to take its capital elsewhere.

Governments can offer a variety of incentives to MNCs to invest. Special terms of taxation and of regulation are common. National and local governments may offer to provide business infrastructure—such as roads, airports, or phone lines—at the government's expense.

MNC relations with host governments contain several sources of potential conflict. One is the potential for governments to break agreements with MNCs regarding taxes, regulations, or other conditions. In the extreme case, nationalization, a host government takes ownership of MNC facilities and assets in the host country (with or without compensation). However, governments hesitate to break their word with MNCs because other MNCs may not invest there in the future. Nationalization of foreign assets is rare now.

Another source of conflict is the trade policies of the host government. Government restrictions on trade seldom help foreign MNCs; more often they help the host country's own industries—which often directly compete with foreign MNCs. Ironically, although they favor global free trade, MNCs may funnel direct investment to states that restrict imports, because MNCs can avoid the import restrictions by producing goods in the host country (rather than exporting from the home country).

Monetary policy also leads to conflicts between MNCs and host governments. When a state's currency is devalued, imports suddenly become more expensive. A foreign MNC selling an imported product (or a product assembled from imported parts) in the host country can be devastated by such a change. Therefore, an MNC making a long-term investment in a host country wants the country's currency to be reasonably stable.

Finally, MNCs may conflict with host governments on issues of international security as well as domestic political stability. When an MNC invests in a country, it assumes that its facilities there operate profitably over a number of years. If a war or revolution takes away the MNC's facility, the company loses not just income but capital—the

IT'S A JOB

Foreign direct investment is often sought by host governments because it stimulates employment and economic growth, though at wages that home countries would not tolerate. Here, Muslim women in Indonesia assemble Barbies at a Mattel factory. Note that along with investment, a host country imports certain cultural trappings of the MNC's activity—such as Mattel's rendition of femininity in its doll. (This is a literal case of what postmodern feminists call the social construction of gender roles.)

standing wealth embodied in that facility. In 2003, ethnic violence in Nigeria led to a costly, weeks-long shutdown of oil production there by ChevronTexaco, Shell, and TotalFinaElf.

In negotiating over these various sources of conflict, MNCs use a variety of means to influence host governments. They hire lobbyists, use advertisements to influence public opinion, and offer incentives to host-country politicians (such as locating facilities in their districts). Such activities are politically sensitive because host-country citizens and politicians may resent foreigners' trying to influence them. Corruption is another means of influence over host governments. Nobody knows the full extent to which MNCs use payoffs, kickbacks, gifts, and similar methods to win the approval of individual government officials for policies favorable to the MNC.

MNCs have a range of conflicts with their home governments as well. Taxation is an important one, as are trade policies. A recurrent complaint of MNCs against home governments is that policies adopted to punish political adversaries—economic sanctions and less extreme restrictions—end up harming the home-country MNCs more than the intended target. Unless ordered to do so, MNCs tend to go on doing business wherever it is profitable, with little regard for the political preferences of their governments.

The location of an MNC's headquarters determines its home nationality. The shareholders and top executives of an MNC are mostly from its home country. But as the world economy becomes more integrated, this is becoming less true. Just as MNCs are increasingly doing business all over the world and assembling products from parts made in many countries, so are shareholders and managers becoming more international in composition.

All business activity takes place in an environment shaped by politics. The international business environment most conducive to the creation of wealth by MNCs is one of stable international security. It is difficult and risky to make money in a situation of international conflict, especially one that threatens to degenerate into violence and war. War destroys wealth, reduces the supply of labor, and distorts markets in many ways. Certainly some businesses profit from international instability and the threat of war—such as arms merchants and smugglers—but these are the exceptions.

Beyond these international security concerns, MNCs favor political stability in the broader rules of the game governing international business. In monetary policy, international business benefits from the stability of rates that the managed float system tries to achieve. In trade policy, business benefits from the stability of tariff levels in the slowly shifting WTO framework. In norms of international law, business benefits from the traditions holding governments responsible for their predecessors' debts and requiring compensation for nationalized foreign assets.

We do not yet live in a world without national borders—by a long shot—but the international activities of MNCs are moving us in that direction. The next chapter considers first the United Nations and its limited supranational role; then the European Union, the most highly developed intergovernmental organization; and finally the structure and norms governing international law and how they are changing the nature of world order.

CHAPTER REVIEW

SUMMARY

- The volume of world trade is very large—about one-sixth of global economic activity—and is concentrated heavily in the states of the industrialized West (Western Europe, North America, and Japan/Pacific) and China.

- Liberal economics emphasizes international cooperation—especially through worldwide free trade—to increase the total creation of wealth (regardless of its distribution among states).

- Mercantilism emphasizes the use of economic policy to increase state power relative to other states. It mirrors realism in many ways.

- Trade creates wealth by allowing states to specialize in producing goods and services for which they have a comparative advantage (and importing other needed goods).

- The distribution of benefits from an exchange is determined by the price of the goods exchanged. With many buyers and sellers, prices are generally determined by market equilibrium (supply and demand).

- Politics interferes in international markets in many ways, including the use of economic sanctions as political leverage on a target state. However, sanctions are difficult to enforce unless all major economic actors agree to abide by them.

- States that have reduced their dependence on others by pursuing self-sufficient autarky have failed to generate new wealth to increase their well-being. Self-reliance, like central planning, has been largely discredited as a viable economic strategy.

- Through protectionist policies, many states try to protect certain domestic industries from international competition. Such policies tend to slow down the global creation of wealth but do help the particular industry in question.

- The World Trade Organization (WTO), formerly the GATT, is the most important multilateral global trade agreement. The GATT was revised in 1995 with the creation of the WTO, which expanded the focus on manufactured goods to consider agriculture and services. Intellectual property is another recent focus.

- In successive rounds of GATT negotiations over 50 years, states have lowered overall tariff rates (especially on manufactured goods). The Uruguay Round of the GATT, completed in 1994, added hundreds of billions of dollars to the global creation of wealth. The Doha Round began in 2003, and textile tariffs were dropped worldwide in 2005.

- Although the WTO provides a global framework, states continue to operate under thousands of other trade agreements specifying the rules for trade in specific products between specific countries, such as regional free trade areas (with few if any tariffs or nontariff barriers) that have been created in Europe, North America, South America, Asia, and Africa.

- International cartels are occasionally used by leading producers (sometimes in conjunction with leading consumers) to control and stabilize prices for a commodity on world markets. The most visible example in recent decades has been the oil producers' cartel, OPEC, whose members control more than half the world's exports of a vital commodity, oil.

- Because there is no world government to enforce rules of trade, such enforcement depends on reciprocity and state power. In particular, states reciprocate each other's cooperation in opening markets (or punish each other's refusal to let in foreign products). Although it leads to trade wars on occasion, reciprocity has achieved substantial cooperation in trade.

- The world economy has generated wealth at an accelerating pace in the past two centuries and is increasingly integrated on a global scale, although with huge inequalities.

- Free trade agreements have led to a backlash from politically active interest groups adversely affected by globalization; these include labor unions, environmental and human rights NGOs, and certain consumers.

- Each state uses its own currency. These currencies have no inherent value but depend on people's belief that they can be traded for future goods and services.

- Gold and silver were once used as world currencies that had value in different countries. Today's system is more abstract: national currencies are valued against each other through exchange rates.

- The most important currencies—against which most other states' currencies are compared—are the U.S. dollar, the euro, and the Japanese yen.

- Inflation, most often resulting from the printing of currency faster than the creation of new goods and services, causes the value of a currency to fall relative to other currencies. Inflation rates vary widely but are generally much higher in the global South and former Soviet bloc than in the industrialized West.

- States maintain reserves of hard currency and gold. These reserves back a national currency and cover short-term imbalances in international financial flows.

- Fixed exchange rates can be used to set the relative value of currencies, but more often states use floating exchange rates driven by supply and demand on world currency markets.

- Over the long term, the relative values of national currencies are determined by the underlying health of the national economies and by the monetary policies of governments (how much money they print). To ensure discipline in printing money—and to avoid inflation—industrialized states turn monetary policy over to semiautonomous central banks such as the U.S. Federal Reserve.

- The World Bank and the International Monetary Fund (IMF) work with states' central banks to maintain stable international monetary relations. Since 1971 the system has used Special Drawing Rights (SDRs)—a kind of world currency controlled by the IMF—rather than gold.

- The IMF operates a system of national accounts to keep track of the flow of money into and out of states. The balance of trade (exports minus imports) must be balanced by capital flows (investments and loans) and changes in reserves.

- International debt results from a protracted imbalance in capital flows—a state borrowing more than it lends—in order to cover a chronic trade deficit or government budget deficit.

- Multinational corporations (MNCs) do business in more than one state simultaneously. The largest are based in the leading industrialized states, and most are privately owned. MNCs are increasingly powerful in international economic affairs.

- MNCs try to influence the international political policies of both their headquarters state and the other states in which they operate. Generally MNCs promote policies favorable to business—low taxes, light regulation, stable currencies, and free trade. They also support stable international security relations, because war generally disrupts business.

KEY TERMS

mercantilism   165
economic liberalism   165
free trade   166
interdependence   166
balance of trade   167
comparative advantage   168
autarky   171
protectionism   172
dumping   173
tariff   173
nontariff barriers   173
World Trade Organization (WTO)   174
General Agreement on Tariffs and Trade (GATT)   174
most-favored nation (MFN)   175
Generalized System of Preferences (GSP)   175
Doha Round   176

North American Free Trade Agreement (NAFTA)   177
cartel   178
Organization of Petroleum Exporting Countries (OPEC)   178
intellectual property rights   180
service sector   181
industrialization   183
centrally planned economy   185
transitional economies   186
state-owned industries   186
mixed economies   186
gold standard   190
exchange rate   190
hyperinflation   191
hard currency   191
reserves   191

fixed exchange rates   192
floating exchange rates   192
managed float   192
devaluation   194
central bank   196
discount rate   196
Bretton Woods system   197
World Bank   197
International Monetary Fund (IMF)   197
Special Drawing Right (SDR)   197
balance of payments   198
Keynesian economics   199
fiscal policy   199
monetary policy   199
multinational corporations (MNCs)   200

ONLINE PRACTICE TEST

Take an online practice test at
www.IRtext.com

❏ **A**
🔖 **B**
❏ **C**
❏ **D**

CRITICAL THINKING QUESTIONS

1. Suppose your state had a chance to reach a major trade agreement by making substantial concessions. The agreement would produce $5 billion in new wealth for your state, as well as $10 billion for each of the other states involved (which are political allies but economic rivals). What advice would a mercantilist give your state's leaders about making such a deal? What arguments would support the advice? How would liberal advice and arguments differ?

2. China seems to have made a successful transition to market economics and is growing rapidly. It is emerging as the world's second-largest economy. Do you think this is a good thing or a bad thing for your state? Does your reasoning reflect mercantilist or liberal assumptions?

3. If you were representing an MNC such as Toyota in negotiations over building an automobile factory in a foreign country, what kinds of concessions would you ask the host government for? What would you offer as incentives? In your report to Toyota's top management regarding the deal, which points would you emphasize as most important? If instead you were representing the host state in the negotiations and reporting to top state leaders, what would be your negotiating goals and the focus of your report?

BACK TO THE BIG PICTURE

To hear a discussion of the "big picture" for this chapter, raised on p. 165, along with an example from recent history, consult the "IR Talk" podcast for Chapter 5 at *www.IRtext.com*

PODCAST

UN peacekeepers in Haiti, 2008.

<table>
</table>

CHAPTER 6

International Organization, Law, and Human Rights

Globalization and Integration

Common to most discussions of globalization is a sense that there are forces in the world bringing us all closer together. Some of these forces are the result of state decisions—as we discussed in Chapter 5, states have attempted to integrate their economies through free trade agreements. Still other forces are factors such as technological changes that influence how states, nonstate actors, and even individual citizens function on a day-to-day basis.

This chapter discusses this "coming together." We focus on state decisions to cooperate in order to create international organizations that are **supranational**—they subsume a number of states and their functions within a larger whole. The UN has some supranational aspects, though they are limited

THE BIG PICTURE

RECIPROCITY

How can countries use rules, rather than force, to settle their conflicts? They build institutions that negotiate, apply, and adjudicate the rules countries use to govern their relations. These institutions generally are founded on the reciprocity principle, treating member states as equal, though dominance and identity also play roles in the functioning of international institutions.

The United Nations (UN) represents the most advanced and most important institution in international security. Decisions by the UN Security Council, based on consensus of its Big Five permanent members, bind all countries. And UN peacekeeping forces play a major role in the waning of war discussed in Chapter 3 (pp. 63–65). But the UN is held back by its member states and lacks adequate funding for its mission.

To hear the authors of this book discuss this issue, with an example from recent history, download the "IR Talk" podcast for Chapter 6 from www.IRtext.com.

PODCAST

by the UN Charter, which is based on state sovereignty. On a regional level, the European Union (EU) is a more supranational entity than the UN; other regional organizations have tried to follow Europe's path as well, but with only limited success. These IOs all contain a struggle between the contradictory forces of *nationalism* and *supranationalism*—between state sovereignty and the higher authority of supranational structures.

In addition to formal IGOs such as the UN and the EU, people are also becoming connected across international borders through the meshing of ideas, including norms, rules, and international laws. Whether the sources of this connection are from states or nonstate actors, the process of integration always involves transnational actors or issues. *Transnational actors* (for example, MNCs and NGOs) bridge national borders, creating new avenues of interdependence among states. *Transnational issues* (for example, global warming or the spread of information technology) are processes that force states to work together because they cannot solve or manage the issues alone.

The rules that govern most interactions in IR are rooted in norms. **International norms** are the expectations actors hold about normal international relations. The attempt to define universal norms follows a centuries-long philosophical tradition. Philosophers such as Kant argued that it was natural for autonomous individuals (or states) to cooperate for mutual benefit because they could see that pursuing their narrow individual interests would end up hurting all. Thus, sovereign states could work together through structures and organizations that would respect each member's autonomy and not create a world government over them. In the 19th century, such ideas were embodied in practical organizations in which states participated to manage specific issues such as control of traffic on European rivers.

Agreed norms of behavior, institutionalized through such organizations, become *habitual* over time and gain *legitimacy*. State leaders become used to behaving in a normal way and stop calculating whether violating norms would pay off. For example, at the turn of the 19th century, U.S. war planners had active war plans for the possibility of a major naval conflict between the United States and Great Britain. Today, such plans seem ridiculous. Over time, states refrain from behavior not just for cost-benefit reasons (as emphasized by realists and liberals) but for normative reasons having little to do with material calculations (as emphasized by constructivists). Legitimacy and habit explain why international norms can be effective even when they are not codified and enforced.

The power of international norms and standards of morality, however, may vary when different states or world regions hold different expectations of what is normal. To the United States, it was a moral imperative to remove Saddam Hussein from power. But from the perspective of Arab populations, the U.S. reinvasion was an unjust violation of territorial sovereignty. In cases of diverging norms, morality can be a factor for misunderstanding and conflict rather than a force of stability. Realists point to examples such as these to suggest that international norms do not hold much sway on important matters of IR. Rather, realists point out, many of the accepted norms were shaped by the powerful states in the system (the dominance principle), and these same powerful states are often responsible for their interpretation. Yet constructivist scholars point out that even if international norms are violated, states (even the United States) go to tremendous lengths to justify behaviors that violate the norm. This suggests that strong norms do exist and are recognized by even the most powerful states.

Roles of International Organizations

International organizations (IOs) include *intergovernmental organizations (IGOs)* such as the UN, and *nongovernmental organizations (NGOs)* such as the International Committee of the Red Cross. The number of IOs has grown more than fivefold since 1945, to about 400 independent IGOs and tens of thousands of NGOs (depending somewhat on definitions). Figure 6.1 illustrates this growth. This weaving together

FIGURE 6.1   States and IGOs in the World, 1815–2000

CRITICAL INTERVENTION

International norms are evolving in such areas as humanitarian intervention versus national sovereignty. These norms help define the roles of international organizations. Here, in 2006, protesters at the UN compound in Ivory Coast object to foreign mediators' decision to dissolve Parliament as part of a postwar settlement, which the protesters call an infringement of sovereignty.

of people across national boundaries through specialized groups reflects world interdependence (see p. 166).

Some IGOs are global in scope; others are regional or just bilateral (having only two states as members). Some are general in their purposes; others have specific functional purposes. Overall, the success of these IGOs has been mixed; the regional ones have had more success than the global ones, and those with specific functional or technical purposes have worked better than those with broad purposes. IGOs hold together because they promote the national interests (or enhance the leverage) of their member states—not because of vague ideals.

Among *regional* IGOs, the European Union encompasses some of the most important organizations, but it is not the only example. Other important regional IGOs are the Association of South East Asian Nations (ASEAN), the Southern Cone Common Market (Mercosur), and the African Union.

Global IGOs (aside from the UN) usually have functional purposes involving coordinating actions of some set of states around the world. The IGO called Intelsat, for example, is a consortium of governments and private businesses that operates communications satellites. Members of the Organization of Petroleum Exporting Countries (OPEC) are major oil producers who meet periodically in Vienna to set production quotas for members in an effort to keep world oil prices high and stable.

NGOs tend to be more specialized in function than IGOs. Many NGOs have economic or business-related functions. The International Air Transport Association coordinates the work of airline companies. Other NGOs have global political purposes—for example, Amnesty International for human rights and Planned Parenthood for reproductive rights and family planning. Still other NGOs have cultural purposes—for example, the International Olympic Committee.

Religious groups are among the largest NGOs—their memberships often span many countries. Both in today's world and historically, sects of Christianity, Islam, Buddhism, Judaism, Hinduism, and other world religions have organized themselves across state borders, often in the face of hostility from one or more national governments. Missionaries have deliberately built and nurtured these transnational links. The Roman Catholic Church historically held a special position in the European international system, especially before the 17th century. NGOs with broad purposes and geographical scope often maintain observer status in the UN so that they can participate in UN meetings about issues of concern.

A web of international organizations of various sizes and types now connects people in all countries. The rapid growth of this network, and the increasingly intense communications and interactions that occur within it, indicate rising international interdependence. These organizations in turn provide the institutional mesh to hold together some kind of world order even when leaders and contexts come and go, and even when norms are undermined by sudden changes in power relations. At the center of that web of connection stands the most important international organization today, the United Nations.

The United Nations

The UN and other international organizations have both strengths and weaknesses in the anarchic international system. State sovereignty creates a real need for such organizations on a practical level, because no central world government performs the function of coordinating the actions of states for mutual benefit. However, state sovereignty also severely limits the power of the UN and other IOs, because governments reserve power to themselves and are stingy in delegating it to the UN or anyone else. The UN has had a mixed record with these strengths and weaknesses—in some ways providing remarkable global-level management and in other ways appearing helpless against the sovereignty of even modest-sized states (not to mention great powers).

The UN System

The UN is a relatively new institution, just over 60 years old. Even newer is the more prominent role that the UN has played in international security affairs since the end of the Cold War. Despite this new prominence, the main purposes of the UN are the same now as when it was founded after World War II.

Purposes of the UN   The UN is the closest thing to a world government that has ever existed, but it is not a world government. Its members are sovereign states that have not empowered the UN to enforce its will within states' territories except with the consent of those states' governments. Thus, although the UN strengthens world order, its design acknowledges the realities of international anarchy and the unwillingness of states to surrender their sovereignty. Within these limits, the basic purpose of the UN is to provide a global institutional structure through which states can sometimes settle conflicts with less reliance on the use of force.

The **UN Charter** is based on the principles that states are *equal* under international law; that states have full *sovereignty* over their own affairs; that states should have full *independence* and *territorial integrity;* and that states should carry out their international *obligations*—such as respecting diplomatic privileges, refraining from

HIGH EXPECTATIONS

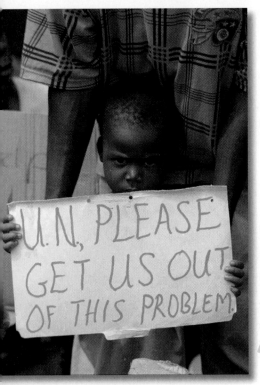

The United Nations has very limited powers and resources, yet the world places great hopes in the UN when national governments cannot solve problems. These Liberians plead for help in ending a seven-year-old civil war, 1996. The UN moves slowly, though, and Liberia fell back into civil war for seven more years until a UN-backed cease-fire (and 15,000 peacekeepers) brought peace in 2003.

committing aggression, and observing the terms of treaties they sign. The Charter also lays out the structure of the UN and the methods by which it operates.

The UN exists not because it has power to force its will on the world's states; it exists because states have created it to serve their needs. A state's membership in the UN is essentially a form of indirect leverage. States gain leverage by using the UN to seek more beneficial outcomes in conflicts. The cost of this leverage is modest—UN dues and the expenses of diplomatic representatives, in addition to the agreement to behave in accordance with the Charter (most of the time).

States get several benefits from the UN. Foremost among these is the international stability (especially in security affairs) that the UN tries to safeguard; this allows states to realize gains from trade and other forms of exchange. The UN is a *symbol* of international order and even of global identity. It is also a *forum* where states promote their views and bring their disputes. And it is a *mechanism* for conflict resolution in international security affairs. The UN also promotes and coordinates development assistance (see Chapter 7) and other programs of economic and social development in the global South. These programs reflect the belief that economic and social problems—above all, poverty—are an important source of international conflict and war. Finally, the UN is a coordinating system for *information* and planning by hundreds of internal and external agencies and programs, and for the publication of international data.

Despite its heavy tasks, the UN is still a small and fragile institution. Compare, for instance, what states spend on two types of leverage for settling conflicts: military forces and the UN. Every year, the world spends about $1.2 trillion on the military, and less than $2 billion on the UN regular budget. The whole budget of UN operations, peacekeeping, programs, and agencies combined is less than $20 billion, or less than 2 percent of world military spending. That proportion is even more extreme in the United States: more than 100 to 1. Each U.S. citizen pays (on average) nearly $2,000 a year for U.S. military spending but only about $15 a year for U.S. payments of UN dues, assessments, and voluntary contributions to UN programs and agencies combined.

Sometimes the UN succeeds and sometimes it fails. The UN deals with the issues that are perhaps the most difficult in the world. If groups of states could easily solve problems such as ethnic conflicts, human rights, refugees, and world hunger themselves, they most likely would have done so. Instead, states turn many of these difficult problems over to the UN and hope it can take care of them.

Structure of the UN   The UN's structure (see Figure 6.2) centers on the **UN General Assembly,** where representatives of all states sit together in a huge room, listen to

FIGURE 6.2   The United Nations

UN Programs	
UNEP	UN Environment Program
UNICEF	UN Children's Fund
UNDRO	Office of the UN Disaster Relief Coordinator
UNHCR	Office of the UN High Commissioner for Refugees
UNRWA*	UN Relief Works Agency [for Palestinian Refugees]
UNDP	UN Development Program
UNITAR*	UN Institute for Training and Research
UNIFEM	UN Development Fund for Women
INSTRAW	UN International Research and Training Institute [for women]
UNCTAD	UN Conference on Trade and Development
WFP	World Food Program
WFC	World Food Council
UNCHS	Human Settlements (Habitat)
UNFPA	UN Population Fund
UNU	UN University
UNDCP	Drug Control Program
ITC	International Trade Center

* Does not report to ECOSOC.

Autonomous Agencies	
IAEA*	International Atomic Energy Agency (Vienna)
WHO	World Health Organization (Geneva)
FAO	Food and Agriculture Organization (Rome)
IFAD	International Fund for Agricultural Development (Rome)
ILO	International Labor Organization (Geneva)
UNESCO	UN Educational, Scientific, and Cultural Organization (Paris)
UNIDO	UN Industrial Development Organization (Vienna)
ITU	International Telecommunications Union (Geneva)
UPU	Universal Postal Union (Berne)
ICAO	International Civil Aviation Organization (Montreal)
IMO	International Maritime Organization (London)
WIPO	World Intellectual Property Organization (Geneva)
WMO	World Meteorological Organization (Geneva)
MIGA	Multilateral Investment Guarantee Agency
IMF	International Monetary Fund (Washington)
IBRD	International Bank for Reconstruction and Development [World Bank] (Washington)
IDA	International Development Association (Washington)
IFC	International Finance Corporation (Washington)
WTO*	World Trade Organization (Geneva)

* Does not report to ECOSOC.

speeches, and pass resolutions. The General Assembly coordinates a variety of development programs and other autonomous agencies through the *Economic and Social Council (ECOSOC)*. Parallel to the General Assembly is the **UN Security Council,** in which five great powers and ten rotating member states make decisions about international peace and security. The Security Council has responsibility for the dispatch of peacekeeping forces to trouble spots. The administration of the UN takes place through the **UN Secretariat** (executive branch), led by the secretary-general of the UN. The *World Court* (International Court of Justice, discussed below) is a judicial arm of the UN.

National delegations to the UN, headed by ambassadors from each member state, work and meet together at UN headquarters in New York City. They have diplomatic status in the United States, which as host country also assumes certain other obligations to facilitate the UN's functioning. For example, the U.S. government has permitted people such as Fidel Castro—normally barred from entry to the United States—to visit New York long enough to address the UN.

A major strength of the UN structure is the *universality of its membership*. The UN had 192 members in 2009. Virtually every territory in the world is either a UN member or formally a province or colony of a UN member. (Switzerland, which traditionally maintains strict neutrality in the international system, joined only in 2003.) Formal agreement on the Charter, even if sometimes breached, commits all states to a set of basic rules governing their relations.

One way the UN induced all the great powers to join was to reassure them that their participation in the UN would not harm their national interests. Recognizing the role of power in world order, the UN Charter gave five great powers each a veto over substantive decisions of the Security Council.

The UN Charter establishes a mechanism for *collective security*—the banding together of the world's states to stop an aggressor. Chapter 7 of the Charter explicitly authorizes the Security Council to use military force against aggression if the nonviolent means called for in Chapter 6 have failed. However, because of the great power veto, the UN cannot effectively stop aggression by (or supported by) a great power. As often happens with the dominance principle, this structure creates resentments by smaller powers. In 2006, Iran's president asked the General Assembly, "If the governments of the United States or the United Kingdom commit atrocities or violate international law, which of the organizations in the United Nations can take them to account?" (None of them, of course, is the answer.) Chapter 7 was used only once during the Cold War—in the Korean War when the Soviet delegation unwisely boycotted the proceedings (and when China's seat was held by the nationalists on Taiwan).

History of the UN   The UN was founded in 1945 in San Francisco by 51 states. It was the successor to the League of Nations, which had failed to effectively counter aggression in the 1930s. Like the League, the UN was founded to increase international order and the rule of law to prevent another world war. A certain tension has long existed between the UN and the United States as the world's most powerful state. (The United States had not joined the League, and it was partly to ensure U.S. interest that the UN headquarters was placed in New York.)

In the 1950s and 1960s, the UN's membership more than doubled as colonies in Asia and Africa won independence. This changed the character of the General Assembly, in which each state has one vote regardless of size. The new members had different concerns from those of the Western industrialized countries and in many cases resented having been colonized by Westerners. Many states in the global South believed that the United States enjoyed too much power in the UN.

Until 1971, China's seat on the Security Council (and in the General Assembly) was occupied by the nationalist government on the island of Taiwan, which had lost power in mainland China in 1949. In 1971 the Chinese seat was taken from the nationalists and given to the communist government. Today, Taiwan—which functions autonomously in many international matters despite its formal status as a Chinese province—is not a member of the UN. But it is the only important nonmember.

Throughout the Cold War, the UN had few successes in international security because the U.S.-Soviet conflict prevented consensus. The UN appeared somewhat irrelevant in a world order structured by two opposing alliance blocs. The General Assembly, with its predominantly third world membership, concentrated on the economic and social problems of poor countries, and these became the main work of the UN. States in the global South also used the UN as a forum to criticize rich countries in general and the United States in particular. By the 1980s, the U.S. government showed its displeasure with this trend by withholding U.S. dues to the UN (eventually more than $1 billion), paying up only years later after UN reforms.

VIDEO

United
Nations
Reform

After the Cold War, the great powers could finally agree on measures regarding international security. The UN had several major successes in the late 1980s in ending violent regional conflicts (in Central America and the Iran-Iraq War) while introducing peacekeepers to monitor the cease-fires. Between 1987 and 1993, Security Council resolutions increased from 15 to 78, peacekeeping missions from 5 to 17, peacekeepers from 12,000 to 78,000, and countries sending troops from 26 to 76.

The new missions ran into serious problems, however. Inadequate funding and management problems undermined peacekeeping efforts in Angola, Somalia, and Cambodia. In the former Yugoslavia in 1993–1995, the UN undertook a large peacekeeping mission before a cease-fire was in place—"peacekeeping where there is no peace to keep." In response to these problems (and to the unpaid U.S. dues), the UN scaled back peacekeeping operations in 1995–1997 (from 78,000 to 19,000 troops) and carried out reductions and reforms in the UN Secretariat and UN programs.

The 2003 Iraq War triggered serious divisions among the great powers that sidelined the UN. After reaching consensus to insist on Iraqi disarmament and send back UN weapons inspectors, the Security Council split on whether to authorize force against Iraq—the United States and Britain in favor; France, Russia, and China against. When France threatened to veto a UN resolution authorizing war, a U.S.-British coalition toppled the Iraqi government without explicit UN backing. UN secretary-general Kofi Annan later called the war "illegal." The UN sent a team to Iraq to help with reconstruction, but suicide truck bombers destroyed it, killing the chief of the mission and dozens of others. Another bomber destroyed the Red Cross headquarters in Baghdad. The UN withdrew its staff from Iraq in 2003, and found itself largely sidelined in the world's most prominent international conflict.

To further aggravate U.S.-UN tensions, documents recovered during the Iraq War showed that high-ranking UN, French, Chinese, and Russian officials (and American oil companies) illegally profited from the UN's $64 billion oil-for-food program for Iraq, which was supposed to ease the civilian suffering caused by economic sanctions in the 1990s. In 2005, an independent investigation found the program corrupt and heavily criticized the UN for mismanagement and poor oversight of the program.

Currently, the UN follows a principle of "three pillars"—security, economic development, and human rights—which are considered mutually necessary for any of them to succeed. In a postwar conflict situation, in particular, the security, economic, and human rights situations reinforce each other.

The UN is in some ways just beginning to work as it was originally intended to, through a concert of great powers and universal recognition of the Charter. In the coming years the UN must continue to grapple with the challenges of its evolving role in a unipolar world, the limitations of its budget, and the strength of state sovereignty.

The Security Council

The Security Council is responsible for maintaining international peace and security and for restoring peace when it breaks down. Its decisions are *binding* on all UN member states. The Security Council has tremendous power to *define* the existence and nature of a security threat, to *structure* the response to such a threat, and to *enforce* its decisions through mandatory directives to UN members (such as to halt trade with an aggressor). In six decades, the Council has passed more than 1,800 resolutions, with new ones added by the week. These resolutions represent the great powers' blueprints for resolving the world's various security disputes, especially in regional conflicts.

The five *permanent members* of the Council—the United States, Britain, France, Russia, and China—are the most important. What they can agree on, generally the world must go along with. Issues on which they disagree can quickly become contentious. In 2008, after the Council failed to decide whether the Serbian province of Kosovo should be independent, Kosovars unilaterally declared their independence from Serbia. Kosovo was quickly recognized by some Security Council members (the United States, France, and Britain), but not others (China and Russia). Angry Serbians rejected Kosovo's declaration.

Substantive Security Council resolutions require 9 votes from among the 15 members. But a "no" vote by any permanent member defeats the resolution—the *veto* power. Many resolutions have been vetoed by the permanent members, and many more have never been proposed because they would have faced certain veto. However, since the early 1990s the use of the veto has dropped abruptly, to just 19 vetoes in the last 13 years—12 of them by the United States, 4 by China, and 3 by Russia.

The Council's ten *nonpermanent members* rotate onto the Council for two-year terms. Nonpermanent members are elected (five each year) by the General Assembly from a list prepared by informal regional caucuses. Usually there is a mix of regions and country sizes, though not by any strict formula. Often, countries lobby vigorously for a seat on the Council, producing books, advertisements, and memos to gain votes from other members of the regional caucuses.

Table 6.1 shows the recent rotations of members onto the Security Council. The system of nomination by regional caucuses has kept the regional balance on the Council fairly constant as individual states come and go. Major regional actors, including those mentioned as candidates for possible new permanent seats, tend to rotate onto the Council more often than do less important states.

The Security Council's power is limited in two major ways, both reflect the strength of state sovereignty in the international system. First, the Council's decisions depend entirely on the interests of its member states (see Figure 6.3). The ambassadors who represent

COUNCIL OF POWER

Collective security rests with the UN Security Council, which has authorized such military interventions as the Gulf War and the 2001 campaign in Afghanistan. Military actions not approved by the Council—such as the 1999 bombing of Serbia and the 2003 U.S.-British invasion of Iraq—tend to be controversial. Here, Serbia's president (left end of table) objects to Kosovo's claim of independence from Serbia, 2008. With the permanent members split on the issue—Russia and China backed Serbia while the United States, Britain, and France recognized Kosovo—the Council did not take action.

those states cannot change a Council resolution without authorization from their governments. Second, although Security Council resolutions in theory bind all UN members, member states in practice often try to evade or soften their effect. For instance, trade sanctions are difficult to enforce. A Security Council resolution can be enforced in practice only if enough powerful states care about it. Even when the Security Council cannot agree on means of enforcement, however, its resolutions shape the way disputes are seen and ultimately how they are resolved.

Proposed Changes The structure of the Security Council is not without problems. Japan and Germany are great powers that contribute substantial UN dues (based on economic size) and make large contributions to UN programs and peacekeeping operations. Yet they have exactly the same formal representation in the UN as tiny states: one vote in the General Assembly and the chance to rotate onto the Security Council (in practice they rotate onto the Council more often than others). As global trading powers, Japan and Germany have huge stakes in the ground rules for international security affairs, and would like seats at the table.

TABLE 6.1　　Regional Representation on the UN Security Council

Region	Permanent Members[a]	NONPERMANENT MEMBERS[b]			Possible Contenders for New Permanent Seats[c]
		2009	2008	2007	
North America	United States				
W. Europe	Britain France	Austria Croatia	Italy Belgium Croatia	Italy Belgium Slovakia	Germany
Japan/Pacific		Japan			Japan
Russia/CIS	Russia				
China	China				
Middle East		Libya Turkey	Libya	Qatar	Egypt?
Latin America		Costa Rica Mexico	Costa Rica Panama	Peru Panama	Brazil, Mexico?
South Asia		Vietnam	Indonesia Vietnam	Indonesia	India, Indonesia?
Africa		Uganda Burkina Faso	South Africa Burkina Faso	South Africa Ghana Congo Republic	Nigeria? South Africa?

[a]The five permanent members hold veto power.
[b]Nonpermanent members are elected for two-year terms by the General Assembly, based on nominations by regional caucuses.
[c]Possible new permanent seats might have fewer if any veto powers.

But including Japan and Germany as permanent Security Council members would not be simple. If Germany joined, three of the seven permanent members would be European, giving that region unfair weight. The three European seats could be combined into one (a rotating seat or one representing the European Union), but this would water down the power of Britain and France, which can veto any such change in the Charter. Japan's bid for a seat faces Chinese opposition. Also, if Japan or Germany got a seat, then what about India, with 20 percent of the world's population? And what about an Islamic country such as Indonesia? Finally, what about Latin America and Africa? Possible new permanent members could include Germany, Japan, India, Brazil, Egypt, and either Nigeria or South Africa. None of these plans has made much progress. Any overhaul of the Security Council would reduce the power of the current five permanent members, any of which could veto the change.

FIGURE 6.3   Divergent Interests on the UN Security Council

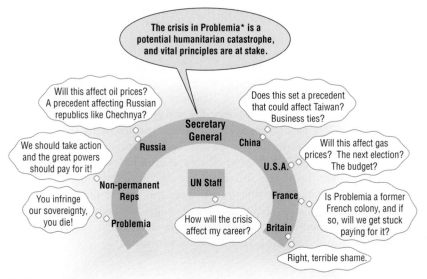

*Problemia could be Kurdish Iraq in 1991 or Darfur, Sudan, in 2007.

Peacekeeping Forces

Peacekeeping forces are not mentioned in the UN Charter. The Charter requires member states to place military forces at the disposal of the UN, but such forces were envisioned as being used in response to aggression (under collective security). In practice, when the UN has authorized force to reverse aggression—as in the Gulf War in 1990—the forces involved have been *national* forces not under UN command.

The UN's *own* forces—borrowed from armies of member states but under the flag and command of the UN—have been *peacekeeping* forces to calm regional conflicts, playing a neutral role between warring forces. These forces won the Nobel Peace Prize in 1988 in recognition of their growing importance and success. However, such neutral forces do not succeed well in a situation in which the Security Council has identified one side as the aggressor.

Peacekeeping Missions   The secretary-general assembles a peacekeeping force for each mission, usually from a few states totally uninvolved in the conflict, and puts it under a single commander. The soldiers are called *blue helmets*. Peacekeeping forces serve at the invitation of a host government and must leave if that government orders them out.

Authority for peacekeeping forces is granted by the Security Council, usually for a period of three to six months that may be renewed—in some cases for decades. *Funds* must be voted on by the General Assembly, and lack of funds is today the single greatest constraint on the use of peacekeeping forces. Special assessments against member states pay for peacekeeping operations. With the expansion of peacekeeping, these expenses far exceed the rest of the UN budget, coming to about $7 billion in 2007.

Recent Missions   In early 2009, the UN maintained more than 90,000 troops (including police and military observers) in 16 separate peacekeeping or observing missions (see Table 6.2).

VIDEO

**UN Aid in
Darfur, Sudan**

The largest peacekeeping mission in 2009 was in Democratic Congo, where more than 18,000 peacekeepers monitored a cease-fire and protected civilians after a civil war. In late 2008, these UN peacekeepers were criticized for not doing enough to protect civilians in refugee camps as the civil war in the eastern portion of the country reignited. UN forces occasionally were attacked by rebels and even by local civilians angry at the UN's failure to protect them. The Secretary General called for thousands of additional troops, but member states were reluctant to bear the cost of providing them. This problem illustrates the limits of the identity principle in solving a collective goods problem, where potential suppliers of peacekeepers face neither rewards for doing so (reciprocity) nor punishment for failing to do so (dominance).

TABLE 6.2   UN Peacekeeping Missions as of January 2009

Location	Region	Size	Annual Cost (million $)	Role	Since
Democratic Congo	Africa	18,500	$1,240	Observe cease-fire; protect civilians	1999
Liberia	Africa	12,700	630	Assist transitional govt.	2003
Sudan	Africa	10,000	860	Support agreement; monitor war	2005
Sudan/Darfur[a]	Africa	11,400	1,570	Protect civilians	2007
Ivory Coast	Africa	9,200	500	Help implement peace agreement	2004
Western Sahara	Africa	230	50	Organize referendum in territory	1991
Central Afr. Rep./Chad	Africa	280	315	Assist in repatriation of refugees	2007
India/Pakistan	South Asia	50	15	Observe India-Pakistan cease-fire	1949
Kosovo	Russia/CIS	1,900	205	Civil administration; relief	1999
Georgia	Europe	150	35	Observe cease-fire in civil war	1993
Lebanon	Middle East	13,000	680	Monitor cease-fire on Israeli border	1978
Syria (Golan Heights)	Middle East	1,000	50	Monitor Israel-Syria cease-fire	1974
Cyprus	Middle East	900	60	Monitor Greek-Turkish cease-fire	1964
Israel	Middle East	150	70	Observe Arab-Israeli truce	1948
Haiti	Latin America	9,000	600	Assist transitional govt.	2004
East Timor	Japan/Pacific	1,600	180	Observe cease-fire; policing	2006
Total		90,060	7,060		

Note: Size indicates total international personnel (mostly troops but some civilian administrators and police).

[a]The Sudan/Darfur force is a joint African Union-United Nations peacekeeping force that has not achieved its authorized strength.

In 2007, the Security Council approved a nearly 20,000-troop peacekeeping force (plus more than 6,000 police) for the Darfur region in Sudan, after several years of resistance from the Sudanese government. The UN troops were to join an already-deployed (but small) African Union contingent. Although the UN deployment was scheduled to occur throughout 2008, Sudanese government objections delayed the operation. By early 2009, only half of the authorized troops had been deployed, owing to continued objections from Sudan. These new deployments are in addition to the 10,000 UN troops enforcing a cease-fire in the southern part of Sudan.

VIDEO

United Nations Operations in Haiti

The UN's other largest peacekeeping operations were in Liberia (maintaining a cease-fire after a civil war), Ivory Coast and Burundi (stabilizing peace agreements), Lebanon (following the 2006 Israeli-Hezbollah war), and Haiti (trying to maintain stability after a military coup). The largest recent missions reflect the resurgence of UN peacekeeping after a shakeout in the mid-1990s.

NATO-led forces largely replaced UN peacekeepers in Bosnia in the late 1990s (and later took military control of Kosovo). UN operations in these countries focus on civilian governmental functions, leaving security matters largely to UN-authorized but independently commanded international forces. The same approach was used in East Timor with an Australian-led force.

At its peak in the early 1990s, the UN ran several large peacekeeping operations in addition to those in the former Yugoslavia and in Lebanon. In Cambodia, 15,000 peacekeepers were coupled with a large force of UN administrators who took over substantial control of the Cambodian government under a fragile pact that ended a long and devastating civil war. The lessons learned in Cambodia helped the UN accomplish a similar mission more easily in Mozambique. These experiences helped the UN respond effectively after civil wars in Sierra Leone, Ivory Coast, and Liberia in 2002–2003. Because of problems with sex-related crimes in UN peacekeeping operations, and the importance of women in postwar societies, the Security Council passed Resolution 1325 in 2000 to focus attention on gender issues in UN peacekeeping and reconstruction (see p. 223).

As UN peacekeeping has become more intensive in recent years, a new generation of missions has expanded the range of what are now broadly called *peace operations*. These operations include not only traditional peacekeeping but also the use of force to protect civilians (as in Democratic Congo), the supervision of elections (as in Liberia), and even running the government while a society gets back on its feet (as in Cambodia, East Timor, and Kosovo). These expanded operations, especially when they entail the use of force rather than relying on the consent of all parties, are called **peacebuilding**. In an effort to provide longer-term support after wars, in 2005 the UN created a Peacebuilding Commission to coordinate reconstruction, institution building, and economic recovery efforts in postwar societies after peacekeeping missions end.

Observing and Peacekeeping   "Peacekeepers" actually perform two different functions: observing and peacekeeping. *Observers* are unarmed military officers sent to a conflict area in small numbers simply to watch what happens and report back to the UN. With the UN watching, the parties to a conflict are often less likely to break a cease-fire. Observers can monitor various aspects of a country's situation—cease-fires, elections, respect for human rights, and other areas.

The function of *peacekeeping* is carried out by lightly armed soldiers (in armored vehicles with automatic rifles but without artillery, tanks, and other heavy weapons). Such forces play several roles. They can *interpose* themselves physically between warring parties to keep them apart (more accurately, to make them attack the UN forces in order to get to their enemy). UN peacekeepers often try to *negotiate* with military officers on both sides. This channel of communication can bring about tactical actions and understandings that support a cease-fire. But the UN forces in a war zone cannot easily get from one side's positions to those of the other to conduct negotiations. Peacekeeping is much more difficult if one side sees the UN forces as being biased toward the other side. When cease-fires break down, UN troops get caught in the middle. More than 2,200 have been killed over the years.

In some conflicts, peacekeepers organized outside the UN framework have been used instead of UN-commanded forces. Some 3,500 French peacekeepers—not under UN command—serve in Ivory Coast alongside 9,000 UN peacekeepers from other countries, monitoring a 2003 cease-fire between the rebel-held north of the country and the government-held south. When government airstrikes killed nine French soldiers in 2004, the French forces retaliated robustly, destroying the government's air force.

Peacekeeping forces have generally been unable to make peace, only to keep it. To go into a shooting war and suppress hostilities requires military forces far beyond those of past UN peacekeeping missions. Thus, peacekeepers are usually not sent until a cease-fire has been arranged, has taken effect, and has held up for some time. Often dozens of cease-fires are broken before one sticks—wars may simmer along for years, taking a terrible toll, before the UN gets its chance.

In the late 1990s, seven countries—Denmark, Norway, Sweden, Poland, the Netherlands, Austria, and Canada—formed a 4,000-troop UN Standby High Readiness Brigade. Headquartered in Denmark and available to deploy to conflict areas in two to four weeks rather than in months, as traditional forces now require, the brigade is controlled by the Security Council. It participated in the UN mission to Ethiopia-Eritrea in 2000–2001. In 2005 the brigade deployed to Sudan to support a peace agreement between northern and southern regions after a long civil war that had killed millions.

The Secretariat

The secretary-general of the UN is the closest thing to a "president of the world" that exists. But the secretary-general represents member states—not the world's 6 billion people. The secretary-general is nominated by the Security Council—requiring the consent of all five permanent members—and must be approved by the General Assembly. The term of office is five years and may be renewed. Secretaries-general have come from various regions of the world but never from a great power.

Secretary-General Ban Ki-moon, a former foreign minister of South Korea, began his term in 2007 focused on UN reform, economic development, human rights, terrorism, proliferation, environmental problems, and HIV/AIDS. His predecessor, Kofi Annan, from Ghana, served ten years and helped reinvigorate the UN, winning the one-hundredth-anniversary Nobel Peace Prize for his efforts.

The Secretariat of the UN is its executive branch, headed by the secretary-general. It is a bureaucracy for administering UN policy and programs. In security matters, the secretary-general personally works with the Security Council; development programs in poor countries are coordinated by a second-in-command, the director-general for Development and International Economic Cooperation. The Secretariat is divided into functional areas, with undersecretaries-general and assistant secretaries-general. The UN staff in these areas includes administrative personnel as well as technical experts and economic advisors working on various programs and projects in the member countries. The staff numbers about 15,000 people, and the total number of employees in the UN system (including the World Bank and IMF) is about 60,000.

One purpose of the UN Secretariat is to develop an *international civil service* of diplomats and bureaucrats whose loyalties lie at the global level, not with their states of origin. The UN Charter sets the secretary-general and staff apart from the authority of national governments and calls on member states to respect the staff's "exclusively international character." The UN has been fairly successful in this regard; the secretary-general is most often seen as an independent diplomat thinking about the whole world's interests, not as a pawn of any state. But in the early 1990s the UN bureaucracy came under increasing criticism for both inefficiency and corruption. These criticisms, coming especially from the United States, which saw itself as bearing an unfair share of the costs, led to a reform program. By the late 1990s, UN staff was reduced by one-quarter compared to a decade earlier, and budgets were scaled back year by year.

The secretary-general is more than a bureaucratic manager. He (it has not yet been a she) is a visible public figure whose personal attention to a regional conflict can move it toward resolution. The Charter allows the secretary-general to use the UN's "good offices" to serve as a neutral mediator in international conflicts—to bring hostile parties together in negotiations.

The secretary-general also works to bring together the great power consensus on which Security Council action depends. The secretary-general has the power under the Charter to bring to the Security Council any matter that might threaten international peace and security, and so to play a major role in setting the UN's agenda in international security affairs. Still, the secretary-general experiences tensions with the Security Council. When the secretary-general asks for authority for a peacekeeping mission for six months, the Security Council is likely to say "three months." If the secretary-general asks for $10 million, he might get $5 million. Thus the secretary-general remains, like the entire UN system, constrained by state sovereignty.

The General Assembly

The General Assembly is made up of all 192 member states of the UN, each with one vote. It usually meets every year, from late September through January, in *plenary session*. State leaders or foreign ministers, including the U.S. president, generally come through one by one to address this assemblage. This global town hall is a unique institution and provides a powerful medium for states to put forward their ideas and arguments. Presiding over it is a president elected by the Assembly—a post without much power.

The Assembly convenes for *special sessions* every few years on general topics such as economic cooperation or disarmament. The Assembly has met in *emergency session* in the past to deal with an immediate threat to international peace and security, but this has happened only nine times and has now become uncommon.

The General Assembly has the power to accredit national delegations as members of the UN (through its Credentials Committee). For instance, in 1971 the delegation of the People's Republic of China was given China's seat in the UN (including on the Security Council) in place of the nationalists in Taiwan. Some political entities that fall short of state status send *permanent observer missions* to the UN, which participate without a vote in the General Assembly; these include the Vatican (Holy See) and the Palestinian Authority.

The General Assembly's main power lies in its control of finances for UN programs and operations, including peacekeeping. It also can pass resolutions on various matters, but these are purely advisory and at times have served largely to vent frustrations of the majority. The Assembly also elects members of certain UN agencies and programs. Finally, the Assembly coordinates UN programs and agencies through its own system of committees, commissions, and councils.

Many of the activities associated with the UN do not take place under tight control of either the General Assembly or the Security Council. They occur in functional agencies and programs that have various amounts of autonomy from UN control.

UN Programs

Through the Economic and Social Council, the General Assembly oversees more than a dozen major programs to advance economic development and social stability in poor states of the global South. Through its programs, the UN helps manage global North-South relations: it organizes a flow of resources and skills from the richer parts of the world to support development in the poorer parts.

The programs are funded partly by General Assembly allocations and partly by contributions that the programs raise directly from member states, businesses, or private charitable contributors. The degree of General Assembly funding, and of operational autonomy from the Assembly, varies from one program to another. Each UN program has a staff, a headquarters, and various operations in the field, where it works with host governments in member states.

The *UN Environment Program (UNEP)* became more prominent in the 1990s as the economic development of the global South and the growing economies of the industrialized world took a toll on the world environment (see Chapter 8). The UNEP grapples with global environmental strategies. It provides technical assistance to member states, monitors environmental conditions globally, develops standards, and recommends alternative energy sources.

UNICEF is the UN Children's Fund, which gives technical and financial assistance to poor countries for programs benefiting children. Unfortunately, the needs of children in many countries are still urgent, and UNICEF is kept busy. Financed by voluntary contributions, UNICEF has for decades organized U.S. children in an annual Halloween fund drive on behalf of their counterparts in poorer countries.

The *Office of the UN High Commissioner for Refugees (UNHCR)* is also busy. It coordinates efforts to protect, assist, and eventually repatriate the many refugees who flee across international borders each year to escape war and political violence. (The longer-standing problem of Palestinian refugees is handled by a different program, the *UN Relief Works Agency*, or *UNRWA*.)

The *UN Development Program (UNDP)*, funded by voluntary contributions, coordinates all UN efforts related to development in poor countries. With about 5,000 projects operating simultaneously around the world, UNDP is the world's largest international agency for technical development assistance. The UN also runs several development-related agencies for training and for promoting women's role in development.

Many poor countries depend on export revenues to finance economic development, making them vulnerable to fluctuations in commodity prices and other international trade problems. The **UN Conference on Trade and Development (UNCTAD)** negotiates international trade agreements to stabilize commodity prices and promote development. Because countries of the global South do not have much power in the international economy, however, UNCTAD has little leverage to promote their interests in trade (see p. 295). The World Trade Organization has become the main organization dealing with trade issues (see pp. 174–176).

In 2006, the UN created a new Human Rights Council, replacing a Human Rights Commission notorious for including human rights abusers as member states. The new council is to have expanded powers and more selective membership. Other UN programs manage problems such as disaster relief, food aid, housing, and population issues. Throughout the poorer countries, the UN maintains an active presence.

Autonomous Agencies

In addition to its own programs, the UN General Assembly maintains formal ties with about 20 autonomous international agencies not under its control. Most are specialized technical organizations through which states pool their efforts to address problems such as health care and labor conditions. The only such agency in international security affairs is the *International Atomic Energy Agency (IAEA)*, headquartered in Vienna, Austria. It was established under the UN but is formally autonomous. Although the IAEA has an economic role in helping develop civilian nuclear power, it mainly works to prevent nuclear proliferation (see p. 156). The IAEA was responsible for inspections in Iraq in 2002–2003, which found no

HELPING WHERE NEEDED

An array of UN programs, operating under the General Assembly, aim to help countries in the global South to overcome social and economic problems. These programs played a crucial role in the massive international assistance effort that followed the 2004 Indian Ocean tsunami, and in the long-term development of the devastated regions. This helicopter from the UN refugee agency, on loan from the Swiss government, delivers supplies in Indonesia, 2005.

evidence of a secret nuclear weapons program. It is involved in monitoring Iran's nuclear program to the extent Iran allows. The IAEA won the 2005 Nobel Peace Prize.

In the area of health care, the Geneva-based **World Health Organization (WHO)** provides assistance to improve conditions and conduct major immunization campaigns in poor countries. In the 1960s and 1970s, WHO led one of the great public health victories of all time—the worldwide eradication of smallpox. Today WHO is a leading player in the worldwide fight to control AIDS (see pp. 330–332).

In agriculture, the *Food and Agriculture Organization (FAO)* is the lead agency. In labor standards, it is the *International Labor Organization (ILO)*. UNESCO—the *UN Educational, Scientific, and Cultural Organization*—facilitates international communication and scientific collaboration. The *UN Industrial Development Organization (UNIDO)* promotes industrialization in the global South.

The longest-established IOs, with some of the most successful records, are specialized agencies dealing with technical aspects of international coordination. For instance, the *International Telecommunications Union (ITU)* allocates radio frequencies. The *Universal Postal Union (UPU)* sets standards for international mail. The *International Civil Aviation Organization (ICAO)* sets binding standards for international air traffic. The *International Maritime Organization (IMO)* facilitates international cooperation on shipping at sea. The *World Intellectual Property Organization (WIPO)* seeks world compliance with copyrights and patents and promotes development and technology transfer within a legal framework that protects such intellectual property. Finally, the *World Meteorological Association (WMA)* promotes the exchange of weather information.

The major coordinating agencies of the world economy (discussed in Chapters 5 and 7) are also UN-affiliated agencies. The World Bank and the International Monetary Fund (IMF) give loans, grants, and technical assistance for economic development (and the IMF manages international balance-of-payments accounting). The World Trade Organization (WTO) sets rules for international trade.

Overall, the density of connections across national borders, both in the UN system and through other IOs, is increasing year by year. These interconnections are furthest developed in the European Union.

The European Union

Like the UN, the **European Union (EU)** was created after World War II and has developed since. But whereas the UN structure has changed little since its Charter was adopted, the EU has gone through several waves of expansion in its scope, membership, and mission over the past 50 years. The EU today has nearly 500 million citizens and surpasses the U.S. economy in GDP.

Integration Theory

The theory of international integration attempts to explain why states choose supranationalism, which challenges once again the foundations of realism (state sovereignty and territorial integrity). **International integration** refers to the process by which supranational institutions replace national ones—the gradual shifting upward of sovereignty from state to regional or global structures. The ultimate expression of integration would be the merger of several (or many) states into a single state—or ultimately into a single world government. Such a shift in sovereignty to the supranational level would probably entail some version of federalism, in which states or other political units recognize the sovereignty of a central government while retaining certain powers for themselves. This is the form of government adopted in the U.S. Constitution.

In practice, the process of integration has never gone beyond a partial and uneasy sharing of power between state and supranational levels. States have been unwilling to give up their exclusive claim to sovereignty and have severely limited the power and authority of supranational institutions. The most successful example of the process of integration by far—though even that success is only partial—is the European Union. The regional coordination now occurring in Western Europe is a new historical phenomenon.

CROSSING THE BORDER

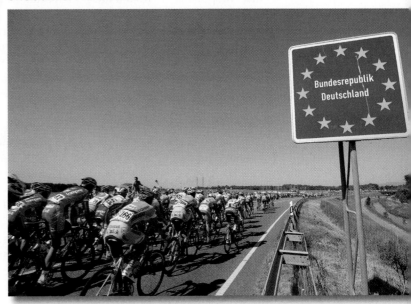

Integration processes in Europe and elsewhere are making state borders more permeable to people, goods, and ideas—increasing interdependence. The European Union is deepening economic integration while expanding eastward. Here, in 2006, the Tour de France crosses into Germany, passing only a road sign where in centuries past great armies faced off across massive fortifications

Until 50 years ago, the European continent was the embodiment of national sovereignty, state rivalry, and war. For 500 years until 1945, the states of Europe were locked in chronic intermittent warfare; in the 20th century alone two world wars left the continent in ruins. The European states have historical and present-day religious, ethnic, and cultural differences. The 27 members of the EU in 2009 spoke 23 different official languages. If ever there were a candidate for the failure of integration, Europe would appear to be it. Even more surprising, European integration began with the cooperation of Europe's two bitterest enemies over the previous 100 years, enemies in three major wars since 1870—France and Germany.

That Western European states began forming supranational institutions and creating an economic community to promote free trade and coordinate economic policies caught the attention of IR scholars, who used the term *integration* to describe what they observed. Seemingly, integration challenged the realist assumption that states were strictly autonomous and would never yield power or sovereignty. These scholars proposed that European moves toward integration could be explained by *functionalism*—growth of specialized technical organizations that cross national borders. According to functionalists, technological and economic development lead to more and more supranational structures as states seek practical means to fulfill necessary *functions* such as delivering mail from one country to another or coordinating the use of rivers that cross borders. As these connections became denser and the flows faster, functionalism predicted that states would be drawn together into stronger international economic structures.

The European experience, however, went beyond the creation of specialized agencies to include the development of more general, more political supranational bodies, such as the European Parliament. **Neofunctionalism** is a modification of functional theory by IR scholars to explain these developments. Neofunctionalists argue that economic integration (functionalism) generates a *political* dynamic that drives integration further. Closer economic ties require more political coordination in order to operate effectively and eventually lead to political integration as well—a process called *spillover*.

Some scholars focused on the less-tangible *sense of community* ("we" feeling) that began to develop among Europeans, running contrary to nationalist feelings that still existed as well. The low expectation of violence among the states of Western Europe created a **security community** in which such feelings could grow. This is a prime example of the identity principle in IR.

Costs of Integration   The new wave of integration in Europe and elsewhere is encountering limits and setbacks. Integration can mean greater centralization at a time when individuals, local groups, and national populations demand more say over their own affairs. The centralization of political authority, information, and culture as a result of integration can threaten both individual and group freedom. Ethnic groups want to safeguard their own cultures, languages, and institutions against the bland homogeneity that a global or regional melting pot would create. As a result, many states and citizens, in Europe and elsewhere, responded to the new wave of integration with resurgent nationalism over the past decade.

Indeed, these forces have set in motion a wave of *disintegration* of states running counter to (though simultaneous with) the integrating tendencies in today's world. The wave of disintegration in some ways began with the decolonization of former European empires after World War II. After the Cold War, disintegration centered on Russia and Eastern Europe—especially in the former Soviet Union and former Yugoslavia. States in other regions—Somalia, Democratic Congo, and Iraq—appear in danger of breaking into pieces, in practice if not formally. A challenge to integration theorists in the future will be to account for these new trends running counter to integration.

Throughout the successful and unsuccessful efforts at integration runs a common thread—the tension between nationalism and supranational loyalties (regionalism or globalism). In the less successful integration attempts, nationalism stands virtually unchallenged, and even in the most successful cases, nationalism remains a potent force locked in continual struggle with supranationalism. This struggle is a central theme even in the most successful case of integration—the European Union.

The Vision of a United Europe

Europe in 1945 was decimated by war. Most of the next decade was spent recovering with help from the United States through the Marshall Plan. But already two French leaders, Jean Monnet and Robert Schuman, were developing a plan to implement the idea of functionalism in Europe—that future wars could be prevented by creating economic linkages that would eventually bind states together politically.

In 1950, Schuman, as French foreign minister, proposed a first modest step—the merger of the French and German steel (iron) and coal industries into a single framework that could most efficiently use the two states' coal resources and steel mills. Coal and steel were key to European recovery and growth. The Schuman plan gave birth in 1952 to the *European Coal and Steel Community (ECSC)*, in which France and Germany were joined by Italy (the third large industrial country of continental Europe) and by three smaller countries—Belgium, the Netherlands, and Luxembourg (together called the *Benelux countries*). These six states worked through the ECSC to reduce trade barriers in coal and steel and to coordinate their coal and steel policies. The ECSC also established a High Authority that to some extent could bypass governments and deal directly with companies, labor unions, and individuals. Britain, however, did not join.

If coal and steel sound like fairly boring topics, that was exactly the idea of functionalists. The issues involved were matters for engineers and technical experts and did not threaten politicians. (Of course, coal and steel were not chosen by accident, since both were essential to make war.) If German and French steel experts had more in common than German and French politicians, this is even truer of scientists. Today the European scientific community is one of the most internationally integrated areas of society. For example, the EU operates the European Space Agency and the European Molecular Biology Laboratory.

Although technical cooperation succeeded in 1952, political and military cooperation proved much more difficult. In line with the vision of a united Europe, the six ECSC states signed a second treaty in 1952 to create a European Defense Community to work toward integrating Europe's military forces under one budget and command. But the French parliament failed to ratify the treaty, and Britain refused to join such a force. The ECSC states also discussed formation of a European Political Community in 1953, but could not agree on its terms. Thus, in economic cooperation, the supranational institutions succeeded, but in political and military affairs, state sovereignty prevailed.

The Treaty of Rome

In the **Treaty of Rome** in 1957, the same six states (France, Germany, Italy, Belgium, the Netherlands, and Luxembourg) created two new organizations. One extended the coal-and-steel idea into a new realm, atomic energy. **Euratom,** the European Atomic Energy Community, was formed to coordinate nuclear power development by pooling research, investment, and management. It continues to operate today with an expanded membership. The second organization was the *European Economic Community (EEC)*, later renamed the *European Community (EC)*.

As discussed briefly in Chapter 5, there are important differences between *free trade areas, customs unions,* and *common markets.* Creating a **free trade area** meant lifting tariffs and restrictions on the movement of goods across (EEC) borders, as was done shortly after 1957. Today the *European Free Trade Association (EFTA)* is an extended free trade area associated with the European Union; its members are Norway, Iceland, Liechtenstein, and Switzerland.

In a **customs union,** participating states adopt a unified set of tariffs on goods coming in from outside the free trade area. Without this, each type of good could be imported into the state with the lowest tariff and then reexported (tariff free) to the other states in the free trade area. The Treaty of Rome committed the six states to creating a customs union by 1969. A customs union creates free and open trade within its member states, bringing great economic benefits. Thus, the customs union remains the heart of the EU and the one aspect widely copied elsewhere in the world.

A **common market** means that in addition to the customs union, member states allow labor and capital (as well as goods) to flow freely across borders. For instance, a Belgian financier can invest in Germany on the same terms as a German investor. Although the Treaty of Rome adopted the goal of a common market, even today it has been only partially achieved.

One key aspect of a common market was achieved, at least in theory, in the 1960s when the EU (then the EC) adopted a **Common Agricultural Policy (CAP).** In practice, the CAP has led to recurrent conflicts among member states and tensions between nationalism and regionalism (see pp. 73–74). To promote national self-sufficiency in food, many governments give subsidies to farmers. The CAP was based on the principle that a subsidy extended to farmers in any member state should be extended to farmers in all EU countries. That way, no member government was forced to alienate politically powerful farmers by removing subsidies, yet the overall policy would be equalized throughout the community in line with the common market principle. As a result, subsidies to farmers today absorb about 40 percent of the total EU budget, with France as the main beneficiary, and are the single greatest source of trade friction between Europe and the United States (see pp. 170–172).

The next step in the plan for European integration, after a free trade area, customs union, and common market, was an *economic and monetary union (EMU)* in which the overall economic policies of the member states would be coordinated for greatest efficiency and stability. In this step, a single currency would replace separate national currencies (see below). A possible future step could be the supranational coordination of economic policies such as budgets and taxes.

To reduce state leaders' fears of losing sovereignty, the Treaty of Rome provides that changes in its provisions must be approved by all member states. For example, France vetoed Britain's application for membership in the EEC in 1963 and 1967. However, in 1973 Britain did finally join, along with Ireland and Denmark. This expanded the organization's membership to nine, including the largest and richest countries in the region.

In 1981, Greece was admitted, and in 1986 Portugal and Spain joined. Inclusion of these poorer countries with less industry and lower standards of living created difficulties in effectively integrating Europe's economies that persist today, as the rich European states give substantial aid to the poorer ones in hopes of strengthening the weak links. Greece, Portugal, Spain, and Ireland were called the *"poor four"* within the EU, but have grown more prosperous, and new "poor" members have now joined from Eastern Europe.

Structure of the European Union

The structure of the EU reflects its roots in technical and economic cooperation. The coal and steel experts have been joined by experts on trade, agriculture, and finance at the heart of the community. The EU headquarters and staff have the reputation of colorless bureaucrats—sometimes called *Eurocrats*—who care more about technical problem solving than about politics. These supranational bureaucrats are balanced in the EU structure by provisions that uphold the power of states and state leaders.

Although the rule of Eurocrats follows the functionalist plan, it has created problems as the EU has progressed. Politicians in member states have qualms about losing power to the Eurocrats. Citizens in some states have become uncomfortable with the growing power of faceless Eurocrats over their lives. Citizens can throw their own political leaders out of office in national elections, but the Eurocrats seem less accountable.

The EU's structure is illustrated in Figure 6.4. The Eurocrats consist of a staff of 24,000, organized under the **European Commission** at EU headquarters in Brussels, Belgium. The Commission has 27 individual members—one from each member state—who are chosen for four-year renewable terms. Their role is to identify problems and

FIGURE 6.4   Structure of the European Union (EU)

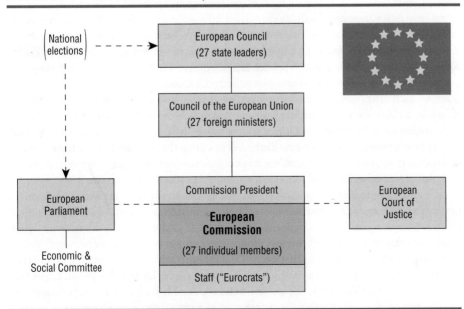

propose solutions to the Council of the European Union. They select one of their members as the Commission president. These individuals are supposed to represent the interests of Europe as a whole (supranational interests), not their own states, but this goal has been only imperfectly met.

The European Commission lacks formal autonomous power except for day-to-day EU operations. Formally, the Commission reports to, and implements policies of, the **Council of the European Union.** The Council is a meeting of the relevant ministers (foreign, economic, agriculture, finance, etc.) of each member state—politicians who control the bureaucrats (or who try to). This formal structure reflects states' resistance to yielding sovereignty. It also means that the individuals making up the Council of the European Union vary from one meeting to the next, and that technical issues receive priority over political ones. The arrangement thus gives some advantage back to the Commission staff. Recall the similar tension between politicians and career bureaucrats in national foreign policy making (see pp. 10–12).

The Council of the European Union in theory has a weighted voting system based on each state's population, but in practice it operates by consensus on major policy issues (all members must agree). On other issues, decisions can be made by qualified majorities, overriding national sovereignty. The Council has a rotating presidency (with limited power). The Council of the European Union must approve the policies of the European Commission and give it general directions.

In the 1970s, state leaders (prime ministers or presidents) created a special place for themselves in the EC, to oversee the direction of the community; this structure again shows state leaders' resistance to being governed by any supranational body. This *European Council* of the 27 state leaders meets with the Commission president twice a year. They are the ones with the power to get things done in their respective national governments (which still control most of the money and power in Europe).

There is a **European Parliament,** which falls somewhat short of a true legislature passing laws for all of Europe. The proposed European constitution would have strengthened it. At present it operates partly as a watchdog over the Commission, but with some power to legislate. It must approve the Commission's budget but cannot control it item by item. The parliament shares power with the Council under a "co-decision procedure" in such areas as migration, employment, health, and consumer protection. It also serves as a debating forum and a symbol of European unity. In 1999, an independent commission created by the parliament found waste and fraud in the Commission, leading all 20 commissioners to resign. Since 1979, voters throughout Europe have directly elected their representatives according to population—785 members representing nearly 500 million citizens. Political parties are organized across national lines.

The *Economic and Social Committee* discusses continent-wide issues that affect particular industries or constituencies. This committee is purely advisory; it lobbies the Commission on matters it deems important. It is designed as a forum in which companies, labor unions, and interest groups can bargain transnationally.

The **European Court of Justice** in Luxembourg adjudicates disputes on matters covered by the Treaty of Rome—which covers many issues. Unlike the World Court (see pp. 243–246), the European Court has actively established its jurisdiction and not merely served as a mechanism of international mediation. The Court can overrule national laws that conflict with EU law—giving it unique powers among international courts. It hears cases brought by individuals, not just governments. In hundreds of cases, the Court has ruled on matters such as discrimination in the workplace and the pensions of Commission staff members.

The Single European Act

European integration has proceeded in a step-by-step process that produces tangible successes, reduces politicians' fears of losing sovereignty, and creates pressures to continue the process. Often major steps forward are followed by periods of stagnation or even reversals in integration. The first major revision of the Treaty of Rome—the 1985 *Single European Act*—began a new phase of accelerated integration. The EU set a target date of the end of 1992 for the creation of a true common market in Europe. This comprehensive set of changes was nicknamed *Europe 1992* and centered on about 300 directives from the European Commission, aimed at eliminating nontariff barriers to free trade in goods, services, labor, and capital within the EC. The issues tended to be complex and technical. For example, a dispute raged for decades over the definition of chocolate, because Belgium—famous for its chocolates—required the exclusive use of cocoa butter but Britain allowed substitution of other vegetable oils. Thus, economic integration sets in motion changes that reach into every corner of society and affect the daily lives of millions of people. The Commission bureaucrats worked to smooth out such inconsistencies and create a uniform set of standards. Each national government had to pass laws to implement these measures.

The 1992 process also deepened a trend toward the EU's dealing directly with provinces rather than the states they belong to—thus beginning to "hollow out" the state from below (stronger provincial governments) as well as from above (stronger Europe-wide government). However, Europe 1992 continued to put aside for the future the difficult problems of political and military integration.

The Maastricht Treaty

The **Maastricht Treaty,** signed in the Dutch city of Maastricht in 1992, renamed the EC as the EU and committed it to further progress in three main areas. The first was monetary union (discussed shortly), in which the existing national currencies were to be abolished and replaced by a single European currency. A second set of changes, regarding justice and home affairs, created a European police agency and responded to the new reality that borders were opening to immigrants, criminals, and contraband. It also expanded the idea of citizenship, so that, for example, a French citizen living in Germany can vote in local elections there. A third goal of Maastricht—political and military integration—is even more controversial. The treaty commits European states to work toward a common foreign policy with a goal of eventually establishing a joint military force.

Some citizens of Europe began to react strongly against the loss of national identity and sovereignty implicit in the Maastricht Treaty. In the end, the EU implemented the Maastricht Treaty, although more slowly and with fewer participating countries than originally hoped. Economic and technical integration, including the monetary union among 12 initial members, maintained momentum.

Europe's economic integration has begun to reshape political economy at a global level. The EU now sets the rules for access to one of the world's largest markets, for a vast production and technology network, and for the world's strongest currency. Europe's new power is illustrated in its environmental initiatives. The U.S. chemical industry operated under U.S. regulations that exempt 80 percent of chemicals. But the EU adopted stricter chemical regulations, requiring tests of health effects of all chemicals used in products, and mandating efforts to substitute for toxic chemicals in everyday products. Similarly, Japanese car manufacturers adapted production processes to meet the EU's requirement that new cars consist of 85 percent recyclable components by 2006. Political and military integration are a bigger problem. The struggle between nationalism and supranationalism seems precariously balanced; the transition to supranationalism has not yet been accomplished in the realms of sovereignty and foreign policy. Even after 50 years of preparation, spillover from economic to political issues is elusive.

EURO ON THE MENU

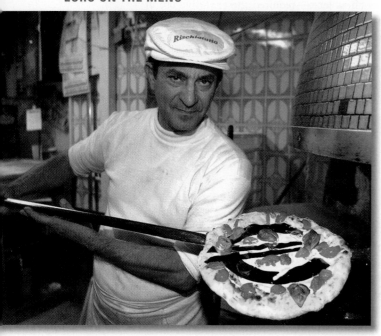

The Maastricht Treaty called for a monetary union with a common currency. In 2002, the euro currency came into effect smoothly in 12 (now 16) countries and, after a year of weakness, gained strength and emerged as a world currency that rivals the U.S. dollar. This Italian chef celebrated the new currency by making a pizza decorated with a euro symbol (€).

Monetary Union

A European currency, the **euro**, has replaced national currencies in 16 EU member states. After several years as an abstract unit like the IMF's SDR (see p. 197), the euro came into full circulation in 2002 and the national currencies ceased to exist. The European Central Bank took over the functions of states' central banks.

Monetary union is difficult for both economic and political reasons. In participating states, fundamental economic and financial conditions must be equalized. One state cannot stimulate its economy with low interest rates (for example, because of a recession) while another cools inflation with high interest rates (because of high economic growth). For example, in 2008 the unemployment rate was 13 percent in Poland but barely 5 percent in the Netherlands. In an integrated economy that is also politically centralized, the central government can reallocate resources, as the United States might do if Texas were booming and Maine were in recession. But the EU does not have centralized powers of taxation or control of national budgets.

One solution is to work toward equalizing Europe's economies. For example, to reduce the disparity between rich and poor EU states, the Maastricht Treaty increased the EU budget by $25 billion annually to provide economic assistance to the poorer members. But the richer EU members pay the cost for this aid—in effect carrying the poor countries as free riders on the collective good of EU integration. Partly for this reason, $25 billion annually was far too small to equalize the rich and poor countries.

The main solution adopted at Maastricht was to restrict membership in the monetary union, at least in the first round, to only those countries with enough financial stability not to jeopardize the union. To join the unified currency, a state had to achieve a budget deficit of less than 3 percent of GDP, a national debt of less than 60 percent of GDP, an inflation rate no more than 1.5 percentage points above the average of the three lowest-inflation EU members, and stable interest rates and national currency values.

This meant hard choices by governments in France, Spain, Italy, and other countries, to cut budgets and benefits and to take other politically unpopular moves. Governments fell to opposition parties in several countries, but the new leaders generally kept to the same course. As a result of their newfound fiscal discipline, all 12 EU members that wanted to participate in the euro ultimately qualified. Slovenia joined in 2007, Cyprus and Malta in 2008, and Slovakia in 2009. Lithuania and Latvia are preparing to adopt the euro next. Britain, Denmark, and Sweden opted to retain their national currencies.

Money is more political than steel tariffs or chocolate ingredients. A monetary union infringes on a core prerogative of states—the right to print currency. Because citizens use money every day, the euro could deepen citizens' sense of identification with Europe—a victory for supranationalism over nationalism. When the euro went into circulation in 2002, people for the first time could "put Europe in their pocket." However, precisely for this reason some state leaders and citizens resisted the idea of giving up the symbolic value of their national currencies.

Conflicts have arisen within the euro zone. In 2004, the European Commission challenged the EU member states for voting to let France and Germany break the euro rules by running high budget deficits. Meanwhile, Greece admitted it had falsified its economic data in order to be admitted. And Latvia's government lost power within six months of the country's joining the EU, under pressure of unpopular budget cuts needed to meet the euro rules within four years. Before the euro even went into circulation, its value slumped (from $1.17 to $0.88) as investor confidence in the experiment initially proved shaky. Having survived its birth, however, the euro gained back its value and more, standing at $1.37 in January 2009. The creation of a European currency is arguably the largest financial overhaul ever attempted in history, and in its first seven years it has been very successful.

Expanding the European Union

The EU's success has attracted neighboring states to join. In 1995, Austria, Sweden, and Finland joined the EU, bringing the total number of members to 15. The EU expanded from 15 members to 27 in 2007, with potentially far-reaching changes in how the EU operates.

The EU's current expansion is guided by the 2000 Treaty of Nice, which came into effect in 2003 after Irish voters reversed an earlier vote and approved it (the last country to ratify it). Ten new members joined in 2004: Poland, Czech Republic, Slovakia, Hungary, Slovenia, Estonia, Latvia, Lithuania, Malta, and Cyprus. The European Commission expanded to 25 members, without the five largest having two seats, and with new voting rules that move away from a requirement for consensus. Romania and Bulgaria's entry in 2007 brought the EU's membership to 27.

Turkey continues to seek membership. Although it rebuffed Turkey in 2002, the EU later agreed to begin formal entry negotiations with Turkey in 2005—the start of a years-long process. Proponents of Turkish membership note that Turkey has made major economic and political changes, including abolishing the death penalty and improving human rights, to try to win EU membership. Granting full membership would reward these changes, keeping an implicit promise to reciprocate Turkey's actions. Turkey's GDP, growing rapidly in recent years, would add about 5 percent to the EU's economy. And Turkish workers could help alleviate a labor shortage in Western Europe. Supporters also argue that Turkey as an EU member would serve as a bridge between Europe and the important but unstable Middle East region, and as an example of secular democracy to other Middle Eastern countries.

Opponents note that Turkey would be the only Muslim country in the EU, yet would be the second most populous EU member after Germany. With 2 million Turks already living in Germany, opponents argue that EU membership would open the floodgates for immigration from a large, poor country, overwhelming the smaller and richer EU members. In France, opposition to Turkey's admission, and to immigration generally, created a backlash. In economic terms, Turkey would be the poorest member, even including the new Eastern European members (see Figure 6.5). Costs to subsidize Turkish farmers and expand social programs could reach tens of billions of euros. Turkey also carries a large debt-to-income ratio, twice as high as any current member. Finally, opponents want Turkey to remove its military forces from Cyprus, where a Greek-Turkish partition has endured for decades (see pp. 125–126).

The EU in the last decade shows signs of dividing into "inner" and "outer" layers—with states such as France and Germany joining a currency union and deepening their integration, and those such as Britain and perhaps the new members operating at the edges of the EU with more autonomy. Still, in some areas, there have been consistent strides toward integration. Since 1995, the EU has established and gradually expanded a zone, called the *Schengen area*, in which border controls have been abolished. Goods and people move freely within the zone without stopping at borders. The agreement also strengthens police cooperation among the member countries. The Schengen countries include the major EU states (except Britain, by its choice). Norway, Iceland, and Switzerland also belong although they are not EU members.

To grapple with the implications of an expanding EU, the 25 leaders signed an EU constitution in late 2004 and the European Parliament gave it a strong vote of support in 2005. To take effect, it was to be ratified by all 25 states, including several requiring referenda. The constitution would establish a stronger president of the EU, as well as a foreign minister, and would replace the requirement for consensus in EU decision making with majority voting in more cases. It also guaranteed fundamental rights to all

FIGURE 6.5   Income Levels of Old and New EU Members, 2005

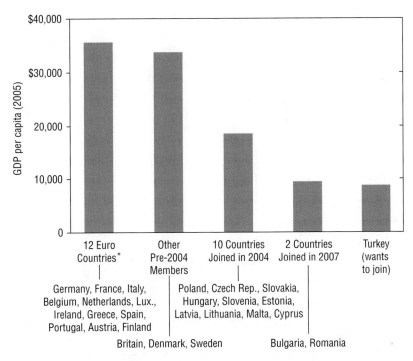

* Slovenia joined the euro in 2007, Cyprus and Malta did so in 2008, as did Slovakia in 2009.

EU citizens. But voters in France and the Netherlands rejected the constitution and the process halted. At the end of 2007, the EU moved forward with another new proposed constitution, the Lisbon Treaty. The treaty was similar to the previous constitution, but faced a popular referendum only in Ireland. In 2008, Ireland rejected the new treaty, but has since said it will vote again in Fall 2009, after several concessions to Ireland were made.

Beyond the EU itself, Europe is a patchwork of overlapping structures with varying memberships (see Figure 6.6). Despite the Single European Act, there are still many Europes. Within the EU are the "inner six," and the new arrivals, each with its own concerns. Around the edges are the EFTA states participating in the European Economic Area. NATO membership overlaps partly with the EU. Russia and even the United States are European actors in some respects. One truly universal intergovernmental organization exists in Europe—the *Organization for Security and Cooperation in Europe* *(OSCE)*. Operating by consensus, with a large universal membership of 56 states, the OSCE has little power except to act as a forum for discussions of security issues. In the late 1990s, the OSCE shifted into new tasks such as running elections and helping political parties.

FIGURE 6.6 Overlapping Memberships of European States

Thus, international integration is not a matter of a single group or organization but more a mosaic of structures tying states together. These various structures of the European political system, centered on the EU, are IGOs composed of states as members. IOs impinge on state sovereignty by creating new structures (both supranational and transnational) for regulating relations across borders. International law and international norms limit state sovereignty in another way. They create principles for governing international relations that compete with the core realist principles of sovereignty and anarchy.

International Law

International law, unlike national laws, derives not from actions of a legislative branch or other central authority, but from tradition and agreements signed by states. It also differs in the difficulty of enforcement, which depends not on the power and authority of central government but on reciprocity, collective action, and international norms.

Sources of International Law

Laws within states come from central authorities—legislatures or dictators. Because states are sovereign and recognize no central authority, international law rests on a different basis. The declarations of the UN General Assembly are not laws, and most do not bind the members. The Security Council can compel certain actions by states, but these are commands rather than laws: they are specific to a situation. Four sources of international law are recognized: treaties, custom, general principles of law (such as equity), and legal scholarship (including past judicial decisions).

Treaties and other written conventions signed by states are the most important source. International treaties now fill more than a thousand thick volumes, with tens of thousands of individual agreements. A principle in international law is that treaties, once signed and ratified, must be observed. In the United States, treaties duly ratified by the Senate are considered the highest law of the land, equal with acts passed by Congress.

Treaties and other international obligations such as debts are binding on successor governments whether the new government takes power through an election, a coup, or a revolution. After the revolutions in Eastern Europe around 1990, newly democratic governments were held responsible for debts incurred by their communist predecessors. Even when the Soviet Union broke up, Russia as the successor state had to guarantee that Soviet debts would be paid and Soviet treaties honored. Although revolution does not free a state from its obligations, some treaties have built-in escape clauses that let states legally withdraw from them, after giving due notice, without violating international law. The United States in 2001 invoked the six-month opt-out provision of the ABM treaty.

Because of the universal commitment by all states to respect certain basic principles of international law, the UN Charter is one of the world's most important treaties. Its implications are broad and far-reaching, in contrast to more specific treaties such as a fishery management treaty. However, the specialized agreements are usually easier to interpret and more enforceable than broad treaties such as the Charter. Another key treaty in international law is the 1949 Geneva Convention (expanding an 1864 convention) defining the laws of war regarding the protection of civilians and prisoners, among related issues.

Custom is the second major source of international law. If states behave toward each other in a certain way for long enough, their behavior may become generally accepted practice with the status of law. Western international law (though not Islamic law) tends to be *positivist* in this regard—it draws on actual customs, the practical realities of self-interest, and the need for consent rather than on an abstract concept of divine or natural law.

General principles of law also serve as a source of international law. Actions such as theft and assault recognized in most national legal systems as crimes tend to have the same meaning in an international context.

The fourth source of international law, recognized by the World Court as subsidiary to the others, is *legal scholarship*—the written arguments of judges and lawyers around the world on the issues in question. Only the writings of the most highly qualified and respected legal figures can be taken into account, and then only to resolve points not resolved by the first three sources of international law.

Often international law lags behind changes in norms; law is quite tradition-bound. Certain activities such as espionage are technically illegal but are so widely condoned that they do not violate international norms. Other activities are still legal but have come to be frowned upon and seen as abnormal. For example, China's shooting of student demonstrators in 1989 violated international norms but not international law.

Enforcement of International Law

Although these sources of international law distinguish it from national law, an even greater difference exists as to the *enforcement* of the two types of law. International law is much more difficult to enforce. There is no world police force. Enforcement of international law depends on the power of states themselves, individually or collectively, to punish transgressors.

Enforcement of international law depends heavily on the reciprocity principle (see p. 67). States follow international law most of the time because they want other states to do so. The reason neither side in World War II used chemical weapons was not that anyone could *enforce* the treaty banning use of such weapons. It was that the other side would probably respond by using chemical weapons, too, and the costs would be high to both sides. International law recognizes in certain circumstances the legitimacy of *reprisals:* actions that would have been illegal under international law may some-times be legal if taken in response to the illegal actions of another state.

A state that breaks international law may face a collective response by a group of states, such as the imposition of *sanctions*—agreements among other states to stop trading with the violator, or to stop some particular commodity trade (most often military goods) as punishment for its violation. Over time, a sanctioned state can become a pariah in the community of nations, cut off from normal relations with others. This is very costly in today's world. Libya suffered for decades from its isolated status in the international community, and decided in 2003 to make a clean break and regain normal status. Libya admitted responsibility for past terrorism, began to compensate victims, and agreed to disclose and dismantle its nuclear, chemical, and biological weapons programs.

Even the world's superpower constrains its behavior, at least some of the time, to adhere to international law. For example, in late 2002 a North Korean freighter was caught en route to Yemen with a hidden load of 15 Scud missiles. The United States, fighting the war on terrorism, had an evident national interest in preventing such proliferation, and had the power to prevent it. But when U.S. government lawyers determined that the shipment did not violate international law, the United States backed off and let the delivery continue.

International law enforcement through reciprocity and collective response depends entirely on national power. Reciprocity works only if the aggrieved state has the power to inflict costs on the violator. If international law extends only as far as power reaches, what good is it? Without common expectations regarding the rules of the game and adherence to those rules most of the time by most actors, power alone would create great instability in the anarchic international system. International law, even without perfect enforcement, creates expectations about what constitutes legal behavior by states. In most cases, although power continues to reside in states, international law establishes workable rules for those states to follow. The resulting stability is so beneficial that usually the costs of breaking the rules outweigh the short-term benefits that could be gained from such violations.

The World Court

As international law has developed, a general world legal framework in which states can pursue grievances against each other has begun to take shape. The rudiments of such a system now exist in the **World Court** (formally called the **International Court of Justice**), although its jurisdiction is limited and its caseload light. The World Court is a branch of the UN. Only states, not individuals or businesses, can sue or be sued in the World Court. When a state has a grievance against another, it can take the case to the World Court for an impartial hearing. The Security Council or General Assembly may also request advisory Court opinions on matters of international law.

The World Court has 15 judges elected for nine-year terms (5 judges every three years) by a majority of both the Security Council and General Assembly. The Court meets in The Hague, the Netherlands. Permanent members of the Security Council customarily have one of their nationals as a judge at all times. Ad hoc judges may be added to the 15 if a party to a case does not already have one of its nationals as a judge.

The great weakness of the World Court is that states have not agreed in a comprehensive way to subject themselves to its jurisdiction or obey its decisions. Almost all states have signed the treaty creating the Court, but only about a third have signed the *optional clause* in the treaty agreeing to give the Court jurisdiction in certain cases—and even many of those signatories have added their own stipulations reserving their rights and limiting the degree to which the Court can infringe on national sovereignty. For example, Iran refused to acknowledge the jurisdiction of the Court when sued by the United States in 1979 over its seizure of the U.S. embassy in Iran. In such cases, the Court may hear the case anyway and usually rules in favor of the participating side—but has no means to enforce the ruling. Justice can also move slowly. In 2007, the Court issued a ruling against Bosnia's case accusing Serbia of genocide, after 14 years of preliminary maneuvering.

In 2002, the World Court settled a long-standing and sometimes violent dispute over an oil-rich peninsula on the Cameroon-Nigeria border. It gave ownership to Cameroon, and Nigeria (which is more powerful) pulled troops out in 2006.

A main use of the World Court now is to arbitrate issues of secondary importance between countries with friendly relations overall. The United States has settled commercial disputes with Canada and with Italy through the Court. Because security interests are not at stake, and because the overall friendly relations are more important than the particular issue, states have been willing to submit to the Court's jurisdiction. In 2004, the court ordered the United States to review death sentences of Mexican nationals to see if their lack of access to Mexican officials had harmed their legal case. Figure 6.7 illustrates one of the Court's current cases, a dispute between Argentina and Uruguay.

Because of the difficulty of winning enforceable agreements on major conflicts through the World Court, states have used the Court infrequently over the years—a dozen or fewer cases per year (about 140 judgments and advisory opinions since 1947).

International Cases in National Courts

Most legal cases concerning international matters—whether brought by governments or by private individuals or companies—remain entirely within the legal systems of one or more states. National courts hear cases brought under national laws and can enforce judgments by collecting damages (in civil suits) or imposing punishments (in criminal ones).

A party with a dispute that crosses national boundaries gains several advantages by pursuing the matter through the national courts of one or more of the relevant states, rather than through international channels. First, judgments are enforceable. The party that wins a lawsuit in a national court can collect from the other party's assets within the state. Second, individuals and companies can pursue legal complaints through national courts (as can subnational governmental bodies), whereas in most areas of international law, states must themselves bring suits on behalf of their citizens. (Even national governments pursue most of their legal actions against each other through national courts.)

Third, there is often a choice of more than one state within which a case could legally be heard; one can pick the legal system most favorable to one's case. Each state's court system must decide whether it has *jurisdiction* in a case (the right to hear it), and courts tend to extend their own authority with a broad interpretation. Traditionally, a national court may hear cases concerning any activity on its national territory, any

FIGURE 6.7   World Court Case of Argentina v. Uruguay

Argentina and Uruguay signed a treaty in 1975 governing the river on their border.

Uruguay brings in foreign companies to build 2 pulp mills across the river from a major Argentine tourist resort.

Yikes, our economy!

Angry Argentines block bridges to Uruguay.

Yikes, <u>our</u> economy!

Make them stop building pulp mills!

Make them stop blocking the border!

Argentina

Uruguay

World Court

Please hold while we review your case. Estimated hold time is until 2009, though the first mill began operations in 2007. We regret any inconvenience. Please continue to hold.

Let's ask the king of Spain to mediate!

Argentina and Uruguay

actions of its own citizens anywhere in the world, and actions taken toward its citizens elsewhere in the world. Noncitizens can use the national courts to enforce damages against citizens, because the national court has authority to impose fines and, if necessary, to seize bank accounts and property.

The United States is a favorite jurisdiction within which to bring cases for two reasons. First, U.S. juries have a reputation for awarding bigger settlements in lawsuits than juries elsewhere in the world (if only because the United States is a rich country). Second, because many people and governments do business in the United States, it is often possible to collect damages awarded by a U.S. court.

There are important limits to the use of national courts to resolve international disputes, however. Most important is that the authority of national courts stops at the state's borders, where sovereignty ends. To bring a person outside a state's territory to trial, the state's government must ask a second government to arrest the person on the second state's territory and hand him or her over for trial. Called *extradition*, this is a matter of international law because it is a legal treaty arrangement between states. If no such treaty exists, the individual generally remains immune from a state's courts by staying off its territory.

Gray areas exist in the jurisdiction of national courts over foreigners. If a government can lure a suspect onto the high seas, it can nab the person without violating another country's territoriality. More troublesome are cases in which a government obtains a foreign citizen from a foreign country for trial without going through extradition procedures.

The principle of territoriality also governs *immigration law*. When people cross a border into a new country, the decision about whether they can remain there, and under what conditions, is up to the new state. The state of origin cannot compel their return. National laws establish conditions for foreigners to travel and visit a state's territory, to work there, and sometimes to become citizens (*naturalization*). Many other legal issues are raised by people traveling or living outside their own country—passports and visas, babies born in foreign countries, marriages to foreign nationals, bank accounts, businesses, taxes, and so forth. Practices vary from country to country, but the general principle is that national laws prevail on the territory of a state.

Despite the continued importance of national court systems in international legal affairs and the lack of enforcement powers of the World Court, it would be wrong to conclude that state sovereignty is supreme and international law impotent. Rather, there is a balance of sovereignty and law in international interactions. The remainder of this chapter discusses particular areas of international law, from the most firmly rooted and widely respected to newer and less-established areas. In each area, the influence of law and norms runs counter to the unimpeded exercise of state sovereignty. This struggle becomes more intense as one moves from long-standing traditions of diplomatic law to recent norms governing human rights.

Laws of Diplomacy

The bedrock of international law is respect for the rights of diplomats. The ability to conduct diplomacy is necessary for all other kinds of relations among states, except perhaps all-out war. Since the rise of the international system five centuries ago, it has been considered unjustifiable to harm an emissary sent from another state as a means of influencing the other state.

The status of embassies and of an ambassador as an official state representative is explicitly defined in the process of **diplomatic recognition.** Diplomats are *accredited* to each other's governments (they present "credentials"), and thereafter the individuals so defined enjoy certain rights and protections as foreign diplomats in the host country. Diplomats have the right to occupy an *embassy* in the host country, within which the host country's laws may not be enforced without the consent of the embassy's country. For this reason, embassies occasionally shelter dissidents who take refuge there from their own governments.

Diplomats enjoy **diplomatic immunity** even when they leave the embassy grounds. The right to travel varies from one country to another; diplomats may be restricted to one city or free to roam about the countryside. Alone among all foreign nationals, diplomats are beyond enforcement of the host country's national courts. If they commit crimes, they may be shielded from arrest. All the host country can do is take away a diplomat's accreditation and expel the person from the host country. However, strong countries sometimes pressure weaker ones to lift immunity so that a diplomat may face trial for a crime.

Because of diplomatic immunity, espionage activities are commonly conducted through the diplomatic corps, out of an embassy. Spies are often posted to low-level positions in embassies, such as cultural attaché, press liaison, or military attaché. If the host country catches them spying, it cannot prosecute them, so it merely expels them. Diplomatic norms (though not law) call for politeness when expelling spies; the standard reason given is "for activities not consistent with his or her diplomatic status." If a spy operates under cover of being a businessperson or tourist, then no immunity applies; the person can be arrested and prosecuted under the host country's laws.

To *break diplomatic relations* means to withdraw one's diplomats from a state and expel its diplomats from one's own state. This tactic is used to show displeasure with another government; it is a refusal to do business as usual. When two countries lack diplomatic relations, they often do business through a third

AGAINST THE LAW

International law prohibits attacks on diplomats. This fundamental principle, like others in international law, can ultimately be enforced only by applying the power of other states (through such leverage as imposing economic sanctions, freezing relations, or threatening military force). Here, a mob burns the U.S. embassy in Serbia in 2008 after the U.S.-backed province of Kosovo declared independence from Serbia. The United States reminded Serbia's government of its responsibility to protect embassies.

country. This is called an *interests section* in the third country's embassy. Thus, the practical needs of diplomacy can overcome a formal lack of relations between states. For instance, U.S. interests are represented by the Swiss embassy in Cuba, and Cuban interests are represented by the Swiss embassy in the United States. In practice, these interests sections are located in the former U.S. and Cuban embassies and staffed with U.S. and Cuban diplomats.

States register lower levels of displeasure by *recalling their ambassadors* home for some period of time; diplomatic norms call for a trip home "for consultations" even when everyone knows the purpose is to signal annoyance. Milder still is the expression of displeasure by a *formal complaint*.

The law of diplomacy is repeatedly violated in one context—terrorism (see pp. 147–149). Because states care so much about the sanctity of diplomats, diplomats make a tempting target for terrorists, and because terrorist groups do not enjoy the benefits of diplomatic law (as states do), they are willing to break diplomatic norms and laws. An attack on diplomats or embassies is an attack on the territory of the state itself—yet can be carried out far from the state's home territory. Many diplomats have been killed in recent decades.

Just War Doctrine

After the law of diplomacy, international law regarding war is one of the most developed areas of international law. Laws concerning war are divided into two areas—laws *of* war (when war is permissible) and laws *in* war (how wars are fought). To begin with the laws of war, international law distinguishes **just wars** (which are legal) from wars of aggression (which are illegal). (We discuss laws in war later in the context of human rights.) This area of law grows out of centuries-old religious writings about just wars (which once could be enforced by threats to excommunicate individuals from the church). Today, the legality of war is defined by the UN Charter, which outlaws aggression. Above and beyond its legal standing, just-war doctrine has become a strong international norm, not one that all states follow but an important part of the modern intellectual tradition governing matters of war and peace that evolved in Europe.

The idea of aggression, around which the doctrine of just war evolved, is based on a violation of the sovereignty and territorial integrity of states. *Aggression* refers to a state's use of force, or an imminent threat to do so, against another state's territory or sovereignty—unless the use of force is in response to aggression. Tanks swarming across the border constitute aggression, but so do tanks massing at the border if their state has threatened to invade. The lines are somewhat fuzzy. But for a threat to constitute aggression (and justify the use of force in response), it must be a clear threat of using force, not just a hostile policy or general rivalry.

States have the right to respond to aggression in the only manner thought to be reliable—military force. Just-war doctrine is thus not based on nonviolence. Responses can include both *repelling* the attack itself and *punishing* the aggressor. Responses can be made by the victim of aggression or by other states not directly affected—as a way of maintaining the norm of nonaggression in the international system. Response to aggression is the only allowable use of military force according to just-war doctrine. The just-war approach thus explicitly rules out war as an instrument to change another state's government or policies, or in ethnic and religious conflicts. In fact, the UN Charter makes no provision for "war" but rather for "international police actions" against aggressors. For a war to be *morally* just, it must be more than a response to aggression; it must be waged for the *purpose* of responding to aggression. The *intent* must be just. A state may not take advantage of another's aggression to wage a war that is essentially aggressive.

Just war doctrine has been undermined by the changing nature of warfare. In civil wars and low-intensity conflicts, it can be hard to identify an aggressor, as the belligerents range from poorly organized militias to national armies, and the battleground is often a patchwork of enclaves and positions with no clear front lines (much less borders). It is harder to identify an aggressor in such situations, and harder to balance the relative merits of peace and justice.

Human Rights

One of the newest areas of international law concerns **human rights**—the rights of human beings against certain abuses of their *own* governments.

Individual Rights versus Sovereignty

The very idea of human rights flies in the face of the sovereignty and territorial integrity of states. Sovereignty gives states the right to do as they please in their own territory: Nobody can tell them how to treat their own citizens.

Thus, a consensus on the most important human rights is difficult to reach. One approach to human rights argues that rights are universal. No matter where a person resides, no matter his or her ethnic nationality, and no matter his or her local religious, ethnic, or clan traditions, that person has certain rights that must be respected. The other approach to human rights is often labeled *relativism*. According to this idea, local traditions and histories should be given due respect, even if this means limiting rights that others outside that local context find important. Efforts to promote human rights are routinely criticized by governments with poor human rights records by Western standards (including China and Russia) as "interference in our internal affairs." This charge puts human rights law on shaky ground and reflects a relativist stance.

The concept of human rights arises from three sources. The first is religion. Nearly every major world religion has at its foundation the idea that humans were created in an image of a higher power and that therefore all humans are to be afforded the dignity and respect that are due that higher power.

Second, political and legal philosophy for centuries has discussed the idea of natural law and natural rights. From Aristotle, to John Locke, to Immanuel Kant, to Jean-Jacques Rousseau, political philosophers have developed the idea that a natural law exists that grants all humans the right to life, liberty, property, and happiness.

Finally, political revolutions in the 18th century, such as the American and French Revolutions, translated the theory of natural law and natural rights into practice. In America, the Declaration of Independence, and in France, the Declaration of the Rights of Man and Citizen, created laws that solidified the idea that humans have certain rights that no state or other individuals can take away.

Of course, criticisms of these ideas of human rights exist, on both a theoretical and a practical level. Theoretically, relativists point out that much of the origin and development of human rights ideas (at least two of the three sources discussed) are Western in origin. Non-Western societies have different philosophical traditions and may choose to emphasize group or family rights, for example, over individual ones. At a practical level, many (especially non-Western) critics are quick to point out that even after the 18th-century revolutions in Europe and America, rights were still not universal. Women, children, and usually nonwhites were not assumed to enjoy the same rights as landholding white males, making the very idea of universal rights misleading.

Partially because of this controversy, there are no globally agreed-upon definitions of the essential human rights. Rights are often divided into two broad types: civil-political and economic-social. Civil-political rights are sometimes referred to as "negative rights" and include what are considered traditional Western rights such as free speech, freedom of religion, equal protection under the law, and freedom from arbitrary imprisonment. These are rights generally thought to be best guaranteed by limiting the power of governments over their people. Economic-social rights are referred to as "positive rights" and include rights to good living conditions, food, health care, social security, and education. These rights are often thought to be best promoted by the expansion of governments to provide minimal standards to their people.

No state has a perfect record on any type of human rights, and states differ as to which areas they respect or violate. When the United States criticizes China for prohibiting free speech, using prison labor, and torturing political dissidents (civil-political rights), China notes that the United States has 40 million poor people, the highest ratio of prison inmates in the world, and a history of racism and violence (economic-social rights). During the Cold War, the United States and its allies consistently criticized the Soviet Union and China for violations of civil-political rights, yet refused to endorse treaties championing economic-social rights. Likewise, communist states encouraged the development of the latter rights, while ignoring calls for the former. Overall, despite the poor record of the world's states on some points, progress has been made on others. For example, slavery—once considered normal worldwide—has been largely abandoned in the past 150 years.

Human Rights Institutions

In 1948, the UN General Assembly adopted what is considered the core international document concerning human rights: the **Universal Declaration of Human Rights (UDHR).** The UDHR does not have the force of international law, but it sets forth (hoped-for) international norms regarding behavior by governments toward their own citizens and foreigners alike. The declaration roots itself in the principle that violations of human rights upset international order (causing outrage, sparking rebellion, etc.) and in the fact that the UN Charter commits states to respect fundamental freedoms. The declaration proclaims that "all human beings are born free and equal" without regard to race, sex, language, religion, political affiliation, or the status of the territory in which they were born. It goes on to promote norms in a wide variety of areas, including banning torture, guaranteeing religious and political freedom, and ensuring the right of economic well-being.

Since the adoption of the UDHR, the UN has opened seven treaties for state signature to further define protections of human rights. Unlike the UDHR, these treaties are legally binding contracts signed by states. Of course, international law is only as good as the enforcement mechanisms behind it. Yet these seven treaties are important in outlining the basic protections for individuals expected by the international community.

Two key treaties are the *International Covenant on Civil and Political Rights* and the *International Covenant on Economic, Social, and Cultural Rights*. These two treaties, both of which entered into force in 1976, codify the promises of the UDHR while dividing the list of rights in the UDHR into civil-political and economic-social rights, respectively. These two covenants, along with the UDHR, are often referred to as the International Bill of Human Rights.

The remaining treaties each deal with a particular group that the international community considers vulnerable. The International Convention on the Elimination of All Forms of Racial Discrimination (ICERD), enacted in 1969, bans discrimination against individuals based on race, ethnicity, religion, or national origin. The ICERD did not include language concerning gender discrimination. The Convention on the Elimination of All Forms of Discrimination against Women (CEDAW), however, fills this void by banning discrimination against women. CEDAW entered into force in 1981.

The Convention against Torture (CAT), which entered into effect in 1987, bans dehumanizing, degrading, and inhumane treatment of individuals even in times of war. The Convention on the Rights of the Child (CRC), which came into force in 1990, promotes children's health, education, and physical well-being (every country in the world except Somalia and the United States has approved the CRC). Finally, the most recent UN human rights treaty is the International Convention on the Protection of the Rights of All Migrant Workers and Members of Their Families (CMW), which entered into force in 2003. The CMW attempts to protect the political, labor, and social rights of the nearly 100 million migrant workers around the globe.

Besides the UN-related human rights treaties, several regional IOs have promoted the protection of human rights. Nowhere is this more true than in Europe, where the European Union, the Council of Europe, and the European Court of Human Rights all work to ensure that human rights are respected by all states in the region (see pp. 187–188). In Latin America as well, the *Inter-American Court of Human Rights* has had some success in promoting human rights, yet it has also been limited by state refusal to abide by its decisions. Finally, the African Union helps support the African Human Rights Commission, but the Commission has been hampered by its lack of monetary and political support from African states.

In the past decade, developed states have begun to use other international organizations to pressure developing states to improve human rights conditions. Free trade agreements (see Chapter 6) frequently contain provisions that condition trade benefits on the respect for human rights, especially workers' rights. Because these treaties provide policies beneficial to the developing states, they create a ready mechanism to punish countries who abuse their citizens. Others argue, however, that limiting economic benefits to countries harms their economic development, which is likely only to make the human rights situation worse.

Today, NGOs play a key role in efforts to win basic political rights in authoritarian countries—including a halt to the torture, execution, and imprisonment of those expressing political or religious beliefs. The leading organization pressing this struggle is **Amnesty International,** an NGO that operates globally to monitor and try to rectify glaring abuses of human rights. Amnesty International has a reputation for impartiality and has criticized abuses in many countries, including the United States. Other groups, such as Human Rights Watch, work in a similar way but often with a more regional or national focus. NGOs often provide information and advocacy for UN and other regional organizations that attempt to promote human rights. They essentially serve as a bridge between the global or regional organizations and efforts to promote human rights "on the ground."

Enforcing norms of human rights is difficult because it involves interfering in a state's internal affairs. Cutting off trade or contact with a government that violates human rights tends to hurt the citizens whose rights are being violated, by further isolating them. And governments shy away from humanitarian interventions using military force to overcome armed resistance by local authorities or warlords and bring help to civilian victims of wars and disasters. However, international norms have increasingly shifted against sovereignty and toward protecting endangered civilians. A major summit of world leaders in 2005 enshrined the concept of the **responsibility to protect,** which holds that governments worldwide must act to save civilians from genocide or crimes against humanity perpetrated or allowed by their own governments.

The U.S. State Department has actively pursued human rights since the late 1970s. An annual U.S. government report assesses human rights in states around the world. In states where abuses are severe or becoming worse, U.S. foreign aid has been withheld from these states or their armed forces. (But in other cases, CIA funding has supported the abusers.) Currently, human rights is one of the two main areas of conflict (along with Taiwan) in China's relationship with the United States. Several practices draw criticism; these include imprisoning political opponents of the government, the use of prison labor, and a criminal justice system prone to abuses. According to Amnesty International, China executed more people than the rest of the world combined—thousands each year—sometimes within days of the crime and sometimes for relatively minor crimes.

War Crimes

Large-scale abuses of human rights often occur during war. Serious violations of this kind are considered **war crimes.** In wartime, international law is especially difficult to enforce, but extensive norms of legal conduct in war are widely followed. After a war, losers can be punished for violations of the laws of war, as Germans were in the Nuremberg trials after World War II. Since the Nazi murders of civilians did not violate German law, the Nuremberg tribunal treated them as **crimes against humanity,** conceived as inhumane acts and persecutions against civilians on a vast scale in the pursuit of unjust ends.

In the 1990s, for the first time since World War II, the UN Security Council authorized an international war crimes tribunal, directed against war crimes in the former Yugoslavia. Similar tribunals were later established for genocide in Rwanda and Sierra Leone. The tribunal on the former Yugoslavia, headquartered in The Hague, the Netherlands, indicted Serbian strongman Slobodan Milosevic in 1999. After Milosevic lost power, the new Serbian government turned him over to the tribunal in 2001.

VIDEO

The Armenian Genocide

His trial continued until his death in 2006. In 2008, the leader of the Bosnian Serbs accused of ordering his forces to kill thousands of Muslims in Bosnia was arrested after 13 years in hiding. He is currently on trial in The Hague, charged with persecuting Bosnian Muslims and Croats, shelling civilian population centers, and destroying property including places of worship.

Following the civil war in Sierra Leone, the government there runs a war crimes tribunal jointly with the UN. In 2003, it indicted the sitting state leader in next-door Liberia, Charles Taylor, for his role in the war's extreme brutality. He fled to Nigeria shortly afterward but was captured there and turned over to the tribunal for trial in 2006.

Following up on the UN tribunals for former Yugoslavia and Rwanda, in 1998 most of the world's states signed a treaty to create a permanent **International Criminal Court**

SORTING OUT WAR CRIMES

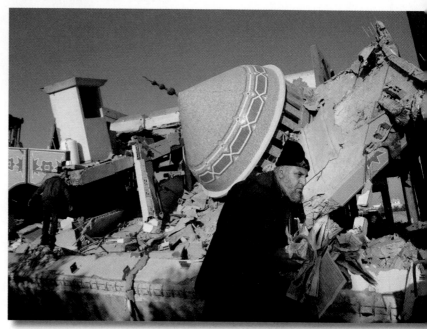

War crimes include unnecessary targeting of civilians and mistreatment of prisoners of war (POWs). Both sides in the 2009 Israeli attack on Hamas in Gaza accused the other of war crimes. Hamas said Israel attacked civilians, as in the airstrike that destroyed this mosque, and used force disproportionate to any military threat it faced. Israel said Hamas targeted civilians with its rocket attacks on Israel, and fought from behind cover of civilians in Gaza, such as by using mosques, schools, and hospitals as military positions.

(ICC). It hears cases of genocide, war crimes, and crimes against humanity from anywhere in the world. The ICC opened for business in 2003 in The Hague, with 18 judges sworn in from around the world (but not the United States). In 2008, the ICC began its first trial, of a militia leader from Democratic Congo accused of drafting children under 15 and killing civilians.

War crimes in Darfur, Sudan—which a UN commission found grave but short of "genocide"—have also been referred to the ICC after the United States dropped its objections in 2005 (when exemptions for U.S. soldiers were restored). The Darfur case is a difficult challenge for the ICC. In 2009, the ICC indicted the sitting Sudanese president, Omar al-Bashir, on charges of war crimes and crimes against humanity, and issued a warrant for his arrest. The indictment angered the Sudanese government, which then expelled humanitarian organizations from Darfur. The ICC faces a difficult balance in holding officials in Sudan accountable, yet being sensitive to efforts to end the violence in Darfur (see p. 119).

VIDEO

War Crimes in Sudan

POLICY PERSPECTIVES

International Criminal Court Chief Prosecutor, Luis Moreno-Ocampo

PROBLEM *How do you balance respect for international legal principles and national interests?*

BACKGROUND For six years, fighting has raged in the western Sudanese province of Darfur. This conflict has been labeled a genocide by many observers. It is estimated that 2.7 million people have been forced from their homes and perhaps 300,000 have died. While some of the violence in Darfur is between warring rebel groups, the Sudanese government has been accused of arming one set of militias and encouraging the violence.

You are the chief prosecutor for the International Criminal Court (ICC). Although Sudan is not a member of the ICC, because the Security Council referred the Darfur case to the ICC, you may choose to begin a case against anyone in the Sudan. The ICC has already issued two arrest warrants for war crimes related to Darfur. In 2009, you obtained an indictment and arrest warrant against Sudan's president, Omar al-Bashir, on charges of war crimes and crimes against humanity. Such a move to prosecute a sitting president of a country in the middle of a civil war was unprecedented.

DOMESTIC CONSIDERATIONS While human rights groups applauded your decision to pursue criminal charges against the Sudanese president, many countries opposed the move. China and Russia, both of which maintain diplomatic ties with Sudan, have expressed disapproval and pressed you to stop prosecutions. Many African Union (AU) countries, which currently deploy peacekeepers in Darfur, have opposed the move, warning that it could lead to a breakdown of the peace process. In fact, after you announced plans to indict al-Bashir, violence did increase in Darfur, including attacks against AU peacekeepers, and after the indictment was announced, Sudan expelled humanitarian NGOs from Darfur, gravely imperiling the population there. The AU has called for you to suspend all ICC proceedings relating to Darfur, and the Arab League has condemned your indictment of Bashir.

The United States and the major European countries support efforts to bring members of the Sudanese government to justice. And while Russia and China have suggested revoking ICC authority to prosecute cases related to Darfur, the United States, France, or Britain could use their Security Council vetoes to stop such an effort. Supporters of the ICC have argued that Darfur represents a crucial case for the future of the legitimacy of the court. This case will set important precedents as to the power of this relatively new body.

SCENARIO Imagine that the Chinese government approaches you and asks you to suspend the indictment of al-Bashir. In return, China agrees to press Sudan both to end violence in Darfur and to allow for more peacekeepers to be deployed there. China has no direct control over Sudan, however, so China's promises may bring little change in behavior on the part of Sudan. On the other hand, China does have some pull with the Sudanese leadership. The United States and its allies would be likely to support such a move if it resulted in a stable cease-fire.

CHOOSE YOUR POLICY Do you suspend your efforts to prosecute the Sudanese leadership, especially the Sudanese president, for war crimes? How do you balance the demands of competing great powers? How do you balance your desire to bring justice to the victims of the conflict in Darfur with the reality of the peace process, which hangs in the balance? Can justice be delayed to save lives in the short term? If justice is delayed, will it ever be achieved?

The most important principle in the laws of war is the effort to limit warfare to the combatants and to protect civilians when possible. It is illegal to target civilians in a war unless there is a compelling military utility to do so. Even then, the amount of force used must be *proportional* to the military gain, and only the *necessary* amount of force can be used.

To help separate combatants from civilians, soldiers must wear uniforms and insignia, such as a shoulder patch with a national flag. This provision is frequently violated in guerrilla warfare, making that form of warfare particularly brutal and destructive of civilian life. If one cannot tell the difference between a bystander and a combatant, one is likely to kill both when in doubt.

In recent years, the unprecedented rise in the use of private military forces in wars, especially in Iraq, has challenged the laws of war (see p. 160). Because these private forces are not members of a country's military, the international laws of war do not necessarily apply to them (only states, not corporations, sign the Geneva Conventions). In Iraq, the U.S. government had granted a waiver to these companies to ensure that they could not be prosecuted for violations of international law, only local law. But because there was no formal Iraqi government, no one could enforce violations of domestic law committed by these companies. Several high-profile incidents (including abuses at the Abu Ghraib prison and several shootings of civilians) led Congress, the UN, and Iraq to hold private forces accountable. A 2008 Iraqi-U.S. agreement on the status of American military forces ended the legal waiver for private contractors beginning in 2009.

Soldiers have the right under the laws of war to surrender, which is to abandon their status as combatants and become *prisoners of war (POWs)*. They give up their weapons and their right to fight, and earn instead the right (like civilians) not to be targeted. POWs may not be killed, mistreated, or forced to disclose information beyond their name, rank, and serial number.

The laws of war reserve a special role for the **International Committee of the Red Cross (ICRC).** The ICRC provides practical support—such as medical care, food, and letters from home—to civilians caught in wars and to POWs. Exchanges of POWs are usually negotiated through the ICRC. Armed forces must respect the neutrality of the Red Cross, and usually they do (again, guerrilla war is problematical). In the war on terrorism, the United States does not consider the "enemy combatants" it detains POWs, but has granted the ICRC access to most (though not all) of them. More controversial is the U.S. policy of "extraordinary rendition," which lets terrorist suspects captured overseas be transferred to other countries, including some that use torture, for questioning.

The laws of warfare impose moral responsibility on individuals in wartime, as well as on states. The Nuremberg Tribunal established that participants can be held accountable for war crimes they commit. German officers defended their actions as "just following orders," but this was rejected; the officers were punished, and some executed.

Changing Context   The laws of warfare have been undermined by the changing nature of war. Conventional wars by defined armed forces on defined battlegrounds are giving way to irregular and "low-intensity" wars fought by guerrillas and death squads in cities or jungles. The lines between civilians and soldiers blur in these situations, and war crimes become more commonplace. In the Vietnam War, one of the largest problems faced by the United States was an enemy that seemed to be everywhere and nowhere. This led frustrated U.S. forces to attack civilian villages seen as supporting the guerrillas. In one infamous case, a U.S. officer was court-martialed for ordering his soldiers to massacre hundreds of unarmed civilians in the village of My Lai in 1968 (he was convicted but given a light sentence). In today's irregular warfare, frequently inflamed by ethnic and religious conflicts, the laws of war are increasingly difficult to uphold.

Another factor undermining laws of war is that states rarely issue a *declaration of war* setting out whom they are warring against and the cause of their action. Ironically, such declarations are historically the exception, not the rule. This trend continues today because declarations of war bring little benefit to the state declaring war and incur obligations under international law.

These new norms still remain unsettled. New expectations are emerging in such areas as human rights, UN peacekeeping, humanitarian interventions, Russia's and China's roles as great powers, and the U.S. role as a superpower. These changes will play out in a world increasingly marked by the gap between rich and poor countries—the subject of Chapter 7.

CHAPTER REVIEW

SUMMARY

- Supranational processes bring states together in larger structures and identities. These processes generally lead to an ongoing struggle between nationalism and supranationalism.

- The UN embodies a tension between state sovereignty and supranational authority. The UN has made sovereignty the more important principle, limiting the UN's power.

- The UN has attracted virtually universal membership of the world's states, including all the great powers.

- Each of the 192 UN member states has one vote in the General Assembly.

- The Security Council has ten rotating member states and five permanent members: the United States, Russia, China, Britain, and France.

- The UN is administered by international civil servants in the Secretariat, headed by the secretary-general.

- UN peacekeeping forces are deployed in regional conflicts in five world regions. Their main role is to monitor compliance with agreements such as cease-fires, disarmament plans, and fair election rules. UN peacekeepers operate under the UN flag and command. Sometimes national troops operate under their own flag and command to carry out UN resolutions.

- International integration partially shifts sovereignty from the state toward supranational institutions.

- The European Union (EU) is the most advanced case of integration. Its 27 member states have given considerable power to the EU in economic decision making. However, national power still outweighs supranational power even in the EU.

- The most important and most successful element in the EU is its customs union (and the associated free trade area). Goods can cross borders of member states freely, and the members adopt unified tariffs with regard to goods entering from outside the EU.

- The EU's Common Agricultural Policy (CAP) equalizes subsidies to farmers within the community. Carrying out the CAP consumes 40 percent of the EU's budget.

- The EU has a new monetary union with a single European currency (the euro) in 16 of the 27 EU states. It is the biggest experiment with money in history and had great success in its first seven years.

- In structure, the EU revolves around the permanent staff of "Eurocrats" under the European Commission. However, member states have power over the Commission.

- The European Parliament has members directly elected by citizens in EU states, but cannot legislate the rules for the community. The European Court of Justice has extended its jurisdiction more successfully than any other international court, and can overrule national laws.

- Twelve new members, mostly Eastern European, joined the EU in 2004 and 2007. The EU's structures and procedures are being adapted as it moves from 15 to 27 members. To some extent the broadening of membership conflicts with the deepening of ties among the existing members.

- International law, the formal body of rules for state relations, derives from treaties (most important), custom, general principles, and legal scholarship—not from legislation passed by any government.

- International law is difficult to enforce but is enforced in practice by national power, international coalitions, and reciprocity.

- The World Court hears grievances of one state against another but cannot infringe on state sovereignty in most cases.

- A permanent International Criminal Court (ICC) began operations in 2003. It hears cases of genocide, war crimes, and crimes against humanity, including war crimes in Sudan.

- Laws of war distinguish combatants from civilians, giving each certain rights and responsibilities. Guerrilla wars and ethnic conflicts have blurred these distinctions.

- International norms concerning human rights are becoming stronger and more widely accepted. However, human rights law is problematic because it entails interference by one state in another's internal affairs.

KEY TERMS

supranational 209
international
  norms 210
international organiza-
  tions (IOs) 211
UN Charter 213
UN General
  Assembly 214
UN Security
  Council 216
UN Secretariat 216
peacebuilding 223
UN Conference
  on Trade and
  Development
  (UNCTAD) 227
World Health
  Organization
  (WHO) 228
European Union
  (EU) 228
international
  integration 229

neofunctionalism 230
security
  community 230
Treaty of Rome 231
Euratom 231
free trade area 232
customs union 232
common market 232
Common Agricultural
  Policy (CAP) 232
European
  Commission 233
Council of the European
  Union 234
European
  Parliament 234
European Court of
  Justice 234
Maastricht Treaty 235
euro 236
World Court
  (International Court
  of Justice) 243

diplomatic
  recognition 247
diplomatic
  immunity 247
just wars 248
human rights 249
Universal Declaration
  of Human Rights
  (UDHR) 250
Amnesty
  International 252
responsibility
  to protect 252
war crimes 252
crimes against
  humanity 252
International Criminal
  Court (ICC) 253
International Committee
  of the Red Cross
  (ICRC) 255

ONLINE PRACTICE TEST

Take an online practice test at
www.IRtext.com

❏ A
❏ B
❏ C
❏ D

CRITICAL THINKING QUESTIONS

1. Suppose you were asked to recommend changes in the structure of the UN Security Council (especially in permanent membership and the veto). What changes would you recommend, if any? Based on what logic?

2. Functional economic ties among European states have contributed to the emergence of a supranational political structure, the EU, which has considerable though not unlimited power. Do you think the same thing could happen in

North America? Could the U.S.-Canadian-Mexican NAFTA develop into a future North American Union like the EU? What problems would it be likely to face, given the experience of the EU?

3. Although international norms concerning human rights are becoming stronger, China and many other states continue to consider human rights an internal affair over which the state has sovereignty within its territory. Do you think human rights are a legitimate subject for one state to raise with another? If so, how do you reconcile the tensions between state autonomy and universal rights? What practical steps could be taken to get sovereign states to acknowledge universal human rights?

BACK TO THE BIG PICTURE

To hear a discussion of the "big picture" for this chapter, raised on p. 210, along with an example from recent history, consult the "IR Talk" podcast for Chapter 6 at *www.IRtext.com*

PODCAST

Children displaced by flood in India, 2007.

North-South Relations

The State of the South

This chapter concerns the world's poor regions—the global South—where most people live. States in these regions are called by various names, used interchangeably: *third world countries, less-developed countries* (LDCs), *underdeveloped countries* (UDCs), or **developing countries.** The chapter first discusses the gap in wealth between the industrialized regions (the North) and the rest of the world (the South), and develops the theories of imperialism introduced in Chapter 3 (pp. 91–92), which try to explain this gap in terms of historical colonization of the South by the North. It then considers international aspects of economic development in the South.

IR scholars do not agree on the causes or implications of poverty in the global South, nor on solutions (if any) to the problem. Thus, they also disagree about the nature of relations between rich and poor states (North-South relations). Everyone agrees, however, that much of the global South is poor, and some of it extremely poor.

In all, about a billion people live in abject poverty, without access to basic nutrition or health care. They are concentrated in Africa, where income levels

THE BIG PICTURE

DOMINANCE

PODCAST

Why are income levels in the global South so much lower than in the North? On average, a person living in the South has less than one-quarter the income of one in the North. Within the South, regions' income levels and rates of economic growth vary, but the bottom billion people remain trapped in extreme poverty, without access to basic necessities.

The history of imperialism weighs heavily on today's gap between rich and poor countries. The South was colonized and developed to suit the colonizer's needs. In this clear example of the dominance principle, capital investment was often concentrated in sectors that exported raw materials to the North, such as oil, mines, and tropical agriculture. In Africa, especially, badly drawn colonial borders left independent states with ethnic conflicts that ignited decades of civil wars. After independence, many former colonies also faced problems of corruption and mismanagement that held back development.

To hear the authors of this book discuss this issue, with an example from recent history, download the "IR Talk" podcast for Chapter 7 from www.IRtext.com.

have lagged for decades. Two decades ago the concentration was as strong in South Asia, but economic growth there has greatly reduced extreme poverty. Still, the average income per person in South Asia—home to 2 billion people—is only $2,600 per year, and in Africa $2,000 (even after adjusting for the lower costs of living in these regions compared to richer ones). Although billions of people are rising out of poverty, because of population growth the number of very poor people nonetheless remains about the same. The bottom line is that every six seconds, somewhere in the world, a child dies as a result of malnutrition. That is 600 every hour, 14,000 every day, 5 million every year. The world produces enough food to nourish these children and enough income to afford to nourish them, but their own families or states do not have enough income. They die, ultimately, from poverty. Meanwhile, in that same six seconds the world spends more than $200,000 on military forces, a thousandth of which could save the child's life. Likewise, people lack water, shelter, health care, and other necessities because they cannot afford them. The widespread, grinding poverty of people who cannot afford necessities is less visible than the dramatic examples of starvation triggered by war or drought, but affects many more people.

The UN in 2000 adopted the **Millennium Development Goals,** which set targets for basic needs measures to be achieved by 2015 and measured against 1990 data. The first of the eight goals is to cut in half the proportion of the world's population living in "extreme poverty," defined as income of less than $1 per day (in 1990 dollars, or about $1.70 in 2009 dollars). For the global South as a whole, that proportion fell from 31 percent to 20 percent between 1997 and 2007. China's rate has already dropped by half (33 to 14 percent), but Africa's is hardly changed, at around 50 percent.

The five regions of the global South differ not only on poverty reduction, but also on income level and growth. As Figure 7.1 shows, the regions experiencing the fastest growth—China and South Asia—are neither the highest- nor the lowest-income regions.

FIGURE 7.1   Income Level and Growth Rate by World Region

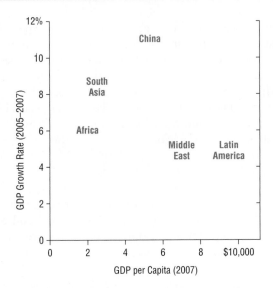

Note: For the global North overall, GDP per capita is $35,000.

**Addressing
Mozambique's
Challenges**

The Middle East is about as developed as China in terms of GDP per capita, but is growing at only half the rate. Later in this chapter we will explore the reasons for these differences in economic growth, but here we note simply that the world's regions vary on both income and growth, with the two dimensions not correlated.

According to the World Bank, between 1990 and 2005 incomes per person (adjusted for inflation, in today's dollars) in the global South as a whole rose from about $3,000 to about $5,000. In the global North they rose from about $20,000 to about $28,000. Does this indicate a slow closing of the gap because the ratio fell from about 6.6 to 5.6 as the result of a higher rate of growth in the South? Or does it indicate a widening of the gap between a person in the North and one in the South because in absolute terms, it increased from $17,000 to $23,000? Each has some truth.

Basic Human Needs

Some countries in the global South have made rapid progress in raising incomes, but others are caught in a cycle of poverty. In order to put economic growth on a firm foundation, the **basic human needs** of most of the population must be met. People need food, shelter, and other necessities of daily life in order to feel secure. Furthermore, as long as people in the global South blame imperialism for a lack of basic needs, extreme poverty fuels revolution, terrorism, and anti-Western sentiments.

Children are central to meeting a population's basic needs. In particular, education allows a new generation to meet other basic needs and move through the demographic transition. Literacy—which UNESCO defines as the ability to read and write a simple sentence—is the key component of education. A person who can read and write can obtain a wealth of information about farming, health care, birth control, and so forth. Some poor countries have raised literacy rates substantially; others lag behind.

Great variation also exists in schooling. Primary school attendance in 2003–2004 was more than 90 percent in most world regions, though only 64 percent for Africa. Secondary education—middle and high school—is another matter. In the North, about 90 percent of secondary-age children are enrolled, but in most of the global South, fewer than two-thirds are. College is available to only a small fraction of the population.

In 2008 in the global South, according to UNICEF, one in four children suffered

STRANDED IN POVERTY

Nearly a billion people in the global South—most of them in Africa and South Asia—live in abject poverty. The majority lack such basic needs as safe water, housing, food, and the ability to read. Natural disasters, droughts, wars, or other events that displace subsistence farmers from their land can quickly put large numbers at risk for their lives. These women in East Timor search for food and clothing in a garbage dump, 2009.

from malnutrition, one in seven lacked access to health care, and one in five had no safe drinking water. The AIDS epidemic is undoing progress made over decades in reducing child mortality and increasing education.

Figure 7.2 shows the variation across regions in two key indicators of children's well-being at different stages—immunizations and secondary-school enrollments. In both cases, achievement of these basic needs for children roughly correlates with the regions' respective income levels. Effective health care in poor countries is not expensive—less than $5 per person per year for primary care. Since 1990, despite the daunting problems of war and the HIV/AIDS epidemic, public health in the global South has registered some important gains. Infant tetanus deaths were halved, and access to safe water was extended to a billion more people. Polio was nearly eliminated, but resistance to vaccination in parts of Nigeria let the disease begin to spread again, with four countries having indigenous virus populations as of 2006. In eight African countries in 2006, following successful trials in several other countries, authorities combined the distribution of insecticide-treated mosquito nets for malaria with

DO THE MATH

Children are a main focus of efforts to provide basic human needs in the global South. Education is critical to both economic development and the demographic transition. Girls worldwide receive less education than boys, and in Afghanistan under the Taliban, they were banned from schools altogether. This math class in Kandahar, Afghanistan, in 2002, followed the Taliban's fall.

measles and polio vaccines, deworming pills, vitamin A supplements, and educational materials—a combined approach proven to work. In the past 25 years, the number of children immunized in developing countries has risen from 5 percent to more than 50 percent. UNICEF reported in 2007 that deaths of children under five worldwide hit a record low, under 10 million, with the rate having dropped by more than half in the last 50 years. Just since 1999 measles deaths had decreased by 60 percent.

Still, the global disparities in access to health care are striking. The 75 percent of the world's people living in the global South have about 30 percent of the world's doctors and nurses. In medical research, less than 5 percent of world expenditures are directed at problems in developing countries, according to the WHO. The biggest killers are AIDS, acute respiratory infections, diarrhea, TB, malaria, and hepatitis. More than 600 million people are infected with tropical diseases—300 to 500 million with malaria alone. Yet, because the people with such diseases are poor, there is often not a large enough market for drug companies (MNCs) in the industrialized world to invest in medicines for them. And when poor countries need medicines developed for rich markets, the drugs may be prohibitively expensive (see pp. 330–332).

Safe water is another essential element of meeting basic human needs. In many rural locations, people must walk miles every day to fetch water. Access to water does not mean running water in every house, but a clean well or faucet for a village. In 2004 (the last year for which data are available), one in six people worldwide, the great majority of them in rural areas, lacked access to safe drinking water. Even among those with access to safe drinking water, many lack sanitation facilities (such as sewers and sanitary latrines). Forty percent of the world's population does not have access to sanitation, and as a result suffers from recurrent epidemics and widespread diarrhea, which kill millions of children each year. The importance of sanitation was underscored in 2008 in Zimbabwe, when an economic collapse led to a shutdown of the water treatment system, quickly sparking a cholera epidemic that killed hundreds. Access to safe drinking water and sanitation has nonetheless improved since 1990, from 78 to 83 percent globally for drinking water and

FIGURE 7.2   Basic Needs Indicators by Region (2005)

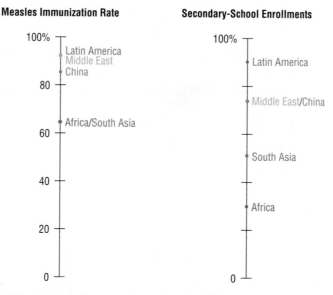

Data Source: World Bank. Regions do not exactly match those used elsewhere in this book.

49 to 59 percent for sanitation. But because of population growth, these improvements leave roughly the same absolute number of people lacking—about a billion for water and more than 2 billion for sanitation.

Shelter is another key basic need. Of the world's 6.6 billion people, about one in six lives in substandard housing or is homeless altogether. For indicator after indicator, we find about a billion people left behind with nothing. The different indicators do not overlap perfectly, but basically the bottom billion of humanity, most living in rural areas, are in desperate poverty. The most important factors keeping these people in desperate poverty appear to be civil war, corruption, the "resource curse" (see p. 277), and landlocked locations without ready access to trade.

War in the global South—both international and civil war—is a leading obstacle to the provision of basic needs. War causes much greater damage to society than merely the direct deaths and injuries it inflicts. In war zones, economic infrastructure such as transportation is disrupted, as are government services such as health care and education. Wars drastically reduce the confidence in economic and political stability on which investment and trade depend.

Figure 7.3 maps the rates of access to safe water and food. The worldwide pattern somewhat resembles the map of wars in progress on p. 111. If indeed there is a relationship between recent or present warfare and a lack of basic needs (in turn correlated with income level), what really causes what? Does being at war keep a society poor and prevent it from meeting its population's basic needs? Or does being poor, with unmet

FIGURE 7.3   Rates of Access to Water and Food, 2005

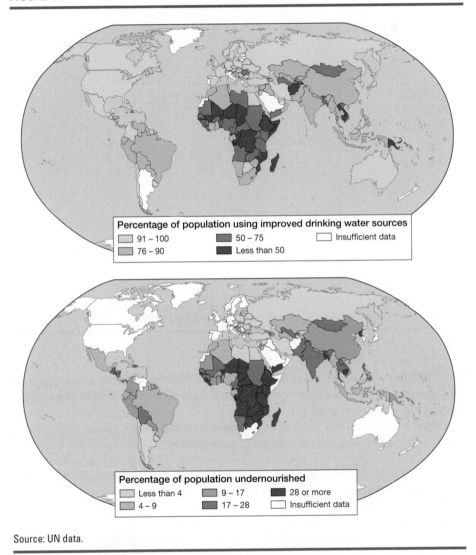

Source: UN data.

basic needs, make a society more war-prone? Probably both are true. War is often part of a vicious circle for states unable to rise out of poverty.

World Hunger

Malnutrition (or malnourishment) refers to the lack of needed foods including protein and vitamins. The term *hunger* refers broadly to malnutrition or outright *undernourishment*—a lack of calories. Hunger does not usually kill people through

TABLE 7.1   Who's Hungry?
Chronically Undernourished People by Region, c. 2007

Region	Number (millions)	Percentage of Population	10 Years Earlier
S. Asia	330	21%	22%
China	140	9%	12%
Africa	210	30%	34%
Latin America	45	8%	11%
Middle East	40	8%	8%
CIS	10	12%	20%
Total	835	13%	14%

Notes: Data are from 2003–2005 and 1995–1997. Chronic undernourishment means failing to consume enough food on average over a year to maintain body weight and support light activity.

Source: Based on Food and Agriculture Organization. *The State of Food Insecurity in the World 2008.* FAO, 2008, pp. 48–50.

outright starvation, but it weakens them and leaves them susceptible to infectious diseases that would not ordinarily be fatal.

Some 920 million people—about one in eight worldwide—are chronically under-nourished (see Table 7.1). At the World Food Summit in 1996, world leaders adopted a goal to cut hunger in half by 2015. But 13 years later there were more hungry people, not fewer. As a proportion of a growing population, however, the rate of hunger dropped from 14 to 13 percent from 1995 to 2005. In 2006, UNICEF reported that China had made great progress in reducing child malnutrition, but progress in South Asia had been very slow and Africa was not moving forward. A quarter of the world's children under age 5—and nearly half those in India—were underweight. Of the world's 150 million underweight children, half lived in India, Pakistan, and Bangladesh. Higher food prices in 2007–2008 led to a particularly large increase in hunger.

Traditionally, rural communities have grown their own food—**subsistence farming.** Colonialism disrupted this pattern, and the disruption has continued in postcolonial times. States in the global South shifted from subsistence to commercial agriculture. Small plots were merged into big plantations, often under the control of wealthy landlords. By concentrating capital and orienting the economy toward a niche in world trade, this process is consistent with liberal economics. But it displaces subsistence farmers from the land. Wars displace farmers even more quickly, with similar results.

Commercial agriculture relies on machinery, commercial fuels, and artificial fertilizers and pesticides, which must be bought with cash and often must be imported. To pay for these supplies, big farms grow **cash crops**—agricultural goods produced for export to world markets. Such crops typically provide little nutrition to local peasants; examples include coffee, tea, and sugar cane. Subsistence farmers end up working on the plantation at very low wages or migrating to cities in search of jobs. Often they end up hungry. Ironically, the higher food prices in 2007–2008 provided increased income for farmers in rural areas, yet at the cost of many being unable to afford food.

International food aid itself can sometimes add to these problems. Agricultural assistance may favor mechanized commercial agriculture. And if an international agency floods an area with food, prices on local markets drop, which may force even more local farmers out of business and increase dependence on handouts from the government or international community. Also, people in a drought or famine often have to travel to feeding centers to receive the food, halting their work on their own land.

Rural and Urban Populations

The displacement of peasants from subsistence farming contributes to a massive population shift that typically accompanies the demographic transition. More and more people move to the cities from the countryside—**urbanization.** This is hard to measure exactly; there is no standard definition of when a town is considered a city. But industrialized states report that about 70–90 percent of their populations live in cities. By contrast, China is only 30 percent urbanized—a level typical of Asia and Africa. Most Middle Eastern states are a bit more urban (45–55 percent), and South American ones are 70–85 percent urban.

Urbanization is not caused by higher population growth in cities than in the countryside. In fact, the opposite is true. In cities, the people are generally better educated, with higher incomes. They are further along in the demographic transition and have lower birthrates than people in the countryside. Rather, the growth of urban population is caused by people moving to the cities from the countryside. They do so because of the higher income levels in the cities and the hope of more chances for an exciting life. They also move because population growth in the countryside stretches available food, water, arable land, and other resources.

Many states have considered policies to break up large land holdings and redistribute land to poor peasants for use in subsistence farming—**land reform.** The main opponents of land reform are large landowners, who often wield great political power because of their wealth and their international connections to markets, MNCs, and other sources of hard currency.

Women in Developing Countries

Economic development in poor countries is closely tied to the status of women in those societies. Most attention for decades had focused on men as supposedly the main generators of capital. Governments and international reports concentrated on work performed by male wage earners. Women's work, by contrast, often is not paid for in money and does not show up in financial statistics. But women in much of the world work harder than men and contribute more to the economic well-being of their families and communities. Women are key to efforts to improve the lot of children and reduce birthrates. In nutrition, education, health care, and shelter, women are central to providing the basic needs of people in poor countries.

Yet women hold inferior social status to men in the countries of the South (even more than in the North). For instance, when food is in short supply, men and boys often eat first, and women and girls get what is left. Similarly, discrimination against girls is widespread in education and literacy. Worldwide, nearly twice as many women as men are illiterate. Throughout Asia, Africa, and the Middle East (though not in Latin America), more boys receive an education, especially at the secondary level, though that gap has closed considerably in recent years. At university level, only 30 percent of students are women in China and the Middle East, a bit more than 20 percent in South Asia and Africa (but 45 percent in Latin America). The Taliban regime in Afghanistan (1996–2001) took extreme measures against women's education, banning all girls from school and all women from paid work.

States and international agencies have begun to pay attention to ending discrimination in schooling, ensuring women's access to health care and birth control, educating mothers about prenatal and child health, and generally raising women's status in society (allowing them a greater voice in decisions). These issues occupied the 1995 UN women's conference in Beijing, China, attended by tens of thousands of state and NGO representatives.

For example, international agencies help women organize small businesses, farms, and other income-producing activities. UNICEF has helped women get bank loans on favorable terms to start up small businesses in Egypt and Pakistan as well as cooperative farms in Indonesia. Women have organized cooperatives throughout the global South, often in rural areas, to produce income through weaving and other textile and clothing production, retail stores, agriculture, and so forth.

Migration and Refugees

The processes just outlined—basic needs deprivation, displacement from land, and urbanization—culminate in one of the biggest political issues affecting North-South relations: **migration** from poorer to richer states. Millions of people from the global South have crossed international borders, often illegally, to reach the North.

Someone who moves to a new country in search of better economic opportunities, a better professional environment, or better access to his or her family, culture, or religion is engaging in migration (emigration from the old state and immigration to the new state). Such migration is considered voluntary. The home state is not under any obligation to let such people leave, and, more important, no state is obligated to receive migrants. As with any trade issue, migration creates complex

WOMEN'S POWER

The status of women in countries of the global South affects prospects for economic development. Women are central to rural economies, to population strategies, and to the provision of basic human needs, including education. Here, a women's cooperative in Mauritania makes small loans to its members, 2006.

VIDEO

Immigration

patterns of winners and losers. Immigrants often provide cheap labor, benefiting the host economy overall, but also compete for jobs with (poor) citizens of the host country. *Remittances*—money sent home by migrants to relatives in their country of origin—are an important source of income for many poor countries with large numbers of emigrant workers, such as Latin Americans working in the United States.

Most industrialized states try to limit immigration from the global South. Despite border guards and fences, many people migrate anyway, illegally. In the United States, such immigrants come from all over the world, but mostly from nearby Mexico, Central America, and the Caribbean. In Western Europe, they come largely from North Africa, Turkey, and (increasingly) Eastern Europe. Some Western European leaders worry that the loosening of border controls under the process of integration (see pp. 228–230) will make it harder to keep out illegal immigrants. Indeed, fear of immigration is one reason why Swiss voters rejected membership in the EU.

International law and custom distinguish migrants from **refugees,** people fleeing to find refuge from war, natural disaster, or political persecution. (Fleeing from chronic discrimination may or may not be grounds for refugee status.) International norms obligate countries to accept refugees who arrive at their borders. Refugees from wars or natural disasters are generally housed in refugee camps temporarily until they can return home (though their stay can drag on for years). Refugees from political persecution may be granted asylum to stay in the new state. Acceptance of refugees—and the question of which states must bear the costs—is a collective goods problem.

The number of international refugees in the world was 16 million in 2007. In addition, 14 million more people are currently displaced within their own countries, and more than 30 million others held some other refugee-related status as a result of either political conflict or natural disaster. An additional 4 million Palestinian refugees fall under the responsibility of the UN Relief and Works Agency (UNRWA). The majority of refugees and internally displaced people have been displaced by wars (see Table 7.2).

TABLE 7.2   Refugee Populations, 2007

Region	Millions	Main Concentrations
Middle East and Asia	13	Afghanistan, Iraq, Pakistan, Nepal, Iran
Palestinians under UNRWA	4	Palestine, Jordan, Lebanon, Syria
Africa	10	Somalia, Uganda, Sudan, D.R. Congo
Latin America	4	Colombia
Europe	3	Former Yugoslavia, Germany[a]
World Total	34	

[a] Various regions of origin.

Note: Includes refugees, asylum seekers, returned refugees, and internally displaced people. Does not include an estimated 30 million refugees not assisted by UNHCR.

Source: UN High Commissioner for Refugees (UNHCR).

The political impact of refugees has been demonstrated repeatedly. The most politicized refugee problem for decades has been that of Palestinians displaced in the 1948 and 1967 Arab-Israeli wars (and their children and grandchildren). They live in "camps" that have become long-term neighborhoods, mainly in Jordan, Lebanon, and the Palestinian territories of Gaza and the West Bank. Economic development is impeded in these camps because the host states and Palestinians insist that the arrangement is only temporary. The poverty of the refugees in turn fuels radical political movements among the inhabitants. The question of Palestinian refugees' right to return to what is now Israel has blocked every attempt at a comprehensive peace settlement for years.

It is not always easy to distinguish a refugee fleeing war or political persecution from a migrant seeking economic opportunity. Illegal immigrants may claim to be refugees in order to be allowed to stay, when really they are seeking better economic opportunities. In recent decades this issue has become a major one throughout the North. In Germany, France, Austria, and elsewhere, resentment of foreign immigrants has fueled upsurges of right-wing nationalism in domestic politics.

Trafficking   In addition to migration and refugees, a growing number of people—estimated at about 700,000 annually—are trafficked across international borders against their will. They include both sex slaves and labor slaves, with each category including females and males, adults and children. Perhaps 20,000 of these people are trafficked to the United States annually. In 2008, the U.S. State Department listed 14 countries making insufficient efforts to stop human trafficking, including friends such as Kuwait and Saudi Arabia.

In general, South-North migration of all types creates problems for the industrialized states that, it seems, can be solved only by addressing the problems of the South itself.

Theories of Accumulation

How do we explain the enormous gap between income levels in the world's industrialized regions and those in the global South? What are the implications of that gap for international politics? There are several very

ON THE MOVE

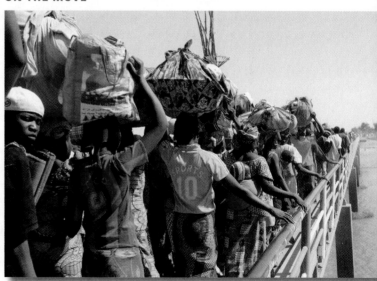

Refugees are both a result of international conflict and a source of conflict. In addition to those fleeing war and repression and those seeking economic opportunity, hundreds of thousands of people each year cross borders as sex and labor slaves. These refugees from war in Chad cross the Cameroon border, 2008.

different approaches to these questions; we will concentrate on two contrasting theories of wealth accumulation, based on more liberal and more revolutionary world views.

Economic Accumulation

A view of the problem from the perspective of capitalism is based on liberal economics—stressing overall efficiency in maximizing *economic growth*. This view sees the global South as merely lagging behind the industrialized North. More wealth creation in the North is a good thing, as is wealth creation in the South—the two are not in conflict.

A different view of things, from the perspective of socialism, is concerned with the distribution of wealth as much as the absolute creation of wealth. It sees the North-South divide as more of a zero-sum game in which the creation of wealth in the North most often comes at the expense of the South. It also gives politics (the state) more of a role in redistributing wealth and managing the economy than does capitalism. Socialism thus parallels mercantilism in some ways. But socialists see economic classes rather than states as the main actors in the political bargaining over the distribution of the world's wealth. And mercantilism promotes the idea of concentrating wealth (as a power element), whereas socialism promotes the broader distribution of wealth.

Capitalist and socialist approaches are rather incompatible in their language and assumptions about the problem of third world poverty and its international implications. The next few sections somewhat favor socialist approaches, focusing on the past history of imperialism and on revolutionary strategies and massive redistribution of wealth as solutions, whereas the sections concluding the chapter lean toward capitalist approaches. In Latin America in recent years, several states have elected leftist presidents committed to changing course away from free market capitalism and toward a socialist philosophy with more state-owned industries.

The World-System

The global system of regional class divisions has been seen by some IR scholars as a **world-system** or a *capitalist world economy*. This view is Marxist in orientation (focusing on economic classes; see Chapter 3) and relies on a global level of analysis. In the world-system, class divisions are regionalized. Regions in the global South mostly extract raw materials (including agriculture)—work that uses much labor and little capital, and pays low wages. Industrialized regions mostly manufacture goods—work that uses more capital, requires more skilled labor, and pays workers higher wages. The manufacturing regions are called the *core* (or *center*) of the world-system; the extraction regions are called the periphery.

The most important class struggle today, in this view, is that between the core and periphery of the world-system. The core uses its power (derived from its wealth) to concentrate surplus from the periphery, as it has done for about 500 years. Conflicts among great powers, including the two world wars and the Cold War, basically result from competition among core states over the right to exploit the periphery.

In world-system theory, the semiperiphery is an area in which some manufacturing occurs and some capital concentrates, but not to the extent of the most advanced areas in the core. Eastern Europe and Russia are commonly considered semiperipheral, as are some of the newly industrializing countries (see p. 280) such as Taiwan and Singapore. The semi-periphery acts as a kind of political buffer between the core and periphery because poor states can aspire to join the semiperiphery instead of aspiring to rebel against domination by the core. Over time, membership in the core, the semiperiphery, and the periphery changes somewhat, but the overall global system of class relations remains.

Semiperiphery regions, which export manufactured products, are just those—China and South Asia—that have been growing very rapidly in recent years (see Figure 7.1 on p. 262). The three periphery regions that engage with the globalizing world economy primarily as raw-material exporters (Africa, the Middle East, and Latin America) are growing more slowly.

Imperialism

Both the disparities in wealth between the global North and South and the specialization in regions' exports have long histories. In Chapter 3 we discussed Marxist theories of imperial-ism, which give a particular kind of explanation for how the North-South gap evolved. Here we review how imperialism affected the South over the centuries and how its aftereffects are still felt around the world. Imperialism, especially in the 16th to mid-20th centuries, struc-tured world order starkly around the dominance principle, with masters and slaves, conquerors and conquered peoples with their land, labor, and treasures. At the same time, imperialism depended on the identity principle to unite the global North around a common racial identity that defined nonwhite people as an out-group. (Although identity issues today are more complex, racism still affects North-South relations.)

European imperialism got its start in the 15th century with the development of oceangoing sailing ships in which a small crew could transport a sizable cargo over a long distance. Portugal pioneered the first voyages of exploration beyond Europe. Spain, France, and Britain soon followed. With superior military technology, Europeans gained control of coastal cities and of resupply outposts along major trade routes. Gradually this control extended further inland, first in Latin America, then in North America, and later throughout Asia and Africa (see Figure 7.4).

These empires decimated indigenous populations and cultures, causing immense suffering. Over time, the economies of colonies developed with the creation of basic transportation and communication infrastructure, factories, and so forth. But these economies were often molded to the needs of the colonizers, not the local populations.

In the 20th century, the world regions formerly dominated by Europe gained inde-pendence, with their own sovereign states participating in the international system. Independence came earlier in the Americas (around 1800). Decolonization continued through the mid-1970s until almost no European colonies remained. Most of the newly independent states have faced tremendous challenges and difficulties in the postcolonial era because of their colonial histories.

FIGURE 7.4 Conquest of the World

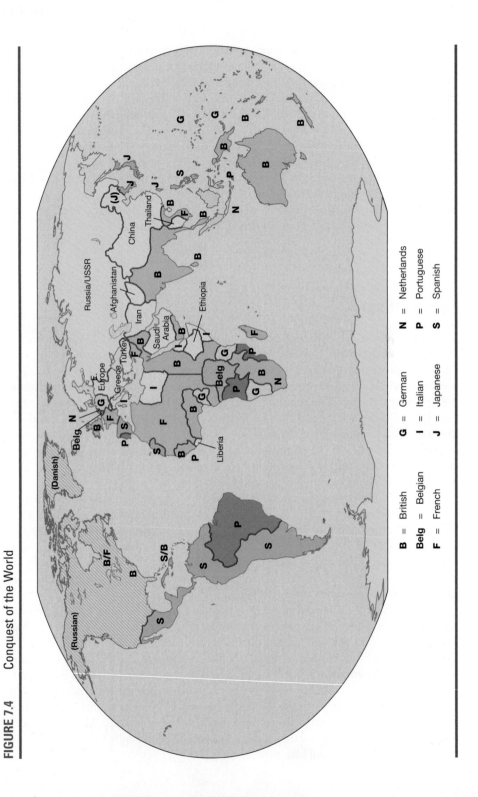

B = British   **G** = German   **N** = Netherlands

Belg = Belgian   **I** = Italian   **P** = Portuguese

F = French   **J** = Japanese   **S** = Spanish

Effects of Colonialism

For most states in the global South, the history of having been colonized by Europeans is central to their national identity, foreign policy, and place in the world. For these states—and especially for those within them who favor socialist perspectives—international relations revolves around their asymmetrical power relationships with industrialized states.

Being colonized has a devastating effect on a people and culture. Foreigners overrun a territory with force and take it over. They install their own government, staffed by their own nationals. The inhabitants are forced to speak the language of the colonizers, to adopt their cultural practices, and to be educated at schools run under their guidance. The inhabitants are told that they are racially inferior to the foreigners.

VIDEO

World's Worst Humanitarian Crises

White Europeans in third world colonies in Africa and Asia were greatly outnumbered by native inhabitants but maintained power by a combination of force and (more important) psychological conditioning. After generations under colonialism, most native inhabitants either saw white domination as normal or believed that nothing could be done about it. The whites often lived in a bubble world separated from the lives of the local inhabitants.

Colonialism also had certain negative *economic* implications. The most easily accessible minerals were dug up and shipped away. The best farmland was planted in export crops rather than subsistence crops. The infrastructure that was built served the purposes of imperialism rather than the local population—for instance, railroads going straight from mining areas to ports. The education and skills needed to run the economy were largely limited to whites.

The economic effects were not all negative, however. Colonialism often fostered local economic accumulation (although controlled by whites). Cities grew. Mines were dug and farms established. Much of the infrastructure that exists today in many developing countries was created by colonizers. In some cases (though not all), colonization combined disparate communities into a cohesive political unit with a common religion, language, and culture, thus creating more opportunities for economic accumulation. In some cases, the local political cultures replaced by colonialism had been oppressive to the majority of the people.

Wherever there were colonizers, there were anticolonial movements. Independence movements throughout Africa and Asia gained momentum during and after World War II, when the European powers were weakened. Through the 1960s, a wave of successful independence movements swept from one country to the next, as people stopped accepting imperialism as normal or inevitable. Within a few decades, nearly all of Africa overthrew white rule (see Figure 7.5).

Although many developing countries gained independence around the same time, the methods by which they did so varied. In India, the most important colony of the largest empire (Britain), Gandhi led a movement based on nonviolent resistance to British rule (see pp. 95–96). However, nonviolence broke down in the subsequent Hindu-Muslim civil war, which split India into two states—India mostly with Hindus, and Pakistan (including what is now Bangladesh) mostly with Muslims. Some colonies—for example, Algeria and Vietnam—won independence through warfare to oust their European masters; others won it peacefully by negotiating a transfer of power with weary Europeans.

FIGURE 7.5   Areas of White Minority Rule in Africa, 1952–1994

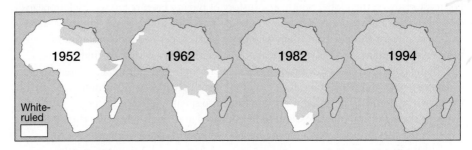

Formal colonialism was swept away over 40 years. However, postcolonial dependency lingers on in many former colonies.

Source: Adapted from Andrew Boyd, *An Atlas of World Affairs.* 9th ed. NY: Routledge, 1992, p. 91.

Postcolonial Dependency

If imperialism concentrated the accumulation of wealth in the core and drained economic surplus from the periphery, one might expect that accumulation in the global South would take off once colonialism was overthrown. Generally, however, this was not the case. A few states, such as Singapore, have accumulated capital successfully since becoming independent. But others, including many African states, seem to be going backward, with little new capital accumulating to replace the old colonial infrastructure. Most former colonies are making only slow progress in accumulation. Political independence has not been a cure-all for poor countries.

One reason for these problems is that under colonialism, the training and experience needed to manage the economy were often limited to white Europeans, leaving a huge gap in technical and administrative skills after independence. Another problem faced by many newly independent states was that their economies rested on the export of one or two products. For Zambia, it was copper ore; for El Salvador, coffee; for Botswana, diamonds. Such a narrow export economy would seem well suited to use the state's comparative advantage to specialize in one niche of the world economy. And having exportable natural resources might seem a big plus for an economy. But in fact the problems of basing economic growth on resource exports have been called the **resource curse.** Dependence on exporting resources distorts an economy, facilitates corruption, and leaves a country vulnerable to price swings. The liberal free trade regime based around the WTO corrected only partially for the North's superior bargaining position in North-South trade. And the WTO has allowed agriculture (exported by the periphery) to remain protected in core states, while promoting liberalization of trade in manufactured goods exported by the core (see pp. 272–273).

The newly independent states inherited borders that were drawn in European capitals by foreign officers looking at maps. As a result, especially in Africa, the internal rivalries of ethnic groups and regions made it very difficult for the new states to implement coherent economic plans. In a number of cases, ethnic conflicts within former colonies led to civil wars, which halted or reversed capital accumulation.

Finally, governments of many postcolonial states did not function very effectively, creating another obstacle to accumulation. In some cases, corruption became much worse after independence (see p. 289). In other cases, governments tried to impose central control and planning on their national economy, based on nationalism, mercantilism, or socialism.

In sum, liberation from colonial control did not transform underlying economic realities. The main trading partners of newly independent countries were usually their former colonial masters. The main products were usually those developed under colonialism. The administrative units and territorial borders were those created by Europeans. The state continued to occupy the same peripheral position in the world-system after independence as it had before. And in some cases it continued to rely on its former colonizer for security.

For these reasons, the period after independence is sometimes called **neocolonialism**—the continuation of colonial exploitation without formal political control. This concept also covers the relationship of the global South with the United States, which (with a few exceptions) was not a formal colonizer. And it covers the North-South international relations of Latin American states, independent for almost two centuries.

Dependency   Marxist IR scholars have developed **dependency theory** to explain the lack of accumulation in the global South. These scholars define dependency as a situation in which accumulation of capital cannot sustain itself internally. A dependent country must borrow capital to produce goods; the debt payments then reduce the accumulation of surplus.

Dependency theorists focus not on the overall structure of the world-system (center and periphery) but on how a peripheral state's own internal class relationships play out. The development (or lack of development) of a poor country depends on its local conditions and history, though it is affected by the same global conditions as other countries located in the periphery.

One historically important configuration of dependency is the **enclave economy,** in which foreign capital is invested in a third world country to extract a particular raw material in a particular place—usually a mine, oil well, or plantation. A different historical pattern is that of nationally controlled production, in which a local capitalist class controls a cycle of accumulation based on producing export products. The cycle still depends on foreign markets, but the profits accrue to the local capitalists, building up a powerful class of rich owners within the country—the local bourgeoisie. After World War II a third form of dependency became more common—penetration of national economies by MNCs. Here the capital is provided externally (as with enclaves), but production is for local markets. For instance, a GM factory in Brazil would produce cars mostly for sale within Brazil. To create local markets for such manufactured goods, income must be concentrated enough to create a middle class. This sharpens disparities of income within the country (most people remain poor).

According to dependency theory, the particular constellation of forces within a country determines which coalitions form among the state, the military, big landowners, local capitalists, foreign capitalists (MNCs), foreign governments, and middle classes. On

MY DOLL, MY SELF

European colonialism worldwide promoted values and norms implying that the colonizer's culture was superior to the indigenous culture. Lingering effects remain in postcolonial societies. This girl displaced by violence in Kenya, a former British colony, plays with a light-skinned doll, 2008.

the other side, peasants, workers, and sometimes students and the church form alliances to work for more equal distribution of income, human and political rights, and local control of the economy. These class alliances and the resulting social relationships are not determined by any general rule but by concrete conditions and historical developments in each country. Like other Marxist theories, dependency theory pays special attention to class struggle as a source of social change. Some people think that under conditions of dependency, economic development is almost impossible. Others think that development is possible under dependency, despite certain difficulties. We will return to these possibilities later in the chapter.

Overall, North-South relations show how difficult it has become to separate political economy from international security. The original political relations contained in European imperialism led to economic conditions in the South—such as high population growth, urbanization, and concentrations of wealth—that in turn led to political movements for independence, and later to revolutions. The various aspects of the North-South gap considered in the first half of this chapter—including hunger, refugees, and the structure of commodity exports—all contain both economic and political-military aspects. The remainder of the chapter turns to the question of how economies in the South can develop the accumulation process and what role the North can play in that process.

Development Experiences

This chapter so far has discussed the situation in the global South and how it came to be. The remainder takes up the question of what to do about it. **Economic development** refers to the combined processes of capital accumulation, rising per capita incomes (with consequent falling birthrates), increasing skills in the population, adoption of new technological styles, and other related social and economic changes. The most central aspect is the accumulation of capital (with its ongoing wealth-generating potential). The concept of development has a subjective side that cannot be measured statistically—the judgment of whether a certain pattern of wealth creation and distribution is good for a state and its people. But one simple measure of economic development is the per capita GDP—the amount of economic activity per person. This measure was the horizontal axis in Figure 7.1 (p. 262), and change in this measure was on the vertical axis.

By this measure, we can trace the successes and failures of the South as a whole and, more important, its regions and countries. The latter is more important because it contains the seeds of possible lessons and strategies that could build on the South's successes in the future. Most of the global South made progress on economic development in the 1970s, but real per capita GDP decreased in the 1980s in Latin America, Africa, and the Middle East, with only China growing robustly. In the 1990s, real economic growth returned across much of the South—about 5–6 percent annual growth for the South as a whole, compared to 2–3 percent in the global North. China stood out among the regions of the South as making rapid progress toward economic development.

In the new century, growth has accelerated in the South and now outpaces the North in growth rate (see Figure 7.6). This growth was still uneven. South Asia joined China in rapid growth of 8–9 percent annually. Because China and South Asia together contain the majority of the population in the global South, this development is very important. Even in Africa, according to the World Bank, economies grew by more than 5 percent annually from 2005 to 2007 (led by, but not limited to, oil- and mineral-exporting nations). Yet, as we discuss later in this chapter, the current global economic downturn threatens some of the economic progress made by the developing world.

FIGURE 7.6   Real GDP Growth of Selected Countries, 2007

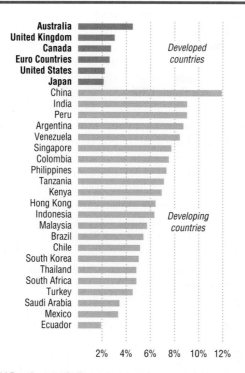

Source: World Bank, *World Development Indicators.*

The Newly Industrializing Countries

Before China took off, a handful of poor states—called the **newly industrializing countries (NICs)**—achieved self-sustaining capital accumulation, with impressive economic growth. These semiperiphery states, which export light manufactured goods, posted strong economic growth in the 1980s and early 1990s (see "The World-System" on pp. 272–273). They suffered a setback in the late 1990s because growth had been too fast, with overly idealistic loans, speculative investments, and corrupt deals (see p. 289). Notwithstanding these setbacks, the NICs resumed growth and have developed much faster than most of the global South.

The most successful NICs are the **"four tigers"** (or *"four dragons"*) of East Asia: South Korea, Taiwan, Hong Kong, and Singapore. Each succeeded in developing particular sectors and industries that were competitive on world markets. These sectors and industries can create enough capital accumulation within the country to raise income levels not just among the small elite but across the population more broadly. Scholars do not know whether the NICs are just the lucky few that have moved from the periphery to the semiperiphery of the world-system or whether their success can eventually be replicated throughout the world. This growth, however, shows that it is possible to rise out of poverty to relative prosperity. South Korea did so, followed by China, and India appears to be starting on the same curve (see Figure 7.7).

South Korea, with iron and coal resources, developed competitive steel and automobile industries that export globally, creating a trade surplus (see pp. 167–168). Taiwan also used a strong state industrial policy, specializing in the electronics and computer industries, and in other light manufacturing. Hong Kong—controlled by China since 1997—also has world-competitive electronics and other light industries, but its greatest strengths are in banking and trade. Singapore is a trading city located at the tip of the Malaysian peninsula—convenient to the South China Sea, the Indian Ocean, and Australia.

For different reasons, each of these states holds a somewhat unusual political status in the international system. South Korea and Taiwan were hot spots of international conflict that came under the U.S. security umbrella during the Cold War. Both were militarized, authoritarian states intolerant of dissent that later became democratic.

Hong Kong and Singapore have a different political profile. They are both former British colonies. They are more city-states than nation-states, and their cities are trading ports and financial centers. Although not as repressive or as militarized as South Korea and Taiwan during the Cold War era, Hong Kong and Singapore were not democracies either. Hong Kong was ruled by a British governor, and Singapore by a dominant individual.

Beyond the four tigers, other South East Asian countries have tried, since the 1980s, to follow in their footsteps. These countries include Thailand, Malaysia, and Indonesia. Because their experiences vary, they are discussed below with other Asian economies (see pp. 285–286).

The Chinese Experience

If there was ever a doubt that the successes of the NICs could be replicated elsewhere and on a larger scale, China ended those doubts. China has 1.3 billion people, and this

FIGURE 7.7   Per Capita GDP of South Korea, China, India, and Ghana

Source: Based on Penn World Tables, World Bank and IMF data.

size alone makes China's efforts to generate self-sustaining accumulation worthy of study. But China has also had the world's fastest-growing economies over the past two decades.

After Mao died in 1976, China under Deng Xiaoping instituted economic reforms and transformed its southern coastal provinces into *free economic zones* open to foreign investment and run on capitalist principles. Peasants worked their own fields, instead of collective farms, and got rich (by Chinese standards) if they did well. Entrepreneurs started companies, hired workers, and generated profits. Foreign investment flooded into southern China, taking advantage of its location, cheap labor, and relative political stability. Other areas of China gradually opened up to capitalist principles as well. The state required more industries to turn a profit and gave more initiative to managers to run their own companies and spend the profits as they saw fit.

However, China has also re-created some of the features of capitalism that Mao's revolutionaries had overturned. New class disparities emerged, with rich entrepreneurs driving fancy imported cars while poor workers found themselves unemployed. Unprofitable state-owned industries laid off 10 million workers in the 1990s, with more coming each year. Indeed, in the countryside, areas bypassed by development still

FLYING HIGH

China's rapid economic growth has raised incomes dramatically, especially for a growing middle class. These successes followed China's opening to the world economy and adoption of market-oriented reforms. China's strong performance in the 2008 Beijing Olympics, both athletically and as the host country, marked a coming of age for China as a leading power in the international community. Now, as exports slow down in a global recession, China must develop its domestic market and consumer spending rather than relying so heavily on exports to fuel growth.

VIDEO

China Rising: The Boom

contain 200 million desperately poor Chinese peasants. Social problems such as prostitution returned, as did economic problems such as inflation (since largely tamed). Most frustrating for ordinary Chinese is the widespread official corruption accompanying the get-rich atmosphere.

Popular resentment over such problems as inflation and corruption led industrial workers and even government officials to join students in antigovernment protests at Beijing's Tiananmen Square in 1989. Authorities used the military to violently suppress the protests, killing hundreds of people and signaling the government's determination to maintain tight political control while economic reform proceeded.

Foreign investors returned quickly after the political disruption of 1989, however, and economic growth roared ahead. Chinese exports grew to over $1 trillion in 2007, aided by China's WTO membership since 2001.

A new generation of Chinese leaders—led by President Hu Jintao—is trying to address the growing inequality between the country's newly rich strata and the hundreds of millions left in poverty in the countryside or laid off from jobs in state-owned industries in the cities (along with migrants from the countryside who cannot find work in the cities). In rural villages, thousands of "mass incidents of unrest" have taken place, ranging from protests to full-scale riots put down by lethal force, as peasants reacted to land seizures, taxes, pollution, and corruption by local officials. The government suppressed news of these protests in mass media and over the Internet.

China's membership in the WTO raises new questions about how the ongoing Chinese opening of its economy to the world can coexist with continued political authoritarianism under communist rule. China's hundreds of millions of new Internet users and cell phone subscribers will be able to communicate with overseas partners, monitor shipments, and follow economic trends globally. They will also be able to bypass government-controlled sources of political information. Some observers expect economic integration in an information era to inexorably open up China's political system and lead to democratization, whereas other experts think that as long as Chinese leaders deliver economic growth, the population will have little appetite for political change.

China's economic success has given it both more prestige in the international system and a more global perspective on international relations far from China's borders. In 2004–2006, President Hu and other Chinese leaders made high-profile visits to resource-rich areas of the global South, notably Africa and Latin America, making large-scale deals for minerals and energy to fuel China's growth, while boosting China's foreign aid to these areas. In 2007, China announced $3 billion in preferential loans to Africa, which, China emphasized, "carry no political conditions" (unlike Western loans, which often demand such policies as respect for human rights or fighting corruption). China's rising international standing was also reflected in the selection of Beijing to host the 2008 Olympics, which were enormously successful.

For years it appeared that China's huge population would supply limitless cheap labor to foreign investors making goods in China. In recent years, however, China's growth has begun to squeeze the available labor force and push wages up somewhat. MNCs have begun to move some light manufacturing to other Asian countries with even cheaper labor, such as Vietnam.

China's economic miracle seemed unstoppable in 2008, but the world economic recession has cast doubt on the prospects for continuing rapid growth. China's exports stopped growing as demand for consumer products dried up in the United States and other industrialized countries. At the same time, China's investments in the United States, made with the trade surpluses China had accumulated over the years, lost a substantial fraction of their value in the financial meltdown of late 2008. Chinese leaders announced a major stimulus package aimed at spurring domestic consumption in China, but this faced problems in the short term, including the cultural problem of getting people with a history of poverty to spend instead of saving, and the economic problem of reorienting an export-driven economy to produce for domestic markets. All these challenges underlined the uncertainty facing China in the latest phase of its development process.

It is unclear what lessons China's economic success over the past decade holds for the rest of the global South. The shift away from central planning and toward private ownership was clearly a key factor in its success, yet the state continues to play a central role in overseeing the economy (even more than in the NICs). These topics are being debated vigorously as China navigates its new era of rising prosperity and rising expectations, finds its way in the newly turbulent world economy, and other poor states look to China's experience for lessons.

India Takes Off

India, like China, deserves special attention because of its size and recent robust growth. From 1996 to 2008, India's average annual growth rate exceeded 7 percent. India's decade of success still does not compare to China's nearly three decades, and India's GDP per person is still not much more than half of China's. But India's success has started it toward what could be, in the coming years, a repetition of China's rise out of poverty.

AT YOUR SERVICE

India has grown rapidly in recent years, using its large, well-educated, English-speaking population to generate export revenues in the service sector—software companies, call centers serving American customers, and professional services in such areas as accounting, architecture, engineering, and medicine. This radiologist in Bangalore, India's technology capital, reads body scans from a U.S. hospital sent via the Internet and discusses the results by phone with the patient's doctor in Connecticut, 2004.

India's economy was for decades based loosely on socialism and state control of large industries but on private capitalism in agriculture and consumer goods. The state subsidizes basic goods and gives special treatment to farmers. Unlike China, India has a democratic government, but a fractious one, with various autonomy movements and ethnic conflicts. India's government has suffered from corruption, although this has improved in recent years.

In the era of globalization, India's niche in the globalized world economy is in the service and information sectors. Whereas South Korea specialized in exporting heavy manufactured goods and China in light manufactured goods, India specializes in exporting information products such as software and telephone call center services. Each country uses its labor force to add value to products that could be exported worldwide, especially to the large American market. In India's case the labor force is well educated and speaks English. India can also use its location to advantage by working during the nighttime hours in North America. Software companies can hand off projects daily for the India shift to work on overnight, and American hospitals can send medical notes for overnight transcription. MNCs widely use India's labor force to answer phone calls from around the world, such as technical support calls for the company's products.

India's future success or failure will bear strongly on several competing theories about economic development. In particular, China has had success under a harsh, centralized political system whereas India has a free-wheeling democracy. If India cannot sustain growth, then maybe authoritarian government helps development, and democracy should wait until a later stage (an argument we discuss shortly). If India continues to succeed, however, then clearly authoritarian government is not a precondition.

Figure 7.8 compares China's and India's progress on two key indicators—infant mortality (a good overall measure of public health) and the fertility rate (see pp. 326–328). In both cases, China was able to make dramatic improvements very quickly because of its authoritarian government, whose control (in theory) extended to every village and every bedroom. In the 1950s, after taking power, China ordered mass campaigns in which

FIGURE 7.8   Comparing Chinese and Indian Development

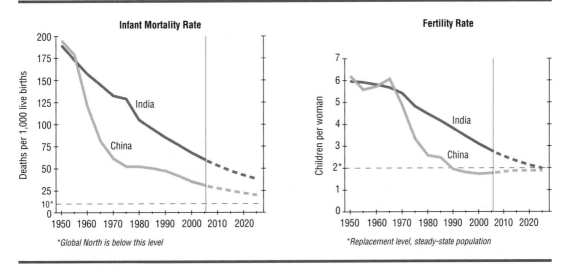

citizens exterminated pests and set up sanitation facilities. As a result, in the 1960s China's rates of epidemic diseases such as cholera and plague dropped, and so did the infant mortality rate. In the 1970s, with its heavy-handed one-child policy, China forced down the fertility rate. Women who objected could be forcibly sterilized. Thus, China relied on the dominance principle to force individuals to take actions that were in society's interest. Its successes in improving public health and lowering fertility provided a foundation for China's subsequent economic success, although obviously at a cost to individual freedom.

India, by contrast, has relied more on the identity principle, getting people to change their preferences and *want* to have fewer children and help improve public health. Without a dictatorship to force compliance, India's progress has been slower. However, over time India is moving toward the same results as China, albeit decades later, and doing so without giving up its own national identity as a democracy.

Other Experiments

Other sizable developing countries have pursued various development strategies, with mixed successes and failures. The best results have come from Asia. Figure 7.9 shows the income levels and growth rates of the 16 largest countries by population in the global South. The graph parallels that for world regions in Figure 7.1. Clearly the large countries of the South vary widely in income level. The five highest-income countries (Turkey, Iran, Thailand, Mexico, and Brazil) come from three of the four regions and are growing at 3–6 percent. The fastest-growing countries (India, Vietnam, Ethiopia, and Democratic Congo) at 7–9 percent were at the lower end of the income scale. (These growth rates declined in 2008 and 2009 as the global economic crisis spread to the developing world.) Clearly China is developing faster than the other 15 large countries of the global South, although all posted

FIGURE 7.9   Largest Countries' Income Levels and Growth Rates, 2007

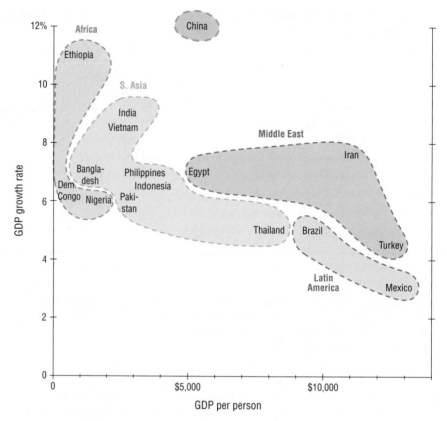

Note: Figure shows the 16 most populous developing countries.

Source: World Bank, *World Development Indicators.*

solid growth, 5–9 percent for most. Clearly, too, regional location makes a difference. The fact that the five regions of the global South can be mapped onto single contiguous zones on this figure shows that whole regions are moving together in distinct patterns.

The largest developing countries are following somewhat different strategies with somewhat different results. But several common themes recur. These themes concern trade, the concentration of capital, authoritarianism, and corruption.

Import Substitution and Export-Led Growth

Throughout the global South, states are trying to use international trade as the basis of accumulation. For the reasons discussed in Chapter 5, a policy of self-reliance or autarky is at best an extremely slow way to build up wealth. But through the creation of a trade surplus, a state can accumulate hard currency and build industry and infrastructure.

One way to try to create a trade surplus, used frequently a few decades ago, is through **import substitution**—the development of local industries to produce items that a country had been importing. These industries may receive state subsidies or tariff protection. This might seem to be a good policy for reducing dependency—especially on the former colonial master—while shrinking a trade deficit or building a trade surplus. But it is against the principle of comparative advantage and has not proven effective in most cases. Some scholars think that import substitution is a useful policy only at a very early phase of economic development, after which it is counterproductive. Others think it is never useful.

More and more states have shifted to a strategy of **export-led growth,** a strategy used by the NICs. This strategy seeks to develop industries that can compete in specific niches in the world economy. The industries may receive special treatment such as subsidies and protected access to local markets. Exports from these industries generate hard currency and create a favorable trade balance. The state can then spend part of its money on imports of commodities produced more cheaply elsewhere. Such a strategy has risks, however, especially when a state specializes in the export of a few raw materials (see pp. 276–277). It leaves poor countries vulnerable to sudden price fluctuations for their exports.

Concentrating Capital for Manufacturing

Manufacturing emerges as a key factor in both export-led growth and self-sustaining industrialization (home production for home markets). To invest in manufacturing, these countries must *concentrate* what surplus their economies produce. Money spent building factories cannot be spent subsidizing food prices or building better schools. Thus the concentration of capital for manufacturing can sharpen disparities in income. Furthermore, because manufacturing industries in poor countries are not immediately competitive on world markets, one common strategy is to first build up the industry with sales to the home market (protected by tariffs and subsidies). But home markets for manufactured goods do not come from poor peasants in the countryside or the unemployed youth in city slums. Rather, wealth must be concentrated in a *middle class* that has the income to buy manufactured goods. These disparities may result in crowds rioting in the streets or guerrillas taking over the countryside.

Capital for manufacturing can come instead from foreign investment or foreign loans, but this reduces the amount of surplus (profit) available to the state in the long term. Another way to minimize capital needs is to start out in low-capital industries. These industries can begin generating capital, which can then be used to move into somewhat more technologically demanding and capital-intensive kinds of manufacturing. A favorite starter industry is *textiles*. The industry is fairly labor-intensive, giving an advantage to countries with cheap labor, and does not require huge investments of capital to get started. In 2005, textile tariffs were removed worldwide, so textile exporters in developing countries gained access to Western markets but faced intensified competition from China.

A related approach to capitalization in very poor countries, growing in popularity in recent years, is **microcredit** (or *microlending*). Based on a successful model in Bangladesh (the Grameen Bank, which won the 2006 Nobel Peace Prize), microcredit uses small loans to poor people, especially women, to support economic self-sufficiency. The borrowers are organized into small groups and take responsibility for each other's success, including repaying the loans. Repayment rates have been high, and the idea has spread rapidly in several regions. In one popular application, village women used small loans to start businesses renting cell phone time. Rural farmers used the phone time to find out market conditions before making a long trek to sell their products. Thus, bringing the information revolution to isolated villages raised incomes for farmers and the entrepreneurial women alike, and the bank got its loans repaid. Microcredit is now being applied on a macro scale. Tens of millions of families have received loans from thousands of institutions worldwide. Microcredit is the opposite of a trickle-down approach—it injects capital at the bottom of the economic hierarchy. A loan to buy a goat or cell phone may do more good, dollar for dollar, than a loan to build a dam.

The World Bank reviewed evidence on the effect of income inequality on economic growth, and concluded that inequality holds back growth by wasting human potential. The Bank recommends extending access to health care, education, and jobs—as well as to political power—to the poorest people in societies of the global South in order to spur faster economic growth.

Authoritarianism and Democracy

Several decades ago, many scholars expected that states in the global South would follow the European and North American states in economic and political development. The gradual accumulation of capital would be accompanied by the gradual extension of literacy and education, the reduction of class and gender disparities, and the strengthening of democracy and political participation. The United States could be a model, in this view. It had gone from poor colony to industrializing state to rich superpower. Political rights (including the vote) had been steadily extended to more segments of the population.

In reality, democracy did not accompany economic development in a systematic way. The fastest-growing states were generally authoritarian states like China, not democracies. But there is no guarantee that, even in early phases of accumulation, authoritarian control leads to economic development. Some successful accumulators, such as Singapore, have maintained tight political control throughout the process. Others, such as South Korea and Turkey, have started with authoritarian rule and evolved into democracies. Still others, such as Costa Rica, Malaysia, and now India, have achieved good economic results while maintaining much democracy and little repression. Similarly, among the countries that have done poorly in economic accumulation are both authoritarian regimes and democratic ones. Therefore, a state's form of political governance does not seem to determine its success in economic development. Future years will show whether China follows South Korea's example, gradually democratizing after decades of successful economic development.

VIDEO

Innovation and Political Reform in China

Corruption

Corruption is an important negative factor in economic development in many states. Corruption centers on the government as the central actor in economic development, especially in its international aspects. Through foreign policy, the government mediates the national economy's relationship to the world economy. It regulates the conditions under which MNCs operate in the country. It enforces worker discipline—calling out the army if necessary to break strikes or suppress revolutions. It sets tax rates and wields other macroeconomic levers of control over the economy. And in most developing countries, it owns a sizable stake in major industries—a monopoly in some cases.

State officials decide whether to let an MNC into the country, which MNC to give leases or contracts to, and what terms to insist on. Corruption adds another player, the corrupt official, to share the benefits. In 2003, a Mobil Oil executive was indicted for paying $78 million to two senior officials in Kazakhstan—with a kickback of $2 million for himself—to secure Mobil's billion-dollar stake in a huge oil field there.

Corruption is by no means limited to the global South. But for several reasons corruption has a deeper effect in poor countries. First, there is simply less surplus to keep economic growth going; accumulation is fragile. And in developing countries dependent on exporting a few products, the revenue arrives in a very concentrated form—large payments in hard currency—presenting a greater opportunity for corruption than in a more diversified economy. This is a major element in the "resource curse" (see p. 277). Furthermore, incomes in developing countries are often so low that corrupt officials are more tempted to accept payments.

Corruption in the global South presents a collective goods problem for states and MNCs in the global North: individually, MNCs and their home states can profit by clinching a deal with a private payoff; collectively, the MNCs and states of the North lose money by having to make these payoffs. This gives an incentive to clamp down on corruption only if other industrialized states do likewise. A Berlin-based NGO, Transparency International, publishes annual surveys showing the countries that business executives consider most corrupt. The top five on the list in 2008 were Somalia, Burma, Iraq, Haiti, and Afghanistan. In 1997, the world's 29 leading industrialized states agreed to forbid their companies from bribing foreign officials. And the Extractive Industries Transparency Initiative, a coalition of states, NGOs, and MNCs launched by Britain in 2002, fights corruption in the especially vulnerable oil, gas, and mineral sectors worldwide by getting companies to release information on payments they make to developing countries.

North-South Capital Flows

Capital from the global North moves to the South and potentially spurs growth there in several forms—foreign investment, debt, and foreign aid. The rest of this chapter discusses these capital flows from North to South.

Foreign Investment

VIDEO

**Developing
Chad's Oil**

Poor countries have little money available to invest in new factories, farms, mines, or oil wells. Foreign investment—investment in such capital goods by foreigners (most often MNCs)—is one way to get accumulation started (see pp. 201–202). Foreign investment has been crucial to the success of China and other Asian developing countries. Overall, private capital flows to the global South totaled roughly $500 billion in 2007— six times the amount given in official development assistance.

Foreigners who invest in a country then own the facilities; the investor, by virtue of its ownership, can control decisions about how many people to employ, whether to expand or shut down, what products to make, and how to market them. Also, the foreign investor can usually take the profits from the operation out of the country (repatriation of profits). However, the host government can share in the wealth by charging fees and taxes, or by leasing land or drilling rights (see pp. 202–204).

Because of past colonial experiences, many governments in the global South have feared the loss of control that comes with foreign investments by MNCs. Sometimes the presence of MNCs was associated with the painful process of concentrating capital and the sharpening of class disparities in the host state. Although such fears remain, they are counterbalanced by the ability of foreign investors to infuse capital and generate more surplus. By the 1980s and 1990s, as models based on autarky or state ownership were discredited and the NICs gained success, many poor states rushed to embrace foreign investment. China has been the most successful of these by far.

One way in which states have sought to soften the loss of control is through *joint ventures*, companies owned partly by a foreign MNC and partly by a local firm or the host government itself. Sometimes foreign ownership in joint ventures is limited to some percentage (often 49 percent), to ensure that ultimate control rests with the host country. The percentage of ownership is usually proportional to the amount of capital invested; if a host government wants more control, it must put up more money. Joint ventures work well for MNCs because they help ensure the host government's cooperation in reducing bureaucratic hassles and ensuring success (by giving the host government a direct stake in the outcome).

MNCs invest in a country because of some advantage of doing business there. In some cases, it is natural resources. Sometimes it is cheap labor. Some states have better *absorptive capacity* than others—the ability to put investments to productive use—because of developed infrastructure and skilled workers. MNCs also look for a favorable *regulatory environment* in which a host state will facilitate, rather than impede, the MNC's business.

MNC decisions about foreign investment also depend on prospects for *financial stability*, especially prospects for low inflation and stable currency exchange rates. If a currency is not convertible, an MNC will not be able to take profits back to its home state or reinvest them elsewhere. Of equal importance in attracting investment is *political stability* (see pp. 203–204). Banks and MNCs conduct *political risk analyses* to assess the risks of political disturbances in developing countries in which they might invest.

Beyond these financial considerations, a foreign investor producing for local markets wants to know that the host country's *economic growth* will sustain demand for the goods being produced. Similarly, whether producing for local consumption or export, the MNC wants the local labor supply—whether semiskilled or just cheap—to be stable. Foreign investors often look to international financial institutions, such as the World Bank and the IMF, and to private analyses, to judge a state's economic stability before investing in it.

Technology transfer refers to a poor state's acquisition of technology (knowledge, skills, methods, designs, and specialized equipment) from foreign sources, usually in conjunction with foreign direct investment or similar business operations. A developing country may allow an MNC to produce certain goods in the country under favorable conditions, provided the MNC shares knowledge of the technology and design behind the product. The state may try to get its own citizens into the management and professional workforce of factories or facilities created by foreign investment. Not only can physical capital accumulate in the country, but so can the related technological base for further development. Of course, MNCs may be reluctant to share proprietary technology.

Most poor states seek to build up an educated elite with knowledge and skills to run the national economy. One way to do so is to send students to industrialized states for higher education. This entails some risks, however. Students may enjoy life in the North and fail to return home. The problem of losing skilled workers to richer countries, called the **brain drain,** has impeded economic development in states such as India, Pakistan, and the Philippines (where more nurses emigrated than graduated nursing school in 2000–2004).

North-South Debt

Borrowing money is an alternative to foreign investment as a way of obtaining funds to prime a cycle of economic accumulation. If accumulation succeeds, it produces enough surplus to repay the loan and still make a profit. Borrowing has several advantages. It keeps control in the hands of the state (or other local borrower) and does not impose painful sacrifices on local citizens, at least in the short term.

Debt has disadvantages too. The borrower must service the debt—making regular payments of interest and repaying the principal according to the terms of the loan. *Debt service* is a constant drain on whatever surplus is generated by investment of the money. With foreign direct investment, a money-losing venture is the problem of the foreign MNC; with debt, it is the problem of the borrowing state, which must find the money elsewhere. Often, a debtor must borrow new funds to service old loans, slipping further into debt. Debt service has created a net financial outflow from South to North in recent years, as the South has paid billions more in interest to banks and governments in the North than it has received in foreign investment or development aid.

Failure to make scheduled payments, called a **default,** is considered a drastic action because it destroys lender confidence and results in cutoff of future loans. Rather than defaulting, borrowers usually attempt **debt renegotiation**—reworking the terms on which a loan will be repaid. By renegotiating their debts with lenders, borrowers seek a mutually acceptable payment scheme to keep at least some money flowing to the lender. If interest rates have fallen since a loan was first taken out, the borrower can refinance. Borrowers and lenders can also negotiate to restructure a debt by changing the length of the loan (usually to a longer payback period) or the other terms. Occasionally state-to-state loans are written off altogether—forgiven—for political reasons, as happened with U.S. loans to Egypt after the Gulf War.

North-South debt encompasses several types of lending relationships, all of which are influenced by international politics. The borrower may be a private firm or bank in a developing country, or it may be the government itself. Loans to the government are somewhat more common because lenders consider the government less likely to default than a private borrower. The lender may be a private bank or company, or a state (both are important). Usually banks are more insistent on receiving timely payments and firmer in renegotiating debts than are states. Some state-to-state loans are made on artificially favorable *concessionary* terms, in effect subsidizing economic development in the borrowing state.

Debt renegotiation has become a perennial occupation of developing countries. Such renegotiations are complex international bargaining situations. For lenders, debt renegotiations involve a collective goods problem: all of them have to agree on the conditions of the renegotiation but each really cares only about getting its own money back. To solve this problem, state creditors meet together periodically as the *Paris Club*, and private creditors as the *London Club*, to work out their terms.

Through such renegotiations and the corresponding write-offs of debts by banks, developing countries have largely avoided defaulting on their debts. However, in 2001, Argentina in effect defaulted. By then, financial institutions had adjusted psychologically to the reality that Argentina could not pay its debt, so the default did not cause a wider panic. Indeed, Argentina recovered—its economy growing 9 percent a year since 2001—and in 2005 offered its creditors a take-it-or-leave-it deal for repayment of less than 30 cents on the dollar. Most took it, showing Argentina's strong position despite the default.

Despite stabilization, developing countries have not yet solved the debt problem. As shown in Table 7.3, the South owes more than $2 trillion in foreign debt, and pays more than $300 billion a year to service that debt. The debt service (in hard currency) absorbs more than a third of the entire hard-currency export earnings in Latin America—the region most affected. Africa's debt is equal to 30 percent of the annual GDP of the region. Some states in Asia are vulnerable to debt problems as well.

TABLE 7.3   Debt in the Global South, 2008

Region	Foreign Debt		Annual Debt Service	
	Billion $	% of GDP[a]	Billion $	% of Exports
Latin America	900	20%	190	18%
Asia	1,165	17	150	5
Africa	275	22	30	5
Middle East	400	21	40	4
Total "South"	2,740	20	360	8

[a]GDP not calculated at purchasing-power parity.

Notes: Regions do not exactly match those used elsewhere in this book. Africa here includes North Africa. Asia includes China.

Source: IMF. *Statistical Appendix to World Economic Outlook*, Sept. 2008, pp. 36–37.

In recent years, activists and NGOs have called for extensive debt forgiveness for the poorest countries, most of which are in Africa. Critics say such cancellations just put more money in the hands of corrupt, inept governments. But G7 members in early 2005 agreed on a new plan to eliminate all debts owed by 37 very poor countries to the World Bank and IMF—cutting almost in half the poorest countries' estimated $200 billion in debt.

IMF Conditionality

The International Monetary Fund (IMF) and the World Bank have a large supply of capital from their member states (see pp. 196–198). This capital plays an important role in funding early stages of accumulation in developing countries and in helping them get through short periods of great difficulty. And, as a political entity rather than a bank, the IMF can make funds available on favorable terms.

The IMF scrutinizes developing countries' economic plans and policies, withholding loans until it is satisfied that the right policies are in place. Then it makes loans to help states through the transitional process of implementing the IMF-approved policies. The IMF also sends important signals to private lenders and investors. Its approval of a state's economic plans is a "seal of approval" bankers and MNCs use to assess the wisdom of investing in that state. Thus, the IMF wields great power to influence the economic policies of developing countries.

An agreement to loan IMF funds on the condition that certain government policies are adopted is called an **IMF conditionality** agreement; implementation of these conditions is referred to as a *structural adjustment program*. Dozens of developing countries have entered into such agreements with the IMF in the past two decades. The terms insisted on by the IMF are usually painful for the citizens (and hence for national politicians). The IMF demands that inflation be brought under control, which requires reducing state spending and closing budget deficits. This often spurs unemployment and requires that subsidies of food and basic goods be reduced or eliminated. Short-term consumption is curtailed in favor of longer-term investment. Surplus must be concentrated to service debt and invest in new capital accumulation. The IMF wants to ensure that inflation does not eat away all progress and that the economy is stable enough to attract investment. In addition, it demands steps to curtail corruption.

Because of the pain inflicted by a conditionality agreement—and to some extent by any debt renegotiation agreement—such agreements are often politically unpopular in the global South. On quite a few occasions, a conditionality agreement has brought rioters into the streets demanding the restoration of subsidies.

MIRACLE OF LOAVES

IMF conditionality agreements often call for reducing subsidies for food, transportation, and other basic needs. In Egypt, bread prices are heavily subsidized, forcing the government to use hard currency to import wheat. But public resistance to bread price increases is so strong that the government has not brought itself to cut the subsidy. Here, bread is delivered in Cairo during the presidential election, 2005.

POLICY PERSPECTIVES

President of Egypt, Hosni Mubarak

PROBLEM   *How do you balance the demands of domestic actors and international institutions?*

BACKGROUND   Imagine that you are the president of Egypt. Your economy is not in the healthiest shape. Unemployment is high, running around 10 percent. Economic growth has been steady but slow, hovering between 3 and 5 percent in recent years. Given your large and growing population, many believe this rate is too low. Your country is saddled with a large debt burden—as of 2006, around $30 billion.

Recently, however, your government has begun to undertake new economic reforms. Led by a new group of young leaders (including your son), the government is selling several large state-owned industries, especially banks, to private investors. In addition, rules governing who can own industries have been relaxed to allow international MNCs to invest in Egypt.

International actors have praised these moves toward reform. The International Monetary Fund (IMF) and the World Bank have extolled your economic plans and suggested an accelerated pace for reform.

In the past, you have been far more cautious in your approach to economic reform. State-owned industries are politically important for you because they employ large numbers of Egyptians. When these industries are privatized, many employees will likely be fired.

DOMESTIC CONSIDERATIONS   Already, the privatization that has occurred has been unpopular. To make up for the new waves of unemployed, you increased food subsidies. These increases led to more public debt, however, as they cost your government billions of dollars. In 2004, your budget deficit was more than $8 billion, which necessitated new loans from the IMF.

Still, you view these subsidies and state-owned industries as an important political tool for ensuring political stability for your government. You are increasingly challenged with calls for political reform, including holding elections and allowing Islamic parties (which you

have outlawed in the past) to participate in politics. In the past, IMF-related programs have led to riots and civil unrest in your country.

SCENARIO   Now imagine that after a particularly difficult year economically, you must return to the IMF for more loans. The IMF, however, demands even further economic reform as a condition for the new loans. Although they praise your efforts so far, IMF negotiators push you to go further. They demand more privatization and the slashing of food subsidies.

Rejecting the IMF demands risks a cut in loans that would threaten your economic stability and frighten foreign investors away. The privatization and reform does seem to be improving the investment environment in your country, which is boosting your economy.

Acquiescing to the IMF conditions carries a large political risk, however. Privatization will lead to unemployment, while a cut in food subsidies will increase hunger.

CHOOSE YOUR POLICY   Do you adopt further reforms, hoping to blame the IMF for your economic troubles with your public? Do you refuse the IMF loans and search for alternate sources of loans? How do you balance your domestic political needs with the demands of international economic institutions and investors?

Sometimes governments have backed out of the agreements or have broken their promises under such pressure. Occasionally, governments have been toppled.

The South in International Economic Regimes

Because of the need for capital and the wealth created by international trade, most states of the global South see their future economic development as resting on a close interconnection with the world economy, not on national autarky or regional economic communities. Thus poor states must play by the rules embedded in international economic regimes, as discussed in Chapter 5.

The WTO trading regime sometimes works against poor states, however, relative to industrialized ones. A free trade regime makes it harder for poor states to protect infant industries in order to build self-sufficient capital accumulation. It forces competition with more technologically advanced states. A poor state can be competitive only in low-wage, low-capital niches—especially those using natural resources that are scarce in the North, such as tropical agriculture, extractive (mining and drilling) industries, and textiles.

Yet just those economic sectors in which developing countries have comparative advantages in world markets—agriculture and textiles in particular—were largely excluded from the free trade rules for decades (see pp. 174–176). Instead, world trade deals concentrated on free trade in manufactured goods, in which states in the North have comparative advantages. As a result, developing countries had to open their home markets to foreign products, against which home industries were not competitive, yet see their own export products shut out of foreign markets. Current WTO negotiations are attempting to remedy this inequity, but so far without success.

Another criticism leveled at the WTO centers on the trade dispute system, in which states may bring complaints of unfair trading practices. Such legal disputes can cost millions of dollars to litigate, requiring expensive lawyers and a large staff at WTO headquarters in Geneva. Few states in the global South can afford this legal process, and therefore few use it to help their own industries knock down unfair barriers to trade. Recall that even if a state wins a WTO dispute, it gains only the right to place tariffs on the offending country's goods in an equal amount. For small states, this retaliation can inflict as much damage on their own economies as on the economies of the offending states.

To compensate for these inequities and to help developing countries use trade to boost their economic growth, the WTO has a Generalized System of Preferences. These and other measures—such as the Lomé conventions in which EU states relaxed tariffs goods from the global South—are exceptions to the overall rules of trade, intended to ensure that participation in world trade advances development. Nonetheless, critics claim that developing countries are the losers in the overall world trading regime.

Countries in the South continue to pursue proposals to restructure world trade to benefit the South through the *UN Conference on Trade and Development (UNCTAD)*, which meets periodically but lacks power to implement major changes in North-South economic relations. Such efforts have left the South dependent on the North.

Foreign Assistance

VIDEO

Rwanda's
Millennium
Villages

Foreign assistance (or *overseas development assistance*) is money or other aid made available to help states speed up economic development or simply meet basic humanitarian needs. It covers a variety of programs—from individual volunteers lending a hand to massive government packages.

Different kinds of development assistance have different purposes, which often overlap. Some are humanitarian, some are political, and others are intended to create future economic advantages for the giver. The state or organization that gives assistance is called a *donor;* the state or organization receiving the aid is the *recipient.* Foreign assistance creates, or extends, a relationship between donor and recipient that is simultaneously political and cultural as well as economic. Foreign assistance can be a form of power in which the donor seeks to influence the recipient, or a form of interdependence.

Patterns of Foreign Assistance

VIDEO

Taking
on Global
Poverty

The majority of foreign assistance comes from governments in the North. Private donations provide a smaller amount, although sometimes a significant one. For instance, the Bill and Melinda Gates Foundation contributes more than $1 billion annually to world health campaigns.

Of the $100 billion in governmental foreign assistance provided in 2008, more than 90 percent came from members of the **Development Assistance Committee (DAC),** consisting of states from Western Europe, North America, and Japan/Pacific. Several oil-exporting Arab countries provide some foreign development assistance and in 2003, transition economies became a net "exporter" of financial aid. Three-quarters of the DAC countries' assistance goes directly to governments in the global South as state-to-state **bilateral aid;** the rest goes through the UN or other agencies as **multilateral aid.** The DAC countries have set themselves a goal to contribute 0.7 percent of their GNPs in foreign aid. But overall they give less than half this amount. Only Norway, Sweden, Denmark, the Netherlands, and Luxembourg are close to the target. In fact, Oxfam International reported that industrialized countries' aid dropped from 0.48 percent of income in 1960–1965 to 0.34 percent in 1980–1985 and then to 0.24 percent in 2003.

The United States gives the lowest percentage of GNP—about two-tenths of 1 percent—of any of the 30 states of the industrialized West that make up the OECD. In total economic aid given ($22 billion), the United States has recently regained the lead over Japan (which cut foreign aid to $12 billion). Germany, Britain, and France each give about $10 billion. U.S. and other decreases brought the world total in foreign assistance down substantially in the 1990s (see Figure 7.10). But after the 2001 terrorist attacks, Britain proposed a $50 billion increase in foreign aid, nearly doubling current levels, and the United States raised its aid budget sharply. In 2002, rock star Bono took U.S. treasury secretary Paul O'Neill on a two-week tour through Africa to argue for increased U.S. foreign assistance. O'Neill lost his job later that year, but the U.S. foreign aid budget rose by more than 15 percent a year in 2003–2005 (although it has since dropped back somewhat).

FIGURE 7.10   Foreign Assistance as a Percent of Donor's Income, 2007 and 1960–2007

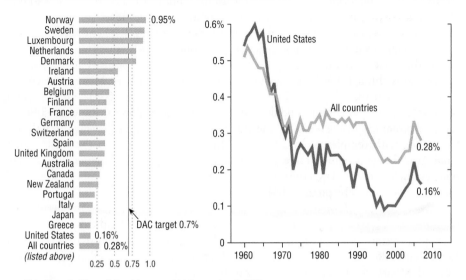

Note: Percent of Gross National Income, which is very close to GDP.

Source: *The New York Times.*

Types of Aid   Bilateral aid takes a variety of forms. *Grants* are funds given free to a recipient state, usually for some stated purpose. *Technical cooperation* refers to grants given in the form of expert assistance in some project rather than just money or goods. *Credits* are grants that can be used to buy certain products from the donor state. For instance, the United States regularly gives credits that can be used to purchase U.S. grain.

Loans are funds given to help in economic development, which must be repaid in the future out of the surplus generated by the development process (they too are often tied to the purchase of products from the donor state). Unlike commercial loans, government-to-government development loans are often on concessionary terms, with long repayment times and low interest rates. Although still an obligation for the recipient country, such loans are relatively easy to service.

Loan guarantees, which are used only occasionally, are promises by the donor state to back up commercial loans to the recipient. If the recipient state services such debts and ultimately repays them, there is no cost to the donor. But if the recipient cannot make the payments, the donor has to step in and cover the debts. A loan guarantee allows the recipient state to borrow money at lower interest rates from commercial banks (because the risk to the bank is much lower).

Military aid is not normally included in development assistance, but in a broad sense belongs there. It is money that flows from North to South, from government to government, and it does bring a certain amount of value into the economies of the global South. If a country is going to have a certain size army with certain weapons, getting them free from a donor state frees up money that can be used elsewhere in the economy. However, of all the forms of development assistance, military aid is one of the least efficient and most prone to impede rather than help economic development. It is also geared almost exclusively to political alliances rather than development needs.

The main agency dispensing U.S. foreign economic assistance (but not military aid) is the State Department's *Agency for International Development (USAID)*, which works mainly through the U.S. embassy in each recipient country. Major recipients of U.S. foreign aid include Israel, Egypt, Turkey, and Iraq (since 2003)—all important strategic allies in the volatile Middle East. Like other great powers, the United States uses the promise of foreign aid, or the threat of cutting it off, as leverage in political bargaining with recipients. In 2004, the United States launched the Millennium Challenge Account, which increases U.S. aid but only to governments with certain policies, such as rule of law, control of corruption, investment in education, and sound fiscal management. The program has been well received.

The U.S. **Peace Corps** provides U.S. volunteers for technical development assistance in developing countries. They work at the request and under the direction of the host state but are paid an allowance by the U.S. government. Started by President Kennedy in 1961, the Peace Corps now sends about 8,000 volunteers to 76 countries, where they participate in projects affecting about a million people.

In foreign aid, the donor must have the permission of the recipient government to operate in the country. This goes back to the principle of national sovereignty and the history of colonialism. National governments have the right to control the distribution of aid and the presence of foreign workers on their soil. Only occasionally is this principle violated, as when the United States and its allies provided assistance to Iraqi Kurds against the wishes of the Iraqi government following the Gulf War. International norms may be starting to change in this regard, with short-term humanitarian assistance starting to be seen as a human right that should not be subject to government veto (see p. 299).

UN Programs   Most of the multilateral development aid goes through *UN programs*. The place of these programs in the UN structure is described in Chapter 6. The overall flow of assistance through the UN is coordinated by the **UN Development Program (UNDP),** which manages 5,000 projects at once around the world (focusing especially on technical development assistance). Other UN programs focus on concentrating capital, transferring technology, and developing workforce skills for manufacturing. UNIDO works on industrialization, UNITAR on training and research. But most UN programs—such as UNICEF, UNFPA, UNESCO, and WHO—focus on meeting basic needs. UN development programs are funded largely through voluntary contributions by rich states. Each program has to solicit contributions to carry on its activities, so the contributions can be abruptly cut off if the program displeases a donor government (see pp. 328–329).

Forms of Development Assistance

The remainder of this chapter discusses three models of development assistance, distinguished by the type of assistance rather than by the type of donor (all three models encompass both government and private aid). The three overlap in real life.

The Disaster Relief Model   The disaster relief model describes the kind of foreign assistance given when poor people are afflicted by famine, drought, earthquakes, flooding, or other such natural disasters. (War is also a disaster.) When disaster strikes a poor state, many people are left with no means of subsistence and often without their homes. **Disaster relief** is the provision of short-term relief to such people in the form of food, water, shelter, clothing, and other essentials.

Disaster relief is very important because disasters can wipe out years of progress in economic development in a single blow. Generally, the international community tries to respond with enough assistance to get people back on their feet. The costs of such assistance are relatively modest, the benefits visible and dramatic. Having a system of disaster relief in place provides the global South with a kind of insurance against sudden losses that could otherwise destabilize economic accumulation.

Disasters generally occur quickly and without much warning. Rapid response is difficult to coordinate. International disaster relief has become more organized and better coordinated in the past decade but is still a complex process that varies somewhat from one situation to the next. Contributions of governments, private charitable organizations, and other groups and agencies are coordinated through the *UN Office of the Disaster Relief Coordinator (UNDRO)* in Geneva. In 2006, the UN set up a $500 million fund to enable it to respond quickly to disasters without waiting to raise funds first each time disaster strikes. Typically, international contributions make up no more than about one-third of the total relief effort, the remainder coming from local communities and national governments in the affected states. The U.S. government's contributions are coordinated by the *Office of Foreign Disaster Assistance (OFDA)*, which is part of USAID.

Disaster relief is something of a collective good because the states of the North do not benefit individually by contributing, yet they benefit in the long run from greater stability in the South. Despite this problem and the large number of actors, disaster relief is generally a positive example of international cooperation to get a job done—and an example of the use of the identity principle to solve a collective goods problem. Food donated by the World Council of Churches may be carried to the scene in U.S. military aircraft and then distributed by the *International Committee of the Red Cross (ICRC)*. Embarrassing failures in the past—of underresponse or overresponse, of duplication of efforts or agencies working at cross-purposes—have been fewer since the 1990s.

The newfound success of the international community in coordinating relief efforts was evident following the December 2004 tsunami disaster in Asia. Within hours, millions lost family members, homes, possessions, safe drinking water, and ways of life. The World Health Organization estimated that 5 million people lacked basic supplies. The world community's response began quite modestly, but after the full extent of the disaster was beamed around the globe and the death toll climbed to staggering numbers, aid poured into the region. More than $7 billion was pledged by states, IOs, and private citizens across the globe.

Both IOs and NGOs quickly mobilized to carry out what has been termed the largest relief effort in human history. The efforts by these organizations were coordinated through a variety of relief agencies, including the International Committee of the Red Cross, the International Organization for Migration, the UNHCR, and Oxfam. Initially, it appeared as though the United States would coordinate its own relief efforts apart from the UN, but after reconsideration, the United States ceded the lead role in relief to the UN. This somewhat spontaneous coordination of states, IOs, and NGOs seems contrary to the anarchical international system.

The relationship between disasters and economic development is complex, and appropriate responses vary according to location, type and size of disaster, and phase of recovery. Appropriate disaster relief can promote local economic development, whereas inappropriate responses can distort or impede such development. International norms regarding states' legal obligations to assist others in time of natural disaster and to accept such assistance if needed are changing. Some have even suggested extending the idea of the responsibility to protect to the area of disaster relief. This idea became particularly relevant in the wake of Cyclone Nargis, which struck Burma in 2008. An estimated 130,000 people died in that natural disaster, yet the repressive government of Burma delayed or denied efforts of the international community to provide assistance to those affected by the cyclone. While aid did eventually flow into Burma, weeks were wasted while the government denied the needed assistance for coping with the cyclone.

The Handout Model   Beyond disaster relief, many governments and private organizations provide ongoing development assistance in the form of projects in local communities in the South administered by agencies from the North to help meet basic needs. Although such efforts vary, one could call the approach a *handout* model because it relies on simply giving food or money without much thought to the broader consequences. Such charitable programs are a useful means by which people in the North funnel resources to people in the South, but may create unanticipated problems. They do not address the causes of poverty, the position of poor countries in the world economy, or local political conditions such as military rule or corruption.

In recent years, aid advocates in the United States have fought a U.S. law requiring that such food sent to hungry people in Africa be grown in the United States and shipped in U.S. vessels. Instead of this simple handout system, they proposed using U.S. funds to buy food locally in Africa, which would save a lot of money, get aid to the hungry people faster, and help African farmers. But the proposal was opposed by the so-called Iron Triangle of food aid—U.S. agribusiness that profits from selling the food to the government, U.S. shipping companies that profit from shipping it, and U.S. charities (including CARE and Catholic Relief Services) that fund a healthy fraction of their budgets by selling in Africa some of the grain they ship from the United States. The charities, by becoming international grain merchants and flooding local markets with cheap food (both sold and given away), compete with local farmers and drive down local prices, harming long-term recovery. Yet because of the Iron Triangle's lobbying power, Congress killed off the proposal to allow purchase of food locally in Africa.

The Oxfam Model   A third model of development assistance can be found in the approach taken by the private charitable group **Oxfam America** (one of seven groups worldwide descended from the Oxford Committee for Famine Relief, founded in 1942 in Britain). Originally devoted to short-term aid to famine victims, and still active in that effort, Oxfam America realized that over the longer term, people need not just handouts of food but the means to feed themselves—land, water, seed, tools, and technical training.

The distinctive aspect of the Oxfam model is that it relies on local communities to determine the needs of their own people and to carry out development projects. Oxfam does not operate projects itself but provides funding to local organizations. Nor does Oxfam call itself a donor and the organizations recipients. Rather, it calls both sides "project partners"— working together to accomplish a task. In this model, a little outside money can go a long way toward building sustained local economic development. Furthermore, projects help participants empower themselves by organizing to meet their own needs.

The Oxfam approach seeks to reconceptualize development assistance to focus on long-term development through a bottom-up, basic needs strategy and the political empowerment of poor people. (The group's philosophy of a "rights-based approach to development" is explored in the special insert section that follows this chapter.) Because of disappointment with the political

MOUTHWASH FOR MAURITANIA

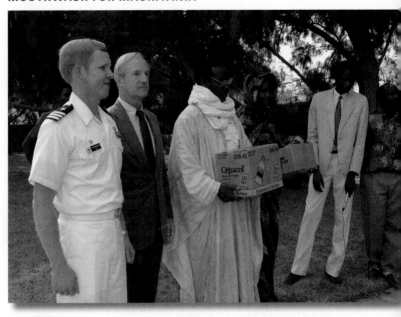

The handout model of foreign assistance contributes goods to third world economies, but often with little understanding of local needs or long-term strategies. Here, free supplies including cartons of mouthwash are delivered by the U.S. ambassador and the captain of a U.S. Navy ship participating in Project Handclasp, 1989.

uses of foreign aid in the past, Oxfam has tried to minimize the role in its projects of governments in both the North and South. For instance, Oxfam does not accept government funds or make grants to governments.

The general goals of the Oxfam model of foreign aid are consistent with a broader movement in the global South toward grassroots *empowerment*. Efforts such as those of Oxfam partners are organized by poor people to gain some power over their situation and meet their basic needs—not by seizing control of the state in a revolution but by means that are more direct, more local, and less violent. The key to success is getting organized, finding information, gaining self-confidence, and obtaining needed resources to implement action plans.

The Oxfam model has the advantage of promoting grassroots empowerment, thereby overcoming the dangers of externally run programs under the disaster relief and handout models. However, the Oxfam model to date has been tested on only a small scale. Although the model may be effective in the local communities it reaches, it would have to be adopted widely and replicated on a much larger scale in order to influence the overall prospects for development. It is unclear whether the principles the model embodies, from a reliance on local community organizers to an avoidance of

PARTNER IN DEVELOPMENT

The Oxfam model of foreign assistance emphasizes support for local groups that can stimulate self-sustaining economic development at a local level. A mutually beneficial North-South partnership is the global goal of such projects. These women show off a mill they purchased with microcredit from an Oxfam-affiliated group in Gambia, 2001.

government involvement, would work on a massive scale.

Confronting the North-South Gap
All three models of development assistance have contributions to make. Perhaps the most important point is for people in the North to be aware of the tremendous gap between North and South and try to address the problem. Poverty can seem so overwhelming that citizens in rich countries can easily turn their backs and just try to live their own lives.

But in today's interdependent world this really is not possible. North-South relations have become a part of everyday life. The integrated global economy brings to the North products and people from the South. The information revolution puts images of poverty on TV sets in comfortable living rooms. The growing role of the UN brings North and South together in a worldwide community. This global integration is especially evident in the areas of environmental management and technological change, which occupy Chapter 8.

CHAPTER REVIEW

SUMMARY

- Most of the world's people live in poverty in the global South. About a billion live in extreme poverty, without access to adequate food, water, and other necessities.

- Moving from poverty to well-being requires the accumulation of capital. Capitalism emphasizes overall growth with considerable concentration of wealth, whereas socialism emphasizes a fair distribution of wealth.

- Most states have a mixed economy with some degree of private ownership of capital and some degree of state ownership. However, state ownership has not been very successful in accumulating wealth.

- Since Lenin's time, many Marxists attribute poverty in the South to the concentration of wealth in the North. In this theory, capitalists in the North exploit the South economically and use the resulting wealth to buy off workers in the North.

- IR scholars in the world-system school argue that the North is a core region specializing in producing manufactured goods and the South is a periphery specializing in extracting raw materials through agriculture and mining. Between these are semiperiphery states with light manufacturing.

- Following independence after World War II, countries of the global South were left with legacies of colonialism, including their basic economic infrastructures, that made wealth accumulation difficult in certain ways. These problems still remain in many countries.

- Wealth accumulation depends on meeting basic human needs such as access to food, water, education, shelter, and health care. Developing countries have had mixed success in meeting their populations' basic needs.

- War has been a major impediment to meeting basic needs, and to wealth accumulation generally, in poor countries.

- Hunger and malnutrition are rampant in the global South. The most important cause is the displacement of subsistence farmers from their land because of war, population pressures, and the conversion of agricultural land into plantations growing export crops to earn hard currency.

- Urbanization is increasing throughout the global South as more people move from the countryside to cities. Huge slums have grown in the cities as poor people arrive and cannot find jobs.

- Women's central role in the process of accumulation has begun to be recognized. International agencies based in the North have started taking women's contributions into account in analyzing economic development in the South.

- Poverty in the South has led huge numbers of migrants to seek a better life in the North; this has created international political frictions. War and repression in the South have generated millions of refugees.

- Economic development in the global South has been uneven. In recent years many poor countries, led by China, have grown robustly. But the 2008–2009 global recession creates new obstacles for development.

- Evidence does not support a strong association of economic growth either with internal equality of wealth distribution or with internal inequality.

- The newly industrializing countries (NICs) in Asia—South Korea, Taiwan, Hong Kong, and Singapore—show that it is possible to rise out of poverty into sustained economic accumulation.

- China has registered strong economic growth in the past 25 years of market-oriented economic reforms. Though still quite poor, China is the world's leading success story in economic development.

- Export-led growth has largely replaced import substitution as a development strategy. This reflects the experiences of the NICs and China as well as the theory of comparative advantage.

- Government corruption is a major obstacle to development.

- Given the shortage of local capital in most poor states, foreign investment by MNCs can be a means of stimulating economic growth. MNCs look for favorable local conditions, including political and economic stability, in deciding where to invest.

- Debt, resulting largely from overborrowing in the 1970s and early 1980s, is a major problem in the global South. Despite renegotiations and other debt management efforts, the South remains $2 trillion in debt to the North.

- The IMF makes loans to states in the South conditional on economic and governmental reforms. These conditionality agreements often necessitate politically unpopular measures such as cutting food subsidies.

- The WTO trading regime works against the global South by allowing richer nations to protect sectors in which the global South has advantages—notably agriculture and textiles. The Generalized System of Preferences tries to compensate by lowering barriers to exports from the global South.

- Foreign assistance, most of it from governments in the North, plays an important part in the economic development plans of the poorer states of the South.

- Most foreign aid consists of bilateral grants and loans from governments in the North to specific governments in the South. Such aid is often used for political leverage and promotes the export of products from the donor state.

- Donors in the global North use various relief models to distribute aid to the developing world, each with advantages and drawbacks.

KEY TERMS

developing countries 260
Millennium Development Goals 261
basic human needs 262
malnutrition 266
subsistence farming 267
cash crops 267
urbanization 268
land reform 268
migration 269
refugees 270
world-system 272
resource curse 276

neocolonialism 277
dependency theory 277
enclave economy 277
economic development 278
newly industrializing countries (NICs) 280
"four tigers" 280
import substitution 287
export-led growth 287
microcredit 288
technology transfer 291

brain drain 291
default 291
debt renegotiation 291
IMF conditionality 293
foreign assistance 296
Development Assistance Committee (DAC) 296
bilateral aid 296
multilateral aid 296
Peace Corps 298
UN Development Program (UNDP) 298
disaster relief 299
Oxfam America 300

ONLINE PRACTICE TEST

Take an online practice test at
www.IRtext.com

☐ A
☐ B
☐ C
☐ D

CRITICAL THINKING QUESTIONS

1. In North and South America, independence from colonialism was won by descendants of the colonists themselves. In Asia and Africa, it was won mainly by local populations with a long history of their own. How do you think this aspect has affected the postcolonial history of one or more specific countries from each group?

2. Currently, incomes in the global North are five times as high, per person, as in the global South. If you could magically redistribute the world's income so that everyone had equal income ($10,000 per person per year), would you? What effects would such a change make in the North and South?

3. Some scholars criticize the IMF for imposing harsh terms in its conditionality agreements with poor states. Others applaud the IMF for demanding serious reforms before providing financial resources. If you were a leader negotiating with the IMF, what kinds of terms would you be willing to agree to and what terms would you resist? Why?

BACK TO THE BIG PICTURE

To hear a discussion of the "big picture" for this chapter, raised on p. 261, along with an example from recent history, consult the "IR Talk" podcast for Chapter 7 at *www.IRtext.com*

PODCAST

Foreword

We have invited Oxfam America, a leading NGO working on issues of poverty in the global South, to present the following special section about their work, in their own words and from the unique perspective of their decades of experience addressing these issues.

Ever since the fall of the East-West divide as a predominant feature of world order, the gap between the global North and South has loomed ever larger in importance. North-South relations shape international security (for example, NATO in Afghanistan), the shifting balance of power (the rise of China), trade (disputes over farm subsidies), business (emerging markets), the United Nations (demands for Security Council reform), and even domestic politics in the United States (immigration and job outsourcing). Yet many college students in the global North, especially Americans, lack fundamental information and perspectives regarding the South.

We hope that this section will give you, the student learning International Relations, a different perspective in thinking about all the issues discussed in this book and allow you to think critically about them with new insight. The section describes how people in various countries and contexts in the global South are working to address such IR-related issues as trade, conflict, and gender in the pursuit of economic development. The lessons from these cases bring home the close connections of global North and South, of economics and politics, and of diverse social spheres such as government, law, business, community life, and family. We hope instructors and students can use these lessons to illuminate and deepen the knowledge they gain in studying the range of subjects in this book.

JOSHUA S. GOLDSTEIN AND JON C. PEVEHOUSE

Empowering the Global South: A Rights-Based Approach to Development

By Oxfam America

I. Introduction: International Development

Why should you, a college student in the global North, be interested in the global South? There are a lot of good answers to that question: because you're a global citizen; because we have a collective responsibility to those with whom we share this planet; or because to do otherwise is shortsighted.

How you live your life has an enormous impact on others. For many, this is common sense. For others, this is a newer notion. Let's look briefly at a story that is unrelated to development but can help us think about how the seemingly unrelated are connected.

DDT, one of the world's most powerful pesticides, became widely available in 1945. Thirteen years later, a former marine biologist with the U.S. Fish and Wildlife Service, Rachel Carson, began research on the effects of DDT. The resultant book, *Silent Spring*, published in 1962, was a best-seller; it changed the way people understood our relationship to the world—and our responsibilities. Carson described how DDT entered the food chain, causing the death of birds and animals. A single application on a crop remained toxic in the environment even after it was diluted by rain-water.

She concluded that DDT had contaminated the global food supply. The book took its title from Carson's vision of an American town in springtime where all the sounds of the season, like robins chirping, had been silenced by the spreading toxin. The image of a "silent spring" made a deep impression on many Americans.

It is not a new message: How we live shapes the lives of all those with whom we share our planet. Carson saw this as an issue "of interrelationships, of interdependence." She explained, "We spray our elms and following springs are silent of robin song, not because we sprayed the robins directly but because the poison traveled, step by step."

Poverty is a toxin of another sort but no less deadly. And recognition of our global interdependence is critical—though many Americans are not raised to think like this. We are raised to value independence. We have a hearty sense of confidence, a belief that we control our own destiny. But imagine that your best efforts weren't enough. You studied hard, but there were no public schools and your family was not wealthy enough to pay school fees. So you never learned to read. Your parents worked 12-hour days on their farm growing cotton but, no matter how diligently they worked, they could not manage to pay their rent and feed the family. The reason? A glut of U.S. cotton (caused by government subsidies) was driving worldwide cotton prices down to such an extent that your parents' crops were worthless. Such cases are not rare. In fact, 40 percent of the people on our planet—more than 2.5 billion—live in poverty, struggling to survive on less than $2 a day.

As you read this section, consider this: Everyone on earth has the same basic needs; it is only our circumstances—where we live and the family and culture into which we're born—that differ. Some of us are born into relative prosperity and security, while millions, through no choice of their own, are born into poverty.

Development is an issue for all of us—even if we have not yet begun to understand our role.

II. Oxfam America and a Rights-Based Approach to Development

The purpose of relief and development organizations is, in the broadest terms, to alleviate suffering. Traditionally relief agencies have provided direct delivery of services, including disaster relief, food aid, and health services. This is a traditional *needs-based approach*. People in emergency situations have urgent needs that must be met. Oxfam pays attention to these needs but also follows a *rights-based approach*.

Oxfam America is an international relief and development organization that creates lasting solutions to poverty, hunger, and injustice. Together with individuals and local groups in more than 120 countries, Oxfam saves lives, helps people overcome poverty, and fights for social justice. "Give a man a fish, he eats for a day. Teach him to fish, and he will eat for a lifetime." So goes the old saying. Oxfam does not simply "dump aid" in poor communities; we try to help people build their own capacity to change their lives. That's our long-term development work. The importance of fighting for social justice can be understood by a variation on the old saying that we often repeat at Oxfam: "Even if you teach a man to fish, if he has no access to the river, he will still go hungry." So, in addition to emergency aid and helping people learn to make long-term changes, it is also crucial to work to change the laws, regulations, and customs that prevent people from overcoming poverty.

Rights-based approach

Oxfam, among other relief and development organizations, has come to understand that what have traditionally been called "basic needs" are in fact human rights, and that the inability of people to meet these needs often stems from violations of human rights. For example, lack of access to safe drinking water is a violation of an economic and social right. Fear of speaking out about injustice is prevalent in contexts where civil and political rights are not respected or protected—in other words, where human rights are violated. This recognition has prompted an evolution from a development model based on temporarily meeting poor people's needs to one in which people are able to claim what is rightfully theirs—a model known as a *rights-based approach*.

Based on a human rights framework, a rights-based approach to development focuses on changing basic power dynamics. To borrow from rights language, there are *rights-holders* and *duty-bearers*. This form of development focuses on building the rights-holders' ability to claim their rights and holding duty-bearers accountable to meet their obligations. Let's look at an example.

Understanding the Rights-Based Approach: Mining in Ghana

Paul Ayensu, a farmer in the small town of Teberebie, had a tiny farm, just a third of an acre cut out of the intense green of Ghana's western rain forest. He grew 12 different crops, including yams, oil palms, cassava, pineapples, and cocoa. "I was growing a lot of food and I was making money," he said. "I spent all of my time there."

Fighting injustice

He had the bad fortune to work a field on top of a gold deposit, so when the government conceded the minerals to an international mining company in 1991, 37-year-old Ayensu, his wife, and four children were displaced. Worse, he later discovered that the payment he was to receive for his land had been arbitrarily cut by two-thirds. "I was not happy and I cried," Ayensu said later. "It was because of this farm that we could eat…Now my

children are out of school. I can't go to my farm ever again."

Ayensu is a *rights-holder*. The Ghanaian government and the mining company are among the *duty-bearers* in this example.

The farmers in Teberebie and many other towns across mining areas of Ghana are struggling to overcome basic injustices without the help of those whose duty it is to represent them in government and protect their rights. Local leaders are co-opted by mining companies and elected officials

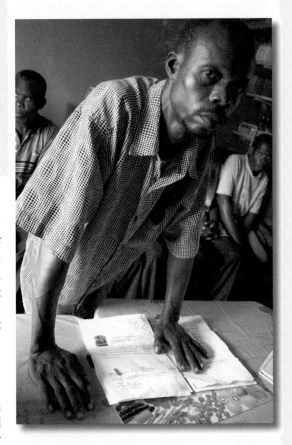

Paul Ayensu shows visitors the two proposals for compensation he received from a mining company. The first proposal offered to pay him for the loss of the cocoa trees and other crops on his small farm. The second proposal, which superseded the first, offered two-thirds less for the farm that he lost to the company. (Photo: Jane Hahn / Oxfam America)

in parliament do not consider the needs of poor farmers. So farmers affected by mining are instead turning to the non-governmental sector and media to air their grievances and build respect for their right to live with dignity and make a decent living.

To help them, Oxfam America is funding the work of WACAM, an organization that teaches villagers about the constitution of Ghana and their rights under the 2006 Minerals and Mining Act. Armed with this information, farmers can then assert their rights to fair compensation for their lands and hold companies responsible for damage to the environment.

The approach is effective in several towns where WACAM has educated citizens and helped them understand how to engage with the mining companies and the media to push for justice. In Prestea, an industrialized mining town since the 1920s, 62-year-old Godfried Ofori said that teaching people about their rights has made a significant impact.

"Most people don't have money," said Godfried Ofori, "but they have their spirit."

Fifteen of the farmers in Teberebie are disputing the compensation packages offered them by the mining company. The Concerned Farmers Association of Teberebie staged a march to a nearby mining center, where they were interviewed on the radio and on television. This brought a lot of visibility to their case, and a proposal to negotiate from the mining company. Unfortunately, it did not lead to an agreement, and the claim is now in the courts.

The farmers know it could be a long time until they get a decision on this case. "When we took the company to court, they said they would prolong the process and frustrate us," Kwame Bentil, one of the plaintiffs, said. It was clear this tactic was a way to force the poor farmers to take the lower compensation offer. So far they have been to court 14 times.

What respect looks like

WACAM also provided training to the community of Abekoase. Nana Molobah Nyamiketh, chief of the village of Abekoase, has a friendly face, but a serious nature. And it was this serious side that went into action the morning of October 16, 2001, when villagers came to him with bad news: Their main source of drinking water, the Asuman River, was full of dead fish, and those people who had come in contact with the water had developed skin problems. "We were alarmed," Nyamiketh said, adding that it was their worst fear: a cyanide spill. "We informed WACAM, as they had been teaching us how to negotiate with the company and understand our rights...and we got some journalists to cover news of the cyanide spill."

As word got out, Nyamiketh did his best to negotiate with the Gold Fields Ghana Corporation, but the discussions did not lead anywhere. The 400 villagers of Abekoase, half of whom had already been displaced by the Gold Fields mine, took the company to court in March 2002. By the end of 2003, Abekoase and Gold Fields had reached a settlement out of court that included a community center building and a development fund.

Nyamiketh said that the villagers are satisfied with the settlement, but that they are even more pleased with the changed relationship with Gold Fields. "People are now better equipped to negotiate with the company," Nyamiketh said, adding that the company now handles them differently too. "They were surprised we took them to court; they thought they would just ride over us. But we scared them...Now, when something happens, they react quickly because people here know their rights."

Chief Nyamiketh looked out the window of his house, into the daily afternoon downpour of a May afternoon, where the rain was smashing down into the red earth and thunder boomed in the distance. "It is a sign of respect," he said.

How change happens

Using rights-based approaches, development actors use a variety of methods—including policy analysis, advocacy, and capacity building—to help poor and marginalized people and communities create lasting change. Rights-based approaches are grounded in the International Bill of Rights, the UN Universal Declaration of Human Rights, and other internationally agreed upon instruments that offer widely accepted standards for what it means to live in dignity. Ultimately, rights-based approaches are aimed at creating the conditions under which people can live in dignity and peace and develop their full potential.

Let's see how this concept shapes some key aspects of Oxfam's work: gender equality; creating and protecting economic opportunities; advocacy for fair trade; and reducing people's vulnerability to disasters.

III. Empowering Women and Families

Poverty is not gender neutral. Seventy percent of the world's poorest people are women and girls. In many societies, women lack even the most basic rights—access to education, property ownership, and lives free from violence—leaving them and their children vulnerable to disease, displacement, famine, and brutality. Oxfam America is helping poor women use their power to transform their lives.

A violent history

Let's look at the role of gender in El Salvador. During the civil war of El Salvador (1979–92), 80,000 people died and 7,000 more disappeared. Women were highly and increasingly victimized over time. Gender roles in the family and society were disrupted. The state became a force of gender oppression. The Salvadoran army, National Police, National Guard, and Treasury Police were all implicated in the use of rape as a systematic method of torture. Ownership and use of guns or machetes became widely associated with male identity. At the end of the war, 66,900 former militants were reintegrated into society during a time of high unemployment. In 1999, it was estimated that half of all Salvadoran households had been directly affected by violent crime. The war had been so long, violent, and widespread that people "normalized" (that is, made normal) the victimization of women. Rates of gender violence remained extremely high. Between 1999 and 2004, seven out of every ten Salvadoran women suffered some kind of gender-based violence.

A campaign for change

In 2005, Oxfam joined with four other organizations to address the vulnerability of Salvadoran women by challenging the government to provide better protection; training and mobilizing women and men to change the *machista* culture; and raising public awareness through a media campaign. What emerged is a movement under the slogan *Entre Vos y Yo: Una Vida Diferente* ("Between You and Me: A Different Life") that calls for new laws to protect women at both the local and national levels, as well as the financial commitment to back it up. In addition, members of the coalition are training public officials such as police officers, judges, doctors, social workers, and even municipal bus drivers to be sensitive to gender violence, recognize the signs of abuse, and take steps to stop crimes against women.

The campaign's first step was to generate a new level of public discussion about gender violence. The theory is that increasing awareness will change attitudes and help build public and political will to prevent violence against women. Another important component of the program is to create forums to discuss male identity within Salvadoran society. These discussions have helped participants to explore concepts of masculinity and gender relationships and to see that perpetuators of gender violence are also victims of historical patterns of societal violence. The program fosters women's leadership and ensures that women and youth are involved in decision making. Finally, the campaign focuses on young people and is targeting students at

50 high schools in the most violent areas of El Salvador. Raising awareness among youth is critical to changing future attitudes about gender and women's rights. Let's look at one woman's story and how the campaign has affected her life.

Breaking the Cycle of Violence: Gender Change in El Salvador

Outside the home of Gilma Molina de Vasquez, 30 women sit patiently on chairs and benches under trees decorated with balloons and colorful paper streamers shaking in the mild wind. Trucks roar past in low gear as the women strain to hear their attorney, who is reading through the articles of incorporation for a new women's organization. When he finishes, each woman signs official documents to be filed with the government. De Vasquez is among the first. The women take turns holding each other's infants to allow the mothers to add their signatures.

De Vasquez worked hard to get the group established. When asked why helping other women is so important to her, she says, "Let me tell you a little about my own life, then you will know."

The details come spilling out, like someone who walks away from a serious car accident describing how lucky she is just to have survived. Mistreated by her father, her mother abused, de Vasquez was married at 14 to a soldier. "I thought it was a way to escape," she says, "but my life got worse." Her husband was violent and his family "used to tell me that my job was to work, have children, and take care of my husband."

But others saw something more in her. When her first child went to school, de Vasquez was chosen to be president of the parents' association. "When I told my husband, he was angry. He told me I was not capable of it. I accepted this; he always told me I was good for nothing. For 11 years it was like that."

Eventually they moved to a rural area and things started to improve. Her husband became an agricultural laborer. De Vasquez started to do more things outside their home. She joined a health training program and, as part of her education with Oxfam's partner organization, she learned about the rights of women.

"I started to listen to talks about preventing violence in the home," de Vasquez said. "I learned about my rights." Taking a huge risk, she decided to try and get her husband involved. "I invited him to go to the... training sessions with me and he became more sensitive." Together, she and her husband questioned the gender roles and attitudes in El Salvador and re-created their relationship.

"Now my husband and I solve problems through dialogue—not violence," de Vasquez says. He recognizes how important it is for her

Gilma Molina de Vasquez (left) assists another woman in signing their new organization's articles of incorporation. (Photo: Claudia Barrientos / Oxfam America)

to use her leadership skills. "If someone asks me to do something, I will do it because I know my husband will not say no."

De Vasquez is committed to the new women's organization. "I would like to get women to know about their rights and duties and to increase their self-esteem." She says there are practical reasons for this: "We need jobs for all women. We can help ourselves and our families, care for our children, and earn income to change our lives." For de Vasquez, respect for women and fighting poverty are part of the same struggle.

Recalling the oppression she faced early in life, de Vasquez says, "I have overcome it—so why can't I help other women? That is my goal: to help many other women."

IV. Making a Living

All people have the right to what the UN Universal Declaration on Human Rights calls a "secure livelihood." In other words, everyone has the right to make a decent living. What does that mean? It means that you have the resources you need to do your work; the skills you need to produce enough to meet your needs while also respecting the environment; and access to a market to sell your wares. You earn enough money for essentials like food and shelter. And, through hard work, you have opportunities to move beyond poverty and toward greater financial security. Unfortunately, many hard-working people are unable to earn a decent living.

Focus on small farmers

From Minnesota to Bolivia, South Carolina to South Africa, farmers work hard to get the most from their land. Growing and harvesting crops is a more than full-time job—and farmers have the right to reap the benefits of their labor. In many countries, though, small-scale farmers face daily challenges in the struggle to get by. Of the 840 million people in the world who are malnourished, 75 percent depend on farming to make a living. These family farmers must contend with prolonged drought, inundated markets, and other factors that challenge their ability to earn a living.

Mozambique contains one of the largest areas of fertile land in southern Africa. With nearly 60 million uncultivated acres, it is a hotspot for enterprising investors. But despite this potential, the central provinces of Mozambique are among the poorest regions in the world—more than 70 percent of the population lives in poverty.

Floods, disease, and a costly recovery from a long civil war keep farming families trapped in poverty, with few opportunities for economic growth. In addition, farmers don't have access to markets where they can get a fair price for their cotton. Many are tied to unfair contracts with large cotton concession companies, leaving them deep in debt. Others struggle to get a fair price in international markets that they cannot control. Meanwhile, the government of Mozambique does little to help—though the farmers keep asking for laws and policies that will help them earn more from their crops.

"Cotton has been one of the most stable cash crops in Mozambique for the last 100 years," says Norberto Mahalambe, director of Mozambique's National Cotton Institute. "There are over 350,000 cotton farmers supporting some 1.5 million dependents on this crop. Income from cotton pays school fees, medical bills, and many other essential expenses."

In Mozambique, Oxfam uses a three-fold approach to help farmers exercise their rights. Local partner organizations train farmers on new methods for growing a more sustainable and productive crop. At the national level, farmers organize into cooperatives and other associations, so they can hold governments and companies accountable. At the global level, Oxfam works to give farmers' concerns a voice in the international cotton marketplace. Let's look more closely at Mozambican cotton farmers' efforts to earn a decent living.

Overcoming Obstacles: Cotton Farming in Mozambique

Two years ago, Alberto Malico was just one cotton farmer struggling to make a living in Mozambique. Today, he is the president of FONPA, the National Cotton Producers Forum, which has organized small cotton farmers to become equal partners with government and industry. FONPA is one of Oxfam America's local partner organizations in Mozambique.

Developing new methods

On a warm July afternoon, Malico met with local farmers to discuss the latest harvest and their concerns. Two representatives of Oxfam's partner organization ABIODES (the Organic Agriculture, Biodiversity, and Sustainable Development Association) came to discuss a pilot project introduced during the last growing season.

The small headquarters of the Naicole Farmers Association is regularly crowded with members of the local Cotton Producers Associations who meet to discuss the cotton crop and plan a better deal for farmers. (Photo: ABIODES)

The project provided seeds, equipment, training, and draft animals to 50 members of three local farmers' associations. The aim was to increase the growing areas and productivity, boost cotton quality and yield, and introduce sustainable agriculture. Isabel Mazive of ABIODES said that the project nearly doubled farmers' productivity.

Women especially welcomed these new growing methods. In Mozambique, women farmers work longer hours than men, make less money, and often suffer from poor health due to exposure to dangerous pesticides. In many households, although women do most of the farm work, men control all the proceeds. For these reasons, Oxfam's Mozambique program has a particular focus on making sure that women farmers have equal economic rights.

Isora Jamal is one of the farmers who benefited from the pilot project. Standing in her family's field, among head-high cotton plants, she was satisfied with this year's crop. "The draft animals have been a big help in preparing the land in time for planting and have allowed me to increase my areas of cultivation. The training and services have definitely improved the amount and quality of my cotton. It saved us women a lot of time and manual labor in the fields," she said.

Breaking the cycle of debt

Malico and FONPA also lobby the government for policies that protect and improve the lives of cotton producers. Most of the small-scale cotton farmers in Mozambique are tied to contracts with privatized concession companies. Under this arrangement, the companies provide seed in return for the cotton crop. The farmers complain that the inputs and services are of poor quality, and many farmers end up owing the companies more than they receive in payment for their crops. This cycle of debt deepens every year. FONPA wants banks to finance cotton production and processing in order to improve the quality of cotton and the small farmers' income.

Oxfam helped establish FONPA in 2005. Mahalambe, the director of the National Cotton Institute, said that Oxfam's support "has been fundamental in assisting farmers to get organized into a national forum, able to negotiate with companies and the government. The farmers no longer stand alone and they are much more informed and capable."

"We are now able to put pressure on government, raise the concerns of the small cotton farmers, and begin to address the imbalance of power relations," said Malico. "By joining together in associations, we have found it easier to negotiate a better price for our cotton and to help each other...to improve our production and harvesting."

A global voice

In addition to working with groups like FONPA at the local and national level, farmers need to have a voice in global trade negotiations. Farmers in Mozambique are particularly concerned about subsidies paid to growers in wealthier countries, which encourage overproduction of crops like cotton and sugar that are then "dumped" on world markets.

Since most farmers in the world do not get government subsidies, they can't compete when these surpluses cause prices to drop below what it costs to grow their crops. Oxfam works to address this problem as part of our global campaign for fair trade.

Helping farmers voice their concerns about global policy and government positions on international trade can have a big impact. Farmer voices have been notably absent in these policy dialogues in recent years. When the farmers are organized into associations, with trained leaders and spokespeople, they are better able to have a say in the economic policies that affect their lives.

In 2005, cotton farmers in Mozambique found a creative way to voice their concerns about unfair trade rules: They staged a "Citizen's Tribunal" in the studios of Radio Mozambique calling for global market reforms to ensure fair prices for their crops. The tribunal was held in Maputo and attended by 50 people from across Mozambique, including cotton farmers and government ministers. The event was broadcast live with commentary for three hours throughout the country the week before the World Trade Organization's Sixth Ministerial Conference, where trade rules for agriculture were on the agenda.

Several farmers testified at the Citizen's Tribunal, including Cecelia Aly Said, a single mother and farmer in Mozambique's northern cotton-growing region. "I have to feed my children, yet I sell at low prices," she said. "Who is going to buy...books for my children's education? Buyers are not helping us. We need better prices to survive."

V. Advocacy and Trade

World trade could be a powerful force for reducing poverty if poor people could sell their products at a decent price. What's stopping them? The world trade system is loaded with unfair trade agreements and agricultural subsidies that favor the interests of the rich and powerful. Making trade fair is a key strategy for helping to end poverty.

Unfair trade

To correct the gross imbalances of the current system requires strategic change. For instance, reforming agricultural subsidies would help end the habit wealthy countries have of overproducing certain commodities and dumping their excesses on world markets. Subsidies paid to U.S. cotton growers encourage them to produce more than they otherwise would. The surplus depresses world prices and has a debilitating effect on more than one million West African households for whom cotton is a central source of income. One recent study found that subsidy reform could increase the income of those African farmers by 8 to 20 percent.

A range of other changes in world trade mechanisms would also help right some of the injustices poor producers face in a system that is stacked against them. One would be to eliminate conditions to International Monetary Fund/World Bank loans that force poor countries to open their markets to foreign goods, regardless of the impact on local producers. The World Trade Organization could also be made more democratic so that poor countries could have a stronger voice in its proceedings. Additionally, national and regional trade policies should give poor people better access to markets—and the benefits of trade that would follow.

But how can all of this come about? It takes a lot of people on a lot of levels, starting with grass roots and stretching to the top tiers of power. It starts with students like you—and the choices you make about the products you buy.

Making trade fair

Fair Trade is a movement designed to provide growers a fair price for their goods—a price that not only covers the cost of their production, but also ensures they earn a decent living. Fair Trade embraces the idea of long-term contracts

and credit that guarantee farmers a measure of security. It's also about knowledge-sharing and skills-sharing so that farmers can hone their understanding of the industry in which they participate and become competitive players in their markets.

Increasingly, you can find Fair Trade products—coffee, tea, chocolate, cocoa, bananas—alongside standard ones on shop shelves. They usually carry a Fair Trade label. That label guarantees that farmers in poor countries will get a decent price for their goods. By choosing to buy Fair Trade products, you are adding your voice to a groundswell of support for poor farmers around the world. Real change requires that more people get involved, speak out, and ask decision makers to change unjust laws and practices.

So, how about that coffee you had this morning? Did it come from Starbucks? Maybe your voice was one of those that helped convince Starbucks, a global brand, to negotiate a win-win solution to benefit farmers who produce some of the coffees on which the company built its reputation. Here's a story about how advocacy—and grassroots gumption—can bring about critical changes that will help improve the lives of countless Ethiopian coffee farmers. It all started with a name and who had rightful ownership of it.

What's in a Name? Starbucks and Ethiopia's Coffee Farmers

Gemede Robe walked to the podium outside the Addis Ababa Sheraton, a white shawl wrapped around his shoulders. An 85-year-old coffee farmer, Robe had come to support Ethiopia's trademark initiative.

He'd left his village for the first time to explain why companies like Starbucks should recognize Ethiopia's ownership of its own coffee brands.

"The names Yirgacheffe, Sidamo, and Harar are as unique to Ethiopia as the flavors of the coffees," he said. "Whoever says these names are not the property of Ethiopia is as crazy as someone who would say the name I gave my first-born son is no longer his."

Robe spoke at this coffee ceremony as a kind of local celebrity. His face—the gray beard, the unflinching stare—had become the iconic

Ethiopian coffee farmer Gemede Robe became the face of Oxfam America's campaign asking Starbucks to sign an agreement recognizing Ethiopia's right to license and distribute its specialty coffees. By recognizing the country's intellectual property rights, the coffee giant could give poor farmers a chance to earn a greater share of the profits. (Photo: Donna Morris / Oxfam America)

image of Oxfam America's Starbucks campaign. Launched in October 2006, the campaign asked that the coffee giant sign an agreement acknowledging Ethiopia's right to license and distribute its fine coffees. By recognizing Ethiopia's intellectual property rights, Starbucks could give poor farmers a chance to earn a greater share of the profits.

Aware of Starbucks's status as a global brand interested in maintaining its socially responsible reputation, Oxfam used grassroots activism and media to draw attention to the issue. Though initially reluctant, Starbucks entered into serious talks with Ethiopia and by mid-2007 had finalized an agreement that could change the coffee industry forever.

"The true victors of this campaign are the 1.5 million coffee farmers in Ethiopia whose lives will improve," said Abera Tola, director of Oxfam America's regional office in Ethiopia. "They have given a glimmer of hope to millions more like them all over the world who deserve recognition for the quality products they generate."

Creating public pressure

Oxfam began negotiating with Starbucks in 2005 when it first learned about Ethiopia's efforts to trademark its fine coffees. After dozens of conversations between our Boston headquarters, the Seattle home of Starbucks, and Ethiopia's Intellectual Property Office in Addis Ababa, it became clear that high-level talks would not be enough to bring the key actors to the table. It was time to enlist the public.

At a grassroots level, Oxfam worked with a coalition of allies to organize members of the Ethiopian diaspora, students, Starbucks employees, and others. By the campaign's end, more than 100,000 people had gotten involved, many of them sending Robe's photo around the world on postcards, fliers, and posters. Robe's face even appeared on Web sites and in newspaper ads during a series of global "days of action" in places like Seattle, Scotland, and Hong Kong. The accompanying message to Starbucks remained simple: Honor your commitments to coffee farmers.

Oxfam tested new ways to engage supporters: a video on YouTube, a petition to Starbucks signed by more than 90,000 people, and a photo petition on Flickr. And Oxfam promoted it on social networking pages such as MySpace and Facebook.

Eventually Oxfam's message reached Starbucks's shareholders. A few sent letters to Starbucks supporting Ethiopia's trademark initiative. And at the Starbucks annual general meeting in April 2007, some joined members of the Ethiopian community in asking pointed questions of both the company CEO and chairman.

With activists combining efforts around the world, Oxfam ramped up the public pressure by focusing on the press. Over the course of the campaign, major media outlets—including NPR, the BBC, CNN, *Time, Fortune,* and *The Wall Street Journal*—featured the David-and-Goliath struggle of the Ethiopian farmers and Starbucks.

"What might have remained a little-noticed bureaucratic dispute became an international affair when Oxfam, a nonprofit relief and development group, began publicizing it in the fall," wrote *The Wall Street Journal*.

Remembering the "ground truth"

Each aspect of the campaign had its impacts. But it just may have been the voice on the ground that resonated loudest with Starbucks. In the end, the company seemed to accept the simple truth: The campaign wasn't about a development agency, a roaster, or a government. It was about people like Robe, the coffee farmer demanding economic justice.

When the old farmer from Afursa Waro village, whose face had launched the entire campaign, made one final appearance, it was in a thank-you video.

Sitting among his fellow farmers in a lush meadow overlooking the Yirgacheffe hills, Robe looked into the camera once again. "We know that Oxfam and many people around the globe are standing by our side in supporting us in this effort," he said. "You, our supporters, have given voice to our cause."

Then Robe stood alongside his fellow farmers and, in unison, offered a series of customary bows. "Gelatoma. Gelatoma. Gelatoma," they said in Oromifa, their region's language. "Thank you. Thank you. Thank you."

VI. Reducing People's Vulnerability

Most of us think that disasters are democratic—we are all equally vulnerable. But the facts suggest otherwise. "The world is hit an estimated 300–500 times per year by natural disasters such as floods, drought, earthquakes, storms, torrential rains, and mudslides. On average about 60,000 people die in these disasters—95 percent of them in developing countries more populous and geographically exposed" (*Financial Times*, January 2005).

The United Nations Office for the Coordination of Humanitarian Affairs (OCHA) is the umbrella agency under which many emergency responses are organized. Its mission is to "mobilize and coordinate effective and principled humanitarian action." This means that under OCHA's guidance, different aid groups work to meet the range of people's basic needs during a crisis. Some organizations offer medical care; others provide food, clean drinking water, decent sanitation, and public health outreach.

Human rights in humanitarian response

At the heart of humanitarian work is the support of people's basic human rights. Oxfam believes that structural injustices are at the core of the suffering that poor people experience in manmade and natural disasters. Essential, also, is respect for several broad humanitarian tenets, including impartiality and independence. Aid groups serious about delivering assistance do so without discrimination in regard to people's nationality, race, religious beliefs, class, or political opinions. That's impartiality. Remaining independent requires aid groups not to operate in support of the political objectives or actions of states.

During disasters, Oxfam's mission is not only to save lives, but to help communities with their rehabilitation efforts. That's why, whenever possible, Oxfam works with local organizations, helping them to build their ability to respond to future challenges.

Internationally accepted guidelines guide humanitarian response efforts. For example, the Sphere Standards spell out basic requirements for things like shelter, food, and water. For water, the standard calls for a little less than four gallons per person per day. That amount, which many Westerners would find difficult to survive on, is meant to cover all washing, cooking, and drinking needs. For food, the Sphere Standard is 2,100 calories per person each day; the shelter guideline is 38 square feet of covered floor area per person.

Reducing risk long-term

As global warming increases, the consequences for millions of people around the world—particularly the poorest—are all too clear to those involved in providing humanitarian assistance. In 2007, floods in Asia affected hundreds of millions of people. Extreme floods are common in South Asia, but climate change models predict even heavier monsoon rainfall—and intense rain in unlikely places. Conversely, the Turkana people of northwest Kenya have experienced a 25 percent drop in annual rainfall over the past 30 years, and experts predict that by 2020, up to 250 million people across Africa could face more severe water shortages. In some countries, the yield from rain-fed crops could be cut in half during that period.

But as these events increase, international aid organizations are beginning to look at the consequences differently, too, and to encourage local, state, and national governments to take concrete steps to prevent severe weather—or other natural events—from spawning disaster. This is one approach to what is called *disaster risk reduction*.

Let's return to the idea that poor people are more vulnerable to disasters.

The term "natural disaster" is familiar to us all. We're accustomed to thinking of it as a dramatic event where nature and humans collide in ways that are both unavoidable and unavoidably tragic. Yet a closer look at how events like earthquakes, droughts, and tsunamis become tragedies reveals that these events of nature, while powerful, trigger disasters only if communities are exposed to their destructive force. A river overflowing its banks is simply a natural phenomenon; it becomes a disaster only if communities located in low-lying areas—perhaps because they have no affordable alternatives—lose their homes, farms, and loved ones to the flooding. Likewise, a volcano that

erupts in an uninhabited area can hardly be called a tragedy. But when people live on the side of a volcano because poverty has left them no other options, an eruption can be disastrous. And the poor lack insurance to provide for them if an earthquake destroys their homes or their means of making a living. As Luis Romano, a risk management specialist from the Humboldt Center puts it, "We cannot say that disasters are natural. Some physical events are natural, but the effects of these events are not natural; they are built on social practices. Disasters are socio-natural events."

What does disaster risk reduction look like in practice? The answer has to do with empowering people and their communities to develop solutions that work for them. The experiences of alpaca herders in the highlands of Peru are a good example.

Reducing Risk: Working at 16,000 Feet in Peru

There's a saying in the Peruvian highlands that describes the remotest of destinations: "the place where the devil lost his poncho"—a place where disaster could strike and the outside world would never know until it was too late to help.

It's the kind of place Oxfam America and its local partner, Asociación Proyección, are working in now—at nearly 16,000 feet above sea level, in air so thin that newcomers lose their breath.

The place is the district of Caylloma, and the people who live here are alpaca herders. The challenge is to make sure that when trouble does come—as it has in the past and surely will again—they will be prepared to cope.

Three years ago, after a severe cold snap wiped out tens of thousands of llamas and alpacas across Peru's southern highlands, Oxfam and Proyección joined forces to find a way to prevent a repeat of the suffering people experienced then. Their proposal—a form of disaster risk reduction—included a range of self-help ideas, a smattering of technology, and the most important tool of all: planning.

Today, acres of barley now grow on the slopes—a buffer against food shortages for livestock. New adobe sheds with metal roofs stand in some of the coldest mountain pockets, offering critical shelter for alpacas that had none before. Gravity-fed sprinklers irrigate enclosed pastures of rye grass, guaranteeing a steady source of nourishment for animals. And a handful of radio towers dot the district, connecting far-flung hamlets with the world at large.

A backup of barley

Chinosiri, a tiny hamlet of stone huts perched about 16,000 feet above sea level in the Peruvian Andes, is the only home alpaca herder Jose Gonzalez Condo has ever known.

At 39, he's content there—even if he doesn't have enough money to build his animals a shed to protect them from the cold and snow. That will come in due time, he says. For now, he's focused on another project that has helped to make his life in these remote mountains a little more secure: the field of barley growing on a steep slope near his hut.

That barley, harvested and carefully stored in a giant pit not far from the field, represents a lifeline for the 100 head of alpaca from which Gonzalez and his family make their living. The nutrient-rich grass will help tide his herd over should severe cold and snow damage their pasturelands again, as it did—with devastating consequences—in the winter of 2004.

"Two-and-a-half years ago we came here because the local government asked us to come, and when we suggested planting barley, everyone said we were crazy," said Arturo Rivera Vigil, the field coordinator for Proyección. Today, small patches of deep green barley and oats dot the mountain plains, a buffer against future disasters.

With the help of the two agencies, villagers planted a total of 110 hectares—about 272 acres—with barley. Family plots are more than half an acre in size—large enough to produce sufficient fodder to help sustain their animals through the roughest weather between May and September. The yield was about 23 tons per family. And since the first successful

season, the families and the wider Caylloma community have been buying the seeds themselves, without the assistance of the two agencies.

Free energy for sprinklers

In Jachaña, another small hamlet in the district of Caylloma, Oxfam and Asociación Proyección have installed three pilot sprinkler systems designed to help herders withstand the hardships of mountain living. In a place where there is no electricity to run a pump, where llamas transport many of the

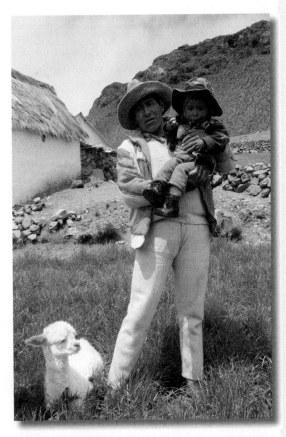

Oxfam America is helping alpaca herders such as Jose Gonzalez Condo learn new ways to prevent disaster from striking. A father of six children, he has lived in this village of Chinosiri his entire life and has learned how to grow barley to tide his alpacas over during the harshest weather. (Photo: Marisol Regis Fuentes / Oxfam America)

goods, and where most people rely on a local spiky grass for their cooking fuel, gravity is the free and abundant energy source that is now powering Simon Ccalachua's sprinkler. And beneath the arc of water it sprays, a new growth of hardy rye grass is now sprouting—the guarantee that Ccalachua's alpacas will have the nourishment they need.

"They used to rely on nature and now they know how to work on channels and sprinkling," said a translator, summarizing the benefits for Ccalachua. "Before this project, the mortality of the animals [was very high]. Now the mortality is 3 to 10 percent."

The sprinkler is irrigating about two-and-a-half acres of Ccalachua's sloped, rocky land. Well-watered and well-fertilized (naturally, with alpaca droppings), a pasture that size is big enough to keep 20 alpacas happily nourished. The trick is to fence off portions of the pasture after the animals have grazed, allowing the grasses to recover. By the time the herd completes a full rotation, the grass where they started will be ready to eat again.

Get Involved!

As a student, you are in a rare position to play a role in international development. The choices you make every day have a profound impact. Do you support small farmers in your choices? Do you buy Fair Trade goods? Do you exercise your rights as a consumer—speaking out on issues like our campaign to influence Starbucks? If you are a U.S. citizen, do you contact your representatives in Congress about issues (such as farm policy) that affect the lives of poor people around the world?

If you'd like to join Oxfam's online community and receive email updates on important issues and breaking news about humanitarian issues, go to www.oxfamamerica.org/join. We also have an extensive outreach program and leadership training for college students; visit www.oxfamamerica.org/change.

Further information about development issues and Oxfam's work in general is at www.oxfamamerica.org or by following the Oxfam links at this book's Web site, IRtext.com, which lead to videos about the Starbucks campaign, students in Darfur, and other materials.

You have a critical role to play in shaping the world in the coming decades. Take action now.

During a Supermarket Day of Action event in Boston, Susan Ngo hands out a recipe for Fair Trade mocha brownies. (Photo: Jesse Ladner / Oxfam America)

Afterword

BY JOSHUA S. GOLDSTEIN AND JON C. PEVEHOUSE

Oxfam America offers a fresh perspective on the issues affecting people living in the global South. You, the readers, are mostly college students in the North, primarily in the United States. Did Oxfam's perspective change your views, reinforce your views, or did you find Oxfam's approach off-target? Did this section make you more or less likely to engage with the lives of people living far away and in very different conditions and cultures from your own? What lessons can you draw from

Oxfam's experiences that might enhance your understanding of the topics in this textbook, such as conflict (Chapter 5), trade (Chapter 8), and especially international development (Chapter 13)?

The following critical thinking questions connect the Oxfam section to the subject of International Relations as discussed elsewhere in this book.

1. IR theorists speak of *levels of analysis* (see p. 15) as a way to think about the multiple influences on outcomes. Oxfam also uses levels of analysis to represent a multifaceted approach to solving problems in international development. The Mozambique cotton example included local initiatives to train farmers in new methods; national actions to organize cooperatives as a counterweight to governments and companies; and global activism to amplify farmers' voices in world trade negotiations. How important do you think it is to study IR on multiple levels of analysis and to work for change on multiple levels as well? Would it be better to concentrate on one (presumably most important) level?

2. Oxfam sometimes confronts corporations, such as the gold mining company in Ghana, but at other times successfully appeals to corporations' enlightened self-interest to use their power for good, as when Starbucks agreed to pay more to Ethiopian coffee growers. Do you think multinational corporations (see pp. 315–319) are a force for good or for bad in international development? Or if both have some truth, what makes the difference from case to case?

3. The partnership of organizations in the global North and global South can, potentially, reflect elements of all three core principles discussed on pp. 3–7. For instance, foreign aid can impose the values and culture of the North on former colonies (dominance); it can give help while opening markets for the North's goods (reciprocity); or it can draw upon a shared sense of humanity (identity). Which principle is most effective in your view? In particular, should the North offer humanitarian assistance with no strings attached, such as providing sprinklers to Peruvian herders, or should it concentrate on mutually beneficial exchanges, such as buying fair-trade coffee? Or, if both approaches work, when and where is each appropriate?

4. Oxfam's work in El Salvador, Democratic Congo, and Sudan grapples with the effects of recent or ongoing wars. How important is peace and conflict resolution in meeting the basic needs (human rights) of desperately poor people? Do you see war as a predominant factor in poverty or as an issue separate from economic development (see Chapter 4)? If war is a central impediment to development, should humanitarian groups such as Oxfam work to reduce violent conflict, or is that job best left to specialized organizations such as international peacekeeping troops?

Whether through Oxfam's approach or another way, we hope that you as students in the global North will see the global South as part of your community, as among your problems and opportunities, and as an integral part of your life. We authors are trying to do the same: For 15 years we have donated more than 5 percent of the royalties from this book to Oxfam America. The important thing, however, is not the particular actions you take or the contributions you make—humanitarian, political, career, volunteer—but that you see the whole world and not just your corner of it as the context for your life. Think globally!

Special thanks to Oxfam America—particularly Jane Huber, Coco McCabe, Anna Kramer, Andrea Perera, Chris Hufstader, and Charles Scott—for writing this section.

To link to Oxfam videos, visit www.IRtext.com

U.S. Farm Subsidies and Mali Farmers (5:51)

Ethiopian Coffee Farmers (1:50)

The Campaign for Oxfam America (10:46)

Youth Ambassador Visits Darfur (5:00)

CHANGE College Leadership Program (3:29)

VIDEO

Windmill and nuclear power plant, Britain, mid-1980s.

CHAPTER **8**

Environment and Technology

Interdependence and the Environment

Global threats to the natural environment are a growing source of interdependence. States' actions regarding pollution, conservation, and natural resources routinely affect other states. Because environmental effects tend to be diffuse and long term and because such effects easily spread from one location to another, international environmental politics creates difficult collective goods problems (see pp. 3–9). A sustainable natural environment is a collective good, and states bargain over how to distribute the costs of providing that good. The collective goods problem arises in each issue area concerning the environment, resources, and population.

For example, the world's major fisheries in international waters are not owned by any state; they are a collective good. The various fishing states must cooperate (partly by regulating nonstate actors such as MNCs) to avoid depleting the stocks of fish. If too many states fail to cooperate, the fish population declines and everyone's catch drops. And indeed, in 1997–2007, catches worldwide declined by about 15 percent. Further declines are

THE BIG PICTURE

RECIPROCITY

Can countries cooperate to prevent future environmental disasters such as global warming? International negotiations about the environment face the challenge of very difficult collective goods problems. Countries share the benefits of a healthy global environment or the costs of an environmental breakdown, regardless of each country's individual contribution to cause or prevent that outcome. Only when costs are low have states effectively solved global environmental problems.

Such is not the case for global warming. The Kyoto Protocol set goals for industrialized countries to slightly reduce emissions of carbon dioxide by 2012. Such reductions are costly because carbon emissions result from a prime motor of industrial economies—fossil fuels (coal, oil, gas). The United States did not ratify the treaty, and the countries of the global South are exempt despite becoming a major source of carbon emissions. Environmental agreements such as the Kyoto Protocol depend on the reciprocity principle, which does not work very well with many actors, high costs, and weak enforcement mechanisms.

To hear the authors of this book discuss this issue, with an example from recent history, download the "IR Talk" podcast for Chapter 8 from www.IRtext.com.

PODCAST

projected for the coming years. Fishers have moved on to new species of seafood after depleting earlier ones, but have already depleted a third of the species, with the rest projected to go by mid-century (see Figure 8.1). Because the world's states did not solve the collective goods problem of world fisheries, they are paying $20 billion a year in subsidies to bankrupt fishing industries in their respective countries.

This depletion occurred because each additional fishing boat—and the MNC that owns it as well as its state of origin—gains by catching an additional fish. The benefits of that fish go entirely to the one catching it, whereas the eventual costs of depleted stocks will be shared by all who fish there. But what is a state's fair quota of fish? No world government exists to decide such a question, so states must enter into multilateral negotiations, agreements, and regimes. Such efforts create new avenues for functionalism and international integration, but also new potentials for conflict and "prisoner's dilemmas."

In 1999, a UN-sponsored agreement among all the world's major fishing states set goals to reduce fleet overcapacity. (Four million fishing boats operate worldwide, of which 40,000 are ships larger than 100 tons.) Participating nations are capping the size of fishing fleets and then scaling them back gradually, while reducing subsidies. The pain of unemployment and economic adjustment should thus be shared. However, the agreement is voluntary, its implementation delayed, and its effect on collapsing fisheries probably too little, too late.

This type of collective goods dilemma has been called the **tragedy of the commons.** Centuries ago, the commons were shared grazing land in Britain. As with fisheries, if too many people kept too many sheep, the commons would be

FIGURE 8.1   Global Loss of Seafood Species

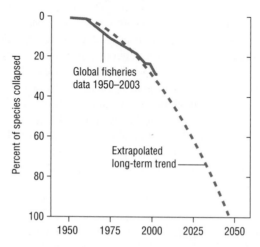

Source: *New York Times,* Nov. 3, 2006: A16.

overgrazed. Yet adding one more sheep was profitable to that sheep's owner. Britain solved the problem by **enclosure** of the commons—splitting it into privately owned pieces on each of which a single owner would have an incentive to manage resources responsibly. The world's states have taken a similar approach to coastal fisheries by extending territorial waters to put more fish under the control of single states (see pp. 324–325). The *global commons* refers to the shared parts of the earth, such as the oceans and outer space.

As in other areas of IPE, the solution of environmental collective goods problems is based on achieving shared benefits that depend on overcoming conflicting interests. *Regimes* are an important part of the solution (see pp. 67–69), providing rules based on the reciprocity principle to govern bargaining over who gets the benefits and bears the costs of environmental protection. Functional IOs specialize in technical and management aspects of the environment.

Increasingly, these IOs overlap with broader communities of experts from various states that structure the way states manage environmental issues; these have been called *epistemic communities* (knowledge-based communities). For example, the transnational community of experts and policy makers concerned with pollution in the Mediterranean is an epistemic community.

In global environmental politics, it is hard to manage collective goods problems because of the large number of actors. Collective goods are easier to provide in small groups, in which individual actions have more impact on the total picture and cheating is more noticeable. The opposite is true with the environment. The actions of nearly 200 states (albeit some more than others) aggregate to cause indirect but serious consequences throughout the world.

Sustainable Development

Sustainable development refers to economic growth that does not deplete resources and destroy ecosystems so quickly that the basis of that economic growth is itself undermined. The concept applies to both the industrialized regions and the global South.

The 1992 Earth Summit produced an overall plan whereby large states in the global South promise to industrialize along cleaner lines (at a certain cost to economic growth) and industrialized states promise to funnel aid and technology to them to assist in that process. The summit also established the *Commission on Sustainable Development*, which monitors states' compliance with the promises they made at the Earth Summit and hears evidence from environmental NGOs such as Greenpeace. But it lacks powers of enforcement over national governments—again reflecting the preeminence of state sovereignty over supranational authority (see pp. 210–213). The commission has 53 member states. The commission's ability to monitor and publicize state actions is supposed to discourage states from cheating on the Earth Summit plan and the follow-up 2002 Johannesburg Plan of Implementation. But progress has been slow.

China and other developing countries in Asia stand at the center of the debate over sustainable development. In the drive for rapid economic growth, these countries have created serious pollution and other environmental problems. Just to clear the air long enough to hold the 2008 Olympics, Beijing had to shut down industry and ban traffic. Because of China's size, any success in developing its economy along Western industrialized lines (for example, with mass ownership of automobiles) could create shocks to the global environment. In recent years China has also been scouring the planet for raw materials—such as imports of 200 million tons of iron a year—to fuel its extraordinary growth. China has begun to switch away from dirty coal, helping ease air pollution, but its thirst for imported oil and gas drove up world oil prices in 2003–2008 before the global recession abruptly curtailed demand.

Managing the Environment

The most global environmental problems are those that involve collective goods for all states and people in the world.

The Atmosphere

Preserving the health of the earth's atmosphere is a benefit that affects people throughout the world without regard for their own state's contribution to the problem or its solution. Two problems of the atmosphere have become major international issues: global warming and depletion of the ozone layer.

Global Warming   Global climate change, or **global warming,** is a long-term rise in the average world temperature. Growing and compelling evidence shows that global warming is a real problem, that it is caused by the emission of carbon dioxide and other gases, and that it will get much worse. The issue of global warming rose high on the political agenda in 2005–2008 because of massive melt-offs of Arctic ice, high oil prices, and devastating hurricanes. In 2007, former U.S. Vice President Al Gore and the UN Intergovernmental Panel on Climate Change won the Nobel Peace Prize, and in 2009 President Obama vowed to redirect U.S. policy and work more closely with other countries to tackle global warming. Unfortunately, the international community has had little success solving the problem.

Over the next few decades, according to most estimates, global temperatures may rise by between 3 and 10 degrees Fahrenheit. The high end of this forecast corresponds with the difference between today's climate and that of the last ice age. Possibly within a few decades the polar ice caps will begin to melt and cause the sea level to rise by as much as a few feet. A study by British researchers in 2008 found the thickness of the Arctic ice decreasing by as much as 20 percent in some regions. Such a rise could flood coastal cities and devastate low-lying areas such as the heavily populated coast of Bangladesh. Urgent calls for action come from island states in the Pacific that will likely disappear this century. Indeed, reflecting an all-too-realistic lack of faith in international action, the low-lying state of the Maldives created a fund to buy land in another country to move its 300,000 residents as its territory disappears.

Global climate change could also alter weather patterns in many regions, causing droughts, floods, freezes, and widespread disruption of natural ecosystems. It is also possible that climate changes could benefit some regions and make agriculture more productive. Melting of polar ice is opening new shipping routes north of Canada and Russia that could potentially cut weeks off the transit time from northern Europe or America to Asia (see Figure 8.2), a huge saving for global business. Furthermore, the Arctic seas are thought to hold large deposits of oil and gas, which would become

FIGURE 8.2   Potential Arctic Shipping Routes

Northwest Passage
8,500 miles

Northern Sea Route
8,000 miles

Panama Canal Route
15,000 miles

Suez Canal Route
13,000 miles

commercially accessible if the ice melts (and, ironically, contribute to even more global warming). Still, overall, sudden environmental changes are usually much more destructive than helpful.

The **UN Environment Program (UNEP),** whose main function is to monitor environmental conditions, works with the World Meteorological Organization to measure changes in global climate from year to year. Since 1989 the UN-sponsored *Intergovernmental Panel on Climate Change* (IPCC) has served as a negotiating forum for this issue. In 2007, the IPCC issued a report from scientists around the world, approved by more than 100 countries, calling global warming "unequivocal" and expressing "very high confidence" that humans are the main cause.

It is costly to reduce the emissions of gases—mainly carbon dioxide—that cause global warming. These gases result from the broad spectrum of activities that drive an industrial economy. They are a by-product of burning *fossil fuels*—oil, coal, and natural gas—to run cars, tractors, furnaces, factories, and so forth. These activities create **greenhouse gases**—so named because when concentrated in the atmosphere, these gases act like the glass in a greenhouse: they let energy in as short-wavelength solar radiation but reflect it back when it tries to exit again as longer-wavelength heat waves. The greenhouse gases are *carbon dioxide* (responsible for two-thirds of the effect), *methane gas, chlorofluorocarbons* (CFCs), and *nitrous oxide*.

Thus reducing the greenhouse effect means curbing economic growth or shifting it onto entirely new technological paths, both of which are extremely expensive. The political costs of such actions—which would likely increase unemployment, reduce corporate profits, and lower personal incomes—could be severe. If Arctic sea ice melts, polar bears may go extinct, but they do not have a seat at the table in international climate negotiations. Neither do today's children, who cannot vote but will live with the long-term consequences of their elders' actions.

For individual states, the costs of reducing greenhouse emissions are almost unrelated to the benefits of a solution. If one state reduces its industrial production or makes expensive investments in new technologies, this will have little effect on the long-term outcome unless other states do likewise. And if most states took such steps, a free rider that did not go along would save money and still benefit from the solution.

Global warming thus presents states with a triple dilemma. First, there is the dilemma of short-term (and predictable) costs to gain long-term (and less predictable) benefits. Second, specific constituencies such as oil companies and industrial workers pay the costs, whereas the benefits are distributed more generally across

MELTING AWAY

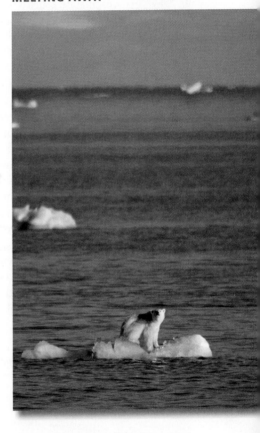

International treaties have been much more successful at addressing ozone depletion than global warming, mostly because the costs of the latter are much higher. A 1997 conference in Kyoto, Japan, set goals for industrialized countries to reduce their outputs of carbon dioxide and related gases modestly over the next decade, but the goals are not being met. If global warming melts polar ice caps in the coming decades, sea levels could rise and devastate many cities. Polar bears are also endangered by the melting Arctic ice.

domestic society and internationally. Third, there is the collective goods dilemma among states: benefits are shared globally but costs must be extracted from each state individually.

This third dilemma is complicated by the North-South divide. How can the industrialization of today's poor countries (China and India in particular) take place without pushing greenhouse emissions to unacceptable levels? Greenhouse gases are produced by each state roughly in proportion to its industrial activity. Eighty percent of greenhouse gases now come from the industrialized countries—25 percent from the United States alone. U.S. carbon dioxide emissions, 20 tons per person annually, are twice the European rate and eight times China's. Yet the most severe impacts of global warming are likely to be felt in the global South. In densely populated countries such as Bangladesh, hundreds of millions of people stand to lose their homes and farmland under a rising sea. Offsetting these North-South divisions, however, is the emerging realization that global climate change could cause environmental catastrophes across both North and South.

All of these elements make for a difficult multilateral bargaining situation, one not yet resolved. The *Framework Convention on Climate Change* adopted at the 1992 Earth Summit set a nonbinding goal to limit greenhouse emissions to 1990 levels by the year 2000. That goal was not met. Western Europe and Japan have been more willing to regulate greenhouse emissions than has the United States (which burns more fossil fuel per person), a situation that may change under the Obama administration.

The 1997 **Kyoto Protocol** adopted a complex formula for reducing greenhouse emissions to 1990 levels in the global North over about a decade. Countries in the global South received preferential treatment because their levels (per capita) were much lower. Yet China, despite its low emissions per person, has total production of carbon dioxide higher than that of the United States, and China's fast-growing, coal-burning economy is a major factor in global warming (see Figure 8.3). China's emissions declined modestly in

VIDEO

Climate Change in the Global South

VIDEO

U.S. Resistance on Climate Change

FIGURE 8.3   Projected U.S. and Chinese Carbon Dioxide Emissions, 1990–2030

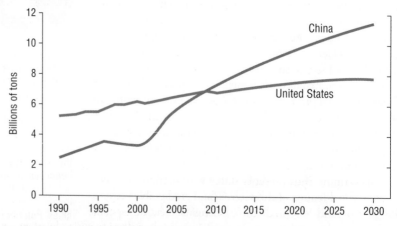

Source: International Energy Agency data.

the late 1990s as China began switching away from its predominant fuel, coal. But China's rapid growth quickly pushed its total up again. India is another large source of carbon dioxide. The U.S. Congress refused to ratify the Kyoto treaty when President Clinton submitted it, and President George W. Bush then declared the treaty "dead."

Moving forward without U.S. support, 160 countries in 2001 agreed to implement Kyoto. The agreement calls for 40 industrialized countries to reduce emissions to 5 percent below 1990 levels, by 2012, with binding penalties for failure. The needed ratifications to put the treaty into effect came when Russia ratified it in 2004, and the treaty entered into effect in 2005. Mandatory carbon cuts under the Kyoto Protocol began in 2008 and expire in 2012. The European Union began operation of markets to trade carbon emission credits among 12,000 industrial facilities across Europe. And internationally the treaty created trading in carbon credits, using free market principles to make reduction in carbon emissions more efficient. For example, a venture in Brazil earned carbon credits by burning methane gas from a garbage dump (to generate electricity) instead of venting it as a strong greenhouse gas. European investors bought the credits and could then sell them to a polluting factory in Eastern Europe.

In 2006, 180 states began negotiations on the question of what happens after 2012 when Kyoto expires. With the United States still opposed, the negotiations stalled, but in 2009 the new U.S. administration rejoined the talks. Meanwhile, about half the states of the United States (notably California), and a number of cities, began taking steps to limit greenhouse emissions. Yet, none of these moves are enough, or soon enough, to decisively reverse the direction of climate change. The dilemma of global warming remains fundamentally unsolved, and with weak enforcement mechanisms, even the states that signed the Kyoto Protocol may not meet their targets by 2012. Indeed, even European states, which have the largest markets for carbon as an attempt to lower emissions, have yet to see any declines in carbon dioxide.

Ozone Depletion   A second major atmospheric problem negotiated by the world's governments is the depletion of the world's **ozone layer.** Ozone high in the atmosphere screens out harmful ultraviolet rays from the sun. Certain chemicals expelled by industrial economies float to the top of the atmosphere and interact with ozone in a way that breaks it down. The chief culprits are CFCs, until recently widely used in refrigeration and in aerosol sprays. (Unfortunately, ozone produced by burning fossil fuels does not replace the high-level ozone but only pollutes the lower atmosphere.) As the ozone layer thins, more ultraviolet radiation reaches the earth's surface. Over Antarctica, a seasonal hole in the ozone grew larger year by year. If ozone levels kept rising, the increased radiation could eventually kill off vegetation, reduce agricultural yields, and disrupt ecosystems.

Clearly, this is another collective goods problem in that one state benefits from allowing the use of CFCs in its economy, provided that most other states prohibit their use. But the costs of replacing CFCs are much lower than the costs of addressing global warming: CFCs can be replaced at modest cost. Furthermore, the consequences of ozone depletion are better understood and more immediate than those of global warming.

Perhaps because of these cost issues, states had much more success in negotiating agreements and developing regimes to manage ozone depletion than global warming. In the 1987 **Montreal Protocol,** 22 states agreed to reduce CFCs by 50 percent by 1998. In

1990, the timetable was accelerated and the signatories expanded: 81 states agreed to eliminate all CFCs by 2000. In 1992, as evidence of ozone depletion mounted, the schedule was again accelerated, with major industrial states phasing out CFCs by 1995. The signatories agreed in principle to establish a fund to help developing countries pay for alternative refrigeration technologies not based on CFCs. Without such an effort, the states of the global South would be tempted to free-ride and could ultimately undermine the effort. These countries were also given until 2010 to phase out production. The Montreal Protocol was revised and strengthened again in 1997 and 1999. Rich countries stopped making CFCs in 1996 and have contributed about $3 billion to the fund. This money, supporting thousands of projects in more than a hundred countries, has helped the global South reduce emissions over the past decade. The ozone hole is projected to slowly shrink back over the coming 50 years if current arrangements continue.

The Montreal Protocol on CFCs is the most important success yet achieved in international negotiations to preserve the global environment. Indeed, UN secretary-general Kofi Annan called it "perhaps the single most successful international agreement to date." It showed that states can agree to take action on urgent environmental threats, can agree on targets and measures to counter such threats, and can allocate the costs of such measures in a mutually acceptable way and actually pay up when the bill comes. But the international cooperation on the ozone problem has not been widely repeated on other environmental issues.

Biodiversity

Biodiversity refers to the tremendous diversity of plant and animal species making up the earth's (global, regional, and local) ecosystems. Because of humans' destruction of ecosystems, large numbers of species are already *extinct*. Extinction results from overhunting, overfishing, and introducing non-native species that crowd out previous inhabitants. But the most important cause is *loss of habitat*—the destruction of rain forests, pollution of lakes and streams, and loss of agricultural lands to urban sprawl. Because ecosystems are based on complex interrelationships among species, the extinction of a few species can cause deeper changes in the environment. For example, the loss of native microorganisms can lead to chronic pollution of rivers or to the transformation of arable land into deserts.

Because ecosystems are so complex, it is usually impossible to predict the consequences of a species' extinction or of the loss of a habitat or ecosystem. Generally, the activities that lead to habitat loss are economically profitable, so real costs are associated with limiting such activities. Species preservation is thus a collective good resembling global warming; the costs are immediate and substantial but the benefits are long term and ill defined.

It has been difficult to reach international agreement on sharing the costs of preserving biodiversity. A UN convention on trade in endangered species has reduced but not eliminated such trade. At the 1992 Earth Summit, a treaty on biodiversity committed signatories to preserving habitats and got rich states to pay poor ones for the rights to use commercially profitable biological products extracted from rare species in protected habitats (such as medicines from rain forest trees). As of 2007, the treaty had

189 member states. However, because of fears that the treaty could limit U.S. patent rights in biotechnology, the United States never ratified it. The United States does, however, participate in other biological treaties, such as a 1971 wetlands convention and the 1973 Convention on International Trade in Endangered Species (CITES).

International regimes to protect whales and dolphins have had limited success. The **International Whaling Commission** (an IGO) sets quotas for hunting certain whale species, but participation is voluntary, and governments are not bound by decisions they object to. Norway dropped out in 1992 when it decided unilaterally that it could increase its catch without endangering the species.

The *Inter-American Tropical Tuna Commission* (another IGO) regulates methods used to fish for tuna, aiming to minimize dolphin losses. The United States, which consumes half the world's tuna catch, has gone further and unilaterally requires—in the Marine Mammal Protection Act—that dolphin-safe methods be used for tuna sold in U.S. territory. Other countries have challenged the act through international trade organizations as an unfair restriction on tuna exports to the United States. Such conflicts portend future battles between environmentalists and free trade advocates. Free traders argue that states must not use domestic legislation to seek global environmental goals.

Thus, unilateral approaches to biodiversity issues are problematic because they disrupt free trade; multilateral approaches are problematic because of the collective goods problem. It is not surprising that the international response has been fairly ineffective to date.

Forests and Oceans

Two types of habitat—tropical rain forests and oceans—are especially important to biodiversity *and* the atmosphere. Both are also reservoirs of commercially profitable resources such as fish and wood. They differ in that forests are located almost entirely within state territory, but oceans are largely beyond any state territory, in the global commons.

Rain Forests   As many as half the world's total species live in *rain forests*, which replenish oxygen and reduce carbon dioxide in the atmosphere—slowing down global warming. Rain forests thus benefit all the world's states; they are collective goods.

International bargaining on the preservation of rain forests has made considerable progress, probably because most rain forests belong to only a few states. These few states have the power to speed up or slow down the destruction of forests—and international bargaining amounts to agreements to shift costs from those few states onto the broader group of states benefiting from the rain forests.

Although some rich states (including the United States) have large forests, most of the largest rain forests are in poor states such as Brazil, Indonesia, Malaysia, and Madagascar. Such states can benefit economically from exploiting the forests—freely cutting lumber, clearing land for agriculture, and mining. Until recently (and still to an extent), leaders of rich states have been most interested in encouraging maximum economic growth in poor states so that foreign debts could be paid—with little regard for environmental damage.

Now that rich states have an interest in protecting rain forests, they are using development assistance as leverage to induce poorer states to protect their forests rather than

POLICY PERSPECTIVES

President of Ireland, Mary McAleese

PROBLEM *How do you balance environmental and economic concerns?*

BACKGROUND Imagine that you are the president of Ireland. Genetically modified organisms (GMOs) are highly controversial in Europe, and this certainly includes your country. In 1997, for example, Ireland reluctantly approved a permit for the global MNC Monsanto to grow sugar beets near Dublin. After several legal attempts to halt the planting of the crop failed, activists destroyed the crop in the ground before it could be harvested.

You have quietly supported several Irish biotechnology firms in the past with joint ventures in research. These have produced a variety of advances that give Ireland a significant advantage in this field over other European states. Several MNCs stand to benefit from this research, providing you with investment and tax income.

DOMESTIC CONSIDERATIONS Unfortunately, your "positive but precautionary" approach is unpopular with the public. Some worry that Ireland's reputation as "the Green Island" will suffer, possibly posing a threat to tourism—a major source of income for your country. Others join the chorus of European opposition to GMOs based on concerns over the possible environmental effects of these products. A recent Eurobarometer poll found that 54 percent of European consumers consider GMO foods "dangerous."

In the spring of 2004, the European Union (EU) approved an end to the moratorium on GMO product sales (with your country voting in the majority), partially under a threat from the United States to enforce a WTO ruling that found the GMO ban illegal. The United States is your largest single trade partner, but other EU states combined are your most significant export market.

SCENARIO Imagine that the balance of power in the EU shifts against GMOs with the admission of new Central European states. Now, the EU will not approve the sale of GMO products within Europe. Thus, although it would still be legal to grow GMO crops, it would not be legal to export them to EU countries.

GMO crops could provide economic benefits to your country. Given your comparative technological advantage in this area, your economy stands to profit from expanding GMO use through increased agricultural output and increased business activity from MNCs. The United States has no regulations concerning the importation of GMO products and would be open to exports of these crops.

GMOs carry possible dangers as well. Some environmentalists warn that GMOs could have negative effects on ecology, wildlife, and human health. Many of your EU partners will shun your GMO products, robbing you of a large export market for these goods. Domestically, expanding the production of GMOs will be controversial.

CHOOSE YOUR POLICY Do you continue to quietly encourage the advance of GMO crops? Do you follow the new EU members in opposing GMOs, out of respect for the long-term environmental concerns raised by these products? Do you work with MNCs to use your comparative advantage for economic gain? How do you balance economic prosperity with a concern for the environment?

exploiting them. In some developing countries burdened by large foreign debts, environmentalists and bankers from rich countries have worked out "debt-for-nature swaps" that cancel debts in exchange for a state's agreement to preserve forests. In 2006, for example, the U.S. government and NGOs helped Guatemala cancel more than $20 million in debts in exchange for expanded conservation programs.

Oceans　The *oceans*, covering 70 percent of the earth's surface, are (like the rain forests) a key to regulating climate and preserving biodiversity. Oceans, like forests, are attractive targets for short-term economic uses that cause long-term environmental damage. Such uses include overfishing, dumping toxic and nuclear waste (and other garbage), and long-distance oil shipments with their recurrent spills. Unlike rain forests, oceans belong to no state but are a global commons. This makes the collective goods problem more difficult because no authority exists to enforce regulations. Preserving the oceans depends on the cooperation of more than a hundred states and thousands of nonstate actors. Free riders have great opportunities to profit. For example, *drift nets* are huge fishing nets, miles long, that scoop up everything in their path. They are very profitable but destructive of a sustainable ocean environment. Most states have now banned their use (under pressure from the environmental movement). However, no state has the authority to go onto the **high seas** (nonterritorial waters) and stop illegal use of these nets.

One solution that states have pursued involves "enclosing" more of the ocean. Territorial waters have expanded to hundreds of miles off the coast (and around islands), so that state sovereignty encloses substantial resources such as fisheries and offshore oil and mineral deposits. This solution has been pursued in the context of larger multilateral negotiations on ocean management.

The **UN Convention on the Law of the Sea (UNCLOS),** negotiated from 1973 to 1982, governs the uses of the oceans. After more than a decade's delay and renegotiation of some of the deep-sea mining aspects, the United States signed UNCLOS in 1994, but has yet to ratify the treaty. The UNCLOS treaty established rules on territorial waters—12 miles for shipping and a 200-mile exclusive economic zone (EEZ) for economic activities, such as fishing and mining. The 200-mile limit placed a substantial share of the economically profitable ocean resources in the control of about a dozen states (see Figure 8.4).

Varying interpretations leave economic rights in dispute in a number of locations. In the East China Sea, China sent five warships in 2005 to back up its claim to an undersea gas field partly claimed by Japan, where China began drilling and Japan granted drilling rights to a Japanese company. China's claim under a Continental Shelf treaty conflicts with Japan's claim of an EEZ.

UNCLOS also developed the general principle that the oceans are a common heritage of humankind. A mechanism was created, through an International Sea-Bed Authority, for sharing some of the wealth that rich states might gain from extracting minerals on the ocean floor (beyond 200 miles).

Antarctica　Like the oceans, *Antarctica* belongs to no state. The continent's strategic and commercial values are limited, however, and not many states care about it. Historically, states have been successful in reaching agreements on Antarctica because

FIGURE 8.4 State-Controlled Waters

Overfishing and similar problems of managing the "commons" of world oceans have been addressed by enclosing the most important ocean areas under the exclusive control of states. Shaded areas are within the 200-mile economic zones controlled by states under terms of the NCLOS treaty.

Source: Adapted from Andrew Boyd, *An Atlas of World Affairs*, 9th ed. New York: Routledge, 1992.

the costs were low and the players few. The **Antarctic Treaty of 1959**—one of the first multilateral treaties concerning the environment—forbids military activity as well as the presence of nuclear weapons or the dumping of nuclear waste. It sets aside territorial claims on the continent for future resolution and establishes a regime under which various states conduct scientific research in Antarctica. The treaty was signed by all states with interests in the area, including both superpowers. By 1991, Greenpeace had persuaded the treaty signatories to turn the continent into a "world park." Antarctica is largely a success story in international environmental politics.

Pollution

Pollution generally creates a collective goods problem, but one that is not often global in scale. Pollution is more often a regional or bilateral issue. With some exceptions—such as dumping at sea—the effects of pollution are limited to the state where it occurs and its close neighbors; U.S. industrial smokestack emissions cause acid rain in Canada but do not directly affect distant states. China's terrible air pollution kills nearly half a million Chinese a year, but few foreigners. Even when pollution crosses state borders, it often has its strongest effects closest to the source. This makes it a somewhat less intractable collective goods problem, because a polluting state can seldom free-ride, and few actors are involved.

In several regions—notably Western and Eastern Europe and the Middle East—states are closely packed in the same air, river, or sea basins. Here, pollution controls must often be negotiated multilaterally. In Europe during the Cold War, the international pollution problem was exacerbated by the inability of Western European states to impose any limits on Eastern ones, whose pollution was notorious.

Several regional agreements seek to limit **acid rain,** caused by air pollution. European states—whose forests have been heavily damaged—have agreed to limit air pollution and acid rain for their mutual benefit. In 1988, 24 European states signed a treaty to limit nitrogen oxide emissions to 1988 levels by 1995. After long negotiations, the United States and Canada signed bilateral agreements to limit such pollution as well. These regional agreements have worked fairly well.

Water pollution often crosses borders as well, especially because industrial pollution, human sewage, and agricultural fertilizers and pesticides all tend to run into rivers and seas. For instance, in 2005, a huge chemical spill in northeast China polluted a river that flows into Russia. Long-standing regional agencies that regulate shipping on heavily used European rivers now also deal with pollution. The Mediterranean basin is severely polluted and difficult to manage because so many states border it. The Great Lakes on the U.S.-Canadian border were heavily polluted in the 1970s. But because the issue affected only two countries, it was easier to address, and the situation later improved.

Toxic and *nuclear wastes* are a special problem because of their long-term dangers. States occasionally try to ship such wastes out of the country. International agreements now ban the dumping of toxic and nuclear wastes at sea (an obvious collective goods problem). But such wastes have been sent to developing countries for disposal, for a fee. For instance, toxic ash from Pennsylvania became material for bricks in Guinea, and Italian nuclear waste was shipped to Nigeria.

Norms have developed in recent years against exporting toxic wastes—a practice seen as exploitive of the receiving country. In 1989, 100 states signed a treaty to regulate shipments of toxic and nuclear wastes and prevent their secret movements under corrupt deals. Forty more countries, in Africa, did not sign the treaty but called for a halt to toxic waste shipments to Africa. Nonetheless, in 2006 a multinational company tried to dispose of toxic waste from a tanker ship in the Netherlands but took it back on finding the cost to run into hundreds of thousands of dollars. Six weeks later, the ship unloaded the toxic sludge in Abidjan, Ivory Coast, where a local company dumped it at locations around the city. Thousands of residents got sick and eight people died. In 2007 the company agreed to pay $200 million to settle claims.

In 1986, a meltdown at the Soviet nuclear power plant at Chernobyl, in Ukraine, created airborne radioactivity that spread over much of Europe, from Italy to Sweden. The accident exemplified the new reality—that economic and technical decisions made in one state can have grave environmental consequences for other countries. Soviet leaders made matters worse by failing to notify neighbors promptly of the accident.

On the various issues of water and air pollution, both unilateral state actions and international agreements have often been feasible and effective. In recent decades, river water quality has improved in most industrialized regions. Market economies have begun to deal with pollution as just another cost of production that should be charged to the polluter instead of to society at large. Some governments have begun to allocate "pollution rights" that companies can buy and sell on a free market.

In the former Soviet bloc, decades of centrally planned industrialization created severe environmental problems. With staggering environmental damage and human health effects, the economically strapped former Soviet republics had to bargain over limiting pollution and repairing the damage. For example, the severely polluted Aral Sea, formerly contained within one state, the Soviet Union, is now shared by two, Kazakhstan and Uzbekistan. Once the world's fourth largest inland sea, it shrank in half, its huge fisheries destroyed, after a Soviet-era mega-irrigation project diverted the Aral Sea's inlet rivers and polluted them with pesticides. Former fishing towns found themselves many miles from the shoreline. After local and international political leaders failed to implement plans to address the problem, local populations suffered from widespread health effects of the disaster.

Natural Resources

The natural environment is not only a delicate ecosystem requiring protection but also a repository of natural resources. The extraction of resources brings states wealth (and hence power), so these resources regularly fuel international conflicts. Because they are mostly located within individual states, however, they do not present a collective goods problem. Rather, states bargain over these vital resources.

Three aspects of natural resources shape their role in international conflict. First, they are required for the operation of an industrial economy (sometimes even an agrarian one). Second, their sources—mineral deposits, rivers, and so forth—are associated with particular territories over which states may fight for control. Third, natural resources tend to be unevenly distributed, with plentiful supplies in some states and an absence in others. These aspects mean that trade in natural resources is extremely profitable; much additional wealth is created by such trade. They also mean that trade in resources is fairly politicized—creating market imperfections such as monopoly, oligopoly, and price manipulation, sometimes by cartels (see pp. 178–179).

World Energy

Of the various natural resources required by states, energy resources are central. The commercial fuels that power the world's industrial economies are oil (about 40 percent of world energy consumption), coal (30 percent), natural gas (25 percent), and hydro-electric and nuclear power (5 percent). The fossil fuels (coal, oil, gas) thus account for 95 percent of world energy consumption. Some energy consumed as electricity comes from hydroelectric dams or nuclear power plants, but most of it comes from burning fossil fuels in electric-generating plants.

Table 8.1 shows energy consumption per person in the nine world regions. The four industrialized regions of the North use much more energy per person than those of the South. North America uses 25 times as much as Asia or Africa. Among industrialized countries there are differences in the *efficiency* of energy use—GDP produced per unit of energy consumed. The least efficient are the former Soviet Republics; North America is also rather inefficient; Europe and Japan are the most energy efficient.

TABLE 8.1   Per Capita Energy Consumption and Net Energy Trade, 2007

	Per Capita Consumption (million BTU)	Total Net Energy Exports[a] (quadrillion BTU)
North America	385	−24
Western Europe	145	−37
Japan/Pacific	175	−23
Russia/CIS	160	+23
China	55	−6
Middle East	125	+42
Latin America	50	+5
South Asia	20	−1
Africa	16	+20
World as a whole	72	

[a]Net exports refers to production minus consumption. Net exports worldwide do not equal net imports for technical reasons.

Source: Calculated from data in U.S. Department of Energy. Energy Information Administration. See http://www.eia.doe.gov/iea/.

International trade in energy plays a vital role in the world economy. As Table 8.1 shows, the regions of the industrialized West are all large net importers of energy. The other six world regions are net exporters of energy. Although all forms of energy are traded internationally, the most important by far is oil, the cheapest to transport over long distances. Russia receives vital hard-currency earnings from exporting oil. Venezuela and Mexico (in Latin America) and Nigeria and Angola (in Africa) are major oil exporters. But by far the largest source of oil exports is the Middle East—especially the countries around the Persian Gulf (Saudi Arabia, Kuwait, Iraq, Iran, and the small sheikdoms of United Arab Emirates, Qatar, Bahrain, and Oman). Saudi Arabia is the largest oil exporter and holds the largest oil reserves (see Table 5.1 on p. 179). The politics of world energy revolve around Middle Eastern oil shipped to Western Europe, Japan/Pacific, and North America.

The importance of oil in the industrialized economies helps explain the political importance of the Middle East in world politics. Not only is energy a crucial economic sector (on which all industrial activity depends), but it is also one of the most politically sensitive because of the dependence of the West on energy imported from the Middle East and the rest of the global South.

To secure a supply of oil in the Middle East, Britain and other European countries colonized the area early in the 20th century, carving up territory into protectorates in which European power kept local monarchs on their thrones. The United States did not claim colonies or protectorates, but U.S. MNCs were heavily involved in the development of oil resources in the area from the 1920s through the 1960s—often wielding vast power. These U.S. and European oil companies kept the price paid to local states low and their own profits high, yet local rulers depended on the expertise and capital investment of these companies.

After World War II the British gave up colonial claims in the Middle East, but the Western oil companies kept producing cheap oil there for Western consumption. Then in 1973, during an Arab-Israeli war, the oil-producing Arab states of the region decided to punish the United States for supporting Israel. They cut off their oil exports to the United States and curtailed their overall exports. This sent world oil prices skyrocketing. OPEC realized its potential power and the high price the world was willing to pay for oil. This 1973 *oil shock* had a profound effect on the world economy and on world politics. Huge amounts of hard currency accumulated in the treasuries of the Middle East oil-exporting countries, which in turn invested them around the world (these were called *petrodollars*). High inflation plagued the United States and Europe for years afterward. The economic instability and sense of U.S. helplessness—coming on top of the Vietnam War—seemed to mark a decline in American power and perhaps the rise of the global South.

In 1979, the revolution in Iran led to a second oil shock. But higher oil prices led to the expansion of oil production in new locations outside of OPEC—in the North Sea (Britain and Norway), Alaska, Angola, Russia, and elsewhere. By the mid-1980s, the Middle East was rapidly losing its market share of world trade in oil. At the same time, industrialized economies learned to be more *energy efficient*. With supply up and demand down, oil prices dropped in the late 1980s to historic lows of less than $20/barrel. A similar cycle saw oil prices climb to $140 a barrel and then collapse in 2008.

In the late 1990s, the Caspian Sea region beckoned as a new and largely untapped oil source (see Figure 8.5). However, the oil must travel overland by pipeline to reach world

FIGURE 8.5   Dividing the Caspian Sea

The Caspian Sea is the world's largest inland body of water. It could be defined under international law as either a lake or a sea.[a] A *lake* has a joint area in the middle (in green on the left panel) that can be exploited only if the countries agree on terms. There are also coastal zones under each country's sole control. In a *sea* less than 400 miles across, the bordering countries' 200-mile Exclusive Economic Zones (EEZs) split up the whole sea (right panel). If the whole area is split as in the map on the right, the sectors can be defined by median lines (dashed line) or by a division into five sectors of equal area (dotted line), giving Iran a larger sector.

In 2009, with major oil development underway in all five countries' coastal areas, the talks to draw final borders remain stalled. Russia had agreed with its neighbors, Azerbaijan and Kazakhstan, to use the median line on the seabed floor, though Russia proposes a different division for fishing purposes. Azerbaijan and Turkmenistan dispute ownership of an oil field along the dividing line between their sectors. Iran still wants one-fifth of the lake, and even sent a warship in 2001 to chase an oil exploration ship from Azerbaijan away from disputed waters. This conflict will not be resolved through dominance, but through reciprocity. Nobody benefits from a war and all five countries benefit from developing their oil resources. Solutions are enormously complicated—in this case factoring in additional elements like shipping, fishing, smuggling, and pipeline routes—and reaching agreement can take a very long time.

[a]Sciolino, Elaine. "It's a Sea! It's a Lake! No. It's a Pool of Oil!" *The New York Times*, June 21, 1998.

markets (the Caspian is an inland sea). But the main pipeline from oil-producing Azerbaijan to the Black Sea (where tanker ships can load) traveled through war-torn Chechnya in southern Russia. The pipeline reopened in 1997, but in 2000 it still carried only a fraction of its capacity. Russia meanwhile built a bypass route around Chechnya that carries a large and growing amount of Caspian oil for export through the Black Sea. Western powers sought other pipeline routes that did not cross Russia, while Turkey sought to control a larger market share and reduce environmental damage to the Bosporus waterway (through which Russian tankers must travel). After long negotiations, states and oil companies agreed to build, in 2002–2004, a large-capacity pipeline costing billions of dollars, through Azerbaijan and Georgia to Turkey's Mediterranean coast.

Violent conflicts make pipeline routes particularly complex. All three countries on the new pipeline route have recently been at war. Meanwhile in 2003, a new $4 billion pipeline began carrying oil from Chad through Cameroon for export, promising to help both countries alleviate poverty, but as rebels based in Sudan attacked in Chad, oil money was diverted to military purposes. Although borders and geopolitics may be less and less important in communications and business, they still matter greatly in such international economic transactions as oil pipelines.

Minerals

To build the infrastructure and other manufactured goods that create wealth in a national economy, states need other raw materials in addition to energy. These include metals, other minerals, and related materials extracted through mining. The political economy of minerals—iron, copper, platinum, and so forth—differs from that of world energy. The value of international trade in oil is many times that of any mineral. Mineral production is distributed more evenly than is oil production—supply is not so concentrated in one region of the world. Industrialized countries have also reduced their vulnerability by stockpiling strategic minerals.

Most important to industrialized economies are the minerals used for industrial equipment. Traditionally most important is iron, used to make steel. The leading producers of steel are the former Soviet Union, Japan, the United States, China, and Germany, followed by Brazil, Italy, South Korea, France, and Britain. Thus, major industrialized countries produce their own steel (Germany and Japan are the leading exporters worldwide). To preserve self-sufficiency in steel production, the United States and others have used trade policies to protect domestic steel industries (such as the U.S. steel tariffs; see p. 183).

For other important industrial minerals such as copper, nickel, and zinc, the pattern of supply and trade is much more diffuse than for oil, and the industrialized countries are largely self-sufficient. Even when states in the global South are the main suppliers, they have not gained the power of OPEC. There is a producer cartel in some cases (copper), a producer-consumer cartel in some (tin), and separate producer and consumer cartels in others (bauxite).

Certain agricultural products have spawned producer cartels such as the Union of Banana Exporting Countries (UBEC) and the African Groundnut Council. Like minerals, some export crops come mainly from just a few countries. These include sugar (Cuba), cocoa (Ivory Coast, Ghana, Nigeria), tea (India, Sri Lanka, China), and coffee (Brazil, Colombia). Despite the concentrations, producer cartels have not been very successful in boosting prices of these products, which are less essential than energy.

Water Disputes

In addition to energy and minerals, states need water. This need increases as a society industrializes, as it intensifies agriculture, and as its population grows. World water use is 35 times that of just a few centuries ago, and grew twice as fast as population in the

20th century. Yet water supplies are relatively unchanging and are becoming depleted in many places. One-fifth of the world's population lacks safe drinking water, and 80 countries suffer water shortages. Water supplies—rivers and water tables—often cross international boundaries; thus access to water is increasingly a source of international conflict. Sometimes—as when several states share access to a single water table—these conflicts are collective goods problems.

Water problems are especially important in the Middle East. For instance, the Euphrates River runs from Turkey through Syria to Iraq before reaching the Persian Gulf. Iraq objects to Syrian diversion of water from the river, and both Iraq and Syria object to Turkey's diversion.

The Jordan River originates in Syria and Lebanon and runs through Israel to Jordan. In the 1950s, Israel began building a canal to take water from the Jordan River to "make the desert bloom." Jordan and its Arab neighbors complained to the UN Security Council, but it failed in efforts to mediate the dispute, and each state went ahead with its own water plans (Israel and Jordan agreeing, however, to stay within UN-proposed allocations). In 1964, Syria and Lebanon tried to build dams and divert water before it reached Israel, rendering Israel's new water system worthless. Israeli air and artillery attacks on the construction site forced Syria to abandon its diversion project, and Israel's 1967 capture of the Golan Heights precluded Syria from renewing such efforts. Thus, the dominance principle comes into play in resolving conflicts over natural resources.

Water contains other resources such as fish and offshore oil deposits. The UNCLOS treaty enclosed more of these resources within states' territory—but this enclosure creates new problems. Norms regarding territorial waters are not firmly entrenched; some states disagree on who owns what. Also, control of small islands now implies rights to surrounding oceans with their fish, offshore oil, and minerals. A potentially serious international dispute has been brewing in the Spratly Islands, where some tiny islands are claimed by China, Vietnam, and other nearby countries (see pp. 135–136).

International Security and the Environment

IR scholars have expanded their studies of environmental politics to systematically study the relationship of military and security affairs with the environment. One side of this relationship is the role of the environment as a source of international conflict. We have seen how environmental degradation can lead to collective goods problems among large numbers of states, and how competition for territory and resources can create conflicts among smaller groups of states. During the 1991 Gulf War, for example, Iraqi forces spilled large amounts of Kuwaiti oil into the Persian Gulf and then, before retreating from Kuwait, blew up hundreds of Kuwaiti oil wells, leaving them burning uncontrollably and covering Iraq and Iran with thick black smoke. Worse still, armies sometimes adopt a "scorched earth policy" to deny sustenance to their adversaries. Fields are burned and villages leveled. Military activity short of war also tends to damage the environment. Military industries pollute. Military forces use energy less efficiently than civilians do. Military aircraft and missiles contribute to ozone depletion. Military bases contain many toxic waste dumps.

Population

World population, 6.8 billion in 2009, is growing by 80 million each year. Forecasting future population is easy in some respects. Barring a nuclear war or an environmental catastrophe, today's children will grow up and have children of their own. For the coming 20 to 30 years, world population growth will be driven, rather mechanistically, by the large number of children in today's populations in the global South. The projected world population in 2030 will be around 8 billion people, and there is little anyone can do to change that projection. Of the increase in population in that period, 96 percent will be in the global South. Currently, half the world's population growth occurs in just six countries: India, China, Pakistan, Nigeria, Bangladesh, and Indonesia. Among the world's poorest countries, population is expected to triple in the next 50 years, whereas many rich countries' populations will shrink in that period.

Projections beyond a few decades have a range of uncertainty (see Figure 8.6). New data in 2002 showed that higher women's status and literacy are reducing population growth more than expected in large, poor countries. The actions of states and IOs *now* will determine the earth's population in 200 years. Two hundred years ago, the British writer Thomas Malthus warned that population tends to increase faster than food supply and predicted that population growth would limit itself through famine and disease. Critics point out that technology has kept pace with population in the past, allowing more food and other resources to be extracted from the environment even as population keeps growing.

The Demographic Transition

Population growth results from a difference between rates of birth (per 1,000 people) and rates of death. In agrarian (preindustrial) societies, both birthrates and death rates are

FIGURE 8.6   World Population Trends and Projections

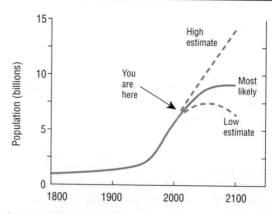

Source: Based on data from the UN Population Office.

FIGURE 8.7   The Demographic Transition

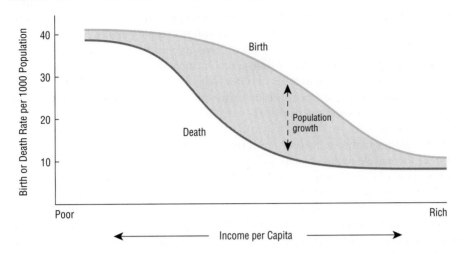

As income rises, first death rates and then birthrates fall. The gap between the two is the population growth rate. Early in the transition, the population contains a large proportion of children; later it contains a large proportion of elderly people.

high. Population growth is thus slow—even negative at times when death rates exceed birthrates (during a famine, for instance).

The process of economic development—of industrialization and the accumulation of wealth on a per capita basis—brings about a change in birthrates and death rates that follows a fairly universal pattern called the **demographic transition** (see Figure 8.7). First, death rates fall as food supplies increase and access to health care expands. Later, birthrates fall as people become educated, more secure, and more urbanized, and as the status of women rises. At the end of the transition, as at the beginning, birthrates and death rates are fairly close to each other, and population growth is limited. But during the transition, when death rates have fallen more than birthrates, population grows rapidly. One reason poor people tend to have many children is that under harsh poverty, a child's survival is not assured. Disease, malnutrition, or violence may claim the lives of many children, leaving parents with no one to look after them in their old age. Having many children helps ensure that some survive.

As a state makes the demographic transition, the structure of its population changes dramatically. At the beginning and middle of the process, most of the population is young. Families have many children, and adults do not have a long life expectancy. Because children are not very productive economically, the large number of children in poor countries tends to slow down the accumulation of wealth. But by the end of the demographic transition, adults live longer and families have fewer children, so the average age of the population is much older. Eventually a substantial section of the population is elderly—a different nonproductive population that the economy must support.

The industrialized countries have completed the demographic transition and now have slow population growth. Russia, Europe, and Japan have shrinking populations. Most developing countries are in the middle of the transition and have rapid population growth.

The dilemma of the demographic transition is this: rapid population growth and a child-heavy population are powerful forces lowering per capita income. Yet the best way to slow population growth is to raise per capita income. Population growth thus contributes to a vicious cycle in many poor states. Where population rises at the same rate as overall wealth, the average person is no better off over time. Even when the economy grows faster than population, so that the *average* income rises, the total *number* of poor people may increase.

The demographic transition tends to widen international disparities of wealth. States that manage to raise incomes a bit enter an upward spiral—as population growth slows, income levels per capita rise more, which further slows population growth, and so forth. Meanwhile, states that do not raise incomes have unabated population growth; per capita incomes stay low, which fuels more population growth—a downward spiral.

Globally, this disparity contributes to the gap in wealth between the North and South (see Chapter 7). Within the South, disparities are also sharpened as a few countries manage to slow population growth and raise incomes while others fail to do so. Even within a single country, the demographic transition sharpens disparities. Cities, richer classes, richer ethnic groups, and richer provinces tend to have low birthrates compared to the countryside and the poorer classes, ethnic groups, and provinces. In countries such as France, Israel, and the United States, wealthier ethnic groups have much slower population growth than poorer ethnic groups.

Recent trends suggest that the global South is splitting into two groups of states. Around 1970, nearly 50 states including China and India entered the phase of the demographic transition marked by falling birthrates. But in nearly 70 other poor states, death rates were still falling faster than birthrates, leading to accelerating population growth. These population trends contributed to disparities within the global South that emerged in the 1990s, notably between Africa and Asia.

Population Policies

The policies that governments adopt—not just economic and demographic conditions—influence the birthrate. Among the most important policies are those regarding birth control (contraception). State policies vary widely.

At one extreme, China uses its strong government control to try to enforce a limit of one child per couple. Penalties for having a second child include being charged for services that were free for the first child and being stigmatized at work. Beyond two children, the penalties escalate. Contraceptives and abortions are free. China's policy has lowered growth rates considerably in the cities but less so in the countryside, where most people still live. Still, in a single decade (the 1970s) China's fertility rate fell from 6 children per woman to about 2.5, a dramatic change. (By 2009 it was 1.7.)

But the Chinese policy has drawbacks. It limits individual freedom in favor of government control. Forced or coerced abortions have been reported. In traditional Chinese society, sons are valued more than daughters. Couples who have a daughter may keep trying until they have a son. In recent years, parents in China (and some places in India) are using ultrasound scans to determine their fetus's gender and abort it if female. China's 2000 census showed a sex difference that amounts to a million "missing" girls per year.

India's policies are less extreme but have been slower to reduce the birthrate, which fell from nearly 6 per woman in 1970 to 2.8 in 2007. India's government, strongly committed to birth control, has tried to make information and means widely available, but as a democracy it does not have China's extreme government control over society. Like China, India and several other countries have widespread sex-selective abortion and imbalanced sex ratios.

At the other extreme from China are governments that encourage or force child-bearing and outlaw or limit access to contraception. Such a policy is called **pronatalist** (pro-birth). Traditionally, many governments have adopted such policies because population was seen as an element of national power. More babies today meant more soldiers later. Today, only a few governments have strongly pronatalist policies, but many do not make birth control or sex education available to poor women. In some such states, population is not considered a problem (and may even be seen as an asset); in other states, the government simply cannot afford effective measures to lower birthrates. According to the United Nations Population Fund (UNFPA), 200 million women do not have access to effective contraception.

Birthrates are heavily influenced by the status of women in society. In cultures that traditionally see women as valuable only in producing babies, great pressures exist against women who stop doing so. Many women do not use birth control because their husbands will not allow them to. These husbands may think that having many children is proof of their manliness. As women's status improves and they can work in various occupations, own property, and vote, women gain the power as well as the education and money necessary to limit the size of their families.

According to the UNFPA, improving the status of women is one of the most important means of controlling world population growth. Government policies about women's status vary from one state to another. International programs and agencies, such as the UN commission on the status of women, are working to address this issue on a global scale.

Disease

Population growth is determined by the death rate as well as the birthrate. People die from many different causes at different ages. In poor countries, people tend to die younger, often from infectious diseases; in richer countries, people live longer and die more often from cancer and heart disease. The proportion of babies who die within their first year is the **infant mortality rate.** It reflects a population's access to nutrition, water, shelter, and health care. In rich countries, infant mortality is 1 percent or less. In the poorest countries, it is as high as 20 percent, and it is even higher in local pockets of extreme poverty.

Although death rates vary greatly from one state or region to another, the overall trends are stable from decade to decade. Wars, droughts, epidemics, and disasters have an effect locally but hardly matter globally. In the poorest countries, which are just beginning the demographic transition, the death rate declined from nearly 30 deaths per thousand population in 1950 to less than 15 since 1990. In the industrialized countries, the death rate bottomed out around 10 per thousand by 1960 (now around 7). These stable trends in mortality mean that the death rate is not a means by which governments or international agencies can affect population growth—worsening poverty may cause famine and a rising death rate, but this is not a realistic way to control population growth. It would mean moving backward through the demographic transition, which would wreck any chance of lowering birthrates. Nor do wars kill enough people to reduce population growth. In short, most of the world is already at or near the end of the transition in *death* rates; the key question is how long birthrates take to complete the transition.

However, three mortality factors—AIDS, other infectious diseases, and smoking—deserve special attention because they exact very high costs even if they do not much affect global population trends. In these cases, actions taken in the short term have long-term and often international consequences, and once again there are short-term costs and long-term benefits.

HIV/AIDS   In the worldwide HIV/AIDS epidemic, one state's success or failure in limiting the spread of HIV (human immunodeficiency virus) affects infections in other states as well. There is a delay of 5 to 10 years after infection by the virus before symptoms appear, and during this period an infected individual can infect others (through sex or blood). AIDS spreads internationally—through business, tourism, migration, and military operations—reflecting the interdependence of states.

By 2008, the HIV/AIDS epidemic had already killed more than 30 million people, and an estimated 33 million more were infected—though most of them did not know it. Two-thirds of them live in Africa and half of the rest in South Asia (see Table 8.2). The

TABLE 8.2   Population and AIDS by World Region, 2008

Region[a]	Population (millions)	Population Growth Rate 1991–2006	HIV Infections (millions)
World	6,600	1.3%	33.0
Global North	1,375	0.3	3.1
Global South	5,225	1.6	29.9
of which:			
China/East Asia	1,350	1.0	0.7
Middle East	425	2.1	0.4
Latin America	575	1.6	1.9
South Asia	2,100	1.9	4.9
Africa (sub-Saharan)	775	2.5	22.0

[a]Regions do not exactly match those used elsewhere in this book.

Source: Calculated from *World Development Indicators.* World Bank, 2007. *AIDS Epidemic Update.* UNAIDS, 2007. In 2007, UNAIDS corrected earlier estimates, resulting in a significant drop in infection rates.

epidemic has also left 15 million orphans. Each year, 2.5 million people are newly infected with HIV, and 2 million die from AIDS, including nearly half a million children.

In Africa, already the world's poorest region, AIDS has emerged as one of several powerful forces driving the region backward into deeper poverty. About 5 percent of adults are infected with HIV, more than half of them women. In the most affected African countries in southern Africa, one in six adults has HIV (one in four for Botswana, the worst case). Infection is also rampant in African armies, with direct implications for international security.

In North America and other industrialized regions, new drug therapies (which keep the virus in check for years) dramatically lowered the death rate from AIDS starting in the late 1990s. But these treatments were too expensive to help much in Africa and other poor regions. India and Brazil began to export cheap generic versions of these drugs, violating patent rights of Western drug companies. The U.S. government threatened to punish South Africa and other countries if they allowed import of these drugs without compensating U.S. corporations holding patents. It filed a complaint against Brazil with the WTO. In response, AIDS activists demonstrated loudly and mobilized public opinion to get the policies changed.

The United States withdrew its complaint against Brazil in 2001. Meanwhile, drug companies began offering lower prices to poor countries, but delivery of the drugs to millions of poor people remained painfully slow. In 2004, the international community finally initiated the large-scale delivery of antiviral drugs to AIDS patients in poor countries. Now, tremendous progress has been made in delivering these drugs. In the past four years, the number of people receiving treatment has increased fivefold, to over 3 million (over 2 million alone in sub-Saharan Africa). Meanwhile, since 2003, the United States has provided nearly $20 billion to combat AIDS, and has pledged $48 billion to combat AIDS, tuberculosis, and malaria in 2009–2014.

In some ways, AIDS has deepened the global North-South division. The 2001 UN session also revealed sharp differences between Western, secular states and a number of Islamic states that objected to any reference to gay people. Catholic authorities, furthermore, objected to programs that encourage condom use. But the most effective prevention measures are public education and the distribution of condoms (especially to prostitutes) and clean needles to drug users. All of these are culturally and politically sensitive issues.

States must cooperate with each other if they are to bring the epidemic under control. These international efforts are coordinated primarily by WHO and funded mainly by the industrialized countries. But the entire WHO budget is equivalent to that of a midsize hospital in the global North. WHO depends on national governments to provide information and carry out policies, and governments have been slow to respond. Some governments falsify statistics to underreport the number of cases (lest tourists be driven away), and many governments do not want to condone or sponsor sex education and distribution of condoms because of religious or cultural taboos.

In recent years, HIV has spread rapidly in South Asia, China, and Russia/Eastern Europe, where prostitution and drug use are growing. In China, the government has been slow to act, and a stigma still prevents effective identification or treatment of the rapidly growing HIV-positive population. China had an estimated 1 million infected people in 2005, with projections of 10 million or more by 2010.

Overall, worldwide, the AIDS epidemic is on track to kill more people in this decade than died in both world wars together—about 100 million people. The international response to the AIDS epidemic is crucial in its ultimate course. AIDS illustrates the transnational linkages that make international borders less meaningful than in the past. Effective international cooperation could save millions of lives and significantly enhance the prospects for economic development in the poorest countries in the coming decades. But once again, a collective goods problem exists regarding the allocation of costs and benefits from such efforts. A dollar spent by WHO has the same effect regardless of which country contributed it.

VIDEO

The Next Flu Epidemic

Other Infectious Diseases AIDS is the most severe epidemic of infectious disease in the world, but not the only concern. Tuberculosis (TB), malaria, hepatitis, dengue fever, and cholera have all reemerged or spread in recent decades, often mutating into drug-resistant forms that are increasingly difficult to treat. TB now kills 1.5 million people per year (in addition to AIDS patients who also contract TB). Malaria sickens hundreds of millions of people and kills more than a million per year, nearly all in Africa. New campaigns have distributed millions of mosquito nets in Africa to reduce malaria—a proven, cost-effective measure. Meanwhile, new and poorly understood diseases have emerged, among them HIV, the Ebola virus, hantavirus, and hepatitis C. Pneumonia, influenza, diarrhea-causing diseases, and measles all continue to be major problems but are not growing or spreading to the same extent. Vaccination programs have reduced the incidence of both polio and measles in recent years. Epidemics among animals, such as mad cow disease and bird flu, have major economic effects. Currently, scientists fear that bird flu could mutate and spread person to person, sparking a global pandemic that could potentially kill millions. In 2009, swine flu spread quickly across the globe, rekindling fears of a global health epidemic and leading various countries to restrict travel to Mexico (where the flu originated).

PANDEMIC PREVENTION

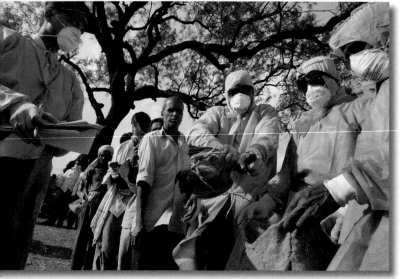

In 2006, avian influenza (bird flu) spread rapidly across much of the world, outpacing the small and poorly funded international institutions devoted to global health, such as the World Health Organization. If bird flu mutates to spread easily from person to person, it could cause a pandemic that could kill millions. Here, in a scene repeated in dozens of countries with millions of domestic birds, health workers in India dispose of infected chickens, 2006. In 2009, an outbreak of swine flu combining pig, bird, and human viruses triggered a world health emergency.

Smoking Worldwide, more than a billion people smoke, five-sixths of them in developing countries, and 5 million people a year die from tobacco-related disease. States that fail to curb the spread of nicotine addiction face high future costs in health care—costs that are just beginning to come due in many poor countries. The costs are largely limited to the state itself; its own citizens and economy pay the price. Nonetheless, the tobacco trade makes smoking an international issue. Tobacco companies' recent marketing campaigns targeting women in the global South could produce a huge increase in smokers in that group, according to the World Health Organization.

In 2001, tobacco companies, with some U.S. support, sought to weaken a new proposed treaty, the Framework Convention on Tobacco Control, but in 2003 the United States dropped its objections and WHO member states adopted the treaty, which entered into force in 2005. Member states will ban tobacco advertising within five years and will be encouraged to raise taxes on tobacco 5 percent a year above the inflation rate. The United States, alone among the world's major powers, still had not ratified the treaty in 2009.

In managing the daunting environmental and disease threats discussed in this chapter, states and NGOs have begun to use new technologies productively. Information technologies, especially, allow scientists to confirm global warming, NGOs to mobilize public opinion, and MNCs to produce more fuel-efficient cars. This information revolution also has far-reaching consequences for world politics far beyond issues of environmental management. The remainder of this chapter discusses these profound, yet still ambiguous, consequences.

The Power of Information

Global telecommunications are profoundly changing how information and culture function in international relations. These technological advances, at the center of globalization, are bringing the identity principle to the fore as communities interact across distances and borders. Newly empowered individuals and groups are creating new transnational networks worldwide, bypassing states.

Networking the World

New international political possibilities are based on technological developments. The media over which information travels—telephones, television, films, magazines, and so forth—shape the way ideas take form and spread from one place to another. The media with the strongest political impact are television, radio, phones, and the Internet.

VIDEO

Obama Addresses the Muslim World

TV and Radio   There are nearly 2 billion TV sets and 3 billion radio receivers in the world. The power of these media lies in their ability to reproduce a single source of information in many copies in many locations. Radio, and increasingly TV, reaches the poorest rural areas of the global South. Peasants who cannot read can understand radio. Shortwave radio—typically stations such as Voice of America (VOA) and the British Broadcasting Corporation (BBC)—is very popular in remote locations. TV is especially powerful. The combination of pictures and sounds affects viewers emotionally and intellectually. Independent TV news channels have attracted large audiences in India, Pakistan, and Nepal.

Ordinary over-the-air TV and radio signals are radio waves carried on specific frequencies. Frequencies are a limited resource in high demand, which governments regulate and allocate to users. Because radio waves do not respect national borders, the allocation of frequencies is a subject of interstate bargaining. International regimes have grown up around the regulation of international communications technologies.

Satellite transmissions bypass the normal over-the-air radio spectrum and transmit signals over a huge area to dish-shaped antennas. This capability, bypassing states' control, fortifies transnational or supranational identity politics by allowing, for example, all Arabs in the world to see Arab satellite TV coverage of the Palestinian issue. The Qatar-based all-news satellite TV network al Jazeera, begun in 1996, has become a force in Middle Eastern politics. It reaches an influential audience across the region and world. In a 2006 poll in six Arab countries, citizens listed al Jazeera as their main source of international news by a large margin over any other satellite TV network.

Images and sounds are being recorded, reproduced, and viewed in new ways through video cameras and cell phone cameras. These tools empower ordinary citizens to create their own visual records, such as videos of political demonstrations in one country that end up on the TV news in another country. In 2007, these capabilities were dramatically demonstrated when a cell phone video of Saddam Hussein's execution (showing him being taunted by Shi'ite guards) spread instantly on the Internet and provoked outrage among Sunni Iraqis.

Telephone and Internet   Even more empowering of ordinary citizens are telephones and the Internet. Unlike TV and radio, these are two-way media through which users interact among themselves without any centralized information source. Telephones, perhaps more than any other technology, make individuals international actors. The minutes of international phone traffic worldwide quadrupled from 1991 to 2004, a clear indicator of globalization.

Growth of phone and Internet use worldwide has been explosive in

LET'S TALK

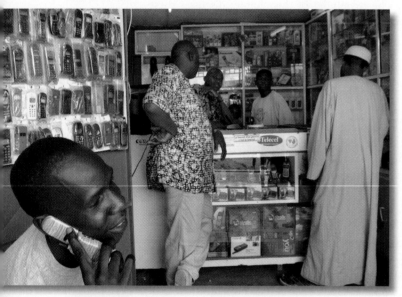

Global communication, a very new capability on the time scale of the international system, is changing the rules of IR and empowering nonstate transnational actors. Telecommunications could change the path of development in poor countries, possibly bypassing traditional infrastructure such as phone lines and leapfrogging to a wireless networked economy. Cheap phones and prepaid calling cards are putting cell phones in reach of a growing segment of the population in the global South. This shop does a brisk business in Abidjan, Ivory Coast, 2001.

FIGURE 8.8   World Phone and Internet Use, 1995–2007

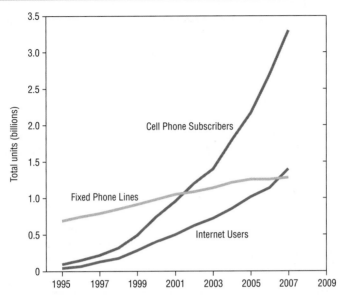

Source: ITU data.

the past decade (see Figure 8.8), with cell phones leading this explosion of connectivity. Nearly 3 billion people had cell phones in 2008, and well over a billion used the Internet—in each case representing a 25-fold increase in a decade.

In Africa, cheap cell phones with cheap prepaid calling cards have let millions of relatively poor individuals bypass the very few land lines previously needed to communicate. In about a decade, sub-Saharan Africa has seen subscribers increase from near zero to more than 200 million. Almost 90 percent of telephone users in Africa use cell phones rather than land lines (versus 60 percent in the United States).

The Digital Divide   Taken on its own, the addition of phone and Internet capability in poor countries is impressive. But in comparison with rich regions, the gap keeps growing (see Figure 8.9). A person living in the global North is four times as likely as a person in the global South to have a land line or cell phone, and eight times as likely to use the Internet. This gap, along with the gap in access to information technologies *within* countries, is known as the **digital divide.**

As the Internet wires parts of the world into a tight network centered on the United States, Europe, and East Asia—where more than 90 percent of Web users live—other regions are largely left out. Poor countries and poor people cannot afford computers, which cost the equivalent of years' worth of wages for a typical person in a poor country. Users of the World Wide Web in 2007 made up nearly 75 percent of the population in the United States, 21 percent in Russia, 7 percent in South Asia, and 5 percent in

FIGURE 8.9   The North-South Digital Divide, 1994–2007

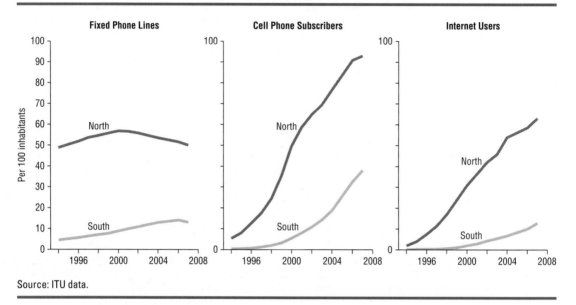

Source: ITU data.

Africa. The explosive growth of Internet use is occurring mainly among the richest strata of the world's people.

Some activists hope that the Internet can transform poor villages in the global South, partly by letting them produce traditional goods locally and market them globally. In one successful experiment in India in recent years, a businessman placed computer screens with pointing and clicking devices and high-speed Internet access in walls and kiosks in very poor slums. In each location, neighborhood kids quickly gathered, taught themselves to browse the Internet, and even invented their own terminology to describe the unfamiliar cursor and icons on the screen. This small-scale "hole-in-the-wall experiment" shows that simple methods can go far to break down the digital divide between the world's rich and poor.

Information as a Tool of Governments

VIDEO

America's Arabic TV Channel

With more information traveling around the world than ever before, information has become an important instrument of governments' power (domestic and interstate). Above all, governments want *access to information*. In 1992, U.S. secretary of state James Baker made his first visit to the newly independent Asian republics of the former Soviet Union. At each stop, one of the first questions Baker was asked by the state leader was, "How do I get CNN?" CNN, state leaders hoped, would tie them directly to the Western world and symbolize their independence from Russia.

With today's information technologies, it is easier for governments to gather, organize, and store huge amounts of information. In this respect, the information revolution empowers governments more than ever. In the past, a wanted criminal, drug lord, or terrorist could slip over the border and take refuge in a foreign country. Today, however, it is more likely that a routine traffic ticket in the foreign country could trigger an instant directive to arrest the person. These technologies are now being mobilized in force to strengthen counterterrorism.

Just as citizens and terrorists find it harder to hide from governments, so are state governments finding it harder to hide information from each other. The military importance of satellite reconnaissance has been mentioned (see p. 145). A powerful state such as the United States can increase its power through information technologies. It can and does monitor phone calls, faxes, data transmissions, and radio conversations in foreign countries.

As the cost of information technology decreases, it comes into the reach of more states. Now small states can gain some of the same capabilities electronically. Even sophisticated information is more available and cheaper—high-resolution satellite photos are now available commercially and cheap or free. These images can be used for both military purposes and natural resource management.

HOT OFF THE PRESS

Information, which easily crosses state borders, is a major factor in both international and domestic politics and may even be laying technological foundations for a global identity. Governments have many ways to try to control information. Here a staff member of Kenya's daily newspaper surveys the damage after police—responding to unfavorable coverage of the president—stormed its offices and burned tens of thousands of copies, 2006.

Most governments (but not the U.S. government) own and operate at least one main TV station, and many hold a monopoly on TV stations. Thus TV signals often rank with military equipment and currency as capabilities so important to a government that it must control them itself. Indeed, in a military coup d'état, usually one of the first and most important targets seized is the television broadcasting facility.

Information as a Tool against Governments

Information can be used against governments as well, by foreign governments, NGOs, or domestic political opponents. Governments, especially repressive ones, fear the free flow of information, for good reason. When they are allowed to circulate among a population, ideas become a powerful force that can sweep aside governments. New information technologies have become powerful tools of domestic opposition movements and their allies in foreign governments. Television coverage fed popular discontent regarding the U.S. war in Vietnam in the 1960s and 1970s, and the Russian war in Chechnya in 1995.

In Iran, millions of people use the Internet to talk about taboo topics such as sex, fashion, and politics. Stores sell prepaid Internet cards good for ten hours of access. More than 100 million Chinese use the Internet, though not uncensored. Both Iran and China want the economic benefits of information on the Internet, despite their governments' usual impulse to control access to information.

In the Philippines in 2001, huge protests that swept a president from office were organized through text messages on cell phones. In Ghana, very popular talk shows on private FM radio programs—allowed after 1995—gave voice to ordinary people who then threw out the ruling party in 2000. The global peace demonstrations preceding the 2003 Iraq War used information technologies to turn out millions of people in dozens of countries on short notice.

To counteract such uses of information, governments throughout the world try to limit the flow of unfavorable information—especially information from foreign sources. For example, China, like several other developing countries, channels all access to the Internet through a few state-controlled service providers and filters the hundreds of billions of text messages exchanged annually among 300 million Chinese cell phone subscribers. The U.S. company Google, complying with Chinese law but angering critics, blocks politically sensitive words from its Chinese search engine.

All in all, the tide of technology seems to be running against governments. Information gets through, and no political power seems capable of holding it back for long. As more and more communication channels carry more information to more places, governments become just another player in a crowded field.

Telecommunications and Global Culture

As the information revolution continues to unfold, it will further increase international interdependence, making actions in one state reverberate in other states more strongly than in the past. Information is thus slowly undermining realists' assumptions of state sovereignty and territorial integrity. At the same time, by empowering substate and transnational actors, information technology is undermining the centrality of states themselves in world affairs.

The information revolution greatly increases *transparency* in international relations. As a result, states do not need to arm against unknown potential threats because they see the real threats. Similarly, the ability to monitor performance of agreements makes collective goods problems easier to resolve because cheaters and free riders can be identified. Moreover, the ability of governments to bargain effectively with each other and to reach mutually beneficial outcomes is enhanced by the availability of instant communications channels. In these ways, the increased transparency allowed by new technologies strengthens the reciprocity principle as a solution to IR conflicts. The complex monitoring and accounting required in international agreements based on reciprocity—from trade deals to arms control—comes much easier in a transparent world.

Telecommunications, with its ability to connect communities beyond geographic space, is also strengthening the identity principle in IR because people's identities have new sources and new avenues of expression that often transcend national borders. In the past, nationalism tapped into the psychological dynamics of group identity in a powerful way that legitimized the state as the ultimate embodiment of its people's aspirations and identity. Now the information revolution may aid the development of transnational or supranational identities. So far, however, nationalism continues to hold the upper hand.

Although a global culture is still only nascent and the most powerful identity is still at the national level, people have begun to participate in specific communities that bridge national boundaries. Journalists, scientists, and church members work in communities spanning national borders. So do members of transnational movements, such as those linking women from various countries, or environmentalists, or human rights activists. The links forged in such transnational communities may create a new functionalism that could encourage international integration on a global scale.

Sports also create transnational communities. Citizens of different states share their admiration of sports stars, who become international celebrities. The Olympics (run by the International Olympic Committee, an NGO) is a global event with a worldwide audience. The U.S.-Chinese rapprochement of 1971 was so delicate that political cooperation was impossible until the way had first been paved by sports—the U.S. table tennis team that made the first official U.S. visit to China.

Finally, tourism also builds transnational communities. International tourists cross borders 500 million times a year. Tourism ranks among the top export industries worldwide. People who travel to other countries often develop both a deeper understanding and a deeper appreciation for them. Added to these contacts are exchange students and those who attend college in a foreign country.

Like international integration and globalization generally, global culture has its downside. The emerging global culture is primarily the culture of white Europeans and their descendants in rich areas of the world (mixed slightly with cultural elements of Japan and local elites in the global South). This cultural dominance has been referred to as **cultural imperialism.** For many people, especially in the global South, the information revolution carrying global culture into their midst is, despite its empowering potential, an invasive force in practice. For example, half of the world's nearly 7,000 languages risk extinction this century.

Above all, the emerging global culture is dominated by the world's superpower, the United States; U.S. cultural influence is at least as strong as U.S. military influence. Culture may be just another economic product, to be produced in the place of greatest comparative advantage, but culture also is central to national identity and politics. The prospect of cultural imperialism thus opens another front in the conflict of liberalism and mercantilism. Even the architecture of cyberspace assumes the United States as the default in such domain names as .gov (U.S. government) and .mil (U.S. military). At the

MAC ATTACK

Some call it "global community"; others, "cultural imperialism." The power of information, opening up a wave of globalization in international business, is bringing together cultures in sometimes incongruous ways. Chinese leaders seemed unsure for years about whether McDonald's brought Western-style prosperity or spiritual pollution—maybe a bit of each.

UN-sponsored World Summit on the Information Society in 2005, Europe and developing countries tried unsuccessfully to break the monopoly held by a U.S. consortium over registering domain names, including country-code domains such as ".uk" (Britain) and ".cn" (China) that states want to control as a matter of national sovereignty.

These supranational cultural influences are still in their infancy. Over the coming years and decades, their shape will become clearer, and scholars will be able to determine more accurately how they influence world politics and state sovereignty.

Conclusion

Ultimately the conflicts and dramas of international relations are the problems of human society—struggles for power and wealth, efforts to cooperate despite differences, social dilemmas and collective goods problems, the balance between freedom and order, and trade-offs of equity versus efficiency and of long-term versus short-term outcomes. These themes are inescapable in human society, from the smallest groups to the world community. The subject of international relations is in this sense an extension of everyday life and a reflection of the choices of individual human beings. IR belongs to all of us—North and South, women and men, citizens and leaders—who live together on this planet.

This book has shown that in IR, more than other social settings, collective goods problems pose formidable challenges to successful cooperation among the large number of independent (state and nonstate) actors. With no central government to enforce order, actors in IR have developed three kinds of solutions to collective goods problems—our three core principles. Countries turn to the dominance principle most often in international security affairs, especially military force (Chapter 4). The identity principle matters most in the remarkable process of integration (Chapters 6 and 8). Most important, however, is the reciprocity principle, which underlies international treaties, law, and organizations from the UN to the WTO. Characteristic solutions based on the reciprocity principle are complicated, take forever to agree upon, and require extensive monitoring of compliance thereafter. But woven together, these reciprocity-based agreements offer the basis for an international system that has moved over centuries from extreme war-proneness to ever stronger peace and prosperity—notwithstanding the world's many serious remaining problems.

One major theme of this book is the nature of the international system as a well-developed set of rules based on state sovereignty, territoriality, and "anarchy"—a lack of central government. Yet the international system is becoming more complex, more nuanced, and more interconnected with other aspects of planetary society. State sovereignty is now challenged by the principle of self-determination. International norms have begun to limit the right of government to rule a population by force against its will and to violate human rights. Territorial integrity is also problematic, because national borders do not stop information, environmental changes, or missiles. Information allows actors—state, substate, and supranational—to know what is going on everywhere in the world to coordinate actions globally.

Technological development is just one aspect of the profound, yet incremental, changes taking place in international relations. New actors are gaining power; long-standing principles are becoming less effective; and new challenges are arising for states, groups, and individuals alike.

Technology is also profoundly changing the utility and role of military force. The power of defensive weaponry makes successful attacks more difficult, and the power of offensive weaponry makes retaliation an extremely potent threat to deter an attack. The 20th-century superpowers could not attack each other without destroying themselves. Today technology plays key roles on both sides in counterinsurgency wars such as in Iraq and the other 12 active wars in the world.

Nonmilitary forms of leverage, particularly economic rewards, have become much more important power capabilities. The post–Cold War era is a peaceful one, yet the peace is fragile. Will this era, like past postwar eras, lapse slowly into the next prewar era, or will it lead to a robust and lasting "permanent peace" such as Kant imagined?

In IPE, we see simultaneous trends toward integration and disintegration among states. People continue to speak their own language, to fly their own flag, and to use their own currency with its pictures and emblems. Nationalism continues to be an important force. At the same time, however, although people identify with their state, they also now hold competing identities based on ethnic ties, gender, and (in the case of Europe) region. In international trade, liberal economics prevails because it works so well. States have learned that to survive they must help the creation of wealth by MNCs and other actors.

Environmental damage may become the single greatest obstacle to sustained economic growth in both the North and South. Because of high costs, the large number of actors, and collective goods problems, international bargaining over the environment is difficult.

Meanwhile, North-South relations are moving to the center of world politics. Demographic and economic trends are sharpening the global North-South gap, with the North continuing to accumulate wealth while much of the South lags. Ultimately, the North will bear a high cost for failing to address the economic development of the South. Perhaps, by using computerization and biotechnology innovations, poor states can develop their economies more efficiently and sustainably than did Europe or North America.

The future is unknowable now, but as it unfolds you can compare it—at mileposts along the way—to the worlds that you desire and expect. For example, you could ask questions such as the following (asking yourself, for each one, why you answer the way you do for your desired future and expected future):

1. Will state sovereignty be eroded by supranational authority?
2. Will norms of human rights and democracy become global?
3. Will the UN evolve into a quasi-government for the world?
4. Will the UN be restructured?
5. Will World Court judgments become enforceable?
6. Will the number of states increase?
7. Will China become democratic? Will it become rich?
8. What effects will information technologies have on IR?
9. Will weapons of mass destruction proliferate?
10. Will military leverage become obsolete?

11. Will disarmament occur?
12. Will women participate more fully in IR? With what effect?
13. Will there be a single world currency?
14. Will there be a global free trade regime?
15. Will nationalism fade out or continue to be strong?
16. Will many people develop a global identity?
17. Will world culture become more homogeneous or more pluralistic?
18. Will the EU or other regional IOs achieve political union?
19. Will global environmental destruction be severe? How soon?
20. Will new technologies avert environmental constraints?
21. Will global problems create stronger or weaker world order?
22. Will population growth level out? If so, when and at what level?
23. Will the poorest countries accumulate wealth? How soon?
24. What role will the North play in the South's development?

The choices you make and actions you take will ultimately affect the world you live in. You cannot opt out of involvement in international relations. You are involved, and year by year the information revolution and other aspects of interdependence are drawing you more closely into contact with the rest of the world. You can act in many ways to bring the world you expect more into line with the world you desire. You can empower yourself by finding the actions and choices that define your place in international relations.

Now that you have completed the studies covered in this book, don't stop here. Keep learning about the world beyond your country's borders. Keep thinking about the world that might exist. Be a part of the changes that will carry this world through the coming decades. It's your world: study it, care for it, make it your own.

CHAPTER REVIEW

SUMMARY

- Environmental problems are an example of international interdependence and often create collective goods problems for the states involved. The large numbers of actors involved in global environmental problems make them especially difficult to solve.

- To resolve such collective goods problems, states have used international regimes and IOs, and have in some cases extended state sovereignty (notably over territorial waters).

- Global warming results from burning fossil fuels—the basis of industrial economies today. The industrialized states are much more responsible for the problem than are states in the global South, but countries such as China and India also contribute to the problem. Solutions are difficult to reach because costs are substantial and dangers are somewhat distant and uncertain.

- Damage to the earth's ozone layer results from the use of specific chemicals, which are now being phased out under international agreements. Unlike global warming, the costs of solutions are much lower and the problem is better understood.

- Many species are threatened with extinction due to loss of habitats such as rain forests. An international treaty on biodiversity and an agreement on forests aim to reduce the destruction of local ecosystems, with costs spread among states.

- The UN Convention on the Law of the Sea (UNCLOS) establishes an ocean regime that puts most commercial fisheries and offshore oil under control of states as territorial waters.

- Pollution—including acid rain, water and air pollution, and toxic and nuclear waste—tends to be more localized than global and has been addressed mainly through unilateral, bilateral, and regional measures rather than global ones.

- Most Western states import energy resources, mostly oil, whereas the other world regions export them. Oil prices rose dramatically in the 1970s, declined in the 1980s, and have been high since 2000. Such fluctuations undermine world economic stability.

- The most important source of oil traded worldwide is the Persian Gulf area of the Middle East. Consequently, this area has long been a focal point of international political conflict.

- World population—now at 6.8 billion—will reach about 8 billion by 2030 and may eventually level out around 9 to 10 billion. Virtually all of the increase will come in the global South.

- Future world population growth will be largely driven by the demographic transition. Death rates have fallen throughout the world, but birthrates will fall proportionally only as per capita incomes go up.

- Government policies can reduce birthrates somewhat at a given level of per capita income. Effective policies are those that improve access to birth control and raise the status of women.

- The global AIDS epidemic will impose huge costs on many poor states in the coming years. Currently, 33 million people are infected with HIV, and 30 million more have died. Most are in Africa, and new infections are growing rapidly in Asia and Russia.

- Supranational relationships and identities are being fostered by new information technologies, though such a process is still at an early stage. Access to these technologies is very unequal between rich and poor countries.

- Government access to information increases the stability of international relationships. Collective goods problems are made less difficult in a transparent world where governments have information about each other's actions.

- The greater and freer flow of information around the world can undermine the authority and power of governments as well. Information technologies can empower ordinary citizens and contribute to transnational and supranational structures that bypass the state.

- Telecommunications are contributing to the development of global cultural integration. Transnational communities are developing in areas such as sports, music, and tourism. However, cultural imperialism may result if such a culture is too strongly dominated by the United States.

KEY TERMS

tragedy of the
  commons   307
enclosure   308
global warming   309
UN Environment
  Program
  (UNEP)   311
greenhouse
  gases   311
Kyoto Protocol   312
ozone layer   313

Montreal
  Protocol   313
biodiversity   314
International Whaling
  Commission   315
high seas   317
UN Convention on the
  Law of the Sea
  (UNCLOS)   317
Antarctic Treaty
  of 1959   319

acid rain   319
demographic
  transition   327
pronatalist   329
infant mortality
  rate   329
digital divide   335
cultural
  imperialism   339

ONLINE PRACTICE TEST

Take an online practice test at
www.IRtext.com

❑ **A**
▸❑ **B**
❑ **C**
❑ **D**

CRITICAL THINKING QUESTIONS

1. Does the record of the international community on environmental management reflect the views of mercantilists, liberals, or both? In what ways?

2. Dozens of poor states appear to be stuck midway through the demographic transition; death rates have fallen, birthrates remain high, and per capita incomes are not increasing. How do you think these states, with or without foreign assistance, can best get unstuck and complete the demographic transition?

3. What are the good and bad effects, in your opinion, of the emergence of global communications and culture? Should we be cheering or lamenting the possibility of one world culture? Does the answer depend on where one lives in the world? Give concrete examples of the effects you discuss.

BACK TO THE BIG PICTURE

To hear a discussion of the "big picture" for this chapter, raised on p. 307, along with an example from recent history, consult the "IR Talk" podcast for Chapter 8 at *www.IRtext.com*

PODCAST

Glossary

acid rain   Rain caused by air pollution that damages trees and often crosses borders. Limiting acid rain (via limiting nitrogen oxide emissions) has been the subject of several regional agreements. (p. 319)

airspace   The space above a state that is considered its territory, in contrast to outer space, which is considered international territory. (p. 137)

alliance cohesion   The ease with which the members hold together an alliance; it tends to be high when national interests converge and when cooperation among allies becomes institutionalized. (p. 50)

Amnesty International   An influential nongovernmental organization that operates globally to monitor and try to rectify glaring abuses of political (not economic or social) human rights. (p. 252)

anarchy   In IR theory, a term that implies not complete chaos but the lack of a central government that can enforce rules. (p. 41)

arms race   A reciprocal process in which two or more states build up military capabilities in response to each other. (p. 56)

autarky   A policy of self-reliance, avoiding or minimizing trade and trying to produce everything one needs (or the most vital things) by oneself. (p. 171)

balance of payments   A summary of all the flows of money into and out of a country. It includes three types of international transactions: the current account (including the merchandise trade balance), flows of capital, and changes in reserves. (p. 198)

balance of power   The general concept of one or more states' power being used to balance that of another state or group of states. The term can refer to (1) any ratio of

power capabilities between states or alliances, (2) a relatively equal ratio, or (3) the process by which counterbalancing coalitions have repeatedly formed to prevent one state from conquering an entire region. (p. 43)

balance of trade   The value of a state's exports relative to its imports. (p. 167)

ballistic missile   The major strategic delivery vehicle for nuclear weapons; it carries a warhead along a trajectory (typically rising at least 50 miles high) and lets it drop on the target. (p. 151) See also *intercontinental ballistic missiles (ICBMs)*.

basic human needs   The fundamental needs of people for adequate food, shelter, health care, sanitation, and education. Meeting such needs may be thought of as both a moral imperative and a form of investment in "human capital" essential for economic growth. (p. 262)

bilateral aid   Government assistance that goes directly to governments as state-to-state aid. (p. 296)

biodiversity   The tremendous diversity of plant and animal species making up the earth's (global, regional, and local) ecosystems. (p. 314)

Biological Weapons Convention (1972) An agreement that prohibits the development, production, and possession of biological weapons, but makes no provision for inspections. (p. 154)

brain drain   Poor countries' loss of skilled workers to rich countries. (p. 291)

Bretton Woods system   A post–World War II arrangement for managing the world economy, established at a meeting in Bretton Woods, New Hampshire, in 1944. Its main institutional components are the World Bank and the International Monetary Fund (IMF). (p. 197)

burden sharing   The distribution of the costs of an alliance among members; the term also refers to the conflicts that may arise over such distribution. (p. 50)

cartel   An association of producers or consumers (or both) of a certain product, formed for the purpose of manipulating its price on the world market. (p. 178)

cash crop   An agricultural good produced as a commodity for export to world markets. (p. 267)

central bank   An institution common in industrialized countries whose major tasks are to maintain the value of the state's currency and to control inflation. (p. 196)

centrally planned economy   An economy in which political authorities set prices and decide on quotas for production and consumption of each commodity according to a long-term plan. (p. 185)

Chemical Weapons Convention (1992)   An agreement that bans the production and possession of chemical weapons and includes strict verification provisions and the threat of sanctions against violators and nonparticipants in the treaty. (p. 153)

civil war   A war between factions within a state trying to create, or prevent, a new government for the entire state or some territorial part of it. (p. 112)

Cold War   The hostile relations—punctuated by occasional periods of improvement, or détente—between the two superpowers, the United States and the Soviet Union, from 1945 to 1990. (p. 24)

collective goods problem   A tangible or intangible good, created by the members of a group, that is available to all group members regardless of their individual contributions; participants can gain by lowering their own contribution to the collective good, yet if too many participants do so, the good cannot be provided. (p. 3)

collective security   The formation of a broad alliance of most major actors in an international system for the purpose of jointly opposing aggression by any actor; sometimes seen as presupposing the existence of a universal organization (such as the United Nations) to which both the aggressor and its opponents belong. (p. 69) See also *League of Nations*.

Common Agricultural Policy (CAP)   A European Union policy based on the principle that a subsidy extended to farmers in any member country should be extended to farmers in all member countries. (p. 232)

common market   A zone in which labor and capital (as well as goods) flow freely across borders. (p. 232)

comparative advantage   The principle that says states should specialize in trading goods that they produce with the greatest relative efficiency and at the lowest relative cost (relative, that is, to other goods produced by the same state). (p. 168)

compellence   The use of force to make another actor take some action (rather than, as in deterrence, refrain from taking an action). (p. 56)

Comprehensive Test Ban Treaty (CTBT) (1996)   A treaty that bans all nuclear weapons testing, thereby broadening the ban on atmospheric testing negotiated in 1963. (p. 158)

conditionality   See *IMF conditionality*.

conflict   A difference in preferred outcomes in a bargaining situation. (p. 113)

conflict and cooperation   The types of actions that states take toward each other through time. (p. 9)

conflict resolution   The development and implementation of peaceful strategies for settling conflicts. (p. 93) constructivism   A movement in IR theory that examines how changing international norms and actors' identities help shape the content of state interests. (p. 87)

containment   A policy adopted in the late 1940s by which the United States sought to halt the global expansion of Soviet influence on several levels—military, political, ideological, and economic. (p. 24)

convertible currency   See *hard currency*.

cost-benefit analysis   A calculation of the costs incurred by a possible action and the benefits it is likely to bring. (p. 57)

Council of the European Union   A European Union institution in which the relevant ministers (foreign, economic, agriculture, finance, etc.) of each member state meet to enact legislation and reconcile national interests. Formerly known as the Council of Ministers. When the meeting takes place among the state leaders, it is called the "European Council." (p. 234) See also *European Commission*.

counterinsurgency   An effort to combat guerrilla armies, often including programs to "win the hearts and minds" of rural populations so that they stop sheltering guerrillas. (p. 140)

coup d'état   The seizure of political power by domestic military forces—that is, a change of political power outside the state's constitutional order. (p. 159)

crimes against humanity   A category of legal offenses created at the Nuremberg trials after World War II to encompass genocide and other acts committed by the political and military leaders of the Third Reich (Nazi Germany). (p. 252) See also *genocide*.

cruise missile   A small winged missile that can navigate across thousands of miles of previously mapped terrain to reach a particular target; it can carry either a nuclear or a conventional warhead. (p. 154)

Cuban Missile Crisis (1962)   A superpower crisis, sparked by the Soviet Union's installation of medium-range nuclear missiles in Cuba, that marks the moment when the United States and the Soviet Union came closest to nuclear war. (p. 26)

cultural imperialism   A term critical of U.S. dominance of the emerging global culture. (p. 339)

customs union   A common external tariff adopted by members of a free trade area; that is, participating states adopt a unified set of tariffs with regard to goods coming in from outside. (p. 232) See also *free trade area*.

debt renegotiation   A reworking of the terms on which a loan will be repaid; frequently negotiated by poor debtor governments in order to avoid default. (p. 291)

default   Failure to make scheduled debt payments. (p. 291)

democratic peace   The proposition, strongly supported by empirical evidence, that democracies almost never fight wars against each other (although they do fight against authoritarian states). (p. 70)

demographic transition   The pattern of falling death rates, followed by falling birthrates, that generally accompanies industrialization and economic development. (p. 327)

dependency theory   A Marxist-oriented theory that explains the lack of capital accumulation in poor countries as a result of the interplay between domestic class relations and the forces of foreign capital. (p. 277) See also *enclave economy*.

deterrence   The threat to punish another actor if it takes a certain negative action (especially attacking one's own state or one's allies). (p. 56) See also *mutually assured destruction (MAD)*.

devaluation   A unilateral move to reduce the value of a currency by changing a fixed or official exchange rate. (p. 194) See also *exchange rate*.

developing countries States in the global South, the poorest regions of the world—also called third world countries, less-developed countries, and undeveloped countries. (p. 260)

Development Assistance Committee (DAC) A committee whose members—consisting of states from Western Europe, North America, and Japan/Pacific—provide 95 percent of official development assistance to countries of the global South. (p. 296) See also *foreign assistance*.

difference feminism A strand of feminism that believes gender differences are not just socially constructed and that views women as inherently less warlike than men (on average). (p. 97)

digital divide The gap in access to information technologies between rich and poor people, and between the global North and South. (p. 335)

diplomatic immunity A privilege under which diplomats' activities fall outside the jurisdiction of the host country's national courts. (p. 247)

diplomatic recognition The process by which the status of embassies and that of an ambassador as an official state representative are explicitly defined. (p. 247)

disaster relief Provision of short-term relief in the form of food, water, shelter, clothing, and other essentials to people facing natural disasters. (p. 299)

discount rate The interest rate charged by governments when they lend money to private banks. The discount rate is set by countries' central banks. (p. 196)

Doha Round A series of negotiations under the World Trade Organization that began in Doha, Qatar, in 2001. It followed the *Uruguay Round* and has focused on agricultural subsidies, intellectual property, and other issues. (p. 176)

dominance A principle for solving collective goods problems by imposing solutions hierarchically. (p. 5)

dumping The sale of products in foreign markets at prices below the minimum level necessary to make a profit (or below cost). (p. 173)

economic classes A categorization of individuals based on economic status. (p. 91)

economic development The combined processes of capital accumulation, rising per capita incomes (with consequent falling birthrates), the increasing of skills in the population, the adoption of new technological styles, and other related social and economic changes. (p. 278)

economic liberalism In the context of IPE, an approach that generally shares the assumption of anarchy (the lack of a world government) but does not see this condition as precluding extensive cooperation to realize common gains from economic exchanges. It emphasizes absolute over relative gains and, in practice, a commitment to free trade, free capital flows, and an "open" world economy. (p. 165) See also *mercantilism* and *neoliberal*.

electronic warfare Use of the electromagnetic spectrum (radio waves, radar, infrared, etc.) in war, such as employing electromagnetic signals for one's own benefit while denying their use to an enemy. (p. 146)

enclave economy A historically important form of dependency in which foreign capital is invested in a developing country to extract a particular raw material in a particular place—usually a mine, oil well, or plantation. (p. 277) See also *dependency theory*.

enclosure The splitting of a common area or good into privately owned pieces, giving individual owners an incentive to manage resources responsibly. (p. 308)

ethnic cleansing Forced displacement of an ethnic group or groups from a particular territory, accompanied by massacres and other human rights violations; it has occurred after the breakup of multinational states, notably in the former Yugoslavia. (p. 134)

ethnic groups Large groups of people who share ancestral, language, cultural, or religious ties and a common identity. (p. 117)

ethnocentrism The tendency to see one's own group (in-group) in favorable terms and an out-group in unfavorable terms. (p. 120)

Euratom An organization created by the Treaty of Rome in 1957 to coordinate nuclear power development by pooling research, investment, and management. (p. 231)

euro Also called the ECU (European currency unit); a single European currency used by 16 members of the European Union (EU). (p. 236)

European Commission A European Union body whose members, while appointed by states, are supposed to represent EU interests. Supported by a multinational civil service in Brussels, the commission's role is to identify problems and propose solutions to the Council of the European Union. (p. 233) See also *Council of the European Union.*

European Court of Justice A judicial arm of the European Union, based in Luxembourg. The court has actively established its jurisdiction and its right to overrule national law when it conflicts with EU law. (p. 234)

European Parliament A quasi-legislative body of the European Union that operates as a watchdog over the European Commission and has limited legislative power. (p. 234)

European Union (EU) The official term for the European Community (formerly the European Economic Community) and associated treaty organizations. The EU has 27 member states and is negotiating with other states that have applied for membership. (p. 228) See also *Maastricht Treaty.*

exchange rate The rate at which one state's currency can be exchanged for the currency of another state. Since 1973, the international monetary system has depended mainly on floating rather than fixed exchange rates. (p. 190)

export-led growth An economic development strategy that seeks to develop industries capable of competing in specific niches in the world economy. (p. 287)

fiscal policy A government's decisions about spending and taxation, and one of the two major tools of macroeconomic policy making (the other being monetary policy). (p. 199)

fissionable material The elements uranium-235 and plutonium, whose atoms split apart and release energy via a chain reaction when an atomic bomb explodes. (p. 150)

fixed exchange rates The official rates of exchange for currencies set by governments; not a dominant mechanism in the international monetary system since 1973. (p. 192) See also *floating exchange rates.*

floating exchange rates The rates determined by global currency markets in which private investors and governments alike buy and sell currencies. (p. 192) See also *fixed exchange rates.*

foreign assistance Money or other aid made available to states in the global South to help them speed up economic development or meet humanitarian needs. Most foreign assistance is provided by governments and is called official development assistance (ODA). (p. 296) See also *Development Assistance Committee (DAC).*

foreign policy process The process by which foreign policies are arrived at and implemented. (p. 78)

"four tigers"/"four dragons" The most successful newly industrialized areas of East Asia: South Korea, Taiwan, Hong Kong, and Singapore. (p. 280)

free trade The flow of goods and services across national boundaries unimpeded by tariffs or other restrictions; in principle (if not always in practice), free trade was a key aspect of Britain's policy after 1846 and of U.S. policy after 1945. (p. 166)

free trade area   A zone in which there are no tariffs or other restrictions on the movement of goods and services across borders. (p. 232) See also *customs union*.

game theory   A branch of mathematics concerned with predicting bargaining outcomes. Games such as Prisoner's Dilemma and Chicken have been used to analyze various sorts of international interactions. (p. 58)

gender gap   Refers to polls showing women lower than men on average in their support for military actions, as well as for various other issues and candidates. (p. 100)

General Agreement on Tariffs and Trade (GATT)   A world organization established in 1947 to work for freer trade on a multilateral basis; the GATT was more of a negotiating framework than an administrative institution. It became the World Trade Organization (WTO) in 1995. (p. 174)

General Assembly   See *UN General Assembly*.

Generalized System of Preferences (GSP)   A mechanism by which some industrialized states began in the 1970s to give tariff concessions to poorer states on certain imports; an exception to the most-favored nation (MFN) principle. (p. 175) See also *most-favored nation (MFN)*.

genocide   An intentional and systematic attempt to destroy a national, ethnic, racial, or religious group, in whole or part. It was confirmed as a crime under international law by the UN Genocide Convention (1948). (p. 119) See also *crimes against humanity*.

geopolitics   The use of geography as an element of power, and the ideas about it held by political leaders and scholars. (p. 40)

globalization   The increasing integration of the world in terms of communications,

culture, and economics; may also refer to changing subjective experiences of space and time accompanying this process. (p. 17)

global warming   A slow, long-term rise in the average world temperature caused by the emission of greenhouse gases produced by burning fossil fuels—oil, coal, and natural gas. (p. 309) See also *greenhouse gases*.

gold standard   A system in international monetary relations, prominent for a century before the 1970s, in which the value of national currencies was pegged to the value of gold or other precious metals. (p. 189)

government bargaining model   A model that sees foreign policy decisions as flowing from a bargaining process among various government agencies that have somewhat divergent interests in the outcome ("where you stand depends on where you sit"). Also called the "bureaucratic politics model." (p. 80)

great powers   Generally, the half-dozen or so most powerful states; the great power club was exclusively European until the 20th century. (p. 44) See also *middle powers*.

greenhouse gases   Carbon dioxide and other gases that, when concentrated in the atmosphere, act like the glass in a greenhouse, holding energy in and leading to global warming. (p. 311)

Gross Domestic Product (GDP)   The size of a state's total annual economic activity. (p. 12)

groupthink   The tendency of groups to validate wrong decisions by becoming overconfident and underestimating risks. (p. 84)

guerrilla war   Warfare without front lines and with irregular forces operating in the midst of, and often hidden or protected by, civilian populations. (p. 112)

hard currency   Money that can be readily converted to leading world currencies. (p. 191) See also *convertible currency*.

hegemonic stability theory   The argument that regimes are most effective when power in the international system is most concentrated. (p. 48) See also *hegemony*.

hegemonic war   War for control of the entire world order—the rules of the international system as a whole. Also known as world war, global war, general war, or systemic war. (p. 110)

hegemony   One state's holding of a preponderance of power in the international system, so that it can single-handedly dominate the rules and arrangements by which international political and economic relations are conducted. (p. 47) See also *hegemonic stability theory*.

high seas   The portion of the oceans considered common territory, not under any kind of exclusive state jurisdiction. (p. 317) See also *territorial waters*.

human rights   The rights of all people to be free from abuses such as torture or imprisonment for their political beliefs (political and civil rights), and to enjoy certain minimum economic and social protections (economic and social rights). (p. 249)

hyperinflation   An extremely rapid, uncontrolled rise in prices, such as occurred in Germany in the 1920s and some poor countries more recently. (p. 191)

idealism   An approach that emphasizes international law, morality, and international organization, rather than power alone, as key influences on international relations. (p. 35) See also *realism*.

identity   A principle for solving collective goods problems by changing participants' preferences based on their shared sense of belonging to a community. (p. 6)

IMF conditionality   An agreement to loan IMF funds on the condition that certain government policies are adopted. Dozens of developing countries have entered into such agreements with the IMF in the past two decades. (p. 293) See also *International Monetary Fund (IMF)*.

import substitution   A strategy of developing local industries, often conducted behind protectionist barriers, to produce items that a country had been importing. (p. 287)

industrialization   The use of fossil-fuel energy to drive machinery and the accumulation of such machinery along with the products created by it. (p. 183)

infant mortality rate   The proportion of babies who die within their first year of life. (p. 329)

information screens   The subconscious or unconscious filters through which people put the information coming in about the world around them. (p. 81) See also *misperceptions, selective perceptions*.

intellectual property rights   The legal protection of the original works of inventors, authors, creators, and performers under patent, copyright, and trademark law. Such rights became a contentious area of trade negotiations in the 1990s. (p. 180)

intercontinental ballistic missiles (ICBMs)   The longest-range ballistic missiles, able to travel 5,000 miles. (p. 151) See also *ballistic missile*.

interdependence   A political and economic situation in which two states are simultaneously dependent on each other for their well-being. The degree of interdependence is sometimes designated in terms of "sensitivity" or "vulnerability." (p. 166)

interest groups   Coalitions of people who share a common interest in the outcome of some political issue and who organize themselves to try to influence the outcome. (p. 73)

intergovernmental organization (IGO)   An organization (such as the United Nations and its agencies) whose members are state governments. (p. 13)

International Committee of the Red Cross (ICRC)   A nongovernmental organization (NGO) that provides practical support, such as medical care, food, and letters from home, to civilians caught in wars and to prisoners of war (POWs). Exchanges of POWs are usually negotiated through the ICRC. (p. 255)

International Court of Justice See *World Court.*

International Criminal Court (ICC) A permanent tribunal for war crimes and crimes against humanity. (p. 253)

international integration The process by which supranational institutions come to replace national ones; the gradual shifting upward of some sovereignty from the state to regional or global structures. (p. 229)

International Monetary Fund (IMF) An intergovernmental organization (IGO) that coordinates international currency exchange, the balance of international payments, and national accounts. Along with the World Bank, it is a pillar of the international financial system. (p. 197) See also *IMF conditionality.*

international norms The expectations held by participants about normal relations among states. (p. 210)

international organizations (IOs) Intergovernmental organizations (IGOs) such as the UN and nongovernmental organizations (NGOs) such as the International Committee of the Red Cross (ICRC). (p. 218)

international political economy (IPE) The study of the politics of trade, monetary, and other economic relations among nations, and their connection to other transnational forces. (p. 10)

international regime A set of rules, norms, and procedures around which the expectations of actors converge in a certain international issue area (such as oceans or monetary policy). (p. 67)

international relations (IR) The relationships among the world's state governments and the connection of those relationships with other actors (such as the United Nations, multinational corporations, and individuals), with other social relationships (including economics, culture, and domestic politics), and with geographic and historical influences. (p. 1)

international security A subfield of international relations (IR) that focuses on questions of war and peace. (p. 10)

international system The set of relationships among the world's states, structured by certain rules and patterns of interaction. (p. 11)

International Whaling Commission An intergovernmental organization (IGO) that sets quotas for hunting certain whale species; states' participation is voluntary. (p. 315)

irredentism A form of nationalism whose goal is to regain territory lost to another state; it can lead directly to violent interstate conflicts. (p. 132)

Islam/Muslims A broad and diverse world religion whose divergent populations include Sunni Muslims, Shi'ite Muslims, and many smaller branches and sects from Nigeria to Indonesia, centered in the Middle East and South Asia. (p. 122)

Islamist Political ideology based on instituting Islamic principles and laws in government. A broad range of groups using diverse methods come under this category. (p. 122)

issue areas Distinct spheres of international activity (such as global trade negotiations) within which policy makers of various states face conflicts and sometimes achieve cooperation. (p. 9)

just wars A category in international law and political theory that defines when wars can be justly started (*jus ad bellum*) and how they can be justly fought (*jus in bello*). (p. 248)

Keynesian economics The principles articulated by British economist John Maynard Keynes, used successfully in the

Great Depression of the 1930s, including the view that governments should sometimes use deficit spending to stimulate economic growth. (p. 199)

Kyoto Protocol (1997) The main international treaty on global warming, which entered into effect in 2005 and mandates cuts in carbon emissions in 2008–2012. Almost all the world's major countries, except the United States, are participants. (p. 312)

land mines Concealed explosive devices, often left behind by irregular armies, that kill or maim civilians after wars end. Such mines number more than 100 million, primarily in Angola, Bosnia, Afghanistan, and Cambodia. A movement to ban land mines is underway; nearly 100 states have agreed to do so. (p. 142)

land reform Policies that aim to break up large land holdings and redistribute land to poor peasants for use in subsistence farming. (p. 268)

League of Nations An organization established after World War I and a forerunner of today's United Nations; it achieved certain humanitarian and other successes but was weakened by the absence of U.S. membership and by its own lack of effectiveness in ensuring collective security. (p. 35) See also *collective security*.

liberal feminism A strand of feminism that emphasizes gender equality and views the "essential" differences in men's and women's abilities or perspectives as trivial or nonexistent. (p. 97)

limited war Military actions that seek objectives short of the surrender and occupation of the enemy. (p. 110)

Maastricht Treaty A treaty signed in the Dutch city of Maastricht and ratified in 1992; it commits the European Union to monetary union (a single currency and European Central Bank) and to a common foreign policy. (p. 235) See also *European Union (EU)*.

malnutrition A lack of needed foods including protein and vitamins; about 10 million children die each year from malnutrition-related causes. (p. 266) See also *undernourishment*.

managed float A system of occasional multinational government interventions in currency markets to manage otherwise free-floating currency rates. (p. 192)

Marxism A branch of socialism that emphasizes exploitation and class struggle and includes both communism and other approaches. (p. 91)

mediation The use of a third party (or parties) in conflict resolution. (p. 93)

mercantilism An economic theory and a political ideology opposed to free trade; it shares with realism the belief that each state must protect its own interests without seeking mutual gains through international organizations. (p. 165) See also *economic liberalism*.

microcredit The use of very small loans to small groups of individuals, often women, to stimulate economic development. (p. 288)

middle powers States that rank somewhat below the great powers in terms of their influence on world affairs (for example, Brazil and India). (p. 46) See also *great powers*.

migration Movement between states, usually emigration from the old state and immigration to the new state. (p. 269)

military governments States in which military forces control the government; they are most common in poor countries, where the military may be the only large modern institution. (p. 159)

Millennium Development Goals UN targets for basic needs measures such as reducing poverty and hunger, adopted in 2000 with a target date of 2015. (p. 261)

misperceptions, selective perceptions The selective or mistaken processing of the available information about a decision; one of several ways—along with affective and cognitive bias—in which individual decision making diverges from the rational model. (p. 81) See also *information screens*.

Missile Technology Control Regime   A set of agreements through which industrialized states try to limit the flow of missile-relevant technology to developing countries. (p. 152)

mixed economies   Economies such as those in the industrialized West that contain both some government control and some private ownership. (p. 186)

monetary policy   A government's decisions about printing and circulating money, and one of the two major tools of macroeconomic policy making (the other being fiscal policy). (p. 199)

Montreal Protocol (1987)   An agreement on protection of the ozone layer in which states pledged to reduce and then eliminate use of chlorofluorocarbons (CFCs). It is the most successful environmental treaty to date. (p. 313)

most-favored nation (MFN)   A principle by which one state, by granting another state MFN status, promises to give it the same treatment given to the first state's most-favored trading partner. (p. 175) See also *Generalized System of Preferences (GSP)*.

multilateral aid   Government foreign aid from several states that goes through a third party, such as the UN or another agency. (p. 296)

multinational corporation (MNC)   A company based in one state with affiliated branches or subsidiaries operating in other states. (p. 200)

Munich Agreement   A symbol of the failed policy of appeasement, this agreement, signed in 1938, allowed Nazi Germany to occupy a part of Czechoslovakia. Rather than appease German aspirations, it was followed by further German expansions, which triggered World War II. (p. 37)

mutually assured destruction (MAD)   The possession of second-strike nuclear capabilities, which ensures that neither of two adversaries could prevent the other from destroying it in an all-out war. (p. 156) See also *deterrence*.

national interest   The interests of a state overall (as opposed to particular parties or factions within the state). (p. 57)

nationalism   Identification with and devotion to the interests of one's nation. It usually involves a large group of people who share a national identity and often a language, culture, or ancestry. (p. 116)

nation-states   States whose populations share a sense of national identity, usually including a language and culture. (p. 11)

neocolonialism   The continuation, in a former colony, of colonial exploitation without formal political control. (p. 277)

neofunctionalism   A theory that holds that economic integration (functionalism) generates a "spillover" effect, resulting in increased political integration. (p. 230)

neoliberal   Shorthand for "neoliberal institutionalism," an approach that stresses the importance of international institutions in reducing the inherent conflict that realists assume in an international system; the reasoning is based on the core liberal idea that seeking long-term mutual gains is often more rational than maximizing individual short-term gains. (p. 66) See also *economic liberalism*.

neorealism   A version of realist theory that emphasizes the influence on state behavior of the system's structure, especially the international distribution of power. (p. 46) See also *realism*.

newly industrializing countries (NICs)   Countries in the global South that have achieved self-sustaining capital accumulation, with impressive economic growth. The most successful are the "four tigers" or "four dragons" of East Asia: South Korea, Taiwan, Hong Kong, and Singapore. (p. 280)

nongovernmental organization (NGO) A transnational group or entity (such as the Catholic Church, Greenpeace, or the International Olympic Committee) that interacts with states, multinational corporations (MNCs), other NGOs, and intergovernmental organizations (IGOs). (p. 13)

Non-Proliferation Treaty (NPT) (1968) A treaty that created a framework for controlling the spread of nuclear materials and expertise, including the International Atomic Energy Agency (IAEA), a UN agency based in Vienna that is charged with inspecting the nuclear power industry in NPT member states to prevent secret military diversions of nuclear materials. (p. 156)

nonstate actors Actors other than state governments that operate either below the level of the state (that is, within states) or across state borders. (p. 13)

nontariff barriers Forms of restricting imports other than tariffs, such as quotas (ceilings on how many goods of a certain kind can be imported). (p. 173)

norms The shared expectations about what behavior is considered proper. (p. 41)

North American Free Trade Agreement (NAFTA) A free trade zone encompassing the United States, Canada, and Mexico since 1994. (p. 177)

North Atlantic Treaty Organization (NATO) A U.S.-led military alliance, formed in 1949 with mainly West European members, to oppose and deter Soviet power in Europe. It is currently expanding into the former Soviet bloc. (p. 51) See also Warsaw Pact.

North-South gap The disparity in resources (income, wealth, and power) between the industrialized, relatively rich countries of the West (and the former East) and the poorer

countries of Africa, the Middle East, and much of Asia and Latin America. (p. 19)

optimizing Picking the very best option; contrasts with satisficing, or finding a satisfactory but less than best solution to a problem. The model of "bounded rationality" postulates that decision makers generally "satisfice" rather than optimize. (p. 83)

organizational process model A decision-making model in which policy makers or lower-level officials rely largely on standardized responses or standard operating procedures. (p. 80)

Organization of Petroleum Exporting Countries (OPEC) The most prominent cartel in the international economy; its members control about half the world's total oil exports, enough to significantly affect the world price of oil. (p. 178)

ozone layer The part of the atmosphere that screens out harmful ultraviolet rays from the sun. Certain chemicals used in industrial economies break the ozone layer down. (p. 313)

Oxfam America A private charitable group that works with local communities to determine the needs of their own people and to carry out development projects. (p. 300)

Peace Corps An organization started by President John Kennedy in 1961 that provides U.S. volunteers for technical development assistance in poor countries. (p. 298)

peace movements Movements against specific wars or against war and militarism in general, usually involving large numbers of people and forms of direct action such as street protests. (p. 95)

peacebuilding The use of military peacekeepers, civilian administrators, police trainers, and similar efforts to sustain peace agreements and build stable, democratic governments in societies recovering from civil wars. Since 2005 a UN Peacebuilding

Commission has coordinated and supported these activities. (p. 223)

positive peace A peace that resolves the underlying reasons for war; not just a cease-fire but a transformation of relationships, including elimination or reduction of economic exploitation and political oppression. (p. 94)

postmodern feminism An effort to combine feminist and postmodernist perspectives with the aim of uncovering the hidden influences of gender in IR and showing how arbitrary the construction of gender roles is. (p. 98)

postmodernism An approach that denies the existence of a single fixed reality, and pays special attention to texts and to discourses—that is, to how people talk and write about a subject. (p. 90)

power The ability or potential to influence others' behavior, as measured by the possession of certain tangible and intangible characteristics. (p. 37)

power projection The ability to use military force in areas far from a country's region or sphere of influence. (p. 143)

Prisoner's Dilemma (PD) A situation modeled by game theory in which rational actors pursuing their individual interests all achieve worse outcomes than they could have by working together. (p. 58)

proliferation The spread of weapons of mass destruction (nuclear, chemical, or biological weapons) into the hands of more actors. (p. 154)

pronatalist A government policy that encourages or forces childbearing, and outlaws or limits access to contraception. (p. 329)

prospect theory A decision-making theory that holds that options are assessed by comparison to a reference point, which is often the status quo but might be some past or expected situation. The model also holds that decision makers fear losses more than they value gains. (p. 83)

protectionism The protection of domestic industries against international competition, by trade tariffs and other means. (p. 172)

proxy wars Wars in the global South—often civil wars—in which the United States and the Soviet Union jockeyed for position by supplying and advising opposing factions. (p. 26)

public opinion In IR, the range of views on foreign policy issues held by the citizens of a state. (p. 74)

"rally 'round the flag" syndrome The public's increased support for government leaders during wartime, at least in the short term. (p. 76)

rational actors Actors conceived of as single entities that can "think" about their actions coherently, make choices, identify their interests, and rank the interests in terms of priority. (p. 57)

rational model A model in which decision makers calculate the costs and benefits of each possible course of action, then choose the one with the highest benefits and lowest costs. (p. 79)

realism A broad intellectual tradition that explains international relations mainly in terms of power. (p. 35) See also *idealism* and *neorealism*.

reciprocity A response in kind to another's actions; a strategy of reciprocity uses positive forms of leverage to promise rewards and negative forms of leverage to threaten punishment. (p. 5)

refugees People fleeing their countries to find refuge from war, natural disaster, or political persecution. International law distinguishes them from migrants. (p. 270)

reserves Hard-currency stockpiles kept by states. (p. 191)

resource curse The difficulties faced by resource-rich developing countries, including dependence on exporting one or a few commodities whose prices fluctuate, as well as potentials for corruption and inequality. (p. 276)

responsibility to protect Principle adopted by world leaders in 2005 holding governments responsible for protecting civilians from genocide and crimes against humanity perpetrated within a sovereign state. (p. 252)

satisficing The act of finding a satisfactory or "good enough" solution to a problem. (p. 83)

secular (state) A state created apart from religious establishments and in which there is a high degree of separation betweeen religious and political organizations. (p. 122)

Secretariat See *UN Secretariat*.

security community A situation in which low expectations of interstate violence permit a high degree of political cooperation—as, for example, among NATO members. (p. 230)

Security Council See *UN Security Council*.

security dilemma A situation in which actions states take to ensure their own security (such as deploying more military forces) are perceived as threats to the security of other states. (p. 42)

service sector The part of an economy that concerns services (as opposed to the production of tangible goods); the key focus in international trade negotiations is on banking, insurance, and related financial services. (p. 181)

Sino-Soviet split A rift in the 1960s between the communist powers of the Soviet Union and China, fueled by China's opposition to Soviet moves toward peaceful coexistence with the United States. (p. 26)

sovereignty A state's right, at least in principle, to do whatever it wants within its own territory; traditionally sovereignty is the most important international norm. (p. 41)

Special Drawing Right (SDR) A world currency created by the International Monetary Fund (IMF) to replace gold as a world standard. Valued by a "basket" of national currencies, the SDR has been called "paper gold." (p. 197)

state An inhabited territorial entity controlled by a government that exercises sovereignty on its territory. (p. 10)

state-owned industries Industries such as oil-production companies and airlines that are owned wholly or partly by the state because they are thought to be vital to the national economy. (p. 186)

state-sponsored terrorism The use of terrorist groups by states, usually under control of a state's intelligence agency, to achieve political aims. (p. 149)

Strategic Defense Initiative (SDI) A U.S. effort, also known as "Star Wars," to develop defenses that could shoot down incoming ballistic missiles, spurred by President Ronald Reagan in 1983. Critics call it an expensive failure that will likely be ineffective. (p. 157)

subsistence farming Rural communities growing food mainly for their own consumption rather than for sale in local or world markets. (p. 267)

subtext Meanings that are implicit or hidden in a text rather than explicitly addressed. (p. 90) See also *postmodernism*.

summit meeting A meeting between heads of state, often referring to leaders of great powers, as in the Cold War superpower summits between the United States and the Soviet Union or today's meetings of the Group of Eight on economic coordination. (p. 26)

supranational Larger institutions and groupings such as the European Union to which state authority or national identity is subordinated. (p. 209)

tariff A duty or tax levied on certain types of imports (usually as a percentage of their value) as they enter a country. (p. 173)

technology transfer Developing states' acquisition of technology (knowledge, skills, methods, designs, specialized equipment, etc.) from foreign sources, usually in conjunction with direct foreign investment or similar business operations. (p. 291)

territorial waters The waters near states' shores generally treated as part of national territory. The UN Convention on the Law of the Sea provides for a 12-mile territorial sea (exclusive national jurisdiction over shipping and navigation) and a 200-mile exclusive economic zone (EEZ) covering exclusive fishing and mineral rights (but allowing for free navigation by all). (p. 136) See also *high seas* and *UN Convention on the Law of the Sea (UNCLOS)*.

total war Warfare by one state waged to conquer and occupy another; modern total war originated in the Napoleonic Wars, which relied on conscription on a mass scale. (p. 110)

tragedy of the commons A collective goods dilemma that is created when common environmental assets (such as the world's fisheries) are depleted or degraded through the failure of states to cooperate effectively. One solution is to "enclose" the commons (split them into individually owned pieces); international regimes can also be a (partial) solution. (p. 307)

transitional economies Countries in Russia and Eastern Europe that are trying to convert from communism to capitalism, with various degrees of success. (p. 186)

Treaty of Rome (1957) The founding document of the European Economic Community (EEC) or Common Market, now subsumed by the European Union. (p. 231)

truth commissions Governmental bodies established in several countries after internal wars to hear honest testimony and bring to light what really happened during these wars, and in exchange to offer most of the participants asylum from punishment. (p. 113)

United Nations (UN) An organization of nearly all world states, created after World War II to promote collective security. (p. 69)

UN Charter The founding document of the United Nations; it is based on the principles that states are equal, have sovereignty over their own affairs, enjoy independence and territorial integrity, and must fulfill international obligations. The Charter also lays out the structure and methods of the UN. (p. 213)

UN Conference on Trade and Development (UNCTAD) A structure established in 1964 to promote development in the global South through various trade proposals. (p. 227)

UN Convention on the Law of the Sea (UNCLOS) A world treaty (1982) governing use of the oceans. The UNCLOS treaty established rules on territorial waters and a 200-mile exclusive economic zone (EEZ). (p. 317) See also *territorial waters*.

UN Development Program (UNDP) A program that coordinates the flow of multilateral development assistance and manages 5,000 projects at once around the world (focusing especially on technical development assistance). (p. 298)

UN Environment Program (UNEP) A program that monitors environmental conditions and, among other activities, works with the World Meteorological Organization to measure changes in global climate. (p. 311)

UN General Assembly A body composed of representatives of all states that allocates UN funds, passes nonbinding resolutions, and coordinates economic development programs and various autonomous agencies through the Economic and Social Council (ECOSOC). (p. 214)

UN Secretariat The UN's executive branch, led by the secretary-general. (p. 224)

UN Security Council A body of five great powers (which can veto resolutions) and ten rotating member states that makes decisions about international peace and security, including the dispatch of UN peacekeeping forces. (p. 216)

Universal Declaration of Human Rights (UDHR) (1948) The core UN document on human rights; although it lacks the force of international law, it sets forth international norms regarding behavior by governments toward their own citizens and foreigners alike. (p. 250)

urbanization A shift of population from the countryside to the cities that typically accompanies economic development and is augmented by displacement of peasants from subsistence farming. (p. 268)

U.S.-Japanese Security Treaty A bilateral alliance between the United States and Japan, created in 1951 against the potential Soviet threat to Japan. The United States maintains troops in Japan and is committed to defend Japan if attacked, and Japan pays the United States to offset about half the cost of maintaining the troops. (p. 53)

war crimes Violations of the law governing the conduct of warfare, such as by mistreating prisoners of war or unnecessarily targeting civilians. (p. 252) See also *just wars*.

Warsaw Pact A Soviet-led Eastern European military alliance, founded in 1955 and disbanded in 1991. It opposed the NATO alliance. (p. 51) See also *North Atlantic Treaty Organization (NATO)*.

weapons of mass destruction Nuclear, chemical, and biological weapons, all distinguished from conventional weapons by their enormous potential lethality and their relative lack of discrimination in whom they kill. (p. 149)

World Bank Formally the International Bank for Reconstruction and Development (IBRD), an organization that was established in 1944 as a source of loans to help reconstruct the European economies. Later, the main borrowers were developing countries and, in the 1990s, Eastern European ones. (p. 197)

World Court (International Court of Justice) The judicial arm of the UN; located in The Hague, it hears only cases between states. (p. 243)

world government A centralized world governing body with strong enforcement powers. (p. 95)

World Health Organization (WHO) An organization based in Geneva that provides technical assistance to improve health conditions in the developing world and conducts major immunization campaigns. (p. 228)

world-system A view of the world in terms of regional class divisions, with industrialized countries as the core, poorest countries as the periphery, and other areas (for example, some of the newly industrializing countries) as the semiperiphery. (p. 272)

World Trade Organization (WTO) An organization begun in 1995 that expanded the GATT's traditional focus on manufactured goods and created monitoring and enforcement mechanisms. (p. 174) See also *General Agreement on Tariffs and Trade (GATT)*.

zero-sum games Situations in which one actor's gain is by definition equal to the other's loss, as opposed to a non-zero-sum game, in which it is possible for both actors to gain (or lose). (p. 58)

Photo Credits

Index

Note: **Boldface** entries and page numbers indicate key terms. Entries for tables and figures are followed by "*table*" and "*fig.*," respectively.

Ambassadors, 72, 248. *See also* Diplomacy; Embassies
American Telephone and Telegraph (AT&T), 200
Americas. *See* Latin America; specific countries
Amnesty International, 212, 252
Analogies, historical, 83
Analysis, of causes of war, 113–116
Anarchy, 41–43, 96
Angola
    ideology and, 130–131
    oil exports from, 322
    UN and, 217
    U.S. military forces in, 27
    warfare in, 31, 64
Animals, epidemics among, 332
Annan, Kofi
    on crimes by UN personnel, 100
    on Montreal Protocol, 314
    receiving Nobel Peace Prize, 224
    on U.S. invasion of Iraq, 217
Antarctica, management of environment in, 317, 319
Antarctic Treaty (1959), 319
Anthony, Susan B., 97
Anti-Americanism, 43, 126
Anticolonial movements, 275
Antitrust policies, monopolies and, 173
Anti-Western sentiment, 124, 126
Appeasement, 36, 83
Appropriateness, logic of, 88–89
Aquino, Corazón, 101 (*table*)
Arab-Israeli conflicts
    border territories and, 135
    Israeli bombing of Syria (2007), 112
    oil exports and, 322
    refugees from, 271
Arab League, 69
Arab oil embargo (1973), 27
Arab world
    caliphate in, 125
    foreign development assistance from, 296
    nuclear proliferation and, 155–156
    oil embargo by, 27
    television network in, 334
Aral Sea, 320
Arbitration, 93, 243–244
Arctic region
    melting in, 31, 310, 311
    potential shipping routes in, 310, 310 (*fig.*)
Argentina
    debt of, 292
    Falkland Islands war and, 76
    financial collapse in, 193

    in Mercosur, 178
    as middle power, 46
    missiles in, 152
    territorial dispute in, 136
Argentina v. Uruguay, World Court case of, 245 (*fig.*)
Aristophanes, 99
Aristotle, 249
Armed forces, 140–145. *See also* Military; Soldiers
    conventional vs. irregular, 139
    Islamist, 126–130, 127 (*table*)
Armenia, 119
Armies, 140, 142
Armor, 140
Arms control, 156–157
Arms race, 56–57
    during Cold War, 57
    Prisoner's Dilemma game in, 59
    reciprocity and, 6, 8–9, 157
Arms trade, 74, 158, 159, 182
Arms Trade Treaty, proposed, 159
ASEAN. *See* Association of South East Asian Nations (ASEAN)
Asia. *See also* specific regions and countries
    debt in, 292
    democracy in, 71
    economic development and, 279
    free-trade area in, 178
    imperialism in, 275
    sustainable development and, 309
    tsunami (2004) in, 299
    United States and, 53
    women in, 268–269
Asia-Pacific IGOs, 178
Assault rifles, 159
Association of South East Asian Nations (ASEAN), 178, 212
Asylum seekers, 270
Atmosphere
    global warming and, 309–314
    ozone depletion and, 313–314
Atomic bombs, 104–105, 150
Atomic energy, Euratom and, 231
Attentive public, in democracy, 75
AU. *See* African Union (AU)
Australia
    as middle power, 46
    military alliances, 53
    troops in Iraq War, 30
Austria
    as early nation-state, 116–117
    in EU, 237
    foreign immigrants in, 271
    UN Standby High Readiness Brigade and, 224
Austria-Hungary, power of, 117
Autarky, 171–172, 286, 290

Authoritarian governments
    concentration of wealth and, 288
    democracy and, 70–71, 288
    economic development under, 288
    fascism as, 117
Authority, for peacekeeping forces (UN), 221–222
Automobiles and automobile industry
    Japanese manufacturers and, 169
    trade in, 169
Autonomous agencies, of UN, 227–228
Autonomy vs. connection, gender issues, 98
Averse to risk, 79–80
Ayatollahs, 126
Azerbaijan, 119, 323–324

Baghdad, bombing of, 144–145, 217
Bahrain, oil exports from, 322
Baker, James, 73, 336
Balance of payments, 198
Balance of power, 43–44
    alliances and, 49–55
    multipolar, 46, 47 (*fig.*)
Balance of trade, 167, 169 (*fig.*), 198
Bali, terrorist bombing in, 129
Balkans, 21. *See also* specific countries
Ballistic Missile Defense (BMD). *See* Strategic Defense Initiative (SDI)
Ballistic missiles, 151–153
    capabilities of, 145
    proliferation of, 12, 152
    system for stopping, 156–158
Baltic region, 28, 53. *See also* specific countries
Banana republics, 14
Bangladesh
    child malnutrition in, 267
    economic development in, 288
    Grameen Bank in, 288
    military government in, 71
    population growth in, 326
    textile exports from, 180
    women in, 288
Banking systems, global, 188–189
Banks and banking, central banks, 196
Bargaining, game theory and, 58
Barriers to trade. *See* Trade
Basic human needs, 262–266
    indicators by region (2005), 265 (*fig.*)
    women and, 268
Battles. *See* specific battles and wars
Bauxite, 324
Bay of Pigs invasion, 26, 160

B-52 bombers, 159
Behavior, norms of, 41
Beijing, 282, 283. *See also*
    Tiananmen protests (1989)
Belarus, 53
Belgium, 231
    chocolate market, 235
    EU headquarters at, 233
    NATO headquarters at, 51
    steel production in, 231
Beliefs, individual decision makers
    and, 81
Bell curves, males and females on,
    103–104, 103 (fig.)
Benefits, distribution of, 57–58,
    166, 167 (fig.), 170
Benelux countries, 231
Berlin, division of, 24
Berlin Wall, 24, 27
Bermuda, 12
Bhutto, Benazir, 30, 101 (table), 129
Bias
    affective, 81
    cognitive, 82–83
    in-group, 120
    normative, 93
Bilateral aid, 296, 297–298
Bilateral alliance
    U.S.-Japanese, 51, 53
    U.S.-South Korea, 31, 53
Bilateral relations, in liberal
    economics, 166
Bilateral trade agreements, 176–177
Bill and Melinda Gates Foundation,
    68, 296
bin Laden, Osama
    al Qaeda and, 129
    September 11, 2001, attacks
    and, 30
Biodiversity, 314–315
Biological weapons, 151, 153–154
**Biological Weapons Convention
    (1972), 154**
Bipolar system, 46, 47 (fig.)
Bird flu, 31, 332
Birth control (contraception), 328,
    329, 331
Birthrates
    demographic transition and,
    326–327
    overpopulation and, 326–327
    in third world countries,
    326–327
Black markets, 190
Black Sea, oil exports and, 323
Blue helmets, UN soldiers as, 221
Bolivia
    cocaine trade and, 139
    as Cuban ally, 93
    territorial dispute in, 132

Bombs and bombings, 144. *See also*
    Atomic bombs; Missiles;
    Nuclear weapons
Bono (singer), foreign aid and, 296
Borders
    colonialism and, 276
    conflicts over, 11, 117,
    118–119, 134
    energy resources and, 322–324
    interstate, 134–135
    of Israel, 135
    pollution and, 319
    secession and, 132–133
    territorial integrity and, 42, 134
    terrorist attacks across, 148
Border wars, 110
Borrowing
    nature of borrower and, 291
    third world and, 287–288,
    291–293
Bosnia. *See also* Serbia
    ethnic cleansing in, 134
    ethnic Serbs in, 28
    EU peacekeepers in, 51
    genocide in, 119
    independence of, 28, 134
    NATO forces and, 51
    public opinion and, 75
    systematic rape in, 103
    warfare in, 64
    World Court and, 244
Bosnian Serbs, war crimes tribunal
    against, 252–253
Bosporus, Russian tankers in, 232
Botswana, 276, 331
Boundaries. *See* Borders
Bounded rationality model, 83
Boys, relations of, 98. *See also*
    Gender; Men
Brain drain, 291
Brazil
    carbon emission credits, 313
    income in, 285
    in Mercosur, 178
    as middle power, 46
    missiles in, 152
    rain forests in, 315
    steel production in, 324
Breaking diplomatic relations, 247
Breeder reactors, 150
Bretton Woods system, 197
Britain. *See* England (Britain)
British Broadcasting Corporation
    (BBC), 333
Brunei, Spratly Islands and, 136,
    136 (fig.)
Brussels, Belgium
    EU headquarters at, 233
    NATO headquarters at, 51
B-2 stealth bomber, 147

Budget
    for UN, 225
    of U.S. intelligence agencies, 146
Budget deficit, EU members, 236–237
Bulgaria, 52, 238
Burden sharing, 50
Bureaucracies, 72–73, 225
Bureaucratic politics model, 80–81
Burma (Myanmar)
    cease-fire in, 64
    corruption in, 289
    disaster relief in, 300
Burundi, 64
Bush, George H.W., 73
Bush, George W.
    appointments, 73
    CTBT Treaty and, 158
    dumping and, 183
    free trade policy of, 177
    international issues and, 49
    Kyoto Protocol and, 29, 313
    rally 'round the flag syndrome
    and, 76, 76 (fig.)
    steel tariffs and, 183
    terrorism and, 29–30
Business, 200–204, 269. *See also*
    Multinational corporations
    (MNCs)

California, 157, 313
Caliphate, Arab, 125
Cambodia, 217, 223
Cameroon, 135, 244, 324
Camp David peace treaty (1978), 135
Canada. *See also* North American
    Free Trade Agreement
    (NAFTA)
    bilateral trade with India, 176
    as middle power, 46
    peacekeeping initiatives, 6
    UN Standby High Readiness
    Brigade and, 224
    U.S.-Canada free-trade
    agreement and, 177
Cancun, Mexico, WTO meeting in,
    19, 180
Capabilities
    power as, 37–38, 41
    strategies for, 56
Capital. *See also* Foreign investment
    concentration of, 287–288, 290
    in enclave economy, 277
    foreign direct investment and,
    201–202
    for manufacturing, 287–288
Capital accumulation, 278
Capital city, of state, 11
Capital flows
    balance of payments and, 198
    North-South, 289–295

Capital goods, 198
Capitalism
    accumulation and, 272–273
    in China, 93, 281–282
    land reform and, 268
    Marxism on, 74, 91, 114
    world economy and, 185, 272–273
Capitalist world economy, 272–273
Carbon dioxide, 311, 312–313,
    312 (fig.)
Carbon emission credits, 313
CARE, 300
Career diplomats, 72
Caribbean, 270
Cars. See Automobiles and
    automobile industry
Cartels, 178–179. See also
    Organization of Petroleum
    Exporting Countries (OPEC)
    agricultural, 324
    cocaine, 139
    joint producer-consumer, 324
    producer cartels, 324
Cash crops, 267
Caspian Sea region
    exclusive economic zones
        (EEZs) in, 323
    oil from, 322–323, 323 (fig.)
Castro, Fidel, 26, 160, 216. See also
    Cuba
Catholic Church, 213, 331
Catholic Relief Services, 300
Cease-fires, UN and, 64, 222, 223
Cell phones, 282, 288, 334–335, 335
    (fig.), 336 (fig.), 338
Central America. See also Latin
    America; specific countries
    migrants from, 270
    UN and, 217
    U.S. free trade with, 178
Central bank, 196, 236
Central Intelligence Agency (CIA)
    covert operations of, 85, 160, 252
    interagency rivalries, 73
Centralization, integration and, 230
Centrally planned economy, 185
Central planning, 185
CFCs. See Chlorofluorocarbons
    (CFCs)
Chad
    coup in (2007), 112
    oil from, 324
    refugees from, 271
Chain of command, 160
Challenge of traditional concepts
    of gender, 97
Chamorro, Violeta, 101 (table)
Charitable programs, foreign
    assistance, 299–300
Chauvinism, national, 117

Chavez, Hugo, 131, 177
Chechnya
    oil pipeline in, 323
    secession of, 28
    Sunni Muslims in, 130
    terrorism and, 130, 148
Checks and balances, on military
    force, 70
Chemical weapons, 151, 153–154
**Chemical Weapons Convention
    (1992), 153**
Chernobyl, 320
ChevronTexaco, 204
Child labor, global trade and, 187
Children
    basic human needs of, 262–263
    malnutrition among, 267
    UN program for, 226, 298
Chile
    bilateral trade with U.S. and, 178
    territorial dispute in, 132
China. See also Hong Kong; Sun Tzu
    AIDS epidemic and, 331
    alignments of, 54
    Angola and, 131
    arms imports, 159
    autarky policy in, 171–172
    balance of power and, 43
    capitalism in, 93, 281–282
    carbon dioxide projected use,
        312 (fig.)
    cheap labor, 177
    child malnutrition in, 267
    class disparities in, 281, 282
    Cold War and, 27
    communism in, 27, 31, 71, 282
    currency of, 193
    economic development in, 261,
        279, 280–283, 285–286
    economy of, 186, 195
    estimated total GDP in, 21
        (table), 45 (fig.)
    foreign aid by, 283
    foreign investment and, 290
    foreign policy of, 56
    as great power, 45–47
    greenhouse emissions and,
        312–313
    HIV in, 331
    Hu Jintao in, 195
    human rights and, 250
    IMF voting power, 197
    India and, 54, 285 (fig.)
    inflation in, 191
    intellectual property piracy in, 181
    Internet use in, 338
    Iraq War and, 217
    Japan and, 136
    Kashmir and, 135
    Kosovo secession and, 133–134

    law of the seas and, 317
    nuclear proliferation and, 155, 157
    per capita GDP in, 279, 279 (fig.)
    pollution in, 309, 319
    population growth in, 326,
        328–329
    pro-democracy demonstrations
        in, 27
    revolution in, 31, 92
    rural vs. urban disparities, 282
    Russian treaty with, 29
    Soviet Union and, 26
    space weapons and, 145
    Spratly Islands and, 136, 136 (fig.)
    steel production in, 324
    strategic actions of, 56
    sustainable development and, 309
    Taiwan and, 12, 56, 217, 280
    Tiananmen Square
        demonstrations in, 27, 242
    trade surplus of, 168 (fig.)
    UN and, 56, 217, 218
    U.S. relations with, 29, 177
    uses of term *hegemony* by, 48
    women in, 269
    world clothing exports from, 180
    in world politics, 31–32
    WTO and, 175, 282–283
Chinese communist revolution
    (1949). See Cultural
    Revolution (China)
Chlorofluorocarbons (CFCs), 311,
    313–314
Chocolate, use of name, 235
Cholera, 264, 285, 332
Christian imperialism, 125
Christianity
    fundamentalists and, 122
    human rights norms and, 89
Churchill, Winston, on iron
    curtain, 24
CIA. See Central Intelligence
    Agency (CIA)
Çiller, Tansu, 101 (table)
CIS. See Commonwealth of
    Independent States (CIS)
Cities. See Urbanization
City-states, Greek, 36
Civilians
    chemical weapons and, 153
    terrorism and, 148
Civilizations, worldwide, 273
Civil-military relations, 159–160
Civil-political rights, as negative
    rights, 250
Civil society, 10
Civil war(s), 112
    Hindu-Muslim, 275
    Liberian struggle against, 121
    trauma of, 112–113

Clans, 112, 120

Class ideology, terrorism and, 147

Class struggle, 91, 272, 278

Client states, 50

Climate, 310, 311. *See also* Environment; Global warming

Clinton, Bill, 313

Clinton, Hillary, as Secretary of State, 73

Coal. *See also* European Coal and Steel Community (ECSC)
Chinese move away from, 309
energy from, 321
gases as byproduct of use, 311, 312–313
greenhouse gases as byproduct of use, 311

Coalitions, power-balancing, 43. *See also* Alliances

Cocaine trade, 139

Cocoa, agricultural cartel in, 324

Coffee cartel, 324

Cognitive balance, 82–83

Cognitive biases, 82–83

Cognitive dissonance, 82–83

Cohen, William, 83

Cold War, 24
arms control during, 157
chemical weapons during, 153
containment in, 31
covert operations in, 160
domestic level of theory of war and, 114
East-West dividing line during, 52, 52 (*fig.*)
end of, 27
Europe and, 29
fall of Berlin Wall and, 27
ideological conflict in, 131
international relations after, 27–32
NATO and, 24–27
nuclear strategy in, 151, 157
regional conflicts during, 26–27
state actors in, 25 (*fig.*)
superpowers in, 24–27
UN during, 217

Collective goods problem, 3
core principles of, 3–9, 5 (*table*)
corruption and, 289
depletion of fisheries as, 306–307
disaster relief as, 299
environmental, 306–309
exchange rate stability and, 196
global warming and, 309–313
overfishing and, 317
pollution as, 319–320
refugees as, 270
in Somalia, 113
tragedy of the commons, 307–308
transparency and, 67, 289

Collective response, enforcement of international law by, 242–243

Collective security, 69–70
UN Charter and, 216
UN Security Council and, 69–70

Colombia, 139

Colonies and colonialism
anticolonial movements in, 275
effects of, 275
European, 92
foreign aid and, 298
former European, 274 (*fig.*)
independence and, 12, 92, 273
Middle East oil and, 322
negative economic implications of, 273, 275
neocolonialism and, 277
postcolonial dependency in former, 276–278
status of former colonies, 12
struggle against, 125

Combat, women in, 99, 101–103

Comfort women, in World War II, 103

Command economy. *See* Centrally planned economy

Commercial agriculture, 267

Commission on Sustainable Development, 309

Common Agricultural Policy (CAP), 232

Common market, 177, 232. *See also* European Economic Community (EEC)

Commons. *See* Global commons

Commonwealth (British). *See* England (Britain); specific countries

Commonwealth of Independent States (CIS)
decline of wars in, 31
estimated total GDP in, 21 (*table*)
formation of, 28
members of, 53

Communication(s), 146–147. *See also* Global communications; Telecommunications

Communism
in China, 26, 27, 71, 186, 282
in Cuba, 26
Marxism and, 91
revolutions and, 91–92

Community, sense of, 230.

Comparative advantage, 168–170, 295

Comparative politics, 9

Compellence strategy, **56**

Competition, market, 166, 172–174

Comprehensive Test Ban Treaty (CTBT) (1996), **158**

Computerization, 15

Computers
digital divide and, 335–336

Concentration of capital, for manufacturing, 287–288

Concert of Europe, 44, 45

Concessionary terms, in economic development, 292

Conditionality agreements, 293, 295

Confidence-building measures, 94

Conflict, 113. *See also* Wars and warfare
of control of governments, 137–138
decline of, 63–65
from drug trafficking, 139
economic, 138–139, 194, 237
ethnic, 116, 117–122
of ideas, 116–131
of interest, 131–139
over home-host country relations, 202–204
over human rights, 252
over interstate borders, 134
over natural resources, 320–325
over self-determination, 117
perceived nation vs. state borders and, 11, 117
rationality and, 57
religious, 122–130
settling through violence, 117

Conflict and cooperation, 9

Conflict resolution, 93
UN as mechanism for, 93, 214
world government and, 95

Congo. *See* Democratic Congo

Congress (U.S.), women in, 100–101

Consensus, 66

Consequences, logic of, 88–89

Conservation, 317. *See also* Environment

Constitution, of EU, 238–239

Constructivism, 87–90

Consulates, 72

Consumer demand, decline in, 186

Container Security Initiative, 153

Containment, 24, 26

Continental Shelf treaty, 317

Contraception, 328, 329, 331

Control, of governments, 137–138

Convention against Torture (CAT), 251

Conventional arms trade, 158

Conventional forces
logistics and intelligence, 145–146

Convention on International Trade in Endangered Species (CITES), 315

peace and, 70–72
public opinion in, 75
transition to, 72
Democratic Congo, 109
dictator overthrow in, 29
disintegration of, 230
economic development in, 285
EU peacekeepers in, 51
ICC and, 253
IGOs in, 71
UN peacekeeping mission in, 222
voting in (2006), 71
warfare in, 29, 65, 119, 153
Democratic peace, 66, **70–72**
Demographics, migration and, 270
Demographic transition, 326–328,
327, 327 (fig.)
Dengue fever, 332
Deng Xiaoping, 281
Denmark, 224, 232, 296
Dependence. *See* Interdependence
Dependency, postcolonial, 276–278
Dependency theory, 277
Depression, in Russia and Eastern
Europe, 186
Deterrence, 56
nuclear, 156–158
wars and, 115
Devaluation, 194
Developed countries, 21, 279 (fig.).
See also North (global)
Developing countries, 260. *See also*
North (global); South
(global); Third world
corruption in, 289
expenditures on medicine in, 264
use of term, 21
women in, 268–269
Development. *See* Economic
development
Development and International
Economic Cooperation, 225
**Development Assistance
Committee (DAC), 296**
Diamonds, 132, 276
Difference feminism, 97
on core assumptions of realism, 98
on feminist practice of
international relations, 100
liberal feminism and, 103–104
peace vs. war and, 99
Digital divide (North-South),
335–336, 336 (fig.)
Diplomacy
laws of, 246–248
norms of, 42–43, 247
terrorism and, 248
Diplomatic corps, 72
Diplomatic immunity, 247
Diplomatic recognition, 247

Diplomatic relations, 247
Diplomats, 72–73, 247–248
Direct foreign investment. *See*
Foreign direct investment
Disarmament, Demobilization, and
Reintegration (DDR), 113
Disaster relief, 299–300
international coordination of,
299–300
by UN, 227, 299
Disasters, refugees from, 270
Discount rate, 196
Discourses, postmodernism and, 90
Discrimination, against girls in
education and literacy, 269
Diseases, 329–333. *See also* AIDS;
specific diseases
bird flu, 31
infectious, 332
malnutrition and, 267
smoking and, 332–333
as transnational concern, 31
tropical, 264
world health, 263–265
Disintegration, 230
Dispute resolution. *See* Wars and
warfare
Disputes. *See* Conflict; Wars and
warfare
Distribution of income. *See* Income
Distribution of power, 46–47
Distribution of wealth. *See also* Wealth
Marxism on, 91–92
mercantilists and, 166
between MNC and host country,
202–203
Diversionary foreign policy, 76
Doha Round, 173, **176,** 178, 180, 181
Dollar (U.S.)
Bretton Woods and, 197
Chinese currency and, 193
euro and, 190
gold standard and, 190, 197
Japanese yen and, 190
relative values of currencies and,
190–193, 197
yuan ratio to, 195
Dolphins, 315
Domain names, 339–340
Domestic policies
public opinion and, 74–76
Domestic politics
bureaucracies and, 72–73
interest groups and, 73–74
legislatures and, 76, 78
military-industrial complex and, 73
public opinion and, 74–76
Domestic (state, societal) level of
analysis, 16–17, 16 (table), 71,
114–115

Dominance, 5
in China's one-child policy, 285
as core principle, 5 (table)
imperialism and, 273
natural resources and, 325
power and, 46
UN Security Council and, 5, 222
Dow Chemical, 200
Drift nets, 317
Drug companies, third world health
care and, 264
Drug trafficking, as illegal trade,
139, 182
Dumping, products into markets,
173, 182–183
Dumping, toxic wastes, 317, 319,
320, 325
Dutch, 92. *See also* Netherlands, The
Duty, 173

Earth Summit (1992), 309, 312, 314
East, in global North, 19
East Asia
countries in, 21
"four tigers" of, 280
free-trade area, 178
use of term, 21
Eastern Europe
disintegration in, 230
economic position of, 185
EU and, 238
in global North, 19
HIV in, 331
migrants from, 270
oil exports from, 324
regional GDP in, 186
states in EU, 238
states in NATO, 31, 51–52
transitional economies of, 186
East Timor, 223, 263
East-West Cold War dividing line,
52, 52 (fig.)
Ebola virus, 332
E-commerce. *See* Internet
Economic accumulation, 272, 277,
278, 287–288. *See also*
Accumulation; Accumulation
theories
Economic and monetary union
(EMU), 232
Economic and Social Committee
(EU), 234
Economic and Social Council
(ECOSOC, UN),
216, 226
Economic classes, 91
Economic community, in Western
Europe, 210, 229–230
Economic conflict, 116,
138–139, 237

Masculinity
  of realism, 98–99
  of war, 99
Massacres, in former Yugoslavia, 28
Material power, 37–38
Mattel, 203
Mauritania, 269
McAleese, Mary, 316
McDonald's, 200, 339
Measles, 264, 332
Mechanization, 183
Media, 75, 333–334
Mediation, 93
Medicine, distribution of health
    care and, 181, 264–265, 265
    (fig.), 331
Mediterranean basin, pollution of, 319
Meir, Golda, 101 *(table)*
Men. *See also* Gender; Masculinity;
    Women
  aggression and, 99
  gender roles and, 96–98
Mercantilism, 165–168
  economic nationalism and, 272
  foreign direct investment and,
    201–202
  foreign policies and, 138
  MNCs and, 201–202
Mercosur. *See* Southern Cone
    Common Market (Mercosur)
Merkel, Angela, 101 *(table)*
Methane gas, 311
Mexico. *See also* North American Free
    Trade Agreement (NAFTA)
  free trade with U.S., 177
  income in, 285
  as middle power, 46
  migrants from, 270
  oil exports from, 322
  World Court and, 244
Microcredit (microlending), **288,** 302
Microeconomics, 166
Middle class, global, 277, 287
Middle East. *See also* Arab-Israeli
    conflicts; Imperialism; specific
    countries
  Arab League in, 69
  countries in, 21
  economic development in, 262
  estimated total GDP in, 21 *(table)*
  Islam and, 122
  oil exports from, 322
  per capita GDP in, 279
  U.S. setbacks in, 27
  water problems in, 325
  weapons sales in, 158
  women in, 269
Middle powers, 46
  alignment of, 55 *(fig.)*
  great powers and, 44–46

Migration, 269–271
Militarism, 94
Military. *See also* Armed forces;
    Military force
  of China, 56
  configuration of, 160
  control of, 159–160
  conventional forces, 139–147
  economics of, 158–159
  EU, NATO, and, 51–52
  institutional interests, 73
  integration of European, 231
  irregular, 112–113, 139, 140 *(fig.)*
  laws of war and, 255
  for leverage, 140 *(fig.)*
  in NATO, 51, 52
  piracy and, 88
  private, 255
  realism and, 39–40
  as response to aggression (just-war
    doctrine), 248–249
  revolution in military affairs
    and, 146
  satellite reconnaissance for, 337
  states and, 158–160
  technology and, 146–147
  terrorism by, 149
  weapons of mass destruction and,
    140 *(fig.)*, 149–158
  women in, 99, 101–103
Military aid, 297–298
Military alliances. *See also* North
    Atlantic Treaty Organization
    (NATO)
  as IGOs, 13
  with South Korea, 26
  with South Korea and Australia, 53
  U.S.-Japan treaty at, 53
Military force. *See also specific wars*
  checks and balances on, 70
  economic conflict and, 138
  gender and, 96, 99, 100
  legislatures and, 78
  leverage of, 114
  militarism and, 94
  power and, 36, 39–40
  proportionality of, 255
  technology and, 146–147
  weapons of mass destruction
    and, 140 *(fig.)*
Military governments, 71, 159
Military industries, 138, 325
Military interventions, explanations
    of, 82
Military power, 46
Military spending
  economics of, 158–159
  great power shares of, 45 *(fig.)*, 46
  UN and, 214
  United States and, 214

Militias
  in Burma, 65
  Hamas, 129
  Hezbollah, 126
  Shi'ite, 126
  Sunni, 129
Millennium Challenge Account, 298
**Millennium Development Goals
    (UN), 261**
Milosevic, Slobodan, 29, 252–253
Minerals, for industrial equipment, 324
Mirror image perceptions, 83, 125
Misperceptions, 81
Missiles. *See also* Nuclear weapons
  aerial, 144
  ballistic, 151–153
  defense against, 156–158
  ranges of Indian and Pakistani,
    152 *(fig.)*
  scud, 154
  from ships, 143–144
  Sputnik and, 26
  standoff distances and, 146
  Stinger, 144
  U.S. intercept system and, 157
**Missile Technology Control
    Regime, 152**
Missionaries, 212–213
Mixed economies, 186
Mixed interest game, 166
MNCs. *See* Multinational
    corporations (MNCs)
Mobil Oil, 289
Moldova, war of secession and, 133
Monetary policy, 193, **199,** 204
Monetary system, 196–198
Monetary union, European, 236–237
Money. *See also* Currency; Dollar
    (U.S.); Euro
  corruption and, 204
  financial positions of states and,
    198–199
  managing, 199
  value of, 189–193
Monnet, Jean, 231
Monopoly, 170, 173
Montenegro, 134
Montreal Protocol (1987), **313**–314
Morality
  international norms and,
    210–211
  power and, 40
  vs. realism, 36
Moral reasoning, gender and, 98
Moreno-Ocampo, Luis, 254
Morgenthau, Hans, 37
Morocco, 124–125, 129, 139
Mortality, 329–330. *See also* Death
    rates
Moslems. *See* Muslims

specialized functions of, 212
types of, 14 *(table)*
Nonmilitary leverage, 140 *(fig.)*
Nonpermanent members, of Security
    Council (UN), 218–219
Non-Proliferation Treaty (NPT)
    (1968), 41–42, **156**
Nonstate actors, 13–15
    information technology and, 334
    intergovernmental organizations
      as, 13
    terrorism by, 147–149
    types of, 14 *(table)*
Nontariff barriers, to trade, **173**
Nonviolence
    of Gandhi, 96, 275
    liability of, 95
    women and, 99
Non-zero-sum games. *See* Zero-sum
    games
Normative bias, 93
Norm entrepreneurs, 89
Norms, 41
    constructivism and, 87
    of diplomacy, 42–43, 247
    international, 67, 88–89,
      210–211, 300
    of international regime
      behavior, 41
    pollution and, 320
    reciprocity as, 39
    sovereignty as, 41–42
    territorial integrity as, 42, 133–134
    terrorist violation of, 148–149
North, Oliver, 85
North Africa, 270
North America. *See also free trade entries*
    AIDS in, 331
    energy efficiency in, 321
    estimated total GDP in, 21 *(table)*
    in global North, 19
    in NATO, 51
North American Free Trade
    Agreement (NAFTA), 177
    industry support for and
      opposition to, 180
North Atlantic Treaty Organization
    (NATO), 51–53
    as alliance, 51–53
    in Bosnia, 28
    Cold War and, 24–27
    expansion of, 51–53, 52 *(fig.)*
    as IGO, 13
    Iraq War and, 52
    in Kosovo, 29, 51, 133, 147
    membership in, 30, 51–52
    Russia and, 51–52
    Serbia and, 52, 160
    Taliban and, 128
    Ukraine and, 52

Northern Ireland, 64, 117
North (global). *See also* specific
    countries
    AIDS and, 330 *(table)*
    capital flows in, 289–295
    concentration of capital in, 288
    economic development in, 279
    GDP in, 21–23 *(table)*
    globalization and, 19–24
    global warming and, 312–313
    Islamist movements and, 125
    in neocolonial period, 276
    North-South debt and, 292 *(table)*
    Oxfam and, 301
    per capita GDP in, 38, 279
    technology transfer and, 291
    trade in, 164
    values in, 17–18
North Korea
    chemical weapons treaty and, 153
    counterfeit U.S. currency in,
      194–195
    Japan and, 77
    military spending by, 158
    missile defense system, 152, 157
    nuclear proliferation and, 155
    nuclear weapons program of, 31,
      41–42, 149, 150, 156, 158
    sanctions against, 243
    weapons of mass destruction
      in, 150
North Sea, oil production in, 322
North-South digital divide,
    335–336, 336 *(fig.)*
North-South gap, 19, 21. *See also*
    Imperialism; North-South
    relations; South (global)
    accumulation theories, 271–273
    development assistance models
      and, 300–302
    in education, 262–263, 269
    pollution from industrialization
      and, 312–313
    skepticism of, 18
    in trade, 295
    wealth disparity and, 91–92
    world-system and, 272–273, 277
    in WTO, 295
North-South relations, 260–305. *See*
    also North-South gap
    debt and, 291–293
    immigration and, 269–271
    Leninism and, 92
Norway
    EU and, 232, 238
    foreign aid from, 296
    North Sea oil and, 322
    UN Standby High Readiness
      Brigade and, 224
    whale hunting in, 315

NPT. *See* Non-Proliferation Treaty
    (NPT) (1968)
NSA. *See* National Security Agency
    (NSA)
Nuclear accident, at Chernobyl, 320
Nuclear power, 306, 321
Nuclear strategy, 156–157
Nuclear wastes, 319–320
Nuclear weapons, 150–151. *See also*
    specific countries
    delivery systems for, 151–153
    as deterrence, 156–158
    IAEA inspection of, 156
    India-Pakistan Prisoner's Dilemma
      matrix and, 59–60, 59 *(fig.)*
    in Iran, 31, 126, 150, 155, 156, 228
    Israel and, 155–156
    in North Korea, 31, 41–42, 149,
      150, 156
    in Pakistan, 155
    prohibitions against, 26
    proliferation of, 8–9
    reduction of, 28
    Security Council (UN), 31,
      156, 158
    sexual terminology for, 104–105
    Soviet development of, 24
    strategy for, 156–157
    terrorist acquisition of, 148
    U.S. development of, 24
Nuremberg Tribunal, 119, 252, 255
Nutrition, 266–268. *See also* Food

OAS. *See* Organization of American
    States (OAS)
Obama, Barack
    Brazilian mask of, 88
    Cabinet appointments, 73
    constructivist theory on election
      of, 88
    draw down of troops in Iraq, 30
    on global warming, 310
    international family heritage of, 126
    multilateral approach to foreign
      policy, 40, 49
    rejoining Kyoto talks, 313
Observation, by UN peacekeepers,
    223–224
Oceans
    environment and, 306–307,
      315, 317
    state-controlled waters in, 317,
      318 *(fig.)*
Office of Foreign Disaster Assistance
    (OFDA), 299
Oil. *See also* Organization of
    Petroleum Exporting Countries
    (OPEC); specific countries
    Arab embargo on, 27
    Arctic, 310–311

381

Petrodollars, 322
Philippines
    brain drain from, 291
    coups in, 73
    protests via cell phones in, 338
    Spratly Islands and, 136, 136 (fig.)
    terrorism in, 129
Pipelines, oil, 322–324
Piracy
    high seas, 88, 142–143, 143 (fig.)
    of intellectual property, 181
de Pisan, Christine, 97
Planned Parenthood, 212
Plenary session (UN), 225
Plutonium, 150, 156
Pneumonia, 332
Poland
    in EU, 238
    as middle power, 46
    in NATO, 51–52
    UN Standby High Readiness
        Brigade and, 224
Polar bears, 311
Polarity, of power distribution, 46
Policies, 78. See also Domestic
        policies; Foreign policy
Policy makers, behaviors of, 9
Polio, 263
Political appointees, diplomats
        as, 73
Political economy. See International
        political economy (IPE)
Political line, Marxist, 186
Political realism. See Realism
Political risk analysis, 290
Political stability, MNCs and, 290
Political systems. See specific systems
Politicians, women as, 100–101,
        101 (table)
Politics. See also Authoritarian
        governments; Democracy
    corruption and, 289
    domestic, 72–78, 93–103
    of economic relationships, 9
    foreign aid and, 296
    global flow of information in, 214
    IMF conditionality agreements
        and, 293, 295
    information as tool against
        governments, 337–338
    information as tool of
        governments, 336–337
    markets and, 170–172
    refugees and, 271
Pollution, 180, 309, 312–314, 317,
        319–320. See also Greenhouse
        gases; specific types
Poor countries, 238, 284–285. See also
        South (global); Third world
"Poor four," in EU, 233

Population, 326–333. See also
        Overpopulation
    age of, 327
    AIDS and, 330–333, 330 (table)
    comparison of world regions
        (2007), 21 (table)
    death rates and, 329–330
    demographic transition and,
        326–328
    diseases and, 329–333
    global, 326
    largest countries, 13 (fig.)
    political policies toward, 328–329
    refugee, 270 (table)
    rural and urban, 268
    size of state and, 12
    trends and projections, 326 (fig.)
    water needs and, 324–325
    women's status and, 329
Portfolio investment, 201
Portugal, 232
Positive affect, 81
Positive balance of trade (trade
        surplus), 167–168
Positive peace, 94–95
Positive rights, 250
Possessions, 12
Post-Cold War era (1990–2009),
        27–32, 159
Postcolonial dependency,
        276–278
Postmodern feminism, 98, 104–105
Postmodernism, 90–91
    deconstruction by, 90–91
    sexual aspects of weaponry and,
        104–105
Poverty. See also Economic
        development; South (global);
        Third world
    in Africa, 260–261
    AIDS and, 331
    in Asia, 261
    basic needs and, 262–266
    capitalist vs. socialist approaches
        to, 272–273
    in China, 261
    economic development and, 280
    in global South, 260–273
    malnutrition, hunger, and,
        266–268, 267 (table)
    North-South gap and, 19, 260–273
Power, 37–40
    balance of, 43–44
    as capability, 37–38, 41
    definition of, 37–38
    distribution of, 46–47
    economics of, 39–40
    elements of, 39–40
    estimating, 39
    GDP as measure of, 38, 39

    geopolitics and, 40
    global disparity of, 295
    hegemony and, 47–49
    of ideas, 38–39
    as influence, 37–38
    of information, 333–340
    long-term resources of, 39
    military and, 39–40
    morality and, 40
    realists on, 35
    of regimes, 68
    relative, 39
    soft, 39
    of UN Security Council, 219
    women and, 104–105, 268–269
Power capabilities, 37–38, 41
Power politics, 35, 82–119
Power projection, 143
Power transition theory, 47, 47
        (fig.), 115
POWs. See Prisoners of war (POWs)
Precious metals, as global currency, 190
Predatory practices, 173
Prices, 166, 267
**Prisoner's Dilemma (PD) game,
        58**–59
    cooperation, neoliberals, and,
        66–67
    India-Pakistan arms race and,
        59–60
    payoff matrix in India-Pakistan
        game, 59–60, 59 (fig.)
Prisoners of war (POWs), 255
Private foreign assistance, 296
Private military forces, 255
Private ownership, 281
Producer cartels, 324
Producer-consumer cartel, 324
Production, nationally controlled, 277
Profit, from food sales to
        government, 300
Project Handclasp, 301
Projection, psychological, 83
Proliferation (weapons of mass
        destruction), **154**–156
Pronatalist (pro-birth), **329**
Propaganda, 75
Property rights, intellectual, 180–181
Proportionality of military force, 255
Prospect theory, 83
Prostitution, AIDS prevention and, 331
Protectionism, 172–174
Protests
    against food subsidies, 293
    against IOs, 18–19
    against Iraq War, 95
    in rural Chinese villages, 282
    in Tiananmen Square, 27, 242, 282
    against UN, 212
    against WTO, 18–19, 176

Ricardo, David, comparative advantage and, 168
Rice, Condoleezza, 73
Rights. *See* Human rights; specific rights
Risk
    decision making and, 79–80
    political risk analysis and, 290
Romania, 52, 238
Rome, Treaty of, 231–233, 235, 236
Roosevelt, Theodore, as internationalist, 48
Rounds, of trade negotiations, 175, 180, 181
Rousseau, Jean-Jacques, 249
Rules
    international regime as, 67
    of trade, 182–183
Rural areas, 268, 288
Russia. *See also* Soviet Union
    after Soviet breakup, 28
    arms sales by, 159
    balance of power and, 43
    Chechnya and, 130, 148
    Chinese treaty with, 29
    CIS and, 53
    decline of wars in, 31
    democratic efforts in, 71
    disintegration in, 230
    economy of, 186
    as energy supplier and power, 38
    estimated total GDP in, 21
        (table), 45 (fig.)
    financial position of, 191
    fishing industry and, 137
    Georgia and, 42, 110, 147
    in global North, 19
    global warming and, 313
    as great power, 45
    HIV in, 331
    IP piracy in, 181
    Iraq War and, 217
    Kosovo secession and, 133–134
    Leninist ideology in, 92
    military capabilities of, 145
    NATO and, 51–52
    nuclear weapons and, 156
    oil from, 322–324
    oil pipeline routes and, 322–324
    republic of, 28
    steel production in, 324
    terrorism in, 129
    transitional economy in, 186
    Ukraine and, 38, 116
    UN and, 218
    U.S. relations with, 29, 157
    wars of secession, 134
    WTO and, 175
Russian Revolution (1917), 92

Rwanda
    genocide in, 29, 119
    systematic rape in, 103
    war crimes and, 252
    warfare in, 31, 64
    women in parliament, 101

Sadat, Anwar, 114
Saddam Hussein
    bombing of Baghdad and, 144–145
    Gulf War and, 126
    Iran and, 130–131
    Iraq War and, 30
    moral standards and, 211
    UN and, 70
    video of execution, 334
al-Sadr, Moqtada, 127
Sanctions
    economic, 171
    international law enforcement and, 242–243
    unilateral by U.S., 149
Sappho, 97
Satellites
    communication by, 334
    military use of, 145
    outer space and, 137
    for TV transmissions, 334
Satisficing, 83
Saudi Arabia
    fundamentalist Islamists in, 128
    human trafficking and, 271
    missiles in, 152
    oil exports from, 169, 178, 322
    terrorism in, 129
Schengen area, 238
Schooling, 262–263, 269
Schuman, Robert, 231
Scorched earth policy, 325
Scud missiles, 154
SDR. *See* Special Drawing Right (SDR)
Seafood, global loss of species, 308 (fig.)
Sea of Japan, missile intercept systems in, 157
Sea of Okhotsk, fishing in, 137
Seas. *See* Oceans
Seattle, WTO meeting in, 18, 176
Sea turtles, 188
Secession, 132–134
Second World War. *See* World War II
Secretariat (UN), UN Secretariat
Secretary-general (UN). *See* UN Secretariat
Secular political organizations, **122**
Security. *See also* Collective security; International security
    military, 138
    MNCs, host countries, and, 203–204
    U.S. initiative for, 153

Security community, 230
Security Council (UN). *See* UN Security Council
Security dilemma, 42–43, 50
Security Sector Reform (SSR), 113
Selective perceptions, 81
Self-Defence Forces, Japan, 53
Self-determination principle, 42, 89, 117
Self-help, 41, 43
Self-reliance, of states, 92–93, 171–172, 286, 290
Semiperiphery, in world-system, 273, 280
Seneca, 113
September 11, 2001, terrorist attacks, 2, 14, 29–30, 148
    congressional approval for use of force, 78
    information screens and, 81
    war on terrorism after, 29–30
Serbia. *See also* Kosovo
    aggression by, 28
    Albanians in Kosovo and, 29, 119, 133
    ethnic cleansing by, 134
    ethnic loyalties in, 120
    UN and, 218
    U.S. bombings of, 144
Serbs
    in Bosnia, 28
    in Croatia, 28, 134
    genocide by, 118–119, 252
Service sector, 181–182, 200, 284
Shah of Iran, overthrow of, 27
Shell, 204
Shelter, 265
Shevardnadze, Eduard, 86
Shi'ite Muslims
    in Iran, 126–128
    in Iraq, 30, 57, 126
    Islam religion of, 122
Shipping companies, 142
Shipping containers, 153
Shipping routes, potential Arctic, 310, 310 (fig.)
Ships, naval, 143–144
Short-range ballistic missiles (SRBMs), 151, 152
Short term
    consumption vs. long-term investment, 293
    power capabilities in, 39–40
Shrimp industry, 188
Sierra Leone
    human rights in, 113
    UN peacekeeping mission in, 223
    war crimes in, 252
    warfare in, 64
Silver, as global currency, 190

Space satellites, 137, 145
Spain
    in EEC, 232, 237
    as middle power, 46
    peace demonstrators in, 95
    terrorism in, 129
    troops in Iraq War, 30
Special Drawing Right (SDR), 197, 236
Special sessions, of UN General Assembly, 226
Species preservation. *See* Biodiversity
Speculation
    in international currencies, 192
Spending. *See* Military spending
Spies, in embassies, 247
Spillover, integration processes and, 230.
Sports, transnational communities in, 339
Spratly Islands, oil drilling rights and fisheries by, 136, 136 *(fig.)*
Sputnik, 26, 186
Sri Lanka, 65, 117, 148
Stability. *See also* Political stability
    of exchange rates, 197
    IMF formula for, 293
Stalin, Joseph, 26, 50, 93
Stalingrad, 115
Standard of living, in transitional economies, 186
Standard operating procedures, in decision making, 80
Standing wealth, 203–204
Starvation, in South, 267
"Star Wars." *See* Strategic Defense Initiative (SDI)
State actors, 10–12
State borders. *See* Borders
Statecraft, 55–57
State level of analysis, 16–17, 16 *(table)*, 115
State-owned industries, 186, 281
State power. *See* Power
State(s), 10
    as actors, 90
    diplomatic norms of, 42–43, 247
    financial positions of, 198–199
    fragmentation of, 117
    head of, 11
    independence of, 117
    and military, 158–160
    nation-states and, 11
    postmodernism and, 90–91
    response to public opinion by, 76, 78
    sovereignty of, 41–42
    stable currency exchange rates and, 193–194
    territorial integrity of, 42, 134–135

terrorism supported by, 149
    as unitary actors, 57
    in world (1815–2000), 211 *(fig.)*
State sovereignty. *See also* National sovereignty; Sovereignty
    human rights and, 249–250
    international law and, 246
    in international system, 41–42
    national vs. world currency and, 193
    UN Charter and, 213
State-sponsored terrorism, 149
Stealth technology, 147
Steam engines, 183–184
Steel
    producers of, 231, 324
    retaliatory tariffs and, 183
Steering process, decision making as, 79, 79 *(fig.)*
Stinger missiles, 144
Stock markets, global, 189
Strategic alignments, 46
Strategic Defense Initiative (SDI), 157
Strategic materials, economic conflict over, 138–139
Strategic weapons, 151
Strategies
    compellence, 56
    deterrence as, 56
    escalation, 56–57
    of export-led growth, 286–287
    nuclear, 165–158
    reciprocity as, 66
    statecraft as, 55–57
Stress, in decision making, 86
Strong leader assumption, 57
Structural adjustment program, 293
Structural realism, 46
Structural violence, 94
Subfields, in IR, 9–10
Subsidies, for domestic industry, 173, 180, 232, 283–285, 293
Subsistence farming, 267
Substate actors, 14–15
Substate nationalism, 11
Subtext, 90
Sudan
    genocide in, 119
    peacekeeping in, 119, 223
    self-determination in, 117
    terrorism supported by, 149
    war crimes in, 253
    warfare in, 31, 64, 129–130
Suffrage movement, 99–100
Sugar cartel, 324
Suicide bombings, 148
Sukarnoputri, Megawati, 101 *(table)*
Summit meeting, 31
    in 1955, 26

in Genoa, 18
    in Quebec, 18
Sunni Muslims
    in Iraq, 30, 57, 126–128, 148
    Islam religion of, 122
Sun Tzu, 36
Superpowers, 12, 24–27, 46. *See also* Cold War; Soviet Union; United States
Supply and demand for currency, 193
Supranational, 209. *See also* International integration
    coordination of economic policies, 232
    cultural influences, 339
    institutions, 17
Supranationalism, 209–210, 339
Supreme Islamic Iraqi Council (SIIC), 127
Surplus. *See* Trade surpluses or deficits
Sustainable economic development, 309
Swaps, debt-for-nature, 317
Sweatshops, 187
Sweden, 224, 237, 296
Swine flu, 332
Switzerland
    embassy interests section, 247
    EU and, 232, 238
    UN membership and, 216, 270
Symbolism, constructivists and, 89
Syria
    chemical weapons treaty and, 153
    Golan Heights and, 325
    Israeli bombing of, 112
    nuclear weapons and, 156
    terrorism supported by, 149
Systemic war, 110

Taba, border dispute at, 132
Tactical weapons, 151
Taiwan
    China and, 12, 56, 217
    economic development in, 280
    nuclear proliferation and, 155
    Spratly Islands and, 136, 136 *(fig.)*
    UN and, 217, 226
Taliban (Afghanistan)
    illicit drug trade and, 139
    as Islamic group, 126–130
    U.S. fight against, 30
    women's education and, 269
Tamils, 148
Tariffs, 173
    GATT, 175
    in global South, 175
    Hawley-Smoot Act, 185
    retaliatory, 182–183
    textile, 287
    trade, 171

U.S.-Chile free-trade agreement, 178
U.S.-Japanese Security Treaty, 51, **53**
U.S.-Mexico free trade, 177
U.S.-Russian Strategic Offensive
    Reductions Treaty (2002), 157
USAID. *See* Agency for
    International Development
    (USAID)
Uzbekistan, 320

Vaccination programs, 263–264, 265
    (fig.), 332
Values
    individual decision makers
        and, 81
    of North (global), 17–18
    of women's contributions, 97
Vatican (Holy See), status of, 12, 226
Venezuela
    anti-American rally in, 177
    coups in, 73
    as Cuban ally, 93
    in Mercosur, 178
    oil exports from, 322
    United States and, 131
Veto, UN, 216
Vietcong guerrillas, 112
Vietnam
    economic development in, 282,
        285
    independence of, 275
    proxy war in, 131
    Spratly Islands and, 136, 136 *(fig.)*
    WTO and, 175
Vietnam War
    decision making in, 82, 83
    guerilla armies in, 112
    laws of warfare in, 256
    public opinion on, 75
    U.S. error in, 27
    U.S.-Japanese alliance and, 53
Violence. *See also* Conflict; Wars
        and warfare
    by conventional forces, 139
    economic conflict and, 138
    human tendency toward, 114
    as leverage, 140 *(fig.)*, 147
    nonviolence and, 95
    structural, 94
    vs. conflict resolution, 93
Voice of America (VOA), 333
Voluntary migration, 269
Voting rights. *See* Elections

Wahhabism, 128, 129
Wajed, Sheikh Hasina, 101 *(table)*
Wal-Mart, 200–201
War crimes, 252–256
    in Bosnian crisis, 252–253
    in Darfur, Sudan, 253

international law and, 252–256
    in Liberia, 253
    in Rwanda, 252
    by Serbs, 252
    UN tribunals against, 29, 252–253
War on terrorism, 29–30, 248. *See
        also* al Qaeda
War Powers Act, 78.
Wars and warfare, 109–116. *See also*
        Conflict; Revolution(s);
        World war; specific wars
    causes of, 113–116
    civil, 112
    constructivists on, 87
    cyberwar, 147
    cyclical theories, 115
    decline of, 31, 63–65
    by democracies, 70
    economy and, 158–159
    electronic (information), 146–147
    gender and, 99–100
    in global South, 265–266
    guerrilla, 112
    hegemonic, 110
    international system and, 24–27,
        25 *(fig.)*, 35–37
    just-war doctrine and, 248–249
    laws of war and changing nature
        of war, 255–256
    liberal theories of, 63–72
    limited, 110
    militarism and, 94
    ongoing in 2009, 111 *(fig.)*
    refugees from, 270–271
    revolution in military affairs
        and, 146–147
    social construction of, 94
    in study of IR, 9
    technological change and,
        146–147
    terrorism and, 147–149
    total, 110
    types of, 110–113
    women and, 100, 101–103
    world war, 110
Warsaw Pact, 24, **51**
Washington, D.C., protests against
        IOs in, 18
Wastes
    dumping, 317, 319, 320, 325
    toxic and nuclear, 319–320
Water
    disputes over, 317, 324–325
    safe drinking water, 264–265,
        266 *(fig.)*
Water pollution, 317, 319
Wealth. *See also* Distribution of
        wealth
    control of, 196
    disparities of, 91–92, 328

North-South gap in, 19
    redistribution of, 272–273
    standing, 203–204
Weapons. *See also* Arms trade;
        specific types
    biological, 153–154
    chemical, 153–154
    electronics and, 146–147
    fission, 150–151
    sexual terminology for, 104–105
    small arms, 159
    smart, 144
    space, 145–146
    strategic, 151
    tactical, 151
    technological change and,
        146–147
Weapons of mass destruction,
    149–158
    ballistic missiles and other
        delivery systems, 145, 151–153
    chemical and biological, 153–154
    as leverage, 140 *(fig.)*
    as military force, 140 *(fig.)*
    North Korea and, 149, 150
    nuclear, 150–151
    proliferation of, 154–156
    terrorist acquisition of, 155
    types of, 150–158
    U.S. security initiative
        against, 153
Weather patterns, 310
Web. *See* Internet
Weighted voting system, in IMF and
        World Bank, 197
West, in global North, 19
West Bank, 129, 135, 271
Western civilization, 273
Western Europe
    in global North, 19
    immigrant labor in, 270
    in NATO, 51
    post-war textbooks in, 120
    supranational institutions in,
        210, 229
Westphalia, Treaty of (1648), 41
Wetlands convention (1971), 315
Whales and whaling, 315
Whites
    effects of colonialism and,
        275, 276
    minority rule in Africa,
        276 *(fig.)*
WHO. *See* World Health
        Organization (WHO)
Will (national), 56
Wilson, Woodrow, 35–36, 48
Wishful thinking, by decision
        makers, 83, 85
Wollstonecraft, Mary, 97

391

Women. *See also* Feminism; Gender;
    Masculinity; Men
  in Afghanistan, 126–130, 269
  in Bangladesh, 288
  birthrates and, 326–327
  in China, 285
  in combat, 99, 101–103
  in developing countries, 268–269
  discrimination against, 268–269
  economic self-sufficiency for, 288
  education for, 269
  in Ethiopia, 302
  fertility rate, 284–285,
    285 *(fig.)*
  forced sterility, 285
  gender gap and, 100
  gender roles and, 96–98
  in global South, 288
  human rights and, 250
  in international relations,
    100–103
  as leaders, 96, 100–101, 101
    (table)
  as military targets, 103
  as peacemakers, 99
  peace organizations of, 99
  power of, 104–105, 268–269
  sexual violence against, 74, 100,
    103, 112, 223, 271
  as soldiers, 100, 101–103
  status in society, 329
  in U.S. Congress, 100–101
  vulnerability in combat, 103
  war and noncombatant, 103
Women's International League for
    Peace and Freedom, 99
Women's Peace Party, 99
Workers
  brain drain and, 291
  in industrialized countries, 187
  socialist views on rights of, 117
World Bank, 197
  conditionality and, 293
  on economic growth in
    Africa, 279
  formation of, 185
  IMF and, 196–198
  on income inequality, 288
  loans by, 228
  missions of, 197–198
  poverty in South and, 262
  weighted voting system of, 197
World civilizations, 273
World Council of Churches, 299

**World Court (International Court
    of Justice),** 135, 216, 234,
    243–244, 245 *(fig.)*
World economic regimes, in global
    South, 295
World economy. *See* Economy
World Food Summit (1996), 267
World government, 95
**World Health Organization
    (WHO), 228**
  AIDS epidemic and, 331–332
  disaster relief and, 299
  foreign assistance from, 298
  medical research
    expenditures, 264
  smoking and, 333
World hunger. *See* Hunger
World Intellectual Property
    Organization (WIPO),
    181, 228
World Meteorological Organization
    (WMO), 228, 311
World order(s)
  authoritarian governments
    and, 288
  distribution of power and, 46–47
  foreign aid and, 296–298
  hegemonic war and, 110
  international law and, 241–249
  international norms and morality
    in, 89, 210–211, 300
  international organizations in,
    212–213
  overpopulation and, 326
  public health and, 263–265
  religion and, 212–213
  revolution in military affairs and,
    146–147
World regions. *See* Region(s)
World Summit on the Information
    Society, 340
World-system, 272–273, 277
World Trade Center
  destruction of, 29, 148
**World Trade Organization (WTO),
    174–176**
  Cancun, Mexico meeting, 19, 180
  China in, 175, 282–283
  consensus in, 66
  Doha Round of, 173, 176, 181
  free-trade regime based on,
    176, 276
  generic drug complaint, 331
  global South and, 295

  Hong Kong Round of, 19, 180
  as IGO, 13
  as IO, 18
  protests against, 18–19, 176
  regional free-trade areas and, 178
  retaliation against trade
    restrictions and, 173, 182–183
  Russia in, 175
  scope of, 228
  Seattle meeting of, 18, 176
  shrimp exports and, 188
  Ukraine and, 175
  Uruguay Round of, 175, 176
  Vietnam and, 175
World War I
  chemical weapons in, 153
  international system and, 35–36
World War II
  biological weapons in, 154
  chemical weapons in, 153
  decolonization after, 275
  economies after, 185
  as hegemonic war, 110
  international system and, 36–37
  nuclear weapons in, 150
  Nuremberg Tribunal after, 119,
    252, 255
  scorched earth policy during, 325
World Wide Web. *See* Internet
WTO. *See* World Trade
    Organization (WTO)

Yeltsin, Boris, 28, 85, 186
Yen (Japan), U.S. dollar and, 190
Yuan (China), 195
Yugoslavia. *See also* Bosnia; Kosovo;
    Serbia
  breakup of, 12, 28, 117
  crimes against humanity and,
    252–253
  disintegration in, 230
  ethnic groups in, 118–119
  Kosovo War and, 51
  secession from, 134
  UN and, 217, 223
  war crimes tribunal against,
    252–253

Zaire. *See* Democratic Congo
Zambia, 276
Zero-sum games, 58
Zhou Enlai, 73
Zimbabwe, 191, 264
Zinc, 324